REVIEWS FOR

TH NEW NATURAL DEATH HANDBOOK

'Gives excellent advice'
Cosmopolitan

'What could be more healthy than bringing society's last taboo
out of the closet?'
The Observer

'Demonstrates to people dissatisfied with conveyor-belt
funerals that there are kinder alternatives'
The Times

'Excellent'
*The British Holistic Medical
Association Newsletter*

'Investigating Natural Death is a cheering experience and I
would recommend it to anyone facing bereavement'
Midweek

'Inspiring'
Church Times

'; trongly recommended for its scope, interest and practicality'
Network

'Full of amazing advice and information'
Sunday Independent

'I'd advise anyone interested to get hold of a copy of *The
Natural Death Handbook*, altogether a very good thing'
Green magazine

The Natural Death Centre is especially grateful to John Bradfield and the A. B. Welfare and Wildlife Trust – the Natural Death Centre largely relies on the Trust for sound information on law and ecology (although the Trust is not responsible for any errors or shortcomings within the text).

Thanks are also due to: Susan Morris, Poppy Aza-Selinger, Francis Bickmore and Neel Mukherjee for their editorial work on the third edition; solicitor Desmond Banks for advice on wills and probate; Joseph Elliot and Gil Elliot for the first draft editions which they prepared of chapters two, three and eleven; Lindesay Irvine for his assistant editorial work on the second edition; Richard Ross-Langley, Lindesay Irvine and Stephen Evans for their proofreading; Richard Doust for his design for the book's layout; Christine Mills for researching the first edition's funerals chapter and for help with other chapters; Yvonne Ackroyd, Mary Bradbury, Roger Knights and Marion Schmidt for their research help; Marcelle Papworth for her translations; Bernd Behr, Nick Laessing, Gillian Roediger, Katherine Davey, Claudia Conway, Helena Thompson, Diana Senior, Josefine Speyer, Yvonne Malik, Mary McHugh, John Wilkey, Maureen Taylor and Milena Petrova for their help; and all those who have suggested improvements, including Heather Albery, Sheila Barratt, Denise Brady, Joanna Gilpin, Christianne Heal, John Horbury, Avril Jackson, Margaret Hayworth, Elizabeth Lawlor, Julian Litten, David Lorimer, Dr Mary Neal, Renée O'Sullivan, Derek Roberts-Morgan, Caroline Sherwood, Jane Spottiswoode, Solveig Taylor, Sheila Thompson and Pam Williams.

THE NEW NATURAL DEATH HANDBOOK

Edited by Nicholas Albery and Stephanie Wienrich
of The Natural Death Centre

RIDER

LONDON · SYDNEY · AUCKLAND · JOHANNESBURG

1 3 5 7 9 10 8 6 4 2

The Natural Death Centre
20 Heber Road
London NW2 6AA, UK
✗ (tel 020 8208 2853; fax 020 8452 6434;
e-mail: rhino@dial.pipex.com: web: www.naturaldeath.org.uk)

All royalties from this book are going to The Natural Death Centre, an educational charity, towards its work in supporting those dying at home. The Centre is grateful to all the many people and publishers who freely contributed items and is apologetic to any whom it failed to trace or acknowledge.

First published by The Natural Death Centre in 1993,
revised edition published by Rider 1997

This revised third edition published in 2000 by Rider, an imprint of Ebury Press, Random House, 20 Vauxhall Bridge Road, London SW1V 2SA
www.randomhouse.co.uk

Random House Australia (Pty) Limited, 20 Alfred Street, Milsons Point, Sydney, New South Wales 2061, Australia

Random House New Zealand Limited, 18 Poland Road, Glenfield, Auckland 10, New Zealand

Random House South Africa (Pty) Limited, Endulini, 5A Jubilee Road, Parktown 2193, South Africa

Random House Group Limited Reg. No. 954009

Papers used by Rider Books are natural, recyclable products made from wood grown in sustainable forests

Printed and bound in Great Britain by CPI Antony Rowe, Chippenham and Eastbourne
record for this book is available from the British Library.

ISBN 0-7126-0576-2

Formal disclaimer: Neither the publisher nor *The New Natural Death Handbook* can accept responsibility for any action taken as a result of reading this book; the reader would be wise to get a second opinion or to consult professional advisers. Please send all corrections, updates and suggested additions to the Centre at the above address.

CONTENTS

Chapter 1

THE NATURAL DEATH MOVEMENT

The idea that launched the Natural Death Centre

The Natural Death Centre is an educational charity, founded in 1991 by three psychotherapists – Christianne Heal, myself and my wife Josefine Speyer. For Josefine and me, the idea for the Centre grew from our experience of the birth of our son. Back in 1975, Josefine was pregnant and I'd taken a long spell off work to help her fulfil a cherished fantasy of travelling by horse and cart. With our horse Patience (on £2 a week rent from the Heavy Horse Preservation Society) and our converted manure tip cart, we meandered our way through the wilder parts of Wales, looking for a cottage for the winter and the birth. Josefine was adamant that she wanted to be at home for the birth. As she put it: 'I'm not ill, why should I go into hospital?' At last we found a place by the river Teifi and a doctor who was willing to come to the farm cottage – 'I don't mind if you give birth on a haystack, I'll come wherever you want,' he told Josefine.

In the event we were very lucky. It was a short, almost painfree and ecstatic labour for Josefine, and all the preparation helped – the Raspberry Leaf tea, the natural birth books and classes, the visualisations and breathing exercises – and the doctor and midwife were like guests in our home for this Leboyer-style birth of low lights and quiet.

In 1988, my father died at home and his death triggered in me a realisation of the need for a natural death movement to parallel the natural childbirth movement, and to spread the tenets of good hospice care to home care for those dying of all causes, not just cancer. It wouldn't suit everybody, but why shouldn't those families who wanted it be fully supported by the NHS in looking after the dying person at home, with adequate financial and other help for carers? Wouldn't more people, if it were possible, prefer to die at home amongst friends rather than in the anonymity of a big and noisy hospital? As with birth, could preparation, exercises and rituals help reduce the anxieties that people feel about dying? Could dying at least for a lucky few become as easy and as ecstatic a process as our experience of birth? Granted that no one can be certain what happens after death, could it be that preparation matters, as the Tibetans argue, to enable the soul at the point of death to merge fearlessly with that bright light reported by many who have recovered from Near-Death Experiences? I remembered how a friend's mother insisted on being given her travelling rug to die with; could the process of dying be the labour pains of the soul, with sometimes the same feeling of expectation and transition as at birth?

Just as many people want to experience birth as consciously as possible, so some people want to face death with minds as unclouded as their circumstances permit. It is here that the analogy between birth and death breaks down somewhat, for drugs are more likely to be necessary to relieve pain for the dying, if only because dying can be a much more long drawn-out labour than giving birth – but nevertheless further research is needed into drugs that are strong enough to relieve terminal pain whilst enhancing alertness.

As related later in this book, Aldous Huxley sat by his wife Maria at her death, urging her with hypnotic repetition to 'go towards the light'. Perhaps many people would like an Aldous Huxley-type figure sitting by them as they go. Perhaps there could be a new profession of 'Midwives for the Dying', people skilled in holistic care of the dying patient's practical, emotional and spiritual needs (and the needs of the family), and more intent on creating a calm and supportive atmosphere than on high-tech medical interventions to prolong life to the utmost. There is a need for such skills in modern life, for as Aldous Huxley wrote: 'The living can do a great deal to make the passage easier for the dying, to raise the most purely physiological act of human existence to the level of awareness and perhaps even of spirituality.'

> *Introduction by Nicholas Albery, co-editor of*
> *'The New Natural Death Handbook'.*

As the sixties-generation Green movement people get older, so the natural death movement will inevitably become a force in health politics, bringing about a redirection of NHS and other resources towards home care and proper provision for carers. The Natural Death Centre aims to be in the vanguard of such changes. It acts as a kind of Society for Home Deaths, and works to implement its long-term plans for Midwives for the Dying, with volunteers to back up the midwife; and does whatever it can to help improve the quality of living and dying. It has founded the Befriending Network, which is now spreading from its bases in north and west London and Oxfordshire. The Befriending Network trains volunteers who visit the home where someone is critically ill, sit with the person who is dying, assist the carer and maintain contact with the carer after the death. Christianne Heal offers Living With Dying workshops for the general public on preparing for dying. Josefine Speyer, who helped develop the training pro-gramme for the Befriending Network volunteers, provides individual counsel-ling for those who are anxious or bereaved. She offers workshops for nurses, doctors and others concerned with looking after people who are dying, and workshops for the public on the theme of 'Accepting Death and Living Fully'.

At present, dying mostly happens 'off stage', as it were, in old people's homes and hospitals, and many people are superstitious enough to believe that the less they think about the subject the longer they will live. Two thirds of the UK adult population have not even taken the first step of writing a will, thus potentially leaving additional problems for their survivors. The Centre wants to make death and dying an unexceptional topic for daily meditation and conversation, and to that end has hosted a series of tea 'salons' and large dinner discussions with candlelit tables and gourmet food and wine on subjects ranging from Near-Death Experiences to care for those who are dying. It also organises a National Day of the Dead celebration for the third Sunday in April each year, inspired by the Mexican Day of the Dead festivities – a day for remembering our friends and relatives who have died and a day to contemplate our own mortality.

Once a family has looked after someone dying at home, they are more likely to want to take care of the dead body themselves too. But whatever the reason, the Centre has found itself submerged in mail from families wanting ecologically sound, inexpensive funerals, without using funeral directors. A great deal of research later, the material for the funeral chapters in this book was assembled. Chapters Four to Six cover not only on how to run a funeral without using a funeral director, at a fraction of the normal cost, but also detail who are the best professionals to approach, should you want help.

The Centre now acts as a consumers' association, available by phone or letter, giving for the first time an in-depth consumer's perspective on the whole funeral trade. It also perforce has had to campaign on behalf of the public with the National Association of Funeral Directors, the Office of Fair Trading and the Department of Trade and Industry, to try to ensure, for instance, that itemised price breakdowns on funerals are available to the public and that cardboard or regular coffins are sold to those people who want to organise a funeral themselves. The kind of changes in policy that seem necessary are outlined in the chapter 'The Politics of Dying' which also includes a Declaration of Rights for the person dying at home.

'The Natural Death Handbook' gives awards to the funeral industry – see Chapter Five for the list of Award winners.

The Natural Death Centre in 1994 launched an Association of Nature Reserve Burial Grounds, in an attempt to ensure that every locality should have its own woodland burial ground, where a tree is planted instead of having a headstone. Already, 90 such grounds are open and 50 more are at the planning stage.

The Centre is financed on a shoestring. It was launched with help from foundations such as the Gulbenkian Foundation and the Nuffield Foundation but nowadays 88% its income comes from the sale of publications. For the rest it survives thanks to members of the public who very kindly become Friends of the Natural Death Centre (£5 per month). This Handbook too requires your assistance if it is to become ever more useful in future editions – if you have a recommendation, update, correction, tip or experience you are willing to share with others, please send it in.

The purpose of this book is not only to collect together all the information that the Centre has gathered to date, but also to introduce readers to the great pioneers of the natural death movement and to the ideas in their writings. The very best books on the subject are marked ✪✪✪ in the Resources chapter; some of these have been published in the United States but deserve a wider readership in the UK. Information for ordering them is at the back of this book and, if not available through your local bookshop, most can be obtained from the publishers. The Centre's own books can be obtained by mail order or credit card from the Centre itself.

Update leaflets for this book – particularly its listings of woodland burial grounds – are available from the Centre for six first class stamps (or a £1·56 cheque). These updates and most of the Centre's books (although not the present volume) are accessible via the Centre's website (www.naturaldeath.org.uk).

What have these other writers had to say about the need for a natural death movement? Douglas Harding has emphasised our resistance to thinking about our own mortality:

The cult of youth-at-all-costs

Our current resistance to such an investigation, to any candour or realism concerning our own mortality, can scarcely be exaggerated. Witness the popular cult of youth-at-all-costs in the worlds of advertising and fashion. Witness those communities of old folk dedicated to being 'as young as you feel' and to avoiding all reminders of old age, sickness, and death. Witness the newspeak and double-talk of 'seventy years young' in place of 'seventy years old' and 'elderly person' or 'senior citizen' in place of 'old man', 'old woman'. Witness the funerary nonsense so tellingly described in Evelyn Waugh's 'The Loved One'. Witness cryonics – the freezing of the newly dead for revival when technology is further developed, thus giving effect to the view that 'death is an imposition on the human race, and no longer acceptable'. Witness the cultists who seriously maintain that death is unnecessary and unnatural, and we can choose to live as long as we wish. How unlike the veneration of old age and the preoccupation with death and the hereafter which are such marked features of some great cultures! And again, what a contrast with the *memento mori* (remember you must die) of earlier centuries of our own civilisation – its human skulls carved on tombstones and displayed on mantelpieces, its countless engravings and paintings confronting the living with the grim spectacle of Death the Reaper and the imagined sequel!

Reproduced by permission of Penguin Books Ltd from 'The Little Book of Life and Death' by D. E. Harding.
For fuller details of all main book references see the booklist in the Resources chapter.

Ivan Illich in 1975 wrote about the torments inflicted on the dying in some hospitals:

The medicalisation of society

Today, the man best protected against setting the stage for his own dying is the sick person in critical condition. Society, acting through the medical system, decides when and after what indignities and mutilations he shall die. The medicalisation of society has brought the epoch of natural death to an end.

From 'Medical Nemesis: The Expropriation of Health'
by Ivan Illich, Calder and Boyars Ltd, 1975.

The isolation of the dying and the bereaved in a centralised society that has lost almost all sense of neighbourhood has been highlighted by Tony Walter:

Neighbours no longer share the loss

Because the elderly person who has died may well not have been widely known by the friends of those left behind, the grief of the bereaved is not shared. When someone dies in Ambridge, or in an African village, or in a police unit, an entire community feels the loss: everyone knew the person and everyone to some degree mourns the loss. But when most old people in Britain die today, only a few close relatives are still in touch to feel the loss.

Nor is this true only when the deceased is elderly. In a relatively isolated nuclear family in which outsiders have played little if any role in child care, the death of a child may be a uniquely isolating experience. Contrast this account by Miller after the destruction of the primary school in Aberfan: 'One bereaved mother told me that when she lost her child the company she sought was not that of other bereaved mothers but of her neighbours. They might not have lost a child themselves, but she realised they had lost her child. It was the neighbours who had helped to bring him up, who had minded him when she went out, had watched him grow and had taken pride in his achievements. In a very real sense they shared her grief.' Usually though, friends and neighbours may be sympathetic, but they do not know the child well enough truly to share the loss. Friends in their thirties or younger may never have experienced any close bereavement.

So the bereaved today often are isolated, and may well report being treated as lepers.

From 'Modern Death: Taboo or Not Taboo?' by Tony Walter,
Sociology, Vol. 25, No. 2.

Tony Walters shares the Natural Death Centre's perception that the Green movement and the natural childbirth movement will tend to lead to the acceptance of death and dying as natural processes to be shared with our family and friends:

Natural childbirth leads to natural death

The Green movement surely must lead to a more realistic acceptance of the fact that human beings are natural creatures who must die. This movement has prompted all of us to question our technological hubris; we all know now that we are part of a delicate natural system; we are less able to split a heroic, rational soul from an inconvenient body.

This new attitude surely underlies the natural childbirth movement. Giving birth may be painful, but it is part of the natural human experience, and many women would not wish it anaesthetised away. Nor do they want to be socially isolated; they want to share this miracle of nature with their partners and their other children.

Death is also a natural part of being human, and therefore I do not wish to be drugged into oblivion: I want the pain to be controlled, but I would like to be conscious and in control as far as is possible. And I would like to share this unrepeatable and important event with my partner and my children.

From 'Funerals and How to Improve Them' by Tony Walter.

Tony Walter pointed out in a letter to the Natural Death Centre that 'natural' does not necessarily mean adopting the practices of pre-technological societies:

The diversity of non-Western, pre-modern death practices is astonishing – many segregate the dying, the Hopi have as many taboos as we do, and the ceremonies of most hunter gatherer societies are as 'thin' as are our own. Not many traditional societies see death as 'natural'.

The historian Roy Porter has shown convincingly that it was doctors in the late 18th century who introduced the idea that death is a natural event, which then eased out older notions of death as ordained by God and as a spiritual passage.

I'm inclined to agree with Arney and Bergen in 'Medicine and the Management of Living' (Chicago, UP, 1984) that it's doctors, not a consumer revolt, that first pushed the demedicalisation, ie naturalisation, of death. Would it all have happened without medics such as Kübler-Ross, Saunders, Parkes and Jolly?

There are, moreover, many kinds of natural death. It is just as much a part of nature to die abruptly or in agony, through accidents or violence or illness, as it is to die with ease and dignity. But even in such circumstances, to feel prepared for any eventuality may help. Gandhi was assassinated, but his almost automatic reaction to the bullets was to chant the name of God. He was prepared, in his own way.

As Jung appreciated:

Death as a goal in old age

Willy-nilly, the ageing person prepares himself for death. Thoughts of death pile up to an astonishing degree as the years increase. That is why I think that nature herself is always preparing for the end. Objectively it is a matter of indifference what the individual consciousness may think about it. But subjectively it makes an enormous difference whether consciousness keeps in step with the psyche or whether it clings to opinions of which the heart knows nothing. It is just as neurotic in old age not to focus upon the goal of death as it is in youth to repress fantasies which have to do with the future.

From 'The Soul and Death' by C. G. Jung in 'The Collected Works, series XX, vol. viii, translated by R. F. C. Hull, Princeton University Press, 1969.

Many people ask: Is it not morbid to think about death and dying earlier in life? No, it is necessary, for preparing for dying is half a lifetime's work. The main preparation is that which the Dalai Lama advises: 'For most of us ordinary people who lead busy lives, what is important is to develop a kind, generous heart to others. If we can do that and live accordingly, we will be able to die peacefully.' And for those who have the opportunity and the necessary circumstances, he adds, there are higher spiritual preparations available through religious and yogic practices. But above all, an awareness of death can sweeten every remaining living moment. Yeats is not the only poet to warn:

'Begin the preparation for your death'

Get all the gold and silver that you can,
Satisfy ambition, animate
The trivial days and ram them with the sun ...

But then:

No longer in Lethean foliage caught
Begin the preparation for your death
And from the fortieth winter by that thought
Test every work of intellect or faith,
And everything that your own hands have wrought,
And call those works extravagance of breath
That are not suited for such men as come
Proud, open eyed and laughing to the tomb.
            From 'Vacillation' by W. B. Yeats.

Ageing to Yeats was a growing of the soul:

An aged man is but a paltry thing,
A tattered coat upon a stick, unless
Soul clap its hands and sing, and louder sing
For every tatter in its mortal dress.
            From 'Sailing to Byzantium'.

Stephen Levine sees death as the graduation ceremony for this cocoon-abandoning soul:

Death as graduation

Death is another transformation through which we move, an adventure to surpass all adventures, an opening, an incredible moment of growth, a graduation.
            From 'Who Dies?' by Stephen Levine.

To adopt this new outlook, we have first to rid ourselves of a great deal of cultural conditioning. Paula Hendrick has surveyed the natural death movement from an American perspective and concludes that our technological mastery of nature and our focus on personal autonomy and self-development have made it very hard for us to accept the inevitability of death:

Natural dying – an American perspective

In the world of nature, death provides a service because it makes room in an ecological niche for a young one. People are part of nature, too, and when people die, they make room for more people. In a time of population explosion, it would be useful to be able to die without making too much of a fuss about it. But we humans, particularly in the affluent cultures of the first world, face the final journey of life with a load of weighty baggage. We avoid talk of death, and we dread the realities of the ageing process.

We as individuals don't necessarily create and lug around this excess baggage on our own. Something pervasive in our society moulds our collective choices. Michael Ignatieff, writing in 'The New Republic', offers this explanation: 'Cultures that live by the values of self-realisation and self-mastery are not especially good at dying, at submitting to those experiences where freedom ends and biological fate begins. Why should they be? Their strong side is Promethean ambition: the defiance and transcendence of fate, the material and social limit. Their weak side is submitting to the inevitable.'

We have become victims of the health care system that our cultural values have created. The dying process has been transformed into a series of wrenching choices. A woman, getting along pretty well after a stroke at age eighty – some confusion, but lots of independence and zest for life – develops increasing heart problems. She has no family support, just a few friends who do the best they can. The doctor recommends a pacemaker. She says no but he persuades her. There are complications during surgery. Now she's totally disorientated and can barely walk even with assistance. Her pacemaker keeps her going.

Out of the apparently needless suffering of countless people has grown a strong movement towards patients' rights and natural death – that is, death with a minimum of medical intervention. Advances are continually – albeit slowly – being made in legislation and public education. The Patient Self-Determination Act, which went into effect in the USA in 1991, requires health care facilities to inform patients of their rights to refuse treatment and to formulate advance directives such as a living will or health care proxy. Difficult moral dilemmas are also being debated on the topic of 'aid-in-dying' or physician-assisted suicide. The goals of the broader 'natural death movement' are to guarantee choice for individuals and to bring about a large-scale cultural shift. An article in The Economist of London describes such a large scale shift this way: 'To civilise death, to bring it home and make it no longer a source of dread, is one of the great challenges of the age ... Gradually, dying may come to hold again the place it used to occupy in the midst of life: not a terror but a mystery so deep that man would no more wish to cheat himself of it than to cheat himself of life.'

Excerpted from In Context magazine No. 31 (c/o Context Institute, PO Box 940, Langley, Washington 98260, USA, tel 001 360 221 6044; web: www.context.org).

Fasting to death

The Natural Death Centre gathers research on the theme of death by fasting. The Hindus who go to die in Benaras in India, for instance, consider ceasing to eat as a natural part of preparing to die – not as a form of passive euthanasia or as a way of accelerating death.

There are examples of pioneering Westerners following a similar path. 'We rarely if ever,' writes Scott Nearing's wife, 'used doctors, pills or hospitals. Yet Scott lived to a hale and hearty 100 and died when he decided to – by fasting for a month and a half at the very end.'

Scott's dying, as Helen describes it, was like nature itself:

Scott Nearing – 'death like a leaf falling from a tree'

He did more than his share of mental and physical work up to his last years. At 98 he said 'Well at least I can still split and carry in the wood.' And when he was close to the end, lying in our living room, his one regret at leaving this Earth plane was on watching me lug in the wood for our kitchen stove, 'I wish I could help with that,' he said. He was a help unto the end.

A month or two before he died he was sitting at table with us at a meal. Watching us eat he said, 'I think I won't eat anymore.' 'Alright,' said I. 'I understand. I think I would do that too. Animals know when to stop. They go off in a corner and leave off food.'

So I put Scott on juices: carrot juice, apple juice, banana juice, pineapple, grape – any kind. I kept him full of liquids as often as he was thirsty. He got weaker, of course, and he was as gaunt and thin as Gandhi. Came a day he said, 'I think I'll go on water. Nothing more.' From then on, for about ten days, he only had water. He was bed-ridden and had little strength but spoke with me daily. In the morning of August 24th, 1983, two weeks before his hundredth birthday, when it seems he was slipping away, I sat beside him on his bed.

We were quiet together; no interruptions, no doctors or hospitals. I said, 'It's alright, Scott. Go right along. You've lived a good life and are finished with things here. Go on and up – up into the light. We love you and let you go. It's alright.'

In a soft voice, with no quiver or pain or disturbance he said, 'All...right,' and breathed slower and slower and slower till there was no movement any more and he was gone out of his body as easily as a leaf drops from the tree in autumn, slowly twisting and falling to the ground.

> *Excerpted from In Context magazine No. 31 (c/o Context Institute, PO Box 940, Langley, Washington 98260, USA, tel 001 360 221 6044; web: www.context.org).*

Caroline Walker, a nutritionist dying of cancer, also decided to stop eating for the weeks before she died:

Caroline Walker – a gentle death by fasting

Caroline was exasperated rather than fascinated by her illness. We did learn a lot, though; enough to make another book. For example, when a doctor says you have cancer he (it's usually a he) will no doubt go on to say what will become of you. Our advice is take note, say thank you, shop around, and take your own decisions. After all, if a builder says you have dry rot, you do not immediately take his word for it, sign his estimate without looking at the small print, shut your eyes and resign yourself to the pickaxes. (No disrespect intended, to doctors or builders.)

There again, just as there are societies to encourage home births, there should be societies for home deaths. Being looked after at home is more trouble, of course, just as home cooking takes more time. But dying in hospital as most people do now, stuck full of tubes in white rooms, surrounded by sufferers and strangers, with those you love kept at the end of a telephone, is a sad and bad ending. Caroline thought being sent to hospital to die is like being put in a skip. (Again, no disrespect to builders or doctors.)

At home in August, Caroline finished planting our garden, with seeds and bulbs identified with little flags, so I would know what to expect the next spring and summer. She gave two interviews: one at the beginning of the month, for the Guardian, on her sense of death, as we ate lunch; the other from her bed, at the end of the month, for 'The Food Programme', on the meaning of her work.

Our home filled with family and friends and flowers. Pain was the only uncertainty. The surgeons had warned me that obstruction caused by the cancer would eventually be horribly painful. Not so; Dr Anne Naysmith, consultant at our local community hospital, a woman about Caroline's age, disagreed; and with a careful cocktail of drugs, Caroline rested at home, and took responsibility for her death, simply by stopping eating, two weeks before she died. Around midnight as her last day began, she foresaw her death. How was it – what did the thought feel like? 'Oh, lovely,' she said; and we laughed. And it was lovely to be with her when she died.

From 'The Good Fight' by Geoffrey Cannon.

That was how Caroline's husband Geoffrey Cannon saw her death. Her friend Judy Sadgrove was the Guardian interviewer:

She was resting after a long conversation in which she described what it was like to die. As she spoke, I could forget her gaunt and fleshless body. I'd known her as the campaigning nutritionist, attacking the food industry and the Government.

The ultimate irony was that Caroline was dying from cancer of the colon. Despite her emaciation, her spirit was still strong. Her campaign now was to urge us to come to terms with death in general. We are all so afraid of death, she said.

There was a phase when every time she shut her eyes, she'd see her own face, pallid, yellowish, grey, empty – already dead. She had visions a religious person might construe as significant. Towering crucifixes reared above her. But to Caroline the crosses were simply the archetypal symbol of death. 'After all, when I was young I went to church every week and gazed at crucifixes. Death in Christian society is mentioned only in association with Jesus. Were I a Muslim I would probably dream up quite another symbol.'

She derived most comfort from the regular presence of a healer, Julian Leech. 'I love seeing him. Not because I think he's going to come up with a miracle cure but because he's so relaxing to talk to. He's used to being with people who are dying and he has tremendous respect for the process, with no rejection or fear.'

'I have to live with it. Why can't other people? I know they find it difficult and disgusting, but whoever said that life was easy? Or that dying was a piece of cake? What do they want? Tinsel and gift-wrapping?' These are the people who said 'Poor you' and bought their way out with flowers. Caroline didn't feel poor. She was consumed by pain, which made her sometimes tense and fractious, but she was not poor. She did not want an Enid Blyton attitude to death. Indeed, she felt she had to be viciously blunt in imposing her death on the world. 'Dying is an alien state. You have to make the effort to communicate otherwise you are totally cut off. And you have to help others come to terms. Although I wasted much precious energy trying to prop up other people, I slowly learned who was important and who wasn't.'

Caroline has shone some light on the mystifying business of dying. She has been brave enough to expose her fear and other people's. We cling to life, avoiding thoughts of death until the very end. Surely that's too late?
From The Guardian (Sept. 7th 1988).

These stories reinforce the accumulating medical evidence that fasting and even dehydration are not necessarily such terrible ways to die. The debate on euthanasia, in Chapter 11, brings in the wider implications of death by fasting.

Near-Death Experiences

Near-Death Experiences (NDEs) are another theme on which the Natural Death Centre gathers research, believing that such experiences can often help people reconcile themselves to their mortality.

While many people who have had NDEs are totally convinced about what has happened to them and the transformations that have occurred in their lives, many sceptics are convinced that the whole phenomenon has nothing to do with life after death, or God, or infinity, but is explicable in simple mechanistic, that is, neurological terms.

Thus Dr Robert Buckman views the sense of peace and tranquillity in an NDE as being caused by substances produced in the brain called endorphins, which are somewhat like painkillers. The nineteenth century explorer, David Livingstone, felt calm, peaceful and painless whilst being crushed across the chest in a lion's jaws. It led him to believe that 'death agonies' may appear so to the onlooker, but may be experienced differently by the patient, protected by a bodily defence mechanism switched on at the approach of death.

Dr Susan Blackmore, a Bristol University psychologist, explains the common NDE vision of a long tunnel with a bright light at the end, as the retina at the back of the eye becoming starved of oxygen, with nerve cells beginning to fire at random. There are more nerve cells in the most sensitive part, the fovea, so a bright spot that looks like the end of a tunnel is seen.

Her explanation is linked to the most common physiological explanation for NDEs, which is that the brain is in receipt of insufficient oxygen (cerebral anoxia). Or that NDEs are the result of temporal lobe seizure. This can produce similar effects to those of some NDEs, without necessarily accounting for the complete range of near-death phenomena. Whereas temporal lobe seizure causes distorted perceptions of the immediate environment, this is not always the case with NDEs.

Whatever the truth of the matter, to know that nature has evolved a way of allowing dying humans to feel blissful can only be reassuring, even for the sceptic who dismisses the visions and feelings as delusionary. It is also reassuring to know that the term 'Near-Death Experience' is in some cases a misnomer – the same, or a seemingly almost identical, experience is accessed by people during 'peak' experiences, by mystics and by others who have not as yet suffered physical harm – such as those falling from a mountain or bridge, who have their NDE before even hitting the ground, when they have been no more damaged than a free-fall parachutist. The difference between the person falling from the mountain and the parachutist is one of expectation of harm and thus degree of shock; and this seems the essence of many experiences of heightened consciousness. The trigger is any severe jolt to our normal consciousness, whether or not physically damaging, which brings about a complete change of perspective and releases us into a world of rich and strange magic (although Tony Lawrence at Coventry University's School of Health and Social Sciences is compiling accounts of negative Near-Death Experiences – hellish experiences, often either of a void or of being dragged down into a pit, and sometimes involving demons).

In the end it comes down to a choice. Do you see consciousness as being contained and confined to the brain? For William James, Ferdinand Schiller and Henri Bergson, for instance, the brain was merely the transmitter of consciousness, necessary for our personal experiencing of consciousness but not its source, just as a radio set is necessary for the reception of programmes but is not their origin:

The brain a transmitter of consciousness not its source

James asked his audience what type of function the brain performed. Does it produce thought, or transmit it? Most, if not all, the major organs of the body are transmitters. The lung takes in air and transmits its nutrients to the rest of the body. There is, therefore, nothing unusual about organs that absorb and transmit; the difficulty would rather be to find an organ which, in any perfect sense, produces. The body neither manufactures the air it breathes nor the food it eats. If we do not manufacture what we eat or what we breathe, why assume that we manufacture, rather than regulate, what we think?

This transmission theory of the brain has the advantage that it solves problems, rather than creating them. The problem of the inrushes experienced in some mental illness, the problem of psychic phenomena and the problem of pure randomness in neo-Darwinism are real difficulties for the scientific world view.

This theory proposes a natural force of intelligence, which is perhaps received and transmitted by the brain, and also influences evolution in the direction of survival. That would restore purpose to nature, but it would also make possible, as James argued, the concept of human survival after death.

From an article by William Rees-Mogg
in The Independent (July 29th 1991).

An NDE account that seems to transcend a simply and solely neurological explanation is Professor Wren-Lewis's story of eating a poisoned sweet in Thailand. Among the more unusual elements in his NDE are that it is still continuing – he can switch back into it by mentally re-focusing on it at any time; that he used a dream-remembering technique – one that seems to help in recapturing the fullness of the NDE on first regaining consciousness; and lastly, that he experienced not the usual white light but rather a black darkness, albeit a radiant one. Here is his eloquent testimony:

The reluctant mystic – an NDE that didn't go away

I had spiritual consciousness thrust upon me in my sixtieth year without working for it, desiring it or even believing in it. The crucial event was a shattering, out-of-the-blue mystical experience in 1983 which, to the astonishment of everyone who knew me, and most of all myself, left me with a permanently changed consciousness, describable only in the kind of spiritual terms I had hitherto vehemently discounted as neurotic fantasy-language.

What happened in 1983 would nowadays be called a 'Near Death Experience', or NDE, though it differed in several notable ways from most of those I'd read about in the rapidly-growing literature on this topic (which I had, incidentally, dismissed as yet another manifestation of the mind's capacity for fantasy). In the first place, I had none of the dramatic visions which have hit the headlines in popular journalism and occupy a prominent place even in serious scholarly studies. As I lay in the hospital bed in Thailand after eating a poisoned sweet given me by a would-be thief, I had no 'out-of-body' awareness of the doctors wondering if I was beyond saving, no review of my life, no passage down a dark tunnel to emerge into a heavenly light or landscape, and no encounter with angelic beings or deceased relatives telling me to go back because my work on earth wasn't yet finished.

I simply entered – or, rather, was – a timeless, spaceless void which in some indescribable way was total aliveness – an almost palpable blackness that was yet somehow radiant. Trying to find words for it afterwards, I recalled the mysterious line of Henry Vaughan's poem 'The Night':

'There is in God (some say) a deep but dazzling darkness.'

An even more marked difference from the general run of NDEs, however, was that I had absolutely no sense of regret or loss at the return into physical life. I lay on the bed, relaxed, and began to take myself back in imagination, in a series of steps, right to the point of coming round. 'Here I am, lying on this bed, with someone asking if I want supper; here I am, just before that, becoming aware of someone shaking my arm; here I am, before that again, with my eyes closed, and ...' Often this process brings back the dream one has forgotten, but what came back this time was nothing like a remembered dream. What came flooding back was an experience that in some extraordinary way *had been with me ever since I came around without my realising it*. It was if I'd come out of the deepest darkness I had ever known, *which was somehow still right there behind my eyes*.

What manifested was simply not the same 'me-experiencing-the-world' that I'd known before: it was 'Everything-that-is, experiencing itself through the bodymind called John lying in a hospital bed'. And the experience was indescribably wonderful. I now know exactly why the Book of Genesis says that God looked upon *all* that He had made – not just beautiful sunsets, but dreary hospital rooms and traumatised sixty-year-old bodies - and saw that it was very good.

What I am trying to describe is no vague feeling of 'good to be alive'. On the contrary, I no longer cared if John lived or ceased to be altogether, and the change of consciousness was so palpable that to begin with I repeatedly put my hand up to the back of my head, feeling exactly as if the doctors had removed the skull and exposed my brain somehow to the infinite blackness of space. Occasionally I still do so, for *the new consciousness has remained with me ever since* – which is the third and most significant difference from what happens in the general run of NDEs, and also from the 'altered states' experienced with psychedelics.

There is in no sense a high from which I can come down. The sense of awe-ful wonder has at the same time a feeling of utter obviousness and ordinariness, as if the marvel of 'everything-coming-into-being-continu-ously-from-the-Great-Dark' were no more and no less than 'just the way things are'. From this perspective, the term *altered* state of consciousness would be a complete misnomer, for the state is one of simple normality.

It seems, rather, as if my earlier state, so-called 'ordinary' human consciousness, represents the real alteration – a deviation from the plain norm, a kind of artificially blinkered or clouded condition wherein the bodymind has the absurd illusion that it is somehow a separate individual entity over against everything else.

In fact I now understand why mystics of all religions have likened the enlightenment-process to waking up from a dream.

As I was walking in the hot sun to the police station to report the poisoned sweet crime I was struck by the sense of loss that the Dark was missing, and my first thought then was: 'Ah, well, you've had the Vision – I suppose now you'll have to join the ranks of all those Seekers who spend their lives trying to attain Higher Consciousness.' And then, to my amazement, I suddenly saw *it was all still there, just waiting, as it were, to be noticed* – the Dark behind my eyes and behind everything else, bringing again the perception that *of course* everything exists by emerging fresh-minted from the Dark now! and now! and now!, with a shout of joy yet also in absolute calm.

The NDE had evidently jerked me out of the so-called normal human state of chronic illusion-of-separateness, into a basic 'wakefulness', interrupted by spells of 'dozing off' – simply forgetting the Dark until the sense of something missing from life brings about instant reawakening with no effort at all.

The key feature of God-consciousness as I know it from my own first-hand experience, is its quintessential ordinariness and obviousness – a feature actually emphasized by many mystics. I know from my own first-hand experience that God-consciousness doesn't abolish human appetites. When I'm in it I don't lose my taste for meat or wine or good company or humour or detective fiction – I actually enjoy them more than ever before. I don't cease to enjoy sexual feelings, nor do I see anything inherently dirty about money.

What the consciousness does bring is the cheerful equanimity of knowing that satisfaction doesn't depend on any of these special preferences of John's bodymind being met; it is inherent simply in being, in the Great Dark which is (in G.K. Chesterton's marvellous phrase) 'joy without a cause'.

Prof. John Wren-Lewis, 1/22 Cliffbrook Parade, Clovelly, NSW 2031, Australia. He has prepared a book for publication on this theme, entitled 'The 9.15 to Nirvana'.

Pagan return to nature

A final thread running through this book is an almost pagan wish to return to the world of nature. This is sometimes expressed by those who are dying as a preference for being outdoors or to be surrounded by plants and flowers. In the following instance, it concerns a 15 year old girl's dying wish to swim with dolphins.

Lee – 'dolphin therapy' for a dying 15 year old

'It's not easy to die when you are 15, but Lee had already accepted her fate,' said Robert. As he spoke, his eyes were full of tears and he could barely keep his voice steady. 'She knew she had an illness that would not spare her. She knew that in spite of their finest efforts the doctors couldn't save her. She suffered a lot but never complained. This particular evening she seemed tranquil and composed but suddenly she said, "Mama, daddy – I think I'm going to die soon and I'm afraid. I know I'm going to a better world than this one and I'm longing for some peace at last but it's hard to accept the idea that I'm going to die at only fifteen."

'We could have lied, telling her of course she wasn't going to die, but we didn't have the heart. Somehow her courage was worth more than our pretence. We just cuddled her and cried together. Then she said, "I always dreamed of falling in love, getting married, having kids ... but above all I would have liked to work in a big marine park with dolphins. I've loved them and wanted to know more about them since I was little. I still dream of swimming with them free and happy in the open sea." She'd never asked for anything, but now she said with all the strength she could muster, "Daddy, I want to swim in the open sea among the dolphins just once. Maybe then I wouldn't be so scared of dying."

'My wife and I talked it over and decided to do everything we could. We had heard of a research centre in the Florida Keys and we phoned them. "Come at once," they said. But that was easier said than done. Lee's illness had used up all our savings and we had no idea how we would be able to afford air tickets to Florida. Then our six year old, Emily, mentioned that she'd seen something on television about a foundation that grants the wishes of very sick children. So I phoned the number and three days later we were all on our way.

'When we arrived at Grass Key, Lee was pale and terribly thin. The chemotherapy she'd been having had made all her hair fall out and she looked ghastly, but she didn't want to rest for a minute and begged us to take her straight away to the dolphins. It was an unforgettable scene. When she got into the water, Lee was already so weak she hardly had the strength to move. We had all put her in a wet suit so she wouldn't get cold, with a life preserver to keep her afloat.

'I towed her out toward the two dolphins, Nat and Tursi, who were frolicking around about thirty feet away from us. At first they seemed distracted and uninterested but when Lee called them softly by name they responded without hesitation. Nat came over first, raised his head and gave her a kiss on the end of her nose. Then Tursi came over and greeted her with a flurry of little high-pitched squeaks of joy. A second later they picked her up with their mighty fins and carried her out to sea with them.

"It feels like flying!" cried Lee, laughing with delight. I hadn't heard her laugh like that since before she became ill. I could hardly believe it was true, but there she was gripping Nat's fin and challenging the wind and the immensity of the ocean. The dolphins stayed with Lee for more than an hour, always tender, always attentive, never using any unnecessary force, always responsive to her wishes.

'There are no words to describe the effect that swim had on her. When she got out of the water it was as if she had been reborn.

'The next day she was too weak to get out of bed. She didn't even want to talk, but when I took her hand she squeezed it and whispered, "Daddy, don't be sad for me. I'll never be afraid again. The dolphins have made me understand that I have nothing to fear." Then she said, "I know I'm going to die tonight. Promise me that you'll cremate my body and scatter my ashes in the sea where the dolphins swim. They have left me with a great feeling of peace in my heart and I know they will be with me on the long journey that lies ahead." Just before dawn she woke and said, "Hold me, daddy, I'm so cold." And she died like that in my arms a few minutes later – passing from sleep to death without a ripple. I only realised her suffering was over because her body became colder and heavier.

'We cremated her as she wanted and went out the next day to scatter her ashes in the ocean amongst the dolphins. We were all crying, I'm not ashamed to say; not just my wife and I and our three other children, but even the sailors on the boat that had taken us out into the bay. Suddenly, through our tears, we saw the great arching silver shapes of Nat and Tursi leaping out of the water ahead of us. They had come to take our daughter home.'

From 'Acquainted with the Night' by Allegra Taylor.
Note: In the UK, the Starlight Foundation (see the Resources chapter) attempts to grant the wishes of critically ill children.

May this present Handbook on improving the quality of all aspects of dying prove a useful contribution to the contemplation of this magnificent and awe-inspiring subject. Above all, may it allow people to 'die in character' as Elisabeth Kübler-Ross puts it. Dr Buckman in his book on how to support a dying person is rightly adamant on this point:

It should be your objective as friend and supporter – as it is my objective when I'm looking after dying patients – to help your friend let go of life *in his own way*. It may not be your way, and it may not be the way you read about in a book or magazine, but it's his way and consistent with the way he's lived his life. You can and should help your friend achieve that.

From 'I Don't Know What To Say – How to Help and Support Someone who is Dying' by Dr Robert Buckman.

Chapter 2

PREPARING
FOR DYING

I am quite terrified of death. Not of dying, but of death itself.

I am a fit pensioner, in my seventies, and for about the last four years I have tried to get people to talk about the subject, with little success. It is very much a taboo subject.

I have spoken to many clergy and they seem uncomfortable about the subject, or else trot out the accepted teaching about the Resurrection. I am familiar with that as I have been a churchgoer all my life. My head accepts the doctrine but my heart is frightened.

There is much bereavement counselling but nothing to prepare one for death.

I am quite terrified and this fear spoils and destroys the quality of my life.

From a letter to The Natural Death Centre.

How can we ever be prepared, either for our own death or the deaths of those around us? How can we 'prepare'?

At first the idea may seem futile, or morbid. Yet most of us find ourselves responsible, at some stage in our lives, for meeting the needs of a dying friend, spouse or relative, and having to learn our way through the difficult process of helping someone who is dying. A wealth of revelations accompany this process, but, more often than not, time, practical considerations and our inability to come to terms with what is happening conspire to leave many things unfinished or unsaid. The same goes for our own death.

How do we want to be cared for? What will be our legacy to our loved ones? Will we have time to find out what needs to be done and then do it? And to what extent are our attitudes towards death and our anxiety about death affecting the quality of our lives now?

As a society we are not geared towards handling death as humanely as we could. The letter above expresses the fundamental problem: we don't want to deal with it until it is inevitable or has already happened. Talking about death, even thinking about it, does not come naturally to many of us. Our fear of death seems to prevent us from coping with it. Indeed, as another letter received by the Natural Death Centre points out:

Fear of living

What has struck me about the majority of people's attitudes towards death is not so much the fear of dying, as an all-consuming fear of actually living.

It seems to me that people are not only afraid of life but also have tremendous difficulty accepting the concept of free choice. Why else would we struggle year after year to maintain dead relationships and unfulfilling jobs?

I was trained as a nurse twenty years ago and my initiation into the dying process at the age of eighteen with little to no experience of death was being told that I was never to mention the subject even if the patient asked, nor was I to speak about it to any relative no matter what the situation. I witnessed some appalling deaths. We were allowed to lay their bodies out, but we were not allowed to talk about it.

From a letter to The Natural Death Centre.

It is important to break the silence: we need to find ways to communicate and share thoughts, feelings and experience. Becoming more aware of the process of dying, and of the demands it makes on us and others, is a practical and valuable undertaking.

This chapter looks at ways of 'training' for dying. We begin with ways of acknowledging the reality of death, and overcoming our fears; and move on to practical considerations of making a will and making our wishes known.

Courses and workshops

A growing number of educational resources exists nowadays for taking care of the practical as well as the philosophical aspects of dying. In the UK three university courses have been launched – at the Open University, the University of Wales at Lampeter and the University of Reading (see Resources chapter for addresses). Here is an extract from the Open University's course information:

The Open University – Death and Dying

In 1990, the Minister of Health made a grant of £484,000 to help create an Open University course on Death and Dying. Very few of the more than one million care workers in Britain, or the many family carers and volunteers, receive any serious education or training for working with dying or bereaved people. Existing courses, however good, reach only a handful of carers each year. At the same time, there is a rising awareness that the process of dying could be made more humane if lessons learned in recent years were shared with carers in hospital and community settings.

The studentship is drawn from those who have regular, extensive contact with dying and bereaved people. Some carers and dying people themselves study the course.

Students will look at how people have in the past dealt with dying, death and bereavement and the issues involved in making legal, ethical and practical decisions. They will study pain relief and other symptoms common in the dying process. Practice-related material will help students to understand the physical and emotional needs of people who are dying or bereaved and how to support them in a multi-cultural society.

While the OU concentrates upon practical considerations for carers, the one-year MA in 'Death and Immortality' at the University of Wales (Lampeter) is philosophical in content:

Death and Immortality Course

All the students at Lampeter take a core course examining the philosophical arguments for and against a future life. Optional modules include Near-Death Experiences' philosophy and reincarnation; death in western popular culture; ending lives; and souls and death.

The one year Reading University course focuses on the social aspects:

MA in Death and Society

A multi-disciplinary postgraduate course that explores how societies – past and present – organise, theorise, symbolise and ritualise the death of their members. There is a compulsory course module on the social context of death, dying and mourning. Optional modules include the modern way of death; medical ethics; and the anthropology of death.

In the future it may well be that going on a course about preparations for dying will become as normal as learning first aid. The Natural Death Centre, as previously mentioned, offers workshops for the general public entitled 'Living with Dying' run by Christianne Heal, and workshops for nurses and others entitled 'Accepting Death and Living Fully' run by Josefine Speyer (for details, please send an SAE to The Natural Death Centre). On the whole death is not an easy or welcome subject for general, informal conversation, and so a setting in which death is discussed and explored is a welcome opportunity, as Christianne Heal explains:

Living with Dying

Death is a crisis, but some view it as a crisis with a point to it. We complete exercises in the workshops that enable people to work out at what stage in the process towards death they are, and how they can feel more comfortable about it. It is the airing of the subject that is important to a lot of people: just being able to talk about it. Participants get a great deal out of it. Some simply want the opportunity to discuss their fears, worries and concerns without someone cutting them off because it is a difficult subject. Some people come because they are dying, others because they have been or are nursing someone who is dying and they don't know how to handle the issue, and others because they are old and near their own death experience. I even had a boy of thirteen come whose father had died before he was born. He needed to talk about this and we gave him the opportunity. I was surprised at just how positive the workshop was for him.

Christianne Heal, interviewed in Counselling News (Sept. 1991).

Linda and Martin, who attended Christianne's workshops, each describe the experience:

Christianne Heal created a safe atmosphere with her sensitive and grounded approach. We first examined our childhood beliefs and experiences of death, and then we sat in pairs, with eyes shut and we took it in turns to be each other's death. 'Hello Ruth, I am your death. I am like the dark side of the moon; you can't see me but you know I'm there. I have known you all your life and now it is time for you to know me, do not be scared, I am nothing to fear.' To hear my death speak was uncanny and this effect is heightened because in the silence you hear all the other deaths in the room quietly talking to their partners. I was amazed how the universality of death drew us closer as a group; we listened, and supported each other.

Linda

Christianne asked us to draw a 'map' and to mark around us all the people who are important to us, living or dead. Then we worked in pairs, one partner listened, while the other had half an hour to say goodbye to all the people he or she had placed on the map. I found this very painful, I think everyone did. It is also beautiful to listen to your partner talking to their friends and family in such a loving and powerful way, expressing the very core of their feelings. Where else would we get the space to say these things to our loved ones, especially those who have died? Funerals only serve this function up to a point, and not at all when it comes to expressing the anger which often accompanies bereavement.

We danced a 'dance of death' to beautiful music with our eyes shut, improvising, imagining death, gently moving amongst each other. We painted death, fascinated by how different all the pictures were – some people started by drawing only black, but then realised that there had to be colour and light there too.

There was an exercise on 'what you would do if you only had six months to live'. Try it some time, take it seriously and you may be surprised at what you reveal to yourself.

We had the opportunity to write our own obituary and were given the freedom to fantasise about the life for which we would like to be remembered.

The difference in people's aspirations was quite lovely: from one person who had built his own chicken shed to another whose assassination at a political rally precipitated world revolution.

At the end one person said: 'I've never laughed so much in a weekend.'

Martin

The Fruits of Life Project

The Fruits of Life Project is an initiative based on prizewinning work conducted by Jozef van der Put, of PRISMA (see the Resources chapter), a Dutch organisation that trains groups of volunteers who then work with individuals.

The project targets people who are experiencing difficulty in accepting and coming to terms with old age and dying. The project's approach is to use personal biography and life history to review the major life events of each individual. The aim is to resolve conflicts or other unfinished business and to gather in 'a harvest of the fruits of each life'.

Where appropriate, a volunteer helps the individual to compile a life story which can be shared with those relatives and friends left behind. For instance, the volunteer may ask the person to write a brief description of a dozen important 'stepping stones' in his or her life, events or decisions that significantly influenced the way the person's life developed; and then to discuss these.

Anxiety about dying

Anxiety about dying can be experienced by people at any age. The Natural Death Centre has designed the scale below to help you to find out how likely you are to be anxious about death and dying when the time comes, if you were to remain as you are at present, and to help you to identify those specific high-scoring, high-anxiety areas that could suggest a focus for 'personal development' or other changes in your approach or lifestyle. There is no need to fake your scoring. There is no one to fool but yourself.

Death-Related Anxiety Scale

Give marks out of 4 to each of the following statements:
Not true at all = 0 / Mainly not true = 1 / Not sure = 2 /
Somewhat true = 3 / Very true = 4

☐ I tend not to be very brave in crisis situations

☐ I am an unusually anxious person

☐ I am something of a hypochondriac and am perhaps obsessively worried about infections

☐ I have never had a semi-mystical, spiritual, out-of-the-body, near-death or peak experience

☐ I tend to be unusually frightened in planes at take off and landing

☐ I do not have a particular religion or philosophy that helps me to face dying

☐ I do not believe in any form of survival of the soul after death

☐ Personally I would give a lot to be immortal in this body

☐ I am very much a city person and not really close to nature

☐ Anxiety about death spoils the quality of my life

- [ ] I am superstitious that preparing for dying might hasten my death
- [ ] I don't like the way some of my relatives died and fear that my death could be like theirs
- [ ] My actual experience of friends dying has been undilutedly negative
- [ ] I would feel easier being with a dying relative if they were not told they were dying
- [ ] I have fears of dying alone without friends around me
- [ ] I have fears of dying slowly
- [ ] I have fears of dying suddenly
- [ ] I have fears of dying before my time or whilst my children are still young
- [ ] I have fears of dying before fulfilling my potential and fully using my talents
- [ ] I have fears of dying without adequately having expressed my love to those I am close to
- [ ] I have fears of dying before having really experienced much 'joie de vivre'
- [ ] I have fears of what may or may not happen after death
- [ ] I have fears of what could happen to my family after my death
- [ ] I have fears of dying in hospital or an institution
- [ ] I have fears of those caring for me feeling overwhelmed by the strain of it
- [ ] I have fears of not getting help with euthanasia when the time comes
- [ ] I have fears of being given unofficial and unwanted euthanasia
- [ ] I have fears of getting insufficient pain control whilst dying
- [ ] I have fears of being over-medicalised and unconscious whilst dying
- [ ] I have fears of being declared dead when not really dead or being buried alive
- [ ] I have fears of getting confused near death or not being able to follow my spiritual practices
- [ ] I have fears of what may happen to my body after death
- [ ] I have fears of mental degeneration near death

☐   Overall I would say that I am unusually anxious about death and
dying

☐   TOTAL

The extremely anxious (scoring over 65 or so) might consider the need for
counselling or therapy; the unusually anxious (scoring over 40) might want to
find a method of meditation, self-hypnotic autogenic training, chant, dance, co-
counselling relationship, therapy workshop, philosophy, spiritual practice or
similar that could help them to experience, explore and accept their feelings; the
averagely anxious (scoring under 40) don't have to be too smug – in certain
respects anxiety can correlate with intelligence; and once the shaman's advice
to 'make friends with one's fear' has been absorbed, anxiety is free to transform
into energy and ecstasy – perhaps there is a Zen Art of Being Anxious, just as
there seems to be a Zen Art of everything else, from archery to flower arranging.

For the record, Nicholas Albery, one of the co-editors of this book, scored an
anxiety rating of 45 – 'no doubt a need to face my anxiety on the subject is what
attracted me to it in the first place,' he says.

The scale is perhaps more interesting for the questions it poses than for the
number it produces. Most of us will recognise that it is possible to be 'overanx-
ious' about death, to the extent that it lessens our enjoyment of life; and indeed
the possibility that we are so anxious about death that we deny any anxiety at all.
It is to be hoped that people who do take the test do not become anxious about
their anxiety rating!

Some people find that their anxiety about death becomes manageable in
unexpected ways, as in these examples:

Da Free John

A contemporary American spiritual teacher Da Free John, reports in his
autobiography, 'The Knee of Listening', how he overcame the fear of death
by 'dying'. When his fear of death became almost overwhelming, he
discovered the ancient wisdom of giving in (which is quite different from
giving up) and cooperating with the process, flowing with the pressure,
letting 'death' take its full and natural course. Here's what happened:

'I was lying home alone in the afternoon. It was as if all my life had
constantly prevented this experience from going to its end. All my life I had
been preventing my death.

'I lay on the floor, totally disarmed, unable to make a gesture that could
prevent the rising fear. And thus it grew in me, but, for the first time, I
allowed it to happen. I could not prevent it. The fear and the death rose and
became my overwhelming experience. And I witnessed the crisis of that
fear in a moment of conscious, voluntary death. I allowed the death to
happen, and I saw it happen.

'When the moment of crisis passed I felt a marvellous relief. The death had occurred, but I had observed it! I remained untouched by it. The body and the mind and the personality had died, but I remained as an essential and unqualified consciousness ... There was just an infinite bliss of being.'

Da Free John quoted in 'Practical Guide to Death and Dying' by John White.

Birth, love, courage and death

It was getting pregnant with my first child ten years ago that started a process within me that revolted against the 'normal', expected, over-medicalised hospital birth. So I set about finding an alternative and by following my instinct (with some determination) I was able to have my first child at home. The experiences of that birth, and the following ones, brought me closer to death than I have ever been – and were comforting for that. I felt I was part of a process that was greater than me and that although it was terrifying in its unknown expectations, it responded to love and courage! I was acutely aware that I would have been unable to function had I not been given the quality of emotional support that I was given. And I thought that if I could die in the same way, I could accept it without too much fear.

I have been afraid of death since I was a very young child and I think the two things that have helped me are giving birth and being in therapy. I hope one day I will be able to welcome death without fear and I fiercely believe that people should die at home if they can and that we should all be able to talk about it.

From a letter by Jehane Markham to The Natural Death Centre.

Death without fear or pain

In our family there has been a strong taboo, or kind of a 'hush' on death as a subject even for mention, and we have had no education or experience. Deaths have occurred but somehow I have always been protected or just not there (when young) and now as an adult I'm all at sea about it.

When our son was on the way, I learned about 'birthing' (the theory) and went to relaxation classes. When he was born I had no fear, hardly any pain (merely discomfort) and he came along almost in record time. I wonder: if we could feel the same way about our deaths, mightn't it help the person involved and everyone else concerned? Perhaps the baby born to an unafraid and relaxed mother might feel better about being born than if the mother is all tense and hurting. Things may go a bit wrong afterwards, but at least she or he has had a fair start. The same could apply to dying.

From a letter to The Natural Death Centre.

The parallels between dying and giving birth are very strong. As Anya Foos-Graber in her book 'Deathing' urges us: 'Look at death's counterpart – fertilization, pregnancy and birth! Not knowing about the 'birds and the bees' doesn't ward off pregnancy! Knowing the process, whether of birth or death, means you can positively utilise it.'

Rehearsal for death

'Philosophy is a rehearsal for death,' says Plato. There is no reason why our everyday activities should not include such rehearsals. Alexander the Great's father, Philip of Macedonia, one of the most powerful men of his time, gave to one of his retinue a single, simple duty: regardless of how much the King protested, raged or grew violent, the man's only task was to approach him every day and say: 'Philip of Macedonia, thou too shall die.' This was a highly dangerous job, as the king often did rage and grow violent; yet he continued to keep the man in his employ. Fortunately for us there are less expensive (and safer) ways of rehearsing.

One stimulating way is to write your own obituary – use a formal newspaper style if you wish, or imagine that you know you are to die within days and complete as many of the following sentences as you find suitably provocative:

D-i-y obituary

• Outside observers would probably say that my main achievements have been ...

• For myself, what I am most pleased with and proud of in my life are ...

• One of the most important lessons that I have learnt during my lifetime is that ...

• During my life I have used my ... [list three positive personal characteristics, for example: imagination, sense of humour and intelligence] through my ... [list three activities, for example: writing, running groups and parenting] with the underlying vision, I now realise, of helping work towards a world in which, one day, ... [describe your long-term Utopia, for example: 'people are kind and sensitive to each other, nature is at ease and magic is alive'].

• The people I have felt closest to in my life have been ...

• One generalisation I could make about the quality of my relationships with others is that ...

• If I regret anything, it is that ...

• If I had known how short a time I had left to live, I would probably have ...

The purpose of this obituary, besides that of evaluating your achievements and failures, is to flush out whether a more acute awareness of your own mortality would lead you to want to make changes in your life, in case you might wish to make them now, rather than being filled with regrets on your deathbed.

Another way of preparing for death is through meditation. Many meditations on dying are to be found in Tibetan traditions, some charming ones as in the first passage below by Stephen Levine, inspired by 'The Tibetan Book of the Dead', and some at least superficially rather gruesome ones, as in the second extract below:

Shining true being

Imagine that your body no longer has the strength, the energy, to maintain its connection with the life-force, with the body of awareness within. And imagine now that you are beginning to experience the process of dissolving out of that body. Sensations from the body no longer so distinct, melting away, leaving just a spaciousness. Dissolving out of the body. Leaving that heavier form behind. Dissolving into consciousness itself.

My friend, listen now, for that which is called death has arrived. So let go gently, gently, of all that holds you back. Of all that pulls you away from this most precious moment. Know that now you have arrived at the transition called death. Open to it. Let go into it.

Recognise the changing experience of the mind as it separates from the body, dissolving.

Dissolving now into the realms of pure light. Your true nature shining everywhere before you.

My friend, maintain an open-heartedness, a spaciousness of being that does not grasp. Let things be as they are without the least attempt to interfere. Grasping at nothing.

Enter the essential nature of your own being shining there before you, a great luminosity. Rest in being. Knowing it for what it is. This light shining, luminous. Your true self.

Let go, gently, gently, without the least force. Before you shines your true being. It is without birth, without death.

Let go of all which distracts or confuses the mind, all that created density in life.

Go gently into it. Do not be frightened or bewildered. Do not pull back in fear from the immensity of your true being. Now is a moment for liberation.

Know that you are well guided by your compassion and love. You are the essence of all things. You are the light.

From 'Who Dies?' by Stephen Levine.

Visualising death

There are both external and internal ways of practice. An external technique is to dwell in a charnel ground and observe the stages of decomposition of the corpses in it, while keeping the mind fixed on the thought that these corpses represent the final destiny of one's own body.

An internal means is to visualise oneself as lying on one's deathbed awaiting the approach of death. Visualise that your parents, relatives and friends surround you, lamenting and upset. The radiance of your countenance has faded and your nostrils have sunk back. Your lips dry, slime begins to form on your teeth and all grace leaves your body. Bodily temperature drops, breathing becomes heavy, and you begin to exhale more deeply than you inhale. All the negative karmas [actions] generated during your life arise within your mind and you become filled with regret. You look to all sides for help, but help does not come.

From 'Tibetan Traditions of Death Meditation'
by Ge-she Nga-wang Dar-gye.

Allegra Taylor describes the way her wishes became clear and focused through participation in a group exercise:

The death bed imagined

... An impromptu drama in which we took it in turns to play the different characters in a deathbed scene: the distraught relative; the voluntary worker; the withdrawn child; the dying person.

As I lay there, my eyes closed, trying to visualise everything I love receding from me, I knew without a shadow of a doubt that what I most wanted was to be treated as I always had been, as me. I felt a need to finish relationships and say my goodbyes calmly. I saw myself as weak and frail but with a last great longing to pass on something of value. I wanted someone to put a baby in my arms for me to hold. A last connection with life – a symbol of love and renewal.

From my family I wanted only closeness, an easy honesty and assurances that they would be all right. From visitors I wanted to know that they would provide a support network for the family after my death. I did not want anyone to take heroic measures to save me or to save my soul. Anyone who spoke to me of spiritual things needed to be supportive of my own beliefs and not a representative of alien ones.

I did rather feel that it was my show, and that the most loving last thing people could do for me would be to set aside their own needs and help me have the kind of death I wanted.

From 'Acquainted with the Night' by Allegra Taylor.

It is through these rehearsals, these meditations, that we begin to develop our own understanding of death, beyond our received ideas. Our anxieties about social status and material possessions seem no longer as important, perhaps we even find death taking on new meanings for us. Relating realistically to impermanence is the essence of both the spiritual life and of living fully. The key point about death is that time runs out – there are no more chances to get it right. As Caroline Sherwood puts it: 'If I live my life "finishing business" by keeping myself up to date and clear in my relationships, living from the deepest truth of myself, working to dissolve the barriers to love in my life – how much more easy my death might be.'

Life is precious for the already-dead

Once someone asked a well-known Thai meditation master: 'In this world where everything changes, where nothing remains the same, where loss and grief are inherent in our very coming into existence, how can there be any happiness?' The teacher, looking compassionately at this fellow, held up a drinking glass which had been given to him earlier in the morning and said, 'You see this goblet? For me, the glass is already broken. I enjoy it, I drink out of it. It holds my water admirably, sometimes even reflecting the sun in beautiful patterns. If I should tap it, it has a lovely ring to it. But when I put this glass on a shelf, and the wind knocks it over or my elbow brushes it off the table and it falls to the ground and shatters, I say, "Of course." But when I understand that this glass is already broken, every moment with it is precious. Every moment is just as it is and nothing need be otherwise.'

When we recognise that, just as that glass, our body is already broken, that indeed we are already dead, then life becomes precious and we open to it just as it is, in the moment it is occurring. When we understand that all our loved ones are already dead – our children, our mates, our friends – how precious they become. How little fear can interpose, how little doubt can estrange us. When you live your life as though you're already dead, life takes on a new meaning. Each moment becomes a whole lifetime, a universe unto itself.

From 'Who Dies?' by Stephen Levine.

Death in Mexico

Most of us Westerners are to an extent estranged from death. By contrast, the Nobel prizewinning writer Octavio Paz explains the Mexican attitude towards death:

Death as a favourite plaything

To the Modern Mexican death doesn't have any meaning. It has ceased to be the transition, the access to the other life which is more authentic than this one. But the unimportance of death has not taken it away from us and eliminated it from our daily lives. To the inhabitant of New York, Paris or London, death is a word that is never uttered because it burns the lips. The Mexican, on the other hand, frequents it, mocks it, caresses it, sleeps with it, entertains it; it is one of his favourite playthings and his most enduring love. It is true that in his attitude there is perhaps the same fear that others also have, but at least he does not hide this fear nor does he hide death; he contemplates her face-to-face with impatience, with contempt, with irony: 'If they're going to kill me tomorrow, let them kill me for once and for all.'

From 'The Labyrinth of Solitude' by Octavio Paz, Penguin, 1985.

Many of the exercises we have seen have been concerned with individual introspection. In the Natural Death Centre's workshops and group exercises there is an added dimension of shared experience. Taking this one step further, the London-based City Dying Group organised candlelit vigils in cemeteries. Each of the participants brought a candle, which they lit one by one, saying goodbye to somebody (or something). The group also organised picnics in cemeteries. Strange as this may seem, it is not unlike the Mexican festival called

'El Dia de los Muertes' (The Day of the Dead) when Mexicans celebrate the memory of lost loved ones with cemetery vigils, dancing and riotous parades, in the (loosely-held) belief that their loved ones return in spirit to join in. Mexico is like most of the world, in that infant mortality and adult illness are much more common than they are here. Death is more a part of life, and perhaps because of this, Mexicans treat it with a healthy mixture of respect and irreverence.

The Mexican Day of the Dead

That a festival to do with the dead should be a joyous occasion perhaps strikes those of us from other cultures with our different perceptions as something hard to come to terms with. The Day of the Dead is just that: a festival of welcome for the souls of the dead which the living prepare and delight in. The souls return each year to enjoy for a few brief hours the pleasures they once knew in life.

In the urban setting of Mexico City and other large towns the celebration is seen at its most exuberant, with figures of skulls and skeletons everywhere. These mimic the living and disport themselves in a mocking modern dance of death. It is not surprising that so colourful an event should have become a tourist event.

Not far away from the tourist routes there is, however, another Mexico. In the rural areas, in every village or small town, the Day of the Dead is celebrated beyond the glare of flashbulbs. Each household prepares its offering of food and drink for the dead to be set out on a table among flowers and candles. The blue smoke of burning copal incense sanctifies the ceremony, just as it has done for centuries. Outside the peace is shattered by the explosions of the rockets set off to mark the fulfilment of an obligation deeply felt. The whole company of the living and the dead share in the flowering and fruiting of the land which both have cultivated.

The Day of the Dead is essentially a private or family feast. It has a public aspect at community level, but the core of the celebration takes place within the family home. It is a time of family reunion not only for the living but also the dead, who, for a few brief hours each year, return to be with their relatives in this world.

From 'The Skeleton At The Feast' by Elizabeth Carmichael and Chloë Sayer, British Museum Press (46 Bloomsbury St, London WC1B 3QQ), 1991, ISBN 0 7141 2503 2, £12-95.

The Day of the Dead is celebrated on October 31st, the eve of All Saints' Day, on which day the same custom of visiting the dead in their last resting places used to be common throughout Christendom, and is still widely observed, in France for example. These practices enable us to commemorate and celebrate our loved ones, and keep our own sense of death in perspective, by giving death and the dead a time as well as a place.

The Natural Death Centre has inaugurated a smaller-scale (UK) National Day of the Dead, for the third Sunday in April of each year. Make contact with the

Centre for the details, or if you have a suitable event to suggest. Each year has different themes and events, which have included: a festival and exhibition; death-related poetry, music and art; a coffin-making workshop; a lunchtime debate on euthanasia; an evening dinner discussion on Near-Death Experiences; an open day at woodland burial grounds around the country; and video workshops where people could prepare their own video messages for their descendants.

Making your will

For those in good health there is one obvious and sensible preparation for death. Make a will! Some of us avoid doing this because it is an admission that we are going to die. For that reason alone it is a valuable spiritual exercise, as well as a highly practical and normalising procedure. Maybe we are not entirely comfortable with our death, maybe we have not fully joined the human race, until we have got hold of that document, filled it in, signed it and have got it witnessed.

In fact, as the Law Society has been campaigning to remind us, only about one in three adults in Britain has a will. This may not matter so much for single people without children, but it can lead to unnecessary financial hardship for many families. If you die without a will ('intestate'), the intestacy rules dictate who receives your estate (the total of your house and its contents, car, various insurance policies and savings accounts may well come to more than you realise). The rules will also decide who should manage the affairs of your estate. It is important to realise that unmarried partners may have no claim on the estate (unless dependant, but this could be expensive to establish; the Law Commission is currently being asked to recommend that cohabiting couples, gay couples included, should have the same succession rights as those who are married). Even a legal wife or husband may have to sell the home to pay the other automatic beneficiaries. Of particular importance in the case of divorced or separated parents, the rules will determine who the legal guardians of your children will be; with a will you can name the person you would like to act as your children's guardian.

The standard way to get a will drawn up is to consult a solicitor (this would be likely to cost from about £50). It is worth familiarising yourself with the procedure before you visit a solicitor as this could save you time, money and possible confusion. There are six simple steps to take before you make a will:

(1) Before you see your solicitor, list all the items you have to leave – house and contents, car, savings accounts, etc, and their rough value.

(2) Consider who you would like to provide for and in what way. (Write down the full names, including middle names, and the addresses of all such people and the dates of birth of all children to be named in the will.)

(3) Consider whether you would like to leave money or property 'in trust' for children or grandchildren until they are grown up and at what age you think they should inherit your gift.

(4) Decide who you would like to receive your sentimental belongings.

These may be of little financial value but you can pass them on to someone you know who will appreciate them.

(5) Consider whether you would like to leave some money to charity (bequests to charities are not liable to inheritance tax).

(6) Choose one or more executors to 'wind up your affairs'. The executors can be spouses or members of the family or friends, although it is as well to get their agreement in advance. If, in the event, they find the task too onerous, as they well may, they can always ask a solicitor to take over.

Adapted from 'The Granada Action Factsheet,
Death: A Practical Guide'.

As a postscript to the above, if you must appoint a professional executor, choose a (cheap and specialist) solicitor rather than a bank, as the latter tends to charge far more. Find a solicitor prepared to forego the standard 'charging clause' in the will – replace this with a statement as to the maximum amount of money chargeable to the beneficiaries for the administration of the estate. Bear in mind that the solicitor will not be under any obligation to take on the task of being the executor when the time comes.

Here is an example of a will for a married man with two children who is concerned to minimise long-term liability to inheritance tax, and with several other unusual features (check their relevance to you with your legal adviser!):

Will for a married man with two children

WILL of Donald Roland Winterton of 26 Oxford Gardens, London W10, made this fourteenth day of April 2000.

1. I revoke all previous Wills and Codicils made by me. I appoint as my executors my brother Arthur Winterton of 48 Book Lane, London N8 (tel 020 8286 2194) and my sister Alice Maples of 12 Montrose Road, London N4 (tel 020 8937 4582) – or if either or both of them is unable or unwilling to act my friend Alan Beam of 12 Corry Close, London WC2 (tel 020 7208 9432) is to be an executor.

2. My funeral wishes are that I be buried in a nature reserve burial ground with a tree planted by the grave instead of having a headstone and I would like my executors to contact an information source such as The Natural Death Centre (tel 020 8208 2853) or A. B. Welfare and Wildlife Trust (tel 01423 530900) to find out the nearest or most suitable such ground after my death.

3. If my wife Rosemary dies before me or does not survive me for thirty days I appoint my sister Alice Maples and her husband Michael Maples as the guardians to the age of eighteen of my son Arthur my daughter Mary and any other children I may have.

4. I give the following bequests free from all taxes and duties payable on or by reference to my death. These bequests and legacies are to lapse automatically if the recipient dies before me or if a total of six letters or telephone calls in any particular case fails to trace him or her within six

months of the first attempt to do so. No advertisement or any other means need be used.

(a) my painting by Emily Young to my friend Amelia Hart of 88 Forge Terrace, Thornhill, Derby (tel 01437 3333)

(b) such motorbike as I may own at my death to my nephew Joseph Lawlor of 33 Warren Street, Church Stretton, Shropshire (tel 01331 3227).

5. I give the following further legacies free from all taxes and duties payable on or by reference to my death:

(a) £1000 to each of my executors who proves my will

(b) £1000 to my secretary Janet Simmonds of 51 Victoria Road, Chesterfield, Derbyshire (tel 01437 34282)

(c) £2000 to the Fourth World Educational and Research Association Trust, 20 Heber Road, London NW2 (tel 020 8208 2853) Registered Charity Number 283040 for the benefit of their project The Natural Death Centre. I declare that the receipt of the charity's treasurer or other person professing to be the duly authorised officer shall be a full and sufficient discharge to my executors.

6. I give free from all taxes and duties payable on or by reference to my death all my interest in the property at 41 Baldwin Lane, Caversham, Reading to my executors as trustees. They are to sell everything not in the form of cash but they may postpone the sale of anything as long as they like. They are to invest or apply what is left in any type of property just as if it were their own money. They may borrow money from institutions in advance of probate if the money is needed to pay the Inland Revenue with the loan to be repaid in due course as my assets become available.

7. My trustees may give to the guardians of my children any part of what is left to enable them to acquire property as needed for my children or to apply for my children's benefit.

8. My trustees are to divide the trust fund (including any income from it) between such of my children as reach the age of eighteen – if more than one then in shares as near to equal as is reasonably practicable. My children are my son Arthur (born 3/1/1986) my daughter Mary (born 28/7/1978) and any other children I may have in future. The trustees may apply the actual assets rather than cash if they think fit without requiring the consent of any other person. Each of these children is to have a contingent rather than vested interest in my estate until he or she has attained the age of 18.

9. If any child of mine dies before me or dies under the age of eighteen leaving children who do reach that age then my trustees are to divide as equally as is reasonably practicable between these grandchildren the share of my estate which their parent would have received if that parent had lived long enough.

10. If my trustees think it proper they may at any time apply for the maintenance education or benefit of any beneficiary under the provisions of the two previous paragraphs any part of the capital of the property to which he or she would have become entitled on reaching eighteen.

11. After the executors have paid my debts any taxes and duties payable on my death and the expenses of my funeral and of administering my estate I give to my wife the whole of the rest of my estate including the contents and furniture at the said 41 Baldwin Lane.

12. The receipt of the guardian or any person professing to be the proper officer of any school college or other education establishment which any of the children are attending at that time shall be a full and sufficient discharge to my trustees in respect of that beneficiary.

13. Any person contesting this will or attempting to set aside any part of it before any court is to be denied any benefit from my estate.

Signed by Donald Roland Winterton
in our presence and then by us in his:
Signature

First witness: Second witness:
Signature   Signature
Name   Name
Address   Address
Occupation   Occupation

Some points about this will:

• On the whole a will can be written in plain English. Avoid any possible ambiguities of meaning.

• In the passages above where it descends into legal gobbledegook it is for a reason, so beware if you make significant changes in such wordings. Beware generally, and seek legal approval of your will if in any doubt. A very useful guide, used in designing the above will, is the 'Which?' book, 'Wills and Probate' edited by the Consumers' Association (for details see under Books in the Resources chapter).

• Always revoke previous wills even if you have never made any.

• Note the absence of commas in the text, except in the addresses, an absence which some lawyers think helps guard against the need for judicial interpretation of the comma's meaning and against fraudulent alteration of a will (in the days of handwritten wills, a comma could easily be added). If the will goes over one side of paper, continue on the back of the paper. If further pages are needed, these should be numbered and you and the witnesses should sign at the bottom of each sheet.

• Those appointed as guardians for children can also be executors of the will, unless you think there could be a conflict of interest – for instance the possibility of the trustees enriching themselves; or, on the contrary, of the trustees not taking enough, through being too diffident to recoup expenses.

• New woodland burial grounds are opening all the time and some may be closer or more appropriate than any currently available, so this document allows for future developments by asking the executors to contact information sources such as the Natural Death Centre after the person's death.

• Inheritance tax was described by Roy Jenkins as 'a voluntary tax, paid only by those who distrust their heirs more than they dislike the Inland Revenue'. The tax raised about £2 billion in 1999-2000. There is no inheritance tax payable when the spouse inherits, but when the spouse in turn dies, then the tax is payable on net assets over £231,000 (the current figure, which alters regularly). To avoid this in advance, the will (above) gives a house to the children, and the contents, furniture, cash, etc, to the wife. This would obviously only be appropriate in a case where the children are to be trusted not to evict or harass the wife and where the house and the rest of the estate are of substantial value.

• Phone numbers and dates of birth are not normally put in a will, with all such details on separate sheets put with the will. But, as long as the details are correct, what harm can it do? Do not, however, fasten information sheets or anything else to the will itself, whether by pins, staples or paperclips.

• The reference to bequests lapsing if the beneficiaries are not readily traceable is to prevent the executors having to go to enormous lengths, including placing ads in the London Gazette, to find beneficiaries – as sometimes happens, especially when a person has lived to a grand old age and lost contact with those remembered in the will.

• A will such as this containing several vital technicalities and creating a 'trust for sale' for the children (which avoids various legal pitfalls and needs careful wording) should at the very least be checked by a solicitor. One way we have done this for free in the past is through one of the house insurance free advice schemes – in this case Frizzell, tel 0345 336 336. Frizzell offer 24 hour free medical, domestic and legal advice service to their clients. Faxing two prototype wills to them provoked a marvellous six page letter of comment from their solicitor in reply.

• The children have a 'contingent' interest – ie contingent in this case upon each reaching the age of eighteen. If the child dies earlier, then that gift will lapse (unless there are children of that child), and the gift will go to the other children. A vested interest on the other hand would have formed part of the child's estate.

• Denying any part of the estate to those contesting your will may not stand up in court, but it could put them off trying – or it could make lawyers rich interpreting the clause! Another way to reduce the risk of dependants from previous relationships contesting the will is to insert a clause that says: 'I have reviewed my obligations to [...] and consider that I have already made adequate and proper provision.'

• John Bradfield, author of 'Green Burial', suggests that if you are asking for something unusual in your will, which your beneficiaries could obstruct, such as a garden burial, you could make all gifts to them in the will conditional on the request being able to be carried out.

• Neither the witnesses nor their spouses should benefit from your will, or they will forfeit any provision made for them. Ideally, witnesses should be traceable after your death, in case there is a dispute as to the will's validity. Desmond Banks, a solicitor in Notting Hill and one of the Natural Death Centre's honorary consultants, suggests that the testator and witnesses should all use the same pen if possible, to help demonstrate that the testator signed the will in the presence of both witnesses and that they then signed in the presence of the testator.

The following points are worth noting about wills in general:

A will could be left in a safe place in the house, along with your other main papers. This would be simpler and quicker than leaving it with a solicitor or depositing it at the bank. Tell your executors, your spouse and your children where you have left it and consider giving them copies (note on the copies who has the original and where; and write at the bottom of the copies: 'We certify that this is a true copy of the original', with signatures from the testator and the witnesses).

If your circumstances are such that the will is not certain to be found, you may like to phone the deposit of wills section at the Probate Registry on 020 7936 6987. They will send you an envelope and a form. You then send them the will and a fee of £15. They hold hundreds of thousands of wills on deposit.

If it is known that there is a will and it cannot be found, those handling your affairs may be required to write to every solicitor in the region, and the bill for this can mount up.

A will is automatically negated by marriage (unless made in anticipation of marriage), so make another one at this time. It is as well to make another one too if you divorce.

Tax can sometimes be saved within two years after death by the beneficiaries of the will entering into a deed to vary its terms.

To repeat: be careful in your use of words in your will. Do not write for instance 'I give all my money to ...' if what you really mean is 'I give everything I own to ...'.

Avoid inadvertently giving your spouse a mere 'life interest' in your property (where the person is only able to get income from the house and no capital). You could make this mistake by specifying what is to happen to the property after the spouse's death. Such considerations should be left for the spouse's own will to deal with.

In Scotland, your spouse and children have rights to one third or more of your estate (other than lands or buildings) whatever your will may say to the contrary.

If a person has property abroad, a will should also be made in that country.

Many more such interesting points are raised in the 'Which?' book mentioned above.

Altering a will by codicil

Typing errors in a will are best avoided. If retained, they must be signed with your signature and that of your witnesses in the margin. To make small changes in a will, one way is to add a codicil, with two new witnesses signing at the end, using the same legal formula as in the main will ('signed by ... in our presence and then ...'). Part of a sample codicil might read:

> This is the first codicil to the will made the fourteenth day of April nineteen ninety seven of me Donald Roland Winterton of 26 Oxford Gardens, London W10.

(1) I revoke the bequest of £1,000 to Janet Simmonds.

(2) In all other respects I confirm my will.

But normally it is safer to make an entire new will rather than to attempt to draft your own codicil.

If you want to find a solicitor or will-writing company to draw up your will, you could phone around in the Yellow Pages for the cheapest and best, or you could ask friends for personal recommendations. Beware that making a solicitor your executor can be like writing a blank cheque.

S. V. Wadsworth & Co, Solicitors, Freepost BM6255, 325 Stratford Road, Shirley, Solihull, West Midlands B90 3BR (tel 0121 745 8550) charges £29 for a will.

The Will Consultancy, Old Bank Chambers, Market Square, Pontypridd, Rhondda Cynon Taff, Wales CF32 2SY (tel 01443 485147) offers a legally-supervised will service for £49 (£74 for a couple). These prices were quoted for London – its consultants can visit you at home.

The charity, Age Concern (see under Organisations in the Resources chapter), offers a will-making service, again based on a questionnaire, for £50 (£70 for a couple).

Roger Garlick of Will Matters, 22 Crane Bridge Road, Salisbury SP2 7TW (tel 01722 337477; e-mail: roger.garlick@virgin.net) charges £69 for a will.

If you or your child suffers from a physical or mental handicap or if you are over 70 and of very modest means with low savings (for instance with less than a thousand pounds in savings, but perhaps owning a house), you may be able to get a will drafted for free under the Legal Help scheme via a law centre, advice centre or by some solicitors.

Inheritance tax information is available from the Inland Revenue's Capital Taxes Office: Ferrers House, PO Box 38, Nottingham NG2 1BB (tel 0115 974 2400). For general information, ask for booklets IR 45 and IHT1. Or you can obtain a helpful and detailed free guide 'Planning for Inheritance Tax' from the financial advisers Chamberlain de Broe (tel 020 7584 3300).

A reminder: if your total estate after debts is likely to be worth over the inheritance tax limit (currently £231,000) then it may be worth taking measures to reduce this figure, such as leaving the first £231,000 of your estate directly to your children – so that your children will not be hit by the tax when your spouse dies. There are ways to set up trusts and to take out life insurance so as to reduce inheritance tax liability. One of the cleverest for a couple seems to be a life assurance investment bond, owned by one partner, who leaves it in trust for the children. It stays in force as long as one of the couple remains alive. The owner may draw income from the bond whilst alive, and the trustees can lend money to the partner after the owner's death (from an article by financial planner Colin McLachland who used to work for the accountancy firm BDO Stoy Hayward – tel 01292 263 277 – which may refund to the client some of the high initial commission charges for such products). Another method, the Home Loan Plan (about which a free pamphlet is available from Speechly Bircham, tel 020 7353 3290) is for the owner to sell their home to a trust set up by the owner, whilst leaving the purchase price outstanding, as an IOU. The IOU can then be given to a separate trust for the children. And the home can be sold later on if the owner wishes to move into a smaller property or a nursing home.

A final warning from the 'Which?' book:

Pitfalls of d-i-y wills

The one thing worse than not making a will at all is making a mess of making a will. Many lawyers would say that they can make more money out of poor home-made wills than they do out of drawing up wills for clients. There is probably some truth in this. There are many ways in which people who prepare and sign their own will can go wrong. This can, later, lead to long and expensive court cases to resolve the matter, with enormous legal costs for the lawyers. This can reduce by staggering amounts the size of the estate to which the beneficiaries are entitled.

A will is a technical legal document; it is not surprising that some laymen go astray when they try to make a will unaided. If you have any doubts, you should seek a solicitor's advice.

From 'Wills and Probate' edited by the Consumers' Association.

Enduring Power of Attorney

At the same time as making a will, it is a good idea to fill in a form entitled 'Enduring Power of Attorney' (available from Oyez Stationery Ltd, 144 Fetter Lane, London EC4A 1BT, tel 0870 737 7370). This enables you to nominate one or more people to represent you at some future stage should you become mentally incapable of handling your financial affairs. Your form would only be officially registered with the Court of Protection if and when required. Filling in such a form in advance could save your relatives up to £1,000 a year or more, as otherwise a receiver would have to be appointed by the court. It could also place a friend between you and any local authority trying to extract money from your account to pay for the cost of your care in a residential home.

In 1999, the government proposed the future introduction of an expanded 'continuing Power of Attorney' whereby you could choose a person to look after not only your financial affairs but also your health care and personal welfare. For instance, the 'attorney' or friend you select could agree to the withdrawal of artificial food and fluid, if you had specifically given them this power, and any disputes would go to a Court of Protection, which could appoint managers to look after your affairs.

A pre-death information dossier

In the same envelope as your will it is worth including a dossier of information that will be helpful for your survivors, including perhaps this book, the Natural Death Centre's forms (Living Will, Death Plan and Advance Funeral Wishes Form) and the Benefits Agency guide 'What to do after a death' (D49) and these details:

Registering a death – details needed

Address and phone number of the local register office (under 'R' in the phone book); your full name (exactly as on birth or marriage certificate); maiden name if a married woman; date and place of birth; home address; (last) occupation; full name and occupation of the husband (and in Scotland, the names and occupations of the spouse, male or female, and of all previous spouses and of the deceased's father; and whether the parents are alive); your NHS number; date of birth of your spouse; information about state or war pensions and allowances. Your birth and marriage certificates and NHS medical card (or at least its number) should also if possible be in this dossier, for taking along to the register office in due course.

Other helpful information you could leave for your relatives after your death could include some of the following:

Addresses, telephone numbers, account numbers, etc for: your bank; landlord; building society; credit cards; standing orders; mortgage; house insurance; council rent department; local Benefits Agency office; local gas, electricity, water and telephone offices; TV licence; life insurance; hire purchase agreements; debts or loans; car and driving licence details; passport office; share certificate details (or the originals of these certificates); premium bonds; pension details; your doctor; your solicitor; your accountant; your stockbroker; your local inspector of taxes and your tax district and tax district reference number; your employers and professional associations; and your main clients.

Protecting your assets from community care charges

For providing care at home, a local authority is allowed to make a 'reasonable' charge. But for providing this care in a residential home there is a national means test. If you have over £16,000 in assets, you will normally pay in full for residential care. Capital under £10,000 will be ignored – but your income will still be assessed. Your home may be at risk – the local authority can place a 'charge' on your home; it can bring bankruptcy proceedings against you – but you may be reassured to know that the value of your house may be disregarded if the house is also lived in by your spouse, your partner or a relative who is incapacitated or over 60. However, if you disburse your assets to avoid the risks of the local authority taking them, then *if* it can show that you did so with avoidance as your main aim, it can force you to pay, however long ago you gave it all away.

You may want to pay your full contribution, in which case no preparation is required, but be aware that the average cost of nursing home care is about £18,000 per year at current prices.

If you do want to shelter your assets, you should get specialist advice, from organisations such as the Carers National Association or the Citizens Advice Bureau (see the Resources chapter) or from solicitors specialising in issues concerning old age, such as Jonathan Wilkey of Gwyn James & Co (Commercial St, Cinderford, Glos GL14 2RR, tel 01594 822277) – the latter is writing a book on this topic, provisionally entitled 'Planning for Death' (ask your library or bookshop to look for it under the author's name). Ironically, however, once you start taking active measures, it would be more sensible to instruct a non-specialist solicitor, as this person's actions are less likely to be construed by the local authority as avoidance tactics than the use of schemes that have been marketed with this in mind. Other small tips include:

• Have a good and legitimate reason for giving away your assets.

• Do so as far ahead as possible.

• Spouses need to consider opening separate bank accounts, so that less remains in the account for assessment once you have begun paying charges.

• Joint owners of houses will be better protected if they sever any Joint Tenancy and create a Tenancy in Common.

• Consider adding the names of those family members living with you to the title deeds of the house, so reducing your part's value for assessment purposes.

• Your children or heirs may prefer to club together to pay your care fees, rather than lose the house.

• Insurance policies are best written in trust, so that the proceeds will not be regarded as your capital.

• Your pension may be used to fund care fees, leaving your dependants in hardship. Options available include taking the maximum lump sum you can, so you can use this money to ensure your spouse's financial security, having the benefits transferred to another person, or going for a deferred annuity or phased retirement, so leaving funds in place for the future.

• Beware that if you give your house away to a relative, this person may die without making provision for you, or may go bankrupt or go through an expensive divorce – or he or she may lose their own entitlement to state benefits. It should also be someone you trust absolutely.

• Ensure that a property remains available for the return of a person from residential or nursing accommodation, so that their stay can be classified as temporary for up to 12 months – in the meantime, the property's value will be disregarded when calculating fees.

A Royal Commission on Long-Term Care may lead to reform in the UK – proposals include that the first £60,000 of your assets should be disregarded; that the value of your home should be disregarded for the first three or four months of residential care; and that personal care should be paid for from general taxation, with only living costs and housing costs being paid for by the resident. Contact the Carers National Association (see Resources chapter) for the latest news on this front.

Simplifying your affairs before death

Anyone who has looked into the complexities of probate (the administration of your estate after death) will know that you can greatly simplify matters, before death and especially if death is imminent, by dividing your assets among the relevant beneficiaries. It should be more enjoyable too, making these gifts whilst still alive. Assets given to the spouse are not liable to inheritance tax (although they may be when the spouse comes to die); nor are small gifts of up to £250 per recipient; nor are gifts up to £3,000 in total per year (you may also be allowed a further £3,000 if your previous year's allowance was not used; and a marriage gift can be up to £5,000 to your own child); nor are assets liable that are given away more than seven years before death (such assets attract a proportion of the tax between three and seven years). If the family home is given to the children, however, the recipients must take up 'genuine possession of the gifted asset' and the donor may either have to vacate the house or take a lease and pay rent, so as not to be benefiting from the gift (although a donor can return to the house 'if effectively forced to due to unexpected hardship arising after the gift' was made). Note too that children who are given a house which is not their principal residence may pay out more as capital gains tax when they sell the house than they would have if they had simply paid inheritance tax instead.

If no precautions are taken, a spouse can be left with access to very little money, as death tends to freeze (non-joint) bank accounts: so, if death is near, it is as well either to take money out of the bank or to open joint bank or building society accounts. Probate on stocks and shares – sending forms to lots of firms and all the minute accounting involved – is excessively complicated: again, if death is imminent, it might be as well to cash them in, or to transfer them into the name of one's spouse (more complicated this – 'Con40' stock transfer forms are obtainable from Oyez Stationery Ltd). In fact your executors may be able to avoid the whole problem of probate altogether if you leave behind you only cash and 'personal effects' (car, furniture, etc), having previously disposed of house, shares, bank accounts, pension arrears, etc.

If you need to maintain a personal store of money in your own name until your death, consider National Savings accounts at the post office, as these do not require a 'grant of probate or letters of administration'. Up to £5,000 in any of these can be handed over to the appropriate relative after death simply by that person filling in form DNS 904 from the post office and sending this in with a death certificate copy and, if relevant, a photocopy of the marriage certificate.

Banks vary in their treatment of accounts awaiting probate. For instance, Lloyds TSB will allow the beneficiary to draw out up to £10,000 (subject to certain conditions such as the production of a certified copy of the death cerfificate); Barclays, Nat West and Nationwide (this last being a building society not a bank) all seem to operate a system whereby a sum of up to £5,000 can be released if a statutory document is signed; and up to £15,000 if further conditions are met; Abbey National on the other hand will only allow the payment of funeral and legal bills. (See also Chapter 4 re payment of inheritance tax from frozen accounts.)

If you can keep the total net worth of your estate (including any jointly owned property) at your death below £100,000 (the current figure, not to be confused with the £231,000 inheritance tax figure), your executors can avoid the Inland Revenue rules demanding a full account of the estate.

If you are taking out life insurance, make sure that it is 'written in trust', so that your beneficiaries can get the money out without waiting for probate.

Living Wills

Jackie Onassis drew up a 'Living Will', setting out that she wished to be allowed to die at home. Her Living Will was respected, and she died peacefully in her own bed, surrounded by friends and family. Here, in contrast is the story of the death of a woman without power or influential friends and who had no Living Will.

What can happen without a Living Will

I have recently had a sad experience with a friend of 86, who was transferred to hospital from the residential home where she had lived for ten years because she was dying. When I went to see her in hospital, I found that she was having many tests and examinations against her will.

When her son arrived from Ireland, he told the doctor to let her die in peace. The doctor told him he had no authority to tell them what to do, unless she had a Living Will – which, of course, she did not have.

Her son was then told that his mother was on the operations list for the next morning to investigate her condition. Fortunately, her son stayed with her and she died that night.

I am 83 years old, a retired nurse and single. I am extremely worried about what may happen to me.

Some of my friends feel like me, it's the quality of life that matters, not the prolonging of it. We want to die naturally and in peace.

From a letter to the Natural Death Centre.

In 1999, the UK government decided against introducing a statute law on Living Wills, but its policy paper on mental incapacity offered a clear statement of the present common law situation regarding Living Wills (also known as Advance Statements):

Living Wills are legally binding

The Government respects the right of people with capacity to be able to define, in advance, which medical procedures they will and will not consent to at a time when that individual has become incapable of making or communicating that decision. The courts have approved this principle and have determined that certain forms of Advance Statement already have full effect at common law. The judgements in Re T, together with those in Airedale NHS Trust v Bland in both the Court of Appeal and the House of Lords indicate that an advance refusal of treatment which is 'clearly established' and 'applicable in all the circumstances' is as effective as the decision of a capable adult.

The British Medical Association's view

In its 1995 booklet, 'Advance Statements About Medical Treatment', the British Medical Association warns doctors that they are legally obliged to obey a patient's advance refusal of medical treatment. Here are extracts from some of the main points and suggestions made:

13.4 If a health professional is involved in the management of a case and cannot for reasons of conscience accede to a patient's request for limitation of treatment, management of that patient must be passed to a colleague.

2.2 Competent, informed adults have an established legal right to refuse medical procedures in advance. An unambiguous and informed advance refusal is as valid as a contemporaneous decision.

6.5 Patients should be reminded about the desirability of reviewing their statements on a regular basis (eds: at least every five years), although a statement made long in advance is not automatically invalidated.

6.6 Patients should be advised to avoid rushing into specifying future treatments when they have only recently received a prognosis or when they may be unduly influenced by others or depressed.

7.4 Women of child bearing age should be advised to consider the possibility of their advance statement or directive being invoked at a time when they are pregnant. A waiver covering pregnancy might be written into the statement.

The BMA suggests that patients who have drafted an Advance Directive carry a card (eds: see the sample card in this chapter) indicating that fact as well as lodging a copy with their doctor.

Religious considerations

Deborah Duda's examination of the religious considerations for the United States is equally relevant to the UK:

> If you are Catholic, you may already be aware that the June 1980 Declaration on Euthanasia concluded: 'When inevitable death is imminent, it is permitted in conscience to take the decision to refuse forms of treatment that would only secure a precarious and burdensome prolongation of life.' The United Methodist Church says, 'We assert the right of every person to die in dignity without efforts to prolong terminal illnesses merely because the technology is available to do so.' The Central Conference of American Rabbis said, 'The conclusion from the spirit of Jewish Law is that while you may not do anything to hasten death, you may, under special circumstances of suffering and helplessness, allow death to come.'

She also reports a study carried out by an American educational council into the effect a Living Will might have on a life insurance policy:

> They reported that signing a Living Will would not invalidate any life insurance policy and would not be construed as an intent to commit suicide. Insurance companies stand to save lots of money if people are not kept alive artificially for months or years in hospitals or nursing homes.

> *Reprinted with permission from 'Coming Home: A Guide to Dying at Home with Dignity', © 1987 Deborah Duda, Aurora Press, PO Box 573, Santa Fe, NM 87504, USA.*

The following Living Will has been adapted by the Natural Death Centre from those put out by the Voluntary Euthanasia Society, the Terrence Higgins Trust and others. The Life Values Statement section is the copyright of Chris Docker, who works at Exit in Scotland, and is an acknowledged expert on Advance Directives around the world.

You would be well advised to discuss your Living Will with your GP and to give or send your GP a copy (photocopy the document once you have filled it out but before signing it and then get each copy signed and witnessed); you may want to change doctor, if yours is particularly hostile to the Living Will concept. You should also leave a copy with your will and with your closest relative or friend. If you go into hospital for any serious reason, you can show it to your doctor or ward sister there and have a copy put in your notes. You may want to update the form every so often, especially if you have a progressive illness – even if just to sign (and to get witnessed) the statement (at the end) to the effect that it still represents your wishes. Strike out any words or phrases which you do not wish to apply to your case, add anything you wish – or write your own version entirely.

The Life Values Statement (Part Two) may help doctors to decide what you would have wanted in circumstances that may not be fully covered by your Living Will. Chris Docker reports (in Exit newsletter, Jan 2000) that current research throws doubt on whether Living Wills – in isolation and without values statements – influence clinical decision making in more than a few cases. The more holistic the process of advance health care planning the better.

If you appoint representatives (see below) these should be people whom you trust absolutely, especially if they would benefit financially from your death.

Living Will & Life Values Statement

TO MY FAMILY, MY DOCTOR, MY HEALTH CARE TEAM, MY SOLICITOR AND ALL OTHER PERSONS CONCERNED. This Living Will and Life Values Statement are made by me at a time when I am of sound mind and after careful consideration. In the event of a clash of interpretations, I wish my Living Will (Part One) to take precedence over my Life Values Statement (Part Two).

Part One: Living Will

I wish to be fully informed about any illness I may have, about treatment alternatives and likely outcomes.

I DECLARE that if at any time the following circumstances exist, namely:

(1) I suffer from one or more of the conditions mentioned in the schedule below; and

(2) I have become unable to participate effectively in decisions about my medical care; and

(3) two independent physicians (at least one a consultant) are of the expert, considered opinion, after a full examination of my case, that I am unlikely to make a substantial recovery from illness or impairment which involve severe distress or incapacity for rational existence,

THEN AND IN THOSE CIRCUMSTANCES my directions are as follows:

(1) that I am not to be subjected to any medical intervention or treatment aimed at prolonging or sustaining my life – such as life support systems; artificial ventilation; antibiotics; surgery; using a kidney machine; or blood transfusion.

(2) that any distressing symptoms (including any caused by lack of food) are to be fully controlled by appropriate analgesic or other treatment, even though that treatment may shorten my life.

(3) that I am not to be tube fed into the stomach or vein; nor artificially hydrated (although I wish my mouth to be kept moistened).

(4) that I wish to be allowed to spend my last days at home if at all possible.

I consent to anything proposed to be done or omitted in compliance with the directions expressed above and absolve my medical attendants from any form of litigation arising out of such acts or omissions.

I wish to be as conscious as my circumstances permit (allowing for adequate pain control) as death approaches. I ask my medical attendants to bear this statement in mind when considering what my intentions would be in any uncertain situation.

I RESERVE the right to revoke this DIRECTIVE at any time, but unless I do so it should be taken to represent my continuing directions.

SCHEDULE

A. Advanced disseminated malignant disease (eg a cancer that has spread considerably).

B. Severe immune deficiency (eg AIDS).

C. Advanced degenerative disease of the nervous system (eg advanced Parkinson's Disease).

D. Severe and lasting brain damage due to injury, stroke, disease or other cause.

E. Senile or pre-senile dementia, whether Alzheimer's, multi-infarct or other.

F. Any other condition of comparable gravity.

My additional instructions (if any, such as pregnancy waiver) are:

....

....

Part Two: Life Values Statement

This Life Values Statement gives indications of the personal value I attach to my life under various circumstances. I ask my health care team to bear these in mind when making decisions about my treatment or non-treatment, especially in situations not covered by Part One above. Where I have indicated that life under such circumstances would be 'much worse than death', this means that I would find the situation totally unbearable and unacceptable, and that I would prefer all life-sustaining treatment to be stopped or withdrawn rather than to exist for the rest of my life in such a state.

[*Instructions. Please give a number to the circumstances below as follows:*

1 = 'Much worse than death: I would definitely not want life-sustaining treatment.'

2 = 'Somewhat worse than death: I would probably not want life-sustaining treatment.'

3 = 'Neither better nor worse than death: I am not sure whether I would want life-sustaining treatment.'

4 = 'Somewhat better than death: I would probably want life-sustaining treatment.'

5 = 'Much better than death: I would definitely want life-sustaining treatment.']

(a) Permanently paralysed. You are unable to walk but can move around in a wheelchair. You can talk and interact with other people.

My number for this is ..... .

(b) Permanently unable to speak meaningfully. You are unable to speak to others. You can walk on your own, feed yourself and take care of daily needs such as bathing and dressing yourself.

My number for this is ..... .

(c) Permanently unable to care for yourself. You are bedridden, unable to wash, feed, or dress yourself. You are totally cared for by others.

My number for this is ..... .

(d) Permanently in pain. You are in severe bodily pain that cannot be totally controlled or completely eliminated by medications.

My number for this is ..... .

(e) Permanently mildly demented. You often cannot remember things, such as where you are, nor reason clearly. You are capable of speaking, but not capable of remembering the conversations; you are capable of washing, feeding and dressing yourself and are in no pain.

My number for this is ..... .

(f) Being in a short term coma. You have suffered brain damage and are not conscious and are not aware of your environment in any way. You cannot feel pain. You are cared for by others. These mental impairments may be reversed in about one week leaving mild forgetfulness and loss of memory as a consequence.

My number for this is ..... .

I have lodged a copy of this declaration with the following doctor, who is/is not my GP, with whom I have/have not discussed its contents :

Name

Address

Tel No

Should I become unable to communicate my wishes as stated above and should amplification be required, I appoint the following person to represent these wishes on my behalf and I want this person to be consulted by those caring for me and for this person's representation of my views to be respected:

Name
Address

Tel No

If this person named above is unable to act in my behalf, I authorise the following person to do so:

Name
Address

Tel No

MY SIGNATURE   Date
My name
My address

WE TESTIFY that the above-named signed this document in our presence, and made it clear to us that he/she understood what it meant. We do not know of any pressure being brought on him/her to make such a declaration and we believe it was made by his/her own wish. We are over 18, we are not relatives of the above-named, nor do we stand to gain from his/her death.

Witnessed by: [two witnesses]
Signature: Signature:
Name: Name
Address   Address:

FOR RENEWING DOCUMENT IN LATER YEARS:
I reaffirm the contents of all my statements above.
MY SIGNATURE   Date
Witnessed by: [two witnesses]
Signature: Signature:
Name: Name:
Address: Address:

If you fill in the part appointing a person to represent your wishes on your behalf, it should be someone whom you trust absolutely, especially if they stand to inherit under your will.

If you would like to see the 'Advance Medical Directive' from which the Living Will is adapted, contact the Voluntary Euthanasia Society (VES), 13 Prince of Wales Terrace, London W8 5PG (tel 020 7937 7770) or Exit in Scotland, 17 Hart Street, Edinburgh EH1 3RN (tel 0131 556 4404). They have further interesting information on this topic on their Internet site (www.euthanasia.org). In Scotland a 'tutor dative', a legally enforceable proxy, can be appointed by the court; and witnesses are not needed, it is sufficient to sign, writing above your signature the words 'adopted as holograph'. The Life Values Statement is © Chris Docker (BM718, London WC1N 3XX, UK) – although the layout in the version above has been altered. The Terrence Higgins Trust Living Will is available from 52-54 Gray's Inn Road, London WC1X 8JU (tel 020 7831 0330). For a copy of the set of forms that includes the above Living Will, please send a minimum £1 donation to: The Natural Death Centre, 20 Heber Road, London NW2 6AA (tel 020 8208 2853; fax 020 8452 6434).

Living Will summary to carry around with your credit cards

> **LIVING WILL:** I have made a Living Will stating, inter alia, that, if terminally ill, I do not wish to have my life prolonged by medical interventions. This Living Will is lodged with Dr..
> Tel...and with my proxy ....
> Tel..

Alongside or instead of the legally-worded version above, you may like to write your own informal Natural Death Instructions. Here, for instance, is a wonderfully idiosyncratic version written by Scott Nearing (and honoured in the event by his wife – see Chapter 1).

Natural Death Instructions

This memorandum is written in order to place on record the following requests:

1. When it comes to my last illness I wish the death process to follow its natural course; consequently:

    a. I wish to be at home not in a hospital.

    b. I prefer that no doctor should officiate. The medics seem to know little about life, and next to nothing about death.

    c. If at all possible, I wish to be outside near the end; in the open, not under a roof.

    d. I wish to die fasting; therefore, as death approaches I would prefer to abstain from food.

2. I wish to be keenly aware of the death process; therefore, no sedatives, painkillers, or anaesthetics.

3. I wish to go quickly, and as quietly as possible. Therefore:

a. No injections, heart stimulants, forced feeding, no oxygen, and especially no blood transfusions.

b. No expressions of regret or sorrow, but rather, in the hearts and actions of those who may be present, calmness, dignity, understanding, joy, and peaceful sharing of the death experience.

c. Manifestation is a vast field of experience. As I have lived eagerly and fully, to the extent of my powers, so I pass on gladly and hopefully. Death is either a transition or an awakening. In either case it is to be welcomed, like every other aspect of the life process.

4. The funeral and other incidental details:

a. Unless the law requires, I direct that no undertaker, mortician, or other professional manipulator of corpses be consulted, be called in, or participate in any way in the disposal of my body.

b. I direct that as soon as convenient after my death my friends place my body in a plain wooden box made of spruce or pine boards; the body to be dressed in working clothes, and to be laid on my sleeping bag. There is to be no ornament or decoration of any kind in or on the box.

c. The body so dressed and laid out to be taken to the Auburn, Maine crematorium of which I am a paid member, and there cremated privately.

d. No funeral services are to be held. Under no circumstances is any preacher, priest, or other professional religionist to officiate at any time or in any way between death and the disposal of the ashes.

e. As soon as convenient after cremation, I request my wife, Helen K. Nearing, or if she predecease me or not be able to, some other friend to take the ashes and scatter them under some tree on our property facing Spirit Cove.

5. I make all these requests in full consciousness and the hope that they will be respected by those nearest to me who may survive me.

Excerpted from 'Loving and Leaving the Good Life', © 1992 by Helen Nearing, with the permission of Chelsea Green Publishing Company, Post Mills, VT 05058, USA.

Choosing the attitude

Most people die at the end of a period of illness. Someone who is going to die has the right, so far as possible, to choose the circumstances, particularly where it will take place. But even when we can no longer control the circumstances of our living and dying, we can still decide on our attitude, as Deborah Duda writes:

Choice of attitude – the ultimate freedom

When we can no longer control the circumstances of our lives, we can still control our attitude about them. We can choose our attitude about dying. We can choose to see it as a tragedy, teacher, adventure, or simply as an experience to be lived. Our attitude will determine the nature of our experience.

When we choose to surrender to life, we are free; and when we are free, we are in control. This paradox lies at the heart of our human existence.

To surrender and to be free we have to accept life as it is instead of holding on to how we think it should be. We can't change something we don't first accept. Surrender and acceptance are not to be confused with resignation and succumbing. Resignation and succumbing are passive – something just overpowered or overcame us and we had no choice but to give up. Resignation is self-pity and believing the illusion that we're powerless. Acceptance and surrender, on the other hand, are positive acts. 'I choose to let go, to give up control and accept life as it is. And there will be things I can change and things I can't.'

If we deny dying and death, we're prisoners to them. When we accept them, we're free and regain the power lost in resisting them. We let go of our resistance by letting go. It's easy to do and can be hard to get ready to do. The choice to let go must be made in the heart. A choice made only in the head, unsupported by the body, feelings and soul, is unlikely to be carried out.

If we remember that choice of attitude, the ultimate freedom, is always available, we make a spacious place in which to experience dying. We can be free whether we are dying ourselves or sharing in the dying of someone we love. We can be free whether we die at home or in a hospital. Choosing our attitude is easier at home than in an atmosphere that unconsciously says dying should be isolated from life and is, therefore, not OK.

Reprinted with permission from 'Coming Home: A Guide to Dying at Home with Dignity', © 1987 Deborah Duda, Aurora Press, PO Box 573, Santa Fe, NM 87504, USA.

More specifically, you can discuss with your family and friends how you would like to die. Henry Tennant, an Aids patient, made up a list of simple demands for how he wanted to die. Some of these he was able to arrange himself, for some he needed his friends and helpers to be aware of his wishes. Allegra Taylor reports her reflections:

'I want to die chanting'

As I become iller, AIDS becomes my life. I long to take a holiday from it – from waking every morning feeling so lousy. But you have to accept the reality of your life and then create maximum value out of what you've got. I'm so much helped by my Buddhism because it gives me a strong and vibrant focal point which is not AIDS.

I want to die in a state of true happiness. I want to die chanting. I want to be in control of my death and have people with me who know what kind of spiritual atmosphere I would like around me.

It's a pity that society's current taboo about death, particularly untimely death, is denying us all an invaluable source of learning and personal development. We need death to savour life. Do what you can in the time you have. You can't expect to be 'normal' again once you're diagnosed with AIDS, but accept the fact that you can be changed by it.

From 'Acquainted with the Night' by Allegra Taylor.

Your wishes may take more specific, personal or light-hearted forms. How would you like to spend your last few weeks? Would you go on one final holiday? Would you take up smoking right at the end? Would you write rude letters to your bank manager? Would you want a bench in your memory? What would you want to say to your family and friends? Is some of it worth saying now? What would your loved ones have to remember you by? A tape of your voice, a home movie? If it enabled you to be utterly decadent for just one month or one week or one day, what would you want to do? Eat at an expensive restaurant? Swim with dolphins? Meet your hero(-ine)?

This is where the death plan comes in – it is similar to a birth plan and indicates what a person would ideally like in terms of atmosphere and environment as he or she lie dying. Of course no one can be sure how they will die or whether such a plan in the event will be of any relevance, and they may change their minds when the time comes; but nevertheless, a death plan may help friends and relatives to know one's orientation and wishes.

In the hope of encouraging readers to improve on the following list, or to send in their sample filled-in versions of this list, or to write a list of their own, here is the Natural Death Centre's Death Plan. Some families have found it helpful and it has also been commended by Age Concern in their 1999 'Debate of the Age' paper on death and dying as an 'important step in the deprofessionalisation of death'. [An A4 copy of this form is part of the Natural Death Centre's set of forms mentioned at the end of the Living Will. Separate sheets can be used for longer responses, using the numbers below to refer your responses back to. Underline or tick or cross out or amplify as relevant. This form can be photocopied for personal use.]

Death Plan

(1) If my condition is terminal I would like to be told the full details / plus implications of treatment and non-treatment / a summary / not to be told at all / other [specify].

(2) If possible, I would / would not like the doctor to tell me a guess as to how much time I might have left, the best and worst cases, and the average.

(3) I imagine I would / would not like every effort to be made to find alternative medicine and approaches / latest medical breakthroughs that might give me a miraculous last-minute remission.

(4) I have / have not made a Living Will, specifying how much high tech medical intervention I wish for when dying and whether or not I wish to be force fed [if yes, the location of this Living Will].

(5) I imagine that I will / will not choose to fast as death approaches.

(6) If possible, when I am dying I would like to be cared for at .... [location, whether hospital, hospice, at home, indoors, outdoors, etc].

(7) I would like to be surrounded by .... [flowers, nature, photos, mementoes, etc].

(8) My next of kin is [name, address, phone number].

(9) If I go into hospital / when I die, what I would like to happen to my pets is ....

(10) I would / would not like for close relatives / friends / everyone to be told that I am terminally ill.

(11) Those friends or relatives who I would most like to be involved in my nursing care are ....

(12) I would like .... to be able to sleep in the same room / bed as me.

(13) I may change my mind, but I imagine I would / would not like visitors when near the end. The ones I would particularly like to visit me · include .... [give addresses and phone numbers if necessary].

(14) I would / would not like to be left as alone as possible when dying.

(15) I imagine that I would / would not like to discuss the fact that I am dying with these visitors, and would / would not like to make explicit the possibility that these are final goodbyes.

(16) My religion / spiritual practice / philosophy is mainly .... and therefore for my dying I would like ....

(17) Depending on my medical condition and feelings at the time, the kind of ministrations I might appreciate when dying include:

(18) Music. My favourite pieces would be .... [state specific music or broad range].

(19) Live singing, chanting, hymns, psalms, particular prayers or texts, etc [as specific as desired].

(20) Physical contact [eg hand held].

(21) Massage.

(22) Aromatherapy [or other such approaches].

(23) The person(s) I would most like to be there at the moment of my death is / are ....

(24) I would like to be as conscious / unconscious as possible as I die, and would like pain control prescribed accordingly. The drugs I imagine I might appreciate include .... [specific or class of drugs].

(25) For the moment of my death I would / would not like all life support machinery and monitors disconnected from my body.

Signed by:

Name

Signature

Date

This signing is witnessed by the two undersigned, neither of whom stand to benefit from the signatory's Will:

Name of first witness
Signature
Witness's occupation and address
Name of second witness
Signature
Witness's occupation and address

Dying wishes

It is worth remembering that 'dying wishes' or messages can assume extreme importance for those you leave behind. It gives them a way of giving to you when you are no longer there. It may be a focus for meaningful or constructive activity when everything is falling to pieces. It can be a creative and humorous act of warmth which proves long-enduring. Death has an uncanny way of freezing certain memories and moments; if they are happy and loving they will prove repeated comfort for the people who mourn you. A difficult request ('I want to be buried in Bolivia') or prohibition ('Don't marry that ghastly man') will stick too!

Your family will have to make certain decisions as to your funeral arrangements: should you be buried or cremated or buried at sea? What sort of casket should they use? What sort of service? What should be the tone of the wake, if there is one? If your spouse, partner or family is aware of your wishes, at least in general, it could save them considerable distress about 'getting it right'.

In her workshops Christianne Heal encourages people to consider the art of funeral preparation.

Imaginative sendoffs

Everyone knew it wasn't the done thing to plan your own funeral, but, said Christianne, most of us put plenty of effort into organising weddings and christening parties, so why did funeral parties have to be such thrown-together, dismal affairs?

Thus prompted, ideas for imaginative sendoffs flowed thick and fast. Bridget wanted a pub crawl for all her friends, followed by a short service at a harbour during which her body would be thrown into the sea. Peter wanted a funeral *al fresco,* preferably on a hillside, with a ragtime band playing his favourite melodies. Monica said she would like a 'green' funeral, with her body buried in a biodegradable bag rather than a tree-wasting coffin. Christianne suggested that anyone with ideas of how they'd want their funeral to be conducted ought to write them down and leave them with a close family member. 'Families have enough to think about after a death without spending hours trying to imagine what the dead person would or wouldn't have wanted at their funeral.'

From an article by Joanna Moorhead,
Weekend Guardian (Aug. 25th 1990).

Some people have used a service called Memorial Messages (see Resources chapter) which helps them to make a videotaped message to be played at their funeral (try to avoid the Oscar speech list of thanks!).

But for others a simple note left with their will may be all they wish to leave to express their funeral wishes, or even to state that funeral arrangements are not important to them. There is no 'right way'.

Advance Funeral Wishes

The following may stimulate you to think of the kind of funeral you might or might not like; and will help to make sure that those who may be responsible in the event will know your wishes. Where sample prices are given below, these are year 2000 prices. Suggested improvements to this form are welcomed. See also The Natural Death Centre's Death Plan form for requirements whilst dying, and the Centre's Living Will form. [Separate sheets can be used for longer responses, using the numbers below to refer your responses back to. Underline or tick or cross out or rewrite or amplify, as relevant. This form can be photocopied for personal use.]

(1) I have / have not written a Will [location.......................... ....] which expresses / does not express my funeral wishes. [If there is such a Will] Please treat this present document as expanding on the wishes expressed in that Will, with the Will taking legal precedence if relevant.

(2) My next of kin is [name, address, phone number].

(3) With this Will / this present document is also added all potentially needed information such as NHS card, birth and marriage certificates, bank account details, credit cards, hire purchase agreements, mortgage and home insurance details, council rent department, local gas, electricity, water and telephone offices, life insurance, car details, share certificate details, premium bonds, pension details, details of doctor, solicitor, accountant, stockbroker, employer, main clients. Also my home address, my last occupation, full name and occupation of spouse and my maiden name [if a married woman]. Plus any deeds to a grave.

(4) I have / do not have any preferences about what happens to my body. [If no preferences] I leave it all entirely in the discretion of ....

(5) I do / do not wish to donate my body / my organs [specify which and to whom, if relevant; those to contact include the Dept. of Health Organ Donor Line, tel 0845 6060 400; and the HM Inspector of Anatomy, tel 020 7972 4342, re body donation].

(6) If possible, I wish my body left undisturbed after my death for .... hours / days.

(7) Nurses attending the death normally lay out the body, but I would like it very much if .... could also assist / do this instead.

(8) If a postmortem after my death requires the consent of my next of kin, I would like them to give it / not to give it.

(9) I would / would not like my body to be brought back to my home after

death / to remain at home until the funeral if I die at home / to remain in the hospital or other establishment's mortuary if possible / to go to a funeral director offering a refrigeration service.

(10) I do / do not wish for my body to be embalmed [incidentally, sea burial is not permitted for embalmed bodies].

(11) I have / do not have a prepaid funeral plan / funeral insurance scheme [if so, please give details and make sure your next of kin are aware of the existence of this plan. Some of what follows may then not be relevant in your case].

(12) The friend(s) or relative(s) I wish to be mainly responsible for arranging my funeral is / are ....

(13) I would / would not prefer for the above-named to arrange it without using a funeral director [if using a funeral director some of what follows may then not be relevant in your case].

(14) If a funeral director is used, I would like it to be .... / I would like someone to phone around the yellow pages for the cheapest / most suitable funeral director's quote / I would like someone to phone The Natural Death Centre (tel 020 8208 2853) to see if they have a recommendation for a helpful funeral director locally.

(15) In general terms, I would like the expenditure on my funeral to be about average [£1,100] / below average / well below average / above average / well above average.

(16) I would like to be cremated / buried [for burial options see (26) below] / deposited in a vault / catacomb / mausoleum.

(17) I would like the cheapest chipboard with veneer coffin [from about £45 to £115 incl. local delivery] / painted coffin [from about £400] / coffin made of recycled wood [about £500] / cardboard coffin [if allowed by the funeral establishment concerned; from about £53] / body bag on plank and covered in drape [if allowed by the establishment concerned; from about £15] / coffin, if possible made by friend or relative or local carpenter [specify any details] / my coffin is already in store waiting [location] / burial shroud / burial sheet / willow coffin [about £400, advance commission advisable] / other.

(18) I would like my body to be transported to the relevant place in our / a friend's large estate car / van [give details where relevant] / I would like a large estate car / small van to be hired for the occasion / I would like a funeral director to be asked to supply a hearse with / without following cars. / I would like a horse-drawn hearse [normally from about £600] / other transport [specify].

(19) I would ideally like .... as the bearers of my coffin.

(20) I would / would not like flowers brought to my funeral / one flower per person / no flowers / donation instead to ....

(21) I would / would not like my death and funeral announced in the following publications ....

(22) I would / would not like a funeral service.

If to be cremated:

(23) I would like my funeral service [if having one] to take place at a church / other venue [specify] before my body is delivered to the crematorium [if a double service in this way, state what if anything is to happen at the crematorium and who is to attend there] / I would like the funeral service to take place at the crematorium.

(24) After cremation, what I would ideally like done with my ashes is ....

(25) [If an urn to be used] The kind of urn I would most like is .... home-made by .... / standard crematorium container / wooden / marble / china [advance commission advisable] / other.

If to be buried:

(26) I do / do not have a burial place reserved / in mind [details if so]. I would like to be buried in a churchyard / cemetery / green burial ground where a tree is planted instead of having a headstone / friendly farmer's land / own garden or land / at sea [please give added details where relevant.] [Note that sea burial is difficult to arrange as the Ministry of Agriculture and Fisheries goes out of its way to discourage it; done through a funeral director it is also very expensive. Contact The Natural Death Centre on 020 8208 2853 for details.]

(27) If own garden or land, although not legally obliged to, I have / have not cleared this with those who will inherit my estate, also / but not with other next of kin / neighbours etc.

(28) If green burial ground, I would / would not like those in charge of my funeral to phone an information source such as The Natural Death Centre (tel 020 8208 2853) or the A. B. Welfare and Wildlife Trust in Harrogate (tel 01423 530900) to find out the nearest or most suitable site at the time of my death [given that so many new ones are opening all the time]. I would prefer such a site to be run by a local authority / farmer / wildlife trust / doesn't matter.

(29) If allowed, I would / would not like .... [names] to help dig my grave / fill my grave.

If having a funeral service:

(30) Amongst those I would most like invited who might otherwise be neglected are .... [names and addresses and phone numbers].

(31) The kind of numbers I would like at my funeral service are .... I see it as ideally a very small family affair / family and friends / all comers.

(32) I would like a funeral service to take account of the fact that my religion / spiritual belief / philosophy is ....

(33) I would like the service led by .... [relative / friend / named or duty priest / minister / rabbi / British Humanist Association officiant / other; plus contact details].

(34) The form of service I would like is ....

(35) The kind of music, hymns, psalms, songs etc I would like include .... [be as specific as you like] played by / sung by ....

(36) The kind of texts / poems I would like include .... read by ....

(37) If possible I would like a main address about my life given by .... or by ....

(38) At this service / at some later occasion [specify] I would / would not like my friends to have a chance to speak up about me.

(39) I would / would not like an open coffin [assuming body is relatively presentable].

(40) Other rituals I would like to see at this time include .... [eg single flowers placed in coffin / grave lined with hay, flowers / football scarf or other identifying symbol placed on or in coffin].

(41) I have / have not left a last message / audiotape / video or other text for my family or friends [if yes, location], and wish for this to be played at the funeral service / some other occasion [specify].

Party or gathering after funeral

(42) I would / would not like a party / gathering after the funeral.

(43) [Assuming one is wanted] In general terms, I would like as much money spent on a gathering after the funeral as on the funeral itself / less money / much less money / more money / much more money.

(44) The form I would like this gathering to take is .... [indoors / outdoors / location / food / drinks / etc].

(45) The rituals I would most like it to include are ....

Memorial service

(46) I would / would not like a memorial gathering some .... months after the funeral.

(47) The form I would like this memorial gathering to take is ....

(48) The rituals I would most like it to include are ....

(49) Those who may not have come to the funeral that I would like invited to the memorial service include ....

(50) I would like the funeral / memorial service announced in the following media ....

Commemoration

(51) I would / would not like a tree / flowers [specify kind of tree or flowers] planted on / near grave / other location, in memory of me.

(52) Memorial objects or ways of commemoration I would ideally like include: entry in memorial book of funeral establishment / plaque / headstone [suggest wording of epitaph] / garden bench / window / book / entry in one of the Internet's online Gardens of Remembrance / endowment [details].

(53) I would / would not like there if possible to be a ritual or remembrance on the anniversaries of my death. Ideally the form this could take would be ....

(54) Amongst things left unsaid to particular people that I would like to say now are: ....

(55) I shall find out for sure in due course, but as a matter of interest, I do / do not believe in an afterlife, which I visualise as ....

Signed by:
Name
Signature
Date
Witnessed by the two undersigned who do not stand to benefit from the signatory's Will:
Names
Signatures
Witnesses' occupations
and addresses

For a copy of a similar set of forms to those in this chapter, please send a minimum £1 donation to: The Natural Death Centre, 20 Heber Road, London NW2 6AA (tel 020 8208 2853).

Widow's budget

Some people choose to leave informal instructions which go beyond funeral arrangements. When Stan Chisman learned that he had cancer, writes his wife Margaret:

His first thought was to draw up a 'Widow's Budget' to see if I would have to sell this house, but with economy and no really bad inflation we found it would be possible for me to continue to live here.

From 'Interim' by Margaret Chisman.

A will covers the legal allocation of your property and the legal guardianship of your children. A Living Will covers your wishes in case of debilitating, intractable illness. There is a wealth of other matters in which you might like a say, or to leave guidance for your family and friends:

Do you have an organ donor card? Does anybody know? (See the Good Funeral Guide chapter on how to offer your body after death.) By contrast, is the idea against your wishes?

Do you want to leave a message for your spouse, family or friends? Letting go of their loss will be a slow and painful process. Is there a simple way of telling them that it's OK to let go?

Are there any obvious conflicts which could be avoided? You will not be able to tell someone how much you love them, to forgive them, or let them know that in fact you weren't as angry with them as you made out. Are you willing to relax some of the views for which you are known after your death? Carrying on with life after losing someone is hard enough, without having to try not to step on their toes!

Can you make it easier for your partner or spouse eventually to move on to a new phase in their life, perhaps changing their job, interests, home or town? Do they know that you don't mind their eventually finding someone else, if that's the case? Compassion exercised from beyond the grave could be a last loving act which spares your circle of loved ones a great deal of distress.

Christianne Heal includes in her workshops exercises to help people focus on what they would want to say.

Rehearsing last goodbyes

Alison, a student in her early twenties, was trying to voice the words she knew she should speak to her mother. They had never been close, she explained. Her mother always seemed distant, more interested in her younger brother than in her. 'I don't know how to begin – we've just never had that kind of conversation,' she said haltingly. Her partner nodded sagely. 'Do it,' she said. 'However hard it is, try to talk to her. My mother and I didn't get on very well, but now she's dead there's so much I wish I'd ...' 'That's it,' said Christianne triumphantly. 'The end of the exercise. Please stop talking straight away. Death, when it comes, won't allow you to finish your sentence.'

From an article by Joanna Moorhead,
Weekend Guardian (Aug. 25th 1990).

I didn't know what to say . . .

So far we have looked at ways of 'preparing' ourselves for death, our own training for dying. What do you say when someone tells you that a loved one of theirs is dying – or that they themselves are dying? Many of us find ourselves caught between the feeling that there's nothing we can really do to help and the fear of upsetting the person by touching their pain, so instead we just gloss over the subject. In the chapter on 'Improving Grieving', we quote Jean Baker explaining how other people's reactions to her husband's death were often to 'cross the road if they saw me coming'. Her advice on how to relate to the recently-bereaved is equally relevant for supporting the dying person and the family: 'The most helpful thing people can do is listen, just let you talk and be compassionate. People think it will hurt you to talk. Or they fear they will be reminding you – as if you had forgotten.'

If you are not someone's close friend or relative, there is a tendency to think that the dying or bereaved person is best looked after by that close network of support, and that it is best not to interfere. There is also perhaps even the fear of being 'landed' with someone else's grief. However, people in such circumstances can experience this as being ostracised. At the time when most they need to be connected to their community, they are hermetically sealed within a bubble of pain, along with the few friends who have the courage to step inside it with them. They may, of course, have chosen to isolate themselves. Either way, the gentle reassurance that you are still there, that you can tolerate their talking about their grief, even that you are not afraid of them, made through words or a gesture, will make a difference and gives them a choice. If you are stuck for words, would a hug not do?

Our wider community

Preparing for dying is not just about ourselves. We have still a long way to go as a society. It is not hard to see that we accord many of the same prejudices, fears and apprehensions to the issues of illness in general, and ageing, that we do to dying. Why is it that so many people assume the role of the 'elderly' when their minds and bodies are fit enough to allow them to expect so much more from life? Why do people hide the terrible suffering of long illness? Why, as a society, do we contract our caring for, and management of, illness and dying out to other people, and then refuse to become involved ourselves? Why is it that some of us deal with the problems of hundreds of dying people, and the rest of us barely see death?

Chapter 3

PRACTICAL CARE
AT HOME

Facts and figures

A recent research report put out by St Christopher's Hospice, based on the work of Professor Irene Higginson and others, looked at how many people actually die at home:

What percentage die at home?

In many countries there has been an increasing trend towards the hospitalisation of death. In England, the proportion of people who died in hospitals increased between 1969 and 1987 from 46% to 50%, whilst the proportion who died in a hospice or other institution increased from 5% to 18%. Meanwhile, the proportion who died at home reduced from 42% to 24%.

In contrast to this trend for reduced home deaths, there is evidence that most members of the general public think that home is the most appropriate place to die, and that the majority of people with cancer would prefer to be cared for and to die at home. Although some patients change their mind as they become more ill, it does seem that many patients who would like to die at home do not currently do so.

This is an important issue for both palliative care providers and the National Health Service because increasing the proportion of home deaths might reduce costs at the same time as meeting patients' wishes.

The report went on to conclude that, at least for cancer deaths, the trend away from home deaths has ended and is now in steady state, at around 26% (the figure for hospitals being now 45% and for inpatient hospices 17%). The finding the many people prefer to die at home is confirmed by a study of home care services as an alternative to hospices:

Information provided by the carers three months after the patient's death indicated that patients who died at home preferred this, while half the patients who died in a hospice or hospital would have preferred to have been at home.

> *From 'Home Care Services – an Alternative to Hospices?' by*
> *Audrey W. M. Ward, in Community Medicine Vol. 9 No. 1.*

A Gallup Poll in America found that no less than 90% of respondents, if faced with a terminal illness, would prefer to die at home.

So why is it that such a large percentage of people are being denied their final wish? Pam Williams discussed this question in her nurse's dissertation:

> As a result of changes in family structure – smaller families, more mobile society, women working, unemployment and poverty – it is harder for families to cope with caring for the dying at home, even though it is generally accepted that most people wish to die in a familiar surrounding, and that the home environment (even with limitations) is the 'ideal' place to die.

The same study cites the aim of the World Health Organisation's 'Global Strategy of Health for All by the Year 2000', that

> Everyone should be afforded dignity and comfort at the time of death. All those dying who are in contact with health and social services should be able to choose where they spend their last days, and, wherever that is, they should be able to expect optimal pain relief, physical comfort and psychological support from professionals.

Of course many deaths are relatively sudden. Here we are concerned with slow deaths, the dying process. Studies show that hospital nurses have more difficulty managing patients who are dying slowly.

The hospice movement offers great expertise in the care of those who are terminally ill, both inside their walls, and through staff such as Macmillan nurses going out into the community to give support to patients and relatives at home. But since the modern hospice owes its being and related service development to major cancer charities, the emphasis until recently has been on support for patients dying of cancer. Yet 75% of people who die do not have cancer.

Hospital attitudes

It is generally accepted that 'in the past many nurses and doctors viewed death as a failure of their skills, and rejected the dying person as a reminder of the limitations of their ability to sustain life' (Pam Williams). Much has been done to improve hospital care of the dying in recent years – for instance with the introduction of hospital palliative care teams and hospital-based Macmillan nurses. Attitudes have dramatically improved, but institutional change can take a long time to show its benefits in practice:

> In 1961, 90% of doctors indicated a preference for not telling patients they had cancer, but in 1979 this was reversed, with 97% indicating a preference for passing on the diagnosis. Yet even today, many nurses are frequently being put on the spot by patients who have been told something ambiguous by the doctor and want more information.
>
> *Pam Williams*

Doctors and nurses have testified to the difficulty of coming close to the dying patient in hospital surroundings (although the small community cottage hospitals have a better reputation). Here are three such accounts, the first by Dr Sean Spence:

Television in hospital

One night in cubicle number one there was a child dying of a rare tumour. She was three years old with her hair short, as if shaven, as a result of chemotherapy. In the corner of the room the television eavesdropped. It played shadows of blue, white and red across the room, silhouetting the bars at the end of the bed and the forms of the parents waiting, its light enough to reflect them in the window opposite me. I could see their tears in that window. It became a mirror in the night. The emotions playing across the room did so without me, carried on around me. My presence was superfluous. No medical intervention would save her now. Curing is easy, but not curing is so hard, an impotence in the soul.

The gathered relatives, extended family, filled the rest of the room. Middle-aged men in suits crouched, sitting on plastic chairs, with tabloid newspapers open before them. They appeared to read the inane headlines by the glow of the artificial light, so that other agencies' realities flooded theirs. Their own state of reality must have been so great – a grandchild about to die – yet they chose to ruminate on external symbols, signs, secrets, intrigues, consumer durables which would not sustain them. When our own internal, subjective world becomes too real, when our own consciousness is too connected, do we then retreat into the external, the objective, the unreal?

From 'Television and the Retreat from Consciousness', by Dr Sean
Spence, in Beshara magazine.

A dying nurse

I am a student nurse. I am dying. I write this to you who are, and will become, nurses in the hope that by sharing my feelings with you, you may someday be better able to help those who share my experience.

We're taught not to be overly cheery now, to omit the 'everything's fine' routine, and we have done pretty well. But now one is left in a lonely silent void. With the protective 'fine, fine' gone, the staff is left with only their vulnerability and fear. The dying patient is not yet seen as a person and thus cannot be communicated with as such.

I know you feel insecure, don't know what to say, don't know what to do. But please believe me, if you care, you can't go wrong. Just admit that you care.

Anon, American Journal of Nursing, 1970.

Doctors withdrawing from the dying

I have recently completed a dissertation, related to how much information terminal patients are offered regarding their diagnosis and prognosis. The results of the study have convinced me that death and dying are over-medicalised, the disease process assuming primacy over the person. Patients within the study firmly located the fear of cancer and dying within their doctors; rather than within themselves. They reported having to 'fight for their diagnosis and prognosis' with very little, if any, information offered voluntarily.

The most disturbing (for me) feature of the study was the reporting by patients that doctors and nurses 'withdrew' from the patient once the patient knew their prognosis. This was despite patients feeling that this was the time they most needed emotional support from their doctors and nurses.

Keith Ward, c/o Wakefield and Pontefract College of Health Studies, Pontefract General Infirmary, West Yorkshire.

In spite of these testimonies, modern hospitals are not soulless machines; doctors and nurses are not ogres. Their fears and withdrawals cannot be wholly blamed on the hospital environment; they are part of the wider 'alienation from death in our age':

Orderly death

The kind of death one would hope for today – that is, to die in one's sleep, ignorant of the event, was, in the Middle Ages and the Renaissance, only wished upon one's enemies.

An orderly kind of death was part of an orderly life, and a number of ceremonies were an intrinsic part of dying. A will was written, psalms were chosen, and the speeches to be held were well prepared: these tasks were well in order long before death actually occurred.

If one fearfully retreats from the new and unknown in life, one will also attempt to flee from death. The need constantly to seek out continuity (non-change) is, in itself, an expression of fear of death.

From 'The Anxiety of the Unknown' by Jorn Beckmann and Henrik Olesen, Odense University Hospital, Denmark, 1988.

Nurses are human too (like the rest of us!) as testified in the next letter from a nurse to The Natural Death Centre, which is followed by a priest's account of visiting an old friend dying in hospital.

Nurses too busy

I do understand the need for a dying patient to be holding someone's hand and for nurses to communicate with them, but most of the time we cannot spare the nurses. Also, some people die quickly and others live for a long time – for one of our patients it was three weeks before he passed on. Many a time I just wanted to sit with patients who are dying for all of my shift, and give them tender loving care– to talk to them, hold their hand and give them the knowledge that someone cares.

From a letter to The Natural Death Centre.

Dedication despite distractions

There was a pulsating machine behind the bed with a digital reading of 30, and which progressively crept up to 35 over the period of my visits. I supposed this to be an oxygen regulator to the pair of tubes which had been inserted into her nostrils. There was another tube emerging from under the bedclothes which was draining off some body fluid and on her wrist a plastic valve had been fitted to enable her to be given subcutaneous injections of antibiotics. On my last visit the nostril tubes had been replaced by a transparent plastic oxygen face mask. There was a perpetual background noise of radio from one of the adjoining beds, so pervasive as to make it difficult to locate its precise origin, and so persistent as to madden one with its inescapably inconsequential form of distraction.

However one might interpret its labours there was no mistaking the sheer dedication of the nursing staff to the wellbeing of the patients. One evening the old black lady was visited by a young, fresh-faced nurse. She chatted with the patient for a few moments and then said, 'Well, good night Amy, I am going off duty now.' And proceeded to plant a firm kiss on the old lady's withered cheek. 'Now give me a kiss,' she continued, 'and have a good night's sleep. Oh no, that's not a proper kiss; now give me a real one. Come on now.' She bent lower over the bed and duly received her benefit. 'That was lovely,' she said, holding the patient's hand, 'Goodnight now, see you in the morning.'

Revd. John Papworth, Editor, Fourth World Review, The Close, 26 High St, Purton, Wiltshire SN5 9AE (tel 01793 772214).

Hospice facilities

Like every institutional movement, the hospice system is shaped by its source of funding and forms of administration. In the United States the first main hospice was founded by Elisabeth Kübler-Ross. Since then, all hospice funding in the States has been done through the medical hospital system, with a few independent exceptions. The UK hospice movement has been going since the mid-nineteenth century, and there are approximately 236 hospices currently operating (including 61 NHS managed units). As noted previously, the source of funding is mainly cancer charities and the emphasis is on patients dying of cancer. However, much current energy and thought is devoted to extending the hospice philosophy to hospitals and people's homes and to providing community facilities, as described in this extract from a letter to The Natural Death Centre from a hospice volunteers' coordinator:

Macmillan Cancer Relief have moved away from the idea of raising money to build bedded hospices because of the vast running costs. They now feel it is more economic to encourage the building of day centres where people can be given both specialised care – eg assisted baths, physiotherapy, aromatherapy, massage – and social activities that keep them in the community and also give their carers a break from looking after them. In this way, people can stay at home longer, taking pressure off scarce hospital and hospice beds. The provision of twenty-four hour care at home is still out of reach in most places, but some people do see that as the ideal. Marie Curie nurses are available in some areas to stay with patients all night. Or, in the Chiltern area, there are Iain Rennie Hospice At Home services who will provide twenty-four hour nursing care if necessary.

From a letter to The Natural Death Centre
by Christine Mills.

The Hospice Information Service, at St Christopher's Hospice, puts out a regular newsletter giving the latest developments on the domestic and international scene, and information about local hospices, etc (see under Organisations in the Resources chapter).

Making the decision

It has been said many times that 'we die alone', but there are degrees of loneliness, and the feeling of being unwanted at the end of life may be the most poignant of all human emotions:

Mother Teresa on being wanted

I have come more and more to realize that it is being unwanted that is the worst disease that any human being can ever experience. For all kinds of diseases there are medicines and cures. But for being unwanted, unless there are willing hands to serve and a loving heart to love, I don't think this terrible disease can ever be cured.

Mother Teresa, quoted in 'Coming Home' by Deborah Duda.

Mother Teresa had a heart pacemaker fitted at the age of 82. Patients who are mentally competent will make such decisions for themselves – the factor of chronological age is an irrelevance, it is more a question of biological age and mental and physical frailty. If the patient is not mentally competent to consent, it will probably be the consultant's decision or that of the hospital's ethics committee whether or not to go ahead with an operation, in consultation with the family. Exit journal in Scotland has published useful 'guidelines for the relatives of patients nearing eighty or more who are faced with a major operation'.

Very elderly patients facing major operations

No operation is undertaken without the expectation of the patient's survival and the policy of treatment is therefore one of 'maximum recovery', even if it involves resuscitation, the use of artificial breathing apparatus, etc.

In general, before consenting on a very elderly patient's behalf, be sure that he or she has a genuine zest for life and will be content to suffer the stresses and struggles of 'maximum recovery'.

For a Declaration of Rights that a person dying at home should have, see Chapter 11, The Politics of Dying.

Deborah Duda summarises some of the arguments for 'coming home', both for the dying person and for the carer:

Easier to adjust at home

Bringing dying people home reassures them that they're wanted and won't be deserted. Dying people fear losing control over their lives. In the hospital, the staff take over and largely dictate what the patient can and cannot do, when you can see them, etc. You and the dying person don't have time to adjust gradually to loss of control. At home, on the other hand, you can help them take a few steps at a time towards giving up control, which makes dying easier.

The feeling of being totally wrenched by an unnatural catastrophe, common in sudden deaths and many hospital deaths, is less likely to occur if they die at home. You know you're doing all you can do. If the thought comes up afterwards, 'Maybe I could have done more,' you're likely to let go of it much more quickly than if you'd been isolated from a loved one dying in a hospital. After caring for someone who dies at home most people report feeling peace as well as loss - a feeling of appropriateness and completion and a greater openness to the new life ahead.

Reprinted with permission from 'Coming Home: A Guide to Dying at Home with Dignity', © 1987 Deborah Duda, Aurora Press, PO Box 573, Santa Fe, NM 87504, USA.

Determining the best interests of a person who cannot express his or her own wishes, or who wishes to go home against the advice of the doctor, may be difficult. Where the level of consciousness is uncertain, it may be possible to confirm their wishes through hand signals: 'Do you want to go home? Squeeze my hand for Yes - blink for No.' It is worth being clear as to who in the family has to make the decision, and how each person might be affected by it. A family discussion to decide, or to talk about the decision once made, may be appropriate. You may want to work out how you might share some of the tasks, and to make others aware of the sort of changes that will be happening. As Deborah Duda points out, 'Once you've made the decision for home, keep in mind that your focus shifts from curing to making comfortable.'

There will be circumstances where dying at home would not be appropriate – for instance if the person wanted to donate organs after death; or if it would involve the carers in overmuch difficulty, anxiety and pure physical exhaustion (especially if there were young children also needing care). Before offering the patient the option of going home, all the factors need to be carefully considered. It is important that those carers who decide that they cannot cope at home for whatever reason should not be made to feel guilty. There may be an insufficiency of family and neighbours to help look after the patient. To be entirely bereft of kith and kin, however, need not always be an insuperable bar to going home, as Dr Elizabeth Lee described in a letter to The Natural Death Centre:

Discharging from hospital against medical advice

I recently talked to my community nurses about the death of one of their patients at home. She was an elderly widow, very strong minded and cantankerous, so much so in fact that neither her family or neighbours offered any practical support for her at home. She took her own discharge from hospital against medical advice and came home to die alone. In spite of her isolation from kith and kin she was able to achieve the death she wanted. She received a tremendous amount of support from her home help, community nurses, GP and night nurses. She was cared for very well at home and had one-to-one attention for many hours a day. She died peacefully one morning when the community nurse was with her. Although I have not added up the hours that she was alone, I am sure it was considerably less than the patients in hospital. Perhaps she knew that by going home to die she would be less isolated and alone than those who die surrounded by professionals in hospital.

The decision to have the dying person at home may sometimes be made in circumstances that place an initial burden on the person making the decision. Here is a moving account of such a case, where a woman in Scotland found there was more support for her decision than she had imagined, in spite of official unhelpfulness.

Sharing the bed at home

My husband had had a pain below his chest for several weeks and finally went to see his GP. At first the doctor thought that he had pulled a muscle, but on a second visit took a blood test. The doctor then decided that my husband should go to a specialist at our local hospital and he was subsequently taken in for a biopsy.

The specialist then told my husband that he had liver cancer and nothing could be done for him. He died ten weeks later. I regret that the specialist told my husband without first telling me or asking me to be present and that he was so blunt about it. I also felt it negative to give no treatment of any kind as I feel there are many alternative treatments that could have been tried and that might have given hope. Soon after my husband told me the result of his biopsy, a friend advised me to get in touch with Macmillan nurses. I went and asked my GP how to contact them and he told me they would not be needed yet and did not seem to know where they were based. I then rang a cancer charity in Edinburgh who told me that they were in the same hospital where the specialist was based and had a part-time cancer doctor working with them.

I got in touch and from that time their support was invaluable. They are in fact not just nurses but specialists in the treatment of cancer and also counsellors. The nurse who called at the house regularly soon realised that my husband was in far more pain than he would admit to the doctor and arranged for him to have increased painkillers. When later he was given drugs to combat sickness, constipation, etc, she was able to tell me whether the way he reacted to them was normal. She gave me her telephone number and I was able to ring her at home any time I needed advice. I find it sad to think that the specialist does not send his patients along the passage to see the Macmillan nurses as soon as he has had to tell them that they have terminal cancer. The doctors appear not to want to recognise that these nurses can help the patients and families more than they can.

We had the choice whether to keep my husband at home or whether he should go to hospital. He was always very attached to his house and family and although we never talked to him about it, I was sure he would wish to stay at home, as we were able to carry on as if he had an illness from which he might recover. I was able to sleep in the same bed with him right until the day he died.

I was lucky enough to have a friend, who had been a nursing nun, with me during the last days, as well as my daughter. It was particularly nice to have somebody whom we all knew and who was a Catholic as we were. However I could have had a Marie Curie nurse daily or nightly if she had not been there. My husband did not need much nursing until the last week. Although he might have been a little more comfortable with a special bed, bed pans, etc, in a hospital and also have had more confidence in a nurse giving him the pills regularly, I am sure the fact that we could be with him most of the time in a normal way, and not as a hospital visit, made up for that.

While my husband was dying we were all able to pray together and I tried to see death as Christianity teaches us. I do feel however that the Church still tends to regard death as a tragedy and not as God's plan. The world makes us feel that dying is unacceptable. Those who live to a great age are congratulated so that conversely those who do not are almost regarded as failures. I have a great belief in another life and also that those who have died are still around in spirit. Both my daughter, who is not a practising Catholic, and I feel that my husband is still looking after us. He was a particularly caring person and, as she said, he has more power to help others now. The book that has helped me more than any Catholic book is 'Who Dies?' by Stephen Levine. I came across it accidentally about a year after my husband died and it made a great difference to me. I understand that it is not even on the reading list for those training as CRUSE counsellors and I feel that it should be more widely known.

From a letter to The Natural Death Centre.

Elizabeth Lawlor in Cheshire has written to the Natural Death Centre. She has no regrets about her decision to bring her husband home to die, despite the lack of support from outside agencies (it has to be said that the palliative care services normally do a tremendously good job).

Dying amidst familiar chaos

My husband Peter died on New Year's Eve 1991. He had been diagnosed with lung cancer in February 1990 – and I think surprised everyone by living so long. He had pneumonia and was admitted to hospital in November. The consultant was not able to face what we realised – that Peter was dying. So at the beginning of December, when our local hospice opened beds for the first time, it was thought to be a good idea for Peter to go there. The doctors were still talking about curing the pneumonia!

Probably because the unit was so new, our experience of the hospice was *not* good and after ten days I 'kidnapped' Peter – they would not organise transport, so I managed to get him into the car somehow. And home into his own bed, with intrusive cats, kid's music reverberating and cobwebs that threaten to garotte the unwary!

The day before he died, the drains blocked and Dyno-Rod spent an unbelievably noisy afternoon. I think that Peter was unconscious, but if there was even a flicker, he would have loved the chaos.

District nurses did their best but were rather limited. The Macmillan nurse never showed up - she was on holiday over Christmas and New Year. We had a Marie Curie nurse for one night – ie 11.30pm to 5am – which was disastrous. But I did have my wonderful doctor friend, who bullied GPs and made sure that Peter had enough heroin at the end.

She and I were with Peter when he died. Brain death had been at about 7.30 in the morning, I think. I was in bed with him – as I had been throughout – and I got a sense that his soul (or whatever one calls it) had detached itself. And at 11am, he quietly stopped breathing.

Mary and I washed him and laid him out, to the disapproval of the funeral director. It was very real, very loving, and I was able to keep literally in touch with Peter. Then I kept him at home, in our bed, until ten minutes before the funeral. We live near the church and the local Coastal Forces veterans' association put the coffin onto the bier (usually used for transport from the church to the grave) and wheeled him round to the church - no hearse.

Now I am again being perhaps a bit difficult and organising the headstone I want and think Peter would have wanted, with the help of Harriet Frazer's Memorials by Artists [see the Resources chapter]. Mottled black marble wasn't Peter's 'thing'! And it is taking time, and I am working through the grieving process in my own time, my own way, with the erecting of the headstone after a year or more as a symbol of letting go.

Elizabeth Lawlor, Furnival Cottage, Acton,
Nantwich, Cheshire CW5 8LD.

Getting an Assessment for Care in the Community

Diana Senior of the Befriending Network describes some of the pitfalls of the UK's 'Care in the Community' programme.

Caring for someone at home should be easier since the introduction of Care in the Community, but this is not always the case. Provision under Care in the Community differs wildly from area to area. Even within the same area, how it works can depend on how clued in, efficient or sympathetic your social worker or GP is, or at what point in the financial year you happen to need it. Jaqueline Worswick, who founded Helen House Hospice, and who has recently had to agree a Care Plan for her now adult daughter says: 'Only two words in that phrase "Care in the Community" bear any resemblance to reality: "in" and "the".'

Theoretically, anybody who needs care can ask for an assessment from their local social services department. (Eds: Beware, however, that if you need residential care, you will be means-tested. Your very home could be at risk – see the section entitled 'Protecting assets from community care charges' in the Preparing for Dying chapter.) A social worker or 'care manager' will come to assess your needs and work out a basic Care Plan with you and your carer. This should take account of your personal needs (help with dressing, washing, food preparation, etc.); your physical needs (physiotherapy, or aids like a wheelchair, ramps, toilet seat, etc). It should also take some into account other needs, including things like recreation or day care. The care manager can also liaise with the GP or district nurse if he or she feels regular visits from them are important to your care. If you have a carer, he or she should get an assessment of their needs as well: time off while you have some respite care; or an unbroken night's sleep courtesy of a night sitter.

The local authority will charge you for your care, but only what it believes you can afford to pay. Hardly any still provide free care, even for those on the lowest incomes. You are likely, for instance, to be asked to contribute a percentage of your Disability Living or Attendance Allowance.

Even if you are in the position of having to pay for the full cost of your care, it could be worth asking for a Care in the Community Assessment, so that you are fully linked in with local resources; and a good care manager, like a good GP, is an invaluable ally. However, if time is limited, do not wait for an assessment. The advice given in 'The Natural Death Handbook' should help you to devise your own Care Plan.

A drawback with Care Plan assessments is that very often you are required to state your needs before you are fully aware of what they will be. Because Care Plans are supposed to be 'needs led' rather than 'resources led', you can often be unaware of what is available if only you'd asked for it. The advice from a carer is: 'Remember, if it has not been offered to you, it does not mean it does not exist.' This principle also applies to getting help from your GP.

If you have or are a carer, a very useful place to get help and advice is your local Carers Centre. Like everything else these vary from area to area. Consult the Carers National Association (see the Resources chapter) for the address of the nearest centre. They should provide up-to-date information on local resources; help with reviewing your Care Plan, and advocacy if things go wrong; a chance to share your feelings with a caring professional or other carers; and much more. The Carers Centre should also be able to provide you with access to charities and grant-giving bodies who will give financial help towards items not covered in your Care Plan.

Anne looked after her husband, Richard (the names have been changed) over five years until his eventual death from multiple sclerosis. Diana Senior describes the Care Plan that was set up for Richard on his discharge from a hospital stay:

A Care Plan in action

The district nurse came every Wednesday, did any nursing tasks, checked on Richard's general health and would call the doctor if anything needed further investigation.

A carer from Crossroads (who have a service agreement with the local social services to care for people with high physical dependency) came every morning, except for Wednesdays, to assist with getting him up.

A night nurse came two evenings per week, and a carer from Crossroads came on the remaining five evenings to help him get to bed. They were able to do this quite late, 10 or 11pm, as this was what Richard preferred.

Meanwhile he also had an assessment from the Occupational Therapist, to work out the sort of chair, bed and other practical aids he needed. The district nurse assessed and provided aids that were necessary for nursing care, for example a hoist and supplies for incontinence.

There is a team of night nurses who will come in and turn the ill person in the night, several times if this is necessary. But Anne avoided the need for turning by getting an air mattress, one that was continually pumped with air, and, once they got used to the noise of the pump, this was wonderful. They hired one, called an Auto Excel Mattress, from a medical supply company, Huntley National Care in Abingdon (tel 01235 533090) for £50 a week plus £30 installation fee. They later bought it from them, at a total cost of about £1,680 (or you can hire them through the Red Cross or borrow one through your district nurse; advice can be sought from a local orthopaedic centre or from the Disabled Living Foundation).

Anne found that Macmillan and Marie Curie nurses were much better than social workers or the GP about making suggestions for life-improving things, both practical aids, and ways of using carers. Unfortunately, their expertise is mainly available only to people with cancer.

Other problems included the lack of reliability of the carers, and lack of reviews of the Care Plan to cope with Richard's increasing needs. Particularly, he should have had regular wheelchair assessments. He finally had a new chair made especially for his needs, and this really made the last weeks much easier, but it was a pity it didn't come earlier.

Luckily they were able to supplement the Care Plan. The two most useful things were: physiotherapy, from a private agency – there was a long waiting list for NHS community physiotherapy; and live-in carers during the last months. This enabled Anne to have regular breaks away.

The first live-in carer was a New Zealander whom they met through

Crossroads. They were so satisfied with this young Antipodean that when she went off on her travels, they advertised for her successor through the expatriate magazine TNT (tel 020 7373 3377). It was hard to define the special quality of these carers: perhaps it was the oomph and curiosity which had led them to go travelling in the first place. All three who lived with Richard and Anne were positive, gentle and worked hard. They were happy to fit in and rough it a bit, but also had lives of their own.

Anne's main tips for other carers would be:

• You must look after yourself, even if this goes against the grain, even if it seems selfish. If you don't look after yourself, you aren't going to be any use as a carer.

• Admit to yourself that you can't do everything. Do not see this as failure.

• It is very important not to become isolated as a carer, and you must accept the help that is offered, or, if you can afford it, buy it in (Eds: see, for instance, under 'Nursing Agencies' in your Yellow Pages.) This seems obvious, but it takes time and effort to organise outside care to fit in with the pattern that suits you and the ill person best, and sometimes this seems too much trouble, it appears easier just to do it yourself. For instance, agency carers (normally offered through the Care Plan) differ enormously, ranging from brilliant to less than useless; they can also be very unreliable, arriving early or late or not at all. A live-in carer or night sitter can invade the little space you have to yourself. But resist the temptation to cancel carers; both you and the ill person will benefit from regular visits from people outside.

• If you have a period of feeling helpless and not being able to do anything, remember just being there helps. And simple physical contact is tremendously important. The odd hug can do more than any amount of medication.

• Acknowledge that you are going to feel angry and trapped quite a lot of the time, and so is the person you are looking after. (Value the good bits, the sharing and the laughs.)

• Recognise the need to let the person go.

Anne said that the instinct to cure and revive was so strong, that she found it hard when her husband became difficult to rouse. She was grateful for the reminder 'You've got to let him go'. At the same time she valued being told that people in a coma often retain their hearing and a sense of their surroundings, so there is no exact point when you stop talking to them, or stop keeping things peaceful and right in the room.

Financial help

Where cost of medication is an important factor, the patient may be entitled to assistance on the grounds of age. Otherwise the patient should apply for exemption from payment because of a 'continuing physical disability'. Free prescription forms (FP91) are available from post offices or doctors' surgeries.

A maze of regulations governs the benefits available to carers and those cared for (again, be sure to read the Preparing for Dying chapter and its warning on means testing) and you might like to consult your local Citizens Advice Bureau or Carers Centre or the Carers National Association (see Resources chapter) for the latest situation. The most underclaimed benefits available are:

• The Disability Living Allowance – a benefit that is tax free, is not means-tested and does not require you to have paid National Insurance contributions. It is for those under 65 and has special rules so that those who are likely to die within six months can get their benefit quickly.

• The Attendance Allowance is a similar benefit, but for those over 65.

• The Constant Attendance Allowance is similar again, but is for those who also receive either an Industrial Injuries Benefit or a War Pension.

Available in addition are:

• Incapacity Benefit. Those who are terminally ill, are of working age and who have paid National Insurance contributions should receive a low rate of nontaxable Incapacity Benefit for the first 28 weeks and thereafter a taxable higher rate.

• A similar benefit, that does not depend on having worked or on National Insurance contributions, is called the Severe Disablement Allowance.

Claimable for the carer rather than the cared-for is:

• Invalid Care Allowance, a grand £40-50 per week. This is for those of up to 60 or 65 years of age, and who are not earning more than £50, after expenses (including National Insurance and tax). One other expense you can deduct is the cost of paying someone to do the caring whilst you are at work. You must be responsible for looking after someone with a severe disability for at least 35 hours a week (and be receiving one of the first three benefits outlined above).

These benefits are all claimed from the Benefits Agency (the current name for the old Department of Social Security – see the Resources chapter). Macmillan Cancer Relief can also give small patient grants to people with cancer who have low incomes and savings.

Support structures

Dr Elizabeth Lee, in her very useful book 'A Good Death – A guide for patients and carers facing terminal illness at home', suggests ways to orchestrate the support structures that may be available. Here is our summary of some of her best tips:

• Explain to the professionals caring for you that you would like your own favourite professional to be your 'key worker' – whether GP, district nurse, social worker or home care specialist nurse.

• 'How long have I got [till I die]?' This is the question that everyone asks and no one answers. The unwritten code of practice among doctors is to reply, 'I would love to give you an answer but the truth is that no one knows'. If you need an answer to this question, you should encourage them to throw caution to the wind and make a best guess. Those who stubbornly refuse can often be pinned down by your asking 'If it was *your* mother who was ill like this, how long would you guess?'

• If you don't get on with your doctor and find her unsympathetic, try not to say that you find her difficult, rather say something like 'Although I appreciate all you are doing, I find that I am very comfortable with Doctor X, and hoped he might be able to visit me more often'.

• You may have a long list of questions for your GP. It may help to write them down before you see her.

NHS services vary in different regions and are sometimes provided in conjunction with voluntary bodies. These include domestic help, delivery of meals at home and special laundry services for bed-linen. In some areas, as already mentioned, night nurses or night attendants may be available.

It is worth exploring the help available from local societies and local voluntary agencies which are experienced in this form of care and may offer technical help and services as well as emotional support.

Individual circumstances vary, and the most crucial area of support in a particular case may range from the official to the highly informal. Here is a checklist of useful services or service providers:

NHS provision (usually free)

- General Practitioner
- Hospital specialist
- District nurse
- Macmillan Nurse
- Marie Curie Nurse
- Occupational therapist (for walking sticks, frames, etc and for some equipment loan – or try Red Cross)
- Physiotherapists
- Dietician

Social Services (means-tested charges for most services)

- Social worker /Care manager – to assess level of care package needed for the following:
- Benefits assessment
- Telephone emergency helpline / piper alarm
- Day centres / respite care
- Carers for personal care eg washing, dressing
- Home help for cleaning, shopping, laundry
- Meals on Wheels

Voluntary organisations and charities

- Local support groups and societies
- Local carer's centre (via Carers National Association)
- Befriending Network volunteer or similar befriending service
- Sitting service such as Crossroads
- Crossroads or Leonard Cheshire Foundation Care At Home

- Charities providing transport
- Charities providing financial help
- Local support groups and societies
- Priest/Vicar/Minister and church groups
- Friends, relatives and neighbours

If you do not know how to contact any of the services on the list, ask those you can contact. See also the list of Organisations in our Resources chapter. It is worth writing down a list of your needs, so that you can ask each source for more information (as well as being a good way of getting them in perspective for yourself). Macmillan nurses are perhaps the key figures in the natural death movement at the present time. They coordinate all the services and they support (and hold the purse strings for) Marie Curie nurses. The latter are qualified cancer nurses for the last few days of life, occasionally the last few weeks. Depending on patchy availability in some areas, they can be available to give support for up to seven nights a week. This is an enormous factor in preventing unnecessary hospital admissions. Otherwise relatives can reach the end of their tether and allow the patient to be admitted to hospital because they know no alternative. Most advisers stress that the carer should not become isolated in the task of looking after someone at home. One recommends that 'there be at least two people at home to take turns supporting the dying person'. This may not always be feasible. If necessary, ask the local priest or doctor to mobilise potentially helpful neighbours on your behalf. Care of the dying can be shared with friends and relatives, and with neighbours too. This is good, not just for the health and wellbeing of the caring person, but, as Ruth I. Johns points out, for the health of society as a whole:

We need the dying in our neighbourhoods and lives

At best, death is very peaceful, quick; at worst, long, protracted and accompanied by illness, pain and suffering. But it is happening to a person and that person matters. The neighbourhood needs – for its own health – to help its members in death and not pass them on to impersonal 'helpers'. In this kind of discussion, some people are always quick to say that they know someone whose life 'was ruined' because of 'having to' care for an elderly person for whom they did not feel any particular affection. To have to appear to care for someone purely out of a sense of duty is never easy and can even be injurious to all concerned; yet this is exactly the way our social systems are designed. Perhaps we have never bothered sufficiently to recognise the immense difference between pseudo-personal care and affectionate personal care? Maybe it is the people who have been 'saddled' with 'caring' for those they did not really care for who have precipitated the increase of the same blight within the formal social helping systems? The people who quietly get on with their affectionate personal care accept it, and, hard work though it may be, feel enhanced by it.

I would venture the suggestion that some of the young people who play with violence are only seeking a substitute for a suppressed and unrealised natural need to be involved in the whole process of life. We protect them (and ourselves) from real death, which is, thereby, devastatingly lonely for the dying.

Perhaps we actually need the inclusion of dying in our lives to use up energies which otherwise can pop up as actual or fantasised aggression?

Being part of the dying of a loved relative or friend makes life more livable and death a reality. The more we push it into the back of our minds, the more it will bounce back to haunt us with substitute fantasies and impersonal aggression.

It is only by becoming deeply personally involved with family, friends and neighbours that we can demonstrate that they mean something to us; thereby we become more at home in ourselves. If we feel whole we can more easily see ourselves as having a niche in the continuing affections of others beyond our own death. Life certainly becomes more tenable once we accept some personal responsibility for death.

> *From 'Life Goes On - Self-help philosophy and practice based on ten years' pioneering work with Family First Trust, Nottingham' by Ruth I. Johns, 1982 (£6 from 'Unknown Publisher', PO Box 66, Warwick CV34 4XE, 1982).*

Of all the people around you, some will want to help 'somehow'. Others will be overwhelmed by the thought of having to deal with it all. Take the statement, 'if there's anything I can do to help, let me know,' at face value, and give them a concrete practical task: walking the dog, making a meal or participating in a round of bridge. These would be manageable favours for them, and it allows them to visit with a specific purpose, rather than just mouth the empty question 'How are you feeling?'

Within the family, how is the responsibility shared? Often it is concentrated in one person, even when the decision has been made to share it. Family members' responsibilities can be split into three components: tasks; time spent in the role of chief carer (shifts); and the feeling of responsibility. The latter is automatically shared if the first two are shared successfully.

The needs of children may have to be taken into account:

Guilt feelings in children

Guilt feelings can be particularly strong in children. They may believe that by some misdemeanour they caused the death of the loved one. Some children will then misbehave more in order to earn the punishment they believe they deserve. It is vital that such feelings are discovered, in order that the child does not go through life burdened and emotionally crippled by such beliefs.

> *From 'Dying at Home' by Harriet Copperman.*

Generally it is believed that it is healthier for children to be involved. Most authorities advise that throughout any terminal illness and following the death, the children should remain an integral part of the family. Children will regard death as abnormal if they are kept away from the scene, and prevented from contact with their relative either just before or just after death. How to tell a child of an approaching death in the family may be discussed with whatever support persons are available. It may be useful to consider how much worse a sudden unexpected death would be for the children than one for which they had been prepared. There are many good books available for children too – some are on the booklist in the Resources chapter or contact The Compassionate Friends (also in the Resources chapter) for their specialist children's book list (they have a postal lending library too).

Befriending services

The Befriending Network (see the Resources chapter), founded by The Natural Death Centre, trains volunteers who visit the homes of those who are critically ill or likely to die within a year from whatever cause, normally for visits of two to three hours each week. The volunteer is there for the person, and will do whatever they can within their particular competence to assist either the patient or the carer, from running errands, to chatting, acting as a counsellor or giving simple massage.

Of all the experts visiting the home whilst the person is dying, the befriender tends to be the only one who is not being paid to be there, who does not have numerous other clients to rush off to and who can spend a substantial time each week with that person, even acting as their intermediary, on occasion, with the other services.

The Befriending Network's aim is also to fill the gaps left by the other disease-specific support groups; and it is often called upon for those who have few members of the family, neighbours or friends to support them.

The Befriending Network is at present focused on Oxfordshire and north and west London but it can refer callers to similar services in other areas.

Those wanting a befriender normally make contact via their discharge nurse in hospital, their social worker or their GP. The Befriending Network urgently needs more volunteers prepared to make the commitment of time required. Each volunteer makes a minimum commitment of one year and takes part in about 50 hours of initial training. Subsequently, besides the two to three hours of visiting each week, there are continuing support groups and supervision sessions.

The Buddhist Hospice Trust have volunteers in their Ananda Network who are prepared to sit with and befriend those who are terminally ill, whether the latter are Buddhists or not (see the Resources chapter).

The Terrence Higgins Trust (see the Resources chapter) can provide 'Buddy' volunteers to visit those with AIDS in Birmingham, Brighton, Cambridge, Leeds, London and Oxford.

Carer's needs

The best advice to carers is to remember that 'we also serve by respecting our own needs'. It is sensible to be aware in advance of the burden that supporting a seriously ill person places on the care-giver, and to anticipate some of the difficult feelings such as resentment and hostility that may arise. This needs to be said more than once:

Carer's resentment...

Your lifestyle may be affected as much as (or even more than) the patient's. You may be spending your time doing things you don't really want to do. You resent that the burden of the relationship may have fallen on your shoulders.

You cannot help but feel resentment. But you can help (both yourself and the patient) by recognising that you do feel some resentment and by not pretending that it does not exist. If you understand that you are feeling this way, you can respond to the patient by saying something like, 'This is really tough and I'm getting very bad tempered' (which is a way of describing your feelings) rather than 'You never do anything except lie there and grumble' (which is a way of exhibiting your feelings, and quite likely to lead to an argument).

From 'I Don't Know What To Say' by Dr Robert Buckman.

...and anger

The most usual and, for many people, the most frightening feeling is anger. If you have very high expectations of being patient and loving every second of the day, it can be upsetting to feel angry and frustrated. But feeling guilty about it will not help – that simply turns the anger on yourself and sooner or later you will start to feel depressed.

Carers have every reason to feel angry and resentful if they are left to cope alone. You may feel tied and trapped by caring, and angry at the opportunities you have missed.

Anger may also be a reaction to loss – witnessing the suffering of someone you are close to can make you feel angry at the injustice of it all. Or it may be a reaction to the anger expressed by the person you look after: carers often bear the brunt of that anger and frustration.

From 'Help at Hand – the Home Carer's Survival Guide'
by Jane Brotchie.

The emotional ups and downs of the situation can cause conflict. The dying person and their family may be going through necessary stages of denial, or experiencing a lot of anger and confusion. Dying does not give one an obvious target for one's anger, and so it is easy to lash out at those nearest to you instead. It can also feel safer to express overwhelming anger in terms of mundane things: a cup of tea which is too hot, or someone else's forgetfulness.

If you can, as Deborah Duda advises, stop before entering the room, and arrest your own 'down' feelings, just for a moment. Relax, breathe in deeply and centre yourself. Touch a place of receptive stillness within that allows the process to unfold as it must. Focus on that aspect of being that is larger than the sick body and the distressing symptoms.

Perhaps a smile is all that is needed to make the difference. The negative side of things is there already, and doesn't need reinforcing. Balancing sadness with cheerfulness and humour can be tricky – if your words are taken the wrong way, stand by what you know you meant. If you feel that the other person is playing emotional games, sidestep them rather than joining in. The oldest technique of them all, and one to use when really riled, is to breathe deeply and count to ten.

Stress can result from many side issues, apart from the obvious, especially if you do not allow yourself apparently selfish feelings. If you can recognise the causes of stress, you are more able to deal with its effects. Jane Brotchie provides the following list of common causes:

My source of stress is...

• not knowing for how long I am going to be giving home care.
• having had the decision of caring forced on me rather than having freely chosen it.
• being of advanced age or having ill-health myself.
• not having the training or information I need to provide care.
• lack of free time for myself.
• loss of freedom.
• changes in family life.
• family conflicts.
• competing demands between my role as a carer and other roles in my life.
• loss of social contacts and social life.
• feelings of guilt.
• financial losses or difficulties.
• having to carry out tasks I find unpleasant or embarrassing.
• changes in the personality of the person I care for.
• lack of sleep.
• needing a complete break from caring.

From 'Help at Hand – the Home Carer's Survival Guide'
by Jane Brotchie.

Most importantly, try not to become too locked into the roles of carer and patient. Remember that you also exist for each other outside those roles and that sometimes you can reverse the roles: the carer may need looking after, and the patient may be able to offer support. Coping is not the care-giver's sole responsibility and an active role for the patient is recommended where possible. It may be worth gently reminding each other of this from time to time: 'Can I speak to John my husband, not John the patient? Just for a minute.'

At times the care-giver will need to escape. Whether this means sharing a worry-free activity with the ill person or getting out of the house to go to the cinema, don't feel guilty about it. Especially at times when you resent the other person, ensure that you get some space and time to yourself.

Enjoy yourself

Do what *you* want and what you think the person you are looking after would want. Then you feel as if you are still in control of your own life, and the person dying is in control of theirs. Everyone is different, so every death is different. There are no 'right' or 'wrong' ways of doing anything within the process.

Ask for what you want or need. You may not get it but there is quite a lot of help around. Conversely, don't accept well-meaning help that makes you feel in any way uncomfortable.

Make sure you (as carer) continue to be as normal as possible. Eat/drink/ laugh/ take the dog for a walk.

Tell people how you feel if it helps you – 'I'm fine' is probably not true!

For me, Peter's dying was very intense emotionally. You can't ever do it again, so *go for it*!

From a letter by Elizabeth Lawlor
to The Natural Death Centre.

The carer may feel extremely lonely, isolated both from the non-care-giving world and from the relative or partner as they knew them. A support group can go some of the way towards filling that gap – who better to talk to than people in your own position? If you need someone to help you find a way through complex problems, you may benefit from seeing a trained counsellor. In the wake of public disasters in recent years, counselling is gradually becoming widely recognised as an important way of coping with life crises. Counselling is completely confidential, and counsellors are trained to help you to clarify and resolve tangled emotions and problems. Contact the British Association for Counselling (see under Organisations in the Resources chapter), or ask your GP or friends who may be able to recommend particular counsellors.

Most carers begin their roles with little experience and inadequate information. Even if we do eventually become near-perfect carers, it is only reasonable to assume that on the way we will have made many mistakes. Over the whole period of time, we will have been only half-perfect! What now follows is a practical guide to looking after someone who is dying at home. If you are reading it in advance of any need to apply it you may get a clearer idea of what dying at home involves and whether you can provide for it. If you are caring for someone it will serve as a primer and resource for the whole process, to be supplemented by local nursing help and expertise. If you are in a rushed situation you may find in places that some advice needs to be discarded as impractical for a short period, and you may find that other advice makes all the difference.

Preparation and equipment

Physical comfort is regarded as the number one priority for the dying patient. Certain needs clearly have to be met before worrying about emotional requirements. If the bed is wet, the sheets must be changed. If the patient is in an awkward position, he or she should be helped to move. If the sheets are tangled, they need rearranging. If the patient is unwashed, he or she may be uncomfortable. Pain and toilet requirements must be dealt with immediately. Here common sense prevails. Physical comfort is basic to a person's dignity and clarity of thought, and is the mainstay of the care which must be provided. Paying close attention to the patient's physical environment and needs is itself a form of emotional care.

A bed downstairs?

Location of the bed may require considerable thought and analysis of the available conditions. Elizabeth Lawlor's sensitive advice is again based upon her own experience of looking after her husband Peter:

Keep everything as normal as possible. If the cat/dog usually sleeps on the bed, let it. And if the bed can stay in its usual place, all the better. It is a way of maintaining a feeling of reality which is comforting when someone is drifting in and out of consciousness. The bed should be accessible on both sides to facilitate moving and turning the patient and the making of the bed, as well as bed-bathing, etc. If possible, a chair by the bed that is easy to transfer into is initially good for morale – the patient can spend the periodic half-hour sitting – which is also useful for the bedmaker. Later on the chair is good for visiting family, etc, and is an accepted piece of furniture in that location.

Other important considerations can be taken into account. If the bedroom is upstairs, the staircase may become an increasingly awkward and frustrating barrier to the rest of the house as the patient becomes less mobile. The experience of negotiating a flight of stairs with little or no strength of one's own is for some an unbearable reminder of their condition, and so the stairs can become a symbol for feelings of isolation and impotence, both for the patient and the carer.

If the patient is moved downstairs then calling for the carer may be less hit-and-miss, and just popping one's head around the door to check may be less tiring. In some cases the same energy expended on coping with stairs could instead be used to get some fresh air outside. This must be balanced with the feasibility of nursing the patient downstairs. Ideally there will be room for a bed and for creating a space which the patient feels is suitably self-contained and private. If this is the living room, the patient may feel invaded by visiting relatives unless there is another room in which they can be greeted and entertained. Are the sleeping arrangements suitable for both partners? Temporary compromises, such as a sofa for the patient, can be quite practical, as long as change will not upset everyone's routine or sense of place. Washing and toilet requirements are also very important.

Ultimately some form of compromise will have to be made. It is important for the carer not to feel guilty that arrangements are not perfect (few people choose a home with all this in mind), just as it is important to make sure that the carer's needs are taken into account. It is easier to be selfless when you have had a few hours' sleep.

Often the sense of what feels right is most important. The care-giver may find unbearable the idea of eventually having to sleep alone in the bed in which their partner spent their last few weeks. Alternatively they may feel that any other way is wrong. The patient may have strong opinions or an obvious need one way or the other: whether to keep everything as normal as possible, or deliberately to create a special environment in which the patient is 'spoiled rotten'. As conditions change a new setup may be required.

Having said all this, what will very probably happen is that events take over and these decisions are made by circumstance! Wherever the bed is, a bedside table is useful for bottles, tissues, flowers and a constant supply of water and juices.

Other practical equipment needed might include the following, which is an extended list based upon suggestions from 'Who Dies?' by Stephen Levine:

Practical equipment list

A rope and a bell by the bed so the patient feels in contact and can summon help; a stand-up bed tray if appropriate; two hot water bottles, one for the feet and one for easing the pain; an ice bucket; a thermos; possibly a hot plate in the room.

A bedpan, slipper bedpan or urinal bottle may be essential, as well as incontinence pads and plastic sheets. Plastic bedpans are less cold to the touch than metal. A plastic washing-up bowl for bed baths may also be useful.

TV, video recorder, radio, walkman according to requirements. With telephone arrangements, bear in mind the needs of both patient and carer for privacy.

Extra nightgowns or pyjamas that are easy to put on and take off, socks and non-skid slippers.

Paper towels and tissues, cotton towels, drinking straws that bend, favourite pictures and photos, a potted plant or bunches of flowers! Bring nature indoors as much as possible.

Consult with your nurse, doctor, or your local physiotherapist to find out about the provision of walking sticks, walking frames and wheelchairs. These can sometimes be borrowed from the Red Cross (see the Resources chapter). Some local councils can provide handrails for toilets, bathrooms and stairs, as well as access ramps for wheelchairs – contact the Benefits Agency department. A shower seat and nonslip bath mats help with bathing. A step-up stool is useful for relatively mobile people.

Bed and bedding

A hospital bed may be preferred (and may be better for the carers if lifting is involved – low divans can wreck lifters' backs) although some patients may be upset at having to give up their own bed. Again, Stephen Levine makes a useful comment:

A hospital bed

A hospital bed with side rails is often quite useful for comfort, because it can be adjusted in so many ways. And the side rails can act as protection during the night so that one does not restlessly or absent-mindedly fall from the bed. Though a hospital bed is very useful, many prefer to die in their own bed and would rather use a foam wedge for support and a few extra pillows than have the up-and-down movement of a strange bed.

From 'Who Dies?' by Stephen Levine.

Special bedding can give extra comfort and prevent bedsores. Sheepskins and pillows are helpful in this respect.

Bedding and comfort

A Spenco mattress helps with preventing sores, as does a fleece. The district nurse should provide that. There should also be a fleece under the heels which should be washed, dried and rubbed regularly to prevent sores.

A wedge of foam under the head of the mattress gives a firmer base than pillows for a half-upright position. The triangular, orthopaedic pillows are also good.

From a letter by Elizabeth Lawlor to The Natural Death Centre.

Special mattresses are available depending on patient requirements (see also above for Diana Senior's information on air mattresses – in 'Care Plan in action'). A large-cell ripple mattress (available via the district nurse) offers protection to pressure areas in cases of severe need. However, this is a highly specialised piece of equipment requiring advice and consultation. A bed cradle, V-shaped pillow, sponge for sitting on, sheepskin squares for sitting or lying on, and sheepskin pads or booties for the feet provide additional comfort. Fresh clean sheets are important, perhaps helped by a rubberised flannel undersheet with a duvet as a comfortable underblanket. You should consult with your nurses or local hospital as to which combination of equipment is best, as well as for details of how to get hold of them (they may themselves be able to provide you with some items). Hospital suppliers are listed in Yellow Pages, although they normally want large orders. There are specialist chemists, such as John Bell & Croyden (see the Resources chapter). Their bed-size sheepskin rugs, for instance, cost from £50 to £100. And the Red Cross, as mentioned, can lend equipment (again see the Resources chapter).

A supply of soft pillows and towels is useful for extra comfort – between or under the knees, behind the back, underneath the patient's book, or at the foot of the bed to lift the top sheet – all according to need. Experts emphasise the need for prevention in dealing with bedsores (see below).

Moving

An EC Directive on 'manual handling of loads' came into force in 1993, whereby employees such as nurses would not normally be expected to lift a patient weighing eight stone or more without a 'mechanical handling device' such as a hoist. Why should carers at home be less well equipped? Introduce a 'no lifting' policy in your home, in imitation of the most progressive hospitals, and insist that your house be fitted with hoists, slings, bath aids, monkey poles, rope ladders, turntables, stair lifts or whatever equipment you may need to protect your back from damage. Take note that one in four qualified nurses has had to take time off for back trouble. And, in an ideal world, there need to be at least two carers at any one time, able to share the strain of moving the patient.

Nevertheless, if you believe that it is well within your capabilities to help say a very light adult or child to move in bed or out of bed, and if you are determined to do so, despite our strong advice above, demonstrations of certain standard moves can perhaps be given by your district nurse (or by the physiotherapist in hospital). Several of these are demonstrated in a now unavailable and somewhat out-of-date video, 'Caring for your relative at home', produced by Marie Curie Cancer Care. The instructions which follow are based on the video, although there is a summary version in the booklet 'Partners in Caring', which can be obtained without charge through your local Marie Curie nurse. Practise these complicated instructions on a friend who is well first, until you feel proficient, rather than on a patient in pain.

So, for the worst case scenario, here are a few basic general guidelines. You are advised to ask a nurse to guide you with these:
 • Make sure that the person understands what you are doing;
 • Allow the person as much independent movement as possible;
 • Make sure that you have a firm footing, and remove any bedclothes that will get in the way;
 • Keep the person warm; cover her or him with a towel or dressing gown if necessary;
 • Take the manoeuvre one step at a time, agreeing or explaining each step before you carry it out together;
 • Take tricky steps, where you have to coordinate moving together, on a count of three;
 • If you find that you are lugging the person, or that she or he is experiencing discomfort, you may need to break the move down into simpler steps;
 • If you are lifting the person, make sure that your back is straight and that your knees are bent;
 • Don't overdo it! You may just have to wait until you can find someone to help you.

Turning in bed

Frequent changes of position are important for comfort, to avoid bedsores, and to facilitate washing. These steps are used to turn someone onto their side from their back. The basic idea is that you turn first the legs, then the arms and shoulders, and then the back:
 • Stand at the side of the bed towards which the person wants to turn;
 • Remove covers and excess pillows;
 • Take hold of the person's far leg (at the knee and ankle), and cross it over the other leg towards you;
 • Take hold of the person's far arm (at the elbow and wrist), and cross it over their chest towards you;
 • Place one hand on the person's hips and the other on their uppermost shoulder, and gently pull their torso towards you.

Moving to a chair or commode

These steps are used to help someone move to a chair from lying down in bed. The basic idea is that you help the person to sit on the edge of the bed, to get up and to shuffle round to a chair behind you.

- Position the chair or commode a few feet from the side of the bed;
- Remove the covers and stand by the bed in front of the chair;
- Help the person to turn towards you (see 'Turning in bed', above);
- Put one arm under the person's lower knee, and the other under the lower ankle. Lift the person's legs and gently pull them towards you, over the side of the bed;
- Put one arm under the person's shoulders, and the other hand on their hips;
- Ask the person to push up with their lower arm, at the same time as you use a rocking motion to bring them up by pulling their shoulders and pressing lightly down on the hips. Have a breather.
- Facing the person, place your feet firmly beside theirs so that you sandwich their feet;
- Bend your knees and keep your back straight;
- Ask the person to put their arms around your shoulders, as you put your arms around their waist;
- Transfer the person to their feet by straightening your knees;
- Stay holding each other and shuffle round slowly to the chair;
- Support the person as they sit down. If using a commode, you may have to help the person lift their nightdress/nightshirt or lower their pyjamas as they sit.

Changing sheets with the person in bed

The basic idea here is that you unmake and make half of the bed at a time:

- Remove the covers. Leave one pillow;
- Help the person to roll onto one side, facing away from the centre of the bed (see 'Turning in bed' above);
- Untuck the free side of the sheet, and roll it up as far as you can towards the person;
- Tuck in the fresh sheet on the same side, and fold up the rest close to the dirty sheet;
- Gently help the person roll over the rolled sheet and the folded part of the fresh sheet onto the clean side of the bed;
- Remove the dirty sheet; tuck in the rest of the clean sheet;
- Change the pillowcases and help the person roll back to the middle of the bed;
- Put on a fresh top sheet and replace the covers.

If many changes of sheets are required, a single sheet lengthwise on a double bed can be changed more easily than a double sheet.

Accidents

If the person falls to the floor, check for obvious signs of injury. If he or she can't move fingers or toes, if tentative movement produces sharp pain, or if you are unsure, assume that there are injuries. If the person is unable to stand up unaided, it is normally best to call for a doctor or ambulance. Make sure that the person moves as little as possible before examination. Make the person comfortable with pillows and blankets. Give reassurance that the situation is being dealt with as well as possible.

Eating

> Peter stopped wanting to eat or drink when he had pneumonia. The hospice tried to bully him into eating which upset him. Once he was home, I would ensure that something that he could manage was always available, but didn't make an issue of eating or drinking. Hence, I think that the actual cause of death was kidney failure. But it meant he didn't need to pass urine very often, and he could have a bit if he wanted. On Christmas Day he managed two sips of whisky!
>
> *From a letter by Elizabeth Lawlor to The Natural Death Centre.*

The above is an extremely unusual occurence. 99% of the time it is the relatives who are trying to make the patient eat. It will probably be necessary to find alternatives to 'three meals a day'. The person is likely to find their appetite waning, and may be too weak to eat more than a small amount at a time anyway. It is important to consult your nurse or doctor about nutrition, but the basic idea is this: offer small and more frequent helpings, and try to make food available to fit the person's sporadic hunger. Liquid food is easier and less tiring to take in: try soups, milk shakes (with a beaten egg for extra nourishment), yoghourt, and so on. Available from chemists, or with a prescription, are a range of nourishing drinks (some very sickly and sweet!), such as Complan, Build Up, Fortisip and Ensure (they do a savoury version of this), which are acceptable if the person is only able to take in small amounts of food, although some are constipating if no bran-type roughage is added. Your doctor can prescribe food supplements, which are taste-free powders that can be sprinkled on food.

Help the person to sit up as much as possible before they eat and immediately after, if possible in a chair. Not being completely flat can help prevent nausea. If they feel dizzy or weak from the movement, they may need a calm moment to recover before eating. If the person feels nauseous, try smaller snacks, a boiled sweet, mineral water or a fizzy soft drink, or dry toast in the morning, or try waiting to give liquids for an hour or two after meals and avoid fried or fatty foods. If nausea is preventing eating, contact your GP for advice.

Cancer BACUP (see the Resources chapter) send free booklets to relatives on 'Diet and the cancer patient'.

IVs and dehydration

Intravenous drips (IVs) are used in non-palliative situations when a person is too weak to take in enough food or liquids to stay alive. Palliative care experts at a recent conference voted 89% in favour of the proposition that 'artificial rehydration is inappropriate in those who are imminently dying'. Many patients have found IVs cumbersome, uncomfortable and alienating, reacting angrily to their use.

If the decision is made to use IV fluids in the last week or so of life, subcutaneous fluids are recommended as these do not involve an IV needle, merely a small needle sitting under the skin.

The alternative is to accept that death is imminent, and to concentrate upon making the dying person's remaining time more comfortable and dignified. Someone who does not take in enough liquid becomes dehydrated. The effect of dehydration is often somewhat anaesthetic, with a sense of mild euphoria. In a 1989 study by Andrews and Levine quoted by Chris Docker in 'The Art and Science of Fasting – Abstinence from food and drink as a means of accelerating death':

> Of the hospice nurses surveyed, 71% agreed that dehydration reduces the incidence of vomiting, 73% agreed that dehydrated patients rarely complain of thirst, 51% reported that there is relief from choking and drowning sensations when fluids are discontinued ... and 82% of the nurses disagreed with the statement that dehydration is painful.

As the American 'Handbook for Mortals' (by Dr Joanne Lunn and colleagues, see the Resources chapter) points out, without IVs there will be less fluid in the throat, less fluid in the lungs, less frequent urination, less pressure on tumours and an increase in the body's natural pain-relieving hormones.

Feelings of thirst and a dry mouth can be alleviated by applying a wet cloth to the lips, filling a drinking straw with water to drip into the mouth, or giving the person crushed ice. Ice can be made with juices or cordials and crushed; or the patient may suck chewing gum or boiled sweets or tinned or fresh pineapple chunks (this last contains an enzyme that makes it a wonderful mouth freshener); or a chemist can prepare artificial saliva concentrate (Luborant or Glandosane in various flavours), which can be diluted and taken in small and frequent doses. Swallowing is easier in general with a slightly raised head.

Mouth care

It is very important to maintain the person's oral hygiene, as otherwise there can be considerable discomfort. If normal teeth brushing, twice a day, is difficult, then a soft toothbrush or cotton wool buds can be used. Failing that, a mouth rinse from the chemist can be used. After eating, a pinch of bicarbonate of soda in a glass of water used as a mouth rinse keeps the mouth clean and fresh. False teeth should be soaked daily in denture-cleansing solution, and brushed with a soft toothbrush. There may come a point when false teeth no longer fit - in which case they should not be used, as they may cause ulcers.

It is important to examine the mouth periodically for ulcers and to watch for the symptoms of thrush. Thrush is a very common fungal infection which shows up as very sore white patches on the tongue, gum and inside the cheek. You should report thrush to your GP.

Washing and hygiene

Bathing

Regular washing is best not skimped, as not washing soon leads to discomfort, sores and infection. It is well worth establishing a routine: ideally a full wash once a day, with either another full wash in the day, or a hands-and-face wash when needed. Where possible, help the person with a bath or shower. Be sensitive as to whether they would enjoy being pampered, or whether it is best to allow them to wash themselves as much as possible.

You may need to ask the GP for referral to the local occupational therapist for bath lifts or shower stools. If against all the Natural Death Centre's advice (see section on Moving above), you are insistent on moving a frail person yourself, the best way to cope with getting a sufficiently light person out of the bath is to get in yourself, stand at her head, put your arms under hers, ask her to bend her knees and then lift her up and forward.

If mobility makes going to the bathroom difficult, then help the person with a bed-bath. Wash all areas of the body in turn: help the person move into the most appropriate position each time, and keep the rest of the body warmly covered. Pay special attention to hidden areas: the back, underarms, buttocks, groin and between the legs, feet, under the breasts and/or folds of skin. As you wash, check for signs of redness or sores. Change the water in the bowl several times during the wash. Make sure that the soap is rinsed off thoroughly and, especially important, that the skin is dried completely. If the skin is too dry in patches, apply an effective moisturising cream such as E45 (available on prescription in big tubs).

Hair care

It is possible to wash hair in bed. You can buy a spray Shampoo such as Batiste from your chemist: this is sprayed on, the hair is massaged for a few minutes and left for a while, then the shampoo is brushed out. For wet washing, your district nurse may be able to supply you with a special bowl with splash attachment. You can use an ordinary plastic bowl: support the person's neck with a rolled towel, and lay plastic sheets or plastic sheeting (a bin liner will do) underneath. Or have the person hang her head over the foot of the bed.

Trim finger and toe nails regularly. Men may of course need help with shaving.

Bedsores and skincare

Special pressure-sore mattresses mean that nowadays the person in bed does not have to be moved and turned so often – depending on the person's condition, sometimes in hospital it will be just once in a nurse's nine hour shift. Careful positioning and avoiding pressure also help. Where two parts of the body touch, such as the thighs or the knees, prolonged pressure leads to impaired circulation which leads to skin breakdown which leads to bedsores. It is important to protect the bones, particularly if the person is very thin. See the 'Beds and bedding' section above. This can also be done with thick cushions, towels and pillows, when seated. The most common pressure points – areas prone to sores – are: the back of the head, shoulder blades, elbows, spine and coccyx (tailbone), hips and heels. These should be checked for signs of redness daily. An obvious time to do this is during washing.

Special dressings are available to prevent bedsores and skin-toughening substances can be used. If the skin does redden and break down, a doctor or nurse should be consulted for suggestions. A review of research (by Buss IC et al in Rehabil. Nurs. 22.5: 229034, Sept 1997) concluded that massage for preventing pressure sores is not to be recommended.

Infected wounds can be very smelly. CancerLink, in their booklet 'Caring for the Very Sick Person At Home', say that the doctor may be able to prescribe special tablets to reduce the smell and they advise that 'concentrated lemon spirit, from the chemists, mixed with a little water' will mask most other smells. Or use joss sticks, scented candles or spray deodorisers; and give the patient a handkerchief dabbed with their favourite scent.

Bowel management

Incontinence

The occasional soiling of bedclothes may be inevitable, is unpleasant, and can be alarming for the patient. It is obviously important to change the sheets and help the person wash immediately. It helps to apply a nappy rash cream, a barrier cream such as Sudocrem. It is also important to be sensitive to what reassurance and affection she or he may need. Ask your district nurse about obtaining disposable incontinence pads from the Incontinence Laundry Service in your area; or the nurse may recommend a catheter (a hollow, flexible tube that drains urine from the bladder into a bag; and that works best if the patient remains unconstipated and drinks plenty of fluids).

Constipation

A blockage in the bowels can cause discomfort and pain and eventually may be life threatening. Constipation is generally caused by inactivity, insufficient fibre in the diet or as a side-effect with certain pain-relieving drugs. Consult a doctor for laxatives. Sometimes it can help if the person drinks plenty of liquids and has a high fibre diet (if tolerated) including, for instance, prunes.

Insomnia

The cares and concerns of a dying person may cause sleeplessness. If your patient has difficulty sleeping, see if you can help without sleeping pills and barbiturates.

Addiction is not a real concern with the dying, but why interfere more with delicate body balances? Some possibilities are to take, before bedtime:

camomile tea, valerian with B-vitamin complex, a warm glass of milk, or tryptophan. Tryptophan is an amino acid in meat, milk and cheese. Turkey is high in tryptophan. Try a warm bath, hot foot bath, a back rub or foot massage, or a guided meditation.

Stroke the hair and scalp and encourage the person to let all thoughts float away and to let the head feel spacious and empty, clouds drifting in and out. When I can't sleep I use the Bach Flower Remedy, Sweet Chestnut. Avoid coffee, black tea and all dark coloured colas before bedtime. They contain eye-opening caffeine. It's also OK not to go to sleep even when someone else thinks it's time. Encourage the person to read, write, watch TV, listen to soothing music or think for a while. If not sleeping continues to trouble the patient, ask a doctor about sleeping medications.

> *Reprinted with permission from 'Coming Home: A Guide to Dying at Home with Dignity', © 1987 Deborah Duda, Aurora Press, PO Box 573, Santa Fe, NM 87504, USA.*

Depression/anxiety

Anxiety will probably be experienced to a greater or lesser degree by most patients.

> Some may become mildly anxious on reaching such a significant point in their lives. Others have always been so anxious with any new event or change of circumstance, however minor, that the advance of debilitating illness and the approach of death, fills them with a terror which is sad to behold. The main treatment is listening, and honest discussion with the patient of the many causes of his anxiety.
>
> Depression, like anxiety, usually involves taking the time to listen to the patient or encouraging him to talk. He may understandably be depressed for many reasons, but if this is the result of boredom or inactivity it should be possible to find a remedy.
>
> *From 'Dying at Home' by Harriet Copperman.*

Consult your doctor, of course, if you feel medication for anxiety or depression may be called for.

Relaxation

A cassette recorder may be particularly useful:

> The person may listen to the wide variety of music and guided meditation tapes available that might encourage investigation and letting go [see under Tapes in the Resources chapter]. Speaking of the process of letting go at two in the afternoon when the patient feels relatively well and is not particularly open to investigating dying may not seem appropriate or even be well received. But a tape about working with pain or preparing for the moment of death, left at the bedside, may be appreciatively absorbed when the patient feels it is the right moment. Perhaps at four in the morning when

sleep has become impossible and the pain in the body has intensified, that individual may then feel prepared, open to hearing what earlier in the day may have seemed beside the point or frightening.

From 'Who Dies?' by Stephen Levine.

Richard Boerstler advocates a meditative Tibetan-inspired breathing technique. The carer copies the patient's breathing pattern, making the sound 'Ah' on the outbreath, strung out as 'Aaaaaaaaaaahhhhhhhh'. The patient may like to make the same sound at least for the first ten breaths or so, or may prefer just to listen. This simplest of exercises can greatly enhance the patient's sense of physical comfort and wellbeing. (See under Boerstler in the books section of the Resources chapter.)

Massage

If you have Lymphoedema, swellings caused by damage to the body's lymphatic drainage system, there is a form of gentle lymph drainage massage you can give yourself on a daily basis (a normal deep massage could be harmful – Lymphoedema massage is always towards the neck, with light circular movements). Ask your nurse for the excellent book 'Living with Lymphoedema – Your Guide to Treatment', published by Marie Curie (see the Resources chapter).

Massage in its various forms is useful in decreasing tension and anxiety whilst deepening personal contact. Simple touching, aromatherapy or foot massage can all be relaxing and encouraging. (Be careful about massaging or applying lotions to skin damaged by radiotherapy.) A personal account of giving scalp massage shows that it can offer many benefits to the dying patient:

Scalp massage

Last year a friend of mine died of cancer. She found it very difficult to open up or to ask for much. I offered to give her scalp massage. She loved it. She said it made her feel wonderful and I did it for her for many of her last days. It made her feel relaxed and cared for and sometimes she talked easily and personally – although I never pushed her to. It was wonderful for me to have something to offer which she really wanted.

This massage offers an easy way to loving physical contact. It gives the patient a relaxing time and I suspect that many will find it a good time to talk: relaxed, loved, but not always looked at. (Some people, as a parallel example, will talk on a car journey where they have company but are not looked at.) It is easy to do once explained: you use your finger tips to move the scalp over the skull. Ask the person you massage to tell you what they like and don't like, and if you are doing it too hard or soft. They should sit or lie comfortably and not 'help' by holding their head in a 'good' position – they should just relax. You move their head gently if necessary. (Try also gentle face massage, as well as neck and shoulders, all places where tension accumulates.) Feedback is the key to getting it right.

I have seen people sitting next to a dying person having run out of things to do, say or offer. I felt that this idea might mean a lot to many people.
From a letter by Margaret Ryder to The Natural Death Centre.

Contact

Simpler than massage is a hug. A spontaneous hug, or ritual 'good morning' hug, may seem out of place for whatever reason. If there is something in the way, you can either offer a hug, which gives the other person the chance to say No, or just surprise them!

Having people going about ordinary activities in the same room is another way of keeping close. While you read a book, eat dinner or watch television, you can just be with your relative. Make sure that everyone in the family is aware of when it would be a good idea to leave the person in privacy.

Making contact can involve simple but valuable actions:

Even when someone is apparently unconscious, do keep talking to them. On a very deep level it is reassuring, and apparently hearing is the last sense to go. Touch and smell are also important.

When my husband was in hospital I started putting a notepad by his bed. Every time I visited, before I left I would write down when I would be back, where I was going, etc – and that I *had* been. Once home, I kept it up so he had a memory prompt. And when he died, I had a record of the last weeks.
From a letter by Elizabeth Lawlor to The Natural Death Centre.

Small gestures mean a lot.

Pain management

Natural pain relief may be useful in addition to any medication the patient is taking.

Breathing and visualisation techniques can be very useful in working with pain. If there's delay in getting a pain reliever, you might try them. In some cases, they may preclude your needing drugs at all. Breathing can be as useful for dying as it is for birthing. When we feel pain, we tense up and tend to stop breathing fully. Our cells don't get the oxygen they need to clean out toxins and keep the nerve signals straight, and the pain gets worse.

One of the first things to do for pain is to keep breathing. Unless someone has had previous experience with breathing consciously, he or she may focus on the pain and fear and forget to breathe. As the helper, encourage the person to breathe deeply, to breathe into the area that hurts, and then down into the toes. Ask the person to relax, to 'soften' around the area that hurts, and open him or herself to the sensation of pain. As the person surrenders, gives up resistance, more oxygen enters the area and the pain may lessen. The body senses that its message is received and relaxes. Keep repeating, 'soften, relax, open'. Paying attention to pain helps relieve it if we don't judge it as bad! It just is.

I find it helpful to combine breathing techniques with hot water bottles and foot massages. While the person is breathing into the area that hurts, partially fill two hot water bottles with hot, not boiling, water. Cover the bottles with a towel so you don't burn the person's skin and place them under the feet and on the area that hurts. If you don't have hot water bottles, put the person's feet into a bucket of medium-hot tap water. Put a hot washcloth on the forehead. Together these seem to keep energy moving through the body so pain is lessened or eliminated. Some people prefer ice packs and cold water. Either is OK. (If the pain is severe and you're unprepared, call a doctor.) If it feels right to you, add a foot massage to further relax the person and to stimulate increased circulation.

Breathing and foot massage are useful techniques for calming anyone in a stressful situation. You might want to take time for them yourself.

I sometimes hear talk in New Age circles that taking drugs for pain is somehow not spiritual. That's baloney. Again, physical pain is a message that something's not working right in the body. The dying get the message loud and clear only this time there's nothing they can do about it. The body can't be fixed. Taking drugs is useful to free us to experience dying on other levels and not to fixate on one level – the body. If we're in pain, the body has our undivided attention. And if dying teaches us anything, it teaches us that we're more than just a body.

If, as many New Age people believe, our essential identity is God, why torture God's body – or anyone else's – by not taking pain medication? That's cruelty. If we truly believe that everything is equally sacred, morphine is just as sacred as the herb from which it's derived.

Reprinted with permission from 'Coming Home: A Guide to Dying at Home with Dignity', © 1987 Deborah Duda, Aurora Press, PO Box 573, Santa Fe, NM 87504, USA.

It is advisable to keep your GP informed about the person's changing pain relief needs. The Beecham Manual of Family Practice advises doctors that many patients 'are given too little analgesia too late'. Strong opioids (such as morphine – or its recent alternatives, with fewer side-effects, such as the new Zydol SR, an opiate analog; and Durogesic fentanyl, applied through a three-day skin patch) are required for most patients with cancer pain – according to the 1994 Working Party on Clinical Guidelines in Palliative Care. Other types of pain may require anti-convulsants or antidepressants, local radiotherapy, nerve blocks, ultrasound, heat or transcutaneous nerve stimulators. If necessary, ask to be referred to the Pain Relief Clinic at your local hospital – they will advise not only on the best medication, but also on additional methods of pain control, such as meditation. Patients dying at home can often have better pain relief than in hospitals, where doctors are loth to use drugs, especially the opiates, appropriately – mainly through ignorance, or fear of legal consequences. In her letter to The Natural Death Centre Elizabeth Lawlor says that she kept a chart of the medication which her husband received, 'partly to see if there was a pattern of when it was most needed, and partly for the doctor to see what was going on'. In this way it may be possible both to pre-empt pain and to establish clear communication about the person's needs. Pain is made worse by fear, loneliness and anticipation of pain to come.

Here is a pain meditation, for the patient to read or that can be read aloud very slowly by a friend. You could record it on a tape – leave up to ten second gaps between each direction, the reason being that the body responds at a much slower rate than the mind. This is a considerably reduced version – see Stephen Levine's book for the text in full and for other equally helpful meditations. (See also under Music,Talks & Films section in the Resources chapter.)

Guided pain meditation:

Sit or lie down in a position you find comfortable. Allow yourself to settle into this position so that the whole body feels fully present where it sits or lies.

Bring your attention to the area of sensation that has been uncomfortable.

Let your attention come wholly to that area. Let the awareness be present, moment to moment, to receive the sensations generated there.

Allow the discomfort to be felt.

Moment to moment new sensations seem to arise.

Does the flesh cramp against the pain? Feel how the body tends to grasp it in a fist, tries to close it off.

Begin to allow the body to open all around that sensation.

Feel the tension and resistance that comes to wall off the sensation.

Don't push away the pain. Just let it be there. Feel how the body tries to isolate it. Tries to close it off. Picture that fist. Feel how the body is clenched in resistance.

Feel how the body holds each new sensation.

Begin gradually to open that closeness around sensation. The least resistance can be so painful. Open. Soften. All around the sensation. Allow the fist, moment to moment, to open. To give space to the sensation.

Let go of the pain. Why hold on a moment longer?

Like grasping a burning ember, the flesh of the closed fist is seared in its holding. Open. Soften all around the sensation. Let the fist of resistance begin to loosen. To open.

The palm of that fist softening. The fingers beginning to loosen their grip. Opening. All around the sensation.

The fist loosening. Gradually opening. Moment to moment, letting go of the pain. Release the fear that surrounds it.

Notice any fear that has accumulated around the pain. Allow the fear to melt. Let tension dissolve, so that the sensations can softly radiate out as they will. Don't try to capture the pain. Let it float free. No longer held in the grasp of resistance. Softening. Opening all around the sensation.

The fist opening. The fingers, one by one, loosening their grip.

The sensation no longer encapsulated in resistance. Opening.

Let the pain soften. Let the pain be. Let go of the resistance that tries to

smother the experience. Allow each sensation to come fully into consciousness. No holding. No pushing away. The pain beginning to float free in the
body.

All grasping relinquished. Just awareness and sensation meeting moment to moment. Received gently by the softening flesh.

The fist opened into a soft, spacious palm. The fingers loose. The fist
dissolved back into the soft, open flesh. No tension. No holding.

Let the body be soft and open. Let the sensation float free. Easy. Gently.
Softening, opening all around the pain.

Just sensation. Floating free in the soft, open body.

From 'Who Dies?' by Stephen Levine.

It may become necessary to relieve pain by means of intravenous or intramus-
cular injections. The latter can be given by the carer once instructed by a doctor
or nurse. Better still might be for your medical helper to obtain a subcutaneous
syringe driver – this has revolutionised pain control at home. It provides a
continuous infusion of painkiller, so that there is no need for injections, and is
thus very practical for home use.

Music

The astounding power of music to soothe a person who is dying has been most
dramatically demonstrated by the work of Therese Schroeder-Sheker in the
United States, who runs the Chalice of Repose project and is bringing harp
music, Gregorian chants and other spiritual music into hospice and other
settings. Here she describes the beginnings of her work:

Musical midwifery for the dying

The first time that I was ever actually present and alone with someone who
was in fact dying is the first time that I ever really experienced silence, and
an indescribably delicate kind of light. The man was struggling, frightened,
unable to breathe. No more respirators, dilators, tracheotomies or medicines could resolve his disintegrated lungs. He could take no more in, could
swallow no more, and in his complete weariness, there was almost nothing
he could return to the world. I climbed into his hospital bed and propped
myself behind him in midwifery position, my head and heart lined up
behind his, my legs folded near his waist, and I held his frail body by the
elbows and suspended his weight. At first I held us both in interior prayer,
but soon began leaning down to his left ear and singing Gregorian chant in
an almost pianissimo.

He immediately nestled in my arms and began to breathe regularly, and
we, as a team, breathed together. The chants seemed to bring him balance,
dissolving fears, and compensating for those issues still full of sting. When
his heart ceased to beat, I stayed still for long moments. Almost twenty years
later, the silence that replaced his struggle and that was present in his room
has continued to penetrate the core of my life.

People ask if a midwife knows fear or sorrow: none of that exists if you are with the dying person. It's their time, not yours. Any burden or sorrow or wounds of your own disappear.

> *From 'The Luminous Wound' by Therese Schroeder-Sheker.*
> *The Chalice of Repose is at 312 East Pine St, Missoula,*
> *MT 59802, USA (tel 001 406 329 2810; e-mail: chalice@*
> *saintpatrick.org; web: www.saintpatrick.org/chalice.html)*

Gilles Bedard has suggested a list of soothing music for a person who is dying, 'music with the power to bring a sense of reverence and comfort to the patient, both emotionally and spiritually', some of it ethereal and inspired by Near-Death Experiences (see the Music, Talks and Films section of the Resources chapter). In the UK the charity Jessie's Fund (see Resources chapter) provides music therapists in a dozen children's hospices.

Memory Boxes

Yvonne Malik suggests the creation of Memory Box personal museums by the elderly or the terminally ill, and has made a beautiful prototype of her own, shoe-box size. She writes:

Many of us have keepsakes – nostalgic mementoes which stimulate our memories, such as old photos, letters, trinkets, holiday souvenirs, scarves, medals. Individually they may seem small or insignificant, but put together in a display, these same objects could become a decorative and pleasing Personal Museum.

The arrangements could be displayed inexpensively in, for instance, sewing boxes, tool boxes, circular tea trays or shallow suitcases.

Memory Boxes leave something precious behind for our relatives and children. They are the opportunity to communicate in nonverbal ways that 'I was here; I did this; I learnt that', or personal letters can be placed there.

> *See under 'Malik' in Chapter 12 for contact details.*

Barnados have now made a Memory Book – a loose-leaf folder – which fits inside a Memory Store – a large colourful fillable box containing a removable tray (for family video, audio cassette and other small treasures) and two compartments (one for documents and photos and the other for bulkier objects). A pack of two Memory Stores costs £15 including p&p, and the Memory Book costs £15 for one, from Dispatch Services, Barnados Child Care Publications, Paycocke Road, Basildon, Essex SS14 3DR (tel 01268 520 224 ext. 267).

The final days

Janet Stevenson wrote to the Natural Death Centre about the death of her Gran:

Passive not active

In a book about childbirth, I read that you need to give the child peace and quiet to be born, without being rushed or troubled. The most important thing at the other end of life is just sitting quietly with the dying and being there, and holding her hand, that was what I learned. Or so it was with Gran. Passive not active.

Josefine Speyer of the Befriending Network describes how each day those who are dying may sleep more and awake less. They may become unable to hold up the head, and be too weary to speak. During sleep, the time between breaths may increase to 12 to 15 seconds. They may appear to be forgetful and muddled. Then, typically, the hands and feet become colder, the colour fades from the skin, the breathing stops, the eyes gaze into space, colour drains from the lips – the person has died. (Do not be alarmed, writes Dr Lee, in 'A Good Death', if there is later a slight gurgling or sighing noise of air escaping from the throat or a sudden shifting of a limb as the muscles relax.)

For some, this can be a moment of great peace and silence, with no rush to leave the bedside – 'this time is immensely precious' writes Josefine Speyer, 'almost sacred and to be respected.'

Chapter 4

Inexpensive, Green Family-Organised Funerals

Almost all those who have tried it advocate looking after at least some aspects of the funeral of a friend or relative oneself, with the assistance of family and neighbours, rather than depending entirely on funeral directors. This chapter, parts of which are not for the squeamish, aims to help you find the courage to organise and design such a funeral by arming you with essential information and tales from some pioneers. The next chapter, however, gives advice about getting the professionals in to help.

D-i-y

In brief, how to organise a funeral for yourself, in the most common of cases, tends to be as follows (many of these points will be amplified later):

If the person died at home, you can normally keep the body there for a couple of days simply by turning off the heating in the room and by opening the windows. The nurse can lay out the body for you.

If the person died in a hospital ward, get the sister there to sign a release form stating that you are doing your own undertaking (these release forms are not a legal requirement but many hospitals seem to use them). Phone the hospital mortuary to arrange a mutually convenient time to collect the body and ask how many assistants, if any, you will need to bring with you and what covering, if any, you will need for the body.

Rent or borrow a transit van or a sufficiently large estate car. Turn up at the arranged time with a coffin, either one you have made or one you have bought. If the coffin and body are very heavy, you may be able to use sawn-off broomstick handles under the coffin to slide it in and out of the van.

Before the funeral, you need in most cases to register the death with a registrar of births, deaths and marriages (under 'R' in the phone book) and to pay for as many copies of the death certificate as you are likely to need for banks and other institutions. You need to decide if you want a cemetery, woodland burial ground or crematorium. For a cremation you will also need three forms from the crematorium (which a good crematorium will no doubt help you to fill in, if you have problems. Their form A needs countersigning by a householder who knows you, the applicant) and two doctors' certificates (for which you will have to pay about £82).

Normally a coffin has six bearers matched in pairs for size, who carry the coffin on their shoulders, not using the handles. If possible, the bearers should practise together beforehand. But some cemeteries and crematoria may have a trolley you can use if you prefer. You may want to cover a cardboard coffin with a drape.

You can have a service, celebration or ritual in whatever venue you prefer, ranging from your living room or a local hall, to the crematorium chapel or the graveside. You can ask a priest or minister to preside over the service or a humanist officiant or perhaps a friend who is able to chair meetings in a sensitive way.

At a crematorium it might be wise to choose the last slot of the day, in case your timing goes slightly out, or to book extra time – and to discuss with them well in advance the music you may want. If a woodland burial ground is being used and it is far from your home, you might prefer to have a service locally, with just one or two members of the family going on with the coffin to the site.

D-i-y advantages

The suggested advantages for a 'd-i-y' funeral are that:

• Participating in this way, according to psychotherapists, helps people to begin to come to terms with their loss.

• You have the option of trying for a greener funeral if you so wish.

• It can be far less expensive – and potentially free, if the body is buried in a shroud on your own land, or from about £200 if cremation is used (whereas a Manchester Unity Friendly Society survey found that the average cost of a burial in 1998 was £1,657, with cremation's average cost at £1,011. The London region was considerably more expensive: £2,391 for a burial, £1,302 for a cremation).

• You have more control over every aspect of the funeral, which can as a consequence be a much more personal and less 'assembly-line' affair.

Below are some of the stories from the front line. First, an extract from an address about d-i-y funerals given by John Bradfield, author of 'Green Burial', at a Cremation Society conference:

Not having the body whisked away

We have helped with informal and formal funerals but all seem to gain from following their own feelings. No one [carrying out a d-i-y funeral] has had regrets about taking control but some do say how difficult it was, when the temptation was to let others take over. We hear how sharing responsibility with friends or relatives strengthened bonds, offering solid comfort – after one bond had been irrevocably broken.

In the case of burials in nature reserves, visits are made beforehand to select the positions of graves, to watch graves being dug, and to do the digging and filling themselves. Purposeful activities directly related to the death are then spread over a number of days. Emotions then move with these events and are less likely to become fixed or frozen. Having the body whisked away and a short, impersonal ceremony a few days later may be harmful for some.

The following letter appeared in The Times from the Reverend Canon Raymond Wilkinson of Warwick, who looks back nostalgically to the past and urges relatives not to hand over funerals entirely to the trade:

Personal involvement in funerals

Two of the ancient parish churches where I served as incumbent (one of them as recently as 1970) still possessed the parish bier, whereon in past days parishioners had themselves placed the body of the deceased member of their family, in a coffin made by the local joiner, before pushing it solemnly to their church. They were then met by the parson at the lychgate before the service in church and the subsequent burial in the churchyard, again performed by friends and relatives.

Undertakers were – and are – neither necessary nor obligatory, but we in this country increasingly divorce ourselves from this last service to our relatives by handing everything over to the professionals – often to the choice of sadly overused hymns.

One of the most memorable funerals I have conducted (from a total of about 5,000) involved no undertakers. The relatives laid out the body; the coffin was made by friends; the family bore it from their own car; after the church service they lowered the coffin into the grave which they had dug.

A few weeks ago (without, of course, the grave) I conducted just such a funeral at the local crematorium. Could it be that an uncommon but godly sense of what funerals are about is returning? Personal involvement may be painful, but it represents reality and personal accountability – as well as a proper reminder of our own mortality.

The dramatic increase in crematorium disposal of the dead in this century is said to be largely in the interests of convenience, cleanliness and conservation. Where convenience is an overriding factor that may well be so. But ashes (Eds: consisting mostly of calcium, with a similar alkaline effect to lime) are useless to growing plants, and I have yet to read of a health risk proven regarding burials.

Churchyards remained relatively small until the 19th century because the usual small wooden memorials decayed, families died out, bones discovered were placed in the charnel-houses built in churchyards, and God's Acre was reused. On the Continent today, such economy of land is general. Grave space there is reused, unless further leases are paid for.

It seems to me that journeys to distant, and often somewhat ugly, crematoria have added expense and detachment where death is concerned. Any enquiry into spiralling costs of undertaking needs to be linked to our increasing detachment from involvement domestically and parochially with our departed friends and relatives.

From a letter to The Times (April 25th 1991) from the Reverend
Canon Raymond Wilkinson, 42 Coten End, Warwick.

The recycled coffin

The parish burials of the past that Wilkinson refers to were originally ecologi-cally-sound affairs. Back in the 15th Century, the body was wrapped in a shroud and the parish coffin, stored in the church, would be reused time and again. Indeed in some parts of the country town councils decreed that funerals should be 'shroud only' with coffins only for the privileged few who could obtain special permission (see the fascinating account in 'The English Way of Death' by Julian Litten, pages 123 to 129). The Natural Death Centre has visions of a similar green funeral service in the future, where the coffin could be reused (and often delivered directly to the next family needing it) with a body covering preventing any leakage into the coffin.

Wilkinson questions whether crematoria are environmentally friendly. So which is better for the environment, being buried or cremated?

Which is greener, burial or cremation?

In the UK cremation was originally presented as the environmentally friendly option, with the anti-burial slogan of 'keeping the land for the living'. Nowadays cemeteries and churchyards help protect the land *from* the living, preventing land being used for development and often acting as a refuge for wildlife. Some of the few bits of green space left in Tokyo are graveyards – although some bodies in Tokyo now have to be kept in special warehouses close to the railway stations until burial space can be found in country graveyards. In some countries in the early days of cremation, the body was taken out of its coffin before being incinerated. Nowadays, however, the coffins are all wastefully burnt and we are in the realms of European regulations concerning the pollution of the atmos-phere and ground water from the glues used, from the plastics in artificial joints and other implants, and from the metals, hydrogen chloride (the cremator's pollution control systems do not catch these emissions), carbon dioxide, formal-dehyde and furans emitted in the burning process. A report from Warren Springs Laboratory in Stevenage found that even one of the crematoria updated to bring it into line with the new standards emitted far more dioxins than permitted. Dioxins can cause cancer and other illnesses even at low concentrations. 12% of UK atmospheric dioxin resulting from combustion comes from crematoria (according to a DTI/EU 'Guide for Household Waste Management'). Ken West, in his report 'Woodland Burial', writes that a heavy concentration of mercury from tooth fillings has been identified around crematoria.

The conclusion must be that burial is a greener option than cremation, particularly if the burial is in a nature reserve, with a tree planted instead of having a headstone, as discussed later in this chapter. If cremation is chosen, coffins entering cremators should contain no substances that will pollute when burnt – for instance, no plastics, PVC, fibreglass, styrofoam, rubber or metals such as zinc.

Jane Spottiswoode, who lives near Bala in North Wales, shares similar doubts to those of Raymond Wilkinson about the encroachments of the funeral industry.

She wrote a spirited book, 'Undertaken with Love', describing the funeral of her husband:

Undertaken with Love

When Jane Spottiswoode's husband Nigel was diagnosed as having lung cancer in 1986, she began to put into operation a plan they had made long before (when both were in perfect health) which was to be buried as cheaply as possible. Indeed her husband had said he would happily be consigned to the compost heap, any funeral money being put towards a slap-up party.

Jane set about arranging Nigel's funeral during his second period in hospital. Immediately, she came across the first of numerous hurdles – that of purchasing a coffin. Armed with the Yellow Pages, she settled down to try to find one but soon met with much hostility. No manufacturer would supply her with one; she was told they only supplied to funeral directors. So she turned to the undertakers themselves, but the results were the same. They would only supply a coffin as part of their full service.

Jane grew cunning. She said that she was a theatrical producer, intending to tour village halls with an amateur production of 'A Scent of Flowers' by James Saunders, a play she knew well and one which had a coffin on the stage throughout. 'Oh no we couldn't possibly supply one of our coffins for that sort of thing!' said the lady on the telephone. 'Why not?' asked Jane. 'It might offend our customers,' came the prim reply. Surely not the audience in distant village halls? 'They are all our potential customers,' said the lady, but before putting down the receiver on this incontrovertible truth, she revealed the name of a firm which Jane will always hold in great regard – that of S. S. Joinery in Stoke on Trent who would supply a coffin in veneer chipboard for £34-50 plus VAT as long as she could collect it herself.

At a total cost of £197-97 against the £700 or so charged by the Co-op, Nigel Spottiswoode's funeral was certainly cheap. But that wasn't the main point. From start to finish she regarded it as an act of affectionate respect, as did his pall-bearing friends. 'My husband was just taken to the crematorium by his friends, instead of employing a stranger to do it. That was all it amounted to, really, and if more people realised how comparatively easy it can be with a little forethought, they might like to consider it for themselves.'

Although in excellent health, Jane Spottiswoode has already purchased her own coffin which she keeps in the loft, tucked away in the shadows behind the water tank to avoid alarming the plumber.

From publicity material for 'Undertaken with Love'
by Jane Spottiswoode.

Incidentally, Jane Spottiswoode subsequently discovered that S. S. Joinery denied all knowledge of having supplied a coffin to her. In China, many elderly people share her desire to have a coffin ready in advance (they get the children to buy one for them). And as for putting the body on the compost heap, a letter writer to The Independent quoted with approval an advertisement in James Joyce's 'Ulysses': 'Well preserved fat corpse, gentleman, epicure, invaluable for fruit garden. A bargain £3-13-6.'

Andrew Kerr has suggested further research into how body composting could work:

Composting bodies

I suggest compost funerals. Animal wastes (and the human body belongs to the animal kingdom) are an integral part of the process by which the vegetable kingdom is sustained. If animal remains are mixed with vegetable wastes to the proportion of one in four, in a controlled system, turned and dampened correctly, the result will be a perfect product to be fed to any kind of plant. Most dangerous pathogens are dealt with in the process.

The corpse could be taken to the Compostorium and placed in a specially constructed autoclave or pressure cooker. The corpse would have already been disembowelled and that material placed into a methane digester; this would have averted the potential danger of pathogens. The gas so generated would contribute to the slow and steady heat required to render the remains to a condition ready to be ground up to a kind of slurry to be 'intimately mixed' with straw and other vegetable wastes.

The whole process would be completed in about twelve weeks or so: a decent time for mourning. The finished compost could then be incorporated into the family memorial garden.

This would be far better than burial which is too deep for aerobic processes, or wasteful incineration which is damaging to the environment.

From a letter from Andrew Kerr, Rectory Cottage, Standlake, near Witney, Oxon OX8 7SG (tel 01865 300125).

Keeping the body at home

Jane Spottiswoode's book about her husband's funeral came in for criticism in the journal of the National Association of Funeral Directors, where the following somewhat value-laden and insensitive comment was made: 'She found that when she needed a mortuary in which to leave her husband until the time of the cremation, she was forced to resort to hijacking the municipal mortuary. Luckily for her she lives in a quiet rural area and as a consequence that facility was otherwise not in use. However, in a busy urban area the use of the municipal mortuary would neither be possible nor desirable.'

Keeping the body cool

So how is the city dweller to manage without the municipal mortuary? Whether or not the person has died in hospital, the hospital mortuary there might be willing to look after the body for a few days, most probably without charge or for a donation; or a funeral director might be willing to provide just this facility without the complete package (certainly many of those listed in the next chapter are willing to do this). If the person has died at home, the body could be kept in a room with the window open, in the coldest room in the house or even in the cellar if preferred. Salt water washing used to be the practice in some cultures. The A. B. Welfare and Wildlife Trust suggests having a refrigerator with its door open and a cover taped around the door to form a tunnel around the body. In rural France a special refrigeration plate is often placed under the body so as to make it possible for the body to remain in the house whilst relatives come to pay their respects. Wrapped ice cubes could be placed by the body (but not placed against bare skin where they may burn). It is more important to keep the trunk of the body cool than the head or limbs. Dry ice (which gradually sublimates to a carbon dioxide mist without leaving a wet puddle) could be bought – it has been used on occasion by mortuaries, when their equipment breaks down, and is widely used in Japan in hot weather to allow the body to remain on a futon at home before the funeral. One supplier in London of dry ice in pellet form is B. O. C. Hackney Ltd, 59 Eastway, London E9 5NS (tel 020 8985 5544), where 10kg, approximately one day's supply, can be collected (from 8-15am to 4-30pm, weekdays only) for £27-48 including VAT, or can be paid for by credit card and sent to you by minicab.

Why keep the body at home?

In some religions, such as Tibetan Buddhism, it is argued that it is best to leave the body undisturbed for several days after death, to allow the complete departure of the soul. And in the West, there are many who emphasise the importance of allowing family members and relatives to see the body – and of giving young children such opportunities, but not insisting on any occasion if they prefer to stay away.

Bereaved parents denied the opportunity to see and touch the bodies of their dead children often deeply regret this. The purpose of concealing grief seems to be to protect other people, not the griever.

The need to hold one's dead child

My child was killed in a road accident. He was 17.

We arrived at the hospital just after 10.15 pm: no one was expecting us. 'Everybody has gone and I should have gone too by now,' a social worker said. My friend and I were put in a small anteroom and the door was closed. We had been put into a box with the lid closed to spare us the sight of panicky people rushing to and fro, telephone calls being made, while the system was reassembled for us.

Apparently there was great rushing about preparing Timothy for viewing. Putting a piece of gauze over a graze on his head was regarded as important so that I should not be offended or frightened or disgusted. We walked along a corridor. We arrived at a door. It was opened. No more hope; no more thinking it might not be Timothy. Incredibly, it was my Timothy, my lovely boy.

He was lying on an altar covered by a purple cloth edged with gold braid and tassels. Only his head was visible. Such was the atmosphere of constraint I either asked or was given permission to enter. I can't remember. I entered alone. The others watched through the open door. I stroked his cheek. He was cold.

Timothy had not ceased to be my child. I desperately needed to hold him, to look at him, to find out where he was hurting. These instincts don't die immediately with the child. The instinct to comfort and cuddle, to examine the wounds, to try to understand, most of all to hold. But I had been told not to do 'anything silly'. They were watching to see that I didn't. So I couldn't move the purple cloth. I couldn't find his hand. I couldn't do anything. I betrayed my instincts and my son by standing there 'not doing anything silly'. I knew that if I did, my watchers would immediately lead me away.

Why? No doubt they thought they were acting for the best. We, as a society, have lost contact with our most basic instincts. We marvel at cats washing and caring for their kittens. We admire the protection an elephant gives her sick calf and are tearful and sympathetic when she refuses to leave her offspring when he dies; when she examines and nuzzles him and wills him to breathe. This is exactly what the human mother's most basic instinct tells her to do. And we deny her. She is being denied her motherhood when in extremis.

We have come to think we are protecting her when we are really protecting ourselves. We have forgotten that this is the mother who has cleaned up the vomit, washed his nappies, cleaned the blood from his wounds, kissed him better and held him in his distress. She has done all this since the day he was born. If he has been in hospital she has possibly fed him by tube, she may have changed his dressings and given injections. She will certainly have washed him, helped him to dress and combed his hair. She will have held him. Who are we protecting when we deny her this last service which she can do for her child? We are not protecting the child. We are not protecting her. The fact of her child's death is not altered by the denial of her instincts.

Having nursed my mother through her last illness, I was privileged to bathe her after death, put clean dressings on her wounds, remove her catheter. It was a tearful and loving last service that my sister and I were privileged to perform for her. It helped to heal our grief. But my lovely boy was draped on an altar, covered with a robe, and all expressions of love and care I had were denied to me. And I don't know when that wound will heal. The caring services should think again about how we serve the bereaved. A cup of tea and an aseptic look at the body does not serve. If it is our wish and instinct to hold and wash the body and to talk to the dead loved one, we should be helped to do this. We will be distressed and may frequently need to stop and wipe the tears, but we will be helped in our healing.

From an article by Sheila Awoonor-Renner
in The Guardian (Mar. 15th 1991).

The same principles hold true when a stillborn baby is involved, as Cathie English made plain in an e-mail to the Natural Death Centre:

Wanting to hold the stillborn baby

When my first daughter, Ruth Cave English, was stillborn, the mortician insisted on embalming, a service, blah, blah, blah, and I said 'no!' – no pearly coffins, no embalming, nothing 'damn it!'. They even wanted us to ride in a white limo! I said 'no'.

We had a 20 minute graveside service and a styrofoam 'box' and a $250 stone without angels or lambs, but *words* – words are important to me: "Whither thou goest, I shall go." We moved a lot, so I needed to know she'd be with us, always.

I also educated the nurses at the hospital where she was stillborn. I don't think they quite knew how to deal with a woman like me. You see, they tried to 'shield' me; they tried to tell me what I wanted. 'You don't want to see your baby. She's dead.' I screamed at them, 'I want to hold my baby!' It's a wonder ... holding a dead, simply beautiful infant came so naturally ... yes, her colouring was dark, etc ... but in five minutes I lived a lifetime. If anything, the juxtaposition of birth and death taught me how natural both are! What a gift to have learned that at 24. Now I don't fear death or living.

Cathie English of Aurora, NE, USA.

Mary Wallace e-mailed the Natural Death Handbook to complain at the first edition's focus on the death of adults:

Death before birth

When I first read the 'Natural Death Handbook', it clarified and crystallised much of my thinking about death. I found the book informative, fascinating and often moving. It caused me to reflect on and prepare for my own death. But it wasn't until I experienced the loss of two babies that I realised that the book concentrates heavily on the death of adults. Given that between 20 and 25 per cent of pregnancies end in miscarriage and a further one per cent in stillbirth or neonatal death, I felt that the book could place more emphasis on this particularly distressing and sometimes lonely experience.

My babies died in the womb during pregnancy – one at around 20 weeks gestation (John), and another, less than a year later, at 14 weeks (Alex). Both were, medically speaking, miscarriages rather then stillbirths.

24 weeks gestation is the point at which the dead baby is referred to as stillborn rather than miscarried. At this point he or she is legally recognised as a baby, unless at an earlier gestation there are signs of life outside the womb. In addition, from 24 weeks, a birth and death certificate must be issued and the baby must be buried or cremated.

Earlier than this, the baby born dead has no legal status as a human being and it is almost as if he or she never existed. This, and the fact that there are sometimes no identifiable remains, make the grieving process all the more difficult. The experience of miscarriage is often more distressing because others, including those in the medical profession, do not always regard it as particularly significant emotionally. It is as if there was no 'real' baby with no 'real' parents.

At one point whilst I was in hospital for example, a midwife asked me about 'the foetus' and I had to tell her that he was my baby and not a foetus. I felt like having a T-shirt printed saying 'I had a baby, not a miscarriage'! To me they were precious little beings – tiny, but fully formed and very beautiful.

In the case of Alex, who died in the womb at 14 weeks, the usual procedure would have been to have had an ERPC (Evacuation of the Retained Products of Conception) on a gynaecological ward. There would have been no identifiable body and disposal would have been in the hospital incinerator, possibly along with other hospital waste.

To me this was barbaric. I gave birth to my tiny babies naturally, held them, photographed them, and in Alex's case, took him home for a few days. My other children, both under seven-years-old at the time, saw and held their little brothers and were filled with wonderment and awe at their beauty and perfection. Before they were born I had been haunted by what they might look like and whether they would be deformed or damaged in some way. I need not have worried, but whatever they had looked like, they were mine and I would have loved them regardless.

I was also adamant that I didn't want other people touching them and we conducted the funerals ourselves, with the help of the hospital chaplain. Whilst we hold no religious beliefs, I needed a ceremony to say goodbye to them properly. The chaplain was a very a special man – kind and warm hearted, with an ability to make an instant emotional connection with people. At no time did he attempt, even subtly, to find out what our religious beliefs were and for this I am grateful.

My husband found solace in making the coffins. It was something he could do at a time when so much was beyond his control. He chose pine and made a simple little box just big enough for them. The boxes were pinned and glued and the lid was inset so that it sat flush. Two brass screws were put into either end of the lid to hold it firm. They were sanded and varnished, with a brass plaque showing the baby's name and date of birth/death – how strange, sad and profound to have death before a birth. Inside we lined the coffin with a quilted fabric. There we lay the babies, wrapped in a little shawl. We each chose a little gift to bury them with – a butterfly brooch, a carved wooden heart, little toys ...

They are buried next to each other in a rose garden especially for babies within one of the city cemeteries. The chaplain said some words and my husband and I also read some poetry. We threw flowers into the grave. We said our goodbyes and we have sad but lovely memories.

We treated their births and deaths with the dignity and respect which I feel should be afforded to any human being, regardless of their age. To me a baby of any gestational age is a baby, and not simply a foetus. Regardless of whether that baby could survive outside the womb, he or she was a living being, and as such deserving of the utmost respect after death.

Since my babies died, I have joined the Humanist Society of Scotland,

and am now training to be an Officiant at non-religious funerals. I have observed and taken part in ceremonies for babies and would be happy to help anyone else who would like a non-religious ceremony.

Mary Wallace (tel 01786 842239; e-mail: mary@wallace.prestel.co.uk).

Even if the bereaved accept that a body is too damaged to be seen, there can be intermediate measures. The Child Bereavement Trust told the Guardian the story of the father of a very damaged stillborn baby. The father had a photograph taken of the baby's hand curling round his fingers – 'it was the most beautiful picture, and having something like that can make the difference to whether you can cope or not.'

From a more academic perspective, one researcher, Therese Rando, has written, with reference to adult deaths as well as children's:

Visits to the body

Give the bereaved adequate private time to be with, touch, caress and hold the body, as time with the deceased may be very critical in helping them settle unfinished business and accept the reality of loss.

Those who did not view the body or had arranged for immediate disposal of the remains (excluding the normal Jewish custom of not viewing the body) reported the greatest hostility following the death, the greatest increase in consumption of alcohol, tranquillisers and sedatives, the greatest increase in tension and anxiety, the lowest positive recall of the deceased and greater problems in adjustment to the death, particularly among male respondents.

From 'Grief, Dying and Death' by Therese Rando (Champaign, USA; Research Press Co., 1984) quoted in 'Caring For Your Own Dead' by Lisa Carlson.

The Natural Death Centre has proposed that the phrase 'visiting the body' could replace 'viewing', as visiting could include the idea of touching the body. As Stephen Briggs has noted, 'the word "view" is coldly impersonal and conveys a sense of distance and slight distaste. It perpetuates the "keep at a distance and do not touch" inclination.'

Fear of being buried alive

A surprising number of people are frightened that they will be buried alive. Indeed this has occasionally happened. Back in 1912, the Funeral Service Journal reported:

In Galicia, the body of George Masug, a rich landowner, was being interred, and the last prayers were being said by the officiating priests at the open grave amid weeping, when, as the bereaved relatives were dropping earth on the coffin, ghastly sounds were heard to proceed from it. The cover was lifted and a panic arose among members of the family when the supposed-dead man was found to be alive. He was at once freed from his terrible position. Masug, who was supposed to have died from apoplexy, soon recovered and was able to walk home with the mourners.

More recently, the same journal told of a case in America:

The Herald Tribune of May 1994 reported that Elenor Marks from New York, apparently dead and being taken in her coffin to the graveside, alarmed the men carrying it by a faint tapping from its interior. When the lid was removed, it was found that the supposed corpse was alive. She was then moved back to her residence and began recovering. She says that she had full knowledge all the time of what was passing, whilst arrangements were made for her burial, but was unable to give any sign of consciousness until the fear of being interred alive roused her to action.

One perhaps over-suspicious correspondent has complained to The Natural Death Centre about 'the unsavoury practice of removing people from nursing homes to undertakers' parlours before being certified or seen by a doctor, even though a qualified nurse may have expressed an opinion that the person was dead. The reason why this is unsatisfactory is that most undertakers either embalm, sew the gums together or refrigerate the person immediately they arrive on the premises. The consequences of a person not being actually dead are horrific.'

These are not wholly unrealistic fears in Western society today, according to a book by Rodney Davies ('The Lazarus Syndrome', published by Robert Hale, 1999) – in 1996, two women in the UK were found alive after being pronounced dead and a study of 150,000 exhumed American war-dead from World War II in Europe it was revealed that no less than 6,000 (4%) showed signs of having been buried alive.

Doctors, if very concerned to avoid, for instance, misdiagnosing a profound barbiturate- or morphine-induced coma as death, are advised to listen to the heart and lungs with a stethoscope for up to five minutes; to feel the carotid pulse at the side of the neck; to shine a light in the eyes (to see if the pupils stay dilated) and to check there is no blink reflex when the eye is touched. Other situations that can lead to mistakes include hypothermia, near-drowning, unconsciousness from electric shocks, alcohol intoxication and shock following blood loss. In any case, keeping the body at home for several days can reassure all concerned that the person is truly dead.

Laying out the body

If you have a nurse helping you, she or he will normally help with laying out the body. Traditionally whoever is attending to the body closes the eyes after death – and coins on the eyelids can help with this. The chin is propped up with a pillow to keep the mouth closed, or a piece of cloth can be tied under the chin and over the head. To prevent seepage from the body, it may in exceptional cases be prudent (depending on the risk of infection, the likely rate of decomposition and the aesthetics of the situation) to plug the natural orifices (rectum, nasal passages, throat). This is simply done with cotton wool using disposable gloves and some lubrication such as soap or KY jelly if required. An alternative, if there is seepage, is to use incontinence pads from the chemist, replacing them as necessary. The correct procedure when laying out is to press upon the lower abdomen thus ensuring that the bladder is drained. A waterproof dressing should be put on any body ulcers or leaking wounds. As soon as the doctor has certified the cause of death, the body can be washed and dressed, as this is easier in the first six hours or so after death, before the body stiffens. The head is left raised on a pillow – as the embalmers put it, 'this helps prevent the expanding internal contents from purging.'

One correspondent wrote to The Natural Death Centre that she felt 'somewhat unnerved' when washing the body of her husband an hour after he had died, 'to see the purple/bluish state of his back and buttocks, due to the blood draining into it, once circulation stopped'.

For some religious communities, such as Sikhs and Muslims, preparing the body for the funeral by gently washing the body is an act of devotion that family members insist on, even if they have to go to do it in the funeral director's premises. For many Jews, the body should remain untouched for twenty minutes after death, with all washing and preparation of the body being the sole prerogative of the Jewish community.

Forms and procedures

The bureaucracy facing newly-bereaved relatives who are arranging a funeral is fairly minimal, although there will be many more forms to fill in for those looking after probate of the estate. The Consumers' Association devotes two books to the subject ('What To Do When Someone Dies' – the 1994 edition is unreliable, especially on the laws surrounding private land burial – and 'Wills and Probate' – which is excellent); and there is a free Benefits Agency booklet 'What To Do After A Death' (see the Resources chapter). We can help the survivors before our own deaths by following the advice in Chapter 2: by leaving a will, telling people where to find it, and putting in the same place all our financial and other details, along with the information and documents that will be needed for the registration of death (again listed in that chapter); and by simplifying our affairs.

When the person is dying at home, it is as well to ensure that the doctor (not just the nurses) sees the patient within 14 days of the death (28 days in Northern Ireland). This will normally avoid the death being referred to the coroner (see below). After the person has died, the doctor will (without charge) fill in a medical certificate as to the cause of death. (If cremation is wanted, the doctor charges for the relevant form – and will need to know about any operations in the past year – and the doctor gets another doctor to fill in a similar form, for a total charge of £82, known in the trade as 'ash cash'; the forms are issued by crematoria and also stocked by funeral directors.)

If the person dies in hospital, you can refuse permission for a postmortem (to learn more about the cause of death) if you wish. The coroner will have to issue a certificate as to the cause of death (and may insist on a postmortem) if there were unusual circumstances surrounding the death. The coroner can issue an interim certificate to allow the executors to begin work on sorting out the deceased's affairs, if an inquest will decide the cause of death at a later date.

Going to the Registry Office

As the next-of-kin or the person arranging the funeral, you take the medical certificate (if the doctor does not send it for you) to the Registrar of Births and Deaths. You are supposed to do this within five days (eight days in Scotland – the five days is extendable to 14 by agreement) or within 42 days in the case of a stillborn child.

Find out which registrar covers the area where the death occurred by looking up under 'R' in the phone book, 'Registration of Births, Deaths and Marriages', and checking by phone which is the nearest office and asking whether or not you can have an appointment. (You can register the death anywhere that suits you but this can add a few days of delay for receiving the death certificate which may be needed to deal with legal matters.) In Scotland the registrar will want to know the time of death as well as the date and place of death.

Make certain the registrar has correctly recorded all the details in the registry as it is complicated getting them altered once it has all been signed.

You can get away with taking with you just the date of birth of the deceased, where the deceased was born and the maiden name of the deceased (and sending on later, if you can find it, the person's NHS number or medical card, so that NHS payments to the GP cease). But ideally take with you not only the full list of items listed in Chapter 2 but also information about the deceased's banks, friendly societies, life insurance and so on, and then the registrar should be able to estimate how many copies of the death certificate you will need to be able to claim these assets. Sometimes, however, banks and other institutions will simply take a copy of the certificate and give you back the original. It is easier and cheaper to obtain at the time (or within a month) as many copies as you may need and an extra one in case, for £3-50 each (£8 Scotland), rather than later when it can cost £6-50 (£13 Scotland).

The basic white certificate that you will also be given is free and contains a social security form for claiming benefit arrears and widow's benefit.

For burial, either a doctor will have issued a free medical cause of death certificate (a white form) or the coroner will have issued a free pink form. One or the other is given to the registrar, who issues a free green form – which must be obtained before the burial goes ahead (in England and Wales). (However, this paragraph does not apply if there is to be an inquest. In such cases, the coroner will issue a free burial order, which again must be obtained before the burial goes ahead.)

Whether you receive the green form burial certificate from a registrar or the free burial order from a coroner, both have tear-off slips which need to be received by the registrar within 96 hours of the burial having taken place.

Cemeteries may want the certificate or order 24 hours before the burial. For burials in private land, give the certificate or order to the landowner or land manager. (The registrar can issue the free burial certificate for the burial to go ahead, before the death has been registered.)

For a cremation, the forms permitting it may be required by a crematorium at least 24 hours in advance of cremation.

Incidentally, the person who paid for the cremation has the right to collect the ashes at any time, even years later. However, if the crematorium gives a fortnight's notice and the ashes are not collected within that time, the ashes can be buried or scattered by the crematorium.

Sudden death

The following is based on notes sent to the Natural Death Centre by PC Rick Jones of the Coroner's Office in Essex.

GPs may issue a death certificate even if they have not seen their patient in the 14 days prior to death, provided that the person died from a disease for which the doctor was previously treating them. This would be acceptable for burial. However, the registrar at the crematorium would generally want a coroner's involvement in such cases. The patient's doctor contacts H. M. Coroner who may then agree to issue a Coroner's 'A' Certificate, a certificate for when there is no postmortem.

Where the person died unexpectedly but 'naturally', the coroner would issue a 'B' Certificate to the Registrar of Births and Deaths, giving the cause of death as found at postmortem. For cremation, the coroner would also issue an 'E' Certificate free of charge (instead of two medical certificates costing about £82).

For so-called 'unnatural' deaths (suicide, road and industrial accidents or deaths from industrial or notifiable diseases), an inquest has to be held. Once this is officially opened (although it may actually take place at a later date), the coroner issues a cremation form 'E' or a Burial Order.

The bodies of those who died abroad of 'unnatural' causes, when repatriated to this country, have to be referred to the coroner.

Anyone seeking to take a body out of England and Wales (even for sea burial) must obtain a coroner's Out of England Certificate.

Moving the body

Jane Spottiswoode had problems moving her husband Nigel's body after he died:

> There was no way that Nigel in his coffin and with the coffin in a horizontal position, could be carried out of the room and around all the corners and down the stairs to where the Volvo was waiting. Since then I have learned that the way it is done by the professionals is in a body bag, which is much easier to handle, and then transferred to a coffin either in the pick-up vehicle or at the undertakers.

From 'Undertaken with Love' by Jane Spottiswoode.

For how to obtain a body bag see the next chapter but note that a strong sheet or curtain works even better.

You may need a van to transport your coffin. For instance, with a 76" coffin the few estate cars it will fit into are the old Volvo 940, the old Vauxhall Carlton and the Ford Scorpio. The A. B. Welfare and Wildlife Trust tends to use a Renault 5 with the passenger seat removed.

If you do not have access to a suitable estate car or van for transport, and cannot find a friend with one, it may be possible to persuade your local funeral director to help or to use a firm that hires out a chauffeur-driven hearse and bearers. See the section on Transport in the next chapter – this is liable to cost from about £90. Alternatively a transit van can be hired through the Yellow Pages for a few hours from about £40.

One correspondent to the Natural Death Centre found that fixing handles on the two ends of the coffin, helped to get it through the living room and front door, for a burial on their own land.

Sheila Page suggests that an ordinary stretcher can perhaps be borrowed from the local Red Cross or St Johns Ambulance to help move a body to the mortuary. Such a stretcher is long, however, and is likely to need a van. Another alternative is to buy the hessian carrier with eight handles which is detailed in the next chapter.

Carrying the coffin

Coffins are normally carried feet first.

Professional pallbearers tend not to use handles, which are decorative. The coffin is lifted from below and carried on the shoulders. However, handles are useful for burial, to thread the lowering webbing or straps through, so as to prevent the coffin from slipping.

When carrying a cardboard coffin with no handles, the A. B. Welfare and Wildlife Trust uses lowering straps, by placing them over and under for a secure hold, or a large curtain or blanket folded up all four sides.

Sheila Page advises that wooden lathes can also be used to carry a coffin, although only with great care and on the flat (unless you have people before and after to prevent the coffin slipping). She writes (from the experience of organising her husband Jan's funeral):

> We bought three four-foot long pieces of planed 2" by 1" wood, sanded down about 6" at the ends. Slipped under the coffin, these provided a very satisfactory way for six of us to carry the coffin...
>
> The gravediggers had put 2" by 2" wooden bars across the grave with the lowering straps laid neatly along these. We lowered the coffin on to these, our own wooden lathes fitting between, and, being only 1" deep, they were slipped out easily by a nominated friend. Then at a word from our previously appointed chief bearer, we picked up the coffin a few inches, using the straps, and the friend removed the wooden bars. At another word from the chief bearer, we gently lowered the coffin on to the bed of cut grass

laid in it by the grave diggers. We placed the ends of the straps by the edge of the grave.

A family organised cremation in Wales

Wales has a reputation as a difficult part of the world in which to organise a funeral without using funeral directors. But Jill Harcourt-Ray managed it:

In memory of my mother Marjorie

My mother died on February 25th 1998 at 3pm in Prince Phillip Hospital, Llanelli, South Wales.

After leaving the hospital, as I was driving home, I thought what now? I then remembered I had sent to the Natural Death Centre some years ago for their information. However, I called into the local undertakers and of course they were nice, they gave me a quote for a basic funeral, but the voice inside told me to go home and contact the Natural Death Centre. I told the undertaker that I would think about it. He was very surprised. I don't think anyone had ever said such a thing to him before.

The following day, I phone the Natural Death Centre and I was very pleased that I did. I was given the telephone number of Narbarth Crematorium here in West Wales. I contacted the superintendent, the Rev Elwyn John, a wonderful man who has a copy of the 'Dead Good Funerals' book in his office. I made an appointment to see him later the same day. He was very encouraging. He also took me to see behind the scenes at the crematorium to look at the ovens. It really was an education – whereas Swansea crematorium are not helpful at all for d-i-y funerals.

The hospital mortuary agreed to keep my mother's body until the Monday following her death, without charge.

We used the Compakta Eco-Coffin. The man at Compakta told us to stuff old pillow cases with newspaper to put around my mother to keep her in place – apparently there was a programme on TV not long ago with regard to d-i-y funerals – and a man used a Compakta coffin for his aunt who was a very small lady and he filled the space around her with soft toys – however, this makes a lot of pollution during the burning.

My daughter has one of the people-mover type vehicles, so, with the seats taken out, it was ideal to transport my mother. The mortician at the hospital was helpful. He assisted us in arranging Marjorie in the coffin and helped to put the coffin in the transport. He remarked how lovely it was to see a family involved in their loved one's funeral preparation.

Rev Elwyn John met us after a 45 mile journey to his crematorium. He and his assistant wheeled the coffin from the transport into the chapel of rest to await the funeral the following day, Tuesday, March 3rd '98.

We had the last slot of the day, just in case anything did not go according to plan. However, all was well and we had a humanist ceremony and celebration of my mother's life.

We draped a gold brocade cloth over the coffin and had a large photograph of my mother on top, with her favourite iris flowers.

We are a very small family but we found doing my mother's funeral ourselves very, very rewarding. It helped so much with the process of grief.

We did not have any opposition to our plans, but we did meet with surprise. When I registered my mother's death, I was handed a green form to give the undertaker. I then said that I was doing the funeral myself and the registrar looked aghast and said "What are you going to do with your mother's body?" So we explained – and she was lost for words.

> • *Jill Harcourt-Ray, Ty Bryn, Mountain Road, Betws, Ammanford, Carmarthenshire SA18 2PL, Wales (tel 01269 593017).*
> • *Rev Elwyn Jon, Parc Gwyn Crematorium, Narberth, Dyfed SA67 8UD (tel 01834 860622; fax 01834 861309).*

Burial on private land

Organising a burial on private land is much simpler than most people tend to think, although it can be hard work physically, as the following account demonstrates.

A grave that took four days to dig

Four weeks before my friend Marcelle died, I asked her: 'Just in case I should live longer than you, and in case I should be asked to help with the funeral arrangements, what is it you would like, as I have absolutely no idea?'

'I would like a community service in St Marks Church over the road,' Marcelle replied, 'and a little service with the 90-year-old priest back in my village in France, for my relatives there. Apart from that, I'm not bothered.'

'Do you want undertakers and a posh coffin?'

'No, I want you to organise it ... But I'm not dead yet you know.'

Marcelle died as she lived, with great fortitude. Her husband John and their three children – Pierre, John-David and Marie, all young adults – along with John-David's girlfriend Stephie, had been on duty in a 24-hour rota caring for Marcelle during her last days, and in the event they proved quite capable of organising everything for the funeral too. John-David and Pierre helped the local furniture maker to make a beautiful coffin out of one-inch pine, with a wooden cross pattern on top and wooden handles wide enough for webbing to slip through, all covered with a light matt varnish. Pierre went down to the piece of land the family owns in the Cotswolds, and there a handful of friends spent no less than four days hacking with pickaxes through stony ground to dig a grave – a grave so deep, John remarked, that there would be room for him too in due course.

John-David collected the death certificate (with six copies for banks and institutions) and we noted the green form's tear-off slip which you have to return with details of where the burial took place and the date. The Gloucestershire County Council planning department confirmed that there was no need for permission from them, and that they had no concerns about a private land burial so long as no archaeological ruins were to be disturbed.

My friend Nicholas drove his Toyota van with me and the boys on board, to the hospital mortuary to pick up Marcelle's body. We had a funeral director's release form which the hospital nurse had given John-David, and which we had filled in with our own names as the funeral directors. The hospital porter had never dealt directly with a family before, so for this special occasion he decided to leave Marcelle's body wrapped like a mummy taped up in their mortuary sheet. He helped us to put the body into the biodegradable body bag which Green Undertakings had sent us and to lift this unexpectedly heavy weight into the coffin.

Now I was glad that we had six strong bearers. We'd had a rehearsal in church with the empty coffin the evening before, when it had all seemed easy. But now we carefully repositioned the bearers so that they were all paired off in size and were all taking some of the weight.

A local woman had typeset the service sheets without charge, and Instant Print had also kindly printed them for free. And so the requiem mass began. 300 people crowded into the church. We followed the bishop in, with the coffin, and we left it in the centre of the chancel, on a low dais. Everyone had been invited to bring one flower only, which they all came up to place in front of the coffin.

Pierre read a bible extract. John, who is an assistant priest, made a moving address about his wife and his family, urging neighbours not to stop dropping by. The bishop outlined some of Marcelle's good works, forgetting to mention that it was largely thanks to her efforts that the beautiful church we were in had been saved from being turned into a block of flats.

The coffin stayed in the side chapel overnight, and the next day, in the afternoon, a small convoy of cars (which would have displeased car-hating Marcelle) drove to the Cotswolds.

We hauled the coffin up the steep hill, using webbing to lift it. Green Undertakings had run out of proper funeral webbing, but John-David had found furniture webbing in John Lewis department store which worked just as well.

John was both the priest conducting the service and husband for this final gathering, with 50 of us crowded round. He read some prayers and he recalled a touching poem by Vikram Seth:

> All you who sleep tonight
> Far from the ones you love,
> No hands to left or right,
> And emptiness above –
>
> Know that you're not alone.
> The whole world shares your tears,
> Some for two nights or one,
> And some for all their years.

Betsy played some Schubert on her flute, people wept and shared their memories of Marcelle and we sang Blake's Jerusalem from memory ('And did those feet ...'). We followed on from John's words 'ashes to ashes, dust to dust ...' with the African custom of everybody helping to fill the grave. We were throwing in very stony soil, which crashed down so hard I feared the coffin would split open.

It was, it is, all very sad. But I think the funeral helped.

From an article in 'Before and After' by Nicholas Albery.

Rural parts of Montana in the United States can include an extreme form of 'recycling' of the body after burial, according to Stephen Levine, who writes:

Fruit tree planted over body

Often, in the back country of Montana, a hole will be dug and the body, in a plain pine coffin or perhaps just wrapped in a tie-dyed cloth, will be lowered into the ground. Instead of a tombstone, a fruit tree is planted over the body. The roots are nourished by the return of that body into the earth from which it was sustained. And in the years to follow, eating the fruit from that tree will be like partaking in that loved one. It touches on the ritual of the Eucharist.

From 'Who Dies?' by Stephen Levine.

In the UK, from the mid 17th century, the early Quakers were often buried in their gardens – indeed William Penn, the founder of Pennsylvania, is buried in the garden of the Friends Meeting House in Jordans, Buckinghamshire. But nowadays, how do people in the UK go about arranging a funeral on their own land? One of The Natural Death Centre's contacts arranged this after the sudden death of her husband from a heart attack by asking her lawyer to set aside a part of the large back garden for the grave, with its own access, so that this part would not be sold with the rest of the house and grounds. Some council officials still do not know how limited the laws are surrounding private burial – see Ian Alcock's struggles, below – so if you approach them for their blessing, go armed with the information in this chapter.

Planning permission for private burial?

Ian Alcock in Aberdeenshire wants himself and his wife to be buried in their wild flower pasture on their own hill in a special conservation area (SSSI). He was told to approach the Nature Conservancy Council for Scotland for initial permission and then had to pay £77 for a planning application for 'change of use of hill land to private burial ground' and £60 for a small ad in the local newspaper under 'developments which may cause concern in the neighbourhood'. 'There is no obligation to seek the approval of neighbours,' he writes; and the environmental health officer confirmed that the burial was not likely to cause pollution.

Alcock has built his own coffin: 'It cost me £40 for the plywood and is big enough for two (in case my wife and I go at the same time) and on account of my lack of carpentry expertise, has a certain "rustic charm". The postman refused to believe that it was a coffin until I put rope handles or slings round it (to avoid the corpse falling out of the bottom) and sprayed "RIP" on it with a black sheep marker. It is now in store in a building awaiting me. The dogs peed on it when it was outside, but I had a strong friend help me to move it. Incidentally, a friend has told me that she has recently paid a £1,000 undertaker's bill (and it is cheaper up here) for the "simplest possible" funeral for her father.'

Ian Alcock, Shannel, Ballogie, Aboyne, Aberdeenshire AB34 5DR
(tel & fax 013398 84207).

Ian Alcock subsequently successfully appealed against the need for planning permission. The Scottish Office, in the person of the Deputy Chief Reporter R. M. Hickman (Ref. P/PPA/GD/342, Nov. 25th 1992), ruled that 'a limited number of unmarked and unfenced graves would not constitute a material change of use and I conclude that the planning consent issued to you by the district council is superfluous'. The decision letter also noted that the square area in the middle of grazing land, identified by Ian Alcock for the burial ground, was about 50 metres by 50 metres, and that Ian and his wife wished to be buried there, and to be able to 'afford this opportunity to another close member of the family, family retainer, or perhaps a close friend. ... As there would be no change in the surface land use, nor any upstanding physical features resulting from the intended burials, I am satisfied that a limited number of private graves would not result in a material change of use. If the ground were to be fenced off to become a cemetery, I would agree with the district council that a material change of use would have occurred. ... I have also considered whether the burials would constitute "engineering ... or other operations in, on, over or under the land" ... However, I am satisfied that the digging of a very limited number of graves by hand ... would not amount to a significant engineering or other operation. If there were a large number of burials, perhaps involving an access track or mechanical excavation, the situation would perhaps be different but that would be a matter of fact and degree to be considered on its merits.'

More cautiously, a spokesman for the Department of the Environment wrote to the Natural Death Centre on May 15th 1994: 'May I confirm that planning permission is not required for the burial of one or two persons in back gardens, it would only be required if there was an intention to bury a larger number of people.'

On one occasion, a case was won on appeal, a Lawful Development Certificate (variously termed either an LDC or a Certificate of Lawfulness or a Certificate of Lawful Use) having been refused. The A. B. Welfare and Wildlife Trust reports that, in May 1996, a man in East Sussex won his appeal to the Department of the Environment against the local authority, who had turned down his application for a Lawful Development Certificate to have two burials in his half acre garden.

Applying to a local authority for a Lawful Development Certificate is a way of determining whether something is legal in planning law, without having to apply for planning permission. John Bradfield of the A. B. Welfare and Wildlife Trust, who has been the Natural Death Centre's main source of information on the laws surrounding funerals, and who is now the UK's acknowledged expert on private land burial law, describes the following two cases in 'Green Burial' (in the out-of-print 1994 edition):

> • No planning consent was required for a private burial ground in the Harrogate area to be used for 'non-commercial' burials. There would be no fences or gravestones, and the site was within an organic smallholding that would continue to be grazed as before.
>
> • No planning consent was required for 'private non-commercial burial of the householder, those resident with her at the time of their deaths and her relatives only' – for burial in a 300 square metre garden also near Harrogate.

This, then, is the Natural Death Centre's conclusion: planning permission is not required for non-commercial sites, for a limited number of burials for family, friends and those living in the house.

In Eire, by contrast, it is claimed that permission is required from the environment ministry. One correspondent writes, however, that people have been taking the law into their own hands: 'In Eire, the way an inexpensive, green and d-i-y funeral is done is that you bury the remains on your own or the deceased person's property.' If the police later take action, with a prosecution and the courts, they will not exhume the corpse. Depending on how long it has been since the burial, a small fine could be imposed, but this would be unlikely.

Legal requirements concerning funerals

The Natural Death Centre published 'Green Burial – The d-i-y guide to law and practice' which is now out of print. John Bradfield, its author, who founded the A. B. Welfare and Wildlife Trust, put an immense amount of research into the two editions of 'Green Burial' and generously donated all the proceeds from sales to the Natural Death Centre. He demolished many legal myths that have surfaced in funeral guides, resulting in changes to the 'Encyclopaedia Britannica', 'Penguin Guide To The Law', the 1994 Which? Consumers' Association book 'What To Do When Someone Dies' and several other books. He has persuaded officials at the highest levels to alter their advice.

What follows is the Centre's understanding of some of the A. B. Welfare and Wildlife Trust's key findings, but readers are advised to refer urgent or complex enquiries to the Trust (tel 01423 5309000 or 868121):

> • Some people organising funerals without using funeral directors have had trouble getting the hospital to give them the body. Unless the coroner is making an investigation into the cause of the death, it is a common law offence for a hospital to refuse to release a body to the executors. As one trial judge put it in 1882: 'executors have a right to the custody and possession of [the] body.'

If you are having problems getting the body released to you, contact the Natural Death Centre and they will willingly send a stiffly-worded fax to any hospital proving obstructive, citing chapter and verse as to their offence and its possible consequences.

• Although cemeteries and crematoria may have their own particular rules or guidelines, there is no law requiring a coffin. It is, however, an offence for a dead body to be exposed naked in a public place if this causes shock or disgust or is intended to do so.

• A body can be transported across county boundaries without permission and no fee is payable. Details can be found in an article by John Bradfield in the Funeral Service Journal. Consent, given free of charge, must be obtained to move a body out of England/Wales (treated as one area), Northern Ireland or Scotland – which includes from one to the other.

• 'Subject to any restrictive covenants affecting the use of the land (see below), a place of burial may be established by any person without statutory authority, in private land, provided no statutory or other 'nuisance' such as smell or pollution is caused ...' (Halsbury's Laws of England, 1975:504, Butterworths). 'The statute law on burial is archaic ... and does not apply ... to private burial grounds' (Hickman, R. M. Deputy Chief Reporter in the Alcock case, see above).

• There may be very rare instances where a property's restrictive covenants prevent the creation of graves, but application can be made for such covenants to be lifted on the grounds that they have ceased to serve their original purpose.

• It is a myth that in England and Wales there must be no neighbours within a hundred yards of a burial – this is a misreading of the 1855 Burials Acts (Ch. 128, S.9 and now repealed; and Ch. 68, S.7 – the latter does apply the 100 yards requirement but only to public burial grounds in Scotland).

• An 1847 Act may apply to some old cities or towns, requiring 30 inches of soil between the coffin top and the ordinary surface of the ground. Council cemeteries are governed by a 1977 Order requirement that there be 2 or 3 feet from the coffin top to the surface. But for any other burial grounds there is no national law specifying a minimum depth.

• There is no requirement to inform the council's environmental health officers of plans for burial on private land, nor do such burials require their advance permission. These officers have no powers to order exhumations. However, they do have legal powers to prevent any 'deposit' which might be 'prejudicial to health or a nuisance'.

The health risks from burial are very remote. Bradfield quotes a professor of forensic pathology and a consultant to the Home Office as concluding that 'the risks [from the] exhumation of ... recent burials are no greater than those of gardening. Antibiotic [precautions are] not required'.

• The Environment Agency (formerly National Rivers Authority) is entitled to carry out works to prevent pollution of 'any controlled waters', but there is no legal obligation to consult it in advance of a burial.

• In England, Wales and Scotland, a burial authorisation must be obtained before the burial takes place.

• In England and Wales, the tear-off slip on the burial authorisation must be completed by the landowner or land manager, giving the date and place of burial, and must be received by the Registrar of Births and Deaths within 96 hours of any burial. This slip will be on a form issued before the burial either by the same Registrar (a 'green form' or Burial Certificate, also known as a Disposal Certificate) or by a coroner, if an inquest will be or has been held (a white form called a Burial Order).

• There must be a land burial register for all graves in England. Unless some other law applies, it is necessary to comply with the 1864 Registration of Burials Act, Ch.97, even for an isolated grave in a garden. It requires that Christian laws be followed, even by non-Christians, on the layout and storage of registers. It is difficult to make proper sense of this law and only if noncompliance is 'wilful' can a prosecution take place. Private burial grounds would be expected by any court to do their utmost to comply.

This durable burials register must record, in columns, the 'Entry No., Christian name and surname in block capitals, Address, Date of Birth, Age, Date of Burial, Plan Ref. No., Officiating Minister', with each entry separated by a printed line. The register must be kept in a specially protected steel cupboard.

• Consecration by the Church of England alters the legal status of the land, whereas consecration by other religions may 'bless' a piece of land but has no legal implications. Even the Church of England is moving away from consecrating its own property.

• There is a common law right for Christians to have a Christian burial, otherwise it is not legally necessary to have a Christian or other religious service or any officiant presiding over a funeral; or to be buried in a formal cemetery or consecrated land.

• 'No Church of England minister' writes John Bradfield, 'can be criticised for holding a religious service in an unconsecrated burial place. This includes a garden or house ... .'

• There are no laws which can force you to move a body in private land from one grave to another.

• No law has ever been passed about the scattering of ashes in public places and the A. B. Welfare and Wildlife Trust has never heard of anyone ever being prosecuted for doing so – nor for the scattering of ashes in rivers.

• Exhumations in England and Wales, unless only from one legally consecrated place to another, require a licence from any Secretary of State (licences are issued by the Home Office for a current fee of £10, maximum fee £20).

• Exhumation from or to legally consecrated land requires a Church of England document called a 'faculty'.

• In theory, a funeral pyre that causes no 'nuisance' (ie pollution or smell) seems to be legal, as long as no construction is made which could be defined as a crematorium. There has been no recent instance of an outdoor cremation. However, according to reports in the Funeral Service Journal, the body of a Nepalese diplomat was cremated on a funeral pyre within the grounds of Brookwood in the 1940s. In the First World War, the bodies of Hindu soldiers who died in the Kitchener Hospital in Brighton were cremated on funeral pyres on a specially prepared site at Patcham, on the Downs.

• Under the Anatomy Act 1984, S.4(9), a hospital, nursing home or other institution has the right to send a body for anatomical use, without consent, if no friend or relative takes possession of the body.

The fear that the bodies of paupers would be used for dissection purposes has haunted the poor ever since the 1832 Anatomy Act (as described by Ruth Richardson in her book 'Death, Dissection and the Destitute' published by Pelican, 1989). It may well be true that hospitals nowadays do not take advantage of this legal power, but it is ethically unacceptable that they should have the potential right to do so.

Burial recommendations (not requirements)

The above summarises the laws. The following are merely the Natural Death Centre's recommendations for good practice:

• Farmland can be used for private land burial. The Ministry of Agriculture has written to the Centre that set-aside land can be used, 'provided there was no return to the farmer in cash or kind ... and the land remains croppable and in good agricultural condition.' Farmers could run green burial grounds in association with wildlife charities, as in the case of Oakfield near Manningtree.

• A large garden can be used for burial. The Natural Death Centre helped one couple in their nineties choose a spot for burial on the edge of their ten acre garden where their beloved boxer dogs were buried, with a way to reach the graves from the public footpath, in case the remainder of the property were later to be sold by the family. The couple also ordered cardboard coffins which they stored in their garage. They felt prepared for their deaths, but their plans were cruelly disrupted when increasing disabilities forced them to move to a residential home, and to sell their home to cover the costs.

The Natural Death Centre advises careful thought before creating a grave in a small urban garden. It is easier to bury a body than it is to exhume it; a garden burial can cause dissension amongst relatives; neighbours may feel offended; and one estate agent has estimated, probably pessimistically, that a back garden burial would substantially reduce the value of a property. In 1995, the body of the playwright Robert Bolt was buried by his family in their garden. It seems possible in such cases that burials of the famous might even increase a property's value.

• You do not need a Lawful Development Certificate. If you nevertheless wish to have one to set your mind at rest, you may want to ask the council to keep the decision-making stage confidential – the outcome, however, must be recorded on a public register. The cost of applying for a Certificate is approximately half the cost of applying for planning permission (the full cost is payable if one or more burials have taken place). If the Certificate is refused or specifies unsatisfactory conditions, a free appeal can be made to the Department of the Environment, although their findings will then definitely be made public.

• In general, the Environment Agency is responsible for the protection and regulation of groundwater and surface water. They have advised the following wording: 'Although there is no formal requirement for authorising private land burials, it is a good idea to contact the Environment Agency by phoning 0645 333111 (Eds: which number should automatically direct you to the nearest area or regional office; if you get no satisfaction you could try phoning Dr Rob Ward of their National Groundwater and Contaminated Land Centre on 0121 711 5841 who is knowledgeable on the issue at the national level). The Environment Agency is unlikely to have any objections provided that the grave is not within 10 metres of any standing or running water, or 50 metres of a well, borehole or spring that supplies water for human consumption. For graveyards or sites of multiple burials a more restrictive view may be taken. The Environment Agency will deal with enquiries sympathetically and will only advise against burial where there is potential for significant pollution to the environment.'

• A suitable grave should have no water at the bottom when first dug.

• It would be wise to avoid burial in very sandy soil, as it is unsuitable for shallow graves and digging a deep grave can be dangerous.

• The burial needs to be deep enough to prevent foraging animals from trying to dig up the body.

• It would be sensible to store a detailed plan of where the body is buried (or a copy of any exhumation licence) with the deeds of your property. One council's Environmental Services Division arranged for an informal notice to be attached to the Land Charges Register so as to inform prospective purchasers of the private graves on the land.

Making the coffin

The Oregon-based novelist Ken Kesey (author of 'One Flew Over the Cuckoo's Nest') wrote to his friends about the death in a traffic accident of his twenty year old son Jed: 'It was the toughest thing any of us has ever had to go through, yet it also had and always will have a decided glory. There was also the support we got from friends and family, from teachers and coaches and schoolmates. Without this support I don't think we would have attempted the kind of funeral we had. A home-made ceremony is legally possible. All you need is the land, the determination and the family.'

Jed Kesey's funeral

We built the box ourselves (George Walker, mainly) and Zane and Jed's friends and frat brothers dug the hole in a nice spot between the chicken house and the pond. Page found the stone and designed the etching. You would have been proud, Wendell, especially of the box – clear pine pegged together and trimmed with redwood. The handles of thick hemp rope. And you, Ed, would have appreciated the lining. It was a piece of Tibetan brocade given Mountain Girl by Owsley fifteen years ago, gilt and silver and russet phoenix bird patterns, unfurling in flames. And last month, Bob, Zane was goose hunting in the field across the road and killed a snow goose.

I told him be sure to save the down. Susan Butkovitch covered this in white silk for the pillow while Faye and MG and Gretch and Candace stitched and stapled the brocade into the box.

It was a double-pretty day, like winter holding its breath, giving us a break. About 300 people stood around and sang from the little hymnbooks that Diane Kesey had Xeroxed – 'Everlasting Arms', 'Sweet Hour of Prayer', 'In the Garden', and so forth. With all my cousins leading the singing and Dale on his fiddle. While we were singing 'Blue Eyes Crying in the Rain', Zane and Kit and the neighbour boys that have grown up with all of us carried the box to the hole. The preacher is also the Pleasant Hill School superintendent and has known our kids since kindergarten. I learned a lot about Jed that I'd either forgotten or never known – like his being a member of the National Honour Society and finishing sixth in a class of more than a hundred.

We sang some more. People filed by and dropped stuff in on Jed. I put in that silver whistle I used to wear with the Hopi cross soldered on it. One of our frat brothers put in a quartz watch guaranteed to keep beeping every 15 minutes for five years. Faye put in a snapshot of her and I standing with a pitchfork all Grantwoodesque in front of the old bus. Paul Foster put in the little leatherbound New Testament given him by his father who had carried it during his 65 years as a minister. Paul Sawyer read from 'Leaves of Grass' while the boys each hammered in the one nail they had remembered to put in their pockets. The Betas formed a circle and passed the loving cup around (a ritual our fraternity generally uses when a member is leaving the circle to become engaged) (Jed and Zane and I are all members, y'unnerstand, not to mention Hagen) and the boys lowered the box with these ropes George had cut and braided. Zane and I tossed in the first shovelfuls. It sounded like the first thunderclaps of 'Revelations'.

The following is adapted from a postscript by George Walker about the making of Jed's coffin.

We selected some clear white boards for the sides and top. Nice looking and easy to work with, pine is also traditional.

It was a very good coffin, as coffins go, very beautiful everybody said, and certainly a labour of love. But I don't really believe that is the point. The real value of that coffin was in the doing, in the building of it ourselves. Not in the coffin, as a thing, but in the act of creating it, as an event. It made us all feel better to do this ourselves, to take charge of things as much as we could, not just the coffin but the burial as well. Perhaps it's because, when we lose someone close, particularly someone young and in the prime of life, we feel more than a little burned that things have been jerked so irrevocably beyond our control. Anything we can do to regain our handle on events is gratifying.

Whatever the reason, all who kept themselves actively involved in getting Jed buried agreed: we all gained something through our efforts. We felt better about it than if we had just turned it all over to the professionals, and gone about our business of feeling bad. So, I would say to anybody who feels that they might want to give it a try when someone close dies, absolutely yes; build it yourself. Even if you can't do basic carpentry, you can nail together a kit. If you do have skills, you can make something that will make you feel good long after it's buried out of sight. It doesn't have to be fancy; simple and neat is just fine, but do make it strong. You'll be surprised by the weight.

> *From an article in CoEvolution Quarterly (Summer 1994);*
> *now called Whole Earth Review,*
> *1408 Mission Ave, San Rafael,*
> *CA 94901-1971, USA; subs. $20).*

The Huelin d-i-y coffins

If expense is the main consideration, it is worth noting that making a coffin yourself will probably work out as expensive just for materials as the cheapest coffin available from a funeral director (see the next chapter). Be careful by the way to make the coffin at least an inch or so longer than the person was tall – a body is longer lying down.

The Huelins, a couple in Oxford, gained a great deal of satisfaction from making their own coffins and found themselves quite a centre of media attention as a result. Barbara Huelin outlines the story:

> My husband (now in his eighties) has built our coffins. We spent a most enlightening few months organising and preparing for our deaths; the idea has caught on amongst our friends in Oxford.
>
> The coffins are made in blockboard at a cost of about £50 each (not including our time). They are painted green and have nautical-looking rope handles (from the boat chandlers). The coffins are stored in the workroom. We have bought a double-decker site in the local Council cemetery for £150 to which we intend that family and friends shall physically bear us. We are leaving the commemorative gravestone for our survivors to add if they wish, so that they have something they can do.

There were a number of interested enquiries from members of the public so her husband David sent the Natural Death Centre the following detailed description and drawings of the design that he used:

> **Materials:** The most convenient, though possibly not the cheapest, material is three quarter inch (18mm) blockboard; it is lighter and stronger than chipboard, and is much easier to work. It is normally sold in sheets measuring 8ft x 4ft (2.44m x 1.22m); each sheet costs about £30 (March 1992). The half inch (12mm) version is cheaper but seems rather flimsy for a coffin, and the one inch (25mm) appears unnecessarily heavy, and costs more.
>
> Three sheets of 8ft x 4ft blockboard are enough for two coffins, with a little fiddling. It is possible, though more difficult, to make one coffin with

Coffin A (woman)

Blockboard sheet 1

Coffin B (Man)

Blockboard sheet 2

Coffins A & B

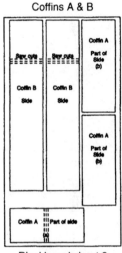

Blockboard sheet 3

a sheet and a half, though it is not always possible to buy half-sheets. The following suggestions are for making two coffins with three sheets of board.

Other Materials (for two coffins):

• 36ft (11m) wood strip 35mm x 10mm (rim round lid)

• 42ft (12.8m) batten 25mm x 25mm; this is not needed if the joining is by dovetailing – see below

• 400 (2 boxes) steel wood-screws, gauge 8 x one and a quarter inch

• 100 panel pins three quarter inch

• 250ml (quarter litre) wood-working glue, e.g. Evo-Stik Wood Adhesive

• 1 litre paint (optional)

• Handles: special subject dealt with separately below.

Tools: A hand-held electric circular saw is invaluable for cutting the basic shapes in the blockboard, which by hand would be arduous work. If dovetailing is intended a coping saw is useful; beyond that, a tenon-saw, chisel, angle-gauge, and sanding equipment for finishing off.

Method: Take the measurements of the future occupant of each coffin, not forgetting the hip width; allow extra space for the possibility of putting on weight before the coffin is needed.

With these measurements the main components for the two coffins can be drawn out on the blockboard: floor and lid, sides and ends (see the illustrations). Since the basic measurements are internal, allowance must be made for the thickness of the wood when drawing the basic shapes.

It is advisable to defer cutting out the lids until the main boxes are built (see below).

Joining: Attaching the sides and ends to the floor of the coffin and to each other, can be done in several ways; the simplest would seem to be one of the following:

1. With internal battens or corner-blocks, using the 25mm x 25mm batten listed above. With plenty of glue and screws this can be quite satisfactory; the batten joining the sides and ends to the floor of the box can be fixed below the floor for extra strength. As the four corners are not right angles, the internal block or batten will have to be shaped to the actual angle.

2. With dovetailing (so called, though it is not true dovetailing); that is by cutting alternating tongues and recesses all along the edges to be joined, so that they fit together. Each tongue and recess can be 3 or 4 inches long; once the whole thing fits snugly together, the joins can be glued and screwed with a one and a quarter inch screw through every tongue. The recesses need to be a whisker over three quarters of an inch (19mm) deep to match the thickness of the board.

This system involves more work and precision than the batten method, but the result is neat and very strong.

Shaped sides: To achieve the bends in the sides of the coffins, the inner surface of the board should have five or six saw-cuts made across it, to a depth of about three quarters of its thickness; it will then bend to the shape of the floor. The saw-cuts can be filled with glue to add to their solidity, but this is not essential. If the batten method is used, the batten itself can be treated in the same way.

In this particular layout for three sheets of board it has been necessary to divide the sides of coffin 'A' into two sections; they can be joined together by dovetailing at the appropriate angle. With four boards this dividing would not be necessary.

Lid: The precise shaping of the lid of each coffin can be left until the main body of the box is complete; this can be placed inverted over the piece of board reserved for the lid, and its outline drawn straight onto the wood. The lid should have a rim or lip all round its edge, made from the 35mm x

10mm strip listed above; this can be fixed with glue and panel pins.

Once it fits nicely, the lid can be drilled for screws, about 8 inches apart, using gauge 8, length one and a quarter inch screws and pilot holes can be drilled in the main box. The thoughtful coffin builder will provide a bag of screws for the purpose, and possibly a screwdriver too.

Headrest: A dead person's head falls back unbecomingly unless it is supported. The coffins should therefore have a small platform across the head end, slightly sloping, some two to three inches from the floor of the box.

Packing: Though not strictly part of the construction, there is the question of packing or lining. A very economical, attractive, and adequately absorbent packing is wood-shavings. If shavings of nice-smelling woods, such as cedar or pitch pine, can be obtained, so much the better. One dustbin-liner-full is probably enough.

Paint: Blockboard is not a very interesting colour; a litre of matt emulsion paint will make the two coffins look much more interesting; they can also be embellished with paintings of flowers or boats or castles, to taste.

Handles: The importance of handles depends on how the coffins are to be carried: if at shoulder height by skilled men, then no handles are required at all (professional bearers never use them). If the intention is that a coffin should be carried by family and friends, with their hands, then the handles are necessary and should be functional.

Metal or tough plastic handles, such as are used on swing and sliding doors, are inexpensive but great care is needed in fixing them. It may be advisable to use one and a half inch screws going through the comparatively soft blockboard into a hardwood block inside. Note that if cremation is chosen, then no large metal parts such as handles should be employed.

Another method is with nylon rope of half inch diameter. Half inch holes, some five inches apart, in three pairs, are to be drilled in the sides of the coffin; the rope (which must be nylon) is cut into lengths of 12 or 13 inches (30 to 33cm) and the ends are threaded into the holes from the outside, so that at least one inch projects on the inside of the box. Next a metal washer with exactly a half inch hole is fitted over the projecting end of rope, which is then melted with a hot-air gun so that it flattens down and spreads over the metal washer; when it cools and hardens it is very firm.

This method is easier than it may seem; it is extremely strong, and the rope loops on the outside of the coffin look attractive and appropriately modest.

Materials: 4 metres (2m each coffin) half-inch nylon rope obtainable at boat chandlers' shops. 24 half-inch washers.

Tool: Hot-air gun.

Barbara and David Huelin, 69 Kingston Road, Oxford OX2 6RJ.

A simple burial box

Ernest Morgan in his excellent book about funerals in the United States, 'Dealing Creatively with Death – A Manual of Death Education and Simple Burial', describes the making of a simple burial box, which has top and sides of quarter inch plywood, and the bottom and ends of three quarter inch plywood. Two reinforcing battens, three quarters of an inch thick, run the length of the box on the inside, attached to the side pieces at the top edge, so the top of the box rests on them – as in this illustration. Ernest Morgan writes:

Using nails or screws (Eds: the latter, say gauge 8, length one and quarter inch, would give extra strength, particularly for the ends. Wood glue, such as Evo-Stik Wood Adhesive, would also give additional strength):

• Attach the reinforcing battens to the side pieces, flush with the edge and the end, making sure to have the good side of the plywood facing outwards.

• Attach the side pieces to the bottom.

• Attach the ends, again with the good sides out, to the bottom and to the side strips.

Four chest handles, two screwed to each end, could be useful for ease of carrying when going through doors (Eds: or rope handles could be used, as in the Huelin coffins, above). The handles could be stored in the box and screwed on when needed. Likewise, the cover could be tacked lightly in place until the box is needed and then when the time comes fixed firmly down.

A birch coffin

For those who would like something finer, and who have the skills, a coffin made of birch or pine planks dovetailed together could look good, with the name carved into the wood and patterns around the edges as desired, and a final polish with beeswax or linseed oil.

Coffins for cremation – avoiding pollution

If the coffin is destined for cremation rather than burial, there are various requirements for avoiding air pollution. The best approach is to check with your intended crematorium as to whether first, they would accept a home-made coffin (see next chapter); second, what the maximum size of the coffin may be – one crematorium in the United States has said that home-made coffins tend to be made larger than they need be (Lisa Carlson in 'Caring for your own Dead' writes that 'two feet wide and 18 inches deep is sufficient for most bodies'); third, whether the particular construction you are planning needs modifying in any way; fourth, whether any lining or handles you are planning for the coffin or clothing for the body are unacceptable (for instance, PVC linings and rubber soled shoes are discouraged); and fifth, whether any medical implants in the body will be problematic. A pacemaker would need to be removed, for instance, in case it explodes during cremation. In 1996, five thousand pounds worth of damage was caused by an exploding pacemaker at the Morden crematorium. A doctor, a mortician at your local hospital or a funeral director can do this, although, writes Lisa Carlson, 'anyone can do it. A pacemaker is about the size of a small coin, embedded just under the skin, usually near the neck or lower on the rib cage. It is attached to wires which should be snipped.' Some crematoria may also not want to burn a body with silicone implants – in Southern California the silicone turned into a sticky goo on the floor of the cremator, although a UK crematorium had no difficulties in a test it ran.

Instructions for funeral directors have been issued by the cremation authorities, many of which would apply to those running a funeral themselves. P. J. Wilson, the secretary of the Federation of British Cremation Authorities, writes to the Natural Death Centre that 'Crematoria invariably require that bodies are conveyed to the building in a reasonable manner. A rigid coffin able to withstand any handling or transportation problems, adequately secured and identified and suitably lined to prevent leakage of fluids or other material will be required.'

Instructions from the Federation of British Cremation Authorities

• *Bearers:* Sufficient bearers should convey the coffin reverently from the hearse to the catafalque.

  • *Coffin construction:* The coffin must be made of a suitable material which, when placed in a cremator and subjected to the accepted cremation processes, is easily combustible and which does not emit smoke, give off toxic gas or leave any retardant smears or drips after final combustion. No metal furniture or fittings whatever shall be used on a coffin for cremation. No metal of any kind shall be used in the manufacture of such a coffin except as necessary for its safe construction and then only metal of a high ferrous content [Eds: eg use ferrous screws]. Cross pieces must not be attached to the bottom of the coffin. If it is desired to strengthen the bottom of the coffin, wooden strips may be placed lengthwise for this purpose. The coffin must not be painted or varnished but may be covered with a suitable cloth [Eds: water-based paints *may* be allowed; for instance, Firwood Paints' Firaqua 482 (tel 01204 525231), a water based acrylic gloss, has been fully crematoria tested, dries fast, is low odour, comes in a range of colours or as a clear finish for natural wood and can be applied by brush or as a spray]. Products containing any chloride or fluorides are prohibited, eg polyvinyl chloride (PVC), melamine. The use of polystyrene must be restricted to the coffin nameplate only, in which case it must not exceed 90 grams in weight.

No coffin shall be accepted unless it bears adequate particulars of the identity of the deceased person therein [Eds: normally this would include the name, age and date of death of the person].

• *Lining of the coffin:* The use of sawdust or cotton-wool must be avoided. If circumstances require, suitable sealing material may be used, but no metal, rubber or polyvinyl chloride (PVC) will be permitted and on no account must pitch or a similar substance be used. [Eds: no lead-lined coffins would be permitted.]

• *Size of the coffin:* Where the external dimensions of a coffin are likely to exceed length 81 inches (206 cm), width 28 inches (71 cm) and depth 22 inches (56 cm) the proper officer of the crematorium must be given advance notice.

• *Cremation of infants:* In cases when bereaved parents desire the cremation of the body of an infant, they should be warned that there are occasions when no tangible remains are left after the cremation process has been completed. This is due to the cartilagineous nature of the bone structure.

If the warning is not given the parents may have been denied the choice of earth burial and thereby been subjected to understandable distress.

• *Cremated remains:* An urn or casket for cremated remains should be of sufficient internal dimension to provide a minimum of 200 cubic inches (3,280 cubic cm) and securely labelled. The container should be strong enough to resist breakage in transit. The lid must fit tightly and the fastening should be strong enough to prevent the lid being forced open by distortion of the container through maltreatment in transit.

Adapted from a text sent by the Federation of
British Cremation Authorities.

Deidre Martin has sent the Natural Death Centre an encouraging description of the funeral of her mother, Dorothy, which they organised themselves and for which they made the coffin. The description, adapted extracts from which appear below, ties together many of the elements previously discussed in this chapter.

In memory of Dorothy Miller – a simple funeral

My mother died in the Royal Sussex Hospital, Brighton, at 11.20am on Friday February 21st, 1992, at the age of 85. Early that morning my husband and I were called to the hospital and she died when we were both present. She was quiet and peaceful and looked very calm. A young nurse and I laid her out, and I placed some flowers by her before we said goodbye.

My mother had always said she wished to be buried 'simply' and we had already told the hospital matron that we would like to make the arrangements ourselves. She was extremely sympathetic and very helpful. She made an appointment for my husband and me to see the hospital registration officer that afternoon and told us the hospital would be able to keep my mother's body until we had made adequate arrangements. She also advised us to speak to the crematorium and to ask them for advice.

At 12.30 pm that day we visited Brighton's Woodvale Crematorium. The staff were marvellous. We asked if we could make the coffin and deal with all the funeral arrangements ourselves. 'Certainly.' They provided us with a leaflet 'Information and specifications for an interment or cremation arranged without the guidance of a funeral director'. [Eds: this present chapter covers everything in the leaflet that is of more than local significance.] They told us how to make the arrangements, but my main worry was what to do with Grandma. They said she can be kept as long as convenient in the borough mortuary for up to three weeks at no charge – after that a small sum would be necessary. I feel this is always a problem with death – everyone seems to want to dispose of the person too soon! The fact that we had time to think, and time to make arrangements was the first step. The staff said they would help with carrying Grandma into the chapel. We went to look at the chapel to see how high the platform was for the body to be placed on. They told us to telephone and come at any time if we wanted more help or information. At 3 pm that afternoon we were with the hospital registrar. She was delighted someone wished to arrange their own funeral – the ward sister had arranged for my mother to be taken to the hospital mortuary, and the registrar spoke to the mortician on our behalf. He was happy to keep my mother until the day of the funeral – no problem – no charge. He gave us the dimensions of the coffin. Width and length: 5' 9" by 18" wide. All we had to do was to let him know the time for collection and they would help us lift her in and to seal the lid. So my mother's last resting place was the hospital mortuary until March 3rd.

This gave us time to make the coffin and sort ourselves out. I telephoned the Natural Death Centre for some information, which came very promptly, and for which I am grateful. Also I wrote to the British Humanist Association who sent me a booklet 'Funerals without God'. It was very reassuring getting information from various sources, showing us that we could do this ourselves, that it would be very personal and that our mother's passing had not been taken away from us and dealt with by strangers. She had very rarely attended a church and we had been to a number of funerals – in 1989 twelve members of our family and friends had died – and none of the funerals seemed to have been satisfactory for the bereaved. Something appeared to be missing.

The coffin was made in our garage in a day. My husband enlisted the help of George Haines, a friend in his seventies, who said he always wanted to make his own coffin, so was delighted to have the chance to practise. Much tea and merriment went into the work, and chipboard and timber arrived from the local yard. Most of the neighbours and friends came to have a look and to try it out.

Really it was the fun bits that started to emerge, such as finding music that my mother liked. On a checkup trip to the crematorium to speak to them about the tapes and how to set them up, they told me they had loads of tapes available. They set all the taping up for us, again giving us every assistance. They also suggested that the funeral should be the last one of the day, to be able to give us assistance and extra time in case we had any hiccups.

The registrar was fascinated; she advised me to take several copies of the death certificate at £2 each as she pointed out that any further copies would cost £5-50 each. That was wise advice as my brothers and the solicitor and crematorium all wanted copies. We dealt with all the paper work which had come from the mortuary, hospital, etc, and that is usually handled by the Funeral Directors – it was simple. We needed burial certificates, doctors' certificates and one or two other certificates mentioned in the interment leaflet from Woodvale, and again we were assisted by everybody.

I tried to involve the family as much as possible. My eldest daughter made a lovely cake for the funeral tea, and also put together a wonderful photographic display, with photos of my mother's life, and the paintings she did in her later years. My brother's estate wagon was measured for the coffin – it would fit in OK. As a precautionary measure, we also hired an estate car for £42 in case of emergencies. Fortunately it was not required to carry the coffin, but it could have been used if necessary. The rest of the family prepared readings from my mother's favourite books and we prepared a programme containing readings, remembrances and music. We timed this for approximately 30 minutes. It was enough. We requested no flowers, but did in fact have a lovely display of everlasting flowers made by my sister-in-law, in a basket, which was placed on the coffin with an Indian rug from my brother, and this looked really great.

So at 4 pm on March 3rd we were ready to conduct the service. What went wrong? Not a lot – one late-arriving relative wanted to view her grand-mother and we did not think to let the mortician know in advance of collecting the body. The body was not prepared and obviously did not look its best for the occasion and there was an upsetting reaction. My husband, the friend who made the coffin, George, my brother from Kent, and his two children (a son and daughter) and another grandson from Wales, all went to fetch the body. Lesson number one – double check who knows who is coming, when and where. At the crematorium it was difficult getting the coffin out of the car – nobody realised quite how heavy it would be. One granddaughter wished to help carry the coffin, which was great, but this needed a rehearsal. The crematorium staff helped and it was OK. We made a mess-up of getting everyone into the chapel, and in the end they went in after the coffin was placed on the rostrum. The staff worked the tape recorder and I compered the show. My husband videoed the event and Mother would have been very, very pleased, because basically it went off OK. And it did – it dealt with a lot of emotions, and people were able to work on their own grief, mainly, I felt, because they had helped to get the show on the road.

We collected the ashes the next day from the crematorium, free of charge. We later gave the mortician a bottle of wine and the crematorium staff a Christmas box, saw to the nurses and staff at the hospital for their Christmas fare and hoped we had not forgotten anyone.

A hundred days after her death we held a Celebration for her death and life at the Chithurst Monastery, where a Dhana was given to the monks, and family and friends came once again to join with us in the memorial.

All this activity has helped me to deal with my grief and my feelings of guilt and resentment at having to look after quite a difficult lady. I feel I was also able to deal with my father's death: he died in 1961 at the age of 54 and the funeral was too quickly dealt with, with little time to realise how we all felt at that time. So I was able to lay to rest some unresolved grief over his loss.

Many people have spoken to us regarding making their own coffins and are surprised at how little we spent. For the record the absolutely necessary expenses were:

Fee for the crematorium £105 (£146 in 2000), fees for the doctors £57 (£82 in 2000), death certificates £8; purchase of chipboard and timber £30. Total: £200 (probably equivalent to about £270 in 2000).

In fact we spent a further £42 on the reserve car, for a grand total of £242. Several people asked, did we do this because we couldn't afford it? The answer to this is, No. I felt doing this ourselves was very rewarding, it helped to deal with our grief and the resentments that we had, and which had built up through the years as a result of some of the difficulties of looking after my mother during her lifetime. The main thought seemed to be that it was just as she would have wanted and this came over very strongly from all who helped and were present.

Dorothy Miller's coffin

Deidre's husband adds this note and the illustration below about the coffin:

We made the coffin from half inch chipboard and 2" by 1" finished battens. First we cut the base and used this as a template for the lid. Although the hospital mortician gave us the width of 18" we erred on the generous side, at 20", to make sure the shoulders would go in all right. On reflection, it would have been ample to make the sides and top with quarter inch chipboard or even hardboard if one really wanted to economise on expense and weight. Below the bottom (and flush with the edges) we fixed battens. We then cut the side pieces 12" high and fixed these on to the battens so that the battens were concealed. Then we fixed battens on the inside of the side pieces a half inch from the top to accommodate a flush-fitting lid. We found it necessary to strengthen the joining to the lid-battens at the junction of the angle at the widest part of the coffin. We pre-drilled the lid so that it was simple to screw down after putting the old lady in at the mortuary.

We used ferrous screws throughout because after the cremation they were removed from the ashes with a magnet. In the foot end we fixed a small rope handle to use in pulling the coffin out of the car. It was not necessary to fit any other handles.

The mortician said that the coffin was one of the best he had seen.

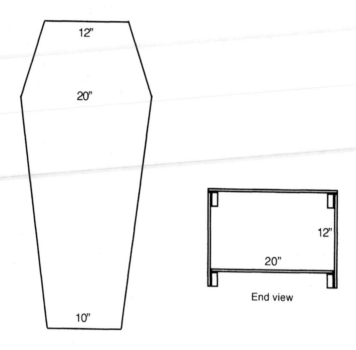

End view

Helping with 'd-i-y' funerals

Several volunteers have offered to give what advice or assistance they can to those organising funerals without funeral directors in their regions:

• Alan Brook offers support, particularly to those in the Northamptonshire and East Midlands areas (tel 01536 534218 w; e-mail: BrooksNN6@aol.com).

• Sheila Page offers support in the Hampshire area (tel Lymington 01590 671205, not after 10pm).

• Deirdre Martin offers support in the Brighton region (tel 01273 507644).

• Steve Stevens offers support in the West Sussex region (tel 01903 230858).

• Carol Davenport offers support in the North West and the Greater Manchester region (tel 0145 787 6155).

• The A. B. Welfare and Wildlife Trust, based in Harrogate, offers support and legal advice on conventional and unconventional funerals (tel 01423 530900 or 868121).

If you have successfully carried out a funeral in this way, please tell the Natural Death Centre if you might be willing to be publicised as part of this network. Please also send in an account of any unusual funeral for publication, again as an encouragement and aid to others, with your tips and advice.

Burial at sea

In theory, burial at sea seems an attractive proposition: the body becomes food for the fish, and it is just a matter of getting a free licence (for England and Wales) from the Ministry of Agriculture, Fisheries and Food (MAFF) and then finding a person with a suitable boat to take the coffin out. In practice, sea burial is mildly discouraged by the authorities (with only about 20 such burials a year) and there are quite complex guidelines. On several occasions, bodies buried off the coast have been washed up on shore. There are concerns about commercial fishing trawling the bodies back up – these are busy shipping lanes and foreign trawlers do not always know the areas to avoid. There are now only three places around the coast where sea burials are now allowed: one near Newhaven, the Needles Spoil Ground, to the West of the Isle of Wight and an area nine miles from the mouth of the Tyne. For the free licence either contact the marine licensing person at MAFF (Matthew Hampshire on 020 238 5869; e-mail: m.hampshire@gsi. maff.gov.uk) or your local fisheries District Inspector:

• *Newhaven, East Sussex:* Angus Radford (tel 01424 424109; fax 01424 444642; e-mail: a.radford@fish.maff.gsi.gov.uk). One of the vessels used for this site is the Tug Meeching (tel Bob Domin, the skipper, on 01273 752625). Local funeral directors in Seaford have used this ground and also Kenyon & Co in London.

• *Poole, Dorset:* Alex Mackenzie (tel 01202 677539; fax 01202 678598; e-mail: a.mackenzie@fish.maff.gsi.gov.uk). His site is the Needles Spoil Ground, shown on Admiralty Chart No 2045, 'Outer Approaches to the Solent'. The vessel normally used for the Needles Spoil Ground is the Island Rose (tel 01590 642500). Funeral directors who have organised sea burials there include: J. Bevis & Son in Southampton (tel Andrew George, 023 9277 2120); Davies Funeral Services of Milford-on-Sea (tel G. R. Davies, 01590 644664); Bennett in Essex (tel Jane Bennett, 01277 210104); the Co-op in Weymouth (tel Allan Quatermain, 01305 772789 – 'our sea burials start from £1,500'); and A. H. Roger (tel 023 8061 2435).

• *North Shields, Tyne and Wear:* Ian Campbell (tel 0191 257 4520; fax 0191 257 1595; e-mail: i.s.campbell@sfi.maff.gov.uk). The site off the mouth of the Tyne has only been open since 1999.

Sea burials organised by funeral directors tend to cost between £1,500 and £4,000.

A private yacht can be used if it has accurate positioning equipment and if its skipper has a yacht master's certificate.

You should tell the registrar when registering the death that you plan a sea burial and you can then obtain from the registrar a 'Coroners Out of England

Form' (Form 104) – and the local coroner's address to which this should be sent.

The Poole Fisheries Officer, Mr Bushell, has dealt with families making their own arrangements, without using funeral directors, and seems helpful. (For a full account of the formidable organisation involved in a 'd-i-y' sea burial, look on the web at: www.globalideasbank.org/ndw/NDW-25.HTML). Guidelines vary slightly between the two regions, but, by talking to Mr Bushell and Mr Radford, and reading the various documents, the following consensus emerges – the aim of these conditions being to ensure that the coffin and body stay down on the sea-bed, that marine life has ready access to the body and that the body is readily identifiable should it be washed up:

• The coffin should not be made of any persistent synthetic material, nor of a species of timber, such as oak, which would endure in the marine environment. It may not include any lead, zinc or copper. (They recommend a solid softwood such as pine – no veneered board, chipboard or solid hardwood – with the coffin as strong as possible, reinforced on the bottom corners, and large enough to fit extra weights. Even the screws must not be zinc.)

• The wooden coffin should be weighted with approximately 200kg (4cwt) of iron, steel or concrete., clamped to the base of the coffin with brackets of 10mm steel bar.

• Holes of at least three quarter inch diameter are to be drilled to allow rapid ingress of water and escape of air, so that the coffin may reach the sea-bed quickly and stay there. (They recommend two dozen holes in both the side and lid.)

• The body should also be weighted. (They recommend that the body should have chain wrapped round it, with the chains weighing about 20 kilos, or about 10% more than the body).

• The coffin should effectively retain the body on the sea-bed without unduly preserving it.

• The body may not be embalmed. (The body may be dressed, although the MAFF specifies a cotton sheet or paper substitute – or a biodegradable body bag may be used, but not a canvas shroud. Biodegradable absorbent padding can be used to contain any leakage of fluids.)

• A certificate of freedom from fever and infection should be obtained from the GP or hospital doctor, and this certificate, together with a copy of the death certificate and the form releasing the body for removal out of England, should be submitted to the district fisheries office.

• The body should have a plastic (or other durable) tag locked to the torso with the telephone number and identity of the licensee.

The MAFF reserves the right to inspect the coffin prior to the burial, although this rarely happens in practice. Normally, the local MAFF office must be informed on the day prior to the date of burial and immediately after. An at-least-verbal amendment to the licence is needed if adverse weather or other circum-stances delay the burial beyond the week of the licence.

Non assembly-line funerals

There are indeed many ways that people have found to prevent funerals from becoming assembly-line affairs, including those events for which funeral directors are used. Below are some examples – and the particularly useful books on this topic detailed in the Resources chapter are Tony Walter's 'Funerals and How to Improve Them', 'The Dead Good Funerals Book' by Sue Gill and John Fox, 'Celebrating Life' by Andrew Hill and 'Funerals Without God' by Jane Wynne Willson.

• **Reminders:** Have something on top of the coffin during the service, as a reminder of the person who has died - such as a favourite hat or scarf.

• **Fires, candles, lanterns**: John Fox of Welfare State International ('the celebratory arts company' – see the Resources chapter under Organisations) suggests a funeral or memorial service outdoors, the space framed with poles, bunting and music, tables decorated with cloth, flowers and papercuts, and the use of fires, candles and lanterns. 'The Dead Good Funerals Book' which he wrote with Sue Gill, demonstrates the flair and genius of his group of 'Engineers of the Imagination' in designing innovative rituals (the book's first edition is unreliable on the legal side). Here, for instance, is John Fox imagining the kind of cremation service he himself would like:

Hanging the crem with banners and papercuts

Wrapped in his favourite blanket we placed his body in a deep blue shiny cardboard coffin painted inside and out. On the lid his daughter painted simple seed and tree designs in white lines. The coffin rested on trestles in the front room of his house for a day or two; we preferred not to have an open coffin.

'No incense', he had requested. So we lit a few candles smelling of honey.

The night before the committal his coffin was driven round Ulverston on a flat bed truck. We visited his works and a couple of pubs accompanied by a wild percussion band, with salsa brass and firecrackers; then returned to the house.

We knew he preferred cremation so we negotiated with the crematorium manager for a double slot at the beginning of the day to gain time to decorate the space and take it all down afterwards. We hung the crem with simple big banners in blue and red suspended from theatrical lighting stands and put marigolds and sunflowers in earthenware vases. We framed it all with strings of small white papercuts cut with fire and bird imagery and made it more cosy with pools of warm lighting. Incidentally, we did have to remove temporarily a crucifix and cover up a statue depicting a sentimental Jesus story about the sheep that escaped.

Rather unconventionally, we arranged the seats in a circle and placed the coffin on trestles in the middle. On the floor was a bright red Persian carpet (which we borrowed from a shop in town). It looked fantastic. The white seed decorations, painted on the top of the coffin, resembled galaxies and the surrounding banners gave the feeling of a womb-like tent.

The service was a bit longer than usual because many people wanted to read poems and tell stories. We gave out photocopied sheets of some of his poems and later made a few handmade books as presents for those who had helped.

The music was great. His son, a musical director, arranged a few tunes for cellos, trombone and trumpet with a small acapella choir who helped us sing along. 'What is the Life of a Man' was hung up on a song sheet! Bryan always said he wanted a song sheet at his funeral because no one ever knows the words of the hymns, but really because he was theatrical and loved pantomimes. Painting the words and hanging the banner took so long we nearly had to abandon the idea but it was worth it

• **One flower each**: You could ask friends not to buy flowers but to bring one flower each, preferably from their garden, and to place it on the coffin. Here is Allegra Taylor's description of how everyone brought one daffodil each to the funeral of Claire, an eight year old girl who died of leukaemia:

A grave lined with moss and leaves like a bird's nest

The funeral, organised magnificently by Margot's husband, was a triumph of life over death. Many children from Claire's old school came, as well as some she'd known in hospital. Their drawings for Claire were stuck up all round the church: drawings of butterflies, flowers and big yellow suns. A few children stood up and read poems. Everyone was given a candle to hold – the place was ablaze with the illuminated faces of children – and a yellow daffodil to throw in the grave.

The minister - a friend of the family - held the little coffin in his arms as he spoke of Claire's courage and of the lightness and joy she'd brought into the world during her short life. The grave was lined with moss and leaves like a nest for a baby bird. We stood with our arms around each other as we threw in an avalanche of daffodils and sang 'The Lord of the Dance' together: 'Dance, dance, wherever you may be ... .' It was the most beautiful funeral I had ever been to and an inspiring example of how it can be. We have begun to reclaim birth and death from the medical profession after generations of abdication - begun to reinstate choice and personal responsibility. Let's do the same with funerals.

From 'Acquainted with the Night' by Allegra Taylor.

• **A child's burial on a farm**: A boy aged five died at home of cancer after a two year struggle. The parents had expected his death and had previously been in touch with the Natural Death Centre for advice. The parents asked a local farmer to allow his land to be used for the burial – the farmer consulted his wife and they gave their permission. The National Rivers Authority (now subsumed within the Environment Agency), having been told the grid reference for the grave, said that there was no danger of it causing pollution. No local council planning permission or permission from the environmental health officer was required.

The father and friends spent all day digging a four foot deep circular grave in the chalky soil. The parents had ordered a woollen burial shroud from the cemetery in Carlisle, and cut this down to child-size, folding it around the boy's body. On the day of the burial, a week after the death, they conducted their own ceremony, with 70 friends of all ages present, including some of the nurses who had cared for him.

As requested, people came wearing ordinary clothes that the boy would have felt comfortable with. They played his favourite music. They had a spiritual circle spreading light into the earth. A friend, whose girl had died some time before, added her cremated ashes to the grave and spoke in her memory. They put flowers and toys into the grave and built a cairn of stones as a burial mound on top.

The funeral director, recommended by the parents' GP, had initially been shocked, but, once satisfied as to the legality of it all, was very helpful. He took the body away and washed it with the essential oils that the parents supplied, so that the body could be visited on his premises by friends. Everything else, such as the transport of the body to the burial place, was organised by the parents.

When the earth has settled over the grave, the parents intend to add a plaque and a rock spiral.

• **Home funerals**: You could get the priest or humanist officiant to conduct the funeral or memorial service in your home or out in the garden. Amongst ministers, Unitarians are particularly willing to conduct a funeral service in your home or elsewhere and will officiate at very personalised or even humanist (that is, atheist or agnostic) funerals. (See Organisations in the Resources chapter). Anglican priests, too, are increasingly willing to conduct 'life-centred' funerals.

The Rosslyn Hill Unitarian Chapel in Hampstead (tel 020 7431 4160) is committed to allowing people to hire the chapel for non-religious funerals, without strict time limits. An organist can be provided.

The following unidentified newspaper cutting in The Natural Death Centre library records a very exuberant funeral that requires very sober non-participant drivers.

Cortège in 250 mile pub crawl

A 20-car funeral cortège set off from Peterborough General Hospital at 8.30am and arrived in Haverfordwest in Wales, 12 hours later. After drinking the Bull Inn there dry, the 100 mourners, mostly Irish travellers, caught the overnight ferry to Rosslare.

The cortège was following the last instructions of Mrs Johanna Connors, who was buried at the end of the trip in New Ross, County Wexford.

• **Humanist funerals**: For a fee similar to that paid to a priest for a funeral, you can get a trained officiant from the British Humanist Association (see Resources chapter) to act as master or mistress of ceremonies for a humanist funeral (the officiant's fee in north west London is currently £85). The officiant will normally ask you beforehand about the life of the person that died, so that their speech will be personalised. Or you or a friend or relative can conduct the service yourselves, perhaps referring to the very helpful pamphlet entitled 'Funerals Without God', by Jane Wynne Willson on how to run such services, with its sample texts and poetry (see Resources chapter). The pamphlet explains how a humanist service tends to divide into distinct parts:

First there is about eight minutes' worth of entry music, which is played until people have settled down in their seats – if an organist is not being used, this music should be recorded on side A only of a tape marked clearly 'Entry Music' and should be presented to the crematorium preferably the day before. The service proper opens with thoughts on life and death; then a tribute to the dead person (perhaps by a relative); followed by the committal (where everyone stands, the officiant turns towards the coffin, 'commits the body to its natural end' and a button is pressed to close the curtains). Up to about 40 seconds of slow and solemn music is sometimes used for the committal, with the person operating the machine cued to switch it on the moment specific words are said (a second tape should be clearly marked 'Committal Music' with the tape in position to deliver music the moment the Play button is pressed); and the service ends with closing words, after which the officiant walks over to the main mourners and leads them out of the exit door; a tape (marked 'Exit Music') can be played for about five minutes from the moment the officiant steps down from the lectern. Be sure to ask the crematorium to play the music loudly, if this is what you want.

Michael Rennie in Dundee used the 'Funerals Without God' book to help him design a secular funeral for his father:

During my father's funeral, after welcoming all present, I dealt with the need to come to terms with death and read some words from Pasternak about the essence of our existence on earth. After a poem by Swinburn about the peace to be found in death, we stood in silence for some moments – moments in which those who had religious faith were asked to pray. I then paid tribute to my father's memory, incorporating anecdotes giving an insight into his character and contribution to life. My daughter played on the violin tunes emphasising my father's links with the sea, with Scotland and with the Tyne, as his coffin was taken from the hall. Later I committed him to the earth, and read a poem by C. Day Lewis, which was sufficiently broad in its humanity to resonate with any secular or religious beliefs.

From a letter to The Independent (Oct. 28th 1991).

• **No service**: A few of those organising a burial themselves on their own land prefer no service at all. As one correspondent wrote to the Natural Death Centre: 'With us the process went on long enough to comprise a kind of rite of its own. Most of the time we were silent. When we had finished we stood for a while more, still in silence, then I played a piece of music and we left.'

• **A New Orleans band**: The Eureka New Orleans Jazz Band (tel 0121 449 0119) plays at funerals. The eight-piece band consists of trumpets, trombone, sousaphone, banjo, clarinet and snare drum. They can play a fanfare inside or outside the chapel, or elsewhere. Prices range from £180 (four-piece) to £350 (eight-piece) for one hour's performance within a 30 mile radius of Birmingham; £300 to £500 for the London area.

• **A string quartet**: Choice Music, based in Birmingham (tel 0121 698 8696; fax 0121 698 8600; e-mail: bookings@choicemusic.co.uk; web: www.choice music.co.uk), can provide a string quartet for a funeral, or a solo vocalist, or even a small orchestra. Prices range from about £80 to £120 per player per hour, depending on location.

• **Longer services**: It may be possible to book two or even three sessions at the crematorium, if the standard time is not enough, and if there are many people who wish to speak; and to book the last service of the day, in case your timing is not as exact as the professionals. Chapter 8 details how much, if anything, each crematorium charges for extra time.

• **Other cultures, other times**: In the UK, two world wars made funerary pomp on the home front seem out of place and accentuated our Puritan heritage of simple funerals. Indeed in 1644 the Puritans directed that the dead were to be interred 'without any ceremony'. In 1648, when the body of King Charles I was brought to the Royal Chapel at Windsor, the governor of the castle refused to let Bishop Juxon read the funeral service from the Book of Common Prayer:

The funeral of King Charles I

The Bishop of London stood weeping by, to tender that his service might not be accepted. Then was Charles I deposited in silence and sorrow in the vacant place in the vault about three of the afternoon; and the Lords that night, though late, returned to London.

> *From 'The History of the Worthies of England' edited by*
> *J. Fuller, Publishers IGWL and WG, 1662, quoted in*
> *'The English Way of Death' by Julian Litten.*

There is a beauty of its own in the simplicity expected at a Quaker funeral today, where the disposal of the body is supposed to be done with no unnecessary expense and with no flowers. But the diversity of funeral practices in other cultures and religions around the world and the beauty or intricacy of some of their rituals can widen our vision of the potential of funerals to 'enchant' the participants, raising their consciousness above the mundane. The Ecuadorians, for instance, are buried with their eyes open so that they can see their way to heaven; the Yanonami Indians of the Amazon believe that it is barbaric that Westerners do not drink the ashes of their relatives; the Merina hold periodic 'dances with the dead' where the women dance with the dried-out remains of their next of kin; rural Greeks tend the graves daily for five years before the corpse is disinterred and placed in a communal ossuary, with clean bones being seen as a reflection of a good life; and for traditional Hindus even the grandchildren are closely involved:

The Hindu rites of death

Hindus should arrange for the dying person to be brought home to die. The dying person should concentrate upon the mantram given at initiation, or if the person is no longer conscious, a family member should chant the mantram softly in his or her right ear.

After death, the relatives place a simple cloth on the person. Each of the relatives comes and applies sesame oil to the deceased's head. The body is bathed with the water from nine kumbhas, and is placed in the coffin. Each of the grandchildren takes a small lighted stick and stands around the body and sings.

> *From 'Death and Dying – A Hindu Point of View', £1-50 from Himalayan Academy Publishers, Rakesh Mathur, 6 Carolyn House, 95 Larkhall Rise, London SW4 6HR.*

A pagan death

Both the Pagan Federation and the Guild of Soul Midwives in the UK offer support to pagans (see the Resources chapter).

Pagans aim to design rituals that bring them very close to nature and the seasons. Here is an eloquent description of a pagan death and memorial ceremony is that by Tony Kelly and his friends, concerning his wife Betty who died from cancer:

> Betty was now lying in a green-covered bed in the sunshine at the window, the window open and the air full of warmth and birdsong, willow and birch branches in front of her and a great leafy birch bough at the foot of the bed and the littler branches by the open window. It looked like a woodland glade and she was pleased. Among all the greenery were two bunches of daffodils in big jars, and jars of dandelions and celandines and yellow polyanthus on the windowsill. And I put a few little branches of silver birch on the bed where she could take hold of them and handle them and feel them in the way she always liked to do ...
>
> I was sitting at Betty's side, speaking to her softly as she dreamed, saying, 'The Goddess loves you,' and other things that I knew would make her happy, and I was holding her hands. Betty stopped breathing ...
>
> We stripped all the alien words and the glitter off the coffin; the wood was beautiful. We laid Betty naked inside it and dressed her with daffodils, tastefully, beautifully, in her hair and about her body, some of them fresh and a few to speak her fading ...
>
> The cremation was without ceremony and we brought her ashes home and kept them with us in the box I made, its lid scalloped like the waves of the sea, till the Hag Moon of Samhain called us to a distant shore ...

The ceremony for the scattering of the ashes took place seven months later, at a remote spot by the sea:

> The Sea-lady came over the grass to where I was standing and she raised the lid of the box, and the ashes, speckled black and grey, lay open to the wide

open sky. As I held the box to my breast and she took the lid into her own two hands I spoke the message that for seven moons my heart had borne:

> I am come, beloved Mabh
> To do a thing for Betty
> And to do the thing for thee
> For love of Betty
> And for love of thee

Each spoke their own devotion and to each the priestess responded with the same words that had been Betty's own spontaneous response when their phone calls had been conveyed to her, and they sang a six-verse song they had composed for the occasion:

> ... Green Lady Earth,
> Deep Lady Sea ...
> Carry the ash ...
> Her life has flown;
> Thou dost abide ...

We joined our hands in a ring, all nine of us, and a kiss from the Green Lady passed from lip to hand all around the ring. 'With thee for always, Mabh,' I spoke as the love of the Goddess moved me. At last we loosened our hands.

Celebration Box

Yvonne Malik (Sweet Briar, 52 Hornby Road, Wray, Near Lancaster LA2 8QN, tel 015242 21767) is a designer by trade and has in the past decorated coffins. She has designed a Celebration Box, which could be placed at the back of the church or crematorium or memorial service, or filled before death, as a kind of miniature art gallery, to be filled by the congregation with photographs, letters, poems, keepsakes and small items. One prototype she put together using an old house-painter's box, as described by Fraser Harrison, in an article in Country Living (June 1996): 'It was dedicated to Lilian and Horace Parker and was filled with mementos of them, his on one side, hers on the other. Every part of the box overflowed with photographs, keepsakes and small items connected with the couple, from the jaunty cigarette holder of Horace's youth to a minute, beaded evening bag belonging to Lilian.' The following is an extract from Yvonne Malik's leaflet seeking commissions to produce Celebration Boxes:

> When a relative or close friend dies, we often find it impossible to find words to express our feelings. We remember special times, events and places which we shared together, or recall good deeds and kindnesses. These keys to our special memories have an intrinsic value only between ourselves and the one who has died.
>
> Using the Celebration Box is an opportunity to express and focus on a new way of saying 'goodbye'. Each box becomes unique and special, giving us the satisfaction of having taken part in filling it, as well as the ultimate feeling of something shared. This is a new way of including family

and friends in a nonverbal act of celebration and comfort – a celebration of the life and shared experiences with the deceased and a later comfort for the bereaved, as well as something to be treasured by the next generation.

Suggested items which have a private or intimate meaning and could be placed in the box include:

Photographs; postcards which reminds us of a special day together; letters, poems, thank-you notes; birthday cards; tickets from a concert which we shared, souvenir from a holiday; button from their favourite jacket, pair of earrings, pipe; copy of a team certificate, club badge, medal; special scarf or cap.

The events and times which we shared require no explanation from us and the tokens placed within the box are private statements. It is something which can be carried out by ourselves, alongside the traditional services of the funeral director.

The Celebration Box can be filled at home prior to the funeral or placed in an accessible situation at the back of the church or chapel and brought home after the final ceremony.

Each Celebration Box is hand decorated and therefore differs from any other. It also has the advantage of being portable, to suit today's more transient lifestyle.

A simpler approach, described by Tony Walter in the Funeral Director (April 1996) – or one which could work in tandem with the Celebration Box – is to place cards in the church pews inviting mourners to leave a sentence or two about the person who has died – for the later comfort of the family.

Public memorial

Remembering the dead begins immediately after death, and continues after the funeral. One suggestion for improving grieving is to set up 'open houses' for bereaved people who can't face going home. Nowadays, many people hold impromptu wakes after the funeral. The wake or after-funeral gathering is common in most cultures, like the wedding feast. However, it is the tone or style of the wake that is all-important. A feast that is too formal might accentuate the loneliness of the bereaved person once the guests have gone home. On the other hand, an informal gathering of mourners who want to share their feelings may begin a sharing process that will come to be of benefit to the bereaved. Laughter and jokes as well as tears are likely to erupt because remembering the dead person is also recalling the richness of life and relationships through stories and anecdotes.

Holding a memorial service at some time, perhaps months after the death and immediate obsequies, may be a way of bringing out the essential cheerfulness and spirit of life with which most of us would like to be remembered. We want to be celebrated as well as mourned. Here is such a celebration, designed by Margaret Chisman for her husband Stan. There is some human instinct that makes us want to be present at such a celebration of people who were our friends.

It is rather like giving wedding gifts. We want to give the gifts, be part of the celebration. Why should we deprive ourselves of being part of such a ceremony, the feasting of a life?

A table of objects to commemorate the person

The celebration and commemoration of Stan was held at our home in the double rooms on the ground floor. About 40 friends and relations were present. It was a beautiful day, the garden was full of flowers and their scent drifted in through the open french doors. After welcoming everyone I took the cloth cover off the table and explained that on it were articles that Stan loved or that exemplified his life.

The first thing that everyone noticed about him was his outstanding physical vigour. By contrast many people seemed only half alive. He was fully and gloriously alive in every fibre of his being. He loved rambling – I held up his walking boots – and whenever he decided to go on a walk he began to get excited and I would know to get his boots out. He loved skiing – I showed his goggles – and sadly had a holiday fixed for January by which time he was too ill. There were several photos amongst those displayed of him enjoying this sport. When living in Ipswich he played in the Post Office Table Tennis Team, and they won the cup one year and each player received a small trophy, here displayed. He also played five-a-side football and his old football boots were still in the cupboard upstairs. He took up sailboarding within the last two years and there were several photos of him displayed. These were taken on our holiday in the South of France. I regret I have no photos of him hang-gliding (whoever heard of a man of 62 taking up hang-gliding?), but George, who also introduced him to this sport describes the last occasion; Stan had become airborne to a height of 50ft and was looking decidedly unhappy but absolutely determined to go through with it.

John White, who could not be present today said that for him he would always remember Stan for playing the glorious voice of Paul Robeson singing 'I thought I saw Joe Hill last night.' We played this record, and as I heard that vibrant voice singing the words of optimism in the face of death I felt once more overcome with grief and loss and wondered whether, despite all my supportive and loving relations and friends, all my active outside interests, my comfortable and satisfying home, I would manage to achieve serenity and full acceptance of his death.

The next part was pure joy. Nearly everyone had an anecdote or memory to share. Some of them were new to me, and I felt as if Stan came alive again for a few minutes.

Alan Mayne commented in the Visitors Book: 'I knew that Stan was a man of many parts but I didn't know how many.'

I asked everyone to end as Stan would have wished – to hug and kiss their neighbours.

From 'Interim', a private newsletter
circulated by Margaret Chisman.

Incidentally, Ernest Morgan warns that those who speak up at memorial services should not allow themselves to be cut short by whoever is conducting the service. 'I have known family members who carried regrets for years that they had been cut-off from speaking because the service was running too long.'

Memorials by Artists

Memorials by Artists helps people to commission individual memorials from the finest designers and lettercutters in Britain. These range from very simple tablets to headstones, boulders, arches, sundials, ceramic tiles, birdbaths, urns, etc. Depending on the individual's needs, the service provides help with the formulation of ideas, finding the most suitable artist, making the introduction, arranging permissions with churchyard or cemetery authorities and administering the project throughout.

Prices range from £900 to over £3,000. An illustrated booklet is available from Memorials by Artists (see the Resources chapter) for £7-50, including postage and packing; also a free illustrated leaflet.

Memorials by Artists was founded in 1988 by Harriet Frazer to help others through the kind of difficulties she experienced over the memorial to her stepdaughter, who died in 1985. There is also an associated charity, The Memorial Arts Charity, to promote memorial arts and crafts.

Elizabeth Lawlor, who used Memorials by Artists for her husband's headstone, commends them to The Natural Death Centre:

> The headstone is up. I wanted a wave on top for symbolic reasons – waves of consciousness, waves being re-absorbed into the ocean, etc – and for my husband's naval and sea-loving connection. The help I received from Memorials by Artists was wonderful.

If you simply need to find a quality person to design the headstone, a free register of artists is kept by the Council for the Care of Churches (tel 020 7638 0971).

A memorial of course need not be a gravestone: you may want to pay for a glass window in church; or to pay for a park bench; or to have a sponsored walk or children sponsored to learn poetry for a recital in aid of the person's favourite charity. If asking for donations to charity, suggest that these be paid by cheque, to help prevent donations going astray.

An astronomer's ashes were sent to the moon by NASA. An exploitative American service to put ashes in orbit (for $12,500) is available from Celestis, Inc (tel 001 713 522 7282; e-mail: celestis@best.com; web: www.celestis.com). More feasible for the average deceased is for their ashes to be launched into the night sky in giant fireworks. None of the UK fireworks manufacturers seem particularly keen to be mentioned, although several have provided this service in the past (one charged £600 for a giant firework with all the ashes on board). You could try approaching them diplomatically (or try approaching firework display firms to ask them to refashion one of their bought-in rockets). Manufacturers include Pains Fireworks (tel 01794 884040), Theatrical Pyrotechnics Ltd (tel 01843 823545), Spectrum (tel 01522 514016) and Kimbolton Fireworks (tel 01480 860988).

A firm called Air Navigation and Trading (tel 01253 345396), based at Blackpool airport, will scatter your ashes over land or sea. They charge £82·25 an hour. A firm called Resting Solutions charges from £400 for the same service (tel 07000 784500; e-mail: restingsolutions@microweb.co.uk; www.microweb. co.ul/restingsolutions).

If you want to plant a tree in a public place in memory of the person, you could ask your local park if this might be possible.

Woodland Creation, Little Bakes, Tredethick, Lostwithiel, Cornwall PL22 0LE (tel 01208 873618) is an unregistered organisation set up by Tim and Nicky Reed where for £20 you can dedicate a tree in new broadleaved woodland in Cornwall. All trees can be located on site and dedications are recorded in a dedication book with a mapped reference number. A certificate is sent out to the sponsor.

Trees for London (Registered Charity), HMS Belfast, Morgans Lane, Tooley Street, London SE1 2JH (020 7407 0888; fax 020 7407 3830; e-mail: treesforlondon@aol.com) say you can sponsor them to plant a young tree for £35 – you can nominate a London Borough and join in with the planting if you wish. Alternatively, you can choose to dedicate a single semi-mature memorial tree with a botanical (black) plaque, recording the Latin and English tree name and a message, for £125. There are only a few sites in London where the tree can be planted: either in South West London, in the Merton Millennium Woodland, near Motspur Park Station, which is to be a 10,000 oak woodland; or in East London, in Tower Hamlets where tree planting is creating a barrier along the Blackwall Tunnel approach road. The most expensive and dashing option is to Plant a Grove: three large trees next to each other in inner London (or about 50 trees together, 'a small wood', outside of London) for £250. A plaque on the tree stakes will bear your name and message.

The National Memorial Arboretum, PO Box 10, Tisbury, Salisbury SP3 6TH (tel 01722 716310) offers dedicatory tree planting for £50 with a label, or for an extra £100, a named plaque. You can propose the type of tree, but the final selection is up to them. There is also a place for the scattering of ashes.

It may have been mainly a publicity gimmick, but a pub in Hereford (The Packhorse) announced a genial offer for regular customers – that of placing their ashes behind tiles in the pub, with a wake in their honour when they die and free drinks all round once a year thereafter, for a price ranging from £50 for a tile in the toilets, to £5,000 for a tile close to the fire. The money was to have been lodged with a local solicitor.

Alternative Urns

John Fox of Welfare State International suggests redecorating the normal small wooden caskets used for ashes: remove the paint with varnish stripper, undercoat with filler and two coats of white wood primer; then paint imagery or words – he uses fluorescent enamel varnish (Brodie and Middleton); re-varnish, allowing 24 hours for the drying. He adds this story:

I commissioned a pottery urn from a friend who specialised in throwing decorative slipware. It was for the ceremony to scatter my father's ashes in the Humber Estuary, where he had earned his living as a sea captain.

We ended up with a dome-shaped circular lidded pot about a foot high and a foot diameter at the base. A little like a tiny bee hive.

The lid had to be surprisingly wide too – about six inches, for the ashes to scatter easily downwind.

In white slip on the dark brown of the pot's surface, we inscribed:

'The last voyage of Captain Fox, MBE. May his spirit be at peace with the sea.'

At the ceremony myself, my wife and our two children then ten and eight played 'Eternal Father' on brass instruments. (My father was a Christian.)

It was memorable and healing for us all.

Welfare State International (artistic director John Fox – see the Resources chapter) offers a consultancy service for those wanting a very special memorial service.

If you might want to buy an artist-designed urn or to inspired by such designs to create your own, see the next chapter.

Probate

In Chapter 2 on Preparing for Dying, under the heading 'Simplifying Your Affairs Before Death', it was outlined how someone could leave their estate so that neither probate, inheritance tax nor Inland Revenue account was required. Probate otherwise involves the executors of the will applying to the probate registry for a grant of probate which confirms their power to process the will (if the person died without a will, or if the executors have died or are unwilling to act, the relatives apply for similar powers, known as letters of administration). Solicitors can do the whole thing for you, but in one typical recent instance they charged a rate of £90 per hour, plus 1% of all the cash, stocks and shares in the estate and 0.5% of the property. To this total they then added 25%. (Banks tend to charge even more for doing probate work.)

Shop around for the cheapest appropriate solicitor you can find – for instance, avoid central London and choose a solicitor who specialises in probate work (they are likely to take less time) – perhaps within such a firm you could get a reduction by asking if a trainee solicitor could handle it for you. You could probably reduce the bill further by doing some of the work yourself, such as gathering in the estate's money from the bank and building society. (Incidentally, if the will names a professional executor and you are determined to do it all yourself, the professional may be willing to surrender the executorship to you for a nominal fee.)

Likely firms of solicitors that we picked almost at random from the London Yellow Pages included: Walford & Co (NW2, tel 020 8452 6644) who charge £120 per hour plus 1.5% of the gross value of the estate (excluding the house). Grant Argent & Co (NW2, tel 020 8452 7651) who charge about £90 per hour;

and a trainee solicitor at Nigel Broadhead Mynard (tel 01245 269909) who charges about £60 an hour. The Will Consultancy, Old Bank Chambers, Market Square, Pontypridd, Rhondda Cynon Taff, Wales CF37 2SY (tel 01443 485147), who can draw up wills, also specialise in probate work nationwide and will tend to quote a fixed price. Likewise Legacies (Will & Probate Services) Ltd, Knight Court, 49 Crown Street, Brentwood, Essex CM14 4BD (tel 0800 496 0 899) quote a fixed price. This they calculate, with a £900 minimum fee, as 3% of the estate for the first £70,000, 2% for the next £70,000 and 1% thereafter – although only half the value of houses which are simply being transferred is included for fee purposes and they have discretion to reduce these fees further in simple cases. Roger Garlick of Will Matters, 22 Crane Bridge Road, Salisbury SP2 7TW (tel 01722 337477; e-mail: roger.garlick@virgin.net) charges a fixed fee of 3% of the estate, with no minimum charge.

But assuming the estate is relatively straightforward (with no business partnership, self-owned business, agricultural land, insurance syndicate or family trusts) it can be done by anyone businesslike, with patience enough to wade through all the fiddly details and to write the many formal letters. Again, as when preparing one's will, the most useful book is the Consumers' Association's 'Wills and Probate'. The following is merely a sketch of what is involved:

You will need forms for a personal application for a 'grant of representation' from your local Probate Personal Application Department – if you were not given this address in a booklet at the time you registered the death, you can find it out from the Probate Registry (see the Resources chapter). The main local offices are also detailed in booklet PA2 (which can be downloaded from the web at: www.courtservice.gov.uk/forms/fmenu_prob.htm) which outlines how to do things without a solicitor – probate offices can supply this booklet and the Citizens Advice Bureau may be able to help you to proceed further. Once you have filled in and returned these forms (PA1, the probate application form; and the account of the estate – IHT205, IHT44), you will be given an appointment to go to your local office in person to swear that the information is true. Before the grant is made you will need to pay the probate fee (a flat fee of £130, although no fee is charged for estates of less than £5,000); you will also need to have paid any inheritance tax owing (although inheritance tax on land or buildings can be paid over a ten year period at a rate of interest that is in line with the average bank base lending rate). There may be a form of inheritance tax self-certification coming in soon, in which case tax issues are likely to be dealt with even before the grant application is made.

If the deceased's funds were in a bank these (above a certain level) may be frozen (see Chapter 2) until after probate is granted (you could try asking the bank to put any current account amount on deposit, so that at least it earns interest; the bank also has discretion to let the executors continue operating the account, if indemnified by the executors against loss). Because an account is frozen, the executors may have to get an expensive overdraft from the same bank to pay the inheritance tax (although a helpful bank may be willing to release money from deceased's accounts – and a prudent person might enquire of their bank before death whether they are helpful in this regard. Thus Barclays, for instance, allow a deceased person's account to be used to pay inheritance tax without imposing any charges, as do National Savings – see CTO leaflet IHT 11; whereas NatWest will require you to set up a loan at 1.5% or more above base rate, with a 1.6% arrangement fee). It is also possible to buy interest-bearing 'certificates of tax deposits' (the prospectus is obtainable from any Inland Revenue Collection Office) as a way of setting aside money for payment of these future tax liabilities.

The executors will also need to deal with the Land Registry to transfer any property (form 56 from an Oyez shop) and with the Income Tax people – their forms Cap 30 (to show that any inheritance tax has been paid), form 59 (an income tax return for the year in which the person died) and form R185E (income tax deduction certificates).

Valuing stocks and shares with the exactitude required for probate purposes (your bank may be willing, without charge, to find out the shares' value at the date of death), filling in the probate schedule of them and handling their transfer or sale are small bureaucratic nightmares. To repeat Chapter 2: any dying person who has accumulated the odd lot of shares would save their executors a great deal of trouble by selling them before death.

Executors will also need to deal with the deceased's mortgage company, house insurance company, district valuer (it is usually acceptable to get sales particulars for similar houses locally and to base your valuation on these), bank, building society, life insurance company, pension company, Benefits Agency and local post office (for forwarding of mail) – plus in some cases advertising in the newspapers for any unknown creditors.

Anyone appointed as an executor who, understandably, cannot face the work involved, can fill in a renunciation form or a form appointing an attorney to do it (both forms are available from an Oyez shop); or you can hand over to a professional part of the way through, but you will have to pay if there are insufficient assets in the estate.

Chapter 5

COFFINS &
PROFESSIONAL SERVICES

Chapter 4 described how people could organise a funeral themselves. This one is for those who want help from the trade. It is for those who may be trying to buy funeral goods – such as a cardboard or a regular coffin; a painted coffin or a recycled coffin; a collapsible coffin, a willow coffin or a coffin as bookcase; an urn; a body bag or lowering webbing. It describes the goods on offer from mail order suppliers and coffin manufacturers. It will also enlighten you if you are seeking just one service rather than a complete package – such as cold storage facilities, or a hearse or horse-drawn carriage you can rent, or the hiring of extra bearers. This chapter serves as an introduction to the detailed listings in the next three chapters and summarises the findings of the Natural Death Centre's nationwide survey of the funeral trade. It describes not only the New Natural Death Handbook Award 2000 Winners, but which local authorities supply a cheaper municipal funeral service; how to get a free funeral; how best to choose a funeral director; why embalming may not be necessary; the snags that go with prepaid funerals (and a woodland burial alternative for Londoners, including collection of the body); and the high standards being laid down by the best funeral directors, crematoria and cemeteries.

New Natural Death Handbook Awards 2000

On Sunday April 16th 2000, as part of the National Day of the Dead ceremonies organised by the Natural Death Centre, the following eight National Awards (and the 32 other Regional Awards detailed in Chapters 6, 7 & 8) will be publicly presented.

National Awards

• The New Natural Death Handbook Award 2000 for the **Best Woodland Burial Ground** in the UK goes to Greenhaven Woodland Burial Ground near Rugby (tel 01788 860604), who provide exceptional value and friendly service – a complete funeral on their farm, including the grave, the digging, a cardboard coffin, a tree and collection from London, costs £570. (See the East Midlands section of Chapter 6 for their details.)

• The New Natural Death Handbook Award 2000 for the **Best Cemetery** in the UK goes, along with the crematorium award, to Carlisle. The Bereavement Manager in charge of both places is Ken West (tel 01228 625310) and the services he and his colleagues provide consistently win awards. Ken West has been the key figure in promoting the excellent Charter for the Bereaved, which recognises the need for nature reserve burial grounds and the right of a family not to use a funeral director. It has already been officially adopted by 35 cemeteries or crematoria and needs to be adopted by all of the remainder. The Carlisle Cemetery makes available not only cardboard and regular coffins, but its own woollen shroud. Ken West writes: 'We know that funerals arranged without a funeral director are at least as good, and often better, than those that take the conventional path.' (See the North West region in Chapter 8 for details.)

• The New Natural Death Handbook Award 2000 for the **Best Crematorium** in the UK goes to the Carlisle Crematorium run by Ken West and his colleagues in Carlisle's Bereavement Services (tel 01228 625310). They offer a reduced fee for those choosing a fuel-saving 'Environmental Cremation', which involves a cardboard coffin and cremation the same day or by the following morning, thus saving on pre-heating of the cremator. They publish excellent guidance for those arranging funerals without funeral directors and can help the public by providing cold storage for the body. They accept a wide variety of body containers from home-made to wicker coffins. They can provide cold storage for the body before the funeral and extra bearers to help the family. (See the North West region in Chapter 8 for details.)

• The New Natural Death Handbook Award 2000 for the **Best Funeral Shop** in the UK goes, as in 1997, to Heaven on Earth in Bristol (tel 0117 926 4999) for their imaginative range of coffin designs and other services. See below in this chapter for details.

• The New Natural Death Handbook Award 2000 for the **Best Funeral Director** in the UK goes to J. E. Gillman & Sons Ltd (tel 020 8672 1557) in Tooting, London SW17. They offer a simple chipboard-based coffin for £45 to families organising a funeral themselves and, as an independent family firm and member of SAIF and NAFD, they provide a superior level of à la carte service. See the London region in Chapter 7 for details.

• The New Natural Death Handbook Award 2000 for the **Best Coffin Manufacturer** in the UK goes to Ted Hodge and his firm E. C. Hodge (MF) Ltd (tel 01945 587477). They were the first mainstream funeral suppliers to make a determined attempt to allow the public to buy coffins direct. Their prices start at £88 for a chipboard oak veneer coffin. (See below in this chapter for their details.)

• The New Natural Death Handbook Award 2000 for the **Best Cardboard Coffin Supplier** in the UK goes to Celtic Casket (tel 01283 521104) who sell a basic brown cardboard coffin in four sizes, with a cremfilm liner and a rigid chipboard base for £53-50 incl. next day delivery; and a more expensive white model.

• The New Natural Death Handbook Award 2000 for the **Best Funeral Supplier** in the UK goes to Thorley Smith Ltd (tel 01942 243331) who will happily supply the general public with body bags, coffin liners, coffin handles, etc – all at reasonable prices.

In making these Awards, the editorial team have relied on their own surveys and investigations and on feedback to the Natural Death Centre from the general public, so as to decide which services were the most helpful, the most innovative and the best value.

Good funeral directors

In our view, the ideal funeral director is a *facilitator,* one who helps the family to do as much of the funeral arranging themselves as they can bear, as exemplified in the following excerpts from an account by an American funeral director about what he learnt from the funeral of his father:

A funeral director helping with his father's funeral

I was sitting on the hospital bed holding my father's hand when he died. I hated the scene but I wouldn't have been anywhere else. Such helplessness and desperation I have never felt at any other time. When he died, we wept.

Two men came with a cot – men I had never seen before. They didn't know me or my profession. My emotion didn't leave room for explanations, so I simply asked them to stand aside. It was my dad and I would do it. Hesitatingly they obliged, while I took the cover from the cot, positioned the cot and gathered Dad's limp body into my arms. It was my job. I was his son. It was our love.

I felt a sense of desertion as I watched those two strangers disappear down the hall with Dad. Dad didn't know them.

One of my best friends, a funeral director from the next town, came to get Dad and did all the embalming work. I did the rest – the death certificate, the notification of newspapers, cemetery, minister, church, family, friends, neighbours, all the scores of details which accompany the task of being a funeral director.

My family did lots of other things: we tucked Dad in (it's rough but it's real) and closed the casket; we took him to church ourselves. My brother, sister and I carried Dad to his grave, we lowered him into his grave with straps and our own muscle power. We closed the vault and shovelled the dirt ourselves. We closed out his life ourselves.

Later, weeks later, I asked myself: how many sons, daughters, parents and spouses had I delayed the grief work for because I had performed all of the tasks for them, because I, as a functionary, had usurped their role as care-giving family members? How many times had I made decisions for a family without their opinion, because I had assumed 'they couldn't take it?' They have a right to be heard. The focus must be on their needs, reactions and prior experience. Immediately, my role in funeral service shifted to being that of a facilitator and it has remained there.

By Roy and Jane Nichols from 'Death – The Final Stage of Growth'
edited by Elisabeth Kübler-Ross.

Buying a coffin

The last chapter dealt with making a coffin. This one, inter alia, tells you how to buy one ready-made – not always an easy purchase, as Jane Spottiswoode discovered. Many funeral directors refuse to sell just a coffin, or do so at grossly inflated prices.

Cardboard coffins

When the Natural Death Centre was launched in 1991, it called for cardboard coffins to be made available in the UK. Nowadays there is a wide variety of models to choose from. The first edition of the 'Natural Death Handbook' in 1993 could identify only a handful of crematoria and cemeteries that would accept cardboard coffins. But by 1994, Jon Luby of The Federation of British Cremation Authorities was writing that 'my advice would be to accept such a coffin if requested'. Now almost every crematorium accepts them; and most funeral directors are willing to obtain a cardboard coffin on behalf of a client, although they will tend to charge a high price.

Cardboard coffins are most regularly used for burials in woodland burial grounds. Some people prefer to use them in conjunction with a body bag, cremfilm, a liquid-proof liner or some other more environmentally-friendly padding or protection for the body such as sawdust, cotton wool, torn-up sheets or old pillows or newspapers (if for cremation, consult the management as to whether the materials you plan to use are acceptable). Some like to paint the coffin (using water-based paints – again ask the crematorium) or to put a drape over the cardboard coffin during the funeral service to hide its unorthodox appearance. It is as well to be aware that if the soil is clay or very stony, the cardboard lid may get smashed open as the grave is filled. Measures that could be taken to avoid this include: placing planks or a mattress-type filling on top of the coffin; dropping a layer of hay or bracken or whatever is to hand on top of the coffin; wrapping the coffin in some covering such as a rug; filling the grave very gently to begin with, using specially gathered loose soil; or filling the grave only when those who would be most upset have left.

If using an estate car, don't forget to check that your cardboard coffin will fit (see Chapter 4 for the relevant makes).

The cardboard coffins available, with the cheapest first, are as follows:

• Danisco Pack Westminster markets the Woodland Coffin. Its dimensions are 72" by 22" by 15". It comes flatpack, in a white oyster (off-white) colour, and assembles into a normal coffin shape. It has a removable lid, but the flaps that hold it together are visible on the outside, so it is perhaps marginally less aesthetically pleasing than some of the other models (see below). It is, however, one of the cheapest cardboard coffins on the market, at £51-41 incl. delivery within England and Wales (be sure to say if your order is urgent). Danisco Pack Westminster, New Road, Sheerness, Kent (tel 01795 580051; fax 01795 66606; web: www.greenburials.com).

• A basic brown cardboard coffin with a cremfilm liner and a rigid chipboard base is available for £53-50 incl. next day delivery. It comes in four sizes: 59" long by 16" wide; 64" by 17"; 69" by 18"; or 74" by 22" (and other sizes for a £5 premium) from Celtic Casket, 40 Monk Street, Tutbury, near Burton-upon-Trent, Staffordshire DE13 9NA (tel 01283 521104; or tel and fax 01283 815992; e-mail: bio.coffins@mcmail.com; web: www.eco.coffins.mcmail.com). Celtic Casket is now also trading as Green Undertakings UK Ltd and states that it is separate from Green Undertakings of Watchet Ltd.

• An elegant cardboard coffin is the Compakta Coffin. It is lightweight, relatively strong and slightly tapered, needs no bolts or clips, and, being white, is suitable for those wishing to paint their cardboard coffin. A longer (77") and more expensive woodgrain-effect version can also be ordered (for £83-37 incl. delivery). The snag with the Compakta is that it is tricky to remove the lid for those wanting access to the body. Internally, it is 72" long by 18" wide and 13.5" deep.

This coffin is available, mainly to the trade, from P. A. Ginns, Compakta Ltd, The Old White Cottage, Desford, Leicestershire LE9 9GS (tel and fax 01455 828642). It can be collected from there or from L. T. & R. Vowles Ltd, Longdon Heath, Upton upon Severn, Worcester WR8 0RL (tel 01684 592212) who deliver the coffin nationwide for Compakta. In urgent cases, the A. B. Welfare and Wildlife Trust (tel 01423 530900 or 868121) may be able to arrange the delivery, adding on no more than £5 to whatever the Trust has to pay the supplier.

Alternatively, members of the public can find out their nearest stockist by phoning the Compakta number or the Natural Death Centre. Compakta's recommended price for the public to pay is £69-32 incl. delivery within England and Wales (£25 extra for overnight delivery; £5 extra for Scotland).

• Larger and less elegant than the Compakta cardboard coffin is the Brighton Casket, also marketed by Danisco Pack Westminster (tel 01795 580051, for full contact details see above). Its dimensions are 74" by 22" by 15". It looks a bit like a giant brown cardboard shoe box with a printed woodgrain-effect on the lid and uses part-plastic bolts to hold it together. It has a 'moisture-protected white liner' inside which gives 'enough protection for a cremation or a burial'. The advantage of both the Brighton Casket and the Woodland Coffin (see above) is that they have removable lids, so they are more suitable for viewing the body than the Compakta.

The Brighton Casket is available flatpack, with instructions for assembly, at a price of £75-79 each incl. delivery within two to three days. Or, a pack of five at £53-46 per coffin; or a pack of ten at £49-94 per coffin incl. delivery. In urgent cases, next day delivery can be organised if there is a coffin ready to go.

• Celtic Casket (tel 01283 521104) also do a smarter, stronger white cardboard coffin with a cremfilm liner, the Celtic, for £77 incl. delivery (or for £75, 'if a person orders directly by telephone without any postal correspondence,' says Alan Goldingay, who runs Celtic Casket). It costs £10 extra for a colour – blue, green or maroon.

• A ready-assembled plain white cardboard coffin from Greenfield Ltd, Braintree, Essex CM7 3JJ (tel 01376 327074; 342 975; e-mail: greenfield@tradprint.demon.co.uk) costs £78-39 incl. next day delivery. It comes fully lined with cremfilm and includes bolts for the lid and a white card nameplate. It is large at 76" by 24.5" by 16.5". A bottle green or wood-effect version costs £104-47 incl. delivery. Both types can be fitted with a range of handles. For example, a white coffin with brass-effect handles costs £91-02 incl. delivery (or £117-10 for a coloured coffin). A white coffin with rope handles, made from 100% cotton and fully biodegradable, costs £92-49 incl. delivery (or £118-57 for a coloured coffin).

• The most expensive cardboard coffin, is the Ecology (Peace Box) coffin. It looks least like a cardboard coffin, with a wood-effect finish, and comes with an elasticated cotton lining, a liquid-proof insert, and a pillow. It is said to be the only one-piece cardboard coffin.

It is the creation of Alexandre Haas, a packaging manufacturer in Lausanne, Switzerland, who writes that it weighs 12 kilos, can carry 200 kilos (although one reader complained to the Natural Death Centre that the coffin's bottom came loose) and resists temperatures from 250 degrees centigrade to minus 180 degrees centigrade. Above all it is kind to the environment, says Haas, 'and it is easily transported and can be slotted together in under five minutes'. (Alexandre Haas, Sondeur Diffusion, CH-1029 Villars-Ste-Croix, Switzerland, tel and fax 00 41 21 634 70 26.)

In the UK, it is distributed flatpack by P. B. UK, Triangle House, 62 Victoria Road, Cirencester, Gloucestershire GL7 1ES (tel 01285 653298; fax 653224; e-mail: ecocoffinpbuk@hotmail.com) for £135-63 incl. delivery. A pack of ten works out at £93-94 each incl. delivery. (A purpose-made carrying belt and metal clips – used when the lid sections of the coffin are folded down for viewing purposes – cost an extra £70-44 incl. delivery and can be reused for each funeral.)

• Some local authority cemeteries and crematoria sell cardboard coffins to members of the public not using their other services. Their prices are reasonable but they will usually require you to collect. They include:

Bretby near Burton-upon-Trent, tel 01283 221505 (either the Compakta or the Celtic model for £70); Brighton, tel 01273 604020 (the Greenfield, sold ready-assembled only, for £58, 'to be collected from the mortuary with a suitable vehicle'); Cardiff, tel 029 2062 3294 (the Compakta for £75, flatpack, no liner); Carlisle, tel 01228 625310 (the Compakta for £62 and others); Hastings, tel 01424 781302 (the Brighton model for £57, flatpack, 'not easy to put together and very big, so bring a large car or van to collect it'); Hexham Town Council in Northumberland, tel 077100 53732 (the Greenfield for £95).

A number of private woodland burial grounds also sell cardboard coffins. They include: Greenhaven near Rugby, tel 01788 860604 (the Compakta for £55); Hinton Park near Christchurch, tel 01425 278910 (£100); South Yorkshire Woodland Burials, tel 01704 821900 (the white Compakta for £90; or the wood-effect for £95). See Chapter 6 for details of other sites selling cardboard coffins.

The many funeral directors around the country who sell cardboard coffins will probably add considerably more mark-up than any of the above sources.

Funeral directors tend to be ferociously opposed to local authorities selling coffins, sometimes getting together to threaten a boycott of those crematoria and cemeteries who do so. In 1996, the Natural Death Centre reported two such cases to the Office of Fair Trading.

Coffins not of cardboard

As detailed below, regular non-cardboard coffins can be obtained from some local funeral directors, direct from a couple of manufacturers, from carpenters or from nationwide funeral suppliers. Wooden coffins can also be collected from several local authorities, such as Carlisle (Carlise is detailed in the North West region in Chapter 8)

Coffins from funeral directors

If you want to buy a coffin that is *not* made of cardboard, your cheapest option may be to approach one of the recommended funeral directors in your local region, as listed in Chapter 7. For instance, UK funeral directors who are prepared to sell their cheapest fully-fitted coffin (fitted with handles and lining) for £60 or under are as follows:

• £50 in Blackpool: from D. Hollowell & Sons (tel 01243 355663). Delivery locally free.

• £50 in Tutbury (Staffordshire): from Green Undertakings UK Ltd, also trading as Celtic Casket (tel 01283 815 992). Delivery free within ten miles.

• £55 in London: from E. M. Kendall (tel 020 7254 6519). Delivery locally £10.

• £60 in Carlisle: from John Simpson (Carlisle) Ltd (tel 01228 512471). Delivery locally £35.

• £60 in Cheltenham: from Beechwood Funeral Services (tel 01242 228208). Delivery locally £10.

• £60 in Liverpool: from Graham J. Clegg Independent Funeral Service (tel 0151 520 3330). Delivery locally free.

Also, not fully-fitted, but good value:

• £45 in London: from Roger Gillman of J.E. Gillman & Sons (020 86721557), a chipboard-based lightly veneered coffin, 'without handles or fancy lining, just cremfilm, using wood from managed sustained-yield forests.' Delivery free within five miles of their premises in Tooting, London SW17.

The Natural Death Centre circulated a questionnaire to 2,400 funeral directors at the end of 1999. Of the 132 (excluding branches of the same firm) who deigned to reply – mostly the small independent firms – all except two were prepared to sell just a coffin, without other services, at prices ranging from £50 to £700 for the cheapest fully-fitted coffin. The resultant average price for a coffin was £137 (11 neglected to give a definitive answer). This is a big improvement since the Centre's 1993 survey, which found a mere 45 funeral directors (53% of all respondents) willing to sell just coffins.

Funeral directors who will supply a coffin to anywhere in the UK are listed under Funeral Suppliers below.

Coffins direct from manufacturers

The following are the cheapest wooden coffins available from those coffin manufacturers who are prepared to deliver directly to a member of the public. Most funeral suppliers remain unwilling to sell directly to the public, often because they are frightened that their main customers, the funeral directors, will object. Indeed in 1993, the Natural Death Centre's survey could not find a single mainstream coffin supplier in the country prepared to sell direct to the public. But now there are a brave few who will do so, although, surprisingly, their prices to the public tend to be higher than those charged by the funeral directors above. The firms with the cheapest coffins are listed first.

• £88-12 for a chipboard oak veneer coffin, fully-fitted with lining, handles and nameplate. Next day delivery £26 nationally. From E. C. Hodge (MF) Ltd, factory at New Drove, Off Weasenham Lane, Wisbech, Cambridgeshire PE13 2RZ (tel 01945 587477; fax 01945 466063); or Norton Road, Stevenage, Hertfordshire SG1 2BB (tel 01438 357341). They can also supply a solid oak coffin for £188, and pet caskets with name plates. 'We have over 100 coffins in stock for next day delivery' (Ted Hodge).

• £120 for an 'oak foil' standard coffin, fitted and lined, for cremation. Overnight delivery locally £20; nationally £50. From Vic Fearn & Co Ltd, Crabtree Mill, Hempshill Lane, Bulwell, Nottingham ND6 8PF (tel 01159 771571; fax 01159 771571); and at Newbarn Farm, Calbourne, Isle of Wight PO30 4JA (tel and fax 01983 531734). 'All our coffins are of superior quality. We sell all funeral items. We refuse no one. Everything we sell is environmentally friendly' (D. G. Crampton).

• £150 for a fully-fitted coffin suitable for burial or cremation – wood veneer on chipboard with a taffeta lining, plastic handles and nameplate. Delivery locally free (not delivered nationally). From Henry Smith (Wandsworth) Ltd, 192-194 Garratt Lane, Wandsworth, London SW18 4ED (tel 020 8874 7622/3). Their solid oak Wandle coffin with solid brass fittings costs £720. 'We are a small family firm and we pride ourselves on our ability to manufacture to any specification very quickly' (John C. Smith, director).

• £265 for an oak finish coffin with lining, handles and nameplate. Delivery nationally £45. From Barry Albin & Sons Ltd, 52 Culling Road, Rotherhithe, London SE16 2TN (tel 020 7237 3637; fax 020 7252 3205). Their top price coffins include the Winchester solid bronze casket for £4,208. 'We are now 217 years old. We sell everything to the trade and to the public. Owned by the family, we accept no pressure [from funeral directors]' (B. Albin).

Coffins from carpenters

Another way of obtaining a coffin, but not normally as cheaply, is simply to ask a local carpenter or to pick one at random from your local Yellow Pages.

The following carpenters have been in touch with the Natural Death Centre, indicating a willingness to provide a coffin:

• No set price – from Stephen Briggs, 42 Vanbrugh Park, London SE3 7AA (tel 020 8293 3365), who needs a week's notice. Price is 'secondary to him', his interest as a cabinet maker is in helping people get the à la carte coffin they want.

• About £150 for making a coffin. Carpenter Paul Sherlock, Units I & B, Collyers Yard Industrial Estate, Lickfield, near Petworth, West Sussex (tel 01798 861601 or mobile 0468 586 290).

• From £200 for a coffin made to order from the 'very flexible' Traditional Funeral Company, 212 Warwick Road, Park Hill, Birmingham B11 2NB (tel 0121 773 9296). Call for more information.

• Artistic coffins made to order from several hundred to several thousand pounds, or less expensive self-assembly (flatpack) pine coffins for about £200, from Bryan Frisby, Sally Clarke and Neil Trinder, Burrowlee House, Broughton Road, Sheffield S6 2AS (tel 0114 2852459 or 2853875).

Coffins from funeral suppliers

There are at present only a few places in the UK which are like shops or mail order funeral suppliers and which sell coffins and other funeral goods to members of the public anywhere in the UK. Often these places can also organise funerals. Their coffins are detailed below.

• The cheapest fully-fitted non-cardboard coffin from Celtic Casket (tel 01283 521104 or see 'Cardboard Coffins' above for more contact details) is £50 incl. free delivery within ten miles. They charge about £70 for an oak veneer coffin.

• The Green Funeral Company, 286 & 288 Church Road, Sheldon, Birmingham B26 3YH (tel 0121 693 0204) charges £70 for an oak, elm or mahogany foil coffin with cremfilm and a coffin plate (or £95 if fully lined and fitted with handles and wreath holders). £83 for an oak, elm, or mahogany veneer with cremfilm and a coffin plate (or £108 fully lined with handles and wreath holders). They also sell solid timber coffins from £370. All prices include delivery locally. See also their entry in the West Midlands region in Chapter 7.

• Undertaken With Love, Unit 1, Mandale Road, Thornaby, Stockton-on-Tees TS17 6AW (24hr tel 01642 606789) charge £120 for the cheapest traditional coffin fully lined with frill and gown (delivery locally free).

• Heaven on Earth shop, run by Paula Rainey Crofts and Simon Dorgan, 18 Upper Maudlin Street, Bristol BS2 8DJ (tel 0117 926 4999) is a rather artistic funeral shop. They charge £130 for a Strandboard coffin without moulding (or £175 with moulding) – a conventionally-shaped shouldered coffin, made of flakes of pine, spruce and larch, fitted with rope handles. An oak veneered coffin costs £225. A reclaimed pine coffin (which can be beeswax finished) costs from £395. Delivery locally free, nationally £50. Also pet coffins from £90.

• Peace Funerals near Sheffield (tel 0114 2530505 or 08457 697822) sell an unfitted chipboard coffin from £30 ('we have helped families to line them with a favourite blanket or sheet or piece of material and to decorate the outside with fabric'). Also, a fully-fitted coffin for £135, or an oak veneer for £160. Delivery locally free. See the North East region in Chapter 7 for more details.

• DIY Funerals (on the web at: www.diyfunerals.co.uk) appears to supply coffins from £95, but the Natural Death Centre has had no reply to its requests for further information.

Coffins for babies

Children's caskets and baby cribs can be obtained from Well's Caskets, Lidwells Yard, North Road, Goudhurst, Kent TN17 1JJ (tel 01580 212040). They range in price from £12 to £123, plus £12-50 for next day delivery.

Compakta (tel 01283 521104 or see 'Cardboard coffins' above for more contact details) sell tiny white-finished cardboard 8" containers for foetal remains for £1-74 each (about £2-50 with postage).

Coffins as bookcases

Heaven on Earth (tel 0117 926 4999 or see full contact details above) sells coffins that can be used as bookcases from £395, made as furniture with mitred joints; and shelves to go inside, with removable brass brackets, for £8 each.

Collapsible coffins

A collapsible coffin, made in Zimbabwe, and available in the UK for £150 from the Heaven on Earth shop in Bristol (tel 0117 926 4999 or see full contact details above), is called the Box. It has only a wooden base which folds down into thirds and a shroud attached to the base. The resulting folded bag can be slung over the shoulder and carried home on a bus.

It is the custom for the urban breadwinner in Zimbabwe to provide a coffin when a relative dies. Private transport is hired for the occasion, since buses will not allow coffins. But with the onslaught of AIDS and thus a high frequency of deaths, the urban dweller's obligations have become prohibitively expensive. The collapsible Box can be carried on a bus, and, besides having potential for a number of developing countries, could perhaps be of service in the UK, since many rail companies have rules against allowing ordinary coffins. People who feel very green and who disdain the use of cars, could then use the train to deliver such a coffin from an urban shop to rural relatives, for their use at the funeral.

The coffin is made by Down to Earth Eco Coffins, PO Box A468, Avondale, Harare, Zimbabwe (tel 00 2634 335 395; fax 0 2634 336 009; e-mail: earthco@africaonline.co.zw) but is sold by them in a minimum quantity of 750 at £10 per unit. (They also sell a painted coffin made from recycled materials at £28 each for a minimum order of 600.)

Earthsleepers and ecopods

Andy Moore of Friends of the Earth and the Community Recycling Network (10-12 Picton Street, Montpelier, Bristol BS6 5QA, tel 0117 9420142), exhibited a psychedelic multicoloured papiermache coffin at the English Day of the Dead exhibition in 1993. This was a one-off, but the designer Andrew Vaccari has since made such coffins commercially available. The earthsleeper – a 'strong and rigid' biodegradable papiermache coffin, with wood studs and an organic lining – is sold flatpack for £350 incl. delivery by Vaccari Design, 27 Prospect Way, Lapford, Devon EX17 6QB (tel 01363 83115; fax 83849; web: www.vaccari.co.uk). It comes in five colours: natural (grey), green, blue, black and red, and Vaccari says it takes 'under five minutes to put together'.

The ecopod is a contoured pod-shaped coffin available from August 2000. It is made from KEF, an entirely recycled and biodegradable material strengthened with cellulose fibres. It carries up to 116 kilos and weighs 14 kilos and thus 'easy to transport'. It is available in blue, red, dark green or cream, and decorated with a Celtic cross, flying doves, or an Aztec sun. It includes a calico mattress. The ecopod costs £290 from Hazel Selina, 37 Western Road, Hove, East Sussex BN3 1AF (tel 01273 746011; fax 734160; e-mail: hselina@aol.com; web: www.ecopod.co.uk).

Coffins made of flax or cork

A company in Germany produces biodegradable coffins and urns. The coffins are made entirely of flax, shaped rather like an insect cocoon. Contact Helmut Hilger, Dürener Sargfabrik, Industriestr. 18-20, 52459 Inden Pier, Germany (tel 00 49 2428 80712; fax 00 49 2428 80722).

Reusable coffins

It is now possible to rent a decorous outer coffin for the funeral service, with only the cardboard inner coffin cremated (normally a thin piece of pine or plywood is placed under the deceased to keep the cardboard rigid).

Green Undertakings UK Ltd/ Celtic Casket in Staffordshire (tel 01283 815992) offers free use of a reusable hardwood Cocoon outer coffin for cremations using their funeral directing service.

Barry Albin & Sons Ltd (52 Culling Road, Rotherhithe, London SE16 2TN, tel 020 7237 3637; fax 020 7252 3205) have a rental scheme whereby you pay £395 for a 'grave liner' and then a rental fee to use a 'superior' coffin that can, for instance, stay overnight in church – the rental fee ranges from £75 for their Victorian Oak coffin to £350 for the American wood casket.

Painted coffins

Ros Clarke (18 The Avenue, Belper, Derbyshire DE56 1WB, tel 01773 82087) will handpaint a cardboard coffin to a client's design, charging from £50 to £100 for her work, and needs at least five days to do the job.

Heaven on Earth (tel 0117 926 4999) will attractively stencil a cardboard coffin for £75, plus £55 for the coffin. Or, from £275 they sell a medium density Fibreboard coffin painted with water-based paints and decorated.

Carol Aston (The Studio, Wistanstow, Craven Arms, Shropshire SY7 8DG, tel 01588 672199 or mobile 0798 0044798) is a decorative artist who handpaints coffins using water-based paints and varnishes suitable for cremation (check with the crematorium) or for green or tradional burial. She is happy to assist with a design or work to a client's own preferences. She specialises in faux marble and verdigris, but takes commissions for religious and secular symbols, football and racing colours, Celtic knotwork, poetry, calligraphy and animal prints. Her prices start from £195 for cardboard coffins to £375 for regular coffins (incl. coffin and handles, plus £30-£100 for the lining). Delivery about £50 for London. Three working days minimum are required, more for extensive art-work.

Susan Kinnear (37 Rainbow Street, London SE5 7TB, tel 020 7703 5830) handpaints coffins from £200 – she can supply the coffin.

Lisette de Roche (164 Westbourne Grove, London W11 2RW, tel 020 7221 8742) accepts independent commissions from members of the public. She can paint a coffin within ten days. You can, if you wish, provide her with a cardboard or regular coffin to paint. Alternatively, her prices (including a coffin) start from £250 for a children's coffin, or from £450 for an adult's coffin. Personal commissions cost from £650.

Vic Fearn coffin manufacturers (tel Nottingham 01159 771571; or Isle of Wight 01983 531734 or see 'Coffins from manufacturers' above for their full contact details) do an artist-designed coffin made from recycled pallets for about £500, and artist-painted coffins using water-based paints suitable for cremation from £350 to £800 depending on the choice of design. Some of their coffins are designed by Lisette de Roche (see above).

Willow coffins

In several cultures, 'the weeping willow is an emblem of grief and a symbol of eternity and immortality. Willows thrive on being pruned.' So runs the argument in favour of the willow coffin, called a 'woven willow chrysalis', which is now being made in Norfolk. It can be ordered either pea-pod-shaped or broad-bean-shaped (for a body to be buried in the foetal position). It is produced within a week to order, in sizes from giant to newborn baby, by Tony Carter (The Willow Weave Company, The Goat Shed, Rowancroft, Kenninghall Road, Banham, Norwich NR16 2HE, tel 01953 887107; fax 01953 456833; mobile 0771 4101567) from about £400 for the larger size, including delivery. About 18 have been made to date, designed by Gemma Nesbitt, who was inspired by the baskets she saw in a West Bengal street market. 'Basket coffins were made in the Middle Ages. Our chrysalis is more natural and informal-looking than a conventional coffin,' writes Nesbitt. 'The body can be wrapped in a coloured shroud and mourners can place their favourite flowers, such as buttercups and daisies or lilies and roses, into the chrysalis, instead of buying expensive wreaths.'

The chrysalis can be kept at home and used for storage. If tightly filled, it can serve as a bench. One bought years in advance 'should be kept completely dry in a large plastic bag' to prevent woodworm. Willow is of varied tints, ranging from white and buff, to green, red and brown, depending on the length of time it is left to steam before being woven.

Peace Funerals (tel 0114 253 0505 or see under Sheffield in the North West region in Chapter 7 for full contact details) now sell their own design of wicker coffin, the Mawdesley Willow, for £399 for the largest adult sizes, down to £75 for smaller sizes up to 24" (delivery locally free). The Mawdesley is more coffin-shaped than the other willow coffins, without pointed ends, which makes it externally slightly shorter than the other designs, but it takes the same size internally. 'They are made in the village where my wife Mary was born in Lancashire. They have a two-part hinged lid, which closes together with a willow stick, attached to toggles on the side of the coffin. We can be very flexible with design and will try and accommodate all requests' (John Mallatratt).

A range of native-grown willow caskets costing from £450 for a rectangular adult casket; £525 for a curved end casket; or from £71 for a baby's crib casket (plus approximately £20 for delivery) are available direct from The Somerset Willow Company, Wireworks Estate, Bristol Road, Bridgwater, Somerset TA6 4AP (tel 01278 424003; fax 446415). Natural linen liners are an extra £50 each, and they can also make caskets to your own size or specifications on request.

Heaven on Earth in Bristol (tel 0117 926 4999 or see full contact details above) sell a willow coffin with a hinged lid for £499.

Coffin handles

Thorley Smith Ltd (Britannia Mill, Clayton Street, Wigan WN3 4DG, tel 01942 243331; fax 821592; e-mail: sales@thorleysmith.com; web: www.thorleysmith.com) supply handles ranging in price from £2-82 for a plastic set to £12-49 for a metal set and upwards. Delivery is extra.

Heaven on Earth (tel 0117 926 4999 or see full contact details above) sell hemp rope handles at £8 each (delivery locally free).

Celtic Casket (tel 01283 815992 or see full contact details above) sell biodegradable cotton webbing handles from £5 for the set, or £10 for 'integrated cotton handles cum lowering webbing'. A set of six cremation-friendly handles, a name plate, six wreath holders and a crucifix costs £20, in brass or chrome effect (delivery extra).

Linings for coffins

Thorley Smith (tel 01942 243331 or see full contact details above) supply patented plastic coffin liners, which can be used as cremfilm, from about £2 each, including a pillow, delivery extra.

Heaven on Earth (tel 0117 926 4999 or see full contact details above) supply coffin linings from £35 (or cremfilm for £1-50 a metre, about £4 per coffin) plus delivery.

Coffin drapes

Heaven on Earth (tel 0117 926 4999 or see full contact details above) have batik throws, to cover a coffin, costing from £118 (delivery locally free).

Shrouds

Carlisle Cemetery Office (tel 01228 625310 or see the North West region in Chapter 6 for full contact details) sell their own design of woollen burial shroud complete with board and ropes for £132 (delivery extra).

Heaven on Earth (tel 0117 926 4999 or see full contact details above) have shrouds or robes in cotton, Indian wool or silk from £5 to £15 or more (delivery locally free).

Body bags

The simplest way to obtain a body bag might be to approach an undertaker local to you listed in Chapter 7. Alternatively, a body bag can be bought from the following:

Thorley Smith (tel 01942 243331 or see full contact details above) sell zipped body bags for £16-57, or unzipped biodegradable ones for £8-47 to £8-83 depending on the size. They also sell clear film bags for £8-46. All prices include delivery.

Celtic Casket (tel 012833 521104 or see full contact details above) sell a body bag for £12 (including delivery).

Heaven on Earth (tel 0117 926 4999 or see full contact details above) sell a cremation body bag for £12 (including delivery); or a heavier biodegradable body bag for burials for £15 (delivery extra).

Lear of London (Bryson House, Horace Road, Kingston Upon Thames, Surrey KT1 2SL, tel 020 8546 2633) sell a wide range of body bags. They have a minimum order of £30 and will deal, reluctantly it would seem, with members of the public.

Peace Funerals (tel 0114 2530505 or 08457 697822 or see under Sheffield in the North West region in Chapter 7 for full contact details) sell a biodegradable body bag with board from £20.

Make sure you get a body bag that is long enough for the body. Heavy duty body bags 7'5" long (ex-Gulf War), semi-opaque and zipped along three sides, are available for £7 (with delivery extra) from RBT (tel 0161 684 1667, ask for Bob or Steve).

Burial stretchers

The Jerrards Hessian Burial Stretcher is a biodegradable hessian burial stretcher which can be carried by four or eight people. It incorporates a fluid-proof inner liner and a 'modesty cover' which rolls out from one end. It is available for £27-50 if it is collected (7.30am to 4.30pm Mon-Thur), or you can pay £6-50 extra for next day delivery, from Jerrards, Tripes Farm, Chelsfield Lane, Orpington, Kent BR6 7RS (tel 08707 304050).

Heaven on Earth in Bristol (tel 0117 926 4999 or see full contact details above) say they have wicker makers who could make a wicker stretcher for £150 or less.

Lowering webbing

Heaven on Earth (tel 0117 926 4999) sell lowering webbing from £15. Furniture webbing from a shop such as John Lewis seems to work well too.

Urns

Danisco Pack Westminster (tel 01795 580051 or see full contact details above) sell containers for ashes made from a material similar to their cardboard coffins, but the minimum quantity they would sell to the public is 25 at £4-75 per pot.

Heaven on Earth in Bristol (tel 0117 926 4999 or see full contact details above) sell urns for ashes, plain or lacquered, from £5 upwards.

Gemma Nesbitt (Wytherston, Powerstock, Bridport, Dorset DT6 3TQ, tel 01308 485 211; fax 01308 485 273) who designed the willow coffin (see above), also designs little clay pots for ashes, in the shape of beehives or mud-huts. These can be commissioned in white or in various colours from Tatina Mallinson (67 Camberwell Grove, London SE5 8JE, tel 020 7703 8080; fax 020 7703 6550; e-mail: wjwm@btinternet.com), a potter and sculptor, who makes little pots from £8 or big ones for about £30.

E. C. Hodge (MF) Ltd (tel Wisbech 01945 587477 or Stevenage 01438 357341, or see full contact details in 'Coffins from manufacturers' above) supply a solid oak casket for ashes from £12.

Tim Hurn, a potter in Dorset (Home Farm House, Bettiscombe, Bridport, Dorset DT6 5NU, tel 01308 868171) makes funerary jars to commission – clay wood-fired stoneware jars for remains – from £25 upwards.

Carol Aston (tel 01588 672199 or see full contact details above) sells ashes caskets handpainted to her own or the client's design, from £45 (pet ashes caskets from £35). Delivery extra.

Rupert Blamire (Ground Floor Unit, Bannerman Buildings, Bannerman Road, Bristol BS5 ORR, tel 01179 39 3914) has designed a striking neoclassical three-foot-high lidded ceramic urn, made of red terracotta clay from Staffordshire. They can be used for housing the ashes or simply as garden ornaments. The 3' urn costs £150, a 4' model is available for £325. Blamire will deliver the urn for about £50 locally.

Transport

If you are arranging a funeral yourselves and providing your own transport, see 'Body, transport' in the Index for advice and make sure that the coffin will fit your vehicle (see the advice in Chapter 4 about particular makes of estate car). If you need to pay for transport, a helpful local funeral director may well be as cheap as a local hire firm. Those who replied to our questionnaire were no doubt the more enlightened members of the profession; almost all of these would supply just transport for the body or coffin without other services – only two refused (19 did not inform us either way). The prices varied greatly, ranging from £27 for an estate car to £250 for a hearse and four bearers; one offered a mileage charge of £1·20 per mile. All the firms and their prices (if given) are detailed in Chapter 7.

Renting a hearse and bearers

Alternatively, you could try a car hire firm that rents out chauffeur-driven hearses, cars and limousines, such as Greens Carriage Masters (tel 020 8692 9200) who charge from £85 for a Daimler hearse; or O'Brien Car Hire (tel 020 8311 9591) who charge £85 for a Daimler hearse for two and a quarter hours and £15 per hour thereafter. Their 'full uniform' chauffeurs can also act as bearers for £10, and extra bearers are available at £25 each. A Daimler limousine is available for £65 for two hours and £15 per hour thereafter. You could find out the phone numbers of other such firms from the main journal in which they tend to advertise, the Funeral Service Journal (tel 0113 2841177; e-mail: info@fsj.co.uk). You can hire an 11-seater stretch limousine for the mourners from Rodeo Drive Limousines (tel 020 8438 9577) for £195 for three hours.

Wheel biers

Those readers who are so green that they cannot accept the idea of motor vehicles of any kind being used to transport the body, could try asking a local church or cemetery if they can lend or rent, with a suitable deposit, a wheel bier. For instance, Maldon Cemetery (see the East Anglia region in Chapter 8) does have such a wheel bier.

Horse-drawn funeral

More feasible, more expensive and more dashing is to arrange for a horse-drawn hearse (which can be hired by the family direct, the use of a funeral director is not obligatory). A number of firms offer such vehicles, complete with black horses: Gibson Carriage Masters (from £500 in the London area and they also have branches in Huntingdon, Nottingham, Bolton and Blackburn, tel 01487 830045); Central Ceremonial Carriages (from £270 plus 50p a mile, based in Bonnybridge, Scotland, tel 01324 812435); Claytons Carriage Masters (from £400, based in Gayton, Northampton, tel 01327 830181); Classic Carriages (from £425, based in London, Kingston and Runcorn, tel 0800 1975125); Foxdell Carriages (from £450 locally to £650 for the London area, based near Bromsgrove, Worcestershire, tel 01527 873865); Mews Carriages (from £550 for the London area, based in Hitchin, Hertfordshire, tel 01438 871622); Peter Taylor (from £600, a funeral director with various branches in East Anglia, tel 01603 760787); Chalfont Carriage Company (from £550, based in Chalfont St Giles, Buckinghamshire, tel 01494 872 304); and T. Cribb & Sons (from £695, a funeral director based in London E16, tel 020 7476 1855).

Mole Valley Green Burial Ground (tel 01769 574512) in South Molton, North Devon (see the South West region in Chapter 6) offer the use of a horse and cart for funerals, free within their site and for £5 to £10 an hour elsewhere.

Trains and canal boats

Peace Funerals (tel 0114 2530505) can help you to arrange a burial in a woodland burial ground at Alfreton in Derbyshire, with arrival there by steam train from the Midland Railway Centre at Ripley in Derbyshire.

The Calder and Hebble Navigation Society took one of their departed members, who lived in Calderdale, on the canal boat 'The Savile' to the crematorium, and were rumoured to be planning to make this a public service, with room on board for a dozen mourners and the coffin. Their phone number is ex-directory, however.

The woodland burial ground in Retford, Nottinghamshire (Cyril Blackshaw, Bassetlaw District Council, tel 01909 533487, or see the East Midlands region in Chapter 6) has boats passing the site along the Chesterfield canal. Mr Blackshaw thinks that it could probably be arranged for a coffin to be delivered by boat.

Cold storage

78% of our progressive respondents were prepared to supply cold storage facilities to families who were not using the funeral director for the funeral. This could be reassuring for those, for instance, who have to wait for relatives arriving from abroad for the funeral. Some of the other funeral directors did not have cold storage facilities, using embalming instead. The price asked for cold storage ranged from no charge at all (in four instances) to £15 per hour, with an average price of just over £15 per day. All the firms and their prices are detailed in Chapter 7.

Embalming

Embalming, which is normally quite unnecessary, involves draining blood from the body, and replacing it with formaldehyde (plus a pinkish dye such as safranine) pumped in under pressure, which has a hardening and disinfecting effect. 'The cheeks become fuller and firmer, and the eyeballs and surrounding skin become harder,' writes Robert Wilkins in 'The Fireside Book of Death'. He describes how the mouth is prevented from hanging open, sometimes by a needle passed from the lower lip up through the nostril, and how the abdomen is suctioned clean. Unlike Egyptian embalmers, modern embalming aims only for a short-term preserving effect. The funeral trade argues that embalming helps prevent the body smelling and removes some of the trauma from the face. As one of our contacts put it: 'I would certainly look better after death pumped full of pink dye, with the lines on my face smoothed away.' Embalming will probably not appeal to those who dislike make-up for the living face; or to those who want the body to be handled only by close family; or to those who want to allow the body to look very evidently dead. But it is, of course, a certain way of ensuring that the deceased is not buried or burnt alive, if you should have this particular fear.

'Do you embalm the deceased as a matter of course or on request?' we asked the funeral directors in our questionnaire. Several firms replied 'Yes, we do embalm as a matter of course', some adding the proviso 'unless asked not to' – so it is important to make your wishes clear in this regard. The majority claimed only to embalm on request, but often again with provisos such as: 'unless the body is to be exported or conveyed long distance' or 'unless the family wishes to view the body'. One firm wrote: 'We embalm when we consider it necessary for hygienic reasons and for viewing purposes. If there is a risk of infection, we will insist on it for our own staff's sake.' At which point, the client may need to insist on a change of funeral directors. Indeed, embalming is not allowed for sea burial or for burial in some of the nature reserve burial grounds.

Using a funeral director

It is hard to find an independent funeral director nowadays – many of the big firms hide behind the name of the small firm they have taken over, and often it takes some persistence to find this out. Many independent firms are members of SAIF, the Society of Allied and Independent Funeral Directors, so look out for their emblem. With other firms, ask outright if the firm's parent company is Service Corporation International (SCI), the American funeral company which has captured more than 18% of the UK market, and has also bought up 21% of the UK's crematoria. SCI are best avoided wherever possible (although Chapter 7 recommends several of their better branches). A BBC TV documentary claimed that this company's internal documents promoted aggressive selling of their most expensive coffins (for instance, they advised their sales force: 'Do not judge the ability of a family to afford a particular coffin by their appearance').

But a bigger problem in choosing a funeral director is that, in the first shock of a relative dying, 97% of people, according to an Office of Fair Trading investigation, sign up with the very first funeral director they contact. Arranging a funeral is not like buying any other consumer service, and people need to be aware that this could lay them open to exploitation, even if most funeral directors are in fact well-meaning and dedicated people. Do not accept, for instance, a funeral director who just happens to be at the hospital, who may have a private 'arrangement' with staff. Ask the staff for a full list of local firms if they have one. Our advice is that you get a friend who is not so emotionally involved to phone around for you and to report back to you when a funeral director has been located who meets your criteria. Do not be wary of looking outside your area – any extra mileage charge is likely to be a small element of the final bill.

It is perhaps worth re-emphasising at this point that, although The Natural Death Centre is campaigning for improvements in the funeral trade, and advocates that families organise funerals themselves wherever possible, it acknowledges that funerals in the UK are as cheap or cheaper than most countries in Europe; they are cheap compared with what the average family is prepared to spend on a wedding; and they are carried out in the main by sensitive professionals doing a difficult and stressful job which most people would not have the courage to do.

All members of funeral associations are supposed to offer a basic funeral, but this needs asking for by name. In response to our questionnaire, several neglected or refused to fill in the questions about prices, but for those who were willing to state them publicly, a basic funeral costs from £318-50 to £890, with an average of £585 – an increase of 10.4% on the £530 figure for 1996. To this £585, which represents the funeral director's charges, need to be added the so-called 'disbursements' paid out on behalf of the client by the funeral director: the cremation fee (averaging £223), doctors' fees (£82) and minister's fee (normally £68), an average extra total for disbursements of £373 (assuming it is a cremation; burial in a Church of England churchyard, for instance, costs £119). Thus the average complete cost for a basic funeral is currently £958.

The best value basic funeral for those in the London area, for instance, seems to be that offered by E. M. Kendall (see the Greater London region in Chapter 7), costing £375. Their cheapest fully-fitted coffin costs only £55.

For those wanting no involvement in the funeral at all, not even to know which crematorium was used, Rowland Brothers (see the Greater London region in Chapter 7) offer what they call a 'disposal service' for £356 (disbursements extra). F. A. Albin & Sons, in London, offer a 'disposal funeral package'; for £519 (incl. disbursements); and J. E. Gillman & Sons Ltd, also in London, offer a similar funeral, more tactfully entitled 'Direct Transfer Service', for £325 (disbursements extra).

If you are genuinely hard-up, many funeral directors are kind-hearted enough to make allowances and will not turn you away. One of our contacts offered a funeral director £400 cash on the spot (the most he could afford) for a £795 funeral and was accepted. The highly commendable and distinctive Islamic funeral service offered by Haji Taslim (see the London region in the Good Funeral Guide), based at the East London Mosque – 95% of their clients are from the Muslim community – offers free burial to the indigent, besides being prepared to give cheap or free help of various kinds to those planning their own funeral.

If you need to complain about a funeral director, you can report the matter to their trade association, if they have one – normally either the National Association of Funeral Directors, the Funeral Standards Council or the Society of Allied and Independent Funeral Directors (see the Resources chapter for their addresses). In practice, you may get more satisfaction by going to your local county court (under 'C' in the phone book) or even to the local media. Or it may be a matter that could be reported to the Trading Standards Officer at your local council. The Natural Death Centre would be interested in receiving any brief written accounts that could help warn others – and in receiving positive feedback about funeral professionals whom you have found to be unusually helpful.

Less expensive funerals for council residents

A very simple but useful scheme has been started by the local authorities in Crewe ('The Local Funeral', tel 01270 212643; web: www.crewe.nantwich. gov.uk/worksservices) and in Nottingham ('The Nottingham Funeral', tel 0115 915 2340). It deserves copying by other councils nationwide. The councils in these cities provide the public with information on the cheapest funeral offered by a funeral director in their area plus a list of the other funeral directors. Nottingham pioneered this in 1996 and as a result, the cheapest funeral price has dropped from £1,000 to £689 – a price that includes a following car and disbursements. The winning funeral director is obliged to take out a certain number of advertisements about the scheme (which is guaranteed for two years, in the second year going up merely by the rate of inflation) and the council also advertises it.

Other councils have made similar agreements with local funeral directors for a special relatively inexpensive funeral package for local residents, but without perhaps the same exclusive focus on price. It may be worthwhile phoning your local council's cemeteries department (eg for Brent, this would mean looking under 'B' for Brent and then under 'Cemeteries' within the list of Brent's services) and asking if your council has made such an agreement (note that the requirement is normally that the deceased should have lived in the borough, not the person organising the funeral, but check this). Often, however, the prices are not that good. In London, the Co-op Funeral Service has for several years provided a not-so-cheap basic funeral for certain boroughs: the CWS Co-op does one for residents of **Southwark** (tel 020 7732 4165), **Lewisham** (tel 020 7698 3244) and **Lambeth** (tel 020 7703 2803) – or try the local councils for details. The cost excluding disbursements for these CWS ones is £1,030 – yet in Southwark and Lewisham, their basic funeral, whether for residents or non-residents, is cheaper than this at £890, although including only a hearse and not the following limousine. The **Hounslow** Council also has a similar arrangement for a 'Hounslow Community Funeral Service' with local funeral directors: Andrew Holmes & Son (tel 020 8572 3277) and Frederick Paine (tel 020 8994 0056) – the price being £550 (disbursements extra). In **Stockport**, the 'Civic Funeral Service' is provided for the council by the United North West Co-operative Society (tel 0161 432 0818). They charge £874 for a cremation (including disbursements); and £1,168 for burial in a new grave (again including disbursements). In **Cardiff**, the local authority funeral service provider is D. Caesar Jones (tel 029 2052 2644), an SCI firm, who charge £390 (disbursements extra). In **Wigan**, the borough council uses the services of a local funeral director, Edwards Funeral Directors (tel 01942 821 215) to offer cremation for £715 (including disbursements) and burial for £940 (including disbursements and the opening of a new grave). An inexpensive service is offered by the **St Helens** council which has an agreement with the local Co-op (tel 01744 23675) whereby cremation costs £663 and burial costs £674, both prices including disbursements. **Bury** Metropolitan Borough Council has an arrangement with Hamers Funeral Directors (tel 0161 797 7133) offering a funeral for £325 (disbursements extra – burial costs an extra £573 or cremation an extra £287).

Memorial Societies

There is scope for religious and neighbourhood groups of one sort or another in the UK to help each other with funeral arrangements, just as within some Jewish communities it is considered an honour to be of service to the deceased in this way. Neighbours could help each other with advice, with transport, by providing bearers, by helping with the making of coffins or even by buying a plot of land for a wildlife cemetery (besides of course helping before death with caring for the dying at home, and after the funeral with reintegrating the bereaved into the life of the neighbourhood). Laurieston Hall, for instance, a large co-operative household near Castle Douglas in Scotland, has prepared a burial ground within its own land for the later use of its currently middle-aged members.

In the United States since the 1940s communities in many local areas have formed their own Memorial Societies which use the power of their membership numbers to make agreements with particular funeral directors for cheaper than normal services (society members tend to pay less than a fifth the average cost of an American funeral). A low lifetime fee is charged, many of the staff are volunteers, and some of the societies offer workshops and meetings and informative leaflets and advice. People who join fill in a prearrangement form which indicates their detailed funeral preferences. Anyone contemplating forming a similar society in the UK – a project which The Natural Death Centre would be happy to help publicise – can find information on the web (at www.funerals.org/famsa/) or can write to P.O. Box 10, Hinesberg, Vt. 05461, USA to get a free copy of a brochure called 'Did you forget the most important part of funeral planning?'

Free funerals

Approximately 8% of the 623,000 deaths per annum in the UK result in claims to the government's Social Fund for help with funeral expenses. Since 1997, new restrictions, denounced at the time as 'mean', have been in force: up to £600 for the funeral will be available from the government (with extra money for 'disbursements' – such as a grave, burial costs, the cremation fee, doctors' certificates and removing a pacemaker; for transporting a body more than 50 miles; and to pay for a return journey for a responsible person who is either arranging or attending the funeral). Claims must be made before or within three months of the funeral and can sometimes be paid out before the funeral takes place, if the invoice is submitted in time. Phone your local Benefits Agency office (under 'Benefits Agency' or 'Social Security' in the phone book) and ask for form SF200. Details and leaflets (but not the claim form) can be obtained from the Benefits Agency Public Enquiry Office (tel 020 7712 2171; e-mail: peo@MS41.dss.gsi.gov.uk; web: www.dss.gov.uk).

The deceased must have been ordinarily resident in the UK at the time of death, although the funeral can in specified circumstances take place anywhere within the European Economic Area. The person organising the funeral must be on Income Support, income-based Jobseeker's Allowance, Family Credit, Housing Benefit, Council Tax Benefit or Disability Working Allowance, although the person's money over £500 (£1,000 if 60 or over) will be used towards the costs. Any money in the estate of the deceased will go towards the costs, as will contributions from relatives, clients or charities. The cheque is usually made out to the funeral directors, not the claimant, but is sent to the claimant to give to them.

Since 1997 a greater attempt has also been made to find a non-estranged partner or relative who could afford to pay for the funeral. As the government puts it, in complex double negatives: 'Where there is no surviving partner, and where a parent, son or daughter of the deceased exists, and neither they nor their partner are in receipt of a qualifying benefit, it will be considered unreasonable for the person in receipt of the income-related benefit to take responsibility for the funeral expenses.'

A claim from an otherwise eligible single parent for the funeral of a child will fail if the absent parent lives abroad or has savings.

The Benefits Agency (see leaflet FB29, 'A Guide to Benefits When Someone Dies') gives out a Widow's Payment of £1,000 if the husband paid enough National Insurance contributions and was not getting retirement pension, and if the widow is under 60. From April 2001 the amount will be raised to £2000 and will be made available to widowers also.

The local authority is obliged (under the Public Health – Control of Disease – Act 1984 Part III Disposal of Dead Bodies Section 46) to arrange for the disposal of the body where 'no suitable arrangements have been made'. A. C. T. Connolly (of 26 Broadfields Avenue, Winchmore Hill, London N21 1AD) decided to test this Act by refusing to arrange for the disposal of a relative's body (which was in the mortuary at the local hospital). He resisted 'wrongful' pressure from the registrar of deaths to take various forms before he would register the death. Finally a helpful official in the council's Social Services department agreed to arrange the funeral and to register the death in the name of the council, with the Connolly family reimbursing the council for the £315 cost. The family were notified in advance of the time for the service and the committal at the crematorium. Mr Connolly concludes: 'It is a legally imposed duty on local authorities to carry out this public health function *no matter what the financial position of the bereaved might be*. Yet very few people indeed know of this local authority option.'

In one recent instance, a local authority took control of a house and its contents in order to recover the cost of a funeral it had provided. The nearest relative was prevented from going into the house to find suitable clothes with which to dress the body. The case was referred by a law centre to John Bradfield, author of 'Green Burial', who is insisting that the local authority be taken to court to prove that relatives cannot be treated in this insensitive way.

Similarly, the ombudsman has issued a report criticising a local authority which tried to define the bodies of old people from private nursing homes as 'industrial waste' (with reference to the 1984 Act mentioned above).

Organ and body donation

Ernest Morgan quotes a poetic statement by Robert Test in favour of organ donation:

Give my sight to the man who has never seen a sunrise

The day will come when my body will lie upon a white sheet tucked neatly under the four corners of a mattress located in a hospital busily occupied with the living and the dying. At a certain moment a doctor will determine that my brain has ceased to function and that, to all intents and purposes, my life has stopped.

When that happens, do not attempt to install artificial life into my body by the use of a machine and don't call this my deathbed. Let it be called the Bed of Life, and let my body be taken from it to help others lead fuller lives.

Give my sight to the man who has never seen a sunrise, a baby's face or love in the eyes of a woman. Give my heart to the person whose own heart has caused nothing but endless days of pain. Give my blood to the teenager who was pulled from the wreckage of his car, so that he may live to see his grandchildren play. Give my kidneys to a person who depends upon a machine to exist from week to week. Take my bones, every muscle, every fibre and nerve in my body and find a way to make a crippled child walk. Explore every corner of my brain. Take my cells, if necessary, and let them grow so that, someday, a speechless boy will shout at the crack of a bat or a deaf girl will hear the sound of rain against her window.

Burn what is left of me and scatter the ashes to the winds to help the flowers grow.

If you must bury something, let it be my faults, my weaknesses and all my prejudice against my fellow man. Give my sins to the devil. Give my soul to God.

If, by chance, you wish to remember me, do it with a kind deed or word to someone who needs you. If you do all I have asked, I will live forever.

'Dealing Creatively with Death' by Ernest Morgan.

If you feel the same way as Ernest Morgan and Robert Test, you need to persuade your next of kin (who will have charge of your body after death), to tell your doctor and your hospital ward and you need to get a donor card from your local library, health centre, doctor or chemist. Or contact the Department of Health Organ Donor Literature Line (tel 0845 6060400) and ask to be sent a form and a donor card. You can choose to donate any part of the body or only the kidneys, heart, liver, corneas, lungs or pancreas. Animal Aid (The Old Chapel, Bradford Street, Tonbridge, Kent TN9 1AW, tel 01732 364 546) issues a Humane Research Donor Card which requests that the body be used for medical and scientific research. Organ donor cards are also available from the British Heart Foundation, Distribution Department, 14 Fitzhardinge St, London W1H 4DH (tel 020 7935 0185). You can also tick the donor box on forms when getting a passport or a driving licence.

The cornea of the eyes is the only part of the body that can wait up to 12 hours for removal; the rest have to be removed immediately after 'brain-stem' death, with machines keeping the body's blood circulating after death. Normally the body is made available for the funeral within less than 12 hours, once the relatives have agreed. Relatives are still asked for their approval, even if a name is on the register.

It is not possible to guarantee a free disposal of your body by leaving it for dissection by medical students. Only a percentage of bodies are accepted. Medical schools generally accept only bodies that are within easy range of the school, unautopsied after death, relatively whole and non-cancerous – although more and more schools are taking cancerous bodies. To offer to donate your body, contact the professor of anatomy at your local medical hospital or HM Inspector of Anatomy, Department of Health, Wellington House, 133-155 Waterloo Road, London SE1 8UG (tel 020 7972 4342 – on call 24 hours); or for those in the London area, contact the London Anatomy Office (tel 020 8846 1216).

People who want to donate their bodies for purposes of medical research only (and not for dissection by medical students) can write to the Histopathology Lab,

Peterborough District Hospital, Thorpe Road, Peterborough PE3 6DA (tel 01733 874000 and ask for the research nurse) for an information pack and consent forms. The hospital makes use of the bodies for drug discovery research. Bodies are returned to the family for a funeral.

Incidentally, whoever is lawfully in possession of the body can donate it to a medical school, even if the person who died made no provision for this, as long as he or she did not object – either in writing or verbally in the presence of two witnesses; and as long as no relative or spouse objects.

Transplants can be authorised as long as there is no reason to believe that the next of kin would object.

Prepaid funerals

It has been estimated that the prepaid funeral market could become as big a business in the UK as it is in the United States, where about three quarters of all funerals are paid for before death. The advantages claimed include: people planning in advance tend to choose simple funerals; it allows for leisurely comparison shopping; in some of the plans you are protected against inflationary price rises; relatives do not suddenly face a big bill at a time of stress; it provides peace of mind for those who are elderly and without relatives; and it would reduce your capital and thus perhaps entitle you to social security benefits you might not otherwise have received.

In our view, the advantages of some of the schemes could be outweighed by the potential disadvantages: prepaid funerals militate against family participation – what if your family decide that they want to make your coffin or to look after your funeral arrangements? Many of the schemes tend to favour the big chains with their assembly-line funerals and to drive the smaller firms to the wall. They encourage TV advertising and other heavy marketing ploys. One firm in the UK went bankrupt. And there has been at least one horror story in the United States where the money was simply pocketed, and the prepaid cremation bodies were stacked in the basement of the mortuary, with others buried in mass graves.

A first step is to consider questions such as: what happens if you do not need a funeral in the UK after all, for instance if you die abroad or if your ship sinks at sea? What happens if you die before completing payments? What happens if you need that capital sum in an emergency? Would you not have done better to put the money into a form of investment that you could recover? What happens if the trust or foundation backing your prepaid scheme goes bust or proves fraudulent? What if whoever attends your dying is not aware of your prepaid arrangement? If you want such an arrangement, would it not be more interesting to discuss your funeral wishes with your most trusted next of kin or partner and to pay money into an account or investment controlled jointly with them? Or, probably a less financially attractive option, to put regular premiums into a funeral insurance scheme (or to top up your life insurance) which would pay a lump sum to your relatives on your death, leaving your relatives with more freedom of action? **Sun Life** (tel 0800 27 21 27), for instance, offers a funeral insurance scheme (Guardian Over 50 Plan) whereby a 70-year-old male, whatever his state of health, pays £18 a month for life, and, if death occurs during the first two years, the premiums plus 50% are paid back; thereafter it pays out £1,920 on death. **Scottish Friendly** (tel 0141 275 5000) and **Tunbridge Wells Equitable** (tel 01892 515353, ask for the Dignity Bond) offer a similar schemes.

Nevertheless, if your circumstances are such that one of the more high profile prepaid plans seems desirable, try to find a scheme which, as well as satisfactorily answering the above questions, is mainly for small independent firms; places at least 90% of the prepaid funds in trust; will not add extras when the time comes; allows a wide range of choice if you move to another part of the country; allows for no-questions-asked cancellation with refund of money *and* interest (less any small administration fees); and returns any unspent money and interest after the funeral. You will not be able to find such a scheme as yet in the UK (although the last two points are required by law in some American states).

The **greenest best buy** for those needing to arrange the funeral in advance might be to set aside sufficient funds in a joint savings account to cover the full costs of one of the less expensive Woodland Burial grounds (described in detail in Chapter 6) which have established arrangements for providing a coffin and for collecting the body. These include: Hinton Park in Dorset (tel 01425 278910), Greenhaven near Rugby (tel 01788 860604) and Oakfield in Essex (tel 01255 503456). But be very cautious about handing over money in advance. It is one thing to buy burial rights, and quite another to hand over money years in advance for digging graves and body collection. It might also be worth approaching the charitable A. B. Welfare and Wildlife Trust in North Yorkshire (tel 01423 530900 or 868121) to see if a special prearrangement can be made for one of their sites. Hinton Park, for instance, charge £975 in advance for a coffin and a plot, including the digging and filling of the grave, the planting of a tree, the provision of a small memorial plaque and the collection of the body (in a green Renault Espace). Extra is charged if the body is collected from beyond a 50 mile radius (collection from London costs about £100 extra). Thus for a London family looking for a site within range of the city, the three feasible sites are Hinton Park, Greenhaven or Oakfield, and the total funeral charges, including collecting the body from London, would be about £1,248-75 for Oakfield; £1,075 for Hinton Park; and £570 for Greenhaven. You will not be able to match Greenhaven's prices in any of the plans described below.

Possibly the least objectionable of the mass market plans is **Golden Charter** (tel 0800 833800), since it is specifically designed for the small, independent funeral directors and their association SAIF, the Society of Allied and Independent Funeral Directors (some of whom are also members of the larger National Association of Funeral Directors). It claims to have over 2,000 participating funeral directors. Golden Charter's cheapest Standard Way plan costs £1,110, which allows £435 towards the costs of disbursements (a sum which increases with the Retail Price Index). If disbursements cost more than this at the time of the plan's purchase, the extra sum can be paid then to ensure full future cover. The Woodland Trust is paid to plant a tree for each plan bought.

Over 120 local funeral directors offer their own prepayment plans, backed by **Funeral Planning Trust** (for referrals to a local firm, phone 01508 532 632).

The next best is probably the **Perfect Assurance Funeral Trust** run by the National Association of Funeral Directors (NAFD) (for details of your local participants, tel 0121 709 0019), which allows you to choose any firm, small or large, that offers the scheme and to tailor-make a plan to your requirements. The firm then pays the money into the presumed safety of the Perfect Assurance trust fund.

The market leader and the first to advertise on TV has been **Chosen Heritage** (tel 0800 525555), whose cheapest Basic Plan funeral costs £1,057 (£330 of disbursements are included, a sum which increases with the Retail Price Index). If the person dies abroad or ends up not needing their funeral, relatives are refunded. All the plan money goes into a trust fund. Chosen Heritage allows cancellations at any time. It has a 'personal choice' option for those wanting a nonstandard package. The snag is that a large number of its 600 funeral directors are part of the giant American SCI company, and such huge chains are to be discouraged.

The Co-op's CRS division (tel 0500 112121) offers a **Co-operative Funeral Bond** Funeral Plan, the price of which will be determined by a quote from your local Co-op funeral director. I asked for the cheapest basic funeral in the Hammersmith area of London (tel 020 8748 2982) and was quoted £1,085, disbursements £326 extra. Once the full cost, including disbursements, is paid, and the plan taken out, there will be no more to pay at the time of the funeral. Cancellation is 'at the discretion of the society and any repayment is subject to an administration fee'.

The Co-op's CWS division (tel 0800 289120) has a **Co-operative Funeral Bond** too. Its Earl cremation plan costs £839 (including disbursements). One unusual feature of this plan is that it allows two people to be named on the form and the plan can eventually pay for either of them.

The scheme **Dignity in Destiny** (tel 0800 269318) is almost completely tied to the big chain SCI and their 580 funeral directors, using independent funeral directors only in those places where it has no coverage itself. Its Primary Plan costs £1,040 including disbursements (cremation fee, minister's fee and doctors' fees) 'however much these rise'.

Crematoria

In our view, most crematoria are to be shunned. Who wants rushed funeral services in buildings which have been described as looking like newspaper reading rooms in public libraries or waiting rooms in airports? Several people of late have suggested a different approach. Rather than, say, a service in church followed by just some of the family going on to a committal at the crematorium, with consequent confusion and disruption for any party or gathering afterwards, both the service and something similar to a committal can be held in the church (or other preferred location), with the coffin borne out towards the end of the service. Then just one member of the family goes with the coffin to the crematorium (or just the vicar goes if a committal service at the crematorium is wanted). Crematoria will prefer this too, suggests funeral director Philip Tomlins in the Funeral Director journal (Nov. 1991), as they then do not have the difficulty of finding a time that fits with the church service.

Perhaps the ideal crematorium would be a building that was designed to allow the mourners to gather round a high-tech version of a funeral pyre. Tony Walter in 'Funerals and How to Improve Them' has suggested a number of slightly less radical design improvements: a coffin visible and central, near floor level throughout the service, which can be touched, kissed, circled round or filed past; a building in which the coffin can be moved by the mourners, possibly by being lowered under the floor; and a building as beautiful and significant as a church, so that the local community will want it for births and marriages too, and which is close to the elements – surrounded by forest and wildlife, rather than manicured lawns and regimented rows of rose bushes.

Of the 114 respondents to our survey of 242 crematoria nationwide, all seem to allow a small group of mourners (by arrangement) to witness the coffin entering the cremator. 9% had flexible seating, which might help those wanting a more participatory 'half-moon' seating arrangement, rather than the 'audience facing the front' style – although changing the seating would no doubt mean paying for extra time.

One off-putting aspect of crematoria is the sense of being led along a factory conveyor belt: In – 30 minutes – Out – Next. However 26 excellent crematoria, as highlighted in Chapter 8, break the 30 minute norm and allow 45 minute services; two superb crematoria, the one in Aberystwyth (see Wales in Chapter 8) and the other in Cinderford (see the West Midlands region in Chapter 8) allow 60 minutes; one outstanding crematorium in Stafford (see the West Midlands region in Chapter 8) has no time limit as such; and most of the other crematoria allow the purchase of extra time at a reduced price.

Contrary to myth, crematoria do burn all the coffins (which is a pity, we feel that they should be reused), and the ashes you get back will definitely be the right ones.

Most crematoria are run by local authorities and have very reasonable fees, although these fees are being sharply increased in many places to finance the cost of new facilities that meet stringent EC anti-pollution requirements. These will cost the average crematorium at least half a million pounds; as a result, some of the local authority operations are beginning to sell out to the larger private firms. For instance, SCI, the American-owned funerals company, already owns 21 (8.7%) of the 242 crematoria in the UK, despite the undesirability of a firm that sells funerals in an area also controlling its crematoria.

At present, the cheapest crematorium that met our other criteria for inclusion was the City of Belfast Crematorium (£95-40 for 30 minutes – see Northern Ireland in Chapter 8). The most expensive was the City of York crematorium (£320 for 30 minutes – see the North East region in Chapter 8). The average price for a cremation was £225, as against £169 in 1997 (an increase of 33%).

Our questionnaire was circulated to all 242 crematoria in the country. Our main interest lay in finding out how helpful they were to people organising a funeral without using a funeral director. Of the 114 who replied, every single one was prepared to deal directly with a family, with no funeral director involvement – whereas in 1993, 8% said that they would deal only with funeral directors. An oppressive 14% said that they would not accept a home-made coffin, even if it met all the anti-pollution requirements and if everything were done 'in a dignified manner without disturbance to other mourners or to staff' – however this was an improvement on the figure of 19% in 1993. Cardboard coffins are now accepted by 96% of all UK crematoria – as against a mere 15% in 1993. 59% of the crematoria would accept wicker coffins; 37% would accept body bags (if supported on a piece of wood and covered with a drape); 34% would accept a body in a shroud (if the shroud were kept rigid with a piece of wood).

The following is the full set of questions and answers given by Ken West, Bereavement Services Manager at the Carlisle Crematorium (address in the North West region of Chapter 8), winner of the New Natural Death Handbook Award 2000 for the Best Crematorium. You can use these questions to select the ones which are relevant to your own situation when approaching your local crematoria, and thus can evaluate the extent to which your local findings match the high standards set by this award winner:

Ken West, who runs both the crematorium and the cemetery, is at the forefront of a campaign to improve local authority funeral provision, and has spearheaded the radical new Charter for the Bereaved, published by the Institute of Burial and Cremation Authorities.

What is your parent organisation if any? Carlisle District Council.

How much time is allotted for each funeral service? 40 minutes.

Can extra time be booked if available? Yes.

If so, at what cost per minute? No charge.

What are your minimum charges for a simple service and cremation? £243, or £217 for an 'Environmental Cremation'. This option requires the use of a cardboard or plastic/chipboard-free container; cremation will be completed either the same day or the following morning. This saves on pre-heating cremators and wasting fossil fuels.

Provided the paperwork is correctly done, and any pacemaker has been removed, will you accept a body directly from the family (no funeral director)? Yes.

Is a home-made coffin acceptable? Yes.

Is a cardboard coffin acceptable? Yes.

Is a wicker coffin acceptable? Yes.

Is a shroud or body bag suitable for cremation and covered with a drape, acceptable, if made rigid with a piece of wood? Yes.

Can mourners view the coffin entering the cremator? Yes.

How many at one time? The room size is the only limit, perhaps 20 maximum.

How would you describe the immediate surroundings of the crematorium? Our crematorium grounds contain four zones: the Peace Garden; the January to December monthly gardens; the Woods; and the Memorial Wall.

How would you describe the architecture and feel of the crematorium building and interior? Non-denominational, no fixed religious symbols. The seating is flexible and we already move seating and put the coffin elsewhere than the catafalque. One family decorated the chapel with posters based on photographs.

In what ways do you feel that your crematorium excels, either in terms of its services, prices, attitudes, practices, architecture or surroundings? Our crematorium excels because it recognises the different needs of the people who desire cremation. Whether they appreciate beautiful gardens, native trees and woodland, memorials or areas without memorials, they can find something to suit them. There is no commercial pressure or bias towards so-called conventional funerals.

Has your crematorium officially adopted the Charter for the Bereaved? Yes.

To this needs to be added that the crematorium publishes very full guidance for families managing on their own, it has a cold storage facility that families can make use of at a very modest charge, and it sells cardboard and other coffins at most reasonable prices – having resisted intense pressure from funeral directors. It also has available for cremations the reusable Carlisle Coffin with an inner Compakta cardboard coffin – only the inner coffin, which slides out, is cremated.

Cemeteries

We wrote to over 800 cemeteries, and of the 171 respondents (some administering several cemeteries) deemed worthy for inclusion in our Good Funeral Guide (Chapter 8) all will accept burial by the family without involving funeral directors. 75% will accept a suitable home-made wooden coffin. 84% will accept one of the manufactured cardboard coffins. 61% will accept wicker coffins. 35% will accept body bags, if supported on a plank and covered with a drape. 40% will accept kaftans or shrouds. One cemetery wrote: 'The majority of Muslims are buried in coffins or caskets, but there are a couple of Muslim communities who bury their dead in kaftans and then the casket or boards are placed over the top'.

The New Natural Death Handbook Award 2000 for the Best Cemetery goes to **Carlisle Cemetery** in Cumbria (who are further detailed in the North West region of Chapter 8). This cemetery also won the Award in 1993 and 1997. And its associated crematorium won the 1997 and year 2000 Awards. The Natural Death Handbook editorial team would have preferred to distribute the Awards more widely, but Carlisle's efforts have been so outstanding that they demand recognition.

The Carlisle Cemetery (and its two nearby associated cemeteries of Upperby and Stanwix) will accept virtually any kind of body container made of biodegradable material. Carlisle Cemetery also has an exceptionally well-run wood-land burial ground. Here are the cemetery's answers to our questionnaire, which, as with the crematorium answers, provide a high standard by which you can judge your own local equivalents:

Does your cemetery have a chapel or meeting room suitable for all faiths? Yes.

How long is allotted for each funeral service? There is no time limit.

How much does a plot cost, including digging and burial? £445.

How long do grave rights last? 50 years.

Maintenance of plot? There is no charge for this.

Provided the paperwork is correctly done, will you accept a body directly from the family? Yes. This is a necessity (Right No. 22) as part of the IBCA Charter for the Bereaved.

Which of the following types of body container are acceptable?

Home-made coffin? Yes, if made of natural materials.

Body bag or shroud? Yes, if made of natural materials.

Cardboard coffin? Yes.

Wicker coffin? Yes.

Has your cemetery officially adopted the Charter for the Bereaved? Yes.

The Cemetery sells the Brighton or Compakta cardboard coffins at £65 each, the Ecology cardboard coffin with cotton liner/pillow at £119 or the traditional type oak-finish chipboard coffin at £135. The Cemetery has also arranged the design and manufacture of a woollen shroud with stiffening board and three cotton carrying ropes, available for £132.

What requirements do you have for a memorial? Traditional graves are not subject to restrictions, lawn memorials must be within size limits. We have added a further choice, the 'recycled' grave, for those who require a simple, inexpensive burial with no memorial.

What are the surroundings like? Parkland in wooded setting with conservation zones. Waterfalls on natural beck, squirrel feeder, lichen reserve, nesting herons, etc.

What is the architecture of the chapel? Attractive, Gothic design. Warm, with seating for 100. Organ available or electronic music. Atmospheric lighting.

How do you feel that your cemetery excels, either in terms of its service, prices, attitudes, practices, architecture or surroundings? We maintain both conservation areas and conventionally attractive cemetery grounds. The secret is in locating conservation areas away from the main drives and putting up signs to explain the purpose of the conservation.

We have arranged many funerals with families and know that funerals arranged without a funeral director are at least as good, and often better, than those that take the conventional path. Indeed, staff members have arranged funerals within their own families using cardboard coffins. Everyone here is committed to improving the participation of the bereaved and listening to their views.

Contrast this approach with the Southern Cemetery in Manchester which has a rule booklet of 56 pages. Articles it prohibits on graves include wooden crosses ('except those supplied by the city council'), sea shells, rockery and other stones. Those bringing the coffin to the cemetery in other than a funeral director's hearse must transfer it at the entrance gate to a wheel bier. Not unreasonably, it also wants to be notified if the coffin size will exceed 6'4" by 22" width, 15" depth (the width measurement must allow for any protruding handles. 'It is difficult and may be dangerous to alter the width of the grave once it has been excavated'. There are occasional stories in the various funeral journals of the embarrassment felt by funeral directors and priests when the coffin will not fit the grave).

The Carlisle Cemetery publishes a leaflet that further demonstrates how seriously it takes its environmental responsibilities:

The greening of a cemetery

Conservation areas. In 1992, Wards 1 and 2 of Carlisle Cemetery were designated as conservation zones. The grass in these areas is mown once each year in October. Reciprocating mowers are used, cutting the grass as if it were hay, and this is raked off and sent to the composting centre. Many wild flowers appeared including pignut, primrose, ox-eye daisy, knapweed and a single cowslip. In 1995, meadow brown butterflies and burnett moths first appeared, and many insects are now evident. Each summer, spotted flycatchers nest and feed in these areas. Unusually, some favourite Victorian plants have flourished. These include the wild daffodil and dog-tooth violet. In these and other areas, bird and bat boxes have been created.

Herbaceous beds. Most beds have been replanted with species favoured by butterflies.

Owls. Residents of Richardson Street have recorded how the owls in the cemetery were regularly heard in the 1950s. They have since declined in number and species, and it is proposed to reverse this trend. Initially, the conservation areas will increase vole numbers, the main prey of owls. Owl boxes are being erected and access given to the roof-space in an old chapel. Since 1996 tawny owls routinely breed in the grounds.

Carved Owl. Artist Linda Watson carved a barn owl from the trunk of an old sweet chestnut. 'Barnie' sits on Ward 3 looking over the conservation area, watching for voles no doubt! She has also carved an 'oak leaf' seat for the woodland grave site.

The Beck. The Fairy Beck runs through the cemetery. Over the years it was straightened, with the banks mown by flymo type machines. This ceased in 1995, and dogrose, hazel and dogwood were planted along the banks in 1996. These are to provide cover for ducks and bank voles. In 1995, a kingfisher was observed on the beck, suggesting that the environment was improving. To help this species, three waterfalls were created in Spring 1996. These will form small pools able to sustain fish and amphibians.

Herons. Herons have nested in the cemetery for some years. We avoid disturbing them during the nesting period. Sadly, the poor spring weather in recent years has killed some of the young birds.

Red Alert. The council are supporting projects to conserve the red squirrel. As red squirrels appear in the cemetery on occasion, a feeding hopper has been erected. This cannot be accessed by the heavier grey squirrel. The woodland burial area is also proposed as a future reserve for red squirrels.

Hedgehogs. Hedgehogs are safe in the cemetery. To help them hibernate, felled trees and timber are placed in 'habitat' piles, under which they can also nest. A local resident also rescues hedgehogs and, after recovery, these are released in the cemetery. We do not use poisons or slug bait in the cemetery, chemicals which can kill these creatures.

Memorials. The memorials in the cemetery date from 1855 to the current time. They are an important social record, as well as an essential substrata for lichens (see below). Unsafe memorials are never removed, except where a repair or sinking deeper in the ground is not possible. Modern memorials are made of foreign stone and the beautiful local sandstones are rarely used. Only a few stones each year are hand carved, most being produced by computer-controlled sandblasting. The development of local sculptors using local stone would be worth promoting.

Lichens. These small plants are composed of a fungus and an algae, and look beautiful under a hand lens. They are disappearing throughout Europe, but grow moderately well in the clean air of Carlisle. Lichens grow on soil, trees and memorials. It is important that memorials are not moved, as the lichens often die in new positions.

Animal vandals. The cemetery sustains wildlife in surprising ways, some of which lead to complaints! Rabbits routinely eat the flowers neatly around the edge of wreaths left at funerals. They also nip off 'pot mums' leaving a neat stub. This leaves the plant looking as if a gardener had clipped the plant with a pair of shears. Carrion crows pull flowers out of vases in order to drink water. The holly berries on Christmas wreaths are also enjoyed by birds. What they think of the plastic berries, it is difficult to know!

Woodland burial. This is the burial option used by those who are concerned with the environment. The graves will create a new oak forest, and, with the planting of Scots pine, will create a red squirrel reserve.

Recycled grave. This option was developed following requests by those concerned about the wastage of land for burial. It is also the least expensive form of burial. These graves are owned by the council and situated in old, often very attractive parts of the cemetery. They have been used for two burials which occurred over 100 years ago. The remains of these burials have now disappeared into the soil. These graves are only suitable for single burials, and, not being 'private', a memorial cannot be placed. A biodegradable coffin must be used and the grave will be reused for burial, some 75 to a 100 years from now. Further details are available.

Biodegradable coffins. The standard coffin used today is made of chipboard and plastics. These cause pollution when cremated and the materials will not degrade into the earth after burial. A selection of biodegradable coffins, some made of recycled floorboards, and a wool burial shroud, can be seen in the old burial chapel. Please ask for details and free leaflets.

Recycling old wreaths. A recycling scheme for old wreath frames was introduced in Autumn 1995. The wreaths are collected from cemetery tip sites by a special needs group. They strip off the old flowers and these are sent for composting. The old frames and plastic trays, etc, are then sold back to the florists for reuse. The scheme has not been totally successful due to adverse criticism from the National Association of Funeral Directors.

Cemetery walks. Cemetery walks occur during the spring and summer. Contact us for current details, or see the East Cumbria Countryside Project walks leaflet.

Just as house prices vary by region, so too do the rights to a burial plot. The Natural Death Centre's survey found that, including the cost of digging the grave, the prices ranged from £118 at Lon Newydd Cemetery in Anglesey (see Wales in Chapter 8) to £3,025 at Highgate Cemetery (see the London region in Chapter 8). The average price for the cheapest individual plot in a cemetery was £524 (incl. digging) as against £504 in 1997 (a 4% increase). Some also charge non-residents either extra, double or even treble the normal price.

Luton Church Cemetery (see the East Midlands region in Chapter 8) is an example of a cemetery with a pleasantly liberal and enlightened approach to memorials, with virtually any design accepted.

Remember to request, if buying burial rights, that ownership is put in the name of the surviving partner, to ensure the eventual right to be buried together.

Chapter 6

WOODLAND BURIAL GROUNDS

All the sites listed in this chapter are either woodland burial grounds – where a tree is planted on or near to the grave instead of having a headstone – or nature reserve burial grounds – which can be wild flower meadows or pastures – where bulbs or flowers can be planted instead of trees.

This is not a Good Funeral Guide to woodland burial grounds, since all woodland burial sites known to the Natural Death Centre, open or planned, are listed, even those not belonging to the Centre's Association of Nature Reserve Burial Grounds. (The Association, which monitors this fast-growing environmental movement, is still at an early stage, relying primarily on the probity of statements made by its members and on feedback from the public, as it does not yet have the resources for site inspections. See Chapter 9 for details of the Association) Abbreviations are as follows:

[**] = Full Association of Nature Reserve Burial Grounds member

[*] = Provisional Association member (applied, having accepted the conditions, but still being assessed)

(**Name of place**) = a site not yet open at the time of going to press

• ✪✪✪ = Winner of a New Natural Death Handbook Award 2000.

Those sites listed as willing to take shrouds normally require the shroud to be made rigid with a plank; likewise body bags, which would also normally need to be covered with a drape of some kind in order to not cause offence to staff or to other members of the public.

Listings are by region, and then by town or nearest town to the site within the region, except in the Greater London region, which has been further subdivided into areas. Please write to The Natural Death Centre (20 Heber Road, London NW2 6AA, tel 020 8208 2853; fax 020 8452 6434; e-mail: rhino@dial.pipex.com) with your experience of using the services of these sites. In your report please complete the following sentences:

Feedback wanted from the public!

(1) The woodland burial ground we used was ...

(2) What we particularly liked was ...

(3) What could perhaps have been better for us was ...

(4) How we would describe the landscape of the ground would be ...

(5) From an ecological point of view, we would say that this ground ...

(6) What satisfied us as to the long-term security of the grave was ...

(7) The total price we paid was (please say what this included) ...

(8) Our impression of the undertaking side of things (which was done by [name and address of firm] ...) was ...

(9) If friends were to ask if we would recommend this burial ground for their family's use, what we would say is ...

(10) If we were organising a funeral again, what we would do differently would be:

(11) My name, address, tel no is ...

(12) *Delete as applies:* You may/may not publish my story anonymously/ with my name; with/without my address; with/without my tel no; and with/ without my e-mail address.

Our listings are otherwise primarily based on information given to us by the sites themselves – the name of the informant is given wherever possible.

For updates to these listings, see the Natural Death Centre's website (www.naturaldeath.org.uk) or send six first class stamps to the Centre saying you have the book and asking for the update sheets.

For statistics and advice on how to set up a woodland burial ground, see Chapter 9.

The North West

Comprising Cumbria, Lancashire, Manchester, Sefton, Wirral, Liverpool, Knowsley, St Helens, Wigan, Bolton, Bury, Rochdale, Salford, Trafford, Manchester, Oldham, Tameside, Stockport and Cheshire.

• **Barrow-in-Furness**: Woodland burial ground in Barrow Cemetery, Devonshire Road, Barrow-in-Furness, Cumbria LA14 5PD (tel 01229 894928); run by Barrow-in-Furness Borough Council. This half-acre site opened in 1998. A grave costs £405 (incl. digging and a natural woodland tree; £501-50 for non-residents). No memorials permitted. Ashes can be interred for £52. A memorial tree on its own costs £52. They will accept home-made, cardboard, or wicker coffins, and body bags or shrouds. Families can arrange a funeral without funeral directors, but will not be allowed to dig or fill the grave. One burial has taken place so far and there is space for 400 graves. 'The site is adjacent to the existing cemetery woodland' (C. R. Pollard).

• **(Blackley)**: Woodland burial area planned for 2001 at Blackley Cemetery, Victoria Avenue, Blackley, North Manchester M9 8JP; run by Manchester City Council. For details contact Paul Burton, Bereavement Services Manager at Longley Lane Depot, Sharston, Manchester M22 4RQ (tel 0161 718 4811; fax 718 4809).

• **Bury**: Woodland burial site within Radcliffe Cemetery, Cemetery Road, Bury, Greater Manchester; run by Bury Metropolitan Borough Council (Maria Swillo, tel 0161 762 9506). A grave costs £792 (incl. digging; tree or seedling to be supplied by the family or friends). They will accept home-made, cardboard, or wicker coffins, and shrouds. Family and friends can help with a token amount of filling the grave. The site is on the perimeter of the cemetery by a housing estate, with fields on the other side.

• **Carlisle**: Woodland Burial Site, Carlisle Cemetery Office, Richardson Street, Carlisle, Cumbria CA2 6AL (tel 01228 625310; e-mail: kenw@carlisle_city.gov.uk); run by Carlisle City Council. A single grave costs £330, a double grave £445 (incl. digging and a tree; £21 extra for non-residents). This, the UK's first woodland burial ground, is a peaceful site looking out towards the river, with cattle in an adjoining field. A local artist has made an oak seat. 162 burials have taken place so far with an average of 44 per year. They will accept home-made, cardboard, or wicker coffins, and body bags or shrouds. Families and friends may help to fill, but not dig, the grave if they wish. They sell Compakta cardboard coffins for £65, Ecology (Peace Box) cardboard coffins for £119, a standard fully-fitted chipboard coffin for £135, the Alverstone wooden coffin with rope handles from £320 and their own Carlisle woollen burial shroud (complete with board and ropes) for £132. A sheepfold has been built of recycled stone and bronze plaques can be placed inside. The site is accessed through the traditional burial ground. 'No chemicals are used. It is proposed as a site for a red squirrel reserve in the future' (Ken West).

• **(Cheshire)**: Woodland burial site planned for five acres of Cheshire agricultural land. Contact J. P. McCormack, Cheshire Woodland, Chestnut Farm, Tarvin Road, Frodsham, Cheshire WA6 6XN for more details.

• **Clitheroe**: Woodland burial ground as part of Clitheroe Cemetery, Waddington Road, Clitheroe, Lancashire; run by Ribble Valley Borough Council, Council Offices, Church Walk, Clitheroe BB7 2RA (tel 01200 425111). A grave costs £216 plus £140 for digging (incl. a tree or bulbs; fees double for non-residents). They will accept cardboard coffins 'if to the required specification'. Families and friends can help in a token way with filling the grave. Trees are planted, about one for every five graves, once a row of graves is completed. Individual memorial trees can also be planted around the perimeter of the site at extra cost. Ashes cannot yet be interred, but the woodland area is to be extended into the next field in the future and there will then be an 'ashes glade' for interment. The site is on the perimeter of the existing cemetery, adjacent to private woodland, in a rural setting overlooking the River Ribble. Over half of the council employees in a survey said that they would prefer this site for themselves. 'The site is managed to ensure maximum tree growth and to create conditions for wild flowers and nature to flourish' (Judith Paliga). (Eds: One funeral director says that this is a 'nice traditional cemetery, with a public footpath' and confirms what is said about the site above. However, another visitor to the site has commented that the site is merely a small field at the back of the cemetery 'with too many oaks in too small an area'. Further reports welcome.)

• **Nr. Manchester**: New Manchester Woodland Cemetery, City Road, Ellenbrook, Worsley, Manchester M28 1BD (tel 0161 790 1300). A privately run concern, this 12-acre site looks across open fields and is surrounded by trees. A new grave costs £700 (incl. digging; a tree from £49 extra; a flat bedstone from £220). Families and friends can fill the grave and can help with a token amount of digging. They will accept home-made, cardboard, or wicker coffins, and body bags or shrouds, and sell coffins to the public 'when available; prices on request'. They also sell other services such as collection of the body – 'quotation on request'. There is a children and babies garden; interment of ashes, memorial bird boxes, name plaques, benches and other facilities are also available. 'Money taken in advance is for purchase of burial plots; a trust scheme is being set up. 170 burials have taken place with a further 40 reserved' (James Broome). (Eds: Reports suggest that this site is well-maintained, if perhaps a little too manicured for some. It is 'mown constantly', but would be 'ideal for those not too concerned about green issues'. The site staff are 'friendly and casual, but informative and efficient'.)

• [*] **Mobberley**: Friends of Nature Burial Ground, Graveyard Farm, Newton Hall Lane, Mobberley, Cheshire WA16 7LJ; run by Mr W. & Mrs M. A. Arnison (tel 01565 880072 or 0161 432 2131). Opened October 1998. £400 for a single grave, £500 for a double, £600 for a treble; digging £200 extra per burial. Ashes interred for £50. Coffins supplied from £90. An advice pack for d-i-y funerals is available. Will help with removals from hospitals and transport or storage, use of chapel etc. 'Graveyard Farm takes its name from a Quaker burial ground on the site which dates from the early 1600s. The site is run with the help of the Cheshire Wildlife Trust' (Mr Arnison). (Eds: Reports suggest that while this is a 'beautiful ideal setting with fields all around,' some families have found the site to be too casual in its approach. All reports, positive or negative, welcome.) [Provisional Association membership requires renewal 22/7/2000.]

• **Morecambe**: Woodland burial ground at the rear of the Torrisholme Cemetery, Westgate Road, Morecambe, Lancashire. Contact Cemeteries Service, Lancaster City Council, Town Hall, Morecambe, Lancashire LA4 5AF (tel 01524 582635). A grave costs £444 (incl. digging and a tree; £548 for non-residents). Unfortunately, funeral directors must be used 'although d-i-y arrangements may be possible at a later date'. Families are also not allowed to assist with digging or filling the grave. An additional woodland burial site is to open in the top corner of Hale Carr Lane Cemetery in Heysham, and one is being considered for Scotforth Cemetery in Lancaster (George Bower).

• [*] ✪✪✪ **Nr. Oldham**: Nature reserve burial ground, with space for 150 graves, as part of Saddleworth Cemetery, Upper Mill, Saddleworth, Oldham; run by Saddleworth Parish Council, Civic Hall, Lee Street, Upper Mill, Oldham OLE 6AE (tel 01457 876665). A grave costs £215-50 (incl. digging and a tree; £323-25 for non-residents). 'This is a fabulous site, high up, in a very rural and hilly area, looking down on at least five villages'. They will accept cardboard coffins and shrouds. Family and friends can help fill the grave and help with a token amount of digging. The woodland burial areas are in long grass (only cut directly near the grave) around a wild copse area, an integral part of the well-designed main cemetery which has been open since 1988 and which won a design competition. 'We want to make this a place that people come to see' (Dave Holland). (Eds: Reports suggest that this is a very attractive and well-run site: 'it really provides a green alternative with understanding and care.') [Provisional Association membership requires renewal 15/1/2000.] Winner of the New Natural Death Handbook Award 2000 for the Best Woodland Burial Ground in the North West.

• [*] **(Nr. Ormskirk)**: West Lancashire Woodland burial ground, Pippin Street, Burscough, near Ormskirk (in the grounds of West Lancashire crematorium). This site, with scope for expansion to 15 acres, is due to open no later than October 2000. Enquiries to Peace Funerals, St Peter's Villa, Ridley Lane, Mawdesley, Nr. Ormskirk L40 3SX (tel 01704 821900/ 08457 697822; fax 0114 2530503; e-mail: peacefuner@aol.com). A grave is expected to cost about £450 (incl. digging and probably a native tree; same for non-residents). York stone memorial plaques will be allowed (at a cost of £85). All coffins and shrouds are accepted. Ashes interred for approximately £135. Memorial tree planted for a person whose funeral was elsewhere also £135. All undertaking services will be offered at cost. Prepaid plan: Golden Leaves. 'Landscaped site in a rural setting. Nearest major housing settlement about one mile away. Families will be able to choose their own plot and tree type' (John Mallatratt, Director). [Provisional Association membership requires renewal 8/12/2000.]

• **Preston**: Woodland burial offered in Preston Cemetery, New Hall Lane, Preston, Lancashire PR1 4SY (Martin Birch, tel 01772 794585); run by Preston Borough Council. A grave costs £233, with digging and burial £233 extra (incl. a tree; no extra for non-residents). The site is in the old cemetery lodge garden, surrounded by trees and shrubs. They will accept strong cardboard coffins. A choice of native species tree is planted for each grave, depending on what type is needed in the area at the time. Mourners may help fill the grave. (Eds: One funeral director has described this site as 'particularly bad, a rundown civil cemetery with the woodland section in a little corner', and there appears to have been only one woodland burial there in four years. Other reports, for or against, would be welcomed.)

• **(Warburton/ Lymm, Cheshire)**: New Memorial Park suitable for the interment of ashes and burials; a peaceful country site on 20 acres of land at Yew Tree Farm, Dunham Road, Warburton/ Lymm, Cheshire WA13 9UY (tel 01925 757832; fax 757744). 'We have decided to take planning to appeal. Enquiries welcome' (Dennis George).

• **(Wigan)**: Cemeteries Section, Wigan Metropolitan Borough Council, Trencherfield Mill, Wallgate, Wigan WN3 4EF (tel 01942 828507). 'The borough has plans to establish one, and possibly two, nature reserve burial areas in the future. Since there is no possibility of expansion at any of our existing sites, the facility will be established in a completely fresh, as yet unknown, location, probably selected from countryside land already owned by the borough. We are unable to say how soon this service will become available' (A. Bassett).

• **The Wirral**: The Woodland Garden at Frankby Cemetery, Frankby Road; run by the Metropolitan Borough of Wirral. Contact the Cemeteries Manager, Landican Cemetery Office, Arrowe Park Road, Birkenhead, Wirral, Merseyside L49 5LW (tel 0151 6772361). Part of an existing cemetery, with enough land available to extend it for many years to come. A grave costs £342 (incl. digging) and mourners can help fill the grave. Trees planted are from native species such as pine, beech and hawthorn. Plots are mainly single graves but adjacent plots may be reserved for partners. Advance purchase of Right of Burial is available. Any type of coffin may be used, but biodegradable ones are preferred.

The North East

Comprising Northumberland, Newcastle-Upon-Tyne, North Tyneside, Gateshead, South Tyneside, Sunderland, Durham, Hartlepool, Stockton-On-Tees, Middlesbrough, Redcar, North Yorkshire, York, East Riding of Yorkshire, Kingston-Upon-Hull, Bradford, Leeds, Calderdale, Kirklees, Wakefield, Barnsley, Sheffield, Rotherham, Doncaster, North Lincolnshire, North East Lincolnshire and Lincolnshire.

• **(Boston, Lincolnshire):** A woodland burial ground planned by Boston Borough Council (tel Martin Potts on 01205 364612) who run Boston Cemetery in Horncastle Road. No details supplied as yet. Home-made, cardboard and wicker coffins are currently accepted at Boston Cemetery.

• **Bradford**: A four-acre woodland burial area opened in 1997 within Thornton Cemetery; run by Bradford City Council. Contact Scholemoor Cemetery, Necropolis Road, Bradford BD7 2PS (tel 01274 571313). A grave costs £771 (incl. digging and a tree; £1156-50 for non-residents). No memorials allowed. Ashes can be interred for £66. They will accept home-made, cardboard, or wicker coffins, and body bags or shrouds, and families are allowed to help fill, but not dig, the grave. Six burials have taken place so far; about two per year. The site is on 'a hillside with some trees' (David Congreve).

• **(Nr. Durham)**: The County Durham Green Burials Partnership has located a couple of possible sites for green burial in the region. The partnership includes local councillors, Durham Wildlife and the Acorn Trust. Contact Maggie Bosanquet, Local Agenda 21, County Hall, Durham DH1 5TY (tel 0191 386 4411) or Samuel Randall, The Vicarage, Holmside Lane, Burnhope, Durham DH7 0DP (tel 01207 529274) for more information.

• **Grantham**: A two-acre green burial site opened in 2000 as an extension to Grantham Cemetery; run by South Kesteven District Council. A grave costs £750 (incl. digging, a choice of tree and a small wooden plaque). Oak, ash, field maple, silver birch, birch, mountain ash, hawthorn, holly, or hazel trees are offered. Only biodegradable coffins are allowed. Families can help with a token amount of filling the grave, but may not dig for health and safety reasons. One burial has taken place so far. Contact: Mr Baxter, Grantham Cemetery, Harrowby Road, Grantham, Lincolnshire NG31 9DT (tel 01476 563083).

• **❂❂❂ Harrogate**: A. B. Welfare & Wildlife Trust (Charity Reg. No. 1037444), 7 Knox Road, Harrogate, North Yorkshire HG1 3EF (tel 01423 530900 or 01423 868121). This combined social work and wildlife charity was launched in 1994. It plans to create new nature reserves through temporary burial projects. Until suitable land becomes available burials are being arranged in existing nature reserves, without damaging the wildlife interest. It is hoped that the major landowning wildlife charities will soon offer what this Trust has pioneered.

The Trust arranges burials or interment of ashes in pastures and wood-pasture. One nature reserve for burials – for benefactors only or for those able to raise substantial sums for the Trust's work – is on eight acres of the Brimham Rocks 400-acre Site of Special Scientific Interest, in the Nidderdale Area of Outstanding Natural Beauty, legally protected for both its geology and wildlife, and with permission for up to 25 burials. The land is named Kate's Fell after Kathleen Davies, one of the first occupational therapists and a modern-day pioneer of the therapeutic value of pets in hospitals. It is a mix of semi-natural woodland with pasture, including bilberry and heather on a warm, west-facing slope looking into the valley of Nidderdale. There are 250 large boulders scattered throughout and each has legal protection.

The second site, and the Trust's main burial project, is Gertrude's Pasture – donations only, but possibly a charge in the future. This is a 3.5-acre site 'teeming with legally protected great crested newts, wild flowers, butterflies, grasshoppers, noctule bats with a wingspan of 355mm, and other wildlife. It is grazed by Hebridean black sheep.' The adjacent river gorge has spectacular walks and views, with more than 100 acres of woodland. Volunteers have health and social services backgrounds and many years of experience in managing nature reserves. One of the Trust's advisers is John Bradfield, probably the UK's leading authority on laws surrounding funerals. He is certainly the source to whom the Natural Death Centre refers people with complex questions.

The Trust can help arrange funerals paid for by the Benefits Agency, or if necessary, a grave can be made available free of charge; other charges are at the Trust's discretion. The land has long-term security being owned by a registered wildlife charity. The Trust accepts home-made, cardboard or wicker coffins, shrouds, or stretchers made of natural materials, but not body bags – 'our experience is that body bags smack of a waste disposal operation'. The Trust can obtain and supply cardboard coffins for the price charged to the Trust plus £5. As for collection of the body or other services, 'all aspects of help can be provided free of charge, depending on circumstances and distance. Donations welcome.' Family and friends can dig and fill the grave. 'Most graves are difficult to see after a few weeks but some are mounded for wild flowers; and others have turfed cairns for great crested newts.' 'Our priority is to meet the needs of those seeking help, whilst creating or helping to protect a wildlife area. We are experienced as conservationists' (John Bradfield). (Eds: This project is probably more for the serious green burial enthusiast. Each grave can be located, but there is little if any obvious marking of most of the graves.) Winner of the New Natural Death Handbook Award 2000 for the Best Nature Reserve Burial Ground in the North East.

• **Harrogate**: For local residents only, a half-acre green burial site at Stonefall Cemetery, Wetherby Road, Harrogate, North Yorkshire HG3 1DE (tel 01423 883523; fax 884151); run by Harrogate Borough Council. A grave costs £879 (incl. digging and burial, no tree; £1319 for non-residents). Families can help fill, but not dig, the grave. They will accept cardboard coffins or shrouds. No trees are planted on the graves, but the area is landscaped and planted with bulbs and flowers and cut twice a year. 'The site opened in 1995, three burials have taken place so far and there is space for 150-200 graves' (Philip Andrew).

• [*] **Hexham**: Woodland burial site on the boundary of St Andrew's Cemetery, set away from the main sections. A west-facing area of grassland overlooking Hexham Golf Course; run by Hexham Town Council. Contact John Thirlwell,

Cemetery Superintendent, St Andrew's Cemetery Lodge, West Road, Hexham, Northumberland NE46 3RR (tel 077100 53732 or 01434 608151). A grave costs £206 (incl. digging, a 'biodegradable burial casket', a numbered flat stone marker, to which 'you may add your own wording', and a broadleafed English tree planted randomly within the woodland burial area in the autumn; double for non-residents). Ashes can be interred for £137-50 (plus £20 for an ashes casket). Families can organise the entire funeral themselves and can help fill the grave, but there will be no reduction in the above fee. A biodegradable casket costs £95 from the Council. The site opened in 1995 and about 25 to 30 burials take place a year. 'The site is in the beautiful Tyne valley with no residential developments nearby. You may plant your own tree if you wish, but must ask the Cemetery Superintendent's permission first' (J. Thirlwell). [Provisional Association membership requires renewal 22/1/2000.]

• **(Huddersfield)**: The Rose Hill Natural Burial Ground is set to open July 1st 2000. It is run by MBF (1954) Ltd, 161 Rose Hill, Birkby Hall Road, Huddersfield HD2 2BS (tel 01484 546 322; fax 546407). The cost of a grave at this site will be unusually high, about £2800. The owners say that 'this is largely dictated by the land value. In addition the site has ... to be properly secured and expensively staffed at all times.' Unfortunately, they also say they will work only with registered funeral directors, and that 'amateurs digging or filling graves is not acceptable under any circumstances.' Only biodegradable coffins will be accepted and no embalmed bodies. 'However cast, this will not suit everybody, and will certainly be too expensive for some!' (Michael Brook).

• **Leeds**: Woodland burial site within Lawns Wood Cemetery, Otley Road, Adel, Leeds LS16 6AH (0113 2673188); run by Leeds City Council. A grave costs £760 (incl. digging and a tree; double for non-residents). This site opened in spring 1997 and two further woodland burial sites in the Leeds area are planned. They will accept home-made or cardboard coffins. Families and friends can fill the grave if they wish. 'The site is a flat area within the cemetery near some mature trees' (Phil Stephenson).

• **Middlesbrough:** Woodland burial area in Acklam Cemetery, Acklam Road; run by Middlesbrough Borough Council. Contact Mr Gitsham, Teesside Crematorium, Acklam Road, Middlesbrough TS5 7HE (tel 01642 817725). A single grave costs £515, or a double £620 (with burial rights for 50 years); plus £230 for the digging for each interment. An oak tree or similar, included in the price, is planted on or next to each grave. Families can help fill, but not dig, the grave. All types of coffins are permitted, but biodegradable ones are preferred. They will consider body bags and shrouds. The woodland burial section lies between two lawn sections in the cemetery extension and can itself be extended. There is currently room for 70 double graves.

• **(Norton Disney, Lincolnshire)**: For locals only. 'Ecoburial' to be offered from late 2000 in the 2.5-acre Hill Holt Wood, south of the A46; run by Nigel Lowthrop, Hill Holt Wood, Norton Disney LN6 9JP (tel 01636 892836; e-mail: econs@supanet.com; web: www.oden.co.uk/hillholtwood). For residents of the parishes, or Friends of Hill Holt Wood and their families (who pay £10 per family per year to join, applications from the address above) only, a grave will cost £450 (incl. digging, a tree and maintenance). Ashes can also be scattered and a memorial tree planted for £150. Trees planted will be from local stock, mainly oak, to form an avenue down the wood's main drive. 'Over 3km of paths cross the wood with plenty of seating to enjoy the wildlife and surrounding farmland. Seven parishes are now represented on the Management Committee' (Nigel Lowthrop).

• [*] **(Ribble Valley, Settle):** Brocklands Woodland Burial, a 1.5-acre site set in pastureland in the Ribble Valley, expected to open late in 2000; run by Julia Weston, Cappleside, Rathmell, Settle, North Yorkshire BD24 0LJ. 500 burials are planned per acre. A oak or hawthorn tree will be planted on each grave (no prices as yet). They hope to sell Compakta, wicker and chipboard coffins, and shrouds; and to offer advance purchase of plots, toilet facilities, and a memorial wall or contemplation area. Families may help with the filling and possibly the digging of the grave along with the gravedigger. 'Rustic yet efficient. Long views across and down the valley, yet secluded. Surrounded by pastureland and small woods. Our own timber and stone will be used on site and graves will be hand-dug. Ideal location.' [Provisional Association membership requires renewal 22/10/2000.]

• [*] **Sheffield**: Wisewood Woodland Burial Ground, Loxley Road; run by Sheffield City Council. Contact Janet Sadler, Bereavement Services, City Road Cemetery, Sheffield S2 1GD (tel 0114 239 6068). This small site is within Wisewood Cemetery, in Sheffield's beautiful Loxley Valley, with a backdrop of trees. Twelve burials have taken place so far, an average of six a year. The cost of a grave is £640 (incl. digging, a tree and a small York stone memorial; same for non-residents). Trees can be alder, silver birch, rowan, mountain ash, whitebeam or ash. Families can help with a token amount of digging and can fill the grave. Comprehensive literature is provided for families organising funerals without funeral directors. Five types of cardboard coffin are on sale from £55 to £114, and traditional coffins from £70. They also accept home-made or wicker coffins and shrouds and will sell a natural fibre shroud for £60. Ashes can be strewn (for £48) or buried (for £381). A biodegradable urn can be supplied free of charge or they sell a range of ashes caskets and urns. They also offer mortuary and washing services (£20 for the first day, £10 per day after this) and transport with an ambulance and driver for £100. [Provisional Association membership requires renewal 18/11/2000.]

• [**] **Nr. Sheffield**: South Yorkshire Woodland Burial Ground, Turnshaw Road, Ulley, Nr. Rotherham; run by Peace Funerals, Gleadless Mount, Sheffield S12 2LN (tel 0114 2530505 or 08457 697822; fax 0114 2530503; e-mail: peacefuner@aol.com). This 2.88-acre site, opened in October 1995 and 100 burials have taken place (about 25 a year). It is surrounded by fields and is located down a lane by a small country village. A stream runs along the boundary with the next field. A hawthorn hedge has been planted. Their tree management policy is guided by a permaculturist and Friends of the Earth Chairman. A grave costs £420 (incl. digging and any native British tree). Rights last for fifty years.

They will accept home-made, cardboard, or wicker coffins, and body bags or shrouds. Family and friends can dig or fill the grave if they wish. A4 size York stone plaques, laid horizontally, are allowed (sold for £85). Ashes can be interred for £125 incl. a tree. There is a group for relatives and friends which discusses the management of the site and acts as a support group. Peace Funerals also sell coffins, from £85 for cardboard ones to £399 for their own design of wicker coffin, the 'Mawdesley Willow'. They will collect the body from hospital for £50. 'A horse and dray can be hired and a restored thatched barn is available nearby for religious or secular ceremonies' (Mary Mallatratt). See also their other 'railway funeral' site near Alfreton, Derbyshire, below. [Association membership requires renewal 14/8/2000.]

• **York**: The York Cemetery Trust, The Warden, The Gatehouse, Cemetery Road, York YO10 5AJ (tel 01904 610578 day; 01759 380267 evening). Prices from £620 (incl. digging). Not a woodland burial ground, since there are traditional headstones too, but 'nature is taking over. This is a Victorian park landscape gone wild and there is an ecological management plan in place to encourage wildlife' (Hugh Goudge). Instead of having a headstone, a tree can be planted near to, but not on the graves, if requested (to be discussed with the warden). All types of cardboard, wicker coffins, and body bags accepted and the warden can help supply these. There is a remembrance garden where an ashes plot for four sets of ashes costs £80, plus £80 for each interment. There is also 'a very fine classical chapel' in working order.

• **North Yorkshire**: The Mowthorpe Independent Garden of Rest, c/o Robert Goodwill, Southwood Farm, Terrington, York YO6 4QB (tel 01653 648459, fax 648225) is a 2.5-acre site with lovely views, adjacent to a wood and an existing cemetery, in an Area of Outstanding Natural Beauty, set on the ridge of the Howardian Hills overlooking the Vale of York. A grave costs £425 (incl. digging). 1,500 trees have been planted. Family and friends can fill the grave if they wish. Memorials less than one metre high are allowed. Undertaken With Love, the funeral directors, charge about £1080 to carry out a funeral here. 'Mowthorpe is part of the 250-acre Southwood Farm at Terrington where the Goodwill family has lived since 1850. The families of all the people buried in Mowthorpe hold shares in the company and can attend the Annual General Meeting.'

Wales

Comprising Flintshire, Wrexham, Denbighshire, Aberconwy and Colwyn, Anglesey, Caernarfonshire and Merionethshire, Powys, Cardiganshire, Pembrokeshire, Carmarthenshire, Swansea, Neath and Port Talbot, Bridgend, Rhondda Cynon Taff, Vale of Glamorgan, Merthyr Tydfil, Caerphilly, Cardiff, Blaenau Gwent, Torfaen, Newport, Monmouthshire.

• ✪✪✪ **Cardiff**: Woodland Burial Glade, Thornhill Cemetery, Thornhill Road, Llanishen, Cardiff, Wales CF14 9UA; run by Cardiff County Council (tel 029 2062 3294; fax 029 2069 2904). The Glade is on the perimeter of the cemetery, overlooked by Wenallt mountain, and looking down over Cardiff Bay. The site has mature oaks. A grave costs £322 (incl. digging, a tree and a marker post with small plaque; £571 for non-residents). The adjoining grave may be prepurchased for £103-50 (£191 for non-residents). They will accept home-made, cardboard, or wicker coffins, and body bags or shrouds, and sell an ecologically designed coffin for £75. Families and friends can fill the grave. The crematorium chapel may be hired for any burial service (religious symbols can be removed or covered by request) for £25. 'It is an excellent site, simply the best' (Roger Swan). Winner of the New Natural Death Handbook Award 2000 for the Best Woodland Burial Ground in Wales.

• [*] **(Nr. Newcastle Emlyn)**: A 4.5-acre woodland burial site owned by Bede David at Coed y Tyddyn, Tyddyn Du Farm, Cwmcoy, Nr. Newcastle Emlyn, Wales. Bede David is appealing against refusal of planning permission and hopes that the site will open in 2002. [Provisional Association membership requires renewal 16/1/2000: Bede David, Engskovvej 16B, 8541 Skødstrup, Denmark (tel and fax [00 45] 86992747).]

• **St Asaph:** Woodland burial at Y Llwyn Cemetery, Mount Road, St Asaph (Llanelwy), Wales. Contact Mrs S. Jones, Cemeteries Officer, Denbighshire County Council, Caledfryn, Smithfield Road, Denbigh, Denbighshire, Wales LL16 3RJ (tel 01824 708461; fax 706787). A grave costs £420 (incl. digging, assistance with lowering if required, a rowan or similar type of tree and wildlife seeds; double for non-residents). Ashes can be interred for £120. Unfortunately, families cannot help dig or fill the grave. 'We will only accept biodegradable coffins – cardboard, home-made or from a funeral director.' The woodland burial ground is a field hedged on three sides at the bottom section of an existing graveyard that is 'very rustic, natural and peaceful' (S. Jones). (Eds: Reports seem to confirm this description: 'A very pleasant traditional, ancient, wild and overgrown cemetery with plenty of character and atmosphere.')

West Midlands

Comprising Shropshire, Staffordshire, Wolverhampton, Walsall, Dudley, Sandwell, Birmingham, Solihull, Coventry, Hereford and Worcester, Gloucestershire.

• [*] **(Nr. Belbroughton)**: A woodland burial ground by Woodfield Lane and Newtown Lane, Bell End, Nr. Belbroughton, West Midlands, in a 6.5-acre site, is still awaiting planning permission. For more information, contact Hourhope Ltd, 23 Market Street, Stourbridge, West Midlands DY8 1AB (tel and fax 01384 373899). [Provisional association membership requires renewal 17/9/1999.]

• **Burton-upon-Trent:** Woodland burial, Stapenhill Cemetery, 38 Stapenhill Road, Burton-upon-Trent, Staffordshire DE15 9AE (tel 01283 508572); run by East Staffordshire Borough Council. Stapenhill is a large traditional cemetery and the woodland burial area is at the far end on sloping ground. A grave costs £299 (incl. digging, a tree and bulbs; double for non-residents). They will accept home-made, cardboard, or wicker coffins, and body bags or shrouds, and sell cardboard coffins for about £70. Family and friends may watch the filling of the grave only. A grave space must be bought if cremated remains are to be buried.

'The woodland burial area is situated on a hillside overlooking the cemetery, above the flood plain of the River Trent. It has been planted with bulbs, wild flowers and a variety of native trees – including ash, oak, cherry, hazel and birch' (Nick French).

• **(Coleshill):** Woodlands Cemetery woodland burial area, Birmingham Road, Coleshill, to be opened in 2002; run by Solihull Metropolitan Borough Council. For more information contact the Robin Hood Cemetery Office, Streetsbrook Road, Shirley, Solihull B90 3NL (tel and fax 0121 744 1121). A grave will cost £645 (incl. digging; triple for non-residents). The interment of ashes will be allowed (no prices yet). Families will be able to help fill, but not dig, the grave. Chapel: 'Built in 1989, with a barn-type appearance.' 'The allocated area within the existing cemetery has eight acres of woodland and a lake. There is a considerable amount of wildlife within the woodland' (Bernard McHale).

• **Coventry:** Lentons Lane Cemetery and Nature Reserve, Lentons Lane, Walsgrave, Coventry; run by the City of Coventry Bereavement Services, The Lodge, Cannon Hill Road, Canley, Coventry CV4 7DF (tel 024 7641 5886 or 024 7641 8055). Cardboard or wicker coffins can be supplied to people using this site. There is no time limit at the graveside. A grave costs from £612 (incl. digging and a biodegradable coffin; no tree – as the woodland is already planted; same prices for non-residents). No memorials allowed. As yet, there is no provision for ashes to be interred within the site. Free advice for families arranging a funeral without undertakers. Families can help dig and fill the grave. 30 burials have taken place so far, about six a year, and there is room for development of this two-acre site. 'The site is part of a larger traditional cemetery on the outskirts of the city, away from residential areas. The area is planted with local trees and there is a wild flower meadow and a pond with frogs and newts' (Allan Charlsworth).

• ✪✪✪ **Craven Arms**: Burial Ground, Westhope Craft College, Craven Arms, Shropshire SY7 9JL (tel 01584 861293). Landowner: Anne Dyer. The college is run by the Westhope Charity. The site is in an ancient orchard, about 1.5 acres, set in a small quiet valley five miles from Craven Arms. Westhope itself is a small widely-scattered Quaker community. A Victorian chapel, rebuilt on the site of a Norman building, is available for ceremonies and for holding bodies before funerals if wished. The orchard is being replanted with memorial apple trees whose species are under threat and there are wild cherry trees along the hedgerows. Ashes may be buried for £50, or scattered in an area beneath some walnut trees. Spring bulbs may be planted on the graves. 12' by 5' plots for coffins cost £200 each and gravedigging costs £100 (the soil is shaley and difficult to dig by hand). An apple tree costs £50 or a cherry tree £40. A small memorial slab costs extra. An oak bench with plaque is £200. Minibus hire costs from £10 or £40 with a driver. Families can organise a funeral without undertakers, but help can only be offered in the form of bearers and general advice. All types of biodegradable coffins, body bags and shrouds are accepted. Families can help dig and fill the grave. The undertakers A. Hoskins (tel 01584 872048) or Funerals Direct (tel 01952 251125) can help with arrangements for inexpensive funerals at this site. 'We have been open since 1996 and about 15 burials take place each year. When I die, the Westhope Charity takes over. There are rare breed trees and sheep and the farm is in conversion to organic' (Anne Dyer). Winner of the New Natural Death Handbook Award 2000 for the Best Woodland Burial Ground in the West Midlands.

• **Dudley**: A woodland burial ground at Gornal Wood Cemetery, Chase Road, Gornal Wood, Dudley DY3 2RL (tel 01384 813970; fax 813971); run by Dudley Metropolitan Borough Council. This small site for up to 34 graves – approximately 300 sq metres – is adjacent to an existing copse of hawthorn and birch trees. Two burials have taken place so far, the first in February 1999. A grave costs £480 (incl. digging, native bulbs planted in the grave and a tree: hawthorn, birch, hazel, or mountain ash; double for non-residents). They will accept home-made, cardboard or wicker coffins. Family and friends can help fill the grave. Free advice for d-i-y funerals. No memorials or flower containers allowed, but a minimum two-line inscription in the Book of Remembrance costs £34. 'There are buildings and grassed areas to one side, a cremated remains area at the front and woodland and seasonal gardens of remembrance to the rear' (Liz Mansell).

• **(Halesowen, Nr. Birmingham)**: A six-acre site for sale in greenbelt country-side, with full planning permission for woodland burials. Offers in excess of £100,000 to Scriven & Co., 821/829 Hagley Road West, Quinton, Birmingham B32 1AD (tel 0121 422 4011; fax 423 2741). The site is at Woodfield Lane, Romsley, Halesowen and is within reach of Birmingham, Kidderminster and the Black Country.

• **Newport, Shropshire**: A two-acre woodland burial ground opened in 1998 as an extension to Newport General Cemetery on Audley Avenue; run by Newport Town Council. A single grave costs £210 (incl. digging; £290 for non-residents). A tree costs from £15 to £25 depending on the species, and can be bought separately for someone whose funeral was elsewhere. Ashes can be interred for £45. Any biodegradable body container is acceptable, including cardboard, but not home-made, or shrouds. Family and friends can help fill the grave. Free advice will be offered to d-i-y families. 'The site is surrounded by open countryside currently used as grazing land. Adjacent to a 150-year-old cemetery with mature trees and a full complement of wildlife. Seven burials have taken place in 14 months. 18 plots have been reserved' (Dee Halliday). Contact the Town Clerk, Newport (Shropshire) Town Council, The Guildhall, High Street, Newport, Shropshire TF10 7TX (tel 01952 814338; fax 825353).

• **Redditch, Worcestershire**: Westall Park Woodland Burial, Holberrow Green B96 6JY (tel 01386 792806). A grave costs £440 (incl. digging). Families can help fill the grave and help is offered for d-i-y funerals. Trees are planted randomly once the burial area is full. Or, a specific memorial tree with wooden name plaque can be planted for an extra £160 (incl. maintenance of the tree). Ashes can be interred from £79 for a plot for up to four interments. Cardboard, wicker, home-made coffins and shrouds are allowed. A 2.5 sq metre plot can be paid for in advance, but no financial safeguards as yet. 'We are out in the country, six miles due south of Redditch, well away from public roads and within sight of the Brecon Hills. The main six-acre field is reached by a private drive and is bowl-shaped with beautiful views. A second five-acre field will eventually be brought into use. There are some very old oak trees, a hundred landscaping trees, and woodpeckers, owls and foxes. I am often congratulated on the site and I am proud of the choice we offer to families. We opened in 1997 and about 30 burials have taken place so far' (Dave Tolly).

• **(Shrewsbury, Shropshire)**: Woodland burial ground in a new cemetery due to open in 2002; run by Shrewsbury and Atcham Borough Council. For more details contact Mrs J. L. Knowles, Cemeteries and Crematorium Registrar, Emstrey Crematorium, London Road, Shrewsbury SY2 6PS (tel 01743 353046).

• [*] **South Perton**: Forest Cemetery at South Perton is a 100-acre woodland cemetery and wildfowl remembrance garden set in an unspoilt area of country-side near Wolverhampton. It is run by Billy and Celia Wilson, Mr Mouse Farm, Jenny Walker Lane, Old Perton, South Staffordshire WV6 7HB (tel 01902 764422; fax 380370). Planning permission has been granted and the site is being landscaped. An unmarked grave costs £395 for South Staffordshire residents (excluding digging; £450 for non-residents). Tree planting costs between £15 and £50 excluding the cost of adequate fencing to protect the sapling (English woodland trees only). Biodegradable coffins and shrouds, not home-made, are welcome. Families can help fill, but not dig, the grave. A natural stone memorial from their own quarry can be engraved from £400 and there is a memorial garden for the scattering of ashes. They hope to offer undertaking services in the future. Pre-payments are safeguarded by a Lloyds/T.S.B. security plan. 'The site is landscaped to garden shrubberies and walks, and surrounded by woodland, lakes, streams, waterfalls and wildfowl wetland.' [Provisional Association membership requires renewal 25/2/2001.]

• **Stafford**: A small 1.5-acre woodland burial ground as part of Stone Cemetery (off the A34); run by Stafford Borough Council, Stafford Burial Grounds, Tixall Road, Stafford ST18 0XZ (tel 01785 242594; fax 228521). This site opened in 1995. A double burial costs £481 (incl. digging and an ash, lime or beech tree; same for non-residents). £61 for interment of ashes in a previously purchased grave. They allow all types of biodegradable coffins, shrouds and will give assistance for d-i-y funerals. Families are permitted to fill graves only. There are plans to erect a memorial wall on the outer boundary. The site is a 'naturalised area with marsh, open fields as a boundary to two sides. Mature trees and shrubs in the old section of the cemetery. Four interments have taken place so far, with four other graves purchased in reserve, and there is space for 300 burials in total' (Anthony Evans).

• **Stroud**: For locals only. Brimscombe woodland burial area, a difficult-to-reach part of a regular cemetery, with no seat to rest on at the top: 'I have never carried a coffin as far under such difficult conditions,' reports one undertaker. It is also rather expensive at £1184 a grave (incl. digging, and a rowan, wild cherry, field maple or birch tree planted between November and March). A grave for ashes costs £992. They specify cardboard or biodegradable coffins or shrouds, but not chipboard coffins. They cannot supply coffins, nor can they actively help d-i-y families. The site is on a hillside adjacent to open country, with views across the valley. Only for those who lived or were born in the area (but if non-residents can show a 'tenable link with the area, individual cases, and costs, will be considered at the discretion of the council'). A plot can be reserved in advance for £460. Contact George Damsell, Housing & Environmental Services, Stroud District Council, Ebley Mill, Westward Road, Stroud GL5 4UB (tel 01453 754425; fax 750932).

• **Telford, Shropshire**: Castle Green Natural Burial Ground, Beeches Road, Ironbridge; run by Telford & Wrekin Council. Contact Rachel Lewis, Countryside Manager, Telford & Wrekin Council, Darby House, Telford TF3 4LA (tel 01952 202228; fax 291585; e-mail: lcc@wrekin.gov.uk) for more details. This 1.5-acre green burial site opened in March 2000. A grave costs approximately £350 (incl. digging, but no tree; double for non-residents). £70 for a plaque on a wooden plinth at the entrance to the site. All types of biodegradable coffins or shrouds are allowed. Ashes can be interred for about £51. Free advice on d-i-y funerals. Families are able to help fill the grave. 'No trees or new planting. The area, an existing meadow enclosed by natural hedges, is already rich in wild flowers including orchids – and will continue to be managed as such.'

• **Worcester**: A wild flower meadow green burial ground at Astwood Cemetery, Tintern Avenue, Worcester WR3 8HA; run by the City of Worcester Council (tel 01905 22633). A grave costs £385 (incl. digging, a memorial inscription and tree planting 'in accordance with the development plan'). They will accept homemade, cardboard or wicker coffins. An inscribed stepping stone in the grass pathway costs £155; a two-line inscription in the nearby crematorium's Book of Remembrance is free. Bird and bat boxes have been put up. Family and friends can fill the grave if they wish and can help in a token way with the digging. 'The site is a wildlife area surrounded by hedges in an old part of the cemetery, with lots of very large established trees nearby. We are currently adopting the Charter for the Bereaved' (David Seaman).

East Midlands

Comprising Derbyshire, Nottinghamshire, Leicestershire, Warwickshire, Northamptonshire, Bedfordshire, Oxfordshire, Buckinghamshire.

• **[*] Nr. Alfreton**: Golden Valley Woodland Burial Ground, Nr. Newlands Road, Riddings, Nr. Alfreton, Derbyshire; run by Peace Funerals, Gleadless Mount, Sheffield S12 2LN (tel 0114 2530505 or 08457 697822; fax 0114 2530503; e-mail: peacefuner@aol.com). This site opened in September 1996 and about 20 burials have taken place (approximately ten per year). A grave costs £300 (incl. a British native tree; digging £145 extra, unless families do their own digging; same for non-residents). York stone memorial plaques with room for fifty characters are sold for £85. All types of coffin and shrouds are accepted. Ashes can be interred for £135 (incl. a tree). Transportation of the coffin and the funeral party can be by steam train to the track-side cemetery (from the Midland Railway Centre at Ripley in Derbyshire). The funeral would then cost about £1300. Full catering options are available on the train. A preserved tin tabernacle near the site can be used for religious or secular funeral ceremonies. The one-acre burial ground can only be reached by train or through the Golden Valley Country Park. 'A lovely secluded setting. Away from any road or housing, with woodland on two sides. Families can choose their own tree type and plot. A friends group meets for mutual support and to advise on policy' (John Mallatratt). Other arrangements as for the South Yorkshire Woodland Burial Ground (see above). Prepaid plan: Golden Leaves. Funds are put in a Trust. [Provisional Association membership requires renewal 8/12/2000.]

• **Bedford**: One-acre woodland burial site at Norse Road Cemetery, 104 Norse Road, Bedford MK41 0RL (tel 01234 353701 or 359986; e-mail: mday@bedford.gov.uk); run by Bedford Borough Council. A grave costs £330 for 75 years (incl. a small granite marker or plaque; £214 for a second interment in an existing grave). Family or friends can plant a native tree, shrub or rose bush at the head of the grave, but approval for the type of plant or tree must be obtained from the Cemetery Registrar prior to purchase or planting. Recycled cardboard coffins are sold at the Norse Road Cemetery office. Embalming is not allowed. 600 burials are planned for the area. 'No chemicals are used in maintaining the area. There is a large wild bird population' (Michael Day).

• **Belper, Derbyshire**: Woodland burial is offered at a 5.7-acre site at Belper Cemetery, Matlock Road, Broadholme, Belper; run by Borough Services, Amber Valley Borough Council, PO Box 18, Town Hall, Ripley DE5 3SZ (tel 01773 841418; fax 841539; e-mail: enquiry@ambervalley.gov.uk; web: www.ambervalley.gov.uk). A grave costs £337 (incl. digging and the planting of a tree or bulbs supplied by the council; £505-50 for non-residents). Families can help fill, but not dig, the grave. Burials should take place in a biodegradable coffin, shroud or other appropriate container (wood coffins should be made from wood obtained from managed forests). Cremated remains can also be buried or scattered in this area for £34. No memorials allowed. 'Please note that each grave is a single plot for one burial only. There is mature woodland on two sides and a mature arboretum' (Paul Martin).

• **(Blidworth, Nottinghamshire)**: Green burial at Undermill Woodland Cemetery; run by Steve Taylor, 14 Dale Lane, Blidworth, Nr. Mansfield, Nottinghamshire, NG21 0TG (tel 01623 798842). Reapplying for planning permission.

• **Buxton, Hope and Thornsett:** Small green burial areas have been created by the High Peak Borough Council within their three cemeteries. Contact Tony Robinson, Environmental Health, High Peak Borough Council, Town Hall, Buxton, Derbyshire SK17 6EL (tel 01298 28404; e-mail: env-health@high peak.gov.uk). A grave costs £272 (incl. digging and a 'contribution towards the planting of trees and bulbs on the grave and continuing maintenance'). Ashes can be interred for £47. No memorials are allowed. Families can arrange a funeral without undertakers, but no assistance will be given. All types of biodegradable coffins and shrouds are accepted. 20 burials have taken place so far, about five a year.

• **Erewash, Derbyshire**: Two woodland burial sites: one located at Park Cemetery, Ilkeston and one at Longmoor Cemetery, Breaston; run by Erewash Borough Council. Contact Caroline Price, Parks Administration Officer, Leisure Services, Town Hall, Long Eaton NG10 1HU (tel 0115 9461321) for more information. A grave costs £217-60 (incl. digging, a sapling and planting).

• **✪✪✪ Gerrards Cross:** Parkside Woodland Burial Ground, Parkside Cemetery, Windsor Road, Hedgerley, Buckinghamshire SL9 8SS (tel 01753 662426); run by the South Bucks District Council. A grave costs £140-79 (double for non-residents) and a digging fee has to be arranged with private contractors, such as Mr Hepburn on 0850 650036. Ashes can be interred for £40-50. A tree costs £44-80 incl. the permit and maintenance for ten years; 'trees are often supplied by the grave owner, we don't object to non-native types'. All sorts of wild flowers, perennials, small shrubs, bulbs etc are allowed, providing they are kept within the confines of the 10' x 5' grave area. They will accept home-made, cardboard, or wicker coffins, and body bags or shrouds. Families and friends can fill the grave if they wish and can help with a token amount of digging. They offer limited assistance to d-i-y families. A small wooden plaque at the bottom of the tree would be possible, if arranged by the family. The two-acre site is an extension of the existing lawn cemetery, with a field with ponies beyond, and woodland behind the field. It opened in 1996. 'Until the woodland matures the area will be treated as a wild flower hay meadow. We allow certain areas of long grass to encourage invertebrates and we are not too tough on brambles and nettles. Many of the wild flowers have naturalised themselves. Our prices are very reasonable for this area. Graves can be prepurchased. The M4 and M40 are readily accessible' (Mr Ian Richens). (Eds: This site, and Mr Richens, seem to be popular with North Londoners who cannot afford London grave prices.) Winner of the New Natural Death Handbook Award 2000 for the Best Woodland Burial Ground in or around London.

• **Hope:** Green burial ground created by the High Peak Borough Council within their cemetery in Hope, Derbyshire. See **Buxton** above for more details.

• **(Kettering):** Green burial ground to be opened as an extension to Rothwell Cemetery. Contact Alan Brook, Burials and Cremations Manager, Kettering Borough Council, East Lodge, Kettering Crematorium, Rothwell Road, Kettering NN16 8XE (tel 01536 534218). An area for 200 single depth graves is proposed. Tree planting will follow a set plan, and not all graves will have their own tree. Prices yet to be determined, but approximately £385 for a grave (incl. digging; double for non-residents). Cardboard coffins will be supplied at cost.

• **Mansfield:** Woodland burial ground as an extension to Mansfield Woodhouse Cemetery; run by Mansfield District Council. Contact Mrs Sally Curtis, Assistant Registrar of Cemeteries, Mansfield and District Crematorium, Derby Road, Mansfield, Notts NG18 5BJ (tel 01623 621811). An adult's grave costs £150, and a child's grave costs from £52 to £78. Plus £138 for the digging. Biodegradable caskets are encouraged, but are not obligatory. There is space for 206 double graves arranged in clusters to permit the development of a woodland copse. Following guidance from the Woodland Trust, oak, ash, birch and rowan trees are planted in appropriate blocks. Graves are sold through a 75 year title deed of right of burial. For maximum encouragement of wildlife, wild flowers and trees, no memorials are allowed on the site. However, the facility of a contoured memorial mound with special plaques is available for those buried in the woodland site. Entries can also be placed in the cemetery's Book of Remembrance.

• **Mappleborough Green**: Wildlife Churchyard, Mappleborough Green, Warwickshire; contact Rev. Richard Deimel, The Vicarage, 3 Manor Mews, Studley B80 7NA (tel 01527 852830). A five-acre meadow with trees situated 15 miles south of Birmingham, with views out onto undulating farmland, and adjoining a Victorian church and churchyard. They accept most kinds of biodegradable body container. A grave costs £175; non-residents £375. Families can either do their own digging and filling of the grave or pay a local digger between about £30 and £50. Families can also provide a tree, although there is a tree planting plan, rather than an individual tree, for each grave.

• **New Mills:** Green burial ground created by the High Peak Borough Council within their cemetery in Thornsett, Nr. New Mills, Derbyshire. See **Buxton** above for details. (Eds: This site has been recommended to the Centre as 'nice enough'.)

• [*] **Nr. Nottingham**: Tithe Green Burial Ground, The Estate Office, Grange Farm, Oxton, Nottinghamshire NG25 ORG (tel Ian Johnson, 01623 882210) This 40-acre site five miles north of Nottingham, near Calverton and the A614, is in peaceful countryside, adjacent to a forest, with a stream, the Dover Beck, running alongside. Memorial trees are planted to form copses, and wild flower seed scattered. A grave costs £250; digging and interment is an extra £100 (families may arrange the digging and filling themselves if they wish) and a native British species tree – ask, oak, lime, wild cherry, hazel or birch – costs £50. Biodegradable coffins are available. Special arrangements can be made to collect a body. A prepaid grave plot costs £225. 'The concept is appropriate as the burial ground is within the boundary of the historic Sherwood Forest' (Ian Johnson). [Provisional association membership requires renewal 10/7/2000.]

• **(Nuthall)**: Woodland burial site planned for 2005 for Nuthall, five miles north of Nottingham; to be run by Broxtowe Borough Council. For updated information contact Alec Thomson, Services Manager, Environmental Services, Wilford Hill Crematorium & Southern Cemetery, Loughborough Road, West Bridgford, Nottingham NG2 7FE (tel 0115 915 6106). If planning permission is approved, the area will initially be three to four acres – with the potential to expand to 20 to 25 acres – out of a new 70-acre cemetery to be built on greenbelt land. Part of the site is already woodland, but trees will probably be planted on individual graves within the woodland burial area, and the rest of the 70 acres will be for conventional graves. (A further 30 acres of the 100-acre site is reserved for new housing developments.)

• [*] **Olney, Buckinghamshire**: A six-acre woodland burial site (with potential to expand) at Yardley Road, Olney MK46 5EH; run by The Green Burial Company, 1a Church Lane, Emberton, Olney MK46 5DD (tel 01234 241808; e-mail: warwickclarke@barclays.net). 160 burials are planned per acre. A 5m x 5m grave costs £750 (incl. digging and a native oak tree; same for non-residents). No memorials permitted. Ashes can be interred for the same price. Families can help dig and fill the grave, subject to supervision. All types of biodegradable coffins, shrouds, body bags, etc allowed. 'The site is on the edge of the wooded Yardley chase, on the side of the Great Ouse Valley, overlooking the country town of Olney. The surrounding countryside is mixed arable pastureland with large tracts of ancient oak woodland. The site will be established as high quality parkland. Attention will be given to visual aspects such as levelling the ground and the quality of the tree planting. This will be a quality operation in all aspects!' (Warwick Clarke). [Provisional Association membership requires renewal 27/ 1/2001.]

• **Oxford:** Hugh Dawson, Cemetery Manager, Wolvercote Cemetery, Banbury Road, Oxford OX2 8EE (tel 01865 513962). Woodland burial plots are located at three cemeteries in Oxford: **Wolvercote** (a corner of the cemetery on the boundary with the recreation ground and sports ground); **Headington** Cemetery (Dunston Road); and **Botley** Cemetery (North Hinksey Lane). A grave costs £391 (incl. digging; double for non-residents). A tree costs £56 extra and bulbs £28 (the same for non-residents). They will accept home-made or cardboard coffins, and possibly wicker coffins, but no body bags or shrouds. Trees are planted between October and May and relatives can help – choosing between a whitebeam, silver birch, hazel, field maple or wild service tree. Individual trees are guaranteed for 20 years and if a tree is lost during that period it will be replaced free of charge. Beyond that period some coppicing and thinning will be required. In addition, a maximum of 100 wild flowers may be planted from a selection of bluebells, snowdrops, wood anemones or wood violets. Relatives may also sponsor a seat with a plaque.

• [*] **Prestwold, Nr. Loughborough:** Natural Burial Ground on 1.56 hectares of scrubland on the Prestwold Estate, a mile east of Loughborough, created by the local environmental charity Environ. Contact David Nicholls or Paul Ginns at The Natural Burial Company, Suite 1, Devonshire House, 26 Bank Street, Lutterworth, Leicestershire LE17 4AG (tel 01455 550099, fax 554855; e-mail: info@naturalburial.co.uk; web: www.naturalburial.co.uk). A grave costs £500 (incl. digging) in the grassland section of the site where wild flowers have already been planted, or in the woodland section where trees are planted randomly as the graves are used. In the memorial section, a grave costs up to £800 (incl. digging and a tree – price varies according to tree type). Ashes can be interred for £150. Four burials have taken place so far. No undertaking services are offered on site and, 'for health and safety reasons', families cannot help dig or fill the grave. There is a car park. [Provisional Association membership requires renewal 6/11/2000.]

• **Retford:** Woodland burial area at The Cemetery, North Road, Retford, Nottinghamshire; run by Cyril Blackshaw, Bassetlaw District Council, Carlton Forest House, Hundred Acre Lane, Carlton, Worksop S81 OTS (tel 01909 533487). The site opened in 1999 with room for 700 burials. A grave costs £383 (incl. digging, a tree and a name plaque; £574-50 for non-residents). Trees are birch, holly, hawthorn, hazel, yew or mountain ash. They will accept home-made, cardboard, or wicker coffins, and body bags or shrouds. Ashes can be interred for £264. This one-acre woodland burial ground is in an old cemetery with established trees. Boats pass up and down the Chesterfield canal and it could probably be arranged for a coffin to be delivered by boat. The grave area is deep enough for single graves without disturbing any remains that may still be there (the last burial was at least 100 years ago). Mourners cannot help with the digging for safety reasons. 'The cemetery has a country park character' (Cyril Blackshaw).

• [**] ✪✪✪ **Rugby:** Greenhaven Woodland Burial Ground at New Clarks Farm is run by Christine Atkin and Nicholas Hargreaves of Yelvertoft Road, Lilbourne, Rugby, Warwickshire CV23 OSZ (tel 01788 860604; e-mail: nichar greaves@hotmail.com; web: www.greenhavenwoodland.com). A grave costs £250 (incl. a tree; family and friends can dig the grave or pay £75 to have it dug for them). They will accept home-made, cardboard, or wicker coffins, and body bags or shrouds. They sell the Compakta coffin from £55 and the Peace Box coffin for £104. They will collect the body at a cost of 90p a mile (eg about £90 for London collections) with a minimum transport fee of about £30. For a Londoner, a basic funeral would cost £570 (incl. the grave, digging, a cardboard coffin, a tree, and collection of the body – £40 less if the family provide their own bearers). Wooden plaques are allowed as memorials. 'The site is situated in an elevated position with good views. It is typical Northamptonshire countryside, at present with not many trees, but lots of old hedges dotted with ash trees and a pond. All our trees are grown from native seeds. Wild flower seeds and bulbs are also planted. Clients' pre-payments are safeguarded as they have a legal deed to their plots and other monies are kept in a separate clients' account. It is a family-run site, very relaxed, with very reasonable prices and very centrally placed' (Christine Atkin). [Association membership requires renewal 6/7/ 2000.] Winner of the New Natural Death Handbook Award 2000 for the Best Woodland Burial Ground in the UK.

• **(Swadlingcote, Derbyshire)**: One or two woodland burial grounds are planned as extensions to existing rural cemeteries. Cardboard coffins will be supplied for around £70. No headstones or memorials will be allowed – flowers and wreaths will be removed two weeks after interment and the grave sites will later be planted with trees and wild flowers. A pilot scheme for one site is currently under consideration. Contact Eileen Mattley, South Derbyshire County Council, Civic Offices, Civic Way, Swadlingcote DE11 0AH (tel 01283 228084).

• **Worksop**: A two-acre woodland burial ground opened in January 1999, attached to Hannah Park Cemetery, Netherton Road, Worksop, Nottingham-shire. One burial has taken place so far and there is room for about 1400 graves. Enquiries to Cyril Blackshaw, Bassetlaw District Council, Carlton Forest House, Hundred Acre Lane, Carlton, Worksop S81 OTS (tel 01909 533487). A grave costs £383 (incl. digging, a tree and a name plaque; £574-50 for non-residents). Trees are birch, holly, hawthorn, hazel, yew or mountain ash. They will accept home-made, cardboard coffins or wicker coffins, and body bags or shrouds (and can advise on where to obtain any of these). Families cannot help with the digging for safety reasons. Ashes can be interred for £284 (but Cyril

Blackshaw comments that 'cremation doesn't really feature in green burial'). A tree can be planted for someone whose funeral was elsewhere for £264. The entrance is through a natural copse of woodland, opening up into an eight-acre cemetery with panoramic views of the town. The site borders and will help to extend the ancient Hannah Park Wood.

East Anglia

Comprising Norfolk, Suffolk, Essex, Cambridgeshire and Hertfordshire.

• **(Barton, Cambridgeshire):** The Church of England has chosen for its first green cemetery a 40-acre site on a quiet hill near Barton. For more information contact the Diocesan Secretary, Matthew Lavis at Bishop Woodford House, Barton Road, Ely CB7 4DX (tel 01353 663579; fax 666148; e-mail: webmaster@ely.anglican.org; web: www.ely.anglican.org). Tree planting has started at the site and the first burial is planned for 2001. A grave will cost £500 (incl. an inscription on a wooden plaque and a tree).

• **(Braintree, Essex):** Woodland burial area proposed as an extension to Braintree Cemetery, London Road, Braintree, Essex. Contact Michael Ashby, Cemeteries Superintendent, Community Services, Braintree District Council, Causeway House, Bocking End, Braintree, Essex CM7 9HB (tel 01376 552523 ext 2324). The present grave price is £420; double for non-residents. Trees will mostly be supplied by the council, but families should be able to plant them. No memorials will be allowed. Only rigid coffins will be accepted, because of the possibility of exhumation. Families will be able to help fill, but not dig, the grave.

• **(Brinkley, Cambridgeshire):** Brinkley Woodland Cemetery, Balsham Lane, off Six Mile Bottom Road, Brinkley; run by Countryside Burials, The Old Courts, 147 All Saints Road, Newmarket, Suffolk CB8 8HH (tel 01638 600693; fax 560869; e-mail: bwc@countryside-burials.co.uk). This 33-acre woodland burial site is set to open summer 2000. An adult grave will cost £350 (or £325 if booked in advance); or £310 for a child and £290 for an infant (all prices incl. digging; same for non-residents). Families can help fill, not dig, the grave. £30 extra for a tree: ash, oak, lime, beech, larch, wild cherry or hazel. They will accept home-made, cardboard, or wicker coffins, and body bags or shrouds. Ashes interred for £120, or scattered for £50. A ground-level flat A4 stone is allowed as a memorial, price to be decided. 'Open rolling countryside interspersed with woodlands. Trees will be planted to build up the woodland area separate from the burial area which will be left as a meadow and only cut twice a year to encourage wild flowers. Part of the cemetery will be consecrated' (Bernard Edge).

• **(Bury St Edmunds, Suffolk):** A woodland burial ground within a new cemetery planned for 2000. Contact Maggie Moss, Cemetery Registrar, St Edmundsbury Borough Council, Angel Hill, Bury St Edmunds IP33 1XB (tel 01284 763 233).

• **(Cambridge):** Green burial area of about an acre included in plans for a new cemetery near the City Crematorium, Huntingdon Road, Cambridge CB3 0JJ

(Cemeteries Manager, David Giles, tel 01954 780681); run by Cambridge City Council. Set to open 2001 or 2002. A grave will probably cost from £645 or from £750 for non-residents. They will accept home-made, cardboard, or wicker coffins, and body bags or shrouds. Families will be able to help dig and fill the grave. Free advice and general guidance will be offered.

• **(Cheshunt, Hertfordshire):** One-acre woodland burial area planned for 2005 at Cheshunt Cemetery, Bury Green, Cheshunt EN7 5AG; run by The Cemetery Office, Broxbourne Borough Council, Bishops College, Churchgate, Cheshunt EN8 9XF (tel 01992 785507; e-mail: broxbournebc@compuserve.com). Current cost of a 'woodland' style grave in the conventional section of the cemetery is £550 (quadruple for non-residents; £50 extra for a native species tree). Families can help with the digging. A brass plaque memorial on a wooden stake costs £60. They will supply cardboard, wicker and other inexpensive coffins for 'trade prices plus 12.5%'. 400 burials per acre are planned.

• [*] **Colney, South Norfolk**: Colney Wood Woodland Memorial Park; run by Melvyn Colby, Colney Hall, Colney, Norwich NR4 7TY (tel 01603 811556; e-mail: james_boddy@lineone.net; web: www.colneywood.com). This 12-acre site near a river, set in a contoured landscape with views out over a lake, opened in 1999. 250 to 300 burials are planned per acre. A grave is expensive at £2000 (incl. digging and a tree; same for non-residents). Wood statuettes are allowed as memorials. Families can help fill the grave if they wish. Transport around the site is environmentally friendly with paths through the site and down along the river. Plots are sold on a 99-year lease and are preferably family-size. Those organising the burial are free to choose any coffin or shroud. Access after the burial is restricted to the bereaved to ensure the site remains private and peaceful. An oriental-style garden is dedicated to the laying of ashes. (Eds: The high cost of a grave at this friendly site may need to be justified to secure full Association membership. The long-term plan is for the site to be electronically controlled, with users needing a swipe card to get in.) [Provisional Association membership requires renewal 16/3/2000.]

• **(Ely, Cambridgeshire):** A woodland burial area planned for Ely Cemetery, Beech Lane, Ely (tel 01353 669659); run by The City of Ely Council. There are no plans to establish a ground as yet, and no prices, but the current cheapest grave price in the conventional part of the cemetery is £163 (incl. digging; double for non-residents). 'Ely Cemetery was a finalist in the Cemetery of the Year Competition in 1998' (Win Hughes, Clerk to the Council).

• **(Harlow, Essex):** Woodland burial planned for late 2000, for Parndon Wood Cemetery, Parndon Wood Road, Great Parndon, Harlow CM19 4SF (tel 01279 423800 or 446199, e-mail: chrisbrown@harlow-gov.uk); run by Harlow District Council. No grave prices yet, but they sell an ecological coffin for £110. All types of cardboard coffin, body bags, shrouds, etc are acceptable. 'We have extended the cemetery and plan to include a natural burial area' (Mrs Chris Brown).

• **Hemel Hempstead**: Woodland burial ground; run by Bill Kynaston, Cemetery Manager, Dacorum Borough Council, Woodwells Cemetery, Hemel Hempstead, Hertfordshire HP2 7HY (tel 01442 252856). This ground opened in 1999.

A grave costs £191-50 (incl. digging; double for non-residents) plus an extra £90 for any one of nine native British species trees. Families can fill the grave if they wish and can help with a token amount of digging. The woodland area is a one-acre patch near the main cemetery, bounded by a fence and trees, on flat ground. 'It is part of what used to be a farm and was bought by the council. It is near the M1 and near a caravan storage area. Averagely attractive.'

• **(Ipswich, Suffolk):** A three-acre site for sale with planning permission for use as a woodland burial ground. The site is part of Home Farm, Thurleston Lane, Whitton, Ipswich IP1 6TH. The agents say: 'The site lies to the north of Ipswich just beyond the borough boundary in the mid-Suffolk District Council administrative area. It is partly wooded and overgrown with a small valley area.' All offers to Beane & Wass, 24 Princes Street, Ipswich, Suffolk IP1 1RJ (tel 01473 212656; fax 231606).

• **Maldon:** Woodland Glades, Maldon Cemetery, London Road, Maldon; run by Maldon District Council Offices, Princes Road, Maldon, Essex CM9 5DL (tel 01621 875836). A grave costs £373 (plus the cost of digging; double for non-residents). They will accept home-made and cardboard coffins. Family and friends can do a token amount of digging and filling of the grave. The woodland site area borders farmland within the walled boundary of an existing mature cemetery. 'On a Day of Dedication held each autumn the bereaved are invited to plant trees and bulbs, and to join the Friends of Woodland Glades who help each other through bereavement and give practical assistance in enhancing the woodland' (David Lobb, Cemeteries Officer).

• ✪✪✪ **Manningtree:** Oakfield Wood Green Burial Ground, Wrabness Hall, Wrabness, Manningtree, Essex CO11 2TQ (tel John Acton 01255 880182). General enquiries and enquiries about new sites planned for Guildford and for Bury St Edmunds to the site agent: Peter Kincaid, Green Woodland Burial Services, 256 High Street, Dovercourt, Harwich, Essex CO12 3PA (tel 01255 503456, fax 504466; e-mail: gburials@talk21.com; web: www.green burials.co.uk). Farmer John Acton manages this seven-acre burial ground overlooking the River Stour, but has given ownership of the land to Essex Wildlife Trust. A grave costs £398-75 for 'perpetuity' (incl. digging, a tree, a wooden plaque, a tree guard, and entry into Register of Burials with an Ordnance Survey grid reference). The £1248-75 all-in price for a funeral, collecting from anywhere within a 100 mile radius of the site, including London, includes a coffin, the burial and collection of the body. Interment of ashes costs £348-75. They will accept home-made, cardboard, or wicker coffins, and body bags or shrouds. Mourners can assist in digging and filling. A native broadleaf tree is planted at every plot in the dormant planting season. The ground is in set-aside farmland. The perimeter is planted with about 22,000 hardwood native hedging plants. Any monies paid in advance go into a Trustee account. 'Our prices are competitive, and it's a special scenic location that will be preserved by a charitable Wildlife Trust' (Peter Kincaid). Winner of the New Natural Death Handbook Award 2000 for the Best Woodland Burial Ground in East Anglia.

• **Peterborough:** Woodland burial area in Fletton Cemetery in Peterborough;

run by Broadway and Eastfield Council Cemeteries, Eastfield Road, Peterborough, Cambridgeshire (tel 01733 262639). Room for 400 graves. A grave costs £555 (incl. digging and an indigenous tree; double for non-residents, less for children). They will accept cardboard coffins or shrouds, and relatives can help fill the grave. 'We have a newly-designed, landscaped woodland burial area with a memorial wall enclosed by a fedge – a living fence of woven willow' (Kate Day).

• **Saxmundham:** A woodland burial ground run by the undertaker Tony Brown, The Funeral Service, New Cut, Saxmundham, Suffolk IP17 1DJ (tel 01728 603108; fax 604346). A grave costs from £1000 (incl. digging, a coffin, transport within Suffolk, but no tree as the site is already planted; plus extra for mileage outside Suffolk, a chapel or graveside service, reception etc). Charles Barnett of the Green Party was the first person to put his name down for an environmentally friendly (Greenwood) burial at this 20-acre site which comprises about a quarter of Racewalk Covert, a private nature reserve in the parish of Farnham, East Suffolk. It has already been planted with deciduous native trees in rows and burial plots are about ten feet square, so a single grave 'will occupy a central position between four trees in about 100 sq feet of land. All wreaths are removed after 14 days, after which a small flat wooden plaque is allowed if required, but the only decoration is to be wild flowers. No marble, metal pots or jam jars are permitted so that the graves integrate with the trees in a natural fashion. There is even a separate area for your pets' (T. Brown). (Eds: Tony Brown has an excellent reputation as a funeral director, but unfortunately this site had to be turned down for Provisional Association membership as families are not permitted to organise the funeral themselves, but must use Tony Brown's services and coffins. The standard grave price is as above, unless you are pre-booking a plot only – for £250 plus £110 for the digging.)

• **Stevenage, Hertfordshire**: A five-acre woodland burial ground at Harwood Park Woodland Cemetery, Watton Road, Stevenage SG2 8XT (tel 01438 815555; fax 817295; e-mail: russell@crematorium.co.uk). A grave costs £600 (incl. digging and an indigenous tree). No memorials, but a plaque can be provided on a memorial wall. Home-made, cardboard, wicker coffins, shrouds and body bags are allowed, subject to approval. Ashes can also be interred and a memorial tree can be planted for someone whose funeral was elsewhere. Free assistance available as required for d-i-y funerals and families can help fill, but not dig, the grave. They will sell coffins and shrouds on application. 'Gently sloping meadowland – formerly arable, to be planted as woodland – situated in the countryside in South Stevenage' (Russell Gadsby, Manager & Registrar).

The South West

Comprising South Gloucestershire, Bristol, Bath and North East Somerset, North West Somerset, Somerset, Dorset, Devon, Cornwall.

• **Bath:** Woodland burial section in Haycombe Cemetery, Whiteway Road, Bath BA2 2RQ (tel 01225 423682; fax 316339; e-mail: reg_greenall@bathnes.gov.uk);

run by Bath and North East Somerset Council. A site with 'rural views'. A grave costs £776 (incl. digging, a tree and a small metal plaque; £1076 for non-residents). Ashes can be interred at a separate site for £380. Advice and help with paperwork is offered (without charge at present) to those not using undertakers. Families can help dig and fill the grave. All types of coffins or shrouds are accepted. 'There is a list of trees suited to the soil here, but any reasonable request will be considered' (R. G. Greenall, Registrar).

• **Bournemouth:** Bournemouth North Cemetery Woodland Burials; run by Bournemouth Borough Council. Contact Julie Dunk, Cemeteries, Bournemouth Community Services, Strouden Avenue, Bournemouth, Dorset BH8 9HX (tel 01202 526238; e-mail: crematorium@bournemouth.gov.uk). A grave costs £440 (incl. digging and the choice of any tree; double for non-residents). They will accept home-made or cardboard coffins. Families and friends can fill the grave. The woodland burial ground has a view of the cemetery grounds and some large trees. Laurel trees have already been planted.

• **Bristol**: Woodland Burial Site, South Bristol Cemetery, Bridgewater Road, Bedminster Down, Bristol BS13 7AS (tel 0117 903 8330; e-mail: simon_westbrook@bristol-city.gov.uk); run by Bristol City Council. A grave for burial or cremated remains costs £790 (incl. digging and a choice of seven native species trees; same price for non-residents). A secluded local authority woodland burial site of several acres overlooking Bristol, the Avon Gorge and the Suspension Bridge. Families and friends can help fill the grave. They will accept home-made, cardboard, or wicker coffins, and body bags or shrouds. 'The site opened in 1996 and 28 burials have taken place so far, about nine per year. Wild flower seeds have been introduced and the grass is cut one or two times a year' (Simon Westbrook). (Eds: One report suggests that this site is set in the grounds of a stark, impersonal 1960s crematorium, with mown lawns and Tarmac. However, the woodland burial area is 'impressive', with trees planted on the graves, and the staff are enthusiastic about the scheme. Further reports welcome.)

• **Nr. Bristol**: Christopher Baker of Rookery Farm, Alveston, (10 miles north of) Bristol BS12 2SY (tel 01454 415495; fax 419081) runs a 20-acre burial ground in the valley. The site is grazing land – small fields with high hedges – with the M5 nearby. Four converted Georgian barns provide a chapel and function rooms. The cost of the grave (incl. digging, a tree, a small concrete plaque and the use of the chapel and party room) is between £500 and £600. Families can help with digging and filling and do not have to use funeral directors.

• **(Canford Magna, Dorset)**: A woodland burial area planned for 2002 or 2003; run by Poole Borough Council, possibly jointly with Bournemouth Borough Council (see entry above). Contact Mr Steve Carter, Manager, Poole Crematorium, Gravel Hill, Poole, Dorset BH17 9BQ (tel 01202 261347). The council has planning permission for a new 28-acre cemetery near Magna Road in Canford Magna, and the periphery will be set aside for woodland burial, with 'dense tree planting'. No more details as yet as funding is still forthcoming.

• **Cleeve, Somerset**: Priory Woodland Burial Ground opened in 1996 next to the residence of the owner, Mrs Almuth Groos, Cleeve Priory, Watchet, Somerset TA23 OJS (tel 01984 631098). About two acres of recently planted woodland, not overlooked from the road, with a view of the Quantox and Brendon Hills. Around 30 burials have taken place so far; about 15 a year. A tree can be planted by or on the grave and a plaque fixed to the supporting pole. Flat-lying stones are also allowed as memorials. A gravesite costs from £320 to £330; a site for an urn costs £50. No grave digging included. Family and friends or funeral directors can arrange the funeral. Any type of biodegradable coffin, body bag or shroud will be accepted. A specially-designed trolley is available to bring the coffin to the grave.

• **Exeter, Devon**: A one-acre woodland burial site on a steeply-sloped part within the boundary of Exwick Cemetery, Exwick Road, Exeter EX4 2BT; run by Exeter City Council. Contact the Cemeteries Registrar, Civic Centre, Paris Street, Exeter EX1 1RQ (tel 01392 665704; fax 665935; e-mail: john.ocallaghan@exeter.gov.uk; web: www.exeter.gov.uk). One burial has taken place and there is room for about 50 more. A grave costs £400 (incl. digging and an English native tree; double for non-residents). £45 for the interment of ashes. Shrouds and biodegradable coffins are preferred, but chipboard or natural wood coffins of timber from managed forests would also be accepted. Families can help dig and fill the grave. 'At the appropriate time of year you may plant an approved tree just off the grave, or maybe wild flowers, as we consider appropriate for the management of the site' (John O'Callaghan).

• **(Falmouth, Cornwall)**: The Falmouth Green Centre, Union Road, Falmouth TR11 4JW (tel 01326 375158) acts as a focus for environmental information, education and action. They are lobbying for more woodland burial grounds locally and throughout Cornwall. 'Offers of support with this campaign are very welcome. We hold up-to-date information on green burials and examples of good practice from other parts of the country' (Philip Pearce).

• [*] ✪✪✪ **Par, Cornwall**: Pontsmill Human Green Burial and Pet Cemetery, c/o Terry Squires, Terraine, Pontsmill Lane, Par PL24 2RR (tel 01726 813975). A two-acre site for about 300 human burials adjoins a cemetery for 1,000 pet burials on a gentle slope looking out onto woodland in this Designated Area of Outstanding Natural Beauty in the Luxulyan Valley. It costs £220 for the grave (incl. an oak tree and a plaque if wanted; same for non-residents) plus £100 for the digging. Ashes can be interred for £40 and a memorial tree can be planted for someone whose funeral was elsewhere for £40. They can also supply coffins (a softwood oak, ash veneer costs £100). Families and friends can help fill or dig the grave. They will supply grass mats for around the grave, tools etc. Owners can have their pets buried with them. Any kind of body container is acceptable. Rules are kept to a minimum. 'Nine burials have taken place so far and 20 plots have been paid for in advance. This area of wooded valley and green fields is regularly visited by the royal family. Mines in the hillside were used by the Phoenicians. There is no through road' (Terry Squires). (Eds: One funeral director highly recommends this site, saying that Terry is a 'lovely bloke, retired' and that Pontsmill is in a beautiful setting. 'Through a country lane you come to a truncated drive, then walk through the pet area, all on sloping ground, higher up to the human cemetery.') [Provisional Association membership requires renewal 10/12/2000.] Winner of the New Natural Death Handbook Award 2000 for the Best Woodland Burial Ground in the South West.

• **Seaton, Devon:** Green Burial Ground, Colyford Road, Seaton; run by Mike Cane and colleagues, c/o The Registrar, Chief Exec Dept, East Devon District Council, Knowle, Sidmouth, Devon EX10 8HZ (tel 01395 516551 ext 376). This site for 160 graves in meadow land, is part of Seaton Cemetery, in an Area of Outstanding Natural Beauty, on a hillside with panoramic views out over the valley, estuary and the sea. They will accept home-made or cardboard coffins. A grave costs only £63 (incl. a tree; double for non-residents), but the digging must also be done and paid for either privately (tel 01297 489530; price £105) or through a funeral director. Friends and family may help with a token amount of digging or filling of the grave. 'Any family-organised funeral must be done properly. A tree or shrub is planted for each grave' (Mr Cane).

• [*] **Shillingstone, Dorset:** Ham Down Woodland Burial Ground, Bere Marsh Farm, Shillingstone DT11 0QY; run by Mrs A. Hughes OBE, Box Bush House, Broadoak, Sturminster Newton DT11 2HD (tel 01258 471370). This two-acre site overlooking the River Stour and Hambledon Hill has room for approximately 350 burials per acre. Please telephone for prices, as none were yet available at the time of going to press. Families will be able to help fill the grave. Trees offered are field maple, silver birch, oak, whitebeam, rowan and small-leaved lime. Wild flowers can also be planted on the graves. A small wooden cross supplied by the relatives of the deceased is allowed as a memorial. 'Over 146 species of birds have been recorded on the farm. Nightingales nest next to the site, and rare butterflies breed in the oaks adjoining the site. A seat will be provided for mourners and there is a small spinney within the site where ashes can be scattered for a nominal sum. We supply a list of county undertakers' (A. W. Hughes). [Provisional Association membership requires renewal 20/7/2000.]

• **South Molton:** Mole Valley Green Burial Ground, Wood House Farm, Queens Nympton, South Molton, North Devon EX36 4JH (tel and fax 01769 574512). Five acres in a 12-acre field adjoining existing woodland, with views over the river valley. A grave costs £400 (plus digging £50-£100). A blackthorn, elder, oak or other type of tree and transport of the coffin costs extra. Full undertaking service available – cost depends on services required – and various coffins and shrouds can be supplied at the retail price. Families can help fill, but not dig, the grave. A small memorial tag is allowed on the tree if supplied by the family. Ashes can be interred for £50. Advance purchase of Right of Burial available. A horse and cart is available free on site, cheap elsewhere. The meadow is planted with local trees and shrubs. 'The site is on an organic farm in rural Devon and is easily accessible via a private lane. There is an unconfirmed ancient woodland, hedgebanks, badgers, deer, birds, hares and foxes. It will be managed with help from Devon Wildlife Trust' (Brian and Jeanne Nicholas).

• [*] (**Nr. Tavistock, Devon**): A four-acre woodland burial site with space for about 500 graves, planned for the year 2000, on pastureland at Stone Park, Walkhampton, Nr. Tavistock. Contact Tania Seldon, Return to Earth Woodland Burials, 23 Bannawell Street, Tavistock PL19 0DJ (tel 01822 618923). A grave will cost £370 (incl. digging and an oak woodland tree seeded from local stock where possible; same price for non-residents). All types of coffins and body bags or shrouds are acceptable, including chipboard coffins, if made from environmentally kind materials. A small wooden or stone memorial plaque will be allowed (cost not yet known). Interment of ashes and nonviable foetuses will be possible. Families and friends will be able to help dig and fill the grave. Free green funeral advice will be offered to those using the site. Reservations will be accepted in local LETS currency (Chips). 'I will seek village involvement in the site so it becomes a community woodland. It is a very peaceful site five minutes walk from a small village up a quiet lane, below a parish church, on a gentle slope with views over Cornwall and the edge of Dartmoor. The hedges are ancient and there are mature trees all around. The pasture will be cut for hay and to maximise flora. It will be unfertilised and planted with local stock. Devon Wildlife Trust have advised me on wildlife management' (Tania Seldon). [Provisional Association membership requires renewal 9/2/2001.]

• **Tavistock, Devon**: Green burial facility offered on two acres of consecrated land at Tavistock Cemetery, 119 Plymouth Road, Tavistock PL19 8BY; run by Teignbridge District Council (contact the Cemetery Superintendent on 01822 612 799). A grave costs £165-50 for parishioners (incl. digging; £344-50 for non-parishioners). Ashes can be interred for £27 (£76 for non-parishioners). Only biodegradable coffins and adornments are allowed. Grass, wild flower seeds or a small native shrub may be planted on the grave, and perhaps an 18" local granite boulder-type of headstone (if wished). One hardwood tree is planted for every eight graves. Six burials have taken place so far. D-i-y funerals allowed, but families cannot help dig or fill the grave. Pre-purchase of a burial plot is possible. 'The site is secluded, surrounded by mature oaks. We hope to contribute to a new sanctuary for wild plants, birds and other wildlife, thus bringing enjoyment to the community and to future generations' (Douglas Parkhouse).

• (**Taunton & Wellington**): A woodland burial ground planned for land close to an existing cemetery at Wellington; run by Taunton & Deane Borough Council. For further details contact Mr P. D. Rayson, Taunton Deane Crematorium, Wellington New Road, Taunton, Somerset TA1 5NE (tel 01823 284811).

• (**Thornbury**): Woodland burial or 'forest' area planned for Thornbury Cemetery, Kington Lane; run by Thornbury Town Council, Town Hall, Old Police Station, High Street, Thornbury, Bristol BS12 2AR (tel G. W. H. Jackson, the Town Clerk, on 01454 412103; fax 281638; e-mail: towncouncil@ thornburytown.freeserve.co.uk). Current conventional grave prices are £265 (incl. digging; £530 for non-residents). The site will be alongside the traditional cemetery, but there are no more details at present.

• **(Torquay)**: Woodland burial is to be offered in the future by Torbay Council, but there are no details as yet. Contact Vivienne Foster, Torquay Cemetery, Hele Road, Torquay, Devon TQ2 7QG (tel 01803 327768) for more details.

• [*] **Nr. Totnes, Devon**: Six acres of newly planted woodland adjacent to the mature Bidwell Wood and farmland; run by Mr Lithgow, Bidwell, Cummings Pond Lane, Rattery, Devon TQ10 9LU (tel 07973 459065). Burials are spaced between existing trees – allowing about 10 square metres per burial. A grave costs £500 (plus digging service as required; trees are already planted). Only biodegradable coffins are allowed. 'To be managed as a high quality timber producing woodland with burials taking place where the trees are wider spaced. This will not be a reserve. ... No memorials, no special trees, just a nice place to remember saying some goodbyes.' [Provisional Association membership requires renewal 15/12/2000.]

• **(Yeovil, Somerset)**: Woodland burial ground planned for land near Yeovil, possibly near the Ham Hill beauty spot; to be run by South Somerset Council. Contact George Smith (tel 01963 435 006) for further details.

The South

Comprising Wiltshire, Berkshire, Surrey, Kent, Hampshire, West Sussex, East Sussex.

• **Ashford**: The Woodland Garden Cemetery, Bybrook Cemetery, Cemetery Lane, Ashford, Kent; run by Christine Smith, Cemeteries Officer, Ashford Borough Council, Civic Centre, Tannery Lane, Ashford, Kent TN23 1PL (tel 01233 637311, ext 472; fax 01233 665413). A grave costs £315 (incl. digging, the provision of a biodegradable cardboard coffin and a tree; no extra for non-residents). £590 for two adjacent spaces. Cremated remains can also be interred for £155 (incl. a biodegradable casket and a tree). The cemeteries office is happy to advise d-i-y families. 'The Woodland Garden Cemetery was started in 1995 to the southern side of Bybrook Cemetery. As with any natural woodland, it will take time to establish and is managed for the benefit of its trees, shrubs and wildlife. A path is maintained for visitors. The area includes two flowering cherry orchards, a wild flower meadow and carefully-placed seating. One tree can be planted on each grave and relatives can choose from a variety of native species. Wooden marker posts and a memorial tag on each tree enables graves to be located easily. If desired, relatives can plant the tree themselves after the ground has settled. For those who want an additional memorial, a bench can be dedicated with a plaque for £375' (Christine Smith). (Eds: One user said of this site in November 1999: 'I cannot speak of it too highly. It is young, and the trees are still small, but in a few years it will be very beautiful and the screening of broad leaved saplings will have hidden the main cemetery from view.')

• **Beaulieu:** Beaulieu Woodland Burial Ground, Grindinstone, Beaulieu, Hampshire; run by Mrs Linda Coote, New Forest District Council, Client Services Division, The Town Hall, Avenue Road, Lymington SO41 9ZG, tel 023 8028 5952). A grave costs £344 (incl. digging and a tree or shrub; £556 for non-residents). They will accept home-made or cardboard coffins. It is a section within an existing cemetery in a rural area. (Eds: One funeral director describes this site as 'an idyllic country churchyard, one mile from the village, with mature trees in the traditional part and the woodland burial ground in the right hand corner, with, as yet, only very small trees. About 25 burials have taken place. Numbered plates only, without names, are placed on the graves; but it is beautiful.')

• [**] **Brighton:** Brighton & Hove Woodland Burial Ground at Bear Road Cemetery, has its office at The Woodvale Lodge, Lewes Road, Brighton, East Sussex BN2 3QB (tel 01273 604020; fax 292320); it is run by Brighton Borough Council. A grave costs £427 (incl. digging and a tree; double for non-residents). This local authority woodland burial site is within a large meadow overlooking Brighton and the sea in one direction and Sussex downland in the other. 160 burials have taken place so far with a further 170 reserved and there is room for over 2,000. Services are tailored to meet individual requirements and assistance is offered to families organising funerals without funeral directors. Family and friends can fill the grave if they wish and can help to plant a tree chosen from nine native species. They sell the Greenfield cardboard coffin for £58 and accept all home-made or cardboard coffins. The meadow is cut only twice a year to encourage wildlife to thrive. No chemicals are used in maintaining the area. 'The site and scheme have won three awards' (Stephen Horlock). [Association membership requires renewal 15/8/2000.]

• **Canterbury**: Green Burial at Canterbury Cemetery, Westgate Court Avenue; run by Mrs Leita Honey, Cemeteries Registrar, Architecture & Engineering, Canterbury City Council, Military Road, Canterbury, Kent CT1 1YW (tel 01227 862490; fax 862020; e-mail: leita.honey@canterbury.gov.uk; web: www.canterbury.gov.uk). A grave at this council-run site costs £280 (incl. digging and the use of a bier; £50 extra to have the grave dug by hand without using petrochemicals; same prices for non-residents, except double the £180 fee to reserve a grave in advance for a 50-year period). Home-made and cardboard coffins are allowed, but not body bags or shrouds. Families cannot help dig or fill the grave. The green burial site is within Section 'H' of Canterbury City Cemetery. No memorials are permitted and no trees are planted on the graves as this 'creates difficulties for providing new graves', but graves are sprinkled with a wild flower mix and bulbs for the spring. For £155 you can dedicate an existing tree anywhere at Canterbury Cemetery, Herne Bay Cemetery – where woodland burial for cremated remains is also being developed – and Whistable Cemetery. A Book of Remembrance and an advice leaflet are also available. No burials have yet taken place in this section of the cemetery. 'Existing young trees and wild flowers will create a sunlit glade attracting wildlife and assisting the selfseeding of flowers. The area will be cut twice a year' (Leita Honey). (Eds: One visitor said of this site: 'This is merely lip service to the green burial movement. There is no discernable difference between this area and any other area in the cemetery.' Further reports welcome.)

• ✪✪✪ **Christchurch**: The Hinton Park Woodland Burial Ground, The Burial

Centre, Hinton, Nr. Christchurch, Dorset BH23 7EJ (tel 01425 278910 or 273640; mobile 0385 390817; fax 01425 278920; e-mail: mikehedger@ woodlandburial.com; web: www.woodlandburial.com). This four-acre site on the Dorset/Hampshire border opened in 1995. It is a peaceful meadow containing about 460 burials, approximately 120 per year, each with a semi-mature tree. It is surrounded by mature oaks and pine, with red deer in an adjoining meadow. Hinton House, an old English manor house, is visible overlooking the lake. Horses, sheep, squirrels, wild deer and pheasants wander round the grounds and there are many species of birds. A grave plot costs £350 and gives a legal right of ownership for 99 years (with an extra £475 for digging and refilling the grave, the provision of a native English tree and the collection of the body within a 30 mile radius). Collection from London, for example, costs about £100 extra. The all-in price for everything including collection of the body from London tends to come to about £1,075. A name plaque costs an extra £55. They will accept home-made, cardboard, or wicker coffins, and body bags or shrouds. Cardboard coffins (£100) or biodegradable polished oak veneer coffins (£125) are sold. Ashes can be interred in a separate area. A church service of any denomination can be arranged for £200 (excluding the ministers', organists' and choir fees). Or a service can be held in the meadow during fine weather. Family and friends can dig and fill the grave if they wish. The graves can be subsequently visited any time during daylight hours. A purpose-built building with lounge and refreshments serves the catering needs of mourners and bed and breakfast can be arranged locally. 'We can collect the body from home, hospital or nursing home and can look after the deceased until the burial (we have a refrigerated mortuary unit). We can make arrangements for newspaper advertisements and flowers. About 80% are pure family burials, doing their own lowering, reading their own thoughts and poems, occasionally prayers and often music. We have had one person saying goodbye alone to her husband, and on another occasion, 300 people saying farewell to a popular nurse from a local hospital' (Mike Hedger, Proprietor). Winner of the New Natural Death Handbook Award 2000 for the Best Woodland Burial Ground in the South.

• **Eastbourne:** Woodland burial at Langney Cemetery; run by Eastbourne Borough Council. Enquires to the Manager, Eastbourne Crematorium, Hide Hollow, Langney, Eastbourne, East Sussex BN23 8AE (tel 01323 761093 or 766536; fax 760637; e-mail: kendry@eastbourne.gov.uk). A single grave costs £425, a double costs £500 (incl. digging, with rights for 75 years). 'The area has already been planted with native trees, wild grasses and flowers and there is space for about 400 graves. Only interments in shrouds, cardboard or wicker coffins will be permitted. Cremated remains can be strewn on specific graves, but not interred, so as to minimise disturbance to the natural habitat' (Kenneth Dry). Advice is offered for families arranging a funeral without a funeral director.

• [*] **East Hampshire**: EarthWorks Trust, Sustainability Centre, Droxford Road, East Meon, Hants GU32 1HR (tel 01730 832166; fax 832168; e-mail: andrew@earthworks.demon.co.uk). The EarthWorks Trust, partially funded by the East Hampshire District Council, has developed a 1.5-acre unconsecrated green burial site for up to 700 graves (10 per year maximum) in a 'pleasant corner of its 55 acres of land on the South Downs, in woodland. Very quiet with a distant sea view.' Funerals cost £650 (incl. digging and an oak, ash, beech or birch tree; £750 for non-residents) if organised through a local undertaker. Or there will be a £100 discount if families organise all the funeral themselves (all burials must be environmentally-friendly). Families can help dig or fill the grave. No other memorials allowed. Ashes can be interred for £150. All biodegradable coffins, shrouds, etc are accepted. Coffins will have to be transported on biers, downhill, for 150 yards or so from the parking area. Mary Vincent of Funeral Services in Petersfield can help supply cardboard coffins and other services. 'We can be very flexible in our approach' (Andrew Braithwaite, Centre Manager). [Provisional Association membership requires renewal 12/11/2000.]

• **Eling:** Eling Woodland Burial Ground, Eling Hill, Totton, Southampton; run by Mrs Linda Coote, New Forest District Council, Client Services Division, The Town Hall, Avenue Road, Lymington, Hampshire SO41 9ZG (tel 023 8028 5952). A grave costs £344 (incl. digging and a tree or shrub; £556 for non-residents). They will accept home-made or cardboard coffins. 'A section within an existing cemetery, in a rural area' (Linda Coote). (Eds: One visitor has described this site as 'really bleak and windswept. Only one burial has taken place.' Other reports from the public, positive and negative, welcome.)

• [*] **Enborne, Nr. Newbury:** Acorn Ridge Natural Burials, Red Hill, Enborne; run by Mrs S. Lynes, Yew Tree Farm, Ball Hill, Newbury, Berkshire RG20 0NG (tel 01635 255441; fax 254018). This 20-acre site set on a hillside overlooking the South Downs leading down to the river Enbourne, had some local opposition, but provisional planning permission was won on appeal. Trees planted are native oak, ash, sycamore, chestnut, beech or elder. Any eco-friendly casket or covering accepted, but burial of embalmed bodies is not be permitted. Approximately £400 per grave (incl. digging; same for non-residents; £50 extra for the tree). £275 for the interment of ashes. Families can help dig and fill the grave. It costs £100 to plant a memorial tree for someone whose funeral was elsewhere. 'The exceptional views and the peace and quiet make this a perfect site for reflection' (Sadie Lynes). [Provisional Association membership requires renewal 10/11/2000.]

• [*] **(Fordingbridge)**: Mrs R. J. Baker of Bustard Farm, East Martin, Fordingbridge, Hampshire SP6 3LJ (tel 01725 519219) plans to set up a woodland burial site on farmland which backs onto Martin Down National Nature Reserve, on the Hampshire/ Dorset border. [Provisional Association membership requires renewal 21/4/2000.]

• [*] **(Gosport, Hampshire)**: Woodland burial ground planned for 2000/2001. Contact Ian Jeffery, 11 Harcourt Road, Gosport PO12 3NR (tel 023 9252 3358; e-mail: burialground@ianrjeffery.co.uk; www.ianrjeffery.co.uk). [Provisional Association membership requires renewal 10/12/2000.]

• **Hastings**: Woodland Burial, Hastings Borough Cemetery, The Ridge, Hastings, East Sussex TN34 2AE (tel 01424 781302); run by Hastings Borough

Council. A grave costs £242 (incl. digging; double for non-residents; £45 extra for use of the chapel). No plots are sold just for cremated remains, although these may be interred or strewn into existing graves. They will accept home-made, cardboard or wicker coffins and sell the Brighton cardboard coffin for £57. Family and friends can fill the grave if they wish. Graves are seeded with wild flowers and have a tree planted on them (silver birch, downy birch, rowan, crab apple, guelder rose or fastigiate hawthorn planted in rotation). 'The site is a peaceful spot on the edge of an existing copse in a quiet corner of an 80-acre cemetery, well shielded by banks and trees' (George Ford).

• **Isle of Wight**: Springwood Woodland Burials run by William Hall, Independent Funeral Directors, Winford Road, Newchurch, Sandown, Isle of Wight PO36 0JX (tel and fax 01983 868688). A single grave costs £475 (incl. digging and a choice of an oak, mountain ash or beech tree). A double grave costs £555. They will accept home-made, cardboard, or wicker coffins, and body bags or shrouds. They sell the Brighton cardboard coffin for £90 or the Alverstone coffin (which 'uses only recycled and reclaimed timber') for £300. Family and friends can help dig or fill the grave if they wish. The five-acre cemetery is in a peaceful setting. Paths lead to a small memorial garden where small bronze plaques can be placed. Extensive tree and bulb planting has taken place and there is a pond with a small marsh area. Bird, bat and kestrel boxes have been erected and a slow worm pit constructed.

• **(St Mary Bourne, Hampshire)**: A one-acre woodland burial site, to be increased in phases, planned for Breach Farm Woodlands, Breach Farm, St Mary Bourne, owned by J. Hirst & Sons. For more details contact: Mrs H. N. Whitehead, Price-Whitehead Chartered Surveyors, Forstal Farm, Tenterden, Kent TN30 7DF (tel 01580 765111; fax 765849; e-mail: B.H.Enterprises@ farming.co.uk). 'New woodland plantations border the site which lies on a gently rolling hill within Bourne countryside on the edge of the picturesque village of St Mary Bourne. Trees will be native deciduous. We aim to provide sustainable, continuous-cover woodlands in this area and throughout the country' (Helen Whitehead, Rural Consultant).

• **Nr. Sevenoaks, Kent**: A woodland burial ground as part of a small cemetery in Otford parish; run by Mrs Barbara Darby, Clerk, Otford Parish Council, School House, 21 High Street, Otford, Sevenoaks, Kent TN14 5PG (tel 01959 524808). Part of the old deer park of Otford Palace, adjacent to new woodland. Established trees include a 600-year-old oak. A grave costs £480 (incl. a native British species tree, normally planted a year after the burial; £600 for non-residents). Graves must be dug by the Parish Council's contractor, for about an extra £150. Coffins may be cardboard, wicker or wood. A small memorial stone may be placed adjacent to the tree. There is no chapel.

• **(Shamley Green, Nr. Guildford)**: A second 18-acre site to be run along the same lines as Oakfield Wood Green Burial Site (see Manningtree in East Anglia above) planned for Surrey, on land between Shamley Green and Cranleigh, near the Gaston Gate Garage. The planning application is with Waverley Borough

Council. Green Woodland Burial Services say: 'Bodies will be buried in cardboard coffins and graves marked by trees with biodegradable plaques.' All enquiries should be directed to the site agent: Peter Kincaid, Green Woodland Burial Services, 256 High Street, Dovercourt, Harwich, Essex CO12 3PA (tel 01255 503456).

• **Tenterden**: Woodland Garden Cemetery, Tenterden Cemetery, Cranbrook Road, Tenterden, Kent. (Contact and pricing information as for the Ashford site above.) A local authority site at the lower end of Tenterden Cemetery which is to be gradually established as a natural woodland. 'The area is bordered by several mature trees and adjoins open farmland with a steam railway running along the boundary. Seating has been placed in quiet areas of contemplation. A natural pond nearby further attracts wildlife' (Christine Smith).

• **(Woking)**: Woodland burial proposed for Brookwood Cemetery, Woking, Surrey GU24 OBL (tel 01483 472222). Current grave prices in the traditional cemetery are around £1500. 'We may develop a woodland burial ground in the future' (R. H. Guney, Director).

• **(Wokingham, Berkshire)**: A separate woodland burial area within an existing cemetery is set to open in June 2000; to be run by Wokingham District Council. Contact Gary Fewkes, Easthampstead Park Cemetery Manager, South Road, Nine Mile Ride, Wokingham RG40 3DW (tel 01344 420314; e-mail: cem.crem@bracknell-forest.gov.uk; web: www.bracknell-forest.gov.uk). No prices as yet. Families will be able to help dig and fill the grave. Free assistance will be offered for d-i-y funerals.

Greater London region

Including old Middlesex. See also South region. Note too that the winner of the New Natural Death Handbook Award 2000 for the Best Woodland Burial Ground in and around London is the Parkside one at Gerrards Cross and that the Best Woodland Burial Ground in the UK award went to Greenhaven near Rugby – the latter charges only £570 for everything, incl. plot, digging, coffin, tree and collection of the body from London. For both these winners see the East Midlands region. With distant sites such as these, many families hold a service locally to them and then just a couple of close relatives go on to the actual burial ground.

• **Brent**: One-acre woodland burial area within 30-acre Carpenders Park Cemetery, Oxhey Lane, Carpenders Park, Watford; run by The Cemetery Office, Brent Council Cemetery Service, Clifford Road, Alperton HA0 1AF (tel 020 8902 2385; fax 020 8795 0273; e-mail: langford@brent.gov.uk; web: www.mortbase.co.uk). Single grave spaces cost £700 (incl. digging, an indigenous tree – hawthorn, oak, rowan, field maple, beech, holly, yew, silver birch, ash, hazel, sloe, sycamore, cherry or hornbeam – and a plaque; £1050 for non-residents). £510 for the interment of ashes. Families can help with the filling of the grave but not with the digging. D-i-y funerals are permitted and advice can be offered, but they say they 'prefer funeral directors, to give a dignified burial'. Only biodegradable coffins are allowed; cardboard coffins can be supplied from £53. Wooden coffins if used must be ecologically sound and made from managed tree forest timber. A wooden plaque can be placed on the grave until the tree is planted. No horticultural chemicals are used in the woodland section. The nearby 'lawn' cemetery allows only flat plaque memorials, not headstones. Three woodland burials have taken place so far. The cemetery opened in 1998 and has 'eight acres of mature woodland, where no burials take place, two lakes and the Hartsbourne stream rolling through. Already the cemetery is a haven for wildlife. Ducks and moorhens nest on small islands in the lakes and kingfishers, jays and herons can be seen quite regularly' (Bob Langford).

• **City of London Cemetery's** woodland burial ground is at Aldersbrook Road, London E12 5DQ (tel 020 8530 2151). New graves with exclusive right of burial cost £996 (incl. digging; £601 for a second interment). Interment in a grave without exclusive burial rights (owned by the corporation, who may carry out a second interment at a later date) costs £448 (incl. digging). All graves are double graves. Ashes could be interred for £83. They accept home-made, cardboard or wicker coffins, and all coffins must be biodegradable. The site already has established trees, so they may not always plant new ones. Families may help fill the grave if they wish. Absolutely no memorials are permitted on the woodland site, although families may sponsor a bench or other memorial elsewhere in the cemetery. 'The site is attached to the existing, world-renowned City of London cemetery, whose 200-acre site has very well-kept grounds and excellent security. We are happy to advise d-i-y families' (Ian Hussain, Director).

• **(Enfield):** A woodland burial area is planned as an extension to Lavender Hill Cemetery at Strayfield Road; run by the London Borough of Enfield. A grave will cost £701 (incl. digging; extra for an oak tree; treble for non-residents). No memorials will be allowed. Ashes can be interred for £100. Free help with lowering the coffin will be offered to d-i-y families. Only cardboard coffins will be allowed. Families will be permitted to help fill, but not dig, the grave. 'The area is conservation greenbelt. Scenic and well-kept despite the poor ground conditions' (Mrs M. Vetere). For more information contact the Cemetery Registrar, London Borough of Enfield, PO Box 58, Civic Centre, Silver Street, Enfield EN1 3XJ (tel 020 8379 3767).

• **Forest Gate**: Woodland burial areas offered within Manor Park Cemetery, Sebert Road, Forest Gate, London E7 0NP (tel 020 8534 1486); run by the Manor Park Cemetery Company. A grave costs £700 (incl. digging, a tree and a small brass plaque). There are several possible areas within the cemetery to choose from. Any native British species tree can be planted. The place already contains mature trees, and has a traditional chapel with spire. There is housing adjoining the site but it is relatively quiet. Biodegradable coffins or shrouds are acceptable. Families can help to fill or dig the grave (Norman Stephens).

• **(Greenford)**: A local authority-run woodland burial ground is expected to open in 2002 in Greenford Park Cemetery, Windmill Lane, Greenford UB6. Contact Elaine Robinson, Cemetery Manager, London Borough of Ealing,

Perceval House, 14-16 Uxbridge Road, London W5 2HL (tel 020 8758 5625) for more information.

• **Hillingdon**: A woodland burial ground in a wild flower meadow with trees, with West Drayton Cemetery to one side and public open space to the other; run by the London Borough of Hillingdon. A grave costs £582 (incl. digging). Families can help fill, but not dig, the grave. Contact David Bryant, Civic Centre, Uxbridge, Middlesex UB8 1UW (tel 01895 250416) for more details.

• **(Islington)**: A woodland burial area is being discussed as part of a feasibility study for Trent Park Cemetery, Cockfosters Road, Cockfosters, also Islington Cemetery Grounds; run by The London Borough of Islington. Contact Mr D. Pryor, Islington Crematorium, High Road, East Finchley, London N2 9AG (tel 020 8883 1230) for more information.

• **(Lewisham)**: A woodland burial area planned for 2001 by The London Borough of Lewisham (Shirley Bishop, tel 020 8697 2555) for its cemetery at Grove Park, London SE12. The current price of a traditional grave is £796 (incl. digging; quadruple for non-residents).

• **Linden Grove:** Woodland burial at Nunhead Cemetery, Linden Grove, London SE15; run by Southwark Council. A half-acre woodland burial area opened in 1998 in association with the Friends of Nunhead Cemetery, extends the existing cemetery. A single grave costs £919 (incl. digging; £2750 for non-residents). £10 extra for a tree. Ashes can be interred for £98 (£291 for non-residents). Mourners may help fill the grave and assistance will be offered with d-i-y funerals at no extra cost. All types of biodegradable coffin or shroud are accepted 'if suitably covered'. 'Strictly no headstones, plastic or wire fences or any other type of memorial permitted, just a tree or shrub (with many varieties to choose from including mountain ash, ash, yew, chestnut, poplar) or seasonal bulbs (bluebell, daffodil, tulip, crocus). The area is very natural and peaceful and the staff are very helpful. The site will be maintained as a meadow when it is full' (T. M. Connor). Five burials have taken place so far. All correspondence should be to Terry Connor, Superintendent, Camberwell New Cemetery, Brenchley Gardens, London SE23 3RD (tel 020 7639 3121; fax 020 7732 3557).

• **Richmond:** The Natural Burial Area, East Sheen Cemetery, Sheen Road, Richmond, Surrey TW10 5BJ (tel 020 8876 4511; fax 020 8878 8118; web: www.richmond.gov.uk/leisure/cemeteries/cems.html); run by the London Borough of Richmond Upon Thames. Single-depth unmarked graves cost £920 (incl. digging; treble for non-residents). Biodegradable coffins are to be used in this small area of the cemetery. The cemetery staff can advise on where to buy a cardboard coffin, and they usually keep a couple in stock (cost £141). Ashes can be interred (up to eight interments in one grave plot). Metal caskets are not permitted. 'The natural burial area is a haven for wildlife and native flowers, at the edge of the cemetery between existing older-style traditional graves and the tree-lined boundary to East Sheen Common. No form of individual memorial, flowers or any other item may be placed here. Trees, shrubs, bulbs etc will be selected and planted by the cemetery's staff. Hedges and bird boxes encourage wildlife' (Natasha Mahon-Smith).

• **(Woolwich)**: 'Very tentative' plans for a woodland burial area in the future at New Woolwich Cemetery; run by Greenwich Council. No details as yet, but the plans are in the hands of Dawn Squires, the Cemeteries Supervisor (tel 020 8856 0100).

Scotland

• **(Aberdeen)**: A steering group of Friends of the Earth members, church members and interested individuals are discussing setting up a woodland burial ground near Aberdeen. Contact Paul Van Midden, Lorieneen, Bridge of Muchalls, Stonehaven, Aberdeen AB39 3RU (tel 01569 731746).

• **(Dumfries & Galloway)**: The natural death and green burial group Another Way is looking for suitable land to provide a woodland burial site in Stewartry. For more information about the proposed site and about Another Way's services contact them c/o SWEAP, 17 Castle Street, Kirkcudbright, Scotland DG6 4JA (tel 01557 331993; e-mail: sweapk@cqm.co.uk). See also Another Way's entry in the Resources Chapter.

• **(Dundee)**: A woodland burial ground to be opened adjacent to Birkhill Cemetery. The site is being landscaped and planted with trees and wild flowers, and the first interments will be late in 2000. A grave may cost about £570. Contact Gary Robertson, Dundee City Council Leisure & Parks, Floor 13, Tayside House, Dundee, Scotland DD1 3RA (tel 01382 433388).

• **Edinburgh:** Woodland Burial Ground, Costorphine Hill Cemetery, Edinburgh; run by City of Edinburgh Council Bereavement Services, Morton Hall Crematorium, Howden Hall Road, Edinburgh, Scotland EH16 6TX (tel 0131 664 4314). A grave costs £875 (incl. digging, a certificate and a tree; same for non-residents). There is a place for memorials on a pathway. They prefer biodegradable coffins, shrouds or body bags. Mourners may help fill the grave. Current graves on the edge of the site are easily accessible; however, visits to the central areas will be discouraged to allow wild flowers to grow. 'There is room for 500 graves. Silver birch trees, bluebells and wild flowers are planted. It is a quiet woodland site' (G. P. Bell).

• **(North Lanarkshire)**: A mixed woodland and traditional lairs cemetery for a 3.5-acre site in Coatbridge; to be run by North Lanarkshire local authority. For further information about the site, which may or may not allow woodland burial style graves with trees, contact Mr McCool, Cemeteries Area Manager, 101 Bank Street, Coatbridge, Scotland ML5 1ET (tel 01236 624051).

• **(Stirling)**: Stirling Council is taking a 'positive' approach to green burial by consulting the community and raising local awareness. So far they say they have had no 'negative feedback' from the public to their proposals, which include woodland burial, memorial gardens and an end to the advance selling of family lairs. For more information contact Jim McBrier, Cemeteries Services, Viewforth, Stirling, Scotland FK8 2ET (tel 01786 442559).

Eire and Northern Ireland

• **(County Cork)**: Tessa Gibson, Dromore, Bantry, West Cork, Ireland (tel 028 31724) would like to establish a woodland burial ground as a small part of thirty acres of land at the holistic centre An Sanctóir, Bawnaknockane, near the coastal village of Ballydehob, West Cork.

• [*] **(County Donegal)**: Kate Morgan of Meenagolan, Bruckless, County Donegal, Ireland (no tel) plans to establish a site in South West Donegal. [Provisional membership of the Association of Nature Reserve Burial Grounds requires renewal 23/4/2000.]

Isle of Man

• **(Isle of Man)**: Pat Kneen of Lhie Ny Greiney, Surby Mooar, Port Erin, Isle of Man IM9 6TD (tel 01624 834104) hopes to open a green burial ground on the Isle of Man. He says there are a group of people interested, but there has been no further progress.

Guernsey

• **(Guernsey)**: Plans for a woodland burial site. For more information contact Phil Sebire, Board of Administration, States of Guernsey, PO Box 43, La Charroterie, St Peter Port, Guernsey GY1 1FH (tel 01481 717000).

United States of America

• **South Carolina**: The Natural Death Centre would like to hear about any woodland burial grounds in the States. One of the first seems to be Memorial Ecosystems' 32-acre Ramsey Creek Preserve at the edge of the Blue Ridge Mountains in Oconee County, Western South Carolina, which opened in 1998. It is rather more expensive than the UK sites (at $1950 for the plot, or $2,300 incl. digging, a biodegradable casket and marker) and it allows engraved natural flat stones as memorials, rather than simply having trees. The same company plans a site for a 500-acre ranch near San Diego, California ('really pretty land, complete with panthers, golden eagles, coyotes, and a host of other bird life') and is negotiating for sites near San Francisco, Boston, Ann-Arbor/Detroit, and Atlanta; 'non-profit preserves providing cemetery functions, not cemeteries working hard to be greener' (Billy Campbell, MD). Find out more from Memorial Ecosystems, 113 Retreat Street, Westminster, SC 29693, USA (tel 001 864 647 7798; fax 001 864 647 7796; e-mail: information@memorial ecosystems.com; web: www.memorialecosystems.com). See also the detailed coverage of this site in the Natural Death Centre's book 'Last Aid Manual', available for £5-95 incl. p&p (tel 020 8208 2853).

Chapter 7

Good Funeral
Directors

Unless otherwise stated, you can assume that all the funeral directors in this nationwide guide provide an à la carte service and will, for instance, sell you just a fully-fitted coffin (for less than £250) without your having to use any of their other services. Abbreviations in bold are as follows:

FD = Funeral director

• **✪✪✪** = Winner of a New Natural Death Handbook Award 2000.

Abbreviations for professional associations are as follows:

BIFD = British Institute of Funeral Directors
BIE = British Institute of Embalmers
CFSA = Co-operative Funeral Services Association
IAFD = Irish Association of Funeral Directors
FOS = Funeral Ombudsman Scheme
FSC = Funeral Services Council
MBIE = Member of the British Institute of Embalmers
NAFD = National Association of Funeral Directors
NAMM = National Association of Memorial Masons
NAPFP = National Association for Pre-Paid Funeral Plans
SAIF = Society of Allied and Independent Funeral Directors

Listings are by region, and then by town within the region, except in the Greater London region, which has not been further subdivided. Here services are listed alphabetically. Please write to The Natural Death Centre (20 Heber Road, London NW2 6AA, tel 020 8208 2853; fax 020 8452 6434; e-mail: rhino@dial.pipex.com) with your experience of using the services of these or other funeral directors, whether positive or negative, and including as much detail as possible; please add if you wish to nominate them for a future Award,. Our listings are otherwise based on information given to us by the services themselves – the name of the informant is given wherever possible.

The North West

Comprising Cumbria, Lancashire, Manchester, Sefton, Wirral, Liverpool, Knowsley, St Helens, Wigan, Bolton, Bury, Rochdale, Salford, Trafford, Manchester, Oldham, Tameside, Stockport and Cheshire.

• **FD Blackpool**: D. Hollowell and Sons, Devonshire House, 287 Devonshire Road, Blackpool FY2 OTW (tel 01253 355663); also at Highfield Funeral Home, 497 Lytham Road, Blackpool FY4 1RE (tel 01253 408886). Cheapest fully-fitted coffin only: £50 (delivery locally free). Cold storage only: Yes, £20 per day. Body transport only: No. Advice for d-i-y: Yes, £15 per hour. Basic funeral: £716, 'including hearse £375, crematorium £185, minister £74 and medical fees £82'. 'We carry out about 20 baby funerals per year with no charge on our side. There is no charge for children to the age of 18' (Andrew Hollowell). Prepaid plan: Golden Charter. Member of FSC.

• **FD Bolton**: Fulton Funeral Directors, 81 Mason Street, Horwich, Lancashire BL6 5QP (tel 01204 694999). Cheapest fully-fitted coffin only: £65 (delivery locally free). Cold storage only: Yes, £30 per day. Body transport only: Yes. Advice for d-i-y: Yes, '£100 flat fee for all help and guidance required'. Basic funeral: £605 – or 'about £400 for cremation with cardboard coffin' (disbursements extra). 'The decor and furnishings are just as you would find in a normal, comfortable domestic house, we have gone to great lengths to get away from what most funeral "homes" aspire to. Where the deceased is female, my wife takes on the embalming and preparation. We have been trading independently since 1998. We are prepared to carry out separate parts of the funeral arrangements as individual items, an aspect of our service that is particularly welcomed by those families wishing to carry out some or most of the details themselves' (John and Samantha Fulton). Prepaid plan: Perfect Assurance. Member of NAFD and BIE.

• **FD Bury**: The Bury Metropolitan Borough Council has an arrangement with Hamers, 7 Rochdale Road, Bury (tel 0161 797 7133) whereby residents can obtain a funeral for £325 (with disbursements extra – burial, for instance, costs an extra £573, cremation an extra 297).

• **FD Carlisle**: John Simpson (Carlisle) Ltd, 1 Blencowe Street, Carlisle, Cumbria CA2 5XP (tel 01228 512471). Cheapest fully-fitted coffin only: £60 (delivery locally £35). Cold storage: Not available. Body transport only: Yes, £35 locally by estate car. Advice for d-i-y people: Yes, 'no charge if providing coffin'. Basic funeral: £520 (disbursements extra) – 'although we prefer to discuss the variety of options'. 'We have carried out woodland burials with the family taking over at the graveside. We will provide as little or as much help as required. Our family business is now into its fourth generation' (Mark Simpson). No prepaid plan. Member of no association.

• **FD Crewe**: The Council has started a scheme called the Local Funeral where you can phone 01270 212643 (or see www.crewe.nantwich.gov.uk/worksservices) and find out the price of the least expensive funeral offered by local funeral directors. In Nottingham, the introduction of a similar scheme has caused prices to drop by a quarter.

• **FD Crewe**: South Cheshire Funeral Services, 6 Brierley Street, Crewe, Cheshire CW1 2AY (tel 01270 582628). Cheapest fully-fitted coffin only: £90 (delivery locally £10). Cold storage only: No. Body transport only: Yes. Advice for d-i-y: Yes, £30 per hour. Basic funeral: £447 (disbursements extra). Does not provide a full price list. 'The same funeral director who interviews the client at home, prepares the coffin and the deceased, digs the grave if required and directs the funeral' (C. L. Harthern). Prepaid plan: Golden Charter. Member of BIE.

• ✪✪✪ **FD Liverpool**: Graham J. Clegg Independent Funeral Service, 7 Dover Road, Maghull, Liverpool L31 5JB (tel 0151 520 3330). Cheapest fully-fitted coffin only: £60 (delivery locally free). Cold storage only: Yes, no charge. Body transport only: Yes. Advice for d-i-y: Yes, no charge. Basic funeral: £500 (disbursements extra). Prepaid plan: Golden Charter. Member of SAIF. (Graham Clegg). Winner of the New Natural Death Handbook Award 2000 for the Best Funeral Director in the North West.

• **FD Manchester**: R. Pepperdine & Sons Ltd, Alexandra House, 5 Manchester Road, Chorlton-cum-Hardy, Manchester M21 9JG (tel 0161 881 5363; web: www.pepperdine.co.uk). Cheapest fully-fitted coffin only: £115 (delivery locally £25). Cold storage only: Yes, £25 per day. Body transport only: Yes, hearse and driver £140. Advice for d-i-y: Yes, £40 per hour. Basic funeral: £695 or £595 using a cardboard coffin (disbursements in both cases extra). 'Independent family firm. Our service is excellent value for money and flexible. What a family wants, a family gets' (Frank Barrett). Prepaid plan: Chosen Heritage, Personal Choice, Perfect Assurance. Member of NAFD.

• **FD Manchester**: S. Wellens and Sons Ltd, 121 Long Street, Middleton, Manchester M24 6DL (tel 0161 643 2677; fax 0161 653 7085). Also branches at: 347 Hollinwood Avenue, New Moston, Manchester M40 OJX (tel 0161 681 4377); and 313 Washbrook, Chadderton, Oldham OL9 8JL (tel 0161 624 4132). Cheapest fully-fitted coffin only: £160 VAT extra (delivery locally 'probably free'). Cold storage only: Yes, £15 per day. Body transport only: Yes, from £27-51. Advice for d-i-y: Yes, £35 to £50 per hour. Basic funeral: £570 (disbursements extra). 'Proudly an independent family firm, established 1870 We have cardboard coffins in stock. We provide a full bereavement support service' (Norman Wellens). Prepaid plan: Golden Charter. Member of NAFD, SAIF and BIE.

• **FD St Helens**: The St Helens Council has an agreement with the Co-op (tel 01744 23675) to provide a municipal funeral for local residents, whereby cremation costs £663 and burial costs £674, both prices including disbursements.

• **FD Stockport**: A 'Civic Funeral Service' is provided by the local authority for residents, run by the United North West Co-operative Society (tel 0161 432 0818). They charge £874 for a cremation including disbursements and £1,168 for a burial in a new grave, again including disbursements.

• **FD Wigan**: Edwards Funeral Directors Ltd, Holmwood, Dicconson Terrace, Wigan WN1 2AA (tel 01942 821215). Cheapest fully-fitted coffin only: £125 (delivery locally £20; nationally 75p per mile). Cold storage only: Yes, £20 per day. Body transport only: Yes. Advice for d-i-y: Yes, £20 per hour. Basic funeral: £715 (including fees for doctors, minister and cremation). Municipal funeral service for local residents only: cremation for £715 (including disbursements) and burial for £940 (including disbursements and opening a new grave). 'Our family has been associated with quality funeral service in the town for over 110 years' (R. B. Edwards). Prepaid plan: Golden Charter. Member of SAIF.

The North East

Comprising Northumberland, Newcastle-Upon-Tyne, North Tyneside, Gateshead, South Tyneside, Sunderland, Durham, Hartlepool, Stockton-On-Tees, Middlesbrough, Redcar, North Yorkshire, York, East Riding of Yorkshire, Kingston-Upon-Hull, Bradford, Leeds, Calderdale, Kirklees, Wakefield, Barnsley, Sheffield, Rotherham, Doncaster, North Lincolnshire, North East Lincolnshire and Lincolnshire.

• **FD Dewsbury**: George Brooke Ltd funeral directors, 27 Bradford Road, Dewsbury, West Yorkshire (tel 01924 454476; e-mail: georgebrooke@email.com). Cheapest fully-fitted coffin only: £255 (delivery locally £35). The firm provides a fully-itemised price list. Cold storage only: Yes, £12-50 per day. Body transport only: Yes. Advice for d-i-y: Yes, 'no charge, we automatically help'. 'We are a small family firm and we try to fulfil a family's requests. We have cardboard coffins in stock' (Helen Wilson). Prepaid plan: Golden Charter. Member of NAFD, BIFD.

• **FD Grimsby**: Kettle Ltd funeral directors, 135 Granville St, Grimsby, N. E. Lincs DN32 9PB (tel 01472 355395); also 110 Kidgate, Louth, Lincs LN11 9BX (tel 01507 600710). Cheapest fully-fitted coffin only: £210 (delivery locally free, nationally 50p per mile). Cold storage only: Yes, £15 per day. Body transport only: Yes (hearse for funeral £95). Advice for d-i-y: Yes, £10 per hour. Basic funeral: £705 (disbursements extra). 'We even supplied handles, plate and linings to a client who had made a coffin for his mother's funeral' (Michael Chevins). Prepaid plan: Golden Charter. Member of NAFD, BIFD and SAIF.

• **F.D. Harrogate**: W. Bowers funeral director, Birstwith Road, Hampsthwaite, Harrogate HG3 2EU (tel 01423 770258; fax 01423 772474; e-mail: Rogerbowers@w-bowers.co.uk; web: www.w-bowers.co.uk). Cheapest fully-fitted coffin only: £95 (delivery £20). Cold storage only: Yes, £8 per day. Body transport only: Yes, £85 for the first 10 miles. Advice for d-i-y: Yes, £25 per hour. Basic funeral: £1,100 (including fees to crematorium, doctors and clergy). Prepaid plans: Golden Charter and Funeral Plans Ltd. Member of no association, although a member of the Small Business Federation. 'We seek to meet individual requirements with sensitivity, care and support. We have been awarded an Oscar for the most customer-focused business by Barclays Bank' (Roger Bowers).

• **FD Hebburn**: Mr Peter Kerrigan, Tynedale Funeral Services, Victoria House, Prince Consort Road, Hebburn, Tyne and Wear NE31 1BE (tel 0191 4281018; e-mail: tfspeter@aol.com.uk). See South Shields below for details.

• **FD Huddersfield**: D. J. Screen & Sons, 222 Bradford Road, Huddersfield HD1 6LJ (tel 01484 452220). Cheapest fully-fitted coffin only: £98 (delivery locally free, nationally 50p per mile). Cold storage only: Yes, £5 per day. Body transport only: Yes Advice for d-i-y: Yes, no charge. Basic funeral: £500 (disbursements extra). 'As a small local family business, we try to assist, barter if required, we are not stuck to fixed prices' (Denis Screen). Prepaid plan: Golden Charter. Dip. F. D.

• **FD Lincoln**: Lincoln Co-operative Funeral Services, 12 Portland Street, Lincoln LN5 7JX (tel 01522 534971). They also have offices in: Gainsborough (tel 01427 612131); Holbeach (Clubley's, tel 01406 422333); Horncastle (M. England, tel 01507 523385); Sleaford (tel 01529 306311); and Spalding (Clubley's, tel 01775 723199). Cheapest fully-fitted coffin only: £195, including a gown (delivery locally free). Cold storage only: Yes, £15 per day. Body transport only: Yes. Advice for d-i-y: Yes, £20 per hour. Basic funeral: £630 (disbursements extra). 'We are a small independent co-op society offering a personal service' (David Bernley). Prepaid plan: Co-operative Funeral Bond. Members of the local society automatically get up to £300 off the funeral price. Member of FSC and FOS.

• **FD Newcastle-on-Tyne**: Phillips Funeral Service, Acron House, 309 Salters Road, Gosforth, Newcastle-on-Tyne NE3 4HN (tel 0191 284 0777). Cheapest fully-fitted coffin only: £135 (delivery locally £30). Cold storage only: 'We do not have cold storage but charge £20 per day to hold a body in our chapel of rest.' Body transport only: Yes, estate car £40, hearse £60. Advice for d-i-y: Yes, £20 per hour. Basic funeral: £520 (disbursements extra); but a 'simple green service would cost from approximately £400, then add £220 for burial for residents of Hexham – £440 for non-residents – in the Hexham woodland burial ground'). 'We are the only independent family funeral service in North Newcastle, for a five mile radius. We advise on green issues and how families can take a more active role in the arrangements themselves' (Philip Harrison). Prepaid plan: Golden Charter. Member of SAIF ('joining in 2000').

• **FD Sheffield**: B & C. Funeral Service, 51 Suffolk Road, Sheffield S2 4BX (tel 0114 276 0211). Parent company: Sheffield Co-operative Society. Cheapest fully-fitted coffin only: £110 (delivery locally £40, nationally 45p per mile). Cold storage only: Yes, £10 per day. Body transport only: Yes. Advice for d-i-y: Yes, £25 per hour or part-hour. Basic funeral: £350 (disbursements extra). 'We work within a 15 mile radius of the city centre at no extra charge' (M. R. Bratton). Prepaid plan: Funeral insurance with vouchers. Member of FSC, CFSA.

• **✪✪✪ FD Sheffield**: Peace Funerals, Gleadless Mount, off Ridgeway Road, Sheffield S12 2LN (tel 0114 253 0505 or 08457 697 822; e-mail: peacefuner@aol.com). Cheapest fully-fitted coffin only: £135 – cardboard £85 (delivery locally free). Cold storage only: Yes, £12 per day. Body transport only: Yes, £50. Advice for d-i-y: Yes, £30 per hour. Basic funeral: £600 (disbursements extra). 'We have our own design of willow basket-work coffins and plain and painted cardboard coffins. We are concerned with empowering the bereaved and providing any funeral choice whatsoever as long as it is legal. We run two woodland burial grounds (see Chapter 6) and have provided woodland burial at over 20 different sites across the UK. We arrange many secular funerals (which we help families to design and implement) and we originated the "Railway Funerals" concept' (John Mallatratt). Prepaid plan: Golden Leaves. Member of no association. (Eds: The Natural Death Centre has received more positive feedback from the public about this firm than any other in the UK). Winner of the New Natural Death Handbook Award 2000 for the Best Funeral Director in the North East.

• **FD South Shields**: Mr Peter Kerrigan, Tynedale Funeral Services, Tynedale House, Stanhope Road, South Shields, Tyne and Wear NE33 4TB (tel 0191 4550904; e-mail: tfspeter@aol.com.uk). Cheapest fully-fitted coffin only: £190 (delivery locally £10, nationally negotiable). Cold storage only: Yes, £10 per day. Body transport only: Yes, £40 one-off payment. Advice for d-i-y: Yes, £15 per hour. Basic funeral: £590 (disbursements extra). 'Full horse-drawn hearse from £450' (Peter Kerrigan). Prepaid plan: Golden Charter. Member of no association.

• **FD Thornaby**: Undertaken With Love, Unit 1, Mandale Road, Thornaby, Stockton-on-Tees TS17 6AW (tel 01642 606789). Cheapest fully-fitted coffin only: £120 (delivery locally free). Storage only: Yes, £15 per day ('not refrigerated'). Body transport only: Yes, from £35. Advice for d-i-y: Yes, £15 per hour. Basic funeral: £890 (including crematorium fees and officiant's fees); or a 'Simple Dignity Funeral' for £590 (including cardboard coffin, crematorium fees, transportation – not in a hearse – and a committal-only ceremony conducted by Martin Cole). Woodland burial at Mowthorpe Garden of Rest in the Howardian Hills or Carlisle cemetery for £1,080 including the grave and digging. 'We will always advise out clients of lower cost options available. We encourage the public to obtain at least three estimates before accepting the final written one. If any person is in genuine need, we will carry out a simple dignified funeral at cost price' (Martin Cole). Prepaid plan: Golden Charter. Member of no association. (Eds: Their published leaflets, whilst generally helpful, are incorrect in several particulars with reference to burial on private land burial – for which topic, the information in the present book is more reliable.)

Wales

Comprising Flintshire, Wrexham, Denbighshire, Aberconwy and Colwyn, Anglesey, Caernarfonshire and Merionethshire, Powys, Cardiganshire, Pembrokeshire, Carmarthenshire, Swansea, Neath and Port Talbot, Bridgend, Rhondda Cynon Taff, Vale of Glamorgan, Merthyr Tydfil, Caerphilly, Cardiff, Blaenau Gwent, Torfaen, Newport, Monmouthshire.

• **✪✪✪ FD Anglesey**: W. O. Williams, Tan Graig, Llanedwen, Anglesey, North Wales LL61 6PX (tel 01248 430312). Cheapest fully-fitted coffin only: £87-50, VAT extra (includes gown; delivery locally £10). Cold storage only: Yes, £14 the first night, £7 per day thereafter. Body transport only: Yes (£30 plus 55p per mile). Advice for d-i-y: Yes, £25. Offers what it terms a 'D-i-y Funeral' for £318-50 (disbursements extra) where 'all the forms and certificates are collected and delivered by the client, there is no embalming included and the client provides own bearers (or pays extra). A fully fitted coffin is supplied and a hearse for up to 20 miles. Reductions made for unrequired services' (W. O. Williams). Prepaid plan: Golden Charter. Member of BIE. Winner of the New Natural Death Handbook Award 2000 for the Best Funeral Director in Wales.

• **FD Cardiff**: A local authority funeral service for Cardiff residents is provided by the firm D. Caesar Jones, 55 Pantbach Road, Rhiwbina, Cardiff (tel 029

20522 644), who charges £390, excluding disbursements. Add to this the crematorium fee of £213 and the doctors' fees of £82. Burial costs £357. Please note that this is an SCI firm, and that in general the Natural Death Centre encourages the use of small independent firms such as those which are members of SAIF.

• **FD Cardiff**: J Pidgeon and Son, 539 Cowbridge Road East, Victoria Park, Cardiff (029 20226 604). Price: £625, excluding disbursements. Add to this the crematorium fee of £213 (non-residents £366) or the cemetery fee of £391-25 (non-residents £782-50); the officiant fee of £38 (plus) and the doctors' fee of £82. They will cut costs to meet small budgets. They will not supply coffin only but will give wholesaler details. Cold storage only: £8 per day. Advice for d-i-y: Yes. 'We have cardboard coffins available, but think our recovered wood chipping Cotswold coffin is more environmentally friendly' (John Pidgeon). Prepaid plan: 'Own plan.' Member of NAFD, SAID and FOS.

• **FD Cardiff:** Green Willow Funerals Ltd, 33 St Isan Road, Cardiff, Wales CF4 4LU (tel 029 2046 2100). See Newport for details.

• **FD Newport:** Green Willow Funerals Ltd, Pillmawr Road, Newport, Wales NP20 6WN (tel 01633 855350; e-mail: john@bettles.fsbusiness.co.uk). Cheapest fully-fitted coffin only: £140 – or £110 for a cardboard coffin (delivery free within 20 miles). Cold storage only: Not available. Body transport only: Yes. Advice for d-i-y: Yes, no charge. Basic funeral: £595 (excluding disbursements). 'The company specialises in tayloring the arrangements for a funeral service to meet the total needs of the family. We can give a full estimate by phone or by post' (John Bettles). Prepaid plan: Golden Charter. Member of no association.

• **FD Tonypandy**: Appletree Funeral Services, Appletree Road, Tonypandy, Rhondda CF40 1JH, Wales (tel 01443 683896); Appletree is the trading name of DCT (Cymru) Ltd. Cheapest fully-fitted coffin only: £125 (delivery locally free) – 'Stock coffin, a cardboard or cheaper coffin would be purchased as a special order if required.' Cold storage only: Not available. Body transport only: Yes, £70 for hearse or limousine for a local funeral. Advice for d-i-y: Yes, first hour free of charge then £45 per hour. Basic funeral: £665 (including hearse and limousine; disbursements and embalming extra). 'We are a new business prepared to accommodate the individual needs of our clients. A full price list is being developed. We are prepared to work within a limited budget, if required, or to offer a funeral ceremony tailored to individual needs' (D. C. Thomas). No prepaid plan. Member of no association.

West Midlands

Comprising Shropshire, Staffordshire, Wolverhampton, Walsall, Dudley, Sandwell, Birmingham, Solihull, Coventry, Hereford and Worcester, Gloucestershire.

• **FD Birmingham**: The Green Funeral Company Ltd, 286 Church Road, Sheldon, Birmingham B26 3YH (tel 0121 6930204). Cheapest fully-fitted coffin only: £70 (including crematorium handles and plate, delivery locally free). Cold storage only: Yes, £10 per day. Body transport only: Yes. Advice for d-i-y: Yes, no charge. Basic funeral: £400 within 50 mile radius of Birmingham (disbursements extra); beyond 50 miles there is a slight additional charge. 'We provide traditional and green funerals in either formal or informal styles all at low cost' (Jon Walker). Prepaid plan: available shortly. Member of NAFD.

• **FD Birmingham**: Jonathan Walker Funeral Directors Ltd, 288 Church Road, Sheldon, Birmingham B26 3YH (tel 0121 7428888). Cheapest fully-fitted coffin only: £70 (including crematorium handles and plate, delivery locally free). Cold storage only: Yes, £10 per day. Body transport only: Yes. Advice for d-i-y: Yes, no charge. Basic funeral: £400 within 50 mile radius of Birmingham (disbursements extra); beyond 50 miles there is a slight additional charge. 'We provide a range of services specifically geared to "what the family wants" rather than pre-packaged funerals. We also provide advice on burial grounds and family organised funerals at no charge' (Jon Walker). Prepaid plan: available shortly. Member of NAFD.

• **FD Birmingham**: Samuel James and Sons, 313 Foxhollies Road, Acocks Green, Birmingham B27 7PS (tel 0121 7082766). Cheapest fully-fitted coffin only: £98 (delivery locally free). Cold storage only: Yes, £4-99 per day. Body transport only: Yes. Advice for d-i-y: Yes, no charge. Basic funeral: £1,200 (including disbursements); £700 (excluding disbursements). 'We opened November 1999. Price lists still to be printed. As a small and new company we try to give the best personal service possible' (T. James & T. Johnson). Prepaid plan: Golden Leaves. Member of no association.

• ✪✪✪ **FD Cheltenham**: Beechwood Funeral Services, 66 Albion Street, Cheltenham, Gloucestershire GL52 2RW (tel 01242 228208; also 01452 722131; fax 01242 579045). They have another branch at 102 Bristol Road, Quedgeley, Gloucestershire GL2 4NA (tel 01452 722131). Cheapest fully-fitted coffin only: £60 (delivery locally £10, nationally negotiable). Cold storage only: Yes, £10 per day. Body transport only: Yes (no fixed price). Advice for d-i-y: Yes, £10 per hour. Basic funeral: £700 (including crematorium and chapel). 'Family business, happy to give concessions where needed. We also have a special "all inclusive" package for £980 – details on application – which covers everything' (Stephen Smith). Prepaid plan: Golden Charter. Member of SAIF. (Eds: We receive positive feedback from the public about this firm.) Winner of the New Natural Death Handbook Award 2000 for the Best Funeral Director in and around the West Midlands.

• **FD Cirencester**: Cowley & Son Ltd, Triangle House, 62 Victoria Road, Cirencester, Gloucestershire GL7 1ES (tel 01285 653298). Cheapest fully-fitted coffin only: £120 (delivery locally £10, nationally negotiable). Cold storage only: Yes, £10 per day. Body transport only: Yes, £50 minimum. Advice for d-i-y: Yes, £50 all in. Basic funeral: £595 (disbursements extra). 'We will do anything the client requires. We are also the main importers of the Peacebox Eulogy coffins into the UK' (Robert Orford). Prepaid plan: Golden Charter. Member of SAIF and NAFD.

• **FD Coventry**: Henry Ison & Sons (Coventry) Ltd, 76-78 Binley Road, Stoke, Coventry CV3 1FQ (tel 024 7645 8665; e-mail: bdpowell@csi.com). They have another branch at 49 Allersley Old Road, Chapel Fields, Coventry CU5 8BU (tel 024 7671 3643). Cheapest fully-fitted coffin only: £135 (delivery locally free). Cold storage only: Yes, £25 per day. Body transport only: Yes, £100 for a hearse. Advice for d-i-y: Yes, £65 per hour. Basic funeral: £585 (disbursements extra). 'A Christian firm offering the highest standards' (B. Powell). Prepaid plan: Golden Charter. Member of SAIF and NAFD.

• **FD Dursley**: L. W. Clutterbuck, 24/26 High Street, Cam, Dursley, Gloucestershire GL11 5LE (tel 01453 542754). Cheapest fully-fitted coffin only: £115, VAT extra (delivery locally £13-60, VAT extra, nationally £13-60 per hour, VAT extra, for the driver, plus 31p per mile). Cold storage only: Yes, £4-99 per day. Body transport only: Yes (no fixed price). Advice for d-i-y: Yes, £13-60 per hour. Basic funeral: 'Funerals are not sold as packages; we start with nought and build up.' 'Family-run, caring service' (K. L. Clutterbuck). Prepaid plan: Golden Charter. Member of no association.

• **FD Nailsworth**: Fred Stevens Funeral Directors, Newmarket Road, Nailsworth, Gloucestershire GL6 ODQ (tel 01453 832188). Cheapest fully-fitted coffin only: £140 (delivery locally £15). Cold storage only: Yes, £8 per day. Body transport only: Yes (private ambulance £60; hearse and driver only – £132). Advice for d-i-y: Yes, no charge. Basic funeral: £740 (disbursements extra). 'We are an independent and family-run company' (J. J. Baker). Prepaid plan: Perfect Assurance. Member of NAFD.

• **FD Stroud**: Lansdown Funeral Service Ltd, 64 Slad Road, Stroud, Gloucestershire GL5 1QU (tel 01453 762276). All other details as for Fred Stevens Ltd (see Nailsworth above) which owns it. Member of NAFD and SAIF.

• **FD Tamworth**: Co-operative Funeral Service, The Mews, Upper Gungate, Tamworth, Staffordshire B79 7NZ (tel 01827 62094). Run by the Tamworth Co-operative Society Ltd which also has offices at: 68 Station Street, Atherstone (tel 01827 712105); 34 High Street, Uttoxeter (tel 01889 565561); and 107 Granville Street, Woodville (tel 01283 217237). Cheapest fully-fitted coffin only: £99 (delivery locally free). Cold storage only: Yes, £5 per day. Body transport only: Yes, £84. Advice for d-i-y: Yes, no charge. Basic funeral: £742 (disbursements extra). 'We are a small independent co-op society offering a personal service' (Amanda Woodward). Prepaid plan: Tamworth Co-op Funeral Bond. Member of FSC.

• **FD Telford**: Wrekin Funeral Services, 6 Whitcurch Road, Wellington, Telford TF1 3AG (tel 01952 251125). Cheapest fully-fitted coffin only: £115, VAT extra (delivery locally £13-60, VAT extra, nationally £13-60 per hour, VAT extra, for the driver, plus 31p per mile). Cold storage only: Yes, £10 per day. Body transport only: Yes, £60 locally. Advice for d-i-y: Yes, no charge. Basic funeral: £595 (disbursements extra). 'We are concerned to meet the needs of the Natural Death Centre and others concerned about current funeral directing and have complete price transparency and individual pricing of components. We provide a free guidance leaflet on independent funerals. We abide by the Charter for the Bereaved' (Suzanne Helm). Prepaid plan: Golden Charter. Member of no association as yet.

• **FD Tutbury**: Green Undertakings UK Ltd, 40 Monk Street, Tutbury, Staffordshire DE13 9NA (tel 01283 815 992 or 01283 521 104; fax 01283 815 992; e-mail: bio.coffins@mcmail.com; web: www.eco.coffins.mcmail.com). Cheapest fully-fitted coffin only: £50 (delivery within 10 miles free). 'We have a complete range of coffins from the basic cremation casket at £20, through a chip casket with rope handles at £43, the basic Celtic (cardboard) Casket at £55, to oak veneered at £70, wicker caskets, stretchers, etc.' Cold storage only: Yes, £5 per day. Body transport only: Yes. Advice for d-i-y: Yes. Basic funeral: £300 (with cardboard coffin, disbursements extra) or £799 at Bretby crematorium (including 'cocoon' outer coffin plus inner cardboard coffin). 'We offer complete choice and not the mysteries and myths perpetuated by contemporary funeral directors. We are opposed to the stereotype, production line funerals which dominate 99% of arrangements offered by funeral directors' (Alan Goldingay). Prepaid plan: 'Own plan, Final Security, in conjunction with NatWest. Client retains control of account and interest.' Member of no association. (Eds: This firm is not to be confused with Green Undertakings of Watchet Ltd in Somerset.)

• **FD Walsall**: Roy Quinton Funeral Directors, 677 Bloxwich Road, Leamore, Walsall, West Midlands WS3 2BD (tel 01922 496800). Cheapest fully-fitted coffin only: £105. Cold storage only: Yes, £30 per day. Body transport only: Yes. Advice for d-i-y: Yes, £30 per hour. Basic funeral: £610 (disbursements extra). 'Our company is a family business, here to meet our clients' needs' (B. Quinton). Prepaid plan: Golden Charter. Member of FSC.

East Midlands

Comprising Derbyshire, Nottinghamshire, Leicestershire, Warwickshire, Northamptonshire, Bedfordshire, Oxfordshire, Buckinghamshire.

• **FD Amersham**: H. C. Grimstead Ltd, 10 Hill Avenue, Amersham, Buckinghamshire HP6 5BG (tel 01494 434393). They offer a cheap basic funeral for £410, disbursements extra – their 'Green Funeral Option' with a cardboard coffin. See Grimstead in the London region, below, for details.

• **FD Beaconsfield**: H. C. Grimstead Ltd, Tilbury House, Shepherds Lane, Beaconsfield, Buckinghamshire HP9 2DU (tel 01494 672668). They offer a cheap basic funeral for £410 (disbursements extra) – their 'Green Funeral Option' with a cardboard coffin. See Grimstead in the London region, below, for details.

• **FD Biggleswade**: Woodman & Son, a branch of Lodge Bros., at 3 Market Square, Biggleswade, Bedfordshire SG18 8AP (tel 01767 315700; web: www.lodgebros.co.uk). See Lodge Bros. in the London region, below, for details.

• **FD Faringdon**: A. E. Baker and Sons Ltd, 5 Park Road, Faringdon, Oxfordshire SN7 7BP (tel 01367 240572; e-mail: geoff@deadman.ghound.net). Cheapest fully-fitted coffin only: £85 (delivery locally £10). Cold storage only: Yes, £10.

Body transport only: Yes. Advice for d-i-y: Yes, £8 per hour. Basic funeral: £660 (disbursements extra). 'Established 1907. We do as much or as little as our clients require' (Geoff Evans). Prepaid plan: Golden Charter. Member of SAIF.
• **FD Nr. Gerrards Cross**: H. C. Grimstead Ltd, Churchfield Lodge, Churchfield Road, Chalfont St Peter, near Gerrards Cross, Buckinghamshire SL9 9EW (tel 01753 891200). They offer a cheap basic funeral (their 'Green Funeral Option' with a cardboard coffin) for £410 (disbursements extra) – . See Grimstead in the London region, below, for details.
• **FD High Wycombe**: G. Smith Ltd, 7 The Green, Woburn Green, High Wycombe HP10 0EE (tel 01628 523 566). Cheapest fully-fitted coffin only: £195 (delivery locally free; nationally courier rates). Body transport only: Yes, £90 per vehicle. Advice for d-i-y: Yes, token fee. Basic funeral: £450 (disbursements extra). 'We will try to fulfil the family's wishes' (Ron Allen, Manager). Prepaid plan: Dignity Plan. Parent company SCI-UK. Member of FSC.
• **FD Luton**: Neville Funeral Service Ltd, Neville House, Marsh Road, Leagrove, Luton LU3 2RZ (tel 01582 490005; web: www.neville-funeral-service.co.uk). Cheapest fully-fitted coffin only: £150 (delivery locally free). Cold storage only: Yes, price on application. Body transport only: Yes. Advice for d-i-y: Yes (free advice). Basic funeral: £615 (disbursements extra). 'We are a family business in a local tradition and offer our clients the opportunity to plan the sort of funeral they want' (Peter Aspinall). Prepaid plan: Chiltern Plan. Member of NAFD and BIE.
• **FD New Mills**: Jeremy Unsworth Funeral Service, 67 Church Road, New Mills, High Peak, Derbyshire (tel 01663 742772; e-mail: j.unsworth@talk21.com). Cheapest fully-fitted coffin only: £180 (delivery locally free). Cold storage only: No. Body transport only: Yes. Advice for d-i-y: No. Basic funeral: £600 (disbursements extra). 'We are here to please' (Jeremy Unsworth). Prepaid plan: Golden Charter. Member of SAIF.
• **FD Nottingham**: The council runs an excellent free scheme called the Nottingham Funeral where you can phone 0115 915 2340 and find out the cheapest funeral director in Nottingham and a list of the others. The cheapest funeral price has dropped as a result from £1,000 to £689 – a price that includes a following car and disbursements.
• **FD Nottingham**: A. W. Lymn, Robin Hood House, Robin Hood Street, Nottingham NG3 1GF (tel 0115 950 5875). Their 13 other offices are: Arnold (tel 0115 967 6777); Beeston (tel 0115 922 0433); Bingham (tel 01949 837211); Bulwell (tel 0115 979 4944); Carlton (tel 0115 961 6180); Clifton (tel 0115 945 6232); Derby (tel 01332 348800); Hucknall (tel 0115 968 0737); Long Eaton (tel 0115 946 3093); Mansfield (tel 01623 623765); Radcliffe (tel 0115 933 2257); Ruddington (tel 01115 921 1075); and West Bridgford (tel 0115 969 6006). Cheapest fully-fitted coffin only: £135, or cardboard £105 (delivery locally £15). Cold storage only: Yes, £5 per day. Body transport only: Yes. Advice for d-i-y: Yes, £140 flat fee. Basic funeral: £710 (disbursements extra). A 'Direct Cremation' is also available for £420 (cardboard coffin, no mourners, no

funeral ceremony, closed vehicle, undisclosed date and time at local crematorium, with cremated remains left in the crematorium grounds). 'Family owned and managed. We encourage distinctive funerals. We are specialists in woodland burials. Fully itemised pricing allows the client to select a number of different options. Many of the coffins are produced locally' (Nigel Lymn Rose). Prepaid plan: A. W. Lymn Prepaid Funerals, Chosen Heritage and Golden Charter. Member of NAFD.

• **☻☻☻ FD Rushden**: A. Abbott & Sons (Rushden) Ltd, Bedford Road, Rushden, Northamptonshire NN10 OLZ (tel 01933 312142 or 410365; fax 01933 410500; e-mail: abbot_funerals@yahoo.co.uk; web: www.abbot funerals.co.uk). Cheapest fully-fitted coffin only: £200 (delivery locally £25; nationally by mileage). Cold storage only: Yes, price negotiable. Body transport only: Yes, £70. Advice for d-i-y: Yes, fee negotiable. Basic funeral: £990 (disbursements extra). 'Family owned and operated. Full bespoke service' (M. Abott). Prepaid plan: Golden Charter. Member of NAFD and SAIF. Winner of the New Natural Death Handbook Award 2000 for the Best Funeral Director in the East Midlands.

• **FD Uppingham**: E. M. Dorman, 10 Main Street, Bisbrooke, Uppingham, Rutland LE15 9EP (tel 01572 823976). Cheapest fully-fitted coffin only: £85 (delivery locally 'at a negotiable price'). Cold storage only: Yes, £11 per day. Body transport only: Yes. Advice for d-i-y: Yes, £12 per hour. Basic funeral: £480 (disbursements extra). 'As a small family-owned funeral director, all arrangements are carried out by myself. It is a family concern that has served the community for over 150 years' (E. M. Dorman). Prepaid plan: Golden Charter. Member of SAIF.

• **FD Whaley Bridge**: J. Williamson Funeral Services, 1 Market Street, Whaley Bridge, Derbyshire (tel 01663 732064; e-mail: j.unsworth@talk21.com). Run by Jeremy Unsworth Funeral Service, see New Mills above for details..

• **FD Winslow**: Heritage & Sons, 63 High Street, Winslow, Buckinghamshire MK18 3DG (tel 01296 713341). Cheapest fully-fitted coffin only: £146 (delivery locally £27; nationally by carrier depending on distance, with a £48 hessian wrapping). Cold storage only: Yes, £20 per day. Body transport only: Yes, £1.20 per mile. Advice for d-i-y: Yes, £35 to cover home visit. Basic funeral: £428 (disbursements extra). 'Quality funerals at reasonable prices, plus our own flexible funeral plan' (David J. Lloyd). Prepaid plan: Our own Heritage & Sons Plan. Member of NAFD.

East Anglia

Comprising Norfolk, Suffolk, Essex, Cambridgeshire and Hertfordshire.

• **FD Clacton-on-Sea**: R. Gwinnell & Sons, 351 Holland Road, Clacton-On-Sea, Essex CO15 6PD (tel 01255 815600). See Manningtree, below, for details.

• **FD Colchester**: R. Gwinnell & Sons, 112 Ipswich Road, Colchester, Essex CO4 4AA (tel 01206 868585). See Manningtree, below, for details.

• **FD Colchester**: Hunnaball Funeral Services, York House, 41 Mersey Road,

Colchester, Essex CO2 7QS (tel 01206 760049; e-mail: hunnaball-funeral@talk21.com; web: www.hunnaball.co.uk). Branches in Ipswich, West Mersea and Manningtree. Cheapest fully-fitted coffin only: from £95; the Ecology cardboard coffin £105. Mortuary storage only: Yes, £60 per day. Advice for d-i-y: Yes, £40 to £50 per hour. Basic funeral: £500 (disbursements extra). 'Independent family business. Non-religious officiants available. Oakfield Wood, Wrabness, is the nearest woodland burial ground' (Trevor Hunnaball). Prepaid plan: Perfect Assurance, Chosen Heritage. Member of NAFD.

• **FD Dovercourt**: R. Gwinnell & Sons, 193 Main Road, Dovercourt, Essex CO12 3PH (tel 01255 241900). See Manningtree, below, for details.

• **FD Great Yarmouth**: Arthur Jary & Sons Ltd, 213/4 Northgate Street, Great Yarmouth, Norfolk NR30 1DH (tel 01493 844363). Also offices at: 43 High Street, Gorleston, Great Yarmouth NR31 6RR (tel 01493 662389); 15 Yarmouth Road, Caister, Great Yarmouth, Norfolk NR30 5DL (tel 01493 722472); Calthorpe Green, Old Road, Acle, Norfolk NR13 3QL (tel 01493 752122). Cheapest fully-fitted coffin only: from £215 including VAT (delivery locally free). Cold storage only: Yes, £40 per day or part-day. Advice for d-i-y: Yes, £20 per hour approximately. Basic funeral: £595 (disbursements extra). 'We are a family-owned company. Our staff go out of their way to be friendly and helpful and nothing is too much trouble. We pay great attention to detail' (Mrs S. Thompson). Prepaid plan: 'Our own, through Funeral Planning Services.' Member of SAIF, FOS.

• **FD Hadleigh**: R. Gwinnell & Sons, 77 High Street, Hadleigh, Essex IP7 5DY (tel 01473 824440). See Manningtree, below, for details.

• **FD Huntingdon**: T. L. Cobbold, a branch of Lodge Bros., at 11 and 13 New Street, St Neots, Huntingdon, Cambridgeshire PE19 1AE (tel 01480 472398; web: www.lodgebros.co.uk). See Lodge Bros. in the London region, below, for details.

• **FD Ipswich**: Farthing, Singleton and Hastings Funeral Service, 650 Woodbridge Road, Ipswich, Suffolk IP4 4PW (tel 01473 272711; e-mail: fsh650@ hotmail.com). Cheapest fully-fitted coffin only: £145 (delivery locally free). Cold storage only: Yes, £15 per day. Advice for d-i-y: Yes, £20 per hour. Basic funeral: £560 (disbursements extra). 'We seek to ensure that the service we provide is second to none. Although we endeavour to keep our fees reasonable, we do not believe that this is the main criterion for a family arranging which funeral director to use' (Luke Farthing). Prepaid plan: Own plan (Golden Security plus NAFD Perfect Assurance). Member of NAFD and SAID.

• **FD Ipswich**: Ipswich Funeral Service, Dove House, 291 Norwich Road, Ipswich IP1 4BP (tel 01473 748808). Contact Melanie Hunnaball. See Hunnaball Funeral Services in Colchester, above, for full details.

• **FD Manningtree**: R. Gwinnell & Sons, 24 High Street, Manningtree, Essex CO11 1AD (tel 01206 391506). Cheapest fully-fitted coffin only: from £100 (delivery dependent on mileage). Cold storage only: Yes, £10 per day. Advice for d-i-y: Yes, basic advice free. Basic funeral: £580 (disbursements extra). 'We are happy to perform any task that is ethically and legally correct' (Roy

Gwinnell). Pre-paid plan: Golden Charter. Member of SAIF and NAFD.
• **FD Manningtree**: Paskell Funeral Service, 15 High Street, Manningtree, Essex CO11 2RS (tel 01206 396709). Contact Saul Hunnaball. See Hunnaball Funeral Services in Colchester, above, for details. Oakfield Wood, Wrabness, near Manningtree, is the local woodland burial ground
• **FD Norwich**: Co-operative Funeral Service, St Stephens Square, Norwich, Norfolk NR1 3QJ (tel 01603 625495). Branches include: Bury St Edmunds (tel 01284 754017); East Dereham (H.H. Aldiss Funeral Service 01362 692233); Felixstowe (01394 670100); Gorleston (tel 01493 440838); Great Yarmouth (tel 01493 842464); Hadleigh (tel 01473 823117); Ipswich (tel 01473 257242); Norwich (tel 01603 483060 & George Bush Funeral Home 01603 764157); Saxmundham (tel 01728 604455); Stowmarket (tel 01449 612765); Sudbury (tel 01787 372736); Woodbridge (tel 01394 385456). Cheapest fully-fitted coffin only: £165 (local delivery free). Cold storage only: Yes, £10 per day. Body transport only: Yes. Advice for d-i-y: Yes, basic advice free. Basic funeral: £600 (disbursements extra). 'We are aware of environmental issues and are able to offer a complete choice to all clients requiring such services, we are also happy to perform any task that is ethically and legally correct' (Chris Doggett). Prepaid plan: Ipswich and Norwich Co-Operative Society Funeral Bond. Member of NAFD.
• **FD Norwich**: Peter Taylor Funeral Services, 85 Unthank Road, Norwich, Norfolk NR2 2PE (tel 01603 760787 or 01603 219216; fax 01603 620298; e-mail: taylors@angliafunerals.co.uk; web: www.angliafunerals.co.uk). Branches include: Holt (tel 01263 711992); Halesworth (tel 01986 872204); Bungay (tel 01986 892178); Long Stratton (tel 01508 531806); Dereham (tel 01362 699484); Watton (tel 01953 881229); Diss (tel 01379 642321); Harleston (tel 01379 853094); Horstead (tel 01603 737729); Wroxham (tel 01603 783797); Aylsham (tel 01263 733176); Wymondham (tel 01953 603138); Thetford (tel 01842 766221); Attleborough (tel 01953 452798); North Walsham (tel 01962 402603). Cheapest fully-fitted coffin only: £100 (delivery locally £20; nationally 60p per mile over 20 miles). Cold storage only: Yes, £10 per day. Body transport only: Yes, £60 locally. Advice for d-i-y: Yes, modest, negotiable fee. Basic funeral: £650 (disbursements extra). 'We also offer a range of ecology funerals, including a cardboard coffin and a craftsman-made woven willow chrysalis. A horse-drawn hearse is available from approximately £600. We have a strong association with, and support, the new local woodland burial ground at Colney Hall, Norwich. We are an Investors in People company.' (Nicholas Taylor). Prepaid plans: 'We have our own with Funeral Planning Services. We are also agents for Chosen Heritage and Age Concern.' Parent company: Anglia Funeral services. Member of NAFD.
• **FD Royston**: Cecil Newling, a branch of Lodge Bros., at 3 Green Drift, Royston, Hertfordshire SG8 5DB (tel 01763 243048; web: www.lodgebros.co.uk) and at Market Hill, Royston, Herfordshire SG8 9LL (tel 01763 243048; web: www.lodgebros.co.uk). See Lodge Bros. in the London region, below, for details.

• **FD Saxmundham**: Tony Brown's Funeral Service, New Cut, Saxmundham, Suffolk IP17 1DJ (tel 01728 603108; fax 01728 604346). (See the description by Libby Purves in Chapter 5.) Would not supply coffin only. Cold storage only: Yes, £10 per day. Body transport only: Yes. 'The charge would depend on distance with a minimum fee of £60 to cover the cost of the limousine hire.' Advice for d-i-y: Yes, no charge. Basic funeral: £650 (disbursements extra). Prepaid plan: No – 'privately if required, but I do not believe in it.' Would not give price breakdowns over the phone and does not have a price list for members of the public to take away. 'I conduct a personal family business I like doing and I object to all unnecessary red tape. I give a very good Christian service and treat everybody the same unless they want something elaborate. We probably know 95 per cent of the people we deal with. We still class ourselves as "your local funeral director".' They also run a green burial site in Blaxhall (Tony Brown).

• ✪✪✪ **FD Southend**: S. Stibbards & Sons Ltd, 4 Common Hall Lane, Hadleigh, Benfleet, Essex SS7 2RN (tel 01702 558717; e-mail: Stibbards@aol.com). Cheapest fully-fitted coffin only: £80 (delivery locally free). Cold storage only: Yes, £10 per day then £20 per day after first 14 days. Body transport only: Yes, £60 per mile round trip from office. Advice for d-i-y: Yes, free. Basic funeral: £460 (disbursements extra). 'We are a genuine fifth generation family business. We are always available to advise people impartially if they wish to discuss arrangements for their own funeral without committing themselves to any expense before the event' (David Coster). Prepaid plan: Golden Charter. Member of NAFD, SAIF and FOS. Winner of the New Natural Death Handbook Award 2000 for the Best Funeral Director in East Anglia.

• **FD Thorpe-le-Soken**: R. Gwinnell & Sons, High Street, Thorpe-le-Soken, Essex CO16 OEA (tel 01255 861818). See Manningtree, above, for details.

• **FD West Mersea**: J. K. May Funeral Service, Blackwater House, Barfield Road, West Mersea, Essex CO5 8JG (tel 01206 382235). Contact John May. See Hunnaball Funeral Services in Colchester, above, for details.

The South West

Comprising South Gloucestershire, Bristol, Bath and North East Somerset, North West Somerset, Somerset, Dorset, Devon, Cornwall.

• **FD Ashburton:** F. Christophers & Son, Bridge House, 9 Kingsbridge Lane, Ashburton, Devon (tel 01364 654065; e-mail: fred@f.christophers.co.uk; web: www.f.christophers.co.uk). Cheapest fully-fitted coffin only: £135 (delivery locally 80p per mile). Cold storage only: Yes, £8 per day. Body transport only: Yes. Advice for d-i-y: Yes, £25 per hour. Basic funeral: £780 (including disbursements of £280). 'Oldest family firm in Devon, established 1846, covering area of Southern Dartmoor' (Frederic Christophers). Member of SAIF.

• ✪✪✪ **FD Bideford**: D. Williams, The Pill, Kingsley Road, Bideford, North Devon EX39 2PF (tel 01237 472108). Cheapest fully-fitted coffin only: £100 (delivery locally £10). Has cold storage facilities. Body transport only: Yes. Advice for d-i-y: Yes, no charge. Basic funeral: £400 (disbursements extra). 'Happy to help people achieve a green burial option' (David Williams). Prepaid plan: Golden Charter. Member of SAIF. Winner of the New Natural Death Handbook Award 2000 for the Best Funeral Director in the South West.

• **FD Bristol:** Heaven on Earth, 18 Upper Maudlin Street, Bristol BS2 8DJ (tel 0117 926 4999). Cheapest fully-fitted coffin only: £165 (delivery locally free). They run the Heaven on Earth funeral shop and have a range of coffins (prices exclude £35 lining): Cardboard from £55; Strandboard from £130; Veneered 'wood' from £225; Painted fibreboard from £275; Bookcase coffins from £395; Reclaimed pine from £395; 'We can make fantasy coffins as required, such as red arrows jet or chess pieces.' Cold storage only: Yes, £5 per day. Body transport only: Yes. Advice for d-i-y: Yes, no charge. Basic funeral: £495 (coffin extra, disbursements extra – 'family involvement can reduce the price'). 'We positively encourage family involvement; for instance, we encourage the family to drive the body themselves. We can recommend pagan, secular, religious or Buddhist celebrants to officiate at funerals' (Paula Rainey Crofts and Simon Dorgan). No pre-paid plan. Member of no association.

• **FD Dawlish:** B. G. Wills & Son, 22 Brunswick Place, Dawlish, Devon EX7 9PD (tel 01626 862426). Cheapest fully-fitted coffin only: £165 (delivery locally 'no charge'; 'we provide cardboard coffins'). Cold storage only: 'Not available, but we would hold body in chapel of rest at £20 per funeral.' Body transport only: Yes, £75 average price. Advice for d-i-y: Yes, £15 per hour. Basic funeral: £495 (disbursements extra). 'We are a small family firm. We are willing to assist in any aspect of the funeral arrangements no matter how small' (G. Wills). Prepaid plan: Golden Charter, Perfect Assurance and own plan. Member of NAFD and SAIF.

• **FD Ilfracombe**: A. D Williams, 31 Portland Street, Ilfracombe, N. Devon (tel 01271 328218). See Bideford above for details.

• **FD Weymouth:** Stockting Funeral Service, 22 Crescent Street, Weymouth, Dorset DT4 7BX (tel 01305 785915; fax 01305 760626; web: www.grassby-funeral.co.uk). Parent company: Grassby & Sons Ltd. Cheapest fully-fitted coffin only: £120 (delivery locally £20; nationally: 'no'). Cold storage only: Yes, £25 per day. Body transport only: Yes. Advice for d-i-y: Yes, £15 per hour. Basic funeral: £610 (disbursements extra). 'We would be prepared to supply a cardboard coffin if requested' (No name given). Member of NAFD.

• **FD Winscombe:** C. V. Gower & Son funeral director, The Square, Winscombe, North Somerset BS25 1BS (tel 01934 842945; fax 01934 843130; e-mail: 106376.3266@compuserve.com). Cheapest fully-fitted coffin only: £150 (delivery locally £10; nationally 50p per mile). Cold storage only: Yes, £5 per day. Body transport only: Yes, basic charge and 50p per mile. Advice for d-i-y: Yes, no charge. Basic funeral: £550 (disbursements extra). Prepaid plan: Golden Charter. Member of SAIF, NAFD, FSC (Marian Gower).

The South

Comprising Wiltshire, Berkshire, Surrey, Kent, Hampshire, West Sussex, East Sussex.

• **FD Chertsey**: Lodge Bros., 104 Station Road, Addlestone, Surrey KT15 2BQ (tel 01932 829929; web: www.lodgebros.co.uk). See Lodge Bros. in the London region, below, for details.

• **FD Banstead**: A branch of W. A. Truelove & Son Ltd at 121 High Street, Banstead, Surrey SM7 2NS (tel 01737 212 160). For details see Sutton, below.

• **FD Battle**: Arthur C. Towner Ltd, 19 Market Square, Battle, East Sussex TN33 OXB (tel 01424 775515). See St Leonards, below, for details.

• **FD Belvedere**: Ashdown Funeral Services, 38 Albert Road, Belvedere, Kent DA17 8PW (tel 020 8294 2115). See Sidcup, below, for details.

• **FD Bexhill-on-Sea**: Arthur C. Towner Ltd, 19-20 Station Road, Bexhill-on-Sea, East Sussex TN40 1RE (tel 01424 733700). See St Leonards, below, for details.

• **FD Burgess Hill**: C & T Radmall Funeral Services, 223 London Road, Burgess Hill, West Sussex RH15 9QU (tel 01444 871212). Cheapest fully-fitted coffin only: £216 (delivery locally £20). Cold storage only: Yes (air conditioned room, not traditional fridges), £20 per day. Body transport only: Yes £45 for collection from hospital. Advice for d-i-y: Yes, £30 per hour. Basic funeral: £950 (including disbursements – doctors' and minister's fees and crematorium; coffin in place at crematorium, no hearse or bearers). 'We can supply cardboard or wicker coffins. We are a small independent family-owned-and-run firm and try our very best to meet any unusual requests' (Matthew Keysell). Prepaid plan: Golden Charter. Member of SAIF.

• **FD Calne**: E. Wooten & Son, a branch of Lodge Bros., at 1 North Street, Calne, Wiltshire SN11 OHQ (tel 01249 812258; web: www.lodgebros.co.uk). See Lodge Bros. in the London region, below, for details.

• **FD Canterbury**: Terry Davis Funerals, Warahay, 2b Jubilee Road, Littlebourne, Canterbury, Kent CT3 1TP (tel 01227 722770 or 720924). Cheapest fully-fitted coffin only: £120 – or £80 cardboard (delivery locally free). Cold storage only: Yes, £15 per day. Body transport only: Yes (£45 for collection from hospital). Advice for d-i-y: Yes, £30 per hour. Basic funeral: £650 (disbursements extra). 'We encourage every bereaved family to make each funeral as unique a celebration of the life of their loved one as possible. It may be appropriate in some cases to arrange the celebration around a particular interest that the deceased had during their life, eg Country and Western music, New Orleans jazz' (Matthew Keysell). No prepaid plan. Member of no association.

• **FD Carshalton**: A branch of J. E. Gillman & Sons at 16 Green Wrythe Lane, Carshalton, Surrey SM5 2DW (tel 020 8669 0483). See their entry in the London region, below, for details.

• **FD Caterham**: A branch of W. A. Truelove & Son Ltd at Leslie House, 187 Croydon Road, Caterham, Surrey CR3 6PH (tel 01883 345 345). For details see Sutton, below.

• **FD Cheam**: A branch of W. A. Truelove & Son Ltd at 31 High Street, Cheam, Surrey SM3 8RE (tel 020 8642 3300). For details see Sutton, below.

• **FD Chertsey**: Lodge Bros., 7 Windsor Street, Chertsey, Surrey KT16 8AY (tel 01932 565980; web: www.lodgebros.co.uk). See Lodge Bros. in the London region, below, for details.

• **FD Couldson**: A branch of W. A. Truelove & Son Ltd at 55 Chipstead Valley Road, Coulsdon, Surrey CR3 2RB (tel 020 8660 2620). For details see Sutton, below.

• **FD Epsom**: A branch of W. A. Truelove & Son Ltd at 14-18 Church Road, Epsom, Surrey KT17 4AB (tel 01372 723 337). For details see Sutton, below.

• **FD Guildford**: J. Monk & Sons, a branch of Lodge Bros., at 3 Artillery Terrace, Guildford, Surrey GU1 4NL (tel 01483 562780; web: www.lodgebros. co.uk). See Lodge Bros. in the London region, below, for details.

• **FD Haywards Heath**: R. A. Brooks and Son, 35 Wivelsfield Road, Haywards Heath, West Sussex RH16 4EN (tel 01444 454391; fax 01444 413751). Cheapest fully-fitted coffin only: £180 (delivery locally free). Cold storage: Yes, small negotiable flat fee. Body transport only: Yes, from £85. Advice for d-i-y people: Yes, free for a limited time. Basic funeral: £680 (disbursements extra). 'As a family-run business, we are totally flexible' (Andrew Brooks). Prepaid plan: Golden Charter. Member of NAFD, SAIF, FOS and MBIE.

• **FD Haywards Heath**: P. & S. Gallagher Funeral Directors, Fraser House, Triangle Road, Haywards Heath, West Sussex RH16 4HW (tel 01444 451166). Cheapest fully-fitted coffin only: £130 (delivery locally £15, nationally at cost). Cold storage: Yes. Body transport only: Yes. Advice for d-i-y people: Yes, £25 per hour. Basic funeral: £595 (disbursements extra). 'A family-run business with complete facilities' (Patrick Gallagher). Prepaid plan: Golden Charter and own plan. Member of SAIF, BIE.

• **FD Henfield**: C & T Radmall Funeral Services, 2 Stanhope House, High Street, Henfield, West Sussex BN5 9JJ (tel 01273 494577). See Burgess Hill above for details.

• **FD Lindfield**: Masters & Son (Lindfield) Ltd, Lewes Road, Lindfield, West Sussex RH16 2LB (tel 01444 482107; e-mail: masters@mistral.co.uk). Cheapest fully-fitted coffin only: £125 (delivery locally £15). Cold storage: Yes, £15 per hour. Body transport only: Yes. Advice for d-i-y people: Yes, £20 per hour. Basic funeral: £595 (disbursements extra). 'An independent family business. Both my wife and I trained as bereavement counsellors with Cruse' (Ian Masters). Prepaid plan: Golden Charter. Member of NAFD and SAIF.

• **FD Mitcham**: A branch of G. E. Gillman & Sons at 205 London Road, Mitcham, Surrey (tel 020 8685 0349). See their entry in the London region, below, for details.

• **FD Mitcham**: Donald Drewett & Sons, a branch of W. A. Truelove & Son Ltd, at 49-51 Upper Green East, Mitcham, Surrey CR4 2PF (tel 020 8648 2905). For details see Sutton, below.

• **FD Newbury**: R. C. Smallbone Ltd, Starwood House, 37 Pound Street, Newbury, Berkshire RG14 6AE (tel 01635 40536). Cheapest fully-fitted coffin only: £120 (delivery locally £10; delivery nationally 'variable'). Cold storage only: Yes, £15 per day. Body transport only: Yes. Advice for d-i-y: Yes, £25 per hour. Basic funeral: £937 (including fee for medical forms, Reading crematorium and CoE minister). 'Small independent family-owned company that strives to carry out every request of the bereaved' (Michael Smallbone).

Prepaid plan: Golden Charter. Member of SAIF.

• **FD Portsmouth**: Co-operative Funeral Directors, 157 Fratton Road, Portsmouth PO1 5EJ (tel 023 9286 3031; e-mail: stevepearce@southerncoops.co.uk). Other Southern Co-op Funeral Directors with the same terms of business at: Andover, Hampshire (Edwards Funeral Directors, tel 01264 334798); Ascot, Berkshire (Lines Bannister & Co Ltd, tel 01344 620266); Basingstoke, Hampshire (A. Monger Funeral Directors, tel 01256 851124); Bognor Regis, West Sussex (tel 01243 865119); Camberley, Berkshire (Camberley & District Funeral Directors, tel 01276 33241); Chichester, West Sussex (tel 01243 782209); Fareham, Hampshire (tel 01329 280249); Farnborough, Hampshire (tel 01252 542236); Fleet, Hampshire (tel 01252 623098); Gosport, Hampshire (tel 023 8258 1032); Havant, Hampshire (tel 023 9248 4499); Overton, Hampshire (tel 01256 770986); Portsmouth, Hampshire (G. Andrew & Sons Funeral Directors, tel 023 9266 2534); Portsmouth (Dashwood & Denyer Ltd, tel 023 9282 3855); Waterlooville, Hampshire (Edwards Funeral Directors, tel 023 9226 6105); Wokingham, Berkshire (J. B. Hall Funeral Directors, tel 01189 793623). Cheapest fully-fitted coffin only: £95 (delivery locally free). Cold storage only: Yes, £30 per day. Body transport only: Yes (£55 for an estate car). Advice for d-i-y: Yes, £30 per hour. Basic funeral: 'The family can pick and choose so it is up to the family' (they do indeed publish a good breakdown of à la carte 'basic charges' and their cheapest complete funeral combination, excluding disbursements but including a hearse and limousine, seems to come to £800). 'We will help the client as much or as little as the client wishes' (Steve Pearce). Prepaid plan: Co-operative Funeral Bond. Member of FSC and FOS.

• **FD St Leonards**: Arthur C. Towner Ltd, 2-4 Norman Road, St Leonards-on-Sea, East Sussex TN37 6NH (tel 01424 436386; web: www.towners.co.uk). Branches in Battle and Bexhill, see above. Cheapest fully-fitted coffin only: £99 (delivery locally free). Cold storage only: Yes, flat fee of £25. Body transport only: Yes. Advice for d-i-y: Yes, £50 per hour. Basic funeral: £566 (disbursements extra). 'We strive always to provide our clients with the funeral they need, not what is most convenient for us to provide' (Edward Towner). Prepaid plan: Golden Charter. Member of SAIF.

• ✪✪✪ **FD Salisbury**: Richard T. Adlem & Stephen Beckwith, 89 Littledow Cottages, Woodcutts, Salisbury, Wiltshire SP5 5RU (tel 01725 552309; e-mail: rtadlem@fairprice.co.uk). Cheapest fully-fitted coffin only: £85 (foil), £95 (veneer), £55+VAT (cardboard), phone for delivery price. Cold storage only: Yes, as long as no other funeral director is involved, no charge for a week and then call for details. Body transport only: Yes, £1.20 per mile, with no minimum charge. Advice for d-i-y: Yes, no charge if they phone or call on us, otherwise a transport charge. Basic funeral: £900 (including church fees, doctors' fees and cremation fee). 'Our large estate car plus wheeled bier etc is available for hire. Families who have used us are willing to discuss the high level of service they have received from us. We do not have to satisfy shareholders or directors so we charge the lowest prices we can afford' (Stephen Beckwith, partner with his wife). Prepaid plan: Golden Charter. Member of no association.

Winner of the New Natural Death Handbook Award 2000 for the Best Funeral Director in the South.

• **FD Sidcup**: Ashdown Funeral Services, 232 Blackfen Road, Sidcup, Kent DA15 8PW (tel 020 8294 2115). Cheapest fully-fitted coffin only: £180 (delivery locally £20). Cold storage only: Yes 'if space available', £10 per day. Body transport only: Yes. Advice for d-i-y: Yes, £10 per hour. Basic funeral: £818 (disbursements extra). 'Having only two premises and three permanent employees, our overheads are small. If our clients wish to add or subtract services, we can do so, and we alter the charges accordingly. Prices will increase by 20 per cent per year' (Mr E. Micallef). Prepaid plan: Golden Charter. Member of SAIF.

• **FD Southsea**: Mayfields Funeral Directors, 90 Elm Grove, Southsea, Hampshire PO5 1LN (tel 02392 875575; fax 02392 751172; e-mail: dcolbourne@linewone.net). Cheapest fully-fitted coffin only: £75 (delivery locally £10, nationally 75p per mile). Cold storage only: Yes, £7 per day. Body transport only: Yes. Advice for d-i-y: Yes, £25 per hour. Basic funeral: £877 (including disbursements). Prepaid plan: Golden Charter. Member of SAIF. 'Small family business with bereavement centre and trained counsellors' (David Colbourne).

• **FD Sutton**: W. A. Truelove & Son Ltd, 118 Carshalton Road, Sutton, Surrey SM1 4RL (tel 020 8642 8211; e-mail: funerals@wa-truelove-and-son.ltd.uk; web: www.wa-truelove-and-son.ltd.uk). They have another Sutton branch at 20 Mulgrave Road, Sutton, Surrey SM2 6LE (tel 020 8642 0089). For other branches, see Truelove (London region, for the Wallington branch), Caterham, Cheam, Coulsdon, Banstead, Epsom and Mitcham. Cheapest fully-fitted coffin only: £150, VAT extra (delivery locally £25). Cold storage only: Yes, £15 per day, subject to availability. Body transport only: No. Advice for d-i-y: Yes, £50 per hour. Basic funeral: £620 (advance payment price, disbursements extra). 'Family owned and run. Eight of our staff are diploma holders, three having won the Harold Rivett Award for excellence. A range of services, simple or elaborate' (Simon Truelove). Prepaid plan: Truelove Funeral Plans Ltd. Member of NAFD and National Selected Morticians.

• **FD Swindon**: A. E. Baker and Sons Ltd, 49/51 Groundwell Road, Swindon, Wiltshire SN1 2LY (tel 01793 433844). For details see Faringdon, above, in the East Midlands region. They also have an office at Brewery Street, Highworth, Wiltshire (tel 01793 764664).

• **FD Swindon**: A. E. Smith & Son, a branch of Lodge Bros., at Queens Drive, Swindon, Wiltshire SN3 1AW (tel 01793 522023; web: www.lodgebros.co.uk). See Lodge Bros. in the London region, below, for details.

• **FD Tonbridge**: Abbey Funeral Services, 173 High Street, Tonbridge, Kent TN9 1BX (tel 01732 360328; fax 01732 773050). Cheapest fully-fitted coffin only: £136 (delivery locally £25). Cold storage only: Yes, £50 per day. Body transport only: Yes, from £92. Advice for d-i-y: Yes, £25 per hour ('form to be provided by client'). Basic funeral: £810 (for deaths attended between 9am and 5pm, and bills settled within 7 days of the funeral, disbursements extra). 'Small independent family business' (Jo Parker). Prepaid plan: Golden Charter.

Member of SAIF and FOS.

• **FD Warminster**: F. Curtis and Son, 11 Portway, Warminster, Wiltshire BA12 8QC (tel 01985 212033). Cheapest fully-fitted coffin only: £100. Cold storage only: Yes, £5 per day. Body transport only: Yes. Advice for d-i-y: Yes, no charge. Basic funeral: £650 to £700 (including disbursements). 'We are straight' (Glen T. Shuttlewood). No prepaid plan. Member of BIFD.

• **FD West Byfleet**: Lodge Bros., 33 Old Woking Road, West Byfleet, Surrey KT14 6LG (tel 01932 355897; web: www.lodgebros.co.uk). See Lodge Bros. in the London region, below, for details.

• **FD Weybridge**: Lodge Bros., 36-38 High Street, Weybridge, Surrey KT13 8AB (tel 01932 854758; web: www.lodgebros.co.uk). See Lodge Bros. in the London region, below, for details.

• **FD Worthing**: TMC Funeral Services (Monumental Company), 92-94 Broadwater Street West, Broadwater Green, Worthing, West Sussex BN14 9DE (tel 01903 235353; e-mail: pennykeen@monumental.co.uk; web: www.monumental. co.uk). Cheapest fully-fitted coffin only: £230 (delivery locally £10 within 10 miles). Cold storage only: Yes, £10 per day. Body transport only: Yes. Advice for d-i-y: free, £25 arrangement fee. Basic funeral: £590 (disbursements extra). 'Privately family-owned and managed' (Penny Keen). Prepaid plan: Golden Charter. Member of SAIF.

Greater London region

Including old Middlesex. See also South region.

• **FD**: **F. A. Albin & Sons** Funeral Directors, Arthur Stanley House, 52 Culling Road, London SE16 2TN (tel 020 7237 3637); also at 164 Deptford High Street, London SE8 3DP (tel 020 8694 1384). Cheapest fully-fitted coffin only: £199 (delivery nationally £52). Basic funeral: £687 for burial at Nunhead cemetery and £822 for cremation at Honor Oak crematorium (both including disbursements). Also offers a 'Disposal Funeral Package' with no viewing, no service and no one in attendance for £519 (including disbursements). For the coffins they sell and the display coffin they rent, see Chapter 5. 'Owned by the family, we are now 217 years old' (B. Albin).

• **FD**: **H. J. Bent & Co** Funeral Directors, 343 Ladbroke Grove, London W10 6HA (tel 020 8969 1170); also at 1c Westminster Court, London NW8 8JN (tel 020 7723 1186); and 3 Pavilion Parade, Wood Lane, London W12 0HQ (tel 020 8743 3338). Cheapest fully-fitted coffin only: £90 approximately. Cold storage only: Yes. Body transport only: Yes. Advice for d-i-y: Yes, £15 per hour. Basic funeral: £650 (disbursements extra). 'We were the first company to be ISO 9002 registered for Funeral Services' (Terry Foreman). Prepaid plan: Chosen Heritage and 'our own'. Member of no association except the Federation of Small Businesses.

• **FD**: **Chelsea Funeral Directors**, 260(b) Fulham Road, Chelsea, London SW10 9EL (tel 020 7352 0008; e-mail: funerals@chelseafunerals.co.uk; web: www.chelseafunerals.co.uk). Cheapest fully-fitted coffin only: £125 (delivery locally £10). Cold storage only: Yes, £15 per day. Body transport only: Yes. Advice for d-i-y: Yes, no charge. Basic funeral: £595 (disbursements extra). 'Independently owned, sensitivity to personalised funeral requests' (Neil Cocking). Prepaid plan: Golden Charter. Member of SAIF.

• **FD**: **T. Cribb & Sons** funeral directors, Victoria House, 10 Woolwich Manor Way, Beckton, London E6 4PA (tel 020 8476 1855; e-mail:johnharris@ looksmart.com). Branches at: 154-155 Barking Road, Canning Town, London E14 4HB; and 112 Rathbone Street, Canning Town, London E16 1JQ. Cheapest fully-fitted coffin only: £153 approx. (delivery locally £10). Cold storage only: Yes, £10 per day. Body transport only: Yes. Advice for d-i-y: Yes, no charge – within reason. Basic funeral: £632 (disbursements extra). 'Our horse-drawn service is still available at £695; we have a probate service. Our phone lines and office are always open to give families advice and help – regardless of the fact that we may or may not be carrying out the full funeral arrrangements' (John Harris). Prepaid plan: Golden Charter. Member of SAIF.

• ❀❀❀ **FD**: **J. E. Gillman & Sons Ltd**, 971 Garratt Lane, Tooting, London SW17 0LW (tel 020 8672 1557; web: www.funeral.org.uk). Branches: Mitcham, Surrey (tel 020 8685 0349); Carshalton, Surrey (tel 020 8669 0483); Battersea, London SW11 (Bassett Funeral Service, tel 020 7228 0360); Balham High Road, London SW12 (tel 020 8673 8719); West Norwood, London SE27 (Wilson Funeral Service, tel 020 8670 4126). A chipboard-based lightly veneered coffin, 'without handles or fancy lining, just cremfilm, using wood from managed sustained-yield forests' is available in a range of sizes for £45, including delivery within 5 miles. Cold storage only: Yes, £10 per day. Body transport only: Yes. Advice for d-i-y: Yes, 'free advice from experienced and flexible staff'. Direct Transfer Service: 'Where there is no service, religious or secular, and no mourners', £325 (disbursements extra). Basic funeral: £725 (disbursements extra). 'Independent family firm, very qualified staff' (Roger Gillman). Prepaid plan: Golden Charter. Member of NAFD and SAIF. Winner of the New Natural Death Handbook Award 2000 for the Best Funeral Director in the UK.

• **FD**: **H. C. Grimstead Ltd**, 58 Swan Road, West Drayton, Middlesex UB7 7JZ (tel 01895 431000). The firm also has branches in Ruislip (tel 01895 623000), Eastcote (tel 020 8866 0688) and Harefield (tel 01895 822297); and see the East Midlands region above for its branches in South Buckinghamshire at Beaconsfield, Amersham and Gerrards Cross. Cheapest fully-fitted coffin only: £210. Cardboard coffin £100. Cold storage only: Yes, £25 per day. Body transport only: Yes, from £60. Advice for d-i-y: Yes, probably no charge. Basic funeral: £410 for the 'Green Funeral Option' with a cardboard coffin (disbursements extra; and £1-45 extra per mile, each way, outside a 10 mile radius); otherwise £480 'excluding the coffin'. 'We are one of the few independent funeral directors, the third generation of the family' (Colin Thompson). Prepaid plan: Own plans and own trust fund.

• **FD**: **Haji Taslim Muslim Funerals**, East London Mosque, 45 Fieldgate Street, London E1 1JU (tel 020 7247 2625 or 020 7247 9583). Cheapest fully-fitted coffin only: £100 approx. Cold storage only: Yes, no charge. Body transport only: Yes, £60 for two hours with a driver within a 25 mile radius. Prices can be reduced for those in financial difficulty. Although 95% of the firm's business is Islamic, it is not exclusively so (Mr Taslim).

• **FD**: **Holmes & Daughters**, 3 Church Road, Ashford, Middlesex (tel 01784 421015). Cheapest fully-fitted coffin only: £95, cardboard coffin £70 (delivery locally £20). Body transport only: Yes, from £78. Advice for d-i-y: Yes, no charge. Basic funeral: £730 (disbursements extra). 'Small independent business. Vintage 1934 hearse no extra cost. Female conductors on request. Many staff are family or longstanding family friends' (David Holmes). This firm publishes a full breakdown of its pricing. Prepaid plan: Golden Charter. Member of SAIF.

• **FD Hounslow**: The local authority in Hounslow has an arrangement with local funeral directors to supply a 'Hounslow Community Funeral Service' to residents at a cost of £550 (disbursements extra). The firms taking part are: The CRS Co-op (tel 020 8570 4741), Andrew Holmes & Son (tel 020 8572 3277) and Frederick Paine (tel 020 8994 0056).

• **FD**: **Indian Funeral Service**, Chani House, Alexander Place, Lower Park Road, London N11 1QD (tel 020 8361 6151; e-mail: chandu@aol.com; web: www.indian-funeral.co.uk). Cheapest fully-fitted coffin only: £180 (delivery locally free). Cold storage only: Yes. Body transport only: Yes, £90. Advice for d-i-y: Yes, no charge. Basic funeral: £700 (disbursements extra). 'The only Asian family-owned funeral directors in London' (Chandu Tailor). Prepaid plan: Golden Charter. Member of SAIF.

• **FD**: **E. M. Kendall** funeral directors, 46 Dalston Lane, London E8 3AH (tel 020 7254 6519 and 020 7249 2884; fax 020 7254 6519). Cheapest fully-fitted coffin only: £55 (delivery locally £10; nationally 'negotiable'). Cold storage only: Yes, £10 per day. Body transport only: Yes. Advice for d-i-y: Yes, £10 per hour. Basic funeral: £375 (disbursements extra). '24 hour service, moderate charges, every assistance given, distance no object' (E. M. Kendall). Prepaid plan: Avalon, Golden Charter and own plan. Member of BIFD and FSC.

• **FD Lambeth**: A municipal funeral service for local residents, by arrangement with the local authority, is provided by the CWS Co-op (tel 020 7703 2803) at a cost of £1,030 (disbursements extra) – note that a basic funeral is available for £890 (no extra for non-residents).

• **FD Lewisham**: A municipal funeral service for local residents, by arrangement with the local authority, is provided by the CWS Co-op (tel 020 7698 3244) at a cost of £1,030 (disbursements extra) – note that a basic funeral is available for £890 (no extra for non-residents).

• **FD**: **Lodge Bros. (Funerals) Ltd**, Ludlow House, Ludlow Road, Feltham TW13 7JF (tel 020 8818 7710; e-mail: info@lodgebros.co.uk; web: www.lodgebros.co.uk). Branches include: Hanworth (tel 020 8894 9731); Northolt (tel 020 8845 0660); Feltham (tel 020 8890 2231); Bedfont (tel 020 8890 7902); Yiewsley (tel 01895 446686); Uxbridge (tel 01895 233018); Sunbury-on-Thames (tel 01932 785402); Shepperton (tel 01932 220081); Hounslow (tel 020 8570 0118); Hillingdon (tel 01895 234011); Hampton Hill (tel 020 8941 4022); Ashford (tel 01784 252226); West Ealing (tel 020 8567

0227); Brentford (tel 020 8560 7499). Cheapest fully-fitted coffin only: £132 . Body transport only: Yes. Advice for d-i-y: Yes, 'free for our d-i-y customers who purchase goods or services.' Economy funeral: £654. Basic funeral: £782 to £857 (varying between branches, disbursements extra). 'Our family business has been established for over 200 years and offers a very full range of services' (John Lodge). Prepaid plan: Family Funerals Trust Ltd. Member of NAFD, BIFD, NAPFP, NAMM. This firm is to be commended for its particularly clear and itemised price lists and for their printed comment on these lists that 'any items listed can be purchased separately by clients wishing to make their own arrangements'.

• **FD**: **Mears & Cotterill**, 169 Merton Road, Wandsworth, London SW18 5EF (tel 020 8874 7698). Cheapest fully-fitted coffin only: £115 (delivery locally £30). Body transport only: Yes. Advice for d-i-y: Yes, £50 set fee. Basic funeral: £420 (disbursements extra). 'We are family owned. We supply coffins, hearse, embalming and advice as required, without insisting that we complete the whole of a funeral' (John William Mears). Prepaid plan: Golden Charter and Golden Leaves. Member of FSC.

• **FD**: **W. G. Miller**, 93-95 Essex Road, Islington, London N1 2SJ (tel 020 7226 3886). Cheapest fully-fitted coffin only: £245 (delivery locally £30). Body transport only: Yes. Advice for d-i-y: Yes. Basic funeral: £850 (disbursements extra). Cold storage only: No. Advice for d-i-y: Yes. 'We are a small family company which still cares for the family's wishes. If there is a need for a particular service we will provide it' (Peter Henry). Prepaid plan: Golden Charter. Member of NAFD and SAIF.

• **FD**: **Rowland Brothers**, 301 Whitehorse Road, West Croydon CR0 2HR (tel 020 8684 1667; e-mail: info@rowlandbrothersinternational.co.uk). Cheapest fully-fitted coffin only: £150 (delivery free locally; nationally £1 per mile). Cold storage only: Yes, £25 per day. Body transport only: Yes, £250 for hearse and four bearers. Advice for d-i-y: Yes, no charge for a quick call, substantial advice £100. Basic funeral: £465 (disbursements extra). 'We also have a disposal service which costs £356 for those who want no involvement at all' (Tony Rowland). Prepaid plan: Golden Leaves. Member of NAFD and SAIF.

• **FD Southwark**: A municipal funeral service for local residents, by arrangement with the local authority, is provided by the CWS Co-op (tel 020 7732 4165) at a cost of £1,030 (disbursements extra) – note that a basic funeral is available for £890 (no extra for non-residents).

• **FD**: **W. A. Truelove & Son Ltd**, a branch at 109 Stafford Road, Wallington, Greater London SM6 9AP (tel 020 8647 1032). See their entry above, under Sutton, South region, above, for details.

• **FD**: **Willow Independent Funeral Service**, 21 Wellington Street, Woolwich, London SE18 6PQ (tel 020 8854 6222). They run another branch at 347 Becksley Road, North Heath, Kent. Cheapest fully-fitted coffin only: £285. Cold storage only: Yes, £5 per day. Body transport only: Yes. Advice for d-i-y: Yes, £15 per hour. Basic funeral: £660 (disbursements extra). 'We are independent and give value for money' (Mr Hopper). Prepaid plan: Golden Charter and own plan. Member of SAIF and OMAS.

Scotland

• **FD**: **Barclay's Funeral Services**, 4 Taylor Gardens, Edinburgh EH6 6TG (tel 0131 553 6818). Parent company SCI (UK). Cheapest fully-fitted coffin only: £250. Cold storage only: Yes, no charge. Body transport only: Yes, £120 hearse, £90 limousine. Advice for d-i-y: Yes, no charge. Basic funeral: £705 (disbursements extra). 'We go above and beyond the call of duty' (Peter Deery). Prepaid plan: Dignity. Member of FSC and FOS.

Eire

• **FD County Leitrim**: Luke Early, Main Street, Mohill, County Leitrim, Eire (tel 00353 78 31081 or 0872 470795; e-mail: earlyfunerals@eircom.net). Cheapest fully-fitted coffin only: £290 (delivery locally £50; anywhere in Eire for £120). Cold storage only: No. Advice for d-i-y: Yes, £15 per hour. Basic funeral: £495 (disbursements extra). 'No parent company, Personal contact with bereaved family' (Luke Early). Prepaid plan: Own plan. Member of IAFD. (Eds: Only firms supplying a fully-fitted coffin for £250 or less have been included in this chapter, but an exception has been made in the case of this firm, since it is the only one in Eire that has come close to meeting the requirements for a listing.)

Chapter 8

GOOD CREMATORIA & CEMETERIES

Unless otherwise stated, you can assume that all the cemeteries and crematoria listed are prepared to deal with families not using funeral directors. Abbreviations in bold are as follows:

Cem = Cemetery
Crem = Crematorium
• ✪✪✪ = Winner of a New Natural Death Handbook Award 2000.

Those crematoria listed as willing to take home-made coffins do so on condition that such coffins meet the anti-pollution requirements of the Federation of British Cremation Authorities, as set out in Chapter 4. Shrouds, if listed as acceptable by either crematoria or cemeteries, are normally required to be made rigid with a plank; likewise body bags, which would also normally need to be covered with a drape of some kind. These institutions do not want to cause offence to staff or to other members of the public.

Listings are by region, and then by town within the region, except in the Greater London region, which has been further subdivided into areas. Please write to The Natural Death Centre (20 Heber Road, London NW2 6AA, tel 020 8208 2853; fax 020 8452 6434; e-mail: <rhino@dial.pipex.com>) with your experience of using your local crematorium or cemetery, whether positive or negative, and including as much detail as possible; please add if you are nominating them for a future award. Our listings are otherwise based on information given to us by the services themselves – the name of the informant is given wherever possible.

The North West

Comprising Cumbria, Lancashire, Manchester, Sefton, Wirral, Liverpool, Knowsley, St Helens, Wigan, Bolton, Bury, Rochdale, Salford, Trafford, Manchester, Oldham, Tameside, Stockport and Cheshire.

• **Cem Accrington**: Accrington (Huncoat) Cemetery, Burnley Road, Accrington, Hyndburn, Lancashire BB5 6HA (tel 01254 232933). Plot (100 years) incl. digging and burial £542. They will accept home-made, cardboard or wicker coffins. Length of funeral service: 30 minutes (extra time can be booked for £62). Chapel: As crematorium below. Grounds: 'Well-tended seating areas.' Memorials: 'Standard headstone style and type, within size restrictions.' 'There are separate plots for different religious denominations and an infant memorial area for foetal remains, stillborn children and small infants. Staff are caring and dedicated' (Janice Tolson).

• **Cem Accrington**: Dill Hall (Church of Clayton-le-Moors) Cemetery, Dill Hall Lane, Church, Near Accrington, Hyndburn, Lancashire (tel 01254 232933). Plot (100 years) incl. digging and burial £429-35. They will accept home-made, cardboard or wicker coffins. Length of funeral service: 30 minutes (extra time can be booked for £62). Chapel: Accrington Crematorium is the nearest available. Grounds: 'A small cemetery with plots for Church of England and Roman Catholics.' Memorials: 'Standard headstone style and type, within size restrictions.' 'A "memorial wall" has been built for the burial and memorial of cremated remains of a loved one' (Janice Tolson).

• **Crem Accrington**: Accrington Crematorium, The Cemetery Office, Burnley Road, Accrington, Hyndburn, Lancashire BB5 6HA (tel 01254 232933). Price: £180. Time allotted: 20 minutes within a thirty minute period (extra time can be booked for £62). They will accept home-made and cardboard coffins. Chapel: 'Church-like; traditional nonconformist, cruciform design, seating 80.' Grounds: 'Burial plots on all sides of the chapel.' 'We are always willing to assist and be flexible to requests. Good disabled access' (Janice Tolson).

• **Cem Alderley Edge**: Alderley Edge Cemetery, Chelford Road, Alderley Edge SK9 7TQ; run by the Macclesfield Borough Council, from Macclesfield Cemetery, Prestbury Road, Macclesfield, SK10 3BU (tel 01625 422330 or 422408 or 504511). Plot (100 years) incl. digging and burial £487 (double for non-residents). They will accept cardboard or wicker coffins. Length of funeral service: 20 minutes (extra time can be booked for £52). No chapel. Grounds: 'Quiet rural setting, with a view of the town and the "edge" ' (John J. Thomas).

• **Cem Askam-in-Furness**: Ireleth Cemetery, Broughton Road, Askam-in-Furness, Cumbria (tel 01229 824928). No Chapel. Grounds: 'A small cemetery next to the local churchyard with superb views of the Duddun estuary' (C. R. Pollard). Other details as for Barrow-in-Furness Cemetery below.

• **Cem Atherton**: Atherton Cemetery, Leigh Road, Atherton, Lancashire. Other details as for Leigh Cemetery below.

• **Cem Nr. Atherton**: Hovebridge Cemetery, Lovers Lane, Near Atherton, Lancashire. Other details as for Leigh Cemetery below.

• **Cem Barrow-in-Furness**: Barrow-in-Furness Cemetery, Devonshire Road, Barrow-in-Furness, Cumbria (tel 01229 894928). Plot (99 years) incl. digging and burial £405. Maintenance: £142. They will accept home-made, cardboard or wicker coffins and body bags or shrouds. Length of funeral service: 45 minutes (extra time can be booked without charge). Chapel: '1960s crematorium chapel.' Grounds: 'On a hillside overlooking the town, with views across the Irish Sea.' Memorials: 'Natural stone, within size restrictions.' 'Several areas are left uncut to encourage wild flowers.' For details of the woodland burial ground see Chapter 6 (C. R. Pollard).

• **Crem Barrow-in-Furness**: Thorncliffe Crematorium, Cemetery Office, Devonshire Road, Barrow-in-Furness, Cumbria LA14 5PD (tel 01229 894928). Price: £214. Time allotted: 45 minutes (extra time can be booked without charge). They will accept home-made or cardboard coffins. Chapel: Modern, non-denominational with flexible seating. Grounds: 'Surrounded by a glade of remembrance and cemetery.' 'Because we are a smaller crematorium the staff offer a more personal, friendly service' (C. R. Pollard).

• **Cem Burnley**: Burnley Cemetery, 93 Rossendale Road, Burnley BB11 5DD (tel 01282 664600 to 664615). Plot (40 years) incl. digging and burial £668 (double for non-residents, although this extra amount is not applicable to former residents who purchased the exclusive Right of Burial when residing within the Borough). They will accept home-made or cardboard coffins. Length of funeral service: Not strictly limited. Chapel: 'Victorian, sombre.' Grounds: 'Woodland to rear. Part of cemetery in tranquil setting.' Memorials: 'Restrictions vary in different sections of the cemetery; no new sidestones, etc allowed; inscriptions not to cause offence, etc.' 'We are currently adopting the Charter for the Bereaved.' 'There are separate plots for different religious denominations, an infant memorial area, and caring and dedicated staff' (John Cummings).

• ✪✪✪ **Cem Carlisle**: Carlisle Cemetery, Richardson Street, Carlisle CA2 6AL (tel 01228 625310; e-mail: kenw@carlisle-city.gov.uk). Plot (50 years) incl. digging and burial £445. They will accept home-made, cardboard or wicker coffins and body bags or shrouds. Length of funeral service: No limit. Chapel: 'Attractive, Gothic design. Warm, with seating for 100.' Grounds: 'Parkland in wooded setting with conservation zones. There are waterfalls on a natural beck, a squirrel feeder, a lichen reserve, nesting herons, etc.' Memorials: 'Traditional graves are not subject to restrictions, lawn memorials must be within size limits.' They have adopted the Charter for the Bereaved. 'Our range of graves and coffins enable us to meet all religious and personal needs without difficulty. We have added a further choice, the 'recycled funeral' for those who require a simple, inexpensive burial with no memorial. We maintain both conservation areas and conventionally attractive cemetery grounds. We have arranged many funerals with families and know that funerals arranged without a funeral director are at least as good, and often better, than those that take the conventional path.' (Ken West). For details of their woodland burial ground, see Chapter 6. Winner of the New Natural Death Handbook Award 2000 for the Best Cemetery in the UK.

• ✪✪✪ **Crem Carlisle**: Carlisle Crematorium, Bereavement Services, Cemetery Office, Richardson Street, Carlisle CA2 6AL (tel 01228 625310; e-mail: kenw@carlisle-city.gov.uk). Price: £217 for 'environmental cremation' in a cardboard coffin, normal fee £243. Time allotted: 40 minutes (extra time can be booked without charge). They will accept home-made, cardboard or wicker coffins and body bags or shrouds. (For their range of coffins see their woodland burial site entry in Chapter 6.) For cremation, a reusable coffin is available, with an inner Compakta cardboard coffin, at a total cost of £90. They can provide cold storage for the body at a charge of £9-25 for up to 24 hours, £12-75 for up to 48 hours or £16 for over 48 hours. Extra bearers to help the family can be supplied at £6 per person. Chapel: 'Non-denominational with flexible seating. One family decorated the chapel with posters based on photographs, so the feel of the chapel can be significantly changed.' Grounds: 'Four different zones ensure that the different needs and beliefs of individuals do not intrude upon others: The Peace

Garden is bedded out and highly-maintained providing the principal view from the Hall of Remembrance; the monthly gardens are planted to a seasonal pattern; the woods are for those who prefer a return to nature and may oppose high maintenance regimes; and the memorial wall offers the only cremation memorial option.' 'The service has adopted with the Charter for the Bereaved, offering both traditional and environmental options. The environmental options also prove far less expensive, offering savings against the cremation fee, and the provision of biodegradable coffins. Our attitude is one of complete openness, giving the bereaved complete access to the information they need in order to obtain a meaningful funeral. There is no commercial pressure or bias towards so-called conventional funerals' (Ken West). Winner of the New Natural Death Handbook Award 2000 for the Best Crematorium in the UK.

• **Cem Cheadle**: Mill Lane Cemetery, Manchester Road, Cheadle; run by Stockport Metropolitan Borough Council, from the Stockport Crematorium, 31a Buxton Road, Heaviley, Stockport SK2 6LS (tel 0161 480 5221; fax 0161 480 6992). Plot (75 years) incl. digging and burial £755 (£675 extra for non-residents). They will accept home-made, cardboard or wicker coffins. Length of funeral service: 45 minutes (extra time can be booked for £55). No chapel. Grounds: 'A lawn cemetery, newly laid out with roads and drives designed for modern corteges; mostly native species trees.' Memorials: 'The site's planning permission allows only flat desk-shaped memorials of granite or slate.' 'The modern layout has made this cemetery very popular. It has a high standard of maintenance' (N. Buckley).

• **Cem Clitheroe**: Clitheroe Cemetery, Waddington Road, Clitheroe, Lancashire (tel 01200 425111; e-mail: sue-walker@ribblevalley.gov.uk); run by the Ribble Valley Borough Council. Plot (100 years) incl. digging and burial £356 (double for non-residents). They will accept cardboard coffins. Length of funeral service: 'No limit at the graveside.' No chapel. Grounds: 'A beautiful rural location.' Memorials: 'Hard stone only. Size restriction in the lawn cemetery. We maintain a high standard of customer care' (Judith Paliga). There is also a woodland burial area on the cemetery's perimeter – see Chapter 6 for details.

• **Crem Crewe**: Crewe Crematorium, Crewe Cemetery Office, Market Close, Crewe, Cheshire CW1 2NA (tel 01270 212643; web: www.crewe-nantwich.gov.uk/worksservices); run by the Crewe and Nantwich Borough Council. Price: £212 (£235 for non-residents). Time allotted: 40 minutes (extra time can be booked for £38). They will accept home-made, cardboard or wicker coffins and body bags or shrouds. Chapel: 'Non-denominational, with flexible seating, for a maximum of 88 people.' Grounds: 'Good grounds and flower beds.' They have adopted the Charter for the Bereaved and have attained the BSI 9002 standard for cemetery and crematorium management. 'There is a woodland area for cremated remains, which is supported by the Cheshire Wildlife Trust' (Mrs Mary M. Slinn).

• **Cem Dalton-in-Furness**: Dalton-in-Furness Cemetery, Cemetery Hill, Newton Road, Dalton-in-Furness, Cumbria (tel 01229 894928). No chapel. Grounds:

'Edge of town with views to the neighbouring countryside. It is an old cemetery with graves dating back to 1800' (C. R. Pollard). Other details as for Barrow-in-Furness Cemetery above.

• **Crem Distington**: Distington Hall Crematorium, Distington, Workington, Cumbria CA14 4QY (tel 01946 830561). Price: £214-90 (£13-50 extra for non-residents). Time allotted: 30 minutes. They will accept cardboard or wicker coffins. Chapel: 'Modern, non-denominational.' Grounds: 'A natural woodland setting.' 'Reasonably priced and well maintained' (Mr S. J. Benn).

• **Cem Great Harwood**: Great Harwood Cemetery, Blackburn Road, Great Harwood, Near Blackburn, Lancashire (tel 01254 232 933). Plot (100 years) incl. digging and burial £504 (double for non-residents). They will accept home-made, cardboard or wicker coffins. No chapel. Grounds: 'Set in a quiet side of town.' Memorials: 'Standard headstone style and materials; there are size restrictions.' 'We are currently considering adoption of the Charter for the Bereaved. The cemetery is well maintained with a caring cemetery foreman' (Mrs Janice Tolson).

• **Cem Hindley**: Hindley Cemetery, Castle Hill Road, Hindley, Near Wigan, Lancashire. Other details as for Leigh Cemetery below.

• **Cem Knowsley**: Knowsley Cemetery, Fox's Bank Lane, Whiston, Knowsley (tel 0151 443 5231); run by the Knowsley Metropolitan Borough Council, 9 West Street, Knowsley L34 1LF. Plot (99 years) incl. digging and burial £424 (£212-50 extra for non-residents). There is no maintenance charge. Length of funeral service: 45 minutes. No chapel. Grounds: 'Open countryside'. Memorials: '3' 3" high, 2' 6" wide' (John Profitt).

• **Cem Knutsford**: Knutsford Cemetery, Tabley Hill Lane, Tabley, Knutsford WA16 OEW; run by the Macclesfield Borough Council, from Macclesfield Cemetery, Prestbury Road, Macclesfield, SK10 3BU (tel 01625 422330 or 422408 or 504511). Plot (100 years) incl. digging and burial £487 (doubled for non-residents). They will accept cardboard or wicker coffins. Length of funeral service: 20 minutes (extra time can be booked for £52). Chapel: 'Fine Victorian octagonal building atop Tabley Hill, compact and airy and light, with space heating.' Grounds: 'The cemetery stands out on top of the hill, overlooking the town.' Memorials: 'Lawn-type memorials only, with size restrictions' (John J. Thomas).

• **Cem Leigh**: Leigh Cemetery, Manchester Road, Leigh, Lancashire (tel 01942 828507). Plot (100 years) incl. digging and burial £420 (£210 extra for non-residents), run by Wigan Borough Council. They will accept home-made, cardboard or wicker coffins. Length of funeral service: 30 minutes (extra time can be booked without charge). No chapel. Memorials: 'Lawn memorials only, within size restrictions.' 'Wigan Borough Council (see under F. D. Wigan below), with the co-operation of a specified reputable funeral director, is now able to offer a low cost, but nevertheless dignified funeral service to local residents' (A Bassett).

• **Cem Lytham St. Annes**: Park Cemetery, Regent Avenue, Lytham St. Annes, Lancashire FY8 4AB (tel 01253 735429). Plot (100 years) incl. digging and burial £495 (£990 non-residents). They will accept home-made, cardboard or wicker coffins. Length of funeral service: 30 minutes (extra time can be booked without charge). Chapel: As crematorium below. Grounds: As crematorium below. Memorials: 'Within size restrictions; no kerbing' (Mr A. Royston).

• **Crem Lytham St Annes**: Lytham Park Crematorium, Park Cemetery, Regent Avenue, Lytham St Annes, Lancashire FY8 4AB (tel 01253 735429). Price: £190. Time allotted: 25 minutes within a 30 minute period (extra time can be booked without charge). They will accept home-made coffins if made from natural wood, cardboard coffins if approved by Federation, or body bags approved for cremation. Chapel: 'Standard 1950s.' Grounds: 'Open view of fields.' 'Saturday services are available' (Mr A. Royston).

• **Cem Macclesfield**: Prestbury Road, Macclesfield SK10 3BU (tel 01625 422330 or 422408 or 504511); run by the Macclesfield Borough Council. Plot (100 years) incl. digging and burial £487 (double for non-residents). They will accept cardboard or wicker coffins. Length of funeral service: 20 minutes (extra time can be booked for £52). Chapel: 'The crematorium chapel is used: a Victorian building, in a quiet and simple style, seating up to 70 persons, centrally heated.' Grounds: 'Near town centre, adjacent to a park and arboretum. The grounds have mature trees and a rhododendron shrubbery.' Memorials: 'Lawn-type memorials only, with size restrictions.' 'Although near the town centre, the area is in a quiet rural setting overlooking the wooded Whitfield Brook Valley, with a view out to the surrounding hills' (John J. Thomas).

• **Crem Macclesfield**: Macclesfield Crematorium, Cemetery Lodge, Prestbury Road, Macclesfield SK10 3BU (tel 01625 422330 or 422408 or 504511); run by the Macclesfield Borough Council. Price: £195. Time allotted: 30 minutes (extra time can be booked for £195). They will accept cardboard coffins. Chapel: 'Fine Victorian nonconformist chapel made from local stone. Movable seating pews.' Grounds: 'Overlooking a pool and stream in an established arboretum valley.' 'We provide a reasonably flexible service' (John J. Thomas).

• **Cem Manchester**: Southern Cemetery, Barlow Moor Road, Chorlton, Manchester M21 7GL (tel 0161 881 2208). Plot (50 years) incl. digging and burial £815 (£1,255 for non-residents). They will accept home-made coffins; or shrouds in the Muslim section. Length of funeral service: 20 minutes in chapel. Chapel: 'Victorian Gothic.'' Grounds: '168-acre site with listed buildings and a great variety of trees and shrubs.' Memorials: A rule booklet of 56 pages. Articles it prohibits on graves include wooden crosses ('except those supplied by the city council'), sea shells, rockery and other stones. Those bringing the coffin to the cemetery in other than a funeral director's hearse must transfer it at the entrance gate to a wheeled bier. Not unreasonably, it also wants to be notified if the coffin size will exceed 6' 4" by 22" width, 15" depth. (The width measurement must allow for any protruding handles. 'It is difficult and may be dangerous to alter the width of the grave once it has been excavated.') 'We will give advice on coffins or anything relating to the cemetery. We pride ourselves on being experienced in all manner of problems associated with burial – and how to solve them!' There is a woodland burial area planned – see Chapter 6 for details (Paul Burton).

• **Crem Manchester:** Barlow Moor Road Crematorium, Chorlton, Manchester M21 7GZ (tel 0161 881 5269), run by the Manchester Crematorium Ltd. Price: £190 (organist or music £12 extra) for 30 minutes in the mornings; or £225 for 40 minutes in the afternoons (extra time can be booked for £77 per half hour). They will accept home-made, cardboard or wicker coffins. Chapels: 'One Romanesque chapel is from the late 19th century and seats 108; the other is a modern one from the late 1950s and seats 60.' Grounds: 'In the suburbs of Manchester with a 168-acre cemetery next door.' 'Families are treated as individually as possible' (Andrew Paul Helsby).

• **Crem Manchester**: Howe Bridge Crematorium, Lovers Lane, Atherton, Manchester M46 OPZ (tel 01942 870811); run by Crematoria Management Ltd. Price: £235. Time allotted: 30 minutes. They will accept home-made or cardboard coffins. Chapel: 'Modern, natural building materials used.' Grounds: 'Open countryside' (P. J. Wilson).

• **Cem Padiham**: Padiham Public Cemetery, St. John's Road, Padiham, Lancashire (tel 01282 425011 or 01282 664602); run by Burnley Borough Council. Grounds: 'No adjacent dwellings.' All other details as for Burnley Cemetery (above) to whom any correspondence should be addressed.

• **Cem Poulton-le-Fylde**: Fleetwood Cemetery, Beach Road, Fleetwood, Lancashire (tel 01253 891000 ext 662; e-mail: envserv@wyre6c.gov.uk); run by Wyre Borough Council, from Cemetery Office, Wyre Civic Centre, Breck Road, Poulton-le-Fylde, Lancashire FY6 7PU. Plot (50 years) incl. digging and burial £397-10 (double for non-residents). They will accept home-made, cardboard or wicker coffins and body bags or shrouds. Time for service: Unlimited. There is no chapel. Grounds: 'Well kept and tidy.' Memorials: 'Memorials must be limited to lawn types; however, the Council will view and consider any other choice of memorial.' 'The constant concern is to try to honour and meet our customer's needs at all times, at a realistic price, with a realistic attitude' (Sonia Neighbour).

• **Cem Poulton-le-Fylde**: Poulton New Cemetery, Garstang Road East, Poulton-le-Fylde, Lancashire (tel 01253 891000 ext 662; e-mail: envserv@wyre6c. gov.uk). Chapel: 'Quaint and simple ' Grounds: 'Well kept, surrounded by trees.' Memorials: 'Memorials must be limited to lawn types; however, the Council will view and consider any other choice of memorial requested by the bereaved.' Other details as for Poulton-le-Fylde above.

• **Cem Preesall**: Preesall Cemetery, Cemetery Lane, Preesall, Lancashire (tel 01253 891000 ext 662; e-mail: envserv@wyre6c.gov.uk). Plot (50 years) incl. digging and burial £397-10 (double for non-residents). They will accept home-made, cardboard or wicker coffins and body bags or shrouds. There is no chapel. Details as for Poulton-le-Fylde above.

• **Cem Preston**: Preston Cemetery, New Hall Lane, Preston, Lancashire PR1 4SY (tel 01772 729485); run by Preston Borough Council. Lawn cemetery plot (75 years) incl. digging and burial £588. They will accept home-made or strong cardboard coffins, 'subject to prior discussion.' Length of funeral service: Unlimited. There is no chapel. Grounds: 'Wooded and Victorian in the old cemetery (opened in 1855), bleakly formal in the new.' 'Memorials of any kind allowed, up to a standard maximum height of 4' 5".' 'We are currently adopting the Charter for the Bereaved' (Mr Martin Birch).

• **Crem Preston**: Preston Crematorium, Longridge Road, Preston; run by Preston Borough Council from New Hall Lane, Preston PR1 4SY, (tel 01772 794585). Price: £214 (incl. £30 environmental surcharge). Time allotted: 30 minutes. They will accept home-made or strong cardboard coffins, 'subject to prior discussion'. Chapel: 'Seats up to 100 people.' Grounds: 'Open parkland at the front, woodlands at the rear. The crematorium was opened in 1962.' 'We are currently adopting the Charter for the Bereaved' (Mr Martin Birch).

• **Crem Southport**: Southport Crematorium, Southport Road, Scarisbrick, Southport PR8 5JQ (tel 01704 533443); run by Sefton Metropolitan Borough Council. Price: £175 (£221 for non-residents). Time allotted: 30 minutes (extra time can be booked for £175). They will accept home-made or cardboard coffins. Chapel: 'Modern, airy, inter-denominational, well-maintained.' Grounds: 'Natural woodland, augmented by ericacious plantings, red squirrels, pheasants, woodpeckers, jays, etc.' 'Our greatest asset has to be our surroundings. Our peat soil provides a magnificent display of rhododendrons and azaleas in May and June and the red squirrel feeding programme has ensured the survival of a healthy colony. They are a delight and comfort to the bereaved' (Carole Sheehan).

• **Cem Stockport**: Highfield Cemetery, Highfield Avenue, Bredbury, Stockport; run by Stockport Metropolitan Borough Council, from the Stockport Crematorium, 31a Buxton Road, Heaviley, Stockport SK2 6LS (tel 0161 480 5221; fax 0161 480 6992). Plot (75 years) incl. digging and burial £675 (double for non-residents). They will accept home-made, cardboard or wicker coffins. Length of funeral service: 45 minutes (extra time can be booked for £55). No chapel. Grounds: 'Wide open, rural aspect, no houses visible nearby.' Memorials: 'Height restriction of 3', restrictions on materials – stone or ceramics.' 'The cemetery is adjacent to Goyt Valley and has fine views, with woods nearby' (N. Buckley).

• **Crem Stockport**: Stockport Crematorium, 31a Buxton Road, Heaviley, Stockport SK2 6LS (tel 0161 480 5221; fax 0161 480 6992); run by Stockport Metropolitan Borough Council. Price: £225. Time allotted: 30 minutes (extra time can be booked for £55 per half hour; £55 surcharge Saturdays; burial chapel available for 45 minutes at basic price). They will accept cardboard 'and other green' coffins. Chapel: 'Built in 1934 in dark brick, in a simple Byzantine style; has a ramped entrance and loop system.' Grounds: 'Crematorium surrounded by walled Gardens of Remembrance.' 'Staff at the crematorium are very flexible and helpful' (N. Buckley).

• **Cem Tyldesley**: Tyldesley Cemetery, Hough Lane, Tyldesley, Lancashire. Other details as for Leigh Cemetery above.

• **Cem Whitehaven**: Whitehaven Cemetery, Low Road, Whitehaven, Cumbria (tel 01946 692329). They also administer Hensingham, Netherwasdale, Millom and St John's Beckermet Cemeteries. Plot (50 years) incl. digging and burial

£461 (£112-75 extra for non-residents). They will accept home-made or card-board coffins. No chapel. Grounds: 'Natural woodland setting.' Memorials: 'Within size restrictions.' 'Reasonably priced and well maintained' (Mr S. J. Benn).

• **Cem Wigan (1)**: Gidlow Cemetery, Wigan Road, Standish, Wigan. Other details as for Leigh Cemetery above.

• **Cem Wigan (2)**: Ince-in-Makerfield Cemetery, Warrington Road, Lower Ince, Wigan. Other details as for Leigh Cemetery above.

• **Cem Wigan (3)**: Westwood Cemetery, Westwood Lane, Lower Ince, Wigan. Other details as for Leigh Cemetery above.

• **Cem Wigan (4)**: Wigan Cemetery, Cemetery Road, Lower Ince, Wigan, (tel 01942 866455). Other details as for Leigh Cemetery above.

• **Crem Wigan**: Wigan Crematorium, Cemetery Road, Lower Ince, Wigan (tel 01942 866455). Price: £175. Time allotted: 30 minutes (extra time can be booked without charge). They will accept home-made or cardboard coffins. Chapel: 'Church-like, converted from a nonconformist cemetery chapel.' Grounds: 'Cemetery with Gardens of Remembrance.' 'We would assist with any part of a funeral arrangement or provide any assistance to a bereaved family' (Anthony Bassett).

• **Cem Wilmslow**: Wilmslow Cemetery, Manchester Road, Wilmslow SK9 2LE; run by the Macclesfield Borough Council, from Macclesfield Cemetery, Prestbury Road, Macclesfield, SK10 3BU (tel 01625 422330 or 422408 or 504511). Plot (100 years) incl. digging and burial £487 (double for non-residents). They will accept cardboard or wicker coffins. Length of funeral service: 20 minutes (extra time can be booked for £52). Chapel: 'Victorian chapel with space heating.' Memorials: 'Lawn-type memorials only, with size restrictions' (John J. Thomas).

The North East

Comprising Northumberland, Newcastle-Upon-Tyne, North Tyneside, Gateshead, South Tyneside, Sunderland, Durham, Hartlepool, Stockton-On-Tees, Middlesbrough, Redcar, North Yorkshire, York, East Riding of Yorkshire, Kingston-Upon-Hull, Bradford, Leeds, Calderdale, Kirklees, Wakefield, Barnsley, Sheffield, Rotherham, Doncaster, North Lincolnshire, North East Lincolnshire and Lincolnshire.

• **Cem Barnsley**: Barnsley Cemetery, Cemetery Road, Barnsley; run by Denis Rhodes, Bereavement Services Manager, Barnsley Metropolitan Borough Council, Barnsley Crematorium, Doncaster Road, Barnsley S71 5EH (tel 01226 206053). The council also runs: Ardsley Cemetery, Hunningley Lane; Bolton Cemetery, Furlong Road; Brierly Cemetery, Church Street; Carlton Cemetery, Royston Lane; Cudworth Cemetery, Church View; Darfield Cemetery, Saltesbrook Road; Dodworth Cemetery, Green Road; Elsecar Cemetery, Church Street; Great Houghton Cemetery, Park Lane; Grimethorpe Cemetery, Cemetery Road; Hemingfield/Jump Cemetery, Cemetery Road; Hoyland Cemetery,

Kirk Balk; Monk Bretton Cemetery, Cross Street; Penistone Cemetery, Thurlstone Road; Royston Cemetery, New Street; Silkstone Cemetery, Cone Lane; Thurgoland Cemetery, Halifax Road; Thurnscoe Cemetery, Southfield Lane; and Wombwell Cemetery, Cemetery Road . Plot (99 years) incl. digging and burial from £629. They will accept cardboard coffins. Length of funeral service: 30 minutes. No chapel. Memorials: 'There are restrictions as to size and offensive wording is not allowed' (Denis Rhodes).

• **Crem Barnsley**: Barnsley Crematorium, Doncaster Road, Ardsley, Barnsley S71 5EH (tel 01226 206053). Price: £242. Time allotted: 30 minutes (extra time can be booked for £91). They will accept coffins approved by the FBCA (see the FBCA anti-pollution requirements in Chapter 4). A member of the public reports that 'they do accept cardboard coffins but seem to prefer chipboard ones, available cheaply locally.' Chapel: 'A mature building built in 1963.' Grounds: 'Peaceful and quiet garden.' 'A service that meets the changing demands of this sensitive subject' (Denis Rhodes).

• **Cem Barrow-on-Humber**: Barrow-on-Humber Cemetery, North Lincolnshire (tel 01724 280289). (All correspondence to Scunthorpe Woodlands Memorial Park address below). No chapel. Grounds: 'A tranquil cemetery with farmland on 2 sides and screened on one side by a belt of mixed trees.' Memorials: 'Headstones, without kerbing, within size restrictions.' All other details as for Cem Scunthorpe (1) below.

• **Cem Barton-upon-Humber**: Barton-upon-Humber Cemetery, Barrow Road, Barton-upon-Humber, North Lincolnshire (tel 01724 280289). (All correspondence to Scunthorpe Woodlands Memorial Park address below.) No chapel. Grounds: 'With farmland on two sides and a fine view across to the Humber Bridge and estuary.' Memorials: 'Headstones, without kerbing, within size restrictions.' All other details as for Cem Scunthorpe (1) below.

• **Cem Boston**: Boston Cemetery, Horncastle Road, Boston, Lincolnshire (vehicular access Marian Road only) (tel 01205 364612); run by the Boston Borough Council. Plot (100 years) incl. digging and burial £480 (£52 extra for non-residents). Maintenance: From £17 (grass only) to £56 (with plants) per annum. They will accept home-made, cardboard or wicker coffins. Length of funeral service: '30 minutes between starts (extra time £100).' Chapel: 'Comfortable 1960s crematorium chapel, with live organ and central heating.' Grounds: 'The original 1850s part is managed for wildlife and is particularly attractive with spring bulbs. There are many varied, mature species of trees.' Memorials: 'No restrictions on kerb sections. The usual restrictions apply to the lawn sections and the cremated remains section.' They have adopted the Charter for the Bereaved. A woodland burial ground is planned – see Chapter 6 for details. 'We are not too restrictive and try to help rather than hinder, whilst balancing this with common sense. The cemetery is a green haven not far from the town centre' (Martin Potts).

• **Crem Boston**: Boston Crematorium, Marian Road, Boston, Lincolnshire PE21 9HA (tel 01205 364612). Price: £187. Time allotted: 25 minutes within a 30 minute period. They will accept home-made or cardboard coffins (must be identified). Chapel: 'Removable Christian symbols'. Grounds: 'Extensive lawns with many trees and formal rosebeds.' 'Our attitude is friendly, and the ambience inviting' (Martin Potts).

• **Cem Bradford**: Scholemoor Cemetery, Necropolis Road, Bradford BD7 2PS (tel 01274 571313). Plot (100 years) incl. digging and burial £316. They will accept home-made, cardboard or wicker coffins and body bags or shrouds. Length of funeral service: No limit. Chapel: As crematorium below. Grounds: 'Maintained to a high standard.' 'Our highly trained staff are committed to delivering a sensitive service to meet the needs of the service user' (David Congreve). They also have a woodland burial area within their Thornton branch cemetery (see Chapter 6 for details).

• **Crem Bradford**: Scholemoor Crematorium, Scholemoor Cemetery, Necropolis Road, Bradford BD7 2PS (tel 01274 571313). Price: £220. Time allotted: 30 minutes (extra time can be booked without charge). They will accept home-made, cardboard or wicker coffins, or shrouds or body bags. Chapel: 'Non-denominational, converted Victorian chapel.' Grounds: 'Well-maintained grounds.' 'Caring, helpful staff' (David Congreve).

• **Cem Brigg**: Brigg Cemetery, Wrawby Road, Brigg, North Lincolnshire (tel 01724 280289). (All correspondence to Scunthorpe Woodlands Memorial Park address below.) No chapel. Grounds: 'On the edge of a pleasant market town, includes an older section with traditional memorials.' Memorials: 'Headstones, without kerbing, within size restrictions.' All other details as for Cem Scunthorpe (1) below.

• **Crem Durham**: Central Durham Crematorium, South Road, Durham, County Durham DH1 3TQ (tel 0191 3848677). Price: £165 (£245 non-residents). Time allotted: 30 minutes (extra time can be booked for £20 per half hour). They will accept home-made or cardboard coffins. Chapel: 'Modern, non-denominational.' Grounds: 'Open parkland with distant views.' 'Our service is dignified and fitting to the needs of individual families. We are happy to arrange any music (within reason) and have recently hosted jazz bands, trumpet solos, etc at services' (Mr Alan S. M. Jose).

• **Crem Great Grimsby**: Great Grimsby Crematorium, Weelsby Avenue, Great Grimsby, North East Lincolnshire DN32 0BA (tel 01472 324868). Price: £220 (£243-50 non-residents). Time allotted: 30 minutes (extra time could possibly be arranged). They will accept home-made or cardboard coffins. 'Only 2 or 3 members of the immediate family permitted to witness coffin entering the cremator, but by prior arrangement.' Chapel: '1950s.' Grounds: 'Attractive landscaped grounds with a memorial garden.' 'We are keen to work closely with the public and have recently been promoting environmentally-friendly coffins and independent funerals' (Mrs Glenis Clover).

• **Crem Harrogate**: Harrogate Crematorium, Stonefall Cemetery, Wetherby Road, Harrogate, North Yorkshire HG3 1DE (tel 01423 883523). Price: £253. Time allotted: 20 minutes within 40 minute period (extra time can be booked for £8). They will accept home-made or cardboard coffins, or others if recommended by FBCA. Chapel: 'Church-like.' Grounds: 'In a well-maintained, traditional cemetery setting'. 'We are in the process of adopting the Charter for the Bereaved.' 'We recognise that bereaved people have differing needs and we accommodate these wherever possible' (Philip Andrew).

• ✪✪✪ **Cem Hexham**: St Andrews Cemetery, West Road, Hexham, Northumberland (tel 07710053732). Plot (99 years) incl. digging and burial £229 (double for non-residents). They will accept cardboard coffins. Length of funeral service: 'As required.' Chapel: 'Victorian.' Grounds: 'In the beautiful Tyne valley with no residential developments nearby' (John Thirwell). For details of their woodland burial area, see Chapter 6. Winner of the New Natural Death Handbook Award 2000 for the Best Cemetery in the North East.

• **Cem Houghton-le-Spring**: Easington Lane Cemetery, Murton Lane, Easington Lane, Houghton-le-Spring, Tyne and Wear (tel 0191 553 1687); run by the City of Sunderland. Plot (99 years) incl. digging and burial £494 (double for non-residents). They will accept cardboard coffins. Length of funeral service: 30 minutes. No chapel. Grounds: 'Small cemetery in a rural area' (John Blyth). They have adopted the Charter for the Bereaved and offer a useful guide for those planning funerals without funeral directors.

• **Cem Houghton-le-Spring**: Hetton Cemetery, Houghton Road, Hetton-le-Hole, Houghton-le-Spring, Tyne and Wear (tel 0191 553 1687); run by the City of Sunderland Council. Plot (99 years) incl. digging and burial £494 (double for non-residents). They will accept cardboard coffins. Length of funeral service: 30 minutes. No chapel. Grounds: 'Small cemetery in a rural area.' They have adopted the Charter for the Bereaved and offer a useful guide for those planning funerals without funeral directors (John Blyth).

• **Cem Houghton-le-Spring**: Houghton Cemetery, Durham Road, Houghton-le-Spring, Tyne and Wear (tel 0191 553 1687); run by the City of Sunderland Council. Plot (99 years) incl. digging and burial £494 (double for non-residents). They will accept cardboard coffins. Length of funeral service: 30 minutes. No chapel. They have adopted the Charter for the Bereaved and offer a useful guide for those planning funerals without funeral directors (John Blyth).

• **Crem Hull**: Chanterlands Crematorium, Chanterlands Avenue, Hull (tel 01482 614976); run by Kingston upon Hull City Council. Price: £283. Time allotted: 40 minutes (extra time can be booked by appointment without charge). They will accept cardboard coffins. Chapel: 'Two modern chapels, one with 30 seats, the other with 120 seats (and an upper balcony for extra capacity)'. Grounds: '23 acres of landscaped grounds. There is a long attractive drive lined with rose bushes' (Terence M. Boulton).

• **Cem Keighley**: Utley Cemetery, Skipton Road, Keighley, Bradford BD20 6EJ (tel 01535 643263). Plot (100 years) incl. digging and burial £316. They will accept home-made, cardboard or wicker coffins and body bags or shrouds. Length of funeral service: No limit. No chapel. Grounds: 'Maintained to a high standard.' 'Our highly trained staff are committed to delivering a sensitive service to meet the needs of the service user' (David Congreve).

• **Crem Keighley**: Oakworth Crematorium, Wide Lane, Oakworth, Keighley, Bradford BD22 0RJ (tel 01535 643263). Price: £220. Time allotted: 30 minutes (extra time can be booked without charge). They will accept home-made, wicker or cardboard coffins and body bags or shrouds. Chapel: 'Non-denominational, converted Victorian chapel.' Grounds: 'Well-maintained countryside.' 'Caring, helpful staff' (David Congreve and J Elsbury).

• **Cem Leeds**: Lawnswood Cemetery, Otley Road, Adel, Leeds LS16 6AH (0113 2673188). Plot for two people (50 years) incl. digging and burial £630 (£1260 for non-residents). They will accept home-made or cardboard coffins. Length of funeral service: 30 minutes. Chapel: 'Dark stone, built in the late 19th century, with seating for 80 people.' Grounds: 'An historic 20-acre cemetery with beautiful old memorials' (Phil Stephenson).

• **Crem Leeds**: Leeds City Council Cemeteries and Crematoria Section, Otley Road, Adel, Leeds LS16 6AH (0113 2673188). Price: £245. Time allotted: 30 minutes (extra time can be booked for £104). They will accept home-made or cardboard coffins. Chapel: 'Church-like, with seating for 80 people.' Grounds: 'A mix of formal and woodland areas' (Phil Stephenson).

• **Cem Middlesbrough**: Acklam Cemetery, Acklam Road, Acklam, Middlesbrough, TS5 7HE. All correspondence to this address. Price: £230 (double for non-residents). Grounds: 'Adjacent to crematorium, open space and Botanic Centre, with views of Cleveland Hills.' Chapel: 'Use of two chapels at adjacent crematorium; both seat 80. One is from the 1960s, with central altar and no windows; the other from the 1980s, with lots of glass' (P. Gitsham). Other details as for Middlesbrough Thorntree Cemeteries below. (For the woodland burial area details see Chapter 6.)

• **Cem Middlesbrough**: Linthorpe Cemetery, Burlam Road, Middlesbrough. Grounds: '52 acres with heavily wooded older areas and a nature conservation area'. There is no chapel. 'A Friends Group has been formed, which arranges walks and talks on the cemetery's history and wildlife' (P. Gitsham). Other details as for Middlesbrough Thorntree Cemeteries below.

• **Cem Middlesbrough**: Thorntree and Thorntree RC Cemeteries, Cargo Fleet Lane, Thorntree, Middlesbrough (tel 01642 817725). Plot (50 years) incl. digging and burial £230 (£460 for non-residents). They will accept home-made, cardboard or wicker coffins and will consider body bags or shrouds. Length of funeral service: Up to 60 minutes. Chapel: 'Seats 30 to 40, 1930s style.' Memorials: 'Natural quarried stones or wooden crosses to Council specifications' (P. Gitsham).

• **Crem Middlesbrough**: Teeside Crematorium, Acklam Road, Acklam, Middlesbrough, TS5 7HE (01642 817725); run by the Middlesbrough Borough Council. Price: £254. Time allotted: 30 minutes (extra time can be booked for £52). They will accept home-made, cardboard or wicker coffins and 'may consider body bags or shrouds.' Chapels: 'One was built in 1961, with a very high ceiling, seating 80; the other is more modern, with a lot of glass windows, light and airy, seating about 100.' Grounds: 'Shrubberies and lawn with views of Cleveland Hills.' They have adopted the Charter for the Bereaved (P. Gitsham).

• **Crem Newcastle-upon-Tyne**: West Road Crematorium, West Road, Newcastle-upon-Tyne (tel 0191 2744 737); run by Newcastle City Council. Price: £237. Time allotted: 30 minutes (extra time can be booked for £56). They will accept home-made, cardboard or wicker coffins and body bags or shrouds. Chapel: 'Very simple and traditional.' Grounds: 'Well-kept gardens.' They will have adopted the Charter for the Bereaved by the end of 2000. 'All family requests by way of music, etc are accommodated whenever possible' (Tracey Harrison).

• **Crem North Shields**: North Shields Crematorium, Walton Avenue, North Shields, North Tyneside (tel 0191 2005861); run by North Tyneside Council. Price: £243-50. Time allotted: 30 minutes (30 minutes extra time can be booked for £35). They will accept home-made or cardboard coffins and all other types would be considered by the registrar. Chapel: 'Church-like, with removable crosses and seating for 60 people.' Grounds: 'Heavily wooded, older part of mature cemetery - one part is a conservation area.' They have adopted the Charter for the Bereaved. 'Very attractive mature woodland surroundings' (Mr Jim Sinley).

• **Cem Scawby**: Scawby Cemetery, Scawby, North Lincolnshire (tel 01724 280289). (All correspondence to Scunthorpe Woodlands Memorial Park address below.) No Chapel. Grounds: 'Tranquil, natural setting in open farmland.' Memorials: Headstones, without kerbing, within size restrictions. All other details as for Cem Scunthorpe (1) below.

• **Cem Scunthorpe**: Crosby Cemetery, Ferry Road, Scunthorpe, North Lincolnshire (tel 01724 280289). (All correspondence to Scunthorpe Woodlands Memorial Park address below.) No chapel. Grounds: 'An old cemetery with traditional memorials.' Memorials: 'Headstones, without kerbing, within size restrictions.' All other details as for Cem Scunthorpe (1) below.

• **Cem Scunthorpe (1)**: Woodlands Memorial Park Cemetery, Brumby Wood Lane, Scunthorpe, North Lincolnshire DN17 1SP (tel 01724 280289; e-mail: jack.startin@northlincs.gov.uk). Administers Brumby, Barrow-upon-Humber, Barton-upon-Humber, Winterton, Brigg, Scawby and Crosby branch cemeteries. Plot (50 years) incl. digging and burial £550. They will accept home-made or cardboard coffins. Length of funeral service: 20 minutes (extra time can be booked for £30). Chapel: See below. Grounds: See below. Memorials: 'No headstones in Sections A and B; only bronze plaques set at an angle, off the ground, in a garden border. Headstones and kerbing permitted in other sections.' There are also plots for cremated remains. They have adopted the Charter for the Bereaved. 'Every effort is made to accommodate the wishes of the deceased and family' (Jack Startin).

• **Cem Scunthorpe (2)**: Brumby Cemetery, Cemetery Road, Scunthorpe, North Lincolnshire (tel 01724 280289). (All correspondence to Scunthorpe Woodlands Memorial Park address below.) No Chapel. Grounds: 'An old cemetery with a mix of traditional kerbs and headstones, plus a lawn section set amongst birch trees.' Memorials: 'Stone headstones, without kerbing, within size restrictions.' All other details as for Cem Scunthorpe (1) above.

• ✪✪✪ **Crem Scunthorpe**: Woodlands Crematorium, Woodlands Memorial Park, Brumby Wood Lane, Scunthorpe, North Lincolnshire DN17 1SP (tel

01724 280289; e-mail: jack.startin@northlincs.gov.uk). Price: £220 (£250 for non-residents). Time allotted: 20 minutes within a 30 minute period (extra time can be booked for £15). They will accept home-made, cardboard or wicker coffins and body bags or shrouds. Chapel: 'Light and airy, the upper portion in glass, with a non-denominational stained glass window.' Grounds: 'Shrubberies, specimen trees and avenues creating long vistas across close-mown lawns.' They have adopted the Charter for the Bereaved. 'We strive to provide an excellent service to all our customers and to help them have the funeral of *their* choice. We have an open door policy, and the public may visit without prior booking for a guided tour' (Jack Startin). Winner of the New Natural Death Handbook Award 2000 for the Best Crematorium in the North East.

• **Cem Shipley**: Nab Wood Cemetery, Bingley Road, Shipley, Bradford BD18 4EW. Plot (100 years) incl. digging and burial £316. They will accept home-made, cardboard or wicker coffins and body bags or shrouds. Length of funeral service: Open. Chapel: As crematorium below. Grounds: 'Maintained to a high standard.' 'Highly trained staff are committed to delivering a sensitive service to meet the needs of the service user' (David Congreve).

• **Crem Shipley**: Nab Wood Crematorium, Bingley Road, Shipley, Bradford BD18 4BG (tel 01274 584109). Price: £220. Time allotted: 30 minutes (extra time can be booked without charge). They will accept home-made, cardboard or wicker coffins and shrouds or body bags. Chapel: Non-denominational, converted Victorian chapel. Grounds: 'Well-maintained grounds.' 'Caring, helpful staff' (David Congreve).

• **Cem Sunderland**: Bishopwearmouth Cemetery, Chester Road, Sunderland SR4 5SU (tel 0191 553 1687); run by the City of Sunderland. Plot (99 years) incl. digging and burial £494 (double for non-residents). They will accept cardboard coffins. Length of funeral service: 30 minutes. Chapel: '1850s building, small and quite pleasant.' Memorials: 'Currently restricted to lawn memorials, although it is intended to make traditional graves available in the future.' They have adopted the Charter for the Bereaved and offer a useful guide for those planning funerals without funeral directors. 'A very large cemetery of 88 acres, dating from 1856' (John Blyth).

• **Cem Sunderland**: Castletown Cemetery, Hylton Castle Road, Castletown, Sunderland (tel 0191 553 1687); run by the City of Sunderland. Plot (99 years) incl. digging and burial £494 (double for non-residents). They will accept cardboard coffins. Length of funeral service: 30 minutes. No chapel. They have adopted the Charter for the Bereaved and offer a useful guide for those planning funerals without funeral directors. 'Small, pleasant, well-tended cemetery' (John Blyth).

• **Cem Sunderland**: Mere Knolls Cemetery, Torver Crescent, Fulwell, Sunderland (tel 0191 553 1687); run by the City of Sunderland. Plot (99 years) incl. digging and burial £494 (double for non-residents). They will accept cardboard coffins. Length of funeral service: 30 minutes. Chapel: 'Victorian, in reasonable condition, fairly pleasant.' Grounds: 'Coastal location, next to the resort of Seaburn.' Memorials: 'Currently restricted to lawn memorials, although it is intended to make traditional graves available in the future'. They have adopted the Charter for the Bereaved and offer a useful guide for those planning funerals without funeral directors. 'Seaside setting. Established 1956. Mature trees along a stream at the northern boundary. A meadow area is under consideration' (John Blyth).

• **Cem Sunderland**: Sunderland (Grangetown) Cemetery, Ryhope Road, Grangetown, Sunderland (tel 0191 553 1687); run by the City of Sunderland. Plot (99 years) incl. digging and burial £494 (double for non-residents). They will accept cardboard coffins. Length of funeral service: 30 minutes. Chapel: 'Victorian building, quite basic' (John Blyth). They have adopted the Charter for the Bereaved and offer a useful guide for those planning funerals without funeral directors.

• **Cem Sunderland**: Ryhope Cemetery, Burdon Lane, Ryhope, Sunderland (tel 0191 553 1687); run by the City of Sunderland. Plot (99 years) incl. digging and burial £494 (double for non-residents). They will accept cardboard coffins. Length of funeral service: 30 minutes. No chapel. Grounds: 'Small established cemetery situated in a conservation area' (John Blyth). They have adopted the Charter for the Bereaved and offer a useful guide for those planning funerals without funeral directors.

• **Cem Sunderland**: Southwick Cemetery, Wembley Road, Witherwack, Sunderland (tel 0191 553 1687); run by the City of Sunderland. Plot (99 years) incl. digging and burial £494 (double for non-residents). They will accept cardboard coffins. Length of funeral service: 30 minutes. Chapel: 'Very basic, seldom used.' They have adopted the Charter for the Bereaved and offer a useful guide for those planning funerals without funeral directors (John Blyth).

• **Crem Sunderland**: Sunderland Crematorium, Chester Road, Sunderland SR4 5SU (tel 0191 5531687). Price: £211 (£69 extra for non-residents). Time allotted: 30 minutes. They will accept home-made or cardboard coffins. Chapels: '1950s design with a fixed catafalque.' Grounds: 'Well-tended grounds, with a small garden of remembrance, adjoining a large cemetery.' They have adopted the Charter for the Bereaved and offer a useful guide for those planning funerals without funeral directors. 'We offer a high quality and flexible service' (John Blyth).

• **Cem Washington**: Washington Cemetery, Glebe Crescent, Washington Village, Tyne and Wear (tel 0191 553 1687); run by the City of Sunderland. Plot (99 years) incl. digging and burial £494 (double for non-residents). They will accept cardboard coffins. Length of funeral service: 30 minutes. Chapel: '1850s building, small and quite pleasant.' Grounds: 'Small established cemetery situated in a conservation area.' Memorials: 'Currently restricted to lawn memorials, although it is intended to make traditional graves available in the future' (John Blyth). They have adopted the Charter for the Bereaved and offer a useful guide for those planning funerals without funeral directors.

• **Crem Whitley Bay**: Whitley Bay Crematorium, Blyth Road, Whitley Bay, North Tyneside (tel 0191 200 8658); run by North Tyneside Council. Price: £243-50. Time allotted: 30 minutes (extra time can be booked for £35). They will accept home-made or cardboard coffins; the acceptance of other types of coffins (wicker coffins and body bags or shrouds) would be at the discretion of the registrar. Chapel: 'Converted church with very attractive domed ceiling, seating for about 60 people. Removable cross.' Grounds: 'Mature cemetery, off a very attractive main drive lined with memorial seats.' They have adopted the Charter for the Bereaved (Jim Sinley).

• **Cem Winterton**: Winterton Cemetery, Cemetery Road, Winterton, North Lincolnshire (tel 01724 280289). (All correspondence to Woodlands Memorial Park address above). No Chapel. Grounds: 'Tranquil cemetery alongside farm-land. A Garden of Remembrance for the scattering of cremated remains.' Memorials: 'Headstones, without kerbing, within size restrictions.' All other details as for Cem Scunthorpe (1) above.

• **Cem York**: York Cemetery, The Gatehouse, Cemetery Road, York YO1 5AJ (tel 01904 610578 day). 'We will take any body container from body bag to home-made coffin, as long as it is all done with dignity.' Plot (99 years) incl. digging and burial £620. Maintenance: £30 p.a. A tree or bulbs can be planted at the request of relatives (with the cost varying, depending on the requirements). Chapel: 'A very fine Grade IIA listed classical chapel, prizewinning decoration, warm feel.' Time for service: Up to one and a half hours if needed. Grounds: 'Formal, wild, wooded. Ecological management plan to encourage wildlife. Memorials should be large and Victorian in style.' 'This is a Victorian park landscape gone wild. There are special butterfly and scented walks and there is a great deal of educational and informal recreational use of the area. We try to put customers' wishes first and empower them so that they can be in control of their funeral' (Hugh Goudge, Warden).

• **Crem York**: City of York Crematorium, Bishopthorpe Road, York YO23 2QD (tel 01904 706096; fax 01904 301569); run by City of York Council. Price: £320. Time allotted: 30 minutes (20 minutes in the chapel; extra time can be booked for £59). They will accept cardboard or wicker coffins. Chapels: 'The main chapel, built in 1962, seats 120; a second, smaller chapel seats from 15 to 20.' Grounds: 'Parkland and trees with a small garden of remembrance' (Mr Milsted).

Wales

Comprising Flintshire, Wrexham, Denbighshire, Aberconwy and Colwyn, Anglesey, Caernarfonshire and Merionethshire, Powys, Cardiganshire, Pembrokeshire, Carmarthenshire, Swansea, Neath and Port Talbot, Bridgend, Rhondda Cynon Taff, Vale of Glamorgan, Merthyr Tydfil, Caerphilly, Cardiff, Blaenau Gwent, Torfaen, Newport, Monmouthshire.

• ✪✪✪ **Crem Aberdare**: Llwydcoed Crematorium, Aberdare, Mid Glamorgan, Wales CF44 0DJ (tel 01685 874115; web: www.yell.co.uk/sites/ llwydcoedcrematorium; e-mail via 'Contact Us' at website). Price: £160. Time allotted: 25 minutes within a 40 minute period (extra time can be booked without charge). They will accept home-made, cardboard or wicker coffins. Chapels:

'The award-winning building fits particularly well into the rural landscape and is in sympathy with the vernacular architecture of the area. Capel Mair seats 120, Capel Tydfil 50.' Grounds: 'Landscaped with trees, shrubs and ornamental pools, and the gardens provide a haven for quiet contemplation in tranquil surroundings.' Llwyncoed stock the Compakta coffin, Ecology Peace coffin and Woodgrain Eco-coffin, and provide a leaflet for those organising cremations themselves (which they have carefully researched, for instance: 'Enquiries have been made at local hospitals and we are informed that the body will be dressed in a shroud and placed in the coffin by mortuary staff. A copy of the Authority for Removal of a Body from the mortuary of local hospitals is attached'). They have adopted the Charter for the Bereaved. 'We try to cater for all needs as far as possible' (Clive G. Lewis). Winner of the New Natural Death Handbook Award 2000 for the Best Crematorium in Wales.

• **Crem Aberystwyth**: Aberystwyth Crematorium, Clarach Road, Aberystwyth, Cardiganshire, Wales SY23 3DG (tel 01970 626 942). Run by the Crematoria Investment Company. Price: £250. Time allotted: 60 minutes (extra time can be booked without charge). They will accept home-made or cardboard coffins. Chapel: 'Modern, with a large window overlooking Cynfelyn Valley. Comfortable furnishings.' Grounds: 'A wooded hillside above the beautiful and peaceful Cynfelyn Valley. The Garden of Remembrance is a rare orchid site, and the sea is visible from parts of the grounds' (P. J. Wilson).

• **Cem Anglesey**: Lon Newydd Cemetery, Lon Newydd, Llangefni, Anglesey, Wales LL77 7TW (tel 01248 723 332); run by the Llangefni Town Council. Plot ('perpetuity') incl. digging and burial £118 (double for non-residents). No maintenance costs. 'No time limit for service.' Re cardboard or unusual coffins: 'Our council would have to decide on a policy on such matters.' Chapel: 'Small, Victorian, nonconformist, well-constructed of local stone.' Grounds: 'Opened in 1867, the cemetery occupies a central position in town. The number buried stands at 2,630.' Memorials: 'Headstone limited to 3' in height, 2' 6" in width.' 'The neat cemetery is a matter of pride to the workers, council and local inhabitants. Our prices are quite low compared to other nearby cemeteries' (M. T. Jones).

• **Crem Bridgend**: Coychurch Crematorium, Coychurch, Bridgend, Wales CF35 6AB (tel 01656 656605); run by Bridgend County Borough Council. Price: £186-30. Time allotted: 30 minutes (extra time can be booked for £41). They will accept home-made or cardboard or wicker coffins. Chapel: 'The main chapel is a Christian chapel with a wooden ceiling and a catafalque of black slate and solid wooden pews; the secondary inter-denominational chapel is built of stone and wood, sheeted both internally and externally with cedar wood. It has a floor of patterned brick and is roofed in copper. The crematorium is built of natural stone taken from old demolished buildings in the area.' Grounds: 'The crematorium is set on a rolling hillside on the dividing line between open countryside and ancient woodland. The grounds extend to 29 acres, of which 15 acres are woodland, within which the car parks are screened. A beautiful natural lake adjoins the main chapel entrance canopy.' 'The tranquil setting coupled with a highly trained and motivated team of staff provides a truly sympathetic environment' (Joanna Hamilton).

• **Crem Cardiff**: City of Cardiff Crematorium, Thornhill Road, Llanishen, Cardiff, Wales CF4 5LA (tel 029 206 23294; fax 029 206 92904). Price: £213 (non-residents £366); run by Cardiff County Council. Time allotted: 20 minutes ('additional 20 minutes at no further cost – simply request this when booking'). They will accept home-made, cardboard or wicker coffins, or shrouds or body bags. Chapels: 'Modern, Portland stone building with wonderful organ. A second small chapel is under construction.' Grounds: 'Formal gardens, informal woods.' They have adopted the Charter for the Bereaved. 'We make every effort to meet the bereaved to ensure they are fully advised rather than relying on the funeral director's "advice" ' (Roger Swan).

• **Cem Mold**: Mold Public Cemetery, Alexandra Road, Mold, Flintshire, Wales CH7 1HJ (tel 01352 753820). Plot incl. digging and burial £250. No time limit for the service. No chapel. Grounds: 'This is the town cemetery with flower borders and trees, surrounded by a football field and playing ground.' Memorials: 'To be made of stone with reverent wording.' 'Friendly management. Family mourners often lower the coffin. The cemetery won a best-kept cemetery award in 1993' (Arfon Llyod Williams-Cooke).

• **Crem Narberth**: Parc Gwyn Crematorium, Narberth, Pembrokeshire, Wales SA6Y 8UD (tel 01834 860622; e-mail: parcgwyn@hotmail.com). Price: £190 incl. organists' fee. Time allotted: 20 minutes (extra time can be booked without charge). They will accept home-made, cardboard or wicker coffins, or shrouds or body bags. Chapel: '1960s, removable cross.' Grounds: 'Beautifully laid out with trees, borders, etc in seven and a half acres of gently rolling countryside.' They have adopted the Charter for the Bereaved. 'A friendly service in accordance with the wishes of the bereaved' (Revd. Elwyn J. John).

• **Cem Newport**: St Woolos Cemetery, Bassaleg Road, Newport NP9 3NA, South Wales (tel 01633 263864); also runs Christchurch Cemetery, Christchurch Road, Newport; and Caerleon Cemetery, Coldbath Road, Caerleon – for both these cemeteries the details are as for St Woolos. Plot (99 years) incl. digging and burial £414 (no extra for non-residents). 'One hour for services plus one hour is left between services.' No chapel in use. Grounds: 'Three old listed buildings in St Woolos and one in Christchurch.' Memorials: 'Headstone limited to 2' 8" in height, 3' in width and 8" in thickness' (N. S. Woodward).

• **Cem Penarth**: Penarth Cemetery, Castle Avenue, Penarth, Wales CF64 3QY (tel 02920 700721; e-mail: townclerk@penarthtowncouncil.fsnet.co.uk). Plot (75 years) incl. digging and burial £192-15 (double for non-residents). No chapel. Grounds: 'Traditional, edge of town location but accessible; elevated position giving views over the town.' Memorials: 'Newer sections – lawn-type; older sections – traditional.' 'Well maintained. Being the local cemetery in a small town, there is a need to be responsive to local views' (Edward J. Vick).

• **Crem Port Talbot**: Margam Crematorium, Longlands Lane, Margam, Port Talbot, Neath and Port Talbot, Wales SA13 2PP (tel 01639 883570). Price: £155 (no extra for non-residents). Time allotted: 30 minutes (extra time can be booked for £13). They will accept cardboard coffins. Chapel: 'Face-the-front seating.' Grounds: 'Natural woodland' (D. Hywel Selway).

• ✪✪✪ **Cem Wrexham**: Wrexham Cemetery, Ruabon Road, Wrexham, Wales LL13 7RE (tel 01978 263159); run by Wrexham County Borough. Plot (99 years) incl. digging and burial £333 (double for non-residents). No maintenance cost. They will accept home-made, cardboard or wicker coffins. Chapel: 'Victorian gothic with spire.' Grounds: 'Preserved Victorian layout, initially described as a garden cemetery. The buildings, chapel and monuments are listed Grade II.' Memorials: 'Maximum 3' 6" height on lawn sections, any design, any colour.' 'Computerised records for family history research. Original landscape preserved. Few prescriptive regulations' (Alan McMahon). Winner of the New Natural Death Handbook Award 2000 for the Best Cemetery in Wales.

• **Crem Wrexham**: Wrexham Crematorium, Pentrebychan, Wrexham, Wales LL14 4EP (tel 01978 840068); run by Wrexham County Borough. Price: £198 (£32 extra for non-residents). Time allotted: 30 minutes (extra time can be booked for £56). They will accept home-made, cardboard or wicker coffins. Chapels: 'Modern from 1960s. Glazed side wall with view of a water feature.' Grounds: 'Riverside walk, ponds, wildlife habitats, woodland. Grounds traversed by Offa's Dyke.' They have adopted the Charter for the Bereaved. 'We aim to preserve and enhance the natural beauty of the setting' (Alan McMahon).

West Midlands

Comprising Shropshire, Staffordshire, Wolverhampton, Walsall, Dudley, Sandwell, Birmingham, Solihull, Coventry, Hereford and Worcester, Gloucestershire.

• ✪✪✪ **Cem Burton-upon-Trent**: Stapenhill Cemetery, 38, Stapenhill Road, Burton-upon-Trent, Staffordshire DE15 9AE (tel 01283 508572); run by East Staffordshire Borough Council. Plot (50 years) incl. digging and burial £345; £331 for a double plot (double for non-residents). They will accept home-made, cardboard or wicker coffins and body bags or shrouds. Length of funeral service: 30 minutes (extra time can be booked without charge). Chapel: 'Victorian, well-maintained, with seating for about 60 people.' Grounds: 'Attractive Victorian cemetery rich in wildlife, overlooking flood plain of River Trent.' Memorials: 'Within size restrictions.' They will have adopted the Charter for the Bereaved by the end of 2000. 'We have a children's burial area and a "forget-me-not" garden' (Nick French). For details of their woodland burial area see Chapter 6. Winner of the New Natural Death Handbook Award 2000 for the Best Cemetery in the West Midlands.

• **Crem Burton-upon-Trent**: Bretby Crematorium, Geary Lane, Bretby, near Burton-upon-Trent, Staffordshire DE15 OQE (tel 01283 221505). Price: £225 (£26 extra if the organ is required). Time allotted: 45 minutes (extra time can be booked for £100). They will accept home-made, cardboard or wicker coffins and body bags or shrouds. Chapels: 'Two chapels, seating 80 and 18 respectively, in a natural and uplifting style using Columbian pine and Welsh slate.' Grounds:

'Maintained as a natural woodland and set in open countryside.' 'The Charter for the Bereaved is in the process of being adopted. The crematorium can supply two types of cardboard coffin and has a positive attitude to informing the public of the choices that are open to them. Awarded the Civic Trust Award in 1978' (Nick French).

• **Crem Cinderford**: Forest of Dean Crematorium, Yew Tree Blake, Speech House Road, Cinderford, Gloucestershire GL14 3HU (tel 01594 826624). Run by Crematoria Management Ltd. Price: £240. Time allotted: 60 minutes (no charge for extra time). They will accept home-made or cardboard coffins. Chapel: 'Simple yet dignified, comfortable, views of the forest.' Grounds: 'Forest location – very attractive' (P. J. Wilson).

• **Cem Coventry**: Canley Cemetery, Cemeteries and Crematorium Office, Cannon Hill Road, Canley, Coventry CV4 7DF (tel 02476 415886 or 02476 418055). Plot (75 years) incl. digging and burial £422. Maintenance: No charge. They will accept home-made or cardboard coffins, and will consider wicker coffins and body bags or shrouds. Length of funeral service: No limit at graveside. Chapels: As Crematorium below. 'A modern lawn-type layout with Garden of Rest and pond' (Mrs S. Turner).

• **Cem Coventry**: London Road Cemetery, London Road, Whitley, Coventry. 'Designed by Sir Joseph Paxton and opened in 1847. 43 acres of landscaped park with many interesting features' (Mrs S. Turner). All other details as for Coventry Canley Cemetery above.

• **Cem Coventry**: Lentons Lane Cemetery, Lentons Lane, Walsgrave, Coventry. 'A new cemetery opened in 1994 includes among other things a wild flower meadow and woodland burial area' (see Chapter 6 for details). 'It is situated to the north of the city next to the countryside. It provides lawn and kerbs; and a Muslim section providing chamber burials' (Mrs S. Turner). All other details as for Coventry Canley Cemetery above.

• **Cem Coventry**: St. Paul's Cemetery, Holbrooks Lane, Coventry. 'Traditional cemetery set in the industrial North of the city' (Mrs S. Turner). All other details as for Coventry Canley Cemetery above.

• **Cem Coventry**: Windmill Road Cemetery, Windmill Road, Foleshall, Coventry. 'A small cemetery serving local people in that part of the city' (Mrs S. Turner). All other details as for Coventry Canley Cemetery above.

• **Cem Coventry**: Walsgrave Cemetery, Woodway Lane, Coventry. 'Small cemetery on outskirts of the city' (Mrs S. Turner). All other details as for Coventry Canley Cemetery above.

• **Crem Coventry**: Canley Crematorium, Cannon Hill Road, Canley, Coventry CV4 7DF (tel 02476 415886 or 02476 418055). Price: £237. Time allotted: 45 minutes (extra time can be booked for £57). They will accept home-made, wicker or cardboard coffins. Chapel: 'Recently modernised to provide second chapel.' Grounds: 'Three acres of Gardens of Remembrance, with rose gardens, pond, seasonal lawns and English woodland.' 'A flexible interpretation of rules and codes is always applied' (G. D. Marshall).

• **Cem Dudley**: Gornal Wood Cemetery, Chase Road, Gornal Wood, Dudley

DY3 2RL (tel 01384 813970); run by Dudley Metropolitan Borough, which also administers cemeteries at Stourbridge, Halesowen, Cradley, Lye and Wollescote, Brierley Hill and Dudley. Plot (75 years) incl. digging and burial £852 (double for non-residents). They will accept home-made or cardboard coffins. Length of funeral service: '30 minutes if in the chapel (which can be booked for £45).' Chapel: 'Modern, light and airy.' Grounds: 'Landscaped setting.' Memorials: 'Only restrictions as regards health and safety.' 'Helpful staff' (Liz Mansell). There is also a woodland burial area within the cemetery (see Chapter 6 for details) (Liz Mansell).

• **Crem Dudley**: Gornal Wood Crematorium, Chase Road, Gornal Wood, Dudley DY3 2RL (tel 01384 813970); run by Dudley Metropolitan Borough. Price: £266. Time allotted: 20 minutes at half-hourly intervals (extra time can be booked for £45). They will accept home-made or cardboard coffins. Chapel: 'Modern, light and airy.' Grounds: 'Pleasant and spacious landscaped setting; helpful staff' (Liz Mansell).

• **Crem Newcastle-under-Lyme**: Bradwell Crematorium, Chatterley Close, Bradwell, Newcastle-under-Lyme, Staffordshire ST5 8LE (tel 01782 635498). Price: £285-50. Time allotted: 30 minutes (extra time can be booked without charge). They will accept home-made, cardboard or wicker coffins; they will consider body bags or shrouds. Chapel: 'Multi-denominational, timber-clad, seating about 100.' Grounds: '13 acres of themed gardens with a multitude of memorial trees and shrubs' (Steve Wells).

• **Cem Newport (Shropshire)**: Newport General Cemetery, Audley Avenue, Newport, Shropshire (tel 01952 814338); run by the Newport Town Council. Plot (50 years) incl. digging and burial £315 (£185 extra for non-residents). They will accept cardboard or wicker coffins and body bags or shrouds. Length of funeral service: 'As long as required.' Chapel: 'Built in 1859 in Gothic style, full restoration underway.' Memorials: 'No restrictions in the new children's burial area. In the main cemetery a maximum height of 2' 10" by 2' 6" wide.' 'There is a reserved area for Jewish burials and a separate area for other faiths' (Miss Dee Halliday). For details of their woodland burial extension, see Chapter 6.

• **Cem Redditch**: Abbey Cemetery, Bordesley Lane, Redditch, Hereford and Worcester B97 5AS (tel 01527 62174; e-mail: ken.elliott@redditchbc.gov.uk); run by the Redditch Borough Council. Plot (50 years) incl. digging and burial £450 (double for non-residents). They will accept home-made, cardboard or wicker coffins and body bags or shrouds. Length of funeral service: 30 minutes (extra time can be booked for £47). Chapel: 'Naturally designed and lit, with the north-facing picture window having an overview of the countryside.' They have adopted the Charter for the Bereaved (Ken Elliott).

• **Crem Redditch**: Redditch Crematorium, Bordesley Lane, Redditch, Hereford and Worcester B97 5AS (tel 01527 62174; e-mail: ken.elliott@redditchbc.gov.uk); run by the Redditch Borough Council. Price: £250. Time allotted: 30 minutes (extra time can be booked for £47). They will accept home-made, wicker or cardboard coffins and body bags or shrouds. Chapel: 'Timber and slate, without religious symbols except a cross on the descending catafalque.' Grounds: 'Spacious, naturally-designed gardens in rolling Worcestershire countryside.' They have adopted the Charter for the Bereaved. 'Our aim is to say "yes" to mourners' needs' (Ken Elliott).

• **Crem Shrewsbury**: Emstrey Crematorium, London Road, Shrewsbury, Shropshire SY2 6PS (tel 01743 359883). Price: £175. Time allotted: 40 minutes (extra time can be booked for £175). They will accept home-made, cardboard or wicker coffins, and body bags or shrouds, subject to FBCA conditions. They publish a basic leaflet for families arranging the funeral without a funeral director or without a minister. Chapel: 'Modern, church-like.' Grounds: 'A quiet restful atmosphere with private formal gardens set in open countryside.' 'The Chapel of Remembrance contains an 'on-screen' memorial cabinet where personalised memorials including photographs and drawings can be viewed' (M. J. Beardall).

• **Cem Solihull**: Robin Hood Cemetery, Streetsbrook Road, Shirley, Solihull, West Midlands (tel 0121 744 1121); run by Solihull Metropolitan Borough Council. Plot (50 years) incl. digging and burial £645 (triple for non-residents). They will accept home-made or cardboard coffins. Chapel: 'Church-like but intimate in size.' Grounds: 'Urban woodlands.' Memorials: 'Maximum 5' height.' 'Well maintained and landscaped' (Bernard McHale). See also the woodland burial area at Woodlands Cemetery, Coleshill, run by Solihull Metropolitan Borough Council, details in Chapter 6.

• **Cem Solihull**: Widney Manor Cemetery, Widney Manor Road, Bentley Heath, Solihull, West Midlands; run by Solihull Metropolitan Borough Council from the Robin Hood Cemetery, Streetsbrook Road, Shirley, Solihull, West Midlands (tel 0121 744 1121). Plot (50 years) incl. digging and burial £645 (triple for non-residents). They will accept home-made or cardboard coffins. No chapel. Grounds: 'Rural.' Memorials: 'Maximum 5' height.' 'Well maintained and landscaped' (Bernard McHale).

• **Crem Solihull**: Solihull Crematorium, Streetsbrook Road, Shirley, Solihull, West Midlands (tel 0121 744 1121); run by Solihull Metropolitan Borough Council. Price: £260. Time allotted: 30 minutes between service times (extra time can be booked for £70). They will accept home-made or cardboard coffins. Chapel: '.Church-like, fixed pews.' Grounds: 'Woodland approach on entrance drive. Well maintained.' 'All services are quality assured to quality system standard BS EN ISO 9002:1994. The buildings have attractive architecture' (Bernard McHale).

• **Cem Stafford**: Stafford Cemetery, Tixall Road, Stafford ST18 0XZ (tel 01785 242594; fax 01785 228521); run by Stafford Borough Council. The council runs two other cemeteries – Eccleshall Cemetery, Eccleshall Road, Stafford; and Stone Cemetery, A34, Stone – to which the following details also apply, unless otherwise stated. Plot (50 years) incl. digging and burial £367 (double for non-residents). They will accept home-made, cardboard or wicker coffins, or body bags or shrouds. Chapel: '1960s, warm.' Grounds: 'From lawn cemeteries to mature old type. Eccleshall Road backs onto Doxey Marches, a recognised wildlife sanctuary.' They have adopted the Charter for the Bereaved. 'Competitive prices. Mature trees and shrubs. Natural areas' (Rachel Lewis). There is a small woodland burial area within Stone Cemetery (see Chapter 6 for details).

• ❂❂❂ **Crem Stafford**: Stafford Crematorium, Tixall Road, Stafford ST18 0XZ (tel 01785 242594; fax 01785 228521); run by Stafford Borough Council. Price: £188. Time allotted: No limit. They will accept home-made, cardboard or wicker coffins and body bags or shrouds 'at the registrar's discretion'. Chapel: 'A warm and inviting chapel, with wooden decor and blue upholstery, with seating for 98 people.' Grounds: 'A parkland effect with slight undulations in a countryside area with mature trees.' They have adopted the Charter for the Bereaved. For details of the woodland burial site see Chapter 6 (Anthony Evans). Winner of the New Natural Death Handbook Award 2000 for the Best Crematorium in the West Midlands.

• **Crem Stoke-on-Trent**: Carmountside Crematorium, Leek Road, Milton, Stoke-on-Trent, Staffordshire ST2 7AB (run by Karen Deaville for Stoke-on-Trent City Council, tel 01782 535050). Price: £245. Time allotted: 30 minutes (extra time can be booked for £55). They will accept cardboard or wicker coffins. Chapel: 'Built in 1930s, seats 175.' Grounds: 'Varied gardens including woodland, garden of remembrance and babies' and children's garden.' The crematorium has a viewing room where up to 12 people can have a sideways view of the coffin entering the cremator. 'Winner of Cemetery and Crematorium of the Year Competition 1999' (Karen Deaville).

• **Crem Stourbridge**: Stourbridge Crematorium, South Road, Stourbridge, West Midlands DY8 3RQ (tel 01384 813985); run by Dudley Metropolitan Borough. Price: £266. Time allotted: 20 minutes at half-hourly intervals (extra time can be booked for £45). They will accept home-made or cardboard coffins. Chapel: 'A converted cemetery chapel with a church-like atmosphere.' Grounds: 'A pleasant, mature, traditional cemetery landscape' (Liz Mansell).

• **Cem Telford**: Castle Green Cemetery, Beeches Road, Ironbridge, Telford; run by Leisure and Community Services, Telford & Wrekin Council, Darby House, Telford TF3 4LA (tel 01952 202754; e-mail: lcc@wrekin.gov.uk). The council runs two other cemeteries – Wellington Cemetery, Linden Avenue, Wellington, Telford; and Wombridge Cemetery, Wombridge, Telford – to which the following details also apply, unless otherwise stated. Plot (75 years) incl. digging and burial £132 (single, unpurchased – purchase price £199) (double for non-residents). They will accept home-made, cardboard or wicker coffins and body bags or shrouds. No chapel. Memorials: 'Maximum 3' 6" height normally – can be taller if fixing method proven to be safe' They have adopted the Charter for the Bereaved. 'Flexible, accommodating service' (Rachel Lewis). They have opened a small wild flower Natural Burial Ground within the Castle Green Cemetery (see Chapter 6 for details).

• **Crem Walsall**: Streetly Crematorium, Little Hardwick Road, Aldridge, Walsall WS9 0SG (tel 0121 353 7228). Price: £225 (£675 for non-residents). Time allotted: 30 minutes (extra time can be booked for £41). They will accept home-made, cardboard or wicker coffins and body bags. Chapel: 'There are two chapels, with interiors in hand-finished straw coloured brickwork and a high, sloping, cedar ceiling. Suitable for small or large non-denominational gatherings.' Grounds: 'A 27-acre site in the greenfield fringe to the East of the borough in a pleasant, rural environment, well separated from residential development.' 'A friendly, flexible and helpful service to all' (Steve Billings).

• **Crem West Bromwich**: West Bromwich Crematorium, Newton Road, West Bromwich B71 3SX (tel 0121 588 2664); run by Sandwell Metropolitan Borough Council. Price: £250. Time allotted: 20 minutes (extra time can be booked for £125). They will accept cardboard coffins. Chapel: 'Modern. Seats 160.' Grounds: 'Landscaped gardens' (Mr K. Howard).

• **Crem Wolverhampton**: Bushbury Crematorium, Underhill Lane, Bushbury, Wolverhampton (tel 01902 554992 or 554993); run by Wolverhampton Borough Council. Price: £230. Time allotted: 30 minutes (extra time can be booked for £55). They will accept home-made, cardboard or wicker coffins. Chapels: 'Modern design. In West Chapel (seating 80) coffin lowers, in East Chapel (seating 50) curtain draws across.' Grounds: '40-acre site with planted flower borders, and a wooded area for placing cremated remains.' 'We have not officially adopted the Charter for the Bereaved but we act within its spirit.' 'Two chapels allow the family to choose the way the coffin is committed, and the East Chapel allows for a more intimate service' (Clare Yardley).

• **Crem Worcester**: Worcester Crematorium, Tintern Avenue, Astwood Road, Worcester WR3 8HA (tel 01905 22633); run by City of Worcester Council. Price: £210. Time allotted: 30 minutes (there would be a £50 charge for extra time – 'a double service is available if we are not busy'). They will accept home-made, cardboard or wicker coffins, 'as long as they have extra support for carrying.' A leaflet is provided for 'd-i-y' families. Chapel: '1960s building with a conventional layout, with seating for 100 people.' Grounds: 'Attractive lawns and borders with a stream running though. The Garden of Remembrance is adjacent to the old cemetery with its many fine old established trees.' 'We will deal with any requests that do not adversely affect other users.' ' We are currently adopting the Charter for the Bereaved' (David Seaman).

East Midlands

Comprising Derbyshire, Nottinghamshire, Leicestershire, Warwickshire, Northamptonshire, Bedfordshire, Oxfordshire, Buckinghamshire.

• **Crem Amersham**: Chilterns Crematorium, Whielden Lane, Amersham, Buckinghamshire HP7 0ND (tel 01494 724263; fax 01494 433065). Price: £190-50. Time allotted: 30 minutes. They will accept home-made or cardboard coffins, and will consider other body containers if they can be inspected in advance. They publish a useful five-page guide for families arranging funerals without a funeral director. Chapel: '1960s brick-built with copper roof.' Grounds: 'A natural woodland setting in open countryside on the edge of the Chiltern Hills'. 'Willing to consider every reasonable request on its merits' (Charles Howlett).

• **Cem Bedford**: Norse Road Cemetery, 104 Norse Road, Bedford, Bedfordshire (tel 01234 353701; e-mail: MDAY@Bedford.gov.uk). Plot (75 years) incl. digging and burial £277. They will accept home-made, cardboard or wicker coffins and body bags or shrouds. Length of funeral service: 45 minutes (extra time can be booked for £30). Chapel: 'Modern, secular.' Grounds: 'Modern, heavily wooded.' Memorials: 'Lawn-type back to back.' They have adopted the Charter for the Bereaved. 'Well-kept' (Michael Day). There is also a one-acre woodland burial area (see Chapter 6 for details).

• **Crem Bedford**: Bedford Crematorium, Cemetery Complex, 104 Norse Road, Bedford, Bedfordshire (tel 01234 353701; e-mail: MDAY@Bedford.gov.uk). Price: £221 (£200 non-residents). Time allotted: 45 minutes (extra time can be booked without charge). They will accept home-made, cardboard or wicker coffins and body bags or shrouds. Chapel: 'Modern, with wall-hangings and oak seating.' Grounds: 'Designed for ease of access and egress.' They have adopted the Charter for the Bereaved. 'Each funeral an individual experience' (Mr Michael Day).

• **Cem Belper**: Belper Cemetery, Matlock Road, Belper, Derbyshire (tel 01773 841418; e-mail: enquiry@ambervalley.gov.uk; web: www.ambervalley.gov.uk); run by Amber Valley Borough Council, Environment and Leisure Department, PO Box 18, Town Hall, Ripley, Derbyshire DE5 3TU. The council also runs five other cemeteries – Alfreton Cemetery, Rodgers Lane, Alfreton; Crosshill Cemetery, Heanor Road, Codnor; Heanor Cemetery, Ilkeston Road, Marlpool, Heanor; Leabrooks Cemetery, Albert Street, Leabrooks; and Ripley Cemetery, Cemetery Lane, Ripley – for all of which the following details apply, unless otherwise stated. Plot (99 years) incl. digging and burial £337 (£405-50 for non-residents). They will accept home-made or cardboard coffins. Length of funeral service: Approximately 40 minutes. Chapel: 'At Leabrooks Cemetery and Heanor Cemetery only.' Memorials: 'Max height 1m, no metal memorials' (Paul Martin). There is also a woodland burial area within Belper Cemetery (see Chapter 6 for details).

• **Crem Bramcote**: Bramcote Crematorium, Coventry Lane, Bramcote, Beeston, Nottingham NG9 3GJ (tel 0115 9221837; fax 0115 9430067); run by the Joint Bramcote Crematorium Committee. Price: £160. Time allotted: 20 minutes (extra time can be booked for £160). They will accept home-made, cardboard, or wicker coffins. 'We will also accept the "Cocoon System", as long as there is a signed statement – this is a new system where both a cardboard coffin and an outer coffin, which a local funeral director can supply, are used; only the cardboard coffin is cremated and the other is given back discreetly.' Chapel: 'Modern, with large window giving view of small enclosed garden, with seating for 95 people.' Grounds: 'Parkland with lots of trees, seats and walks with no plaques as well as immaculate gardens.' They have adopted the Charter for the Bereaved. 'We aim to make each service very personal, and keep costs low to help families' (Mrs Richards).

• **Crem Kettering**: Kettering Crematorium, East Lodge, Rothwell Road, Kettering, Northamptonshire NN16 8XE (tel 01536 534218); run by Kettering Borough Council. Price: £225 (£250 for non-residents). Time allotted: 45

minutes (extra time can be booked for £30). They will accept home-made, cardboard or wicker coffins and shrouds. Chapels: 'One modern, non-denominational, the other church-like; one seats 105, the other 50.' Grounds: 'Pleasant gardens with mature woodland areas.' 'Advice and assistance to those wanting more involvement with funeral arrangements is freely given – funerals are viewed as the family's, not ours.' They are establishing a woodland burial ground – see Chapter 6 for details (Sue Williams).

• ✪✪✪ **Crem Leamington Spa**: Mid-Warwickshire Crematorium, Oakley Wood, Bishops Tachbrook, Leamington Spa, Warwickshire CV33 9QP (tel 01926 651 418); run by Warwick District Council. Price: £160 (£185 for non-residents). Time allotted: 30 minutes (extra time can be booked for £30 per 30 minutes). They will accept home-made, cardboard or wicker coffins and body bags or shrouds. Chapels: 'Modern. The North Chapel seats 20 people; the South Chapel seats 80 and has an organ. There is a music system and collection in both chapels.' Grounds: 'Informal woodland.' They have adopted the Charter for the Bereaved. 'Our crematorium must be one of the most flexible and helpful crematoria in the UK. The atmosphere is extremely peaceful and the woodland is home to many forms of wildlife. We are planning to open a woodland memorial garden. There is no commercialism' (Andrea Barnet). Winner of the New Natural Death Handbook Award 2000 for the Best Crematorium in the East Midlands.

• **Cem Leicester**: Gilroes Cemetery, Groby Road, Leicester, Leicestershire LE3 9QG (tel 0116 287 2292 fax; 0116 222 8706; e-mail: doohj001@leicester.gov.uk); run by Leicester City Council, from the Cemeteries Office, New Walk Centre, Welford Place, Leicester LE1 6ZG. They also run Saffron Hill Cemetery, Stonesby Avenue, Leicester; Welford Road Cemetery, Welford Road, Leicester; and Belgrave Cemetery, Red Hill Way, Leicester. Plot (99 years) incl. digging and burial £442 (double for non-residents). Length of funeral service: 30 minutes (extra time can be booked for £24). They will accept home-made, cardboard or wicker coffins and body bags or shrouds. Chapel: 'Traditional, Gothic-cum-Tudor, seating 85 people, with large Assembly Hall attached. There are also music facilities.' Grounds: 'As well as the architecture, the Assembly Hall is a distinguishing feature of particular interest to Hindu, Sikh and Jain families.' Memorials: 'No kerbsets. Nothing above 4' 6"high.' 'We will give as much assistance to families not using a funeral director as they require '(John Dooher).

• **Crem Leicester**: Gilroes Crematorium, Groby Road, Leicester, Leicestershire LE3 9QG (tel 0116 287 2292 fax; 0116 222 8706; e-mail: doohj001@ leicester.gov.uk); run by Leicester City Council, from the Cemeteries Office, New Walk Centre, Welford Place, Leicester LE1 6ZG. Price: £176 (£186 for non-residents). Time allotted: 30 minutes (extra time can be booked for £24). They will accept home-made, cardboard or wicker coffins and body bags or shrouds. Chapel: 'Traditional, Gothic-cum-Tudor, seating 85 people, with large Assembly Hall attached. There are also music facilities.' Grounds: 'In the middle of a cemetery. As well as the architecture, the Assembly Hall is a distinguishing feature of particular interest to Hindu, Sikh and Jain families.' 'We will give as much assistance to families not using a funeral director as they require' (John Dooher).

• ✪✪✪ **Cem Luton**: Luton Church Cemetery, 26 Crawley Green Road, Luton, Bedfordshire (tel 01582 722874); run by Luton Church Cemetery Trustees. Plot £150 (single) £175 (double) – prices for the digging vary. Maintenance: £55 p.a. 'We positively encourage home-made, cardboard or wicker coffins and body bags or shrouds.' Length of funeral service: No time limit, given four days' notice. Chapel: 'A traditional, high Victorian Chapel currently being redecorated. It is private, small and functional.' Grounds: 'A varied site with chalk grassland, copses and a wild flower meadow. Within it can be found 180 different species of plants, 3 species of orchid and 12 endangered plants.' Memorials: 'Absolutely no restrictions.' 'Understanding and helpful staff' (Sean MacDonald). Winner of the New Natural Death Handbook Award 2000 for the Best Cemetery in the East Midlands.

• **Crem Luton**: Luton Crematorium, The Vale, Butterfield Green Road, Stopsley, Luton, Bedforshire LU2 8DD (tel 01582 23700 or 30761); run by Luton Borough Council. Price: £203 (£213 non-residents). Time allotted: 45 minutes between services (extra time can only be booked by paying for a double slot). They will accept home-made, cardboard or wicker coffins. Chapel: 'Modern and functional, with seating for 120 people.' Grounds: 'Pleasant semi-rural setting.' 'Helpful staff' (N. Schonewald).

• **Crem Mansfield**: Mansfield and District Crematorium, Derby Road, Mansfield, Nottinghamshire NG18 5BJ (tel 01623 621811). Price: £180 (£30 extra for non-residents). Time allotted: 20 minutes, with services at 45 minute intervals (extra time can be booked for £39). They will accept cardboard or wicker coffins. Chapels: 'Two chapels, one traditional and church-like, seating 80; the other light wood and glass, modern.' Grounds: 'Surrounded by woodland, pleasant gardens. No chemicals used unless absolutely necessary.' They have adopted the Charter for the Bereaved. 'Easily accessible by motorway, train, etc. We are forward thinking and open to suggestions' (Sally A. Curtis).

• **Cem Oxford**: Wolvercote Cemetery, Banbury Road, Oxford OX2 8EE (tel 01865 513962); run by Oxford City Council. Administers branch cemeteries at Headington, Rosehill, and Botley, of similar design and with same pricing and practice. Plot (75 years) incl. digging and burial £388, (double for non-residents). Maintenance: £46 p.a. They will accept home-made, cardboard or wicker coffins. Length of funeral service: 30 minutes (extra time can be booked for £27). Chapel: 'Victorian, with fully-equipped organ.' Grounds: 'Late Victorian; wide variety of trees.' Memorials: 'No kerbs.' They have adopted the Charter for the Bereaved. 'Service to the public is paramount. We received the IBCA and MAB Cemetery of the Year Award, 1999' (H. P. Dawson). See also details of their woodland burial areas in Chapter 6.

• **Cem Retford**: The Cemetery, North Road, Retford, Nottinghamshire; run by Bassetlaw District Council, Leisure Services, Grove House, 27 Grove Street, Retford, Nottinghamshire DN22 6JP (tel 01909 533487). Plot (99 years) incl.

digging and burial £217 (£108-50 extra for non-residents). They will accept home-made, cardboard or wicker coffins and body bags or shrouds. Length of funeral service: 'As required.' No chapel. Grounds: 'It is like a country park, with about 1,000 trees and the Chesterfield Canal running through it.' Memorials: 'Maximum 3' high on lawn sections. Kerb memorials are allowed on some sections.' 'We provide a fully comprehensive service for the bereaved, with a close association with local bereavement care groups' (Cyril Blackshaw). For details of the woodland burial area see Chapter 6.

• **Cem Wigston**: Wigston Cemetery, Welford Road, Wigston, Leicestershire (tel 0116 2880942). Plot (100 years) incl. digging and burial £230. Chapel: Victorian . Grounds: 'Neatly laid out.' Memorials: 'None above 2' 6" in height and no kerbs.' (N. R. Coy).

• **Cem Worksop**: Hannah Park Cemetery, Netherton Road, Worksop, Nottinghamshire; run by Bassetlaw District Council, Leisure Services, Grove House, 27 Grove Street, Retford, Nottinghamshire DN22 6JP (tel 01909 533487). Plot (99 years) incl. digging and burial £217 (£108-50 extra for non-residents). They will accept home-made, cardboard or wicker coffins and body bags or shrouds. Length of funeral service: 'As required.' Chapel: 'Made in 1900 from large, Yorkshire stone bricks.' Grounds: 'Adjoining woodland, with a panoramic view of the town.' Memorials: 'Maximum 3' high on lawn sections. Kerb memorials are allowed on some sections.' 'One price for all adult burials and one price for grave purchases' (Cyril Blackshaw). For details of the woodland burial area see Chapter 6.

East Anglia

Comprising Norfolk, Suffolk, Essex, Cambridgeshire and Hertfordshire.

• **Crem Basildon**: Basildon and District Crematorium, Church Road, Bowers Gifford, Basildon, Essex SS13 2HG (tel 01268 584411). Run by Crematoria Management Ltd. Price: £248. Time allotted: 30 minutes. They will accept home-made or cardboard coffins. Chapel: 'Modern, natural wood used, organ or tape music.' Grounds: 'Open countryside' (P. J. Wilson).

• **Cem Braintree**: Braintree Cemetery, London Road, Braintree, Essex; run by Community Services, Braintree District Council, Causeway House, Bocking End, Braintree, Essex CM7 9HB (tel 01376 552523 ext 2324). The council runs three other similar cemeteries – Bocking Cemetery, Church Lane, Bocking; Halstead Cemetery, Colchester Road, Halstead; and Witham Cemetery, Manor Road, Witham – to which the following details also apply, unless otherwise stated: Plot (100 years) incl. digging and burial £420 (double for non-residents). Maintenance: £52-88. Length of funeral service: 'Up to approximately one hour.' Chapel: 'There are chapels at Braintree, Bocking and Witham.' Memorials: 'Varying restrictions depending on the area.'. 'Families can reserve or select a grave space at no extra cost' (Michael Ashby). A woodland burial area is planned at Braintree Cemetery (see Chapter 6 for details).

• **Crem Bury St Edmunds**: West Suffolk Crematorium, Near Risby, Bury St.

Edmunds, Suffolk IP28 6RR (tel 01284 755118). Run by Crematoria Management Ltd. Price: £255. Time allotted: 45 minutes between services. They will accept home-made or cardboard coffins. Chapel: 'Design based on old Suffolk barn.' Grounds: 'Peaceful rural setting.' 'A small staff work as a team, united to help the funeral directors and bereaved' (Royna Brunskill).

• **Cem Cambridge**: Cambridge City Cemetery, Newmarket Road, Cambridge (tel 01954 780681). Plot (50 years) incl. digging and burial £645 (£750 extra for non-residents). They will accept home-made, cardboard or wicker coffins and body bags or shrouds. Length of funeral service: No set limit. Chapel: 'Traditional, church-like.' Grounds: 'No exceptional features.' Memorials: 'Traditional sections graves are not restricted, but must be agreed; headstone/vase only in the lawn section.' 'Well-established cemetery with identified areas for special religious groups, and a separate infants/children's section. It has space for new graves only to about 2003. A new cemetery, adjacent to Cambridge City crematorium (see below) is in the planning stage, and will incorporate a woodland/green burial area' (see Chapter 6 for details) (David Giles).

• **Crem Cambridge**: Cambridge City Crematorium, Huntingdon Road, Cambridge CB3 0JJ (tel 01954 780681). Price: £295. Time allotted: 45 minutes (extra time can be booked for £140). They will accept home-made, cardboard or wicker coffins; they would consider shrouds or body bags. Chapel: 'A more traditional East chapel from 1938 and a modern West chapel from 1991.' Grounds: 'Crematorium situated in open countryside of Cambridge green belt.' 'A total flexibility' (David Giles).

• **Cem Cheshunt**: Cheshunt Cemetery, Bury Green, Cheshunt, Herts EN7 5AG; run by Broxbourne Borough Council, Cemetery Office, Bishops College, Churchgate, Cheshunt, Herts EN8 9XF (tel 01992 785507; e-mail: broxbournebc@compuserve.com). Plot (100 years) £370 – or £150 for an 'unpurchased plot' (both charges are quadruple for non-residents). Maintenance: 'No maintenance charge in lawn sections, elsewhere an optional £44 (£88 including plants).' They will accept home-made, cardboard or wicker coffins and body bags or shrouds. Length of funeral service: 'Unlimited. Over one hour by arrangement.' Chapel: 'Plain white walls, full carpet, with wooden panelled and beamed ceilings. Central heating. No organ, but taped music and PA facility.' Grounds: 'Half urban, half rural in feel. Quiet. Many trees. Extensive wildlife. Well maintained.' Memorials: 'Lawn graves maximum height 3'. Conventional graves maximum height 4' 6". Any natural stone. No restrictions on inscriptions (within public decency). No memorial fees charged.' They have adopted the Charter for the Bereaved. 'A woodland burial ground is planned for 2005 (see Chapter 6 for details). Meanwhile, individual woodland graves are possible. Chartermark Award 1999. No charges for use of chapel; rose petals provided for mourners at interments; rain shelter over graves where necessary. Maximum number of customer choices – the customer is always right' (Jim Duncan).

• **Cem Clacton-on-Sea**: Clacton Cemetery, Burrs Road, Clacton-on-Sea, Essex (tel 01255 831108; e-mail: weeleycrem@netscapeonline.co.uk); run by Tendring

District Council. Plot (99 years) incl. digging and burial £388. They will accept home-made, cardboard or wicker coffins. Length of funeral service: 45 minutes for the chapel and graveside (extra time is charged at £42). Chapel: 'Late 19th century, small but compact, with seating for 44 people.' Grounds: 'Lawned areas neat and tidy, with rose bushes in between headstones.' Memorials: 'Within size restrictions.' 'The grounds are neat and the staff caring' (Jerry Howe).

• **Cem Colchester**: Colchester Cemetery, Mersea Road, Colchester, Essex CO2 8RU (tel 01206 282950); run by Colchester Borough Council. Plot (50 or 100 years) incl. digging and burial £413 (50 years), £557 (100 years); (extra £85 for non-residents). Maintenance: £20 p.a. They will accept home-made or cardboard coffins. Length of funeral service: 20 minutes. Chapel: 'Small Victorian Gothic.' Grounds: 'Victorian, with a variety of long-established trees.' Memorials: 'Within size and materials restrictions.' A woodland burial area is planned – see Chapter 6 for details (C. Ryland).

• **Crem Colchester**: Colchester Crematorium, Mersea Road, Colchester, Essex CO2 8RU (tel 01206 282950); run by Colchester Borough Council. Price: £212. Time allotted: 20 minutes (an extra 20 minutes can normally be booked for £70). They will accept home-made or cardboard coffins. 'We will also accept the "Cocoon System", where only the inner cardboard coffin is cremated and the outer coffin is given back discreetly.' Chapel: 'Modern, non-denominational.' Grounds: 'Formal gardens in attractive 1850s cemetery with fine, mature specimen trees. The gardens have recently been enhanced by further tree planting' (C. Ryland).

• **Cem Ely**: Ely Cemetery, Beech Lane, Ely, Cambridgeshire (tel 01353 669659); run by the City of Ely Town Council, 72 Market Street, Ely, Cambridgeshire. Plot (99 years) incl. digging and burial from £163 (double for non-residents). They would consider cardboard or unusual coffins 'if requested'; likewise, funerals by families not using funeral directors. No time limit on funeral services. Chapel: 'Brick and stone, completed in 1856.' Grounds: 'Rural setting. Relatives can put bulbs and plants on graves.' Memorials: 'Must not exceed 4' in height and no new kerbstones.' The concept of a woodland burial ground is under consideration. 'Ely cemetery was a finalist in the Cemetery of the Year Competition in 1998' (Win Hughes).

• **Cem Frinton-on-Sea**: Kirby Cross Cemetery, Holland Road, Kirby Cross, Frinton-on-Sea, Essex (tel 01255 831108; e-mail: weeleycrem@ netscapeonline.co.uk). Plot (99 years) incl. digging and burial £388. They will accept home-made, cardboard or wicker coffins. Length of funeral service: 45 minutes for the chapel and graveside (extra time can be booked without charge). Chapel: 'Late 19th century, small but compact, with seating for 44 people.' Grounds: 'Lawned areas neat and tidy.' Memorials: 'Within size restrictions.' 'The grounds are neat and the staff caring' (Jerry Howe).

• **Cem Harlow**: Parndon Wood Cemetery, Parndon Wood Road, Harlow, Essex CM19 4SF (tel 01279 423800 or 446199; e-mail: chrisbrown@harlow.gov.uk); run by Harlow Council. Plot (50 years) incl. digging and burial £1,082. They will accept home-made, cardboard or wicker coffins, and body bags or shrouds.

Length of funeral service: 30 minutes. Chapel: 'Non-denominational.' Grounds: 'Tranquil woodland setting.' Memorials: 'Within size restrictions; no kerbing.' 'Having BSI registration shows that we give an excellent service' (Mrs Chris Brown). For details of the natural burial area, see Chapter 6.

• **Crem Harlow**: Parndon Wood Crematorium, Parndon Wood Road, Harlow, Essex CM19 4SF (tel 01279 423800 or 446199; e-mail: chrisbrown@ harlow.gov.uk); run by Harlow Council. Price: £205. Time allotted: 30 minutes (extra time can be booked for a variable charge). They will accept home-made, cardboard or wicker coffins and body bags or shrouds. Chapel: 'Non-denominational, with removable cross.' Grounds: 'Lovely woodland area.' 'A separate baby and children's area. We have extended the cemetery and it will soon include a natural burial area' (Mrs Chris Brown).

• **Cem Harwich**: Dovercourt Cemetery, Main Road, Dovercourt, Harwich, Essex (tel 01255 831108; e-mail: weeleycrem@netscapeonline.co.uk). Plot (99 years) incl. digging and burial £388. They will accept home-made, cardboard or wicker coffins. Length of funeral service: 45 minutes for the chapel and graveside (extra time can be booked without charge). Chapel: 'Late 19th century, small but compact, with seating for 44 people.' Grounds: 'Lawned areas neat and tidy.' Memorials: 'Within size restrictions.' 'The grounds are neat and the staff caring' (Jerry Howe).

• **Cem Hoddesdon**: Hoddesdon Cemetery, Warr Road, Hoddesdon, Herts EN11 9AE; run by Broxbourne Borough Council, Cemetery Office, Bishops College, Churchgate, Cheshunt, Herts EN8 9XF (tel 01992 785507; e-mail: broxbournebc@compuserve.com). All details the same as Cheshunt Cemetery above, except that 'since the site is nearly full, with only sufficient virgin ground until about 2006, plots are only available for residents, unless it is for a very close relative of a resident, in which case the interment fee is quadrupled'. The chapel: 'Red brick walls with oak beamed and pannelled ceiling, centrally heated, music playback and P. A.' (Jim Duncan).

• ✪✪✪ **Crem King's Lynn**: Mintlyn Crematorium, Lynn Road, Bawsey, King's Lynn, Norfolk PE32 1HB (tel 01553 630533); run by the Borough of Kings Lynn and West Norfolk. Price: £209. Time allotted: 45 minutes (extra time can be booked for £41-18). They will accept home-made, cardboard or wicker coffins and body bags or shrouds. Chapel: 'Modern with lowering catafalque, with seating for 100 people.' Grounds: 'Mature woodland glades set with memorial shrubs and trees.' They have adopted the Charter for the Bereaved (Colin Houseman). Winner of the New Natural Death Handbook Award 2000 for the Best Crematorium in East Anglia.

• ✪✪✪ **Cem Maldon**: Maldon Cemetery, London Road, Maldon, Essex (information from Maldon District Council Offices, Princes Road, Maldon, Essex CM9 5DL, tel 01621 875836). Plot (100 years) £373 (double for non-residents). A family organising a funeral themselves would need to make a private arrangement with one of the gravediggers locally (the cemetery can provide a list) – the cost is likely to be about £150. Maintenance: No charge. They will accept home-made and cardboard coffins. Length of funeral service: 'Any reasonable time is allowed.' Chapel: 'Simple Victorian chapel, refurbished 1996, seats 40 people. Available without extra charge.' Grounds: 'Rural, on the edge of town, surrounded by farmland.' Memorials: 'All types of memorial are permitted in the traditional cemetery area. Our Victorian hand pull bier has been renovated and brought into service' (John Hughes). There is also a Primrose Garden for children's burials and a woodland burial ground (see Chapter 6 for details). Winner of the New Natural Death Handbook Award 2000 for the Best Cemetery in East Anglia.

• **Crem Norwich**: St Faiths Crematorium, 75 Manor Road, Horsham St Faith, Norwich NR10 3LF (tel 01603 897727); run by SCI (UK). Price: £278. Time allotted: 30 minutes (extra time can be booked for £80). They will accept home-made, wicker or cardboard coffins and body bags or shrouds. Chapel: '1930s, church-like, with seating for 100; it has a PA system, a hearing loop system and a catafalque with curtains.' Grounds: '26 acres. Our Gardens of Remembrance are of particular peace and beauty.' 'Saturday and Sunday services; opening hours may be extended to accommodate client preferences. No reasonable request is refused' (Mrs A Jarvis).

• **Cem Peterborough**: Broadway and Eastfield Cemeteries, Eastfield Road, Peterborough, Cambridgeshire (tel 01733 262639; web: www.peterborough. gov.uk); run by Peterborough Bereavement Services. Also administers the Woodston, Stanground and Fletton cemeteries under the same pricing, burial and memorial policy. Plot (100 years) incl. digging and burial £580 (double for non-residents). They will accept home-made, cardboard or wicker coffin and body bags or shrouds. No chapel facilities. Grounds: 'Broadway cemetery has a conservation area and a superb range of wild flowers.' Memorials: 'Lawn and traditional type.' They have adopted the Charter for the Bereaved. 'We work to ensure that each service is as individual and meaningful as possible' (Kate Day). See also details of their woodland burial area at Fletton Cemetery in Chapter 6.

• **Crem Peterborough**: Peterborough Crematorium, Mowbray Road, North Bretton, Peterborough, Cambridgeshire PE6 7JE (tel 01733 262639; web: www.peterborough.gov.uk); run by Peterborough Bereavement Services. Price: £215. Time allotted: 30 minutes (extra time can be booked for £124). They will accept home-made, cardboard or wicker coffins (subject to full details in advance). Chapel: 'Modern, church-like; side wall of glass looking out to semi-woodland.' Grounds: 'Semi-woodland.' They have adopted the Charter for the Bereaved. 'Our attitude is that if we are asked for something out of the usual we consider "why not" rather than just plain "no". One gentleman organised a d-i-y funeral – he stayed to watch throughout the whole, three-hour cremation process. This had been his uncle's wish. This is an example of how we will go out of our way to help' (Kate Day).

• **Cem Southend-on-Sea**: Sutton Road Cemetery, Sutton Road, Southend-on-Sea, Essex SS2 5PX (tel 01702 603907); run by Southend Borough Council. Plot (50, 75 and 100 years) incl. digging and burial £777 (no extra for non-residents). Maintenance: 'Fees for contracts.' They will accept home-made or cardboard coffins. Length of funeral service: 30 minutes (extra time may be booked for

£44). Chapel: 'Stone church built in 1902, new seating for 30; a non-denominational stone chapel is also available.' Grounds: 'Over 40 acres, with traditional and lawn sections.' Memorials: 'Must be lawn headstone type.' 'Picturesque cemetery with knowledgeable staff. No interment fees for children up to the age of 16' (G. Green).

• **Crem Southend-on-Sea**: Southend-on-Sea Crematorium, Sutton Road, Southend-on-Sea, Essex SS2 5PX (tel 01702 215018); run by Southend Borough Council. Price: £236. Time allotted: 40 minutes (extra time can be booked for £76). They will accept home-made or cardboard coffins. Chapels: 'Two chapels, one church-like, the other modern. Good acoustics, loop system installed, easy access, wheelchairs available on request.' Grounds: 'Gardens back onto open fields. Woodland memorial garden, densely planted with native trees, underplanted with hollies, ferns and dog-roses. A small stream emanates from a rock pool, through gardens into a large pond. However, there is a busy road at the front and small industrial area to the south.' 'Environmental awareness and support for conservation and the general quality and appearance of the crematorium. No cremation fees for children up to the age of 16' (G. Green).

• **Crem Upminster**: South Essex Crematorium, Okendon Road, Corbets Tey, Upminster, Essex RM14 2UY (tel 01708 222188); run by London Borough of Havering. Price: £230 (with recorded music), £253 (with organ music). Time allotted: 30 minutes (extra time can be booked for £61-50). They will accept home-made, cardboard or wicker coffins. Chapels: 'The South chapel has flexible seating for about 100 people.' Grounds: 'Established formal garden.' They have adopted the Charter for the Bereaved. 'We are flexible to clients' wishes as long as they are not disturbing others' (Sharon Herbert).

• **Crem Weeley**: Weeley Crematorium, Colchester Road, Weeley, Essex CO16 9JP (tel 01255 831108; e-mail: weeleycrem@netscapeonline.co.uk); run by Tendring District Council. Price: £233. Time allotted: 45 minutes for the service (extra time £88 for 45 minutes). They will accept home-made, cardboard or wicker coffins. Chapel: 'Modern, non-denominational, brick walls with wood seating and roof.' Grounds: 'Park-like grounds. Fish pond with waterfall and fountain.' Tape recordings of services can be ordered for £11-75. 'We are a small team like a family. I hope that friendliness and a caring attitude are conveyed to our visitors' (Jerry Howe).

The South West

Comprising South Gloucestershire, Bristol, Bath and North East Somerset, North West Somerset, Somerset, Dorset, Devon, Cornwall.

• ✪✪✪ **Crem Barnstaple**: North Devon Crematorium, Old Torrington Road, Barnstaple, Devon EX31 3NW (tel 01271 345431; fax 01271 328116); run by North Devon and Torridge District Council. Price: £214. Time allotted: 30 minutes (extra time can be booked for £44 per half hour). Provided they conform to regulations, they will accept home-made, cardboard or wicker coffins and body bags or shrouds. Chapel: 'Opened in 1966, with a serene atmosphere and seating for up to 100 people.' Grounds: 'Seven acres of secluded grounds with woodland on two sides.' 'Staff on duty 365 days of year for advice and information' (Mr Graham Bailey). Winner of the New Natural Death Handbook Award 2000 for the Best Crematorium in the South West.

• **Cem Bath**: Haycombe Cemetery, Haycombe Cemetery, Whiteway Road, Bath BA2 2RQ (tel 01225 423682; e-mail: reg-greenall@bathnes.gov.uk); run by the Bath and North East Somerset Council. Plot (75 years) incl. digging and burial £600 (£300 extra for non-residents). They will accept home-made, cardboard or wicker coffins and body bags or shrouds. Length of funeral service: 30 minutes. Chapel: 'Built in the 1930s of Bath stone – it is dignified but light and airy, and was refurbished in 1993.' Grounds: 'Overlooks a rural valley.' Memorials: 'Restrictions vary in different sections of cemetery – in some areas there are no restrictions.' Also has a woodland burial section (see Chapter 6 for details). (R. G. Greenall).

• **Crem Bath**: Haycombe Crematorium, Whiteway Road, Bath BA2 2RQ (tel 01225 423682). Price: £255 (no extra for non-residents). Time allotted: 30 minutes (extra time can be booked for £144). They will accept home-made, cardboard or wicker coffins and body bags or shrouds. Chapel: 'Modern, with a glass wall overlooking rural valley'. Grounds: 'Open countryside with beautiful views.' 'The staff have mostly been here for a long time and take great pride in providing a good service to the public' (R. G. Greenall).

• ✪✪✪ **Cem Bournemouth**: North Cemetery, Strouden Avenue, Bournemouth, Dorset BH8 9HX (tel 01202 526238; e-mail: crematorium@ bournemouth.gov.uk); run by Bournemouth Borough Council. Plot (50 years) incl. digging and burial £440 (double fees for non-residents). Maintenance: £44 p.a. They will accept home-made, cardboard or wicker coffins and body bags or shrouds. Length of funeral service: 60 minutes. Chapels: 'One chapel is small and intimate; the other large, more formal, housed within an attractive stone building forming part of the crematorium complex.' Grounds: 'Many established trees, nicely landscaped.' Memorials: 'Currently only natural stone is allowed but this is being reviewed.' They have adopted the Charter for the Bereaved. 'Regulations are regularly reviewed to ensure that as many requests as possible are met' (Julie Dunk). The council also runs three other cemeteries, for which the above details apply, except where stated: East Cemetery, Gloucester Road, Boscombe, Bournemouth (which has a Late Victorian chapel); Kinson Cemetery, South Kinson Drive, Bournemouth (which has a modern chapel); and Wimborne Road Cemetery, Wimborn Road, Bournemouth (which has 'a Late Victorian chapel with fine stained glass windows'). Winner of the New Natural Death Handbook Award 2000 for the Best Cemetery in the South West.

• **Crem Bournemouth**: Bournemouth Crematorium, Strouden Avenue, Bournemouth, Dorset BH8 9HX (tel 01202 526238; e-mail: crematorium@ bournemouth.gov.uk); run by Bournemouth Borough Council. Price: £209·80. Time allotted: 30 minutes (double time can be booked for £209·80). They will accept home-made, wicker or cardboard coffins and body bags or shrouds. Chapels: 'Two non-denominational chapels with modernised fittings and disabled access, with seating for 30 in one chapel and 80-90 in the other.' Grounds: 'These have glades, seats, rosebeds and a columbarium.' They have adopted the Charter for the Bereaved (Julie Dunk).

• **Cem Bristol**: Canford Cemetery, Canford Lane, Westbury-on-Trym, Bristol BS9 3PQ (tel 0117 9038280; e-mail: simon_westbrook@bristol-city.gov.uk); run by Bristol City Council. Plot incl. digging and burial £265. They will accept home-made, cardboard or wicker coffins and body bags or shrouds. Chapel: 'A traditional chapel, seating 100 people.' Grounds: 'Traditional.' Memorials: 'We try to maintain a flexible approach.' They have adopted the Charter for the Bereaved (Simon Westbrook).

• **Crem Bristol**: Canford Crematorium, Canford Lane, Westbury-on-Trym, Bristol BS9 3PQ (tel 0117 9038280; e-mail: simon_westbrook@bristol-city.gov.uk); run by Bristol City Council. Price: £260. They will accept home-made, cardboard or wicker coffins and body bags or shrouds. Chapel: 'A traditional chapel, seating 100 people.' Grounds: 'Traditional.' They have adopted the Charter for the Bereaved (Simon Westbrook).

• **Crem Bristol**: Westerleigh Crematorium, Westerleigh Road, Westerleigh, Bristol BS37 8QP (tel 01179 374619). Run by Crematoria Management Ltd. Price: £260. Time allotted: 30 minutes (no charge for extra time, if available). They will accept home-made or cardboard coffins. Chapel: 'Modern.' Grounds: 'Open countryside' (P. J. Wilson).

• **Cem Dorchester**: Dorchester Cemetery, Weymouth Avenue, Dorchester, Dorset DT1 2EN (tel 01305 266861); run by the Dorchester Joint Burial Committee. Plot (100 years) incl. digging and burial £474 (non-residents double). Length of funeral service: No time limit. Chapel: 'Victorian, with pews and stained glass window – seats 70 people.' Grounds: 'Well-maintained, secure and pleasant site.' Memorials: 'No restrictions, subject to approval.' 'If current demand continues, the cemetery will be full by 2001, at which point new premises will be sought' (Sue Cheeseman).

• **Cem Exeter**: Exwick Cemetery, Exwick Road, Exeter, Devon EX4 2BT. Chapel: 'Seats 70; volcanic stone and brick. Light and airy inside.' Grounds: 'Some fine angels. Attractive hillside setting in the newer areas with views across the valley to the cathedral and the city centre.' 'A special section for stillborn and pre-term babies. Facilities for Muslim and Jewish burials available' (John O'Callaghan). All other details as for Higher Cemetery below. For details of the woodland burial area see Chapter 6.

• **Cem Exeter**: Higher Cemetery, St. Marks Avenue, Heavitree, Exeter, Devon EX1 2PX (tel 01392 265707, e-mail: john.ocallaghan@exeter.gov.co.uk; web: www.exeter.gov.uk). Plot (75 years) incl. digging and burial £312. They will accept home-made, cardboard or wicker coffins and shrouds. Length of funeral service: 60 minutes. Chapel: 'Seats 50, £37 per hour. Of distinctive red-hued Heavitree stone. Old but cosy.' Grounds: '1860s urban cemetery with a Commonwealth war graves section, an older section laid out as a "quiet garden" and a small area for wildlife. St Marks cemetery is featured in the local historical society's trail.' Memorials: 'Within size restrictions' (John O'Callaghan). They have adopted the Charter for the Bereaved.

• **Cem Exeter**: Topsham Cemetery, Elm Grove Road, Topsham, Exeter, Devon EX3 OEJ. Chapel: 'Seats 60; light, airy and comforting atmosphere with lovely stained glass window.' Grounds: 'A typical small town cemetery.' 'Small site with old-established trees and nearby allotments make this a very tranquil spot' (John O'Callaghan). All other details as for Higher Cemetery above.

• **Cem Paignton**: Paignton Cemetery, Colley End Road, Paignton (tel 01803 327768, e-mail: viviennefoster@torbay.gov.uk). Plot (100 years) incl. digging and burial £536 (double for non-residents). They will accept home-made or cardboard coffins. Length of funeral service: 'As required.' Chapel: 'Seats 31; traditional church setting.' Grounds: 'Mature trees, sea views, sense of space.' Memorials: 'No kerbs, no wood, no metal.' 'Staff endeavour to make funerals as personal as possible' (Vivienne D. Foster).

• **Cem Plymouth**: Efford Cemetery, Efford Road, Plymouth, Devon PL3 6NG (tel 01752 304857, e-mail: palmerg@plymouth.gov.uk). Plot (25 years) incl. digging and burial £831-50. They will accept home-made, cardboard or wicker coffins. Length of funeral service: 30 minutes (extra time can be booked for £23). Chapel: 'Seats 100; Edwardian.' Grounds: 'Formal, with some wooded areas.' Memorials: 'Approved natural stone only, with no kerbing and within size restrictions.' They have adopted the Charter for the Bereaved. 'We produce an advisory leaflet for families organising d-i-y funerals' (Mrs Aitchison).

• **Crem Plymouth**: Efford Crematorium, Efford Road, Plymouth, Devon PL3 6NG (tel 01752 304857). Details as for Weston Mill below.

• **Cem Plymouth**: Weston Mill Cemetery, Ferndale Road, Plymouth, Devon PL2 2EP (tel 01752 304837). Details as for Efford Cemetery above.

• **Crem Plymouth**: Weston Mill Crematorium, Ferndale Road, Plymouth, Devon PL2 2EP (tel 01752 304837). Price: £222-50 (non-residents £253-50). Time allotted: 30 minutes (extra time can be booked for £23 per half hour). They will accept home-made, wicker or cardboard coffins. Chapel: 'Seats 100; 1920s, traditional.' Grounds: 'Secluded Garden of Rest within cemetery grounds.' They have adopted the Charter for the Bereaved. 'Experienced, caring staff' (Brian Howells).

• **Crem Poole**: Poole Crematorium, Gravel Hill, Poole, Dorset BH17 9BQ (tel 01202 602582); run by Poole Borough Council. Price: £233. Time allotted: 20 minutes in a 30 minute period (extra time can be booked). They will accept home-made or cardboard coffins at the discretion of the registrar. Chapel: 'Established in 1986. It has disabled access and seating for 80, with room for 50 standing. There is an organist and a recorded music selection.' Grounds: 'A woodland area with drift planting'. 'We have a woodland scattering area themed to the four seasons, available free to users of the crematorium' (Mrs Sue Gotobed).

• **Cem South Bristol**: South Bristol Cemetery, Bridgewater Road, Bedminster Down, Bristol BS13 7AS (tel 0117 9038330; e-mail: simon_westbrook@bristol-city.gov.uk); run by Bristol City Council. Plot incl. digging and burial £265. They will accept home-made, cardboard or wicker coffins and body bags or shrouds. Chapel: 'Seats 100 people.' Grounds: 'Open plan, with picturesque views.' Memorials: 'We try to maintain a flexible approach.' They have adopted the Charter for the Bereaved (Simon Westbrook).

• **Crem South Bristol**: South Bristol Crematorium, Bridgewater Road, Bedminster Down, Bristol BS13 7AS (tel 0117 9038330; e-mail: simon_westbrook@bristol-city.gov.uk); run by Bristol City Council. Price: £260. They will accept home-made, cardboard or wicker coffins and body bags or shrouds. Chapel: 'Seats 100 people.' Grounds: 'Open plan, with picturesque views.' They have adopted the Charter for the Bereaved (Simon Westbrook).

• **Cem Tavistock**: Tavistock Cemetery, 119 Plymouth Road, Tavistock, Devon PL19 8BY (tel 01822 612799). Plot ('perpetuity') incl. digging and burial £165-50 (£344-50 extra for non-residents). There is a chapel. Grounds: 'The entry to the cemetery is through a large archway, with a view to the chapel along an avenue of trees. There are many mature trees and shrubs.' Memorials: '18" local granite boulder-type headstone are used.' They have adopted the Charter for the Bereaved (Douglas Parkhouse).

• **Cem Thornbury**: Thornbury Cemetery, Kington Lane, Thornbury, South Gloucestershire (tel 01454 412103; e-mail: towncouncil@ thornburytown.freeserve.co.uk). Plot (50 years) incl. digging and burial £265 (£530 for non0residents). Maintenance: £27-50 to £36-75 p.a. They will accept home-made, cardboard or wicker coffins and body bags or shrouds. Length of funeral service: No limit. Chapel: 'Small and intimate.' Grounds: 'Very well-maintained in rural surroundings.' Memorials: Designs are subject to approval as being 'appropriate.' No kerbing. 'One of the best kept cemeteries in the West of England. A woodland burial ground is under consideration. 'We are working towards adopting the Charter for the Bereaved' (G. W. H. Jackson).

• **Cem Torquay**: Torquay Cemetery, Hele Road, Torquay, Devon TQ2 7QG (tel 01803 327768; e-mail: vivienne.foster@torbay.gov.uk); run by Torbay Council. Plot (100 years) incl. digging and burial £536 (£1,072 for non-residents). They will accept home-made or cardboard coffins. Length of funeral service: 'As required.' Chapel: 'Modern, churchlike.'. Grounds: 'Mature trees, clear views.' Memorials: 'No kerbs, no wood, no metal.' They have adopted the Charter for the Bereaved. 'Staff endeavour to make funerals as personal as possible. A woodland burial area is at the very earliest stages of planning' (Vivienne D. Foster).

• **Crem Torquay**: Torquay Crematorium, Hele Road, Torquay, Devon (tel 01803 327768 or 329977; e-mail: vivienne.foster@torbay.gov.uk); run by Torbay Council. Price: £230. Time allotted: 25 minutes (extra time can be booked without charge). They will accept home-made or cardboard coffins. Chapel: 'Modern non-denominational with moveable seating.' Grounds: 'Set at the top of a hill. Tree-lined drive approach surrounded by lawns and gardens.' They have adopted the Charter for the Bereaved (Vivienne D. Foster).

• **Cem Weston-super-Mare**: Ebdon Road Cemetery, Ebdon Road, Worle, Weston-super-Mare, North Somerset BS22 9NY (tel 01934 511717); run by the North Somerset Council. Administers branch cemeteries at Milton Road, Clevedon, and Portishead. Double plot (80 years) incl. digging and burial £575 (double for non-residents). Subject to inspection, they will accept home-made, cardboard or wicker coffins and body bags or shrouds. Length of funeral service: 30 minutes in chapel, no time limit at graveside. Chapel: See crematorium chapel below. Grounds: 'Attractive, well-maintained grounds with farmland on two sides.' Memorials: 'Within size restrictions.' 'Will do their utmost to facilitate special requests.'.For details on plans for a woodland burial facility see Chapter 6 (Paul Wheeler).

• **Crem Weston-super-Mare**: Weston-super-Mare Crematorium, Ebdon Road, Worle, Weston-super-Mare, North West Somerset BS22 9NY (tel 01934 511717). Price: £260 (extra time can be booked for £130). Time allotted: 20 minutes for the service, ten minutes for entry and exit (extra time can be booked). They will accept cardboard coffins. The crematorium opened in 1966. Chapel: 'Seats 75.' Grounds: 'Set in attractive well-maintained grounds with farmland on two sides.' 'Staff will do their utmost to facilitate special requests' (Paul Wheeler).

• **Crem Weymouth**: Weymouth Crematorium, Quibo Lane, Weymouth, Dorset DT4 0RR (tel 01305 786984; fax 01305 767 804); run by the Weymouth and Portland Borough Council. Price: £237. Time allotted: 30 minutes (extra time can be booked for £22-10). They will accept home-made, cardboard or wicker coffins. Chapel: 'Church-like – seating 80 people.' Grounds: 'Large, lawned Gardens of Remembrance with trees and rose beds.' 'Being a relatively quiet crematorium we can spend time on details and go out of our way to meet the family wishes.' They have adopted the Charter for the Bereaved (Ian Morton).

• **Cem Yeovil:** Yeovil Cemetery, Preston Road, Yeovil, Somerset (tel 01935 76718 or 01935 476718); run by the Yeovil Cemetery and Crematorium Committee. Plot (75 years) incl. digging and burial £417 (£834 for non-residents) Maintenance: £25 p.a., for basic upkeep; £12 extra for twice-yearly planting. They will accept home-made or cardboard coffins and body bags or shrouds. Length of funeral service: No limit. Chapel: 'It is in keeping with the cemetery, with seating for 50 people and a ramp for disabled access.' Grounds: 'Formal.' They have adopted the Charter for the Bereaved (Joy Coombs).

• **Crem Yeovil**: Yeovil Crematorium, Bunford Lane, Yeovil, Somerset (tel 01935 476718); run by the Yeovil Cemetery and Crematorium Committee. Price: £210. Time allotted: 20 minutes in a 30 minute period (extra time may be booked for £102-50). They will accept home-made, cardboard or wicker coffins and body bags or shrouds, if contacted prior to the cremation. Chapel: 'It has a stained glass window with seating for 70 people; also disabled access and a braille box for the blind.' Grounds: 'Set in a 10-acre site.' They have adopted the Charter for the Bereaved (Joy Coombs).

The South

Comprising Wiltshire, Berkshire, Surrey, Kent, Hampshire, West Sussex, East Sussex.

• **Cem Arundel**: Arundel Cemetery, Ford Road, Arundel, West Sussex. Grounds: 'Attractive view.' No chapel. Memorials: 'No restrictions.' All other details as for Littlehampton Cemetery below.

• **Cem Basingstoke**: Worting Road Cemetery, Worting Road, Basingstoke, Hampshire RG21 8YZ (tel 01256 321737). Plot (75 years) incl. digging and burial £233 (double for non-residents). They will accept home-made, cardboard or wicker coffins and body bags or shrouds. Length of funeral service: 'At least an hour (and as long as time allows).' Chapel: 'Mainly Old English. Grounds.' Memorials: 'Lawn sections – headstone only up to 3' high (up to 5' for additional fee); also size restrictions on kerb sections.' They have not adopted the Charter for the Bereaved 'but one based on this Charter is due to be agreed shortly.' 'Our cemetery is well kept and excels in its service to people, its attitudes, its practices and its prices (which are usually close to the cheapest in Hampshire' (Roger Fear).

• **Crem Basingstoke**: Basingstoke Crematorium, Manor Farm, Stockbridge Road, North Waltham, Basingstoke RG25 2BA (tel 01256 398 783); run by SCI (UK). Price: £260 Time allotted: 45 minutes (an extra 45 minutes can be booked for £130). They will accept home-made, cardboard or wicker coffins and may consider body bags or shrouds. Chapel: 'A brand-new chapel with a PA system and seating for 120 people (100 seated and 20 standing).' Grounds: 'Also very new with a rose garden and an ornamental lake.' 'We have not officially adopted the Charter for the Bereaved but we follow the spirit of it' (Maureen Waddell).

• **Crem Beckenham**: Beckenham Crematorium, Elmers End Road Beckenham, Kent BR3 4TD (tel 020 8658 8775; fax: 020 8663 3242); run by SCI (UK). Price: £296. Time allotted: 30 minutes (no limit at graveside). They will accept home-made or cardboard coffins, and will consider wicker coffins. Chapel: 'A very old-fashioned, Victorian chapel, with seating for 70 people, and room for 100, standing.' Grounds: '32 acres of land, with two mausoleums at the entrance, of which 5 acres are for a Garden of Remembrance and the rest are for graves.' 'Services are available on both Saturdays and Sundays. There are very few restrictions and we will offer whatever the families want so long as it's legal' (Mr Nashfold).

• **Cem Beckenham**: Beckenham Cemetery, Elmers End Road, Beckenham, Kent BR3 4TD (tel 020 8658 8775; fax 020 8663 3242); run by SCI (UK). Plot (100 years) incl. burial and digging £560. Time allotted: 30 minutes (no limit at graveside). They will accept home-made, cardboard or wicker coffins and body bags or shrouds. All other details as for Beckenham Crematorium above.

• **Cem Bognor**: Bognor Cemetery, Town Cross Avenue, Bognor Regis, West Sussex. All other details as for Littlehampton Cemetery below.

• **Cem Bognor**: Chalcraft Cemetery, Chalcraft Lane, Bognor Regis, West Sussex. Grounds: 'Attractive views and peaceful setting.' No chapel. Memorials: 'Lawn-type.' All other details as for Littlehampton Cemetery below.

• ✪✪✪ **Crem Brighton**: Woodvale Crematorium, Lewes Road, Brighton, East Sussex BN2 3QB (tel 01273 604020); run by Brighton Borough Council. Price: from £146. Time allotted: 45 minutes (extra time can be booked without charge). They will accept home-made or cardboard coffins. Chapels: 'One consecrated church and one non-denominational, both with movable seating, in a Victorian flint building.' Grounds: 'Pleasantly landscaped with rockery, water courses,

gardens with flower beds, benches etc. Awarded Charter Mark 1994 and 1997.'
'Services are tailored to meet individual requirements and assistance will be
given to families organising funerals without funeral directors. A free self-help
guide is also available. Full facilities for the disabled are provided' (Stephen
Horlock). Woodvale also runs a woodland burial ground overlooking Brighton
(see Chapter 6 for details). Winner of the New Natural Death Handbook Award
2000 for the Best Crematorium in the South.

• **Cem Canterbury**: Canterbury City Cemetery, Westgate Court Avenue,
Canterbury, Kent; run by Cemeteries Registrar, Architecture & Engineering,
Canterbury City Council, Military Road, Canterbury, Kent CT1 1YW (tel 01227
862490; fax 862020; e-mail: leita.honey@canterbury.gov.uk; web:
www.canterbury.gov.uk). The council runs two other cemeteries – Herne Bay
Cemetery, Canterbury Road, Herne, Herne Bay; and Whitstable Cemetery, Mill
Strood Road, Whitstable – for both of which most of the following details also
apply. Plot (50 years) incl. digging and burial £180 (double for non-residents).
They will accept home-made or cardboard coffins. Length of funeral service: '30
minutes in chapel, 20 to 30 minutes going to and being beside the grave.' Chapel:
'Gothic but warm and well decorated.' Grounds: 'Tree arbours and colourful
bedding.' Memorials: 'No restrictions except on lawn and green burial graves.
We welcome customer-designed stone memorials as long as safely fixed. A
newly planted tree can be dedicated with a plaque for £155, covering a 20-year
period.' 'Direct, friendly, helpful service providing explanatory advice and
information' (Leita Honey). The cemetery contains a small green burial area (see
Chapter 6 for details).

• **Crem Chatham**: Medway Crematorium, Robin Hood Lane (Upper), Chatham,
Kent ME5 9QU (tel 01634 861639; e-mail: paul.edwards@medway.gov.uk).
Run by Medway Council. Price: £230 (double for non-residents). Time allotted:
40 minutes between services. They will accept home-made, cardboard or wicker
coffins. 'Body bags and shrouds may be accepted by arrangement'. Chapel:
'Churchlike, with movable seating for 60-70 people.' Grounds: 'Semi-formal
rose gardens and woodland.' 'We aim to meet all cultural, religious and personal
preferences where possible' (Paul Edwards).

• **Cem Crawley**: Snell Hatch Cemetery, The Dingle, West Green, Crawley,
West Sussex (tel 01293 528744 ext 2503); run by Crawley Borough Council.
Plot (50 years) incl. digging and burial £336 (double for non-residents). They
will accept home-made, cardboard or wicker coffins and body bags or shrouds.
No chapel. 'Helpful and caring' (Barbara Conley).

• **Crem Crawley**: Surrey and Sussex Crematorium, Balcombe Road, Crawley
RH10 3NQ (tel 01293 882345); the parent company is SCI. Price: £296. Time
allotted: 30 minutes (extra time can be booked for £148). They will accept home-
made or cardboard coffins. Chapels: 'Church-like, 1950s architecture.' 1990.
Grounds: 'Attractive woodland glades' (Peter Mitchell).

• **Cem Dorking**: Dorking Cemetery, Reigate Road, Dorking, Surrey (tel 01306
879299; e-mail: carole.broug@mole-valley.gov.uk); run by Mole Valley District Council. Plot (50 years) incl. digging and burial £540 (trebled for non-

residents). They will accept home-made, cardboard or wicker coffins. Length of funeral service: 'No limits.' Chapel: 'Built in 1855 of local materials, a fine example of Victorian Gothic architecture.' Grounds: 'The cemetery contains native and exotic trees and is sited at the foot of Box Hill, the famous Surrey landmark in the beautiful Mole Valley.' Memorials: 'Headstone up to 3' high.' 'An area of peace and tranquillity little changed since 1855' (Carole Brough).

• **Cem Eastbourne**: Langney Cemetery, Hide Hollow, Langney, Eastbourne, East Sussex BN23 8AE (tel 01323 766536; fax 01323 760637; e-mail: kendry@eastbourne.gov.uk). Plot (75 years) incl. digging and burial £750. They will accept home-made, cardboard or wicker coffins and suitable shrouds. Length of funeral service: No time limit. Chapel: 'Victorian, seats 45, with tape and CD facilities available.' Grounds: 'Parkland with mature trees.' Memorials: 'Regulations on request.' 'In 1995 the service was awarded a Charter Mark for excellent service to the public' (Kenneth Dry). For details of the woodland burial area, see Chapter 6.

• **Cem Eastbourne**: Ocklynge Cemetery, Willingdon Road, Eastbourne, East Sussex BN21 1TL. Grounds: 'Downland cemetery.' All other details as for Eastbourne Langney Cemetery above.

• **Crem Eastbourne**: Eastbourne Crematorium, Hide Hollow, Langney, Eastbourne, East Sussex BN23 8AE (tel 01323 761093; fax 01323 760637; e-mail: kendry@eastbourne.gov.uk). Price: £250. Time allotted: 30 minutes within a 45 minute period (an extra 45 minute period can be booked for £60). They will accept home-made, cardboard or wicker coffins. Chapels: 'Both chapels were opened in 1960 and have CD and tape facilities and induction loops and facilities for those with disabilities. The main chapel seats 80, the family chapel seats 30.' Grounds: 'Designed to have the effect of rolling Sussex downland.' 'In 1995 the service was awarded a Charter Mark for excellent service to the public' (Kenneth Dry).

• **✪✪✪ Cem Forest Row**: Forest Row Cemetery, Priory Road, Forest Row, East Sussex (tel 01342 822661); run by Forest Row Parish Council, Community Centre, Hartfield Road, Forest Row, East Sussex RH18 5DZ. Plot (50 years) incl. digging and burial £151 (double for non-residents). No maintenance charge. They will accept home-made, cardboard or wicker coffins and shrouds or body bags. Length of funeral service: 'No limit.' Chapel: 'Stone, church-like.' Grounds: 'Peaceful surroundings, well maintained.' Memorials: 'We allow all sorts – wood, rocks, rough carvings, etc, although approval by committee required.' (Gwen Pritchett). Winner of the New Natural Death Handbook Award 2000 for the Best Cemetery in the South.

• **Crem Guildford**: Guildford Crematorium, Broadwater, New Pond Road, Godalming, Surrey, GU7 3DB (tel 01483 444711; fax 01483 532 637); run by Guildford Borough Council. Price: £230. Time allotted: 30 minutes (extra time can be booked for £115). They will accept home-made, cardboard or wicker coffins. Chapel: 'Modern, non-denominational, with seating for 100 people.' Grounds: 'Open-fronted, well-maintained.' They follow the spirit of the Charter for the Bereaved (Keith Hendry).

• **Cem Hastings**: Hastings Borough Cemetery, The Ridge, Hastings, East Sussex TN34 2AE (tel 01424 781302). Plot (50 years) incl. digging, burial and use of chapel £467. They will accept home-made, cardboard or wicker coffins. Length of funeral service: 20 minutes (extra time can be booked for £45 per 20 minutes). Chapel: Church-like. Grounds: As Crem below. Memorials: 'Headstones only, within size restrictions.' 'Unrivalled views' (George Ford). There is a woodland burial area in a quiet corner of the site (see Chapter 6 for details).

• **Crem Hastings**: Hastings Crematorium, 234 The Ridge, Hastings, East Sussex TN34 2AE (tel 01424 781302). Price: £225. Time allotted: 20 minutes (extra time can be booked for £45). They will accept home-made or cardboard coffins. Chapel: 1850s. Grounds: 'Trees, lawns and flower beds in 80 acres of cemetery grounds.' 'On a hillside overlooking Rye Bay to the East, and the Sussex countryside to the North and West' (George Ford).

• **Crem Isle of Wight**: Isle of Wight Crematorium, Station Lane, Whippingham, East Cowes, Isle of Wight PO32 6NJ (tel 01983 882288 fax; 01983 883010); run by the Isle of Wight Council. Price: £286. Time allotted: 30 minutes (extra time can be booked for £60). They will accept home-made, cardboard or wicker coffins. Chapel: 'A typical 1960s chapel with room for 120 people.' Grounds: 'Rural, wooded, peaceful.' They are in the process of adopting the Charter for the Bereaved (Mrs B Thompson).

• **Cem Littlehampton**: Littlehampton Cemetery, Horsham Road, Littlehampton, West Sussex; run by Arun District Council, Bognor Town Hall, Clarence Road, Bognor Regis, West Sussex PO21 1LD (tel 01243 863141). Plot (75 years) incl. digging and burial £237 (£474 extra for non-residents). They will accept home-made, cardboard or wicker coffins, or shrouds or body bags. Length of funeral service: 45 minutes . Chapel: 'Plain.' Grounds: 'Daffodils and crocuses are an attraction.' Memorials: 'Restrictions only on lawn section.' (Sheila Berry).

• **Cem Maidstone**: Sutton Road Cemetery, Sutton Road, Maidstone, Kent (tel 01622 738172). Plot (100 years) incl. digging and burial £380. They will accept home-made, cardboard or wicker coffins and shrouds. Length of funeral service: 90 minutes (extra time may be booked without charge). Chapel: 'Built in 1850, with typical gargoyles, stained glass, spire, etc.' Grounds: '49 acres of parkland with mature trees and a variety of lawn and general sections.' Memorials: 'Lawn section allows for headstone only, general section permits headstone, kerbs and vase - both are subject to size restrictions.' 'We are working towards being able to adopt the Charter for the Bereaved. Good location, experienced staff and reasonable prices. A tree memorial may be sponsored, without plaques, and not adjacent to the grave' (Tim Jefferson).

• **Crem Maidstone**: Vintners Park Crematorium, Bearsted Road, Maidstone, Kent ME14 5LG (tel 01622 738172). Price: £220. Time allotted: 30 minutes (extra time can be booked for £69). They will accept cardboard coffins. Chapel: 'Modern, formal, bright, accommodating 80'. Grounds: 'Surrounded by a conservation area, with formal gardens and a woodside walk area.' 'We are working towards being able to adopt the Charter for the Bereaved.' Large, well-laid out, interesting' (Tim Jefferson).

• **Crem Morden**: North East Surrey Crematorium, Lower Morden Lane, Morden, Surrey SM4 4NU (tel 020 8337 4835; fax 020 8337 8745). Price: £230. Time allotted: 30 minutes (extra time can be booked for £70). They will accept cardboard or wicker coffins. Chapel: 'Converted late Victorian church.' Grounds: '400-yard, poplar-lined drive and 3.5 acres of gardens.' 'We have our own trained staff (no contractors) who take pride in their work and helping relatives' (J. E. Skinner).

• **Crem Portchester**: Portchester Crematorium, Upper Cornaway Lane, Portchester, Hampshire PO16 8NE (tel 01329 822533); run by Portchester Crematorium Joint Committee. Price: £205. Time allotted: 30 minutes (extra time can be booked by negotiation). They will accept home-made or wicker coffins. Chapels: 'There are two chapels, one built in 1958 and one in the 1980s, both have organ music available at extra charge; they seat 80 and 44 people respectively.' Grounds: 'Natural gardens.' They have adopted the Charter for the Bereaved (J. Clark).

• **Cem Reading**: Henley Road Cemetery, All Hallows Road, Caversham, Reading, Berkshire RG4 5LP (tel 0118 9472433 or 9474102). Plot (75 years) incl. digging and burial £625 (£676 extra for non-residents). They will accept home-made or cardboard coffins. Length of funeral service: '30 minutes (extra time £75 per half hour)'. Chapel: 'Same chapels as for Reading crematorium. Grounds: 'No traffic noise, park and farmland to the rear, mansion on the hillside.' Memorials: 'Tablet and headstone size restrictions for new graves in Park Cemetery.' They provide seven pages of guidance notes for families arranging funerals without funeral directors. 'Graves are individually numbered, making finding graves very easy' (Mrs Ruth Winch).

• **Crem Reading**: Reading Crematorium, All Hallows Road, Caversham, Reading, Berkshire RG4 5LP (tel 0118 9472433 or 9474102). Price: £235. Time allotted: 30 minutes (extra time can be booked for £75). They will accept home-made or cardboard coffins. Chapels: 'Large 1930s chapel is not church-like, and seats 108 with excellent organ and interior of dome visible. Small, modern brick and pine chapel seats 26.' Grounds: 'Set in centre of 50-acre cemetery, with 5-acre Gardens of Remembrance secluded by tall hedges.' They provide seven pages of guidance notes for families arranging funerals without funeral directors. 'We aim to meet all cultural, religious and personal preferences where possible' (Mrs Ruth Winch).

• **Cem Sutton**: Sutton Cemetery, Alcorn Close, off Sutton Common Road, Sutton, Surrey SM3 9PX (tel 020 8644 9437). Plot (50 years) incl. digging and burial £566. Maintenance: £82. They will accept home-made, cardboard or wicker coffins and body bags or shrouds. Length of funeral service: 60 minutes between bookings (extra time free with sufficient notice). Chapel: 'Victorian Gothic, warm and intimate with seating for 50-60.' Grounds: 'Well-maintained, secure and pleasant site.' Memorials: 'Approved natural stone only, within size restrictions.' 'Experienced and caring staff with our priorities given to the bereaved and the funeral service. Grave site viewing and selection very welcome – by appointment please' (Mr Don Ward).

• **Crem Trowbridge**: West Wiltshire Crematorium, Devizes Road, Semington, Trowbridge BA14 6HL (tel 01380 871101). Run by Crematoria Management Ltd. Price: £235. Time allotted: 30 minutes (no charge for extra time). They will accept home-made or cardboard coffins. Chapel: 'Natural stone. Comfortable.' Grounds: 'Open countryside' (P. J. Wilson).

• **Cem Warlingham**: Greenlawn Memorial Park cemetery, Chelsham Road, Surrey; run by the London Borough of Croydon, Cemeteries and Crematorium Office, Mitcham Road, Croydon CR9 3AT (tel 020 8684 3877; e-mail: mark.healy@croydon.gov.uk). Plot (50 years) incl. digging and burial £698 (no extra for non-residents). Maintenance: Not available. They will accept home-made, cardboard or wicker coffins and body bags or shrouds. Length of funeral service: '90 minutes (extra time may be feasible at no extra cost).' No chapel. Grounds: 'A lawn cemetery established as a park.' Memorials: 'Only bronze memorials laid flush to the ground are permitted.' They have adopted the Charter for the Bereaved. 'This is an unusual cemetery based on the American lawns concept and maintained to the standards of a park. A section has been set aside for use by our Muslim community. Dedicated and responsible staff with an innovative approach to customer service' (Mark Healy).

• **Cem Woking**: The Brookwood Cemetery, Cemetery Pales, Woking, Surrey GU24 OBL (tel 01483 472222; fax 01483 2223); run by the Woking Borough Council. Plot (50 years) incl. digging and burial £1,450 (prices may vary according to the plot). Maintenance: £150 p.a. They will accept home-made, cardboard or wicker coffins and body bags or shrouds. Length of funeral service: As long as needed. Chapel: 'The Chapel seats up to 50 people.' Grounds: 'Vast 420 acre cemetery with beautiful trees, many areas overgrown, Victorian monuments.' Memorials: 'Virtually any design of memorial is accepted up to 3ft.' 'All graves remain undisturbed for ever, there being so much unused land at Brookwood Cemetery. It is the one of the oldest cemeteries not to use old ground.' For details of the woodland burial ground see Chapter 6 (R. H. Guney).

• **Cem Wokingham**: Easthampstead Park Cemetery, Nine Mile Ride, Wokingham, Berkshire RG40 3DW (tel 01344 420314; e-mail: cem.crem@bracknell-forest.gov.uk); run by Bracknell Forest Borough Council. Plot (75 years) incl. digging and burial £319 (£638 extra for non-residents). Maintenance: No charge. They will accept home-made, wicker or cardboard coffins, and body bags or shrouds. Length of funeral service: 30 minutes (extra time can be booked for £120). Chapel: 'Modern chapel with wood panelling, seating 98 people. Organ, CD and tape machine.' Grounds: 'Set in 22 acres of landscaped grounds, with pergolas and hanging baskets separating the lawned and traditional sections.' Memorials: 'Maximum height 3'.' 'Charter Mark winners in 1996. We provide a staff member at every burial to oversee the funeral. The cemetery is set in Berkshire countryside. It is of a lawned style, offering traditional memorials and flat tablets, with a woodland burial area from June 2000' (see Chapter 6 for details) (Gary Fewkes).

• **Crem Wokingham**: Easthampstead Park Crematorium, Nine Mile Ride,

Wokingham, Berkshire RG40 3DW (tel 01344 420314; e-mail: cem.crem@ bracknell-forest.gov.uk); run by Bracknell Forest Borough Council. Price: £250. Time allotted: 30 minutes (extra time can be booked for £120). They will accept home-made, cardboard or wicker coffins and will consider body bags or shrouds. Chapels: 'Modern and well-lit, seating 98 and 16 respectively.' Grounds: 'Set in 22 acres of Berkshire countryside. Extensive memorialisation available, Charter Mark winners in 1996' (Gary Fewkes).

• **Cem Worthing**: Findon Cemetery, Findon By-Pass, Findon, Worthing, West Sussex. Grounds: 'Attractive views and peaceful setting.' No chapel. Memorials: 'No restrictions.' All other details as for Littlehampton Cemetery above.

• **Crem Worthing**: Worthing Crematorium, Horsham Road, Findon, West Sussex BN14 0RQ (tel 01903 872678; e-mail: Worthing.Crematorium@ Virgin.net). Price: £251. Time allotted: 40 minutes (extra time can be booked for £25). They will accept home-made, cardboard or wicker coffins and body bags or shrouds. Chapel: '1960s, Swedish-style, non-denominational.' Grounds: 'Wildlife sanctuary.' 'We have not officially adopted the Charter for the Bereaved but we do work to it' (Ian Rudkin).

Greater London region

Including old Middlesex. See also South region.

• **Cem: Alperton** Cemetery, Clifford Road, Alperton HA0 1AF (tel 020 8902 2385; fax 020 8795 0273; e-mail: langford@brent.gov.uk; web: www.mortbase. co.uk); run by the London Borough of Brent. Plot (50 years) incl. digging and burial £1,500 (£750 extra for non-residents). Maintenance 'Nil. £82 if grave to be planted with flowering plants twice yearly.' They will accept cardboard or home-made coffins, wicker coffins or shrouds. Length of funeral service: 'As much time as required.' No chapel. Grounds: 'A very pretty cemetery, bordering a canal and a golf course.' Memorials: 'Bronze plaques only in the lawn cemetery.' They have adopted the Charter for the Bereaved. 'Fees are fair and in line with competing cemeteries. Very peaceful, with an abundance of wildlife.' (Bob Langford).

• **Cem: Bedfont** Cemetery, Bedfont Road, Bedfont, Middlesex; run by the London Borough of Hounslow, Community Initiatives Partnership, Civic Centre, Lampton Road, Hounslow, Middlesex TW3 4DN (tel 020 8583 4677). Plot (60 years) incl. digging and burial £473 (treble for non-residents). Maintenance: £52. Length of funeral service: 45 minutes (no charge for additional time). No chapel. Memorials: 'Few restrictions in traditional areas; lawn areas are fairly restrictive' (Alan Rice).

• **Cem: New Brentford** Cemetery, Sutton Road, Hounslow; run by the London Borough of Hounslow. Details as for Bedfont Cemetery above.

• **Cem: Camberwell** New Cemetery, Brenchley Gardens, London SE23 3RD (tel 020 7639 3121). Plot (50 years) incl. digging and burial £919 (£2,750-50 for non-residents). They will accept home-made, cardboard or wicker coffins. Length of funeral service: 30 minutes (extra time can be booked for £50).

Chapel: 'Church-like.' Grounds: 'Formal gardens.' Memorials: 'Headstone only. Natural stone, within size restrictions.' (Terry Connor). There is now a woodland burial area within Nunhead Cemetery, Linden Grove, London SE15 (run from Camberwell New Cemetery) – for details see Chapter 6.

• **Cem: Carpenders Park** Lawn Cemetery, Oxhey Lane, Nr Watford; run by the London Borough of Brent, Brent Cemetery Service, Clifford Road, Alperton HA0 1AF (tel 020 8902 2385; fax 020 8795 0273; e-mail: langford@brent.gov.uk; web: www.mortbase.co.uk). Plot (50 years) incl. digging and burial £1,500 (£750 extra for non-residents). Maintenance 'Nil. £82 if grave to be planted with flowering plants twice yearly.' They will accept home-made, cardboard or wicker coffins and shrouds. Length of funeral service: 'As much time as required.' No chapel. Grounds: 'Countryside with mature woodland, a lake and a pond.' Memorials: 'Bronze plaques only in the lawn cemetery.' They have adopted the Charter for the Bereaved. 'Fees are fair and in line with competing cemeteries. Very peaceful, with an abundance of wildlife. ' (Bob Langford). There is also a one-acre woodland burial area within the cemetery (see Chapter 6 for the details).

• **Cem: Charlton** Cemetery, Cemetery Lane, London SE7 8DZ; run by the London Borough of Greenwich, Greenwich Direct Services, Sun Yard, Archery Road, Eltham, London SE9 1HA (tel 020 8856 0100). Plot (50 years) incl. digging and burial £516 (£1,831 extra for non-residents). Maintenance £34-55 p.a., planting £69-10 p.a. Length of funeral service: 20 minutes (extra time £15 for 10 minutes). Chapel: 'Small Victorian chapel with original fixtures and fittings.' Grounds: 'Well maintained.' Memorials: '2' 6" wide by 4' high; kerbs 6' 6" by 2' 6".' 'No new graves except in the children's section.' (Dawn Squires).

• **Cem: Chingford** Mount Cemetery, Old Church Road, Chingford, London E4 6ST (tel 020 8524 5030; fax 020 8523 7944); run by the London Borough of Waltham Forest. Plot (75 years) incl. digging and burial £745 (new graves for residents only; double fees for non-residents in existing graves). They will accept wicker or wooden home-made coffins. Length of funeral service: 30 minutes (extra time can be booked without charge). No chapel. Grounds: 'Large, older cemetery with lots of trees.' Memorials: 'Lawn-type headstones only, within size restrictions.' 'We will accommodate all the wishes of all families to the best of our abilities within the limits of cemetery regulations' (John Billson).

• **Cem: Chiswick** 'New' Cemetery, Staveley Road, Chiswick; run by the London Borough of Hounslow. Details as for Bedfont Cemetery above.

• **Cem: Chiswick** 'Old' Cemetery, Corney Road, Chiswick; run by the London Borough of Hounslow. Details as for Bedfont Cemetery above.

• **Cem: City of London** Cemetery, Aldersbrook Road, London E12 5DQ (tel 020 8530 2151; fax 020 8530 1563; e-mail: ian.hussein@corpoflondon.gov.uk); run by the Corporation of London. Plot (50 years) incl. digging and burial £1,136. Memorials: 'Lawn-type only, in hard stone and within size restrictions.' 'Nine options for burial ranging from catacomb and vault to lawn and woodland' (Lynn Heath). See woodland burial entry in Chapter 6. Other details as for City of London Crematorium (see next entry).

• **Crem: City of London** Crematorium, Aldersbrook Road, London E12 5DQ (tel 020 8530 2151; fax 020 8530 1563; e-mail: ian.hussein@ corpoflondon.gov.uk); run by the Corporation of London. Price: £266. Time allotted: 45 minutes in the traditional chapel, 30 minutes in the modern chapels (extra time can be booked without charge). They will accept home-made, cardboard or wicker coffins and body bags or shrouds (subject to approval). Chapels: 'Three chapels, the traditional one, built in Gothic style, has seating for a hundred people; the two modern multi-faith chapels accommodate 200 mourners (100 seated). Each of the three has a sound system, induction loop, organ, tape and CD facilities.' Grounds: 'The grounds and buildings are English Heritage Grade 2 listed and security patrolled. 32-acre memorial garden, within a cemetery of 200 acres in all.' They have adopted the Charter for the Bereaved. 'Renowned for its not-for-profit service and its care of the bereaved' (Lynn Heath).

• **Cem: Croydon** Cemetery, Mitcham Road, Croydon CR9 3AT (tel 020 8684 3877; e-mail: mark.healy@croydon.gov.uk); run by the London Borough of Croydon, which also administers the Greenlawn Memorial Park cemetery in Surrey (see 'Warlingham' in South region above). Plot (50 years) incl. digging and burial £698 (no extra for non-residents). Maintenance: £42. They will accept home-made, cardboard or wicker coffins and body bags or shrouds. Length of funeral service: '90 minutes (extra time may be feasible at no extra cost).' Chapel: 'Traditional with modern music options.' Grounds: 'Traditional cemetery and service chapel.' Memorials: 'Full memorials welcomed. No restrictions.' They have adopted the Charter for the Bereaved. 'Centrally located and aiming to meet the needs of the whole community. Dedicated and responsible staff with an innovative approach to customer service' (Mark Healy).

• **Crem: Croydon** Crematorium, Mitcham Road, Croydon CR9 3AT (tel 020 8684 3877; e-mail: mark.healy@croydon.gov.uk); run by the London Borough of Croydon. Price: £255. Time allotted: 30 minutes (extra time can be booked without charge). They will accept home-made, cardboard or wicker coffins and body bags or shrouds. Chapels: 'One churchlike and one modern.' Grounds: 'Landscaped, with award-winning water gardens'. They have adopted the Charter for the Bereaved. 'A caring and professional service for all members of the community who are bereaved' (Mark Healy).

• **Cem**: **Mill East Finchley** Cemetery, East End Road, London N2 0RZ (tel 020 8567 0913; e-mail: hanwell@cemcrem.com); managed on behalf of the City of Westminster by Cemetery Management Ltd (based at Hanwell Cemetery, see above). Plot (75 years) incl. digging and burial £825 (£1,440 extra for non-residents). They will accept home-made and cardboard coffins. Length of funeral service: '30 minutes in chapel and then 30 minutes at graveside – extra time £52 per hour.' Chapel: 'Victorian, totally refurbished inside in 1992.' Grounds: 'Monumental memorials, Victorian architecture, exclusive location.' Memorials: 'Up to 2' 6" in width, 3' in height.' 'Interesting architecture' (James Evans).

• **Cem: East London** Cemetery (Company), Grange Road, Plaistow, London

E13 OHB (tel 020 7476 5109; e-mail: supt@elond-cemetery.demon.co.uk; web: www.elond-cemetery.demon.co.uk). Plot (50 years) incl. digging and burial £1,100 (no extra for non-residents). They will accept home-made, cardboard or wicker coffins. Length of funeral service: 30 minutes. Chapel: 'Traditional church, refurbished 1999 to include central heating, CD sound system, new seating, etc.' Grounds: 'Intimate, park-style atmosphere in the centre of the East End of London.' Memorials: 'No lawn section. Traditional memorials only. There are a number of regulations concerning these. Memorial benches are also available for dedication.' They have adopted the Charter for the Bereaved (Paul Mallatratt).

• **Crem**: **East London** Crematorium, Grange Road, Plaistow, London E13 OHB (tel 020 7476 5109; e-mail: supt@elond-cemetery.demon.co.uk; web: www.elond-cemetery.demon.co.uk); run by the East London Cemetery Company. Price: £220. Time allotted: 30 minutes (extra time can be booked – £75 charged 'during busy periods'). They will accept home-made, cardboard or wicker coffins. Chapels: 'Modern, non-denominational, very comfortable. Recently refurbished. Seating – flexible arrangement if desired.' Grounds: 'See our web site' (Paul Mallatratt).

• **Cem**: **East Sheen** Cemetery, Sheen Road, Richmond, Surrey TW10 5BJ (tel 020 8876 4511; fax 020 8878 8118). Administers similar cemeteries in Hampton, Mortlake, Teddington and Twickenham. Plot (50 years) incl. digging and burial £790 (£2,370 for non-residents). They will accept home-made, cardboard or wicker coffins (subject to approval of cemeteries manager). Length of funeral service: As long as required. Chapel: 'Seats 80; non-denominational.' Grounds: 'Rural in an urban environment.' Memorials: 'Natural stone, within size restrictions. Can be either lawn-style or traditional kerbed.' 'We provide assistance and cardboard coffins (for £121 plus VAT)' (Natasha Mahon-Smith).

• **Cem**: **Edmonton** Cemetery, Church Street, Edmonton, London N9 9HP (tel 020 8360 2157); managed on behalf of the London Borough of Enfield. Plot (100 years) incl. digging and burial £701 (£1,333 extra for non-residents). Length of funeral service: 30 minutes (extra time may only be booked if the chapel is used, for an additional fee of £33). Chapel: 'Victorian – Porte cochere.' Grounds: 'Well-kept.' Memorials: 'Lawn type, back to back or single rows; traditional head stones and kerbs on other older sections.' 'The cemetery is extremely well-kept and the staff have a caring attitude. We have a very low number of complaints' (Mrs M Vetere).

• **Cem**: **Eltham** Cemetery, Rochester Way, Eltham, London SE9 2RF; run by the London Borough of Greenwich, Greenwich Direct Services, Sun Yard, Archery Road, Eltham, London SE9 1HA (tel 020 8856 0100). Plot (50 years) incl. digging and burial £516 (£1,831 extra for non-residents). Maintenance £34-55 p.a., planting £69-10 p.a. Length of funeral service: 20 minutes (extra time £15 for 10 minutes). Chapel: 'Brick Gothic.' Grounds: 'A flat site with trees and plants on the edge of the pathways and edges of the grounds – which also contain Eltham Crematorium. Well maintained.' Memorials: '2' 6" wide by 4' high; kerbs 6' 6" by 2' 6"' (Dawn Squires).

• **Crem: Enfield** Crematorium, Great Cambridge Road, Enfield, London EN1 4DS (tel 020 8363 8324); run by the London Borough of Haringdey. Price: £235. Time allotted: 20 minutes (extra time can be booked for £100). They will accept home-made, cardboard or wicker coffins; 'shrouds and body bags would be considered'. Chapels: 'Pre-war, red brick, both seating 100 people.' Grounds: 'Attractive rock and water gardens'. 'The best possible service given the very restricted budget available.' They are currently in the process of adopting the Charter for the Bereaved (Nigel Morgan).

• **Cem: Feltham** Cemetery, Ashford Road, Feltham; run by the London Borough of Hounslow. Details as for Bedfont Cemetery above.

• **Cem: Hanwell** Cemetery, 38 Uxbridge Road, London W7 3PP (tel 020 8567 0913; e-mail: hanwell@cemcrem.com); managed on behalf of the City of Westminster by Cemetery Management Ltd. Plot (75 years) incl. digging and burial £710 (£1,190 extra for non-residents). They will accept home-made or cardboard coffins. Length of funeral service: '30 minutes in chapel and then 30 minutes at graveside – extra time £52 per hour.' Chapel: 'Renovated in 1994. Hammer beam roof.' Grounds: 'Grand avenue of cedars lining the main drive, grounds kept to a high standard.' Memorials: 'Up to 2' 6" in width, 3' in height.' 'There are always staff available 365 days a year to help with queries and to provide a safe atmosphere for families' (James Evans).

• **Cem: Hatton** Cemetery, Faggs Road, Feltham; run by the London Borough of Hounslow. Details as for Bedfont Cemetery above.

• **✪✪✪ Crem: Hendon** Crematorium, Holders Hill Road, London NW7 1NB (tel 020 8346 0657); run by the London Borough of Barnet. Price: £189. Time allotted: 45 minutes (extra time can be booked for £45). They will accept home-made, cardboard or wicker coffins and body bags or shrouds. Chapels: 'Two traditional chapels seating 75 and 55 people respectively.' Grounds: 'Country churchyard set in 40 acres of naturally wooded cemetery grounds.' 'Practical, sympathetic and sensible service to the recently bereaved' (Morris Salmon). Winner of the New Natural Death Handbook Award 2000 for the Best Crematorium in London.

• **Cem Highgate** Cemetery, Swains Lane, London N6 6PJ (tel 020 8340 1834). Plot (70 years) incl. digging and burial £3,025. They will accept home-made or cardboard coffins. No chapel. Grounds: 'One of the most famous cemeteries in the world, with many eminent Victorians buried in grand style in a beautiful woodland setting.' Memorials: 'Any memorial installed must reflect some sympathy with Highgate's historic status.' 'As a privately-run charity, Highgate is able to offer a much more flexible service than most. For instance, within the limits imposed by limited space, we would arrange woodland burial on individual request' (Mr Richard Quirk).

• **Crem: Honor Oak** Crematorium, Brockley Way, London SE23 3RD (tel 020 639 3121; fax 020 7732 4075); run by the London Borough of Southwark. Price: £233 (organist £26 extra). Time allotted: 30 minutes. They will accept home-made, cardboard or wicker coffins and body bags or shrouds. Chapel: 'A listed building in a Grecian style built in 1939, with seating for 100 people. Christian symbols can be covered if desired.' Grounds: 'Formal gardens, shrubbery, wooded area, Garden of Remembrance, sports field and cemetery.' 'The coffin is lowered on a catafalque to symbolise the lowering of a coffin in a grave.' They are in the process of adopting the Charter for the Bereaved (Terry Connor).

• **Cem: Hounslow** Cemetery, Hanworth Road, Hounslow, Middlesex; run by the London Borough of Hounslow. Details as for Bedfont Cemetery above.

• **Cem: Isleworth** Cemetery, Park Road, Isleworth, Middlesex; run by the London Borough of Hounslow. Details as for Bedfont Cemetery above.

• **Crem: Islington** Crematorium, High Road, East Finchley, London N2 9AG (tel 020 8883 1230; fax 020 8883 2784); run by the London Borough of Islington. Price: £205 (£25 extra with organ music). Time allotted: 30 minutes (extra time can be booked for £100). They will accept home-made, cardboard or wicker coffins. Chapel: 'A light and warm 1930s building, with movable seating for 85 people.' Grounds: 'Garden of Remembrance.' Memorials: 'Various forms of memorial are permissible.' 'Families are left to do their own thing.' The crematorium follow the guidelines of the Charter for the Bereaved for improvement of their services, although they have not officially adopted it. They are in the process of opening a woodland burial ground – for details see Chapter 6 (D Pryor).

• **✪✪✪ Cem: Kensal Green** (All Souls) Cemetery, Harrow Road, London W10 4RA (tel 020 8969 0152). Plot (perpetuity) incl. digging and burial from £1,420. Maintenance if required from £44 p.a., VAT extra. They will accept home-made, cardboard or wicker coffins and body bags or shrouds. Length of funeral service: 'Up to an hour, or longer if no following service.' Chapel: 'Greek style (Doric) with a grandiose 'feel' and Victorian ambience.' Grounds: 'Much wildlife; Gothic, with a honeycomb of catacombs underground.' Memorials: 'Very few restrictions, except in two lawn grave areas where size and type of stone are regulated.' They have adopted the Charter for the Bereaved. 'Beautiful setting, historic architecture, polite and friendly staff. For families organising funerals without funeral directors, we provide as full co-operation and advice as possible. There is no extra charge for this' (David Burkett). (See also West London Crematorium.) Winner of the New Natural Death Handbook Award 2000 for the Best Cemetery in London.

• **Cem: Lavender Hill** Cemetery, Cedar Road, Enfield, London EN2 OTH (tel 020 8363 0608); managed on behalf of the London Borough of Enfield. Plot (100 years) incl. digging and burial £701 (£1,333 extra for non-residents). Length of funeral service: 30 minutes (extra time may only be booked if the chapel is used, for an additional fee of £33). Chapel: 'Victorian, Gothic.' Grounds: 'Green belt.' Memorials: 'Lawn type, back to back or single rows; traditional head stones and kerbs on other older sections.' 'The cemetery is extremely well-kept and the staff have a caring attitude. We have a very low number of complaints.' A woodland burial area is planned – see Chapter 6 for details (Mrs M Vetere).

• **Cem Lewishan: Hither Green** Cemetery, Verdant Lane, London SE6 1TP (tel 020 8697 2555); also **Grove Park** Cemetery, Marvels Lane, London SE12; and **Ladywell** Cemetery, Ladywell Road, London SE13; and **Brockley** Cemetery,

Brockley Road, London SE4; all run by the London Borough of Lewisham. Plot (50 years) incl. digging and burial £796 (quadruple for non-residents). They will accept home-made, cardboard or wicker coffins, or – at Grove Park only – shrouds, if transported in coffins. Length of funeral service: 60 to 90 minutes (extra time negotiable if commitments allow). Chapel: 'Victorian at Hither Green and Ladywell. Grove Park is from the 1930s; Ladywell and Brockley have no chapels available at present.' Grounds: 'All the cemeteries have an abundance of wildlife and a tranquil atmosphere.' Memorials: 'Restrictions on sizes for headstones and for full memorials.' There are plans for a woodland burial ground. 'We are actively working towards meeting the needs of the community' (Shirley Bishop).

• **Crem: Lewisham** Crematorium, Verdant Lane, Catford, London SE6 1TP (tel 020 8698 4955). Price: £235. Time allotted: 30 minutes, extra time can be booked for £235. They will accept home-made, cardboard or wicker coffins. Chapel: 'Non-denominational.' Grounds: 'Landscaped Gardens of Remembrance, featuring central pond which attracts wide variety of wildlife.' 'We will always try to accommodate specific requests' (Shirley Bishop).

• **Crem: Manor Park** Crematorium, Manor Park Cemetery Company Ltd., Sebert Road, Forest Gate, London E7 0NP (tel 020 8534 1486). Run by the Manor Park Cemetery Company Ltd. Price: £240. Time allotted: 30 minutes (extra time can be booked). They will accept home-made or cardboard coffins. Chapels: 'Free church design.' Grounds: 'Wide drive-through cemetery. Large area for flowers. Florist on site. Night security patrol' (Norman Stephens).

• **Cem: Mill Hill** Cemetery, Milespit Hill, Mill Hill, London NW7 2RR (tel 020 8567 0913; e-mail: hanwell@cemcrem.com); managed on behalf of the City of Westminster by Cemetery Management Ltd (based at Hanwell Cemetery, see above). Plot (75 years) incl. digging and burial £710 (£1,190 extra for non-residents). They will accept home-made and cardboard coffins. Length of funeral service: '30 minutes in chapel and then 30 minutes at graveside – extra time £52 per hour.' Chapel: 'Modern redbrick.' Grounds: 'Peaceful setting, includes the grave of Billy Fury.' Memorials: 'Up to 3' or 3' 6" in height. Portland stone is banned.' 'Comprehensive memorial survey undertaken in 1997/8' (James Evans).

• **Crem: Mortlake** Crematorium, Kew Meadow Path, Richmond, TW9 4EN (tel 020 876 8056). Price: £170. Time allotted: 30 minutes (extra time for £170). They will accept home-made, cardboard or wicker coffins. Chapels: 'Comfortable ambience, non-sombre atmosphere.' Grounds: 'Overlooks River Thames.' 'Approximately 2,500 cremations per year. The 145,000 cremations since the opening in 1939 include the funerals for Sir Michael Redgrave and Paul Eddington' (Bob Coates).

• **Crem: New Southgate** Crematorium, Brunswick Park Road, London N11 1JJ (tel 020 8361 1713; e-mail: nsg@cemcrem.com); run by the New Southgate Cemetery and Crematorium Ltd, with all profits ploughed back into the site. Price: £240. Time allotted: 20 minutes (extra time can be booked for £75). They will accept home-made, cardboard or wicker coffins and body bags or shrouds.

'There is a new refrigerated coffin store and the new cremators can accommodate coffins up to 36" wide.' Chapels: 'Built 1858, with a high steeple and (screenable) ornate oak altar.' Grounds: 'One of best selections of conifer in London, together with native trees. Mature trees can be dedicated with natural rock memorials alongside, for £235.' 'Mourners are encouraged to donate flowers for our chapel walls so that other funerals can benefit. The crematory has been decorated in a style which offers warmth and comfort to the bereaved to allow those who wish to see the cremation process to attend in a fitting environment. There is a remembrance service in November and a Christmas carol service' (Richard Evans).

• **Cem**: **New Southgate** Cemetery, Brunswick Park Road, London N11 1JJ (tel 020 8361 1713; e-mail: nsg@cemcrem.com); run by the New Southgate Cemetery and Crematorium Ltd, with all profits ploughed back into the site. Plot (50 years) incl. digging and burial £1,825. Maintenance: 'Range of services from £5 (plus cost of bouquet of flowers) to £145.' They will accept home-made, cardboard or wicker coffins and body bags or shrouds. Length of funeral service: 30 minutes (extra time £50). Chapel: 'The use of the chapel for burial services costs £70. It was built in 1858, with a high steeple and (screenable) ornate oak altar.' Grounds: 'One of best selections of conifer in London, together with native trees. Cemetery used by Jews (Reformed) and the Cypriot community. There are new Roman Catholic and Greek Orthodox sections. The shrine of Shogi Effendi in Bahai section has 100,000 visitors a year.' Memorials: 'All new memorials must be supplied by the cemetery for safety reasons. The cemetery will make contributions of up to £2,000 for memorial designs with particular artistic merit.' 'All graves have flower heads covering the bottom of the grave and flowers on the surface at the head and at the corners. Clean dry soil and flower petals provided for strewing. Special facilities provided as and when required, such as tables for traditional Cypriot food and wine' (Richard Evans).

• **Cem: Paddington** Cemetery, Willesden Lane, London NW6; run by the London Borough of Brent, Brent Cemetery Service, Clifford Road, Alperton HA0 1AF (tel 020 8902 2385; fax 020 8795 0273; e-mail: langford@brent.gov.uk; web: www.mortbase.co.uk). Plot (50 years) incl. digging and burial £1,500 (£750 extra for non-residents). Maintenance: 'Nil. £82 if grave to be planted with flowering plants twice yearly.' They will accept home-made, cardboard or wicker coffins and shrouds. Length of funeral service: 'As much time as required.' Chapel: 'Gothic, 14th century style.' Grounds: 'Well laid out, wildlife area, children's play and quiet area, beehives. Dog walkers are permitted.' Memorials: 'No restrictions. A tree with memorial plaque can be planted and maintained for 15 years for £250.' They have adopted the Charter for the Bereaved. 'Fees are fair and in line with competing cemeteries. Very peaceful, with an abundance of wildlife. It is a green haven amidst the harsh urban environment' (Bob Langford).

• **Cem: Plumstead** Cemetery, Cemetery Road, Wickham Lane, Abbeywood, London SE2 0NS; run by the London Borough of Greenwich, Greenwich Direct Services, Sun Yard, Archery Road, Eltham, London SE9 1HA (tel 020 8856

0100). Plot (50 years) incl. digging and burial £516 (£1,831 extra for non-residents). Maintenance £34-55 p.a., planting £69-10 p.a. Length of funeral service: 20 minutes (extra time £15 for 10 minutes). Chapel: 'Original Victorian chapel, well maintained, with polished wooden floors and stained glass.' Grounds: 'Well maintained. Sited on a hillside. From the arched gateway the main path ascends to the chapels. The ground around the chapels undulates and at one point is carved out of the hillside to create a cliff.' Memorials: '2' 6" wide by 4' high; kerbs 6' 6" by 2' 6".' There are plans for a woodland burial ground (Dawn Squires).

• **Crem: Putney Vale** Crematorium, Stag Lane, Putney, London SW15 3DZ (tel 020 8788 2113 or 020 8789 8734; fax 020 8785 3448); run by the London Borough of Wandsworth. Price: £231 (non-residents £282). Time allotted: 20 minutes (extra time can be booked for £100). They will accept home-made or cardboard coffins, 'by prior arrangement'. Chapels: 'There are two traditional chapels converted in 1938, both seating 80 people.' Grounds: 'Formal garden, fountain, lily ponds, extending into a wooded glade' (Peter Tutt).

• **Crem: South London** Crematorium, The Garden of Remembrance, Rowan Road, London SW16 5JG (tel 020 8679 4164); run by SCI (UK). Price: £281. Time allotted: 45 minutes (an extra 45 minutes can be booked for £100). They will accept cardboard or home-made coffins, and will consider wicker coffins. Chapels: 'Edwardian, churchlike, with seating for 60, and room for 100 standing.' Grounds: 'Formal gardens with mausoleums at the front of the building.' 'Services are available on both Saturdays and Sundays. There are very few restrictions and we will offer whatever the families want so long as it's legal' (Mr Nashfold).

• **Crem: South West Middlesex** Crematorium, Hounslow Road, Hanworth, Feltham, Middlesex TW13 5JH (tel 020 8894 9001). Price: £155. Time allotted: 30 minutes (extra time can be booked for £85). They will accept home-made or cardboard coffins and body bags. Chapel: 'Three traditional chapels seating 25, 80 and 120 respectively.' Grounds: 'Both formal and informal.' They have adopted the Charter for the Bereaved. 'Very striking architecture and the grounds give a feel of tranquillity and peace' (Peter Alan Cronshaw).

• **Crem: West London** Crematorium, Kensal Green Cemetery, Harrow Road, London W10 4RA (tel 020 8969 0152). Price: £215. Time allotted: 20 minutes within a 30 minute period (extra time can be booked for £110). They will accept home-made, cardboard or wicker coffins (home-made coffins must comply with FBCA standards); they would need to see shrouds or body bags first. Chapels: 'A beautiful classical building. The East Chapel is in art deco style with oak pews and solid marble catafalque; the West is modern and light with light oak fixtures and catafalque.' Grounds: 'Surrounded by beautiful Gardens of Remembrance, with over 4,000 dedicated roses, and columbaria in the colonnades at the rear of the building.' They have adopted the Charter for the Bereaved. 'The superintendent is a qualified funeral director who will assist people to arrange funerals without recourse to a funeral director. There are no extra costs for this' (David Burkett).

• **Cem Whitton**: **Borough** Cemetery, Powdermill Lane, Whitton, Middlesex; run by the London Borough of Hounslow. Details as for Bedfont Cemetery above.

• **Cem: Willesden New** Cemetery, Franklyn Road, London NW10; run by the London Borough of Brent, Brent Cemetery Service, Clifford Road, Alperton HA0 1AF (tel 020 8902 2385; fax 020 8795 0273; e-mail: langford@brent.gov.uk; web: www.mortbase.co.uk). Plot (50 years) incl. digging and burial £1,500 (£750 extra for non-residents). Maintenance: 'Nil. £82 if grave to be planted with flowering plants twice yearly.' They will accept home-made, cardboard or wicker coffins and shrouds. Length of funeral service: 'As much time as required.' No chapel. Grounds: 'Old established cemetery.' Memorials: 'No restrictions. A tree with memorial plaque can be planted and maintained for 15 years for £250.' They have adopted the Charter for the Bereaved. 'Fees are fair and in line with competing cemeteries. Very peaceful, with an abundance of wildlife.' (Bob Langford).

• **Cem: Woolwich** Cemetery, Kings Highway, Plumstead, London SE18 2DS; run by the London Borough of Greenwich, Greenwich Direct Services, Sun Yard, Archery Road, Eltham, London SE9 1HA (tel 020 8856 0100). Plot (50 years) incl. digging and burial £516 (£1,831 extra for non-residents). Maintenance £34-55 p.a., planting £69-10 p.a. Length of funeral service: 20 minutes (extra time £15 for 10 minutes). Chapel: 'Brick Early English style chapel sits on the brow of the hill.' Grounds: 'The cemetery is divided into two sections. The old cemetery is an excellent example of how a Victorian cemetery can be adapted successfully into something like a country park whilst preserving its main features. The newer cemetery is on flat ground with very little landscaping but does have a Muslim section.' Memorials: '2' 6" wide by 4' high; kerbs 6' 6" by 2' 6"' (Dawn Squires).

Scotland

• **Crem Edinburgh**: Mortonhall Crematorium, 30, Howdenhall Road, Edinburgh EH16 6TX (tel 0131 664 4314). Price: £280. Time allotted: 30 minutes (extra 30 minutes can be booked for £55). They will accept cardboard coffins. Chapels: 'The two chapels were both designed by Sir Basil Spence. The main one seats 300 and has high ceilings and a piped organ; the small chapel seats 60.' Grounds: 'Mature woodland, lawns and mounds.' 'Memorial woodland plaques available from £400' (George Bell).

• **Crem Masonhill**: Masonhill Crematorium, Masonhill, By Ayr, South Ayrshire KA6 6EN (tel 01292 266051). Price: £242. Time allotted: 30 minutes (an extra slot will cost £242). They will accept home-made, cardboard or wicker coffins and shrouds. Chapel: '1960s non-denominational, seating 154.' Grounds: 'In open country with established trees.' 'The service will adapt to meet the needs of the bereaved' (Martin Cole).

• **Crem Perth**: Perth Crematorium, Crieff Road, Perth PH1 2PE (tel 01738 625068). Price: £289. Time allotted: 45 minutes between each service (extra time can be booked for £60). They will accept rigid containers as long as draped with a cloth. Chapel: 'The chapel, built in 1962, has wooden beams, wooden floors, and seats for 160.' Grounds: 'Formal and wooded.' 'This is the most unusual crematorium in Scotland. The gates in the chapel by the coffin close manually, so the family can ceremonially close the gates at the committal if they so wish' (Donald Martin).

Northern Ireland

• **Crem Belfast**: City of Belfast Crematorium, 129 Ballygowan Road, Crossnacreevy, Belfast, Northern Ireland BT5 7TZ (tel 028 9044 8342). Price: £95-40 (non-residents £190-60). Time allotted: 30 minutes (extra time can be booked without charge). They will accept home-made, cardboard or wicker coffins and body bags or shrouds. Chapel: 'Modern, church-like – but without religious symbolism.' Grounds: 'Beautiful lawns and memorial trees.' 'Nothing is too much trouble for our staff and every family regardless of their circumstances or background is treated with courtesy and respect. Families who wish to carry out their loved ones' funeral arrangements themselves are given help and encouragement by all the staff' (Mrs Sharon McCloy).

Chapter 9

How to Set Up a Woodland Burial Ground

The Natural Death Centre, the A. B. Welfare and Wildlife Trust, Ken West at the Carlisle Cemetery and others have for several years publicly promoted the concept of woodland burial grounds – where a tree is planted by the grave instead of having a headstone. Such a site provides a very elegant solution to a number of problems:

• Cemeteries in many areas are filled to capacity – and when visits to graves cease, the cemeteries could be destroyed to make way for building development.

• It would not be desirable to continue for centuries into the future covering the countryside with row upon row of headstones. Furthermore, headstones can become dangerous to children and are very costly to maintain.

• Burial has become pricier than cremation, particularly in and around cities.

• Cremation causes pollution and adds to the greenhouse effect.

• Crematoria are bleak places in which to hold funerals.

• Woodland burial grounds are less costly to develop than crematoria.

• The planet needs more trees and the UK has a policy of increasing its forest cover.

• People are seeking less expensive funerals.

• Woodland burials organised and controlled by family and friends, without necessarily using funeral directors, are more therapeutic for those who are grieving than a short impersonal service in a crematorium.

• Farmers need to diversify to bring in more sources of income – many have land for which they are paid very little under the set aside scheme.

• People would like beautiful rural settings for the burial of their family and friends.

• Woodland burial grounds provide a refuge for wildlife.

• The Green generation as it gets older – Friends of the Earth supporters and the like – will not want to cause pollution with their deaths. They will be attracted by the concept of 'giving the body back to nature'. As Jonathon Porritt puts it: 'The combination of built-in fertiliser, plus unlimited tender loving care from the relatives, would pretty well guarantee a thriving woodland in next to no time.'

The Centre made these points in a number of media interviews from 1993 onwards. Farmers were not slow to respond to the challenge. The Centre also gave a talk to the Institute of Burial and Cremation Authorities, urging that every local authority should follow the example of Carlisle and set up a green burial ground within its area. Again, progress has been rapid.

It was also hoped that charitable and non-profit bodies such as local church groups, the National Trust, the Woodland Trust, the Forestry Commission and the new planned national forests would all start making provision for memorial groves. In this instance, however, progress has been more cautious, with the Woodland Trust, for example, deciding not to develop any such burial grounds within its land for the time being.

Incidentally, 'woodland burial grounds' has become the popular term for these new sites, but it should be noted that woodland is just one sort of habitat and that 'green burial grounds' or 'nature reserve burial grounds' better conveys the diversity of meadows and pastures that are being used.

The Carlisle woodland burial ground

As mentioned, the first woodland burial ground was the one set up by the City of Carlisle. Ken West, the manager there, wrote during the planning stages in 1993:

> The creation of a memorial woodland resource would benefit the environ-ment and could be returned to the community after the expiry of grave rights. It could then form part of a country park or a green lung, for walking, pony trekking or similar. Part of the intangible benefits are a return to nature and the need to encourage insects, birds and mammals.
>
> For the layout of the graves, I prefer a double grave with burials side by side, at a depth of 4' 3". This allows, after a burial, the planting of a tree on the used portion of the grave. There will be space for 537 graves to the acre, about 46% less than our current setting out. This is more than compensated for by the reduced excavation costs, drainage problems, backfilling, rein-statement of sunken graves, etc. Additionally, the cost of a traditional new graveyard had to include new roads, deep drainage, etc, which will not apply in the same degree with this scheme.
>
> People choosing the woodland concept before death will have gained a real psychological benefit – a piece of woodland and a real, living memorial instead of a dull, dead stone. Perhaps the test of any product is 'Would you use it yourself?' I can state clearly that I would and refer you to these lines from 'Drummer Hodge' by Thomas Hardy:
>
>> His homely Northern breast and brain
>> Grow to some Southern tree
>> And strange eyed constellations reign
>> His stars eternally.

Adapted extracts from an article by Ken West,
Carlisle Bereavement Services Manager.

The rate at which new woodland burial grounds are opening is impressive. In January 1996, there were 17 such grounds known to the Natural Death Centre; by July, there were 33; by January 1997 there were 52; by January 2000 there were 90.

Of these 90 woodland burial grounds (all of which are detailed in Chapter 6), 59 are run by councils, 30 are run as businesses by farmers or private individuals, and one is run as a non-profit concern asking for donations to a wildlife trust. At least 52 more sites are about to open, or are at various planning stages (including two Church of England sites). The cost of a grave, including the digging and usually a tree, ranges from £165·50 at Tavistock in Devon to £1,184 at the Brimscombe woodland burial ground in Stroud. The average cost is £517. The average cost for the council-run sites is £492 (with most charging considerably more for non-residents); for the sites run as businesses the average cost is £573.

Association of Nature Reserve Burial Grounds

In 1994, the Natural Death Centre set up an Association of Nature Reserve Burial Grounds in order: (a) to put forward a Code of Practice for its members to adhere to, so that potential clients approaching such a burial ground can be more confident that it reaches these standards; (b) to help full and provisional members through planning and other hurdles; (c) to help reassure neighbours of potential sites that they have nothing to fear; (d) to refer members to legal, ecological and other advice; (e) to provide information for members on obtaining coffins and other funeral supplies; (f) to promote the concept of using land for Nature Reserve Burial Grounds; (g) to provide publicity leaflets, information and a referral service for the public concerning individual sites, including maintaining an information area on this subject on the Internet; (h) to help publicise and defend the movement in the media and with the government and local authorities.

Membership, whether full membership or provisional applicant membership, costs £20 per annum (with cheques payable to 'NDC') although members are also encouraged to pay 1 per cent of the ground's gross income to the Natural Death Centre charity.

To be allowed to become a full member of the Association, a green burial ground must be willing to allow the use of cardboard coffins; it must allow families to organise a funeral without a funeral director if they so wish; it must safeguard funds paid in advance; it must guarantee long-term security for the graves; and it must manage its site ecologically.

The Association is still at a very early stage, relying primarily on the probity of statements made by its members and on feedback from the public, as it does not yet have the resources for site inspections.

Code of Practice

The following is the Code of Practice (updated February 3rd 2000):

• Association members agree to take all reasonable steps for the conservation of local wildlife and archaeological sites and to manage their sites according to sound and consistent ecological principles. (Written evidence must be provided to the Association that the views of local or national bona fide wildlife and archaeological organisations have been sought and that plans have been modified as necessary to take account of any objections.)

• Association members must be in a position to guarantee the long-term security of both the graves and the wildlife, and have a satisfactory plan for when the site reaches its capacity. (Except for local authority sites, written evidence must be provided as to freehold ownership, any mortgages on the site, the legal title that clients receive, any planned transfer of the site to a wildlife charity or other relevant factors. Give full details of the long-term security offered to clients.)

• Association members other than local authority sites must satisfy the Association as to the quality, financial probity and non-indebtedness and relevant qualifications of their directors, trustees, managing body or similar. (Adequate references must also be provided.)

• Association members accept for burial bodies whether wrapped in a shroud or placed in a cardboard or wooden coffin or alternative container or wrapping, provided these are environmentally acceptable.

• Association members will not require that a funeral director be used. Those using the Nature Reserve Burial Ground will be informed that they may organise the funeral themselves, including conducting any service. They may dig a single depth grave, subject to any equipment, training, safety or regulatory constraints; and they may help with filling in the grave.

• Association members will keep a permanent record of exactly where each grave is. A copy of the burial ground register entry will be made available to the client and the register will be open for public inspection.

• Association members will either sell coffins and shrouds to clients or provide information as to where these can be obtained.

• Association members, whose charges must be fair and reasonable, will provide fully itemised price lists for potential clients on request, and will also reveal these prices on the telephone on request.

• Association members will provide a copy of this Code of Practice to clients using their services, and will have copies available on request for others.

• Association members will provide each client using their services with a feedback form, either the site's own form or the Association's form, asking for the client's comments on the service provided and for any suggested improvements, with a request that a copy of the feedback form be sent direct to the Association. This feedback form is to include the address and phone number of the Association and to note that any complaints can be sent to the Association.

• Association members, if taking money in advance, agree to abide by the Office of Fair Trading's recommendations on prepaid funerals.

• Association members accept that in the event of a complaint from a client that is not dealt with to the Association's satisfaction within three months of the complaint being made, the Nature Reserve Burial Ground's membership will cease without refund. A serious complaint may result in immediate suspension of membership whilst the complaint is investigated.

• Before membership is granted or renewed, the Association may require further evidence on the above or any other relevant matters.

• Provisional Association members must provide the information required to convert to full membership within a year of their site opening.

The Association of Nature Reserve Burial Grounds, c/o The Natural Death Centre, 20 Heber Road, London NW2 6AA (tel 020 8208 2853; fax 020 8452 6434; e-mail: rhino@dial.pipex.com; web: www.naturaldeath.org.uk).

Advice for those setting up green burial grounds

The main obstacle facing any farmer, company, charity or individual wanting to set up a relatively large scale green burial ground is likely to be obtaining planning permission. Several grounds have only won permission on appeal. Local objections can be ferocious and irrational, fuelled by fear of death and the taboos surrounding the whole subject. Applicants who want to spare themselves a long-drawn out process and the hostility of their neighbours would do well to choose a site not overlooked by neighbours and where neighbours will not even see the funeral cars. Even to be invisible may not help them sufficiently however: the landscape officer in one application reported that even though the site could not be seen from the road, the mere knowledge that the site was there, would make driving past it a 'depressing experience' – what a contrast with Victorian days when to have picnics in cemeteries was a quite normal occurrence.

Applicants might also be well advised, if they have a choice between forecasting for 700 burials a year or for 50 burials, to go for the smaller number initially; likewise, if there is a choice between applying for the whole property of 50 acres to become a burial ground, or for a mere 7 acre field within it, to apply for the smaller site. The burial ground will take many years to fill up and by then the momentum in favour of such developments will be that much greater than it is now. In the meantime, a small site may arouse fewer passions.

Applicants should also choose a site where the council cannot claim that access from the road will be dangerous or the car-parking inadequate and they should seek the advice of council officers at an early stage.

But even when the council officers support an application, the applicant should be wary if there is local opposition. Local petitions and letters against the applicant need to be matched by petitions and letters in favour.

It could also be good tactics to arrange a five-minute individual meeting with every councillor on the relevant planning committee to show them your plans, to answer any doubts that they may have and to let them see that you are not the devil incarnate.

Produce a detailed landscaping plan and illustrate how the site will look when the trees are mature. At one planning meeting a site was rejected, with one councillor remarking: 'The trees are small, it doesn't look like a wood', not seeming to realise that it is in the nature of trees to grow bigger.

To find a green burial site to buy, it might be worth approaching an agent dealing in woodland such as John Clegg & Co (tel 01844 215800) or the Woodlands Centre (tel 020 8693 4000).

John Bradfield of the A. B. Welfare and Wildlife Trust in Harrogate (see Resources chapter for address) is wary of commercial burial projects, 'as some have unsound foundations and most commercial cemeteries started in the 19th century became bankrupt'. He will give free advice to credible wildlife charities, thinking of starting nature reserve burial projects. 'Initial enquiries should always be in writing,' he stresses, 'giving the charity registration number'.

Questions from local people

The following are some of the typically probing questions that a proposed woodland burial ground aroused and that were sent in by local objectors to their planning department. The list will give those proposing to set up grounds food for thought.

• What are the management plans for the site, who will retain the long-term maintenance of the site, what assurances are there against the site falling into disrepair, who will look after the site when it reaches capacity?

• Will be the gates be opened or locked? Will there be any form of security?

• How many people will be employed at the site? How will the graves be dug?

• Where will the machinery and tools be stored?

• Are there any buildings, structures (eg storage buildings), shelters, benches, memorials, etc, proposed for the future?

• How do the bodies get from the car park to the graves and what are the bodies carried in?

• Is it only for human remains or would animals and pets be buried on the site?

• What evidence do you have of only one burial per fortnight? How long will the site take to reach its full level?

• What boundary fencing is proposed? How will the grass be cut? Who will see to the removal of dead flowers and rubbish?

• What evidence is there of the demand or need for this site?

• What is the total number of graves that the site will hold?

• From where will the site be administered?

• Will the scattering of ashes occur on the site, if so exactly where?

• What evidence have you to demonstrate that there will be no contamination of any watercourses?

• What external lighting is proposed?

• What civil law exists over the establishment and use of the cemetery?

• What is the proposed tree planting density for the site? (The indicative plans do not allow the trees to reach full maturity.)

• The site does not benefit from public transport provision. Have any plans been made or provided to reduce the need for everyone visiting the site to use a private vehicle?

• What signage is proposed for the site?

Advice from existing sites

Additional tips have been sent in by existing green burial grounds:

One correspondent to the Natural Death Centre suggests that the first person to get on your side is the local vicar, then the chair of the parish council, before approaching bodies like the Environment Agency. Once you have an outline letter from the latter saying that they cannot see any immediate objection, you can then spend the money on a planning application.

Mr Rodney Hill, the Wigan Cemetery Registrar, adds that, at the earliest opportunity, groups should meet not only with council people and local clergy but with the local authority cemetery and crematorium people – you need to explain that you are not in competition but are offering an alternative service. When choosing a site, groups should consider whether the area floods or has water problems. Have a colour plan drawn up and put on display, with permission, in local authority buildings and the town hall, hold meetings with the press and public to smooth out problems before a planning application is submitted.

James Broome of the New Manchester Woodland Cemetery has slightly different advice on timing, suggesting that just before the planning application is lodged, or within one week of doing so, make sure local people are aware of your plans. They must clearly understand the difference between your scheme and a traditional cemetery. If you rely on the standard notices sent out by the local authority to inform people, it gives a chance for substantial opposition to arise, and you may find a local do-gooder organising a petition against you. 'While the planning committee tend to ignore petitions,' Broome writes, 'they do take notice of well-constructed logically argued objections in the form of an individual letter, and some of these will no doubt also enter the system.'

In their own case, once they had addressed these problems and had arranged a meeting on site with a cross-section of local people – giving a project presentation followed by a question and answer session – opposition dwindled.

Another correspondent advises that the site you choose is acceptable to the Environment Agency (which has taken over the National Rivers Authority). Apply for a change to mixed use if the site is presently farmland. She emphasises the points made above that 'local people need to know what is happening or they will imagine the worst – always!' and that access must be easy and acceptable to the highway authorities.

Jeanne and Brian Nicholas of the Mole Valley Green Burial Ground stress the importance of the legal aspects – contracts for pre-purchased plots, securing rights of access in the future and ensuring perpetuity.

Bernard Edge, director of Brinkley Wood Cemetery, suggests taking up the grants that may be available for early development tree planting and hedging.

Philip Andrew, who manages the woodland area within Stonefall Cemetery in Harrogate, notes that the site must be large enough to allow trees to be planted, and needs some form of memorialisation such as plaques on trees. He adds that 'two cuts per year are essential to give some control, and yet to maintain a wild area'.

Bob Langford of Carpenders Park Cemetery has been precise about the trees to be planted for their woodland area and for the lower levels.

Tania Thornley, who is planning a woodland burial ground near Tavistock in Devon, writes:

> I do not feel that a fake grass covering for the mound of earth (before the grave is filled) will be in keeping with my site and I will try other ideas such as a covering of greenery from the field.
>
> In order to reduce the couch grass and other invasive weeds on the back-filled grave, while encouraging the wild flowers and herbs, I was given the tip that one should mix the topsoil and subsoil.

Tania Thornley also tackles the problem of double graves:

> Market research suggests individuals often wish to be buried next to their loved ones, and this can be a problem for a woodland burial site for two main reasons. Firstly, the excavation of a grave next to one that has been filled (up to 40 years previously) could disturb the tree roots of neighbouring trees; and secondly, as the area will by then be a wildlife woodland, access through the undergrowth could be difficult.
>
> On my site, double burials will not be permitted on top of each other, but double burials could be acceptable if a separate area were provided with a slightly different management regime – for instance, a native shrub (guilder rose, dog rose, spindle tree or honeysuckle) could be planted on the first interment and a long-life tree only on the second interment.

Tania Thornley goes on to wonder how her site will be rated:

> Will the woodland burial site be rated under agriculture (in which case no rates are payable) or business? There seem to be no set rules applying to woodland burial grounds, and the Regional Rates Valuation Officer will not come up with an answer until the site is up and running. Once a burial has taken place the grave area becomes woodland; and before this it is grazed or cut for hay. Because none of the land therefore lends itself to being a definite business (except the car park area) it has been implied that I will be rated on the land that looks like a business – ie areas with paths, etc.

John O'Callaghan of Exwick Cemetery says that you need to think very carefully about methods of shoring up the grave, particularly if the family wish to back-fill.

Anne Dyer of the burial ground at Craven Arms writes: 'Don't try to hard sell – the site should sell itself. Have a roof, lavatory and tea-making nearby.'

Michael Day of the Norse Road Woodland Cemetery just says to listen and to learn from those who desire this woodland form of burial.

Billy Campbell at Memorial Ecosystems Ramsey Creek Preserve in South Carolina, the first nature reserve burial ground in the States, writes that to begin with they were completely opposed to inorganic grave markers:

Are grave markers ever appropriate?

We decided that any grave markers should be made of stone from the same geological strata as the preserve.

It turns out that stones do have a very important ecological role in most temperate forests. Ants in particular benefit from an ample supply of stones. According to Holldobler and Wilson (1990), stones provide cover for establishing colonies, and (when flat and shallow) are important for colony thermoregulation, and overall colony success. Ants are now understood to be major players in forests, with impressive total biomass/ acre. They are important distributors of certain wild flower seeds. In fact, Pudlo et al (1980) reported that ants might distribute "as much as 70 per cent" of the flora of mesic forests of the temperate areas of the world.

Our preserve consulting biologist, Dr L. L. Gaddy, published a report based on his research in our area of the US that gives credence to Pudlo's conjecture (Gaddy, 1986). Ants do more than just spread seed and are involved in plant pollination and protection as well (Beattie, 1985). They are also important for some other invertebrates and host the larva of the lycaenid butterflies (blues and hairstreaks). I understand that in the UK, the big blues are pretty much extirpated, and I wonder what role the enclosure acts (and subsequent stone gathering) had on them. It is interesting that in certain ecological restoration efforts in the US, ant diversity has lagged, perhaps because we have not paid enough attention to restoring the forest and prairie floor structure.

In any event, we have come to the conclusion that, at least in the case of Ramsey Creek, returning stones to the forest floor is a good thing ecologically.

From Billy Campbell's e-mail to the Natural Death Centre.

Charitable green burial grounds

The trailblazing green burial charity has been the A. B. Welfare and Wildlife Trust in Harrogate (see the North East region of Chapter 6 for their full details and the Index at the back for other references to the Trust and to its founder John Bradfield). In 1993, John Bradfield said: 'I believe that by being able to select burial in land in which nature has a prior claim, there will be a qualitative shift in emotional experience, away from the "warehousing of the dead" in cemeteries and churchyards.' In letters to The Natural Death Centre, John Bradfield has added:

The A. B. Welfare and Wildlife Trust

I'm concerned that we should be able to take *full* control over dying and death. This means being able to avoid the use of funeral directors (et al) or to buy only those services required from them. It could mean digging the grave oneself having chosen the location, or digging it with a group of friends and relatives. Health and safety factors need to be fully taken account of, but are not barriers in themselves. Risks can be reduced by making shallow graves, which are also more environmentally benign.

There is no minimum depth for graves in national laws for private land, unless the Towns Improvement Clauses Act 1847 applies, in which case the minimum is 30 inches from the ground level to the top of the coffin, if a coffin is used. The minimum for public cemeteries is 24 inches and we know of a hospital burial ground, closed in 1969, where coffins were at ground level.

I'm also keen that coffins not be used unless environmentally benign, such as second-hand timbers from doors, floors and pallets. A ban will be placed on tropical hardwoods, even those from assumed sustainable sources. A coffin is wrongly said by some to be required for transporting the body, but a choice may be exercised simply to use a shroud, the person's own clothes, or some other alternative, such as basket from willow or sustainable osier beds, cardboard or carpet.

Burials are arranged by the Trust in existing nature reserves and there are plans to create others. As a combined social work and wildlife charity, it is a tangible example of a seamless voluntary service based on 'joined-up' thinking.

It is the only charity in the country able to give sound advice about dying, death and funerals. By now it should be having a major impact on the health and welfare services, cemeteries, crematoria and wildlife charities. If the government ever sets up an agency to go in search of pioneering work – work which could transform standards in the public services – this Trust should be at the top of the government's list for scrutiny. But in fact further progress is being hindered by a bureaucratic stranglehold imposed by the planners and by the failure of politicians to help.

For a donation of £5, the A. B. Welfare and Wildlife Trust will send any group trying to start a charitable nature reserve burial ground a copy of its constitution – or no doubt a copy could be obtained from the Charity Commission library at 57 Haymarket, London SW1 (tel 020 7210 4477). The Trust is also seeking donations of land and money to run further burial grounds under its own aegis.

John Bradfield noted in 'Green Burial' that the Charity Commission agreed that the trustees of the Harrogate Trust for Wildlife Protection had power to allow a small numbers of burials within its nature reserves, without having to mention burials in its constitution. Such burials have since taken place.

A Lawful Development Certificate or 'LDC' (also known as a Certificate of Lawfulness), he adds, which costs about half the fee for applying for planning permission, could be sought to ascertain how many graves your local authority would permit without requiring planning permission.

If the graves are dug by hand, and there are none of the various identifying signs of a cemetery, such as roads, sale of burial rights, gravestones and large fencing, John Bradfield argues in 'Green Burial' that there will have been no 'substantial' or 'material' change of use and therefore the local authority should not require planning permission to be sought. Woodland burial grounds should make it clear that they have no interest in setting up cemeteries.

John Bradfield prefers to rely, not on tree planting, but on allowing woods naturally to plant themselves, or using a good seed supply from near at hand, thus promoting local strains and genes, and conserving genetic diversity. Burials should be on parts of the site with the least ecological importance, rather than in areas of existing wildlife value such as old woods with woodland flowers, bogs, marshes or wild flower meadows or pasture. 'It is too easy to overlook important wild flower areas, so it is worth asking someone with a trained eye to study the area between early Spring and late Autumn.'

John Bradfield warns that if the burial ground is on old meadow land that has interesting wild flowers, trees should not be planted. It should, however, continue to be mown. He also warns that wild bluebells have been given extra legal protection and should not be dug up for replanting in burial grounds.

Burials should happen only exceptionally, Bradfield adds, in Sites of Special Scientific Interest – but even these may have areas with little ecological value such as old refuse tips or nettle beds, areas once churned up by heavy machinery, large areas of bracken, old bonfire sites, areas where topsoil may need to be stripped off, or agriculturally 'improved' grassland where the aim is to recover some degree of species diversity.

In one planning appeal by a burial ground in Oswestry, monitored by John Bradfield, the inspector pointed out that 'cemeteries are not "inappropriate" development in terms of the guidance on Green Belts (contained in Planning Policy Guidance note 2 (PPG2) or local planning policies)'.

The A. B. Welfare and Wildlife Trust has sent in a number of other tips for those seeking to set up charitable green burial grounds:

Persuade a local and well-established wildlife charity to agree to one or more burials in existing nature reserves, so as to begin the process and start changing attitudes (see 'Green Burial' 1994, page 61) but to avoid complex charity law, do not sell access or burial rights.

Work with a local wildlife charity to extend an existing nature reserve, by purchasing adjacent land for burials. Ask that charity to agree, from the outset, to take over the project after a number of years (as the Essex Wildlife Trust will do at Wrabness) or when burials have ceased.

Even if an established wildlife charity is wary of involvement, it is still worth buying land which it is likely to accept as a gift at some distant date.

Don't accept unsuitable land just to get started, as the land can't be sold or exchanged for a better site – burials are permanent. Small life rafts of wildlife in seas of barley and sugar beet, will be of no interest to most wildlife charities. They would take over small sites if adjacent to existing nature reserves, so the total area is increased.

Don't start until the long-term security of both graves and wildlife can be guaranteed.

If you are aiming for more than a handful of burials in the long-term, decide whether or not to have a few burials first, before applying for planning permission.

You must get a Lawful Development Certificate or planning permission, if graves will be sold in advance of need, to make the arrangement watertight.

To avoid complex charity law, it can be easier for an individual or non-charitable group to own the land and agree to burials, if reasonable donations are made to a named charity, with ownership passing to that or some other charity at a later date (as with Kate's Fell, which is owned by John Bradfield, but with all money going to the A. B. Welfare and Wildlife Trust).

So that there is no doubt when questions are asked, have a clear and long-term plan from the outset on (a) the protection of graves, (b) access to the land for visits to graves, and (c) the conservation of existing wildlife or how wildlife will be established and managed over time.

Perpetual rights and perpetual protection cannot be guaranteed by non-charitable landowners, unless covered by some aspect of law, such as the Cemeteries Clauses Act 1847. The maximum length of time in law which public cemeteries and the Church of England can guarantee is 100 years, but even these rights can be ended if the correct steps are taken.

The A. B. Welfare and Wildlife Trust will not accept embalmed bodies. It has also banned hearses for its Kate's Fell site, partly to keep the planners happy (no one will know a funeral is taking place if no hearses are around) and partly to encourage people to use their own vehicles.

> A. B. Welfare and Wildlife Trust (Charity Reg. No. 1037444), 7 Knox Road, Harrogate, North Yorkshire HG1 3EF (tel 01423 530900 or 868121). For further details, see under John Bradfield and A. B. Welfare and Wildlife Trust in the Index at the back of this book.

A woodland burial network for the bereaved

The following is adapted from letters and a leaflet sent to the Natural Death Centre.

A nationwide network of local groups called Friends of Woodland Glades is being formed to bring together those families and friends who have made use of a woodland burial ground. Taking the original Friends group in Essex as an example, the one centred on the Maldon woodland burial ground, activities for group members can include:

• Establishing bark pathways within the woodland.

• Assisting with the annual day of dedication. Each year, a day of dedication is offered to family and friends of the deceased, which involved them in the planting of trees and bulbs, with refreshments served afterwards in the chapel.

• Providing assistance with the placing of woodland memorial seats.

• Assisting with the aftercare of tree plantings.

• Providing additional planting days for bulbs.

• Providing talks to people on a variety of topics.

Such a group offers the opportunity for the development of friendship between people who have been brought together through bereavement and through an interest in the woodland burial concept.

Each group will have its own committee. In Maldon, the district council's role has been very much in the background, providing meeting rooms, materials and the printing of newsletters.

There is no subscription fee, but any group would have to pay for its own outings or out-of-pocket expenses.

In due course, there could be a network magazine.

David Lobb, the Cemeteries and Parks Development Officer at Maldon District Council, seems to have been the key person behind this imaginative initiative and he is happy to accept enquiries from other woodland burial sites wishing to set up such groups. The Maldon group is refining its constitution which can be made available to other groups for adapting to their needs.

For further information contact: David Lobb, the Cemeteries and Parks Development Officer, Maldon District Council, Princess Road, Maldon, Essex CM9 5DL (tel 01621 854477; fax 01621 852575).

Local authority woodland burial grounds

Dawn Eckhart, the Community Development Officer at the Seaton cemetery in Devon, suggests that the quickest and simplest way for a local authority to begin a woodland burial ground is to set it up as a pilot project within an existing cemetery. The cemetery will already have planning permission and so there are no negotiations needed with other agencies about health and safety or water pollution. If Dawn Eckhart had more time, she would like to research a source of coffins produced from local and sustainably-managed forests.

The disadvantage of a small scheme, she says, is not being able to allow people to buy adjacent plots in advance. The site has no sign of the graves on the surface, so graves are being dug in sequence to avoid error.

Brendan Day, who runs the Thornhill Cemetery in Cardiff, advises that a woodland burial section is a good way of utilising cemetery ground where only a depth of 4'6" can be obtained. Families do not expect two depth graves in a woodland burial ground, once they are aware of the need for the body to be as close to the surface as possible so as to encourage the bacterial action and decay. Thus a local authority may be able to make use of a site with a relatively high water table or with a rocky layer beneath it.

Hugh Dawson, Oxford Cemeteries Manager, writes that all register records are now kept on computer, with many packages available. The woodland burial grounds, he comments, will design themselves, depending on the types of trees which families select to be planted on the graves.

David Lobb, Maldon Cemeteries Officer, wrote in the Funeral Service Journal (November 1996) that their woodland burial glades are being created within an existing mature cemetery. Families choose a grave space within burial islands. Each island consists of between 20 to 40 graves, and the islands will eventually link up together. Pathways constructed from bark with log edgings will be developed as the need arises. The grounds are managed as wild flower meadow. For the wild flower planting, they use pre-grown plant plugs, 'these being of much more immediate impact and far easier to establish. Species include red campion, ragged robin, white campion, harebell and oxeye daisy'.

John Bradfield of the A. B. Welfare and Wildlife Trust cautions, however, against indiscriminate use of wild flower seed – 'no wild flowers should be grown without obtaining advice from a credible wildlife charity on the species and genetic origin.'

The 'Good Bulb Guide', available free in return for an SAE from Fauna and Flora International, Great Eastern House, Tenison Road, Cambridge CB1 2DT (tel 01223 571000) details companies that have pledged never to sell wild-collected bulbs but buyers would still need to satisfy themselves as to their provenance. Some experts argue strongly for local provenance:

> Too often wild flower seed is imported from the Netherlands or raised by nurseries from European sources. ... Many of the wild hyacinth or English bluebell strands have become seriously introgressed by pollen from garden introductions, resulting in hybrid stock. Common sources of seed homogenise the flora and threaten our floral genetic inheritance. If cemetery planners could take account of these concerns by ensuring only indigenous plant material is encouraged in situ it could go some way to prevent the erosion of our native genetic resources.
>
> *From a letter to the Natural Death Centre from Alan Fairweather.*

This chapter ends with suggestions and adapted extracts from a long feasibility study and update prepared by Ken West, the pioneer of woodland burial. The full book-length set of papers, entitled 'Woodland Burial – A Return to Nature', is available for £20 from Carlisle Cemetery, The Cemetery Office, Richardson Street, Carlisle CA2 6AL (tel 01228 625310).

The Woodland Burial – A Return to Nature

• Local authority cemeteries all lose money. In Carlisle, for instance, all cemetery income simply covers the grave digging and associated administrative costs. There is no surplus whatsoever for subsequent grave maintenance – a deficit of £273,500 for a recent financial year. The woodland burial site, by contrast, will have insignificant maintenance costs and long term liabilities. Income from coffin sales and plaques on the Memorial Wall offers the possibility of woodland cemeteries actually making a profit.

• The format of the funeral has been changed by those favouring the woodland concept. The number of secular funerals is slightly above average. One funeral has already occurred with the family requesting that all staff attending, both from the cemetery and the funeral director, should wear jeans and tee-shirts. A further funeral is being planned along these lines for the future. I have not previously experienced this request in my 35 years in this work.

• Chipboard coffins are lined with a plastic sheet. Expert opinion suggests that although chipboard acts like a sponge and breaks down very quickly in damp or wet soil, the plastic wraps itself around the body and may cause mummification. This will be avoided if a biodegradable coffin is used.

• Woodland burial is perceived as being much more successful than it really is. Woodland burial represents only 1.5% of the total funerals we complete, including cremation ... (although), for the period October 1995 to March 1996, 19% of our grave sales were in the woodland, and by January 2000, 30% of new grave sales were in the woodland.

• If a new woodland burial scheme reduces memorial or other sources of income, either to the funeral director or associated memorial outlet, it may be opposed. An advance reservation scheme for graves may defeat negative advice the bereaved may receive from funeral directors at the time of death.

• Graves are marked with a concrete block sunk level with the ground, engraved with a number from 1 upwards. Each twentieth grave marker will be erected 24" high to facilitate measurement to locate other grave markers in dense vegetation.

• The graves take up more space than in conventional cemeteries, as two coffins are put side by side. But the graves are shorter length and width per coffin than usual, because they are dug to a shallow depth and collapse will not become a problem.

• We initially planted many of the unused graves with an oak whip, mainly to give the site a 'woodland' appearance. Subsequently, we find that these trees are easily moved and replanted onto graves which have recently been used for burial. This is useful as it generally allows the partner or family to plant the tree on their grave during the summer months.

• Reports of some other woodland burial schemes have been disappointing. One had graves located around cemetery perimeters, creating a line of trees rather than woodland. Another was situated on a compost heap formed by the cemetery grass mowings accumulating over years. At another location, the staff had little idea about the concept.

The woodland should replicate the type of woodland which exists naturally in the area. One woodland scheme offers a choice of three tree species, one of which is Mountain Ash (.). Unfortunately, most people using the scheme are choosing this and creating a Mountain Ash wood. Such a wood is rarely found naturally, particularly in lowland, and these trees are often short lived.

Other schemes are using the typical garden centre type tree, the 'lollipop' tree, with a cleared stem up to (say) 4' to 5' and the branches radiating from a single apical point. These trees never attain the typical forest tree appearance and they often possess structural weaknesses. They may also be grown from European rather than native seed.

In Carlisle, we located some landowners who have been growing Oaks from acorns harvested from old trees growing on their land. These young trees cost £1 each and are about 2' to 2'6" high and with a good fibrous root system. Any seed trees you use should be old enough to predate the period of potential introduction from abroad. About 100 years should suffice.

Oak offers many benefits – the number of insect species found on the oak is 284, which exceeds any other tree. Oak is not suited, however, to chalk soils or industrial spoils.

• Tree shelters (translucent polypropylene tubes) would look unattractive across burial areas. Spiral guards (loosely coiled plastic tubes which wrap around the stem) are used instead. They are only suitable on feathered whips with a stem diameter of at least 25mm.

• Weeds around the tree are controlled by mulching using black polythene mulching mats (600mm by 600mm square), minimum 500 gauge with ultra violet inhibitor. The mat is dug in around its edges and covered by leaf mould or wood chips.

• Evidence from existing crematoria memorial planting schemes shows that trees, which, on the woodland burial ground will be only 1.5 metres apart, can be thinned after five years, with few, if any people, concerned.

• The Forestry Commission 'Woodland Grant Scheme' gives money per hectare for Oak woodland, if a minimum 0.25 hectare is planted within a five year period. This figure can be reached by including shelter and other types of planting achieved for the opening of the burial area.

• 20 weeks after burial (depending on the time of year), the grave will be forked/rotovated and levelled approximately 75mm below the normal ground surface. Approximately 210 bluebell bulbs will be laid evenly over the grave surface, covered by 75mm of top soil. The Oak tree whip will be planted and the plastic mulch mat at its base will be covered with 65mm of leaf mould. The remaining soil surface will be levelled.

• Environment Agency objections to the setting up of a cemetery may be based on reports of watercourse pollution from cemeteries in the USA. This is apparently due to the high percentage of bodies treated with embalming fluid, and formaldehyde has been found in the water. If this objection arises, it might be sensible to prohibit the embalming of bodies accepted for burial for the woodland burial site.

• The types of people using the woodland graves include those who seek an alternative to cremation; those who like the no-memorial anonymity; single people who do not need to buy the conventional double grave space; the broadly green – gardeners and those who love birds, countryside, trees and wild flowers; those who like the low cost aspect; and those wanting secular or independent funerals.

• A dedication ceremony can formally open the burial area. This involves a religious ceremony jointly performed by representatives of all the churches.

• Although I coined the phrase 'return to nature', other fertile minds are already improving on this. I particularly like 'leave the world a better place', devised by a funeral director operating his own woodland site in the Isle of Wight.

Chapter 10

'Improving' Grieving

Anything written about grieving is unlikely to suit everybody because grief is an intensely personal emotion. It can be bewildering and surprising and make us do unexpected things. Grief can knock us sideways. The absence of grief, too, can be stunning. It is not always there when we expect it and need it. Grief is a volatile emotion: one moment we are engulfed in it, the next we are coping with everyday life, driving the car, calling on a friend, laughing at jokes over lunch. Like being in love, grief is something that is just there; it happens, it makes us feel we are somehow different from people who are not in that condition. For that reason, anyone who is suffering bereavement might read this chapter differently from someone who isn't. The title, for example: of course we cannot 'improve' your grieving. But society can improve the way it reacts to those who are grieving, and there are certain attitudes and practices, some of them reported below, which obstruct the natural expression of feeling and which could be improved upon, and certain evolving customs in modern life that may be worth sharing.

This chapter is built around the experience of grieving. Academic references and sources are given a secondary position. See also the Organisations listed in the Resources chapter – for in many particularly hard bereavements, such as when grieving over the loss of a child, a support group can be a great help in gradually learning to cope.

The different levels of grief we experience can be very surprising. A dear friend dies and after the funeral we resume normal existence with an appetite that makes us almost guilty. Where has that person gone? Why don't we feel it more? We probably will experience the sorrow when reminders of past times crop up, but meanwhile the fact that life just goes on as before can seem almost unreal. And then someone dies who has shared our most intimate life and it is as if a part of the self has been removed without warning. Hence the wisdom of saying that when we mourn the other, we mourn the self. Such grief reaches into the part of us where the roles played in our identity by the self and the other – the partner, the mother, the child – seem indistinguishable. One mourner, just when he thought he was recovering from his wife's death, broke out in a violent rash. It took him a further eighteen months to realise what had happened:

Debilitating grief

I was much debilitated; the body had to excrete the accumulated stress of several years. Some mourners, I was to discover, are prey to nervous breakdowns, ulcers and much much worse: chronic arthritic conditions, heart attacks, even cancer. This is probably what accounts for so many instances, in centuries gone by, of persons dying of grief or 'a broken heart'.

From an article by Libby Purves in The Times (April 3rd 1992).

The potential phases of grieving are recorded in many textbooks, the results of professional and academic study of individual experiences. But here is Margaret Chisman's own personal and courageous account. In the first extract she expresses her immediate reaction to the death of her husband Stan.

Picking up the threads

When the hospital phoned at 3am on March 24th to say he had died I was alone in the house as my daughter, by chance, was away that night. After a short bout of numbed weeping I phoned near relatives and then made a cup of tea – remembering to add extra sugar for shock. I asked myself what I should do with the rest of my life now that the bottom had dropped out of it, and told myself that the most important thing was how to get through the rest of the night, and the next few weeks.

Later she wrote about the emotions of the first week:

During the first week after his death I made myself, in the privacy of my home, keep on saying out aloud 'My husband is dead and I'm a widow' until I could say it without weeping.

I am still weeping daily but it is mercifully lessening as I begin to pick up the threads again just a little.

After a few months she was able to write about the experience in a structured way and to begin to share with others and include a view of the future:

It is probable that most survivors experience similar phases of grief. First comes a numb inability to believe it. The reality of the loved one's presence is still so strong inside you that you know they are still alive and that they will return.

This is gradually replaced by an agonising acceptance of irretrievable loss bringing with it almost overwhelming grief. Never again to see, to hear or to touch your loved one. Oh, the unbearable pain of it all! You cry a lot, your face crumples uncontrollably, your whole torso shakes with hollowness, your throat aches with constriction and grief holds you in its iron grip.

Gradually the incidence of these attacks lessen; your horizon begins to open up a little and you begin to enter phase three. This is shot through with conflicting emotions. It is similar to the early stages of convalescence after a major accident or operation (such as the loss of a limb or of a sense resulting in blindness or deafness). You may feel resentment, 'Why should this happen to me?' You may try to reject the whole thing and suppress your feelings; you may be filled with self pity. There is one thing certain, however, about phase three, you have to fight! You have to confront your anger, resentment, rejection, self-pity – to realise that you won't get through to phase four unless you take these negative reactions and, with determination, turn them into something positive. This could include doing some things in a different way, doing new things, taking up a new hobby – you may have to fight a sense of disloyalty. Towards the end of this phase you feel you want to hurry things along, like a child picking away at its scab, only to be dismayed at the still unhealed flesh below. In many life processes there seems to be a natural flow that cannot be hastened, but neither should it be thwarted. You have to steer between nurturing grief beyond its proper bounds, and yet encouraging the first new shoots of post-bereavement independence, not feeling disloyalty to your loved one when you do something different or new.

Phase four shows a calm and serene acceptance of your bereavement and a need to build for the future, but even here there will be occasions when a trigger flashes fiercely your grief into life again – 'They're playing our tune,' a verse of poetry, a flower, a turn of phrase will bring your memories flooding back – even when your love is but a dream on the horizon of the past.

I see the process of bereavement, grief and recovery in pictorial terms. The black centre is the death of your loved one, phase one is shown in purple, two in red, three in orange and four in green. The grey smudge round the edge is your own death which, with the spiral revolution of time, will coalesce into a dense black dot at the centre of someone else's grief. The lesson we would do well to learn is that no previous phase is ever completely finished. You will get flashes of phase 1 even after years of being in phase four, but it is the balance that changes one phase to the next.

Time does heal if we let it. The scar will always be there, but we must not become like medieval beggars who hawked their festering cicatrices. We must do all we can in phases three and four to help the natural healing processes in ourselves and others.

From 'Interim', a private newsletter
circulated by Margaret Chisman.

How long does it take to 'overcome' grief? Margaret Chisman quotes one widower in her newsletter:

How long till grief is 'overcome'?

You say that I am further along the path to recovery as my wife died over three years ago. I was told that it would be six months before I would get over the grief. It was much longer than that, about eighteen months before I stopped bursting spontaneously into tears, when driving, preparing lectures, etc. Now after three and a half years the emotions are still there, but more controlled. No doubt other people respond differently.

From 'Interim' by Margaret Chisman.

There is an element of grief we should perhaps not even try to overcome but instead build into our lives. If there is a meaning to life, it is amply demonstrated in the emotions we feel for that which we have lost. Yes, there was a meaning after all, if only I could have seen it at the time! What is missing in our lives is not meaning but the ability to perceive it while it is there.

The academic structuring of grief does, after all, have a purpose. It may help us to deal with the overpowering aspects of the emotions we experience in that strange country. Other people have been there before us. We have not been singled out. There are maps. There is a geography of grief and loss:

A tentative 'map' of grieving

Grieving takes place after any sort of loss, but most powerfully after the death of someone we love. It is not just one feeling, but a whole succession of feelings, which take a while to get through and which cannot be hurried.

Although we are all individuals, the order in which we experience these feelings is very similar for most of us. Grief is most commonly experienced after the death of someone we have known for some time. However, it is clear that people who have had stillbirths or miscarriages, or who have lost very young babies suffer a similar experience of grieving and need the same sort of care and consideration.

In the few hours following the death of a close relative or friend, most people feel simply stunned, as though they cannot believe it has actually happened. They may feel like this even if the death had been expected. This sense of emotional numbness can be a help in getting through all the important practical arrangements that have to be made, such as getting in touch with relatives and organising the funeral. However, this feeling of unreality may become a problem if it goes on too long. Seeing the body of the dead person may, for some, be an important way of beginning to overcome this. Similarly, for many people, the funeral or memorial service is an occasion when the reality of what has happened really starts to sink in. It may be distressing to see the body or attend the funeral, but these are ways of saying goodbye to those we love. At the time, these things may seem too painful to go through and so are not done. However, this often leads to a sense of deep regret in future years.

Soon though, this numbness disappears and may be replaced by a dreadful sense of agitation, of pining or yearning for the dead person. There is a feeling of wanting somehow to find them, even though this is clearly impossible. This makes it difficult to relax or concentrate and it may be difficult to sleep properly. Dreams may be extremely disturbing. Some people feel that they 'see' their loved one everywhere they go – in the street, the park, around the house, anywhere they had spent time together. People often feel very angry at this time – towards doctors and nurses who did not prevent the death, towards friends and relatives who did not do enough, or even towards the person who has left them.

Another common feeling is guilt. People find themselves going over in their minds all the things they would like to have said or done. They may even consider what they could have done differently that might have prevented the death. Of course, death is usually beyond anyone's control and a bereaved person may need to be reminded of this. Guilt may also arise if a sense of relief is felt when someone has died after a particularly painful or distressing illness. This feeling of relief is natural, extremely understandable and very common.

This state of agitation is usually strongest about two weeks after the death, but is soon followed by times of quiet sadness or depression, withdrawal and silence. These sudden changes of emotion can be confusing to friends or relatives but are just part of the normal way of passing through the different stages of grief.

Although the agitation lessens, the periods of depression become more frequent and reach their peak between four and six weeks later. Spasms of grief can occur at any time, sparked off by people, places or things that bring back memories of the dead person. Other people may find it difficult to understand or embarrassing when the bereaved person suddenly bursts into tears for no obvious reason. At this stage it may be tempting to keep away from other people who do not fully understand or share the grief. However, avoiding others can store up trouble for the future and it is usually best to try to start to return to one's normal activities after a couple of weeks or so. During this time, it may appear to others as though the bereaved person is spending a lot of time just sitting, doing nothing. In fact, they are usually thinking about the person they have lost, going over again and again both the good times and the bad times they had together. This is a quiet but essential part of coming to terms with death.

As time passes, the fierce pain of early bereavement begins to fade. The depression lessens and it is possible to think about other things and even to look again to the future. However, the sense of having lost a part of oneself never goes away entirely. For bereaved partners there are constant reminders of their new singleness, in seeing other couples together and from the deluge of media images of happy families. After some time it is possible to feel whole again, even though a part is missing. Even so, years later you may sometimes find yourself talking as though he or she were still here with you.

These various stages of mourning often overlap and show themselves in different ways in different people. Most recover from a major bereavement within one or two years. The final phase of grieving is a letting-go of the person who has died and the start of a new sort of life. The depression clears completely, sleep improves and energy returns to normal. Sexual feelings may have vanished for some time, but now return – this is quite normal and nothing to be ashamed of.

Having said all this, there is no 'standard' way of grieving. We are all individuals and have our own particular ways of grieving.

> *From the Royal College of Psychiatrists' free leaflet on*
> *'Bereavement' (available for SAE from 17 Belgrave Square,*
> *London SW1X 8PG; or see www.rcpsych.ac.uk).*

This basic structure is fleshed out in many books. Some of it has, however, been questioned by five different studies of widows and widowers, studies which have found that between a quarter and two thirds of the bereaved are not greatly distressed, and that severe depression need not necessarily follow a loss. Dr

Camille Wortman, a psychologist at the University of Michigan who has reviewed the relevant research in an article in the (American) Journal of Clinical and Consulting Psychology, comments that the absence of extreme distress 'can be a sign of resilience. Many have world views – often a spiritual outlook – that lets them see the loss in a way they can accept.' Those who are most upset after a loss tend also to be among the most upset a year or two later – findings which question the widespread assumption that a period of severe distress leads to a more balanced adjustment. Dr Barnardo of the Catholic University of America reported in the Journal of Personality and Social Psychology that, of the 42 people in his study, those who tended to 'let their grief feelings out' had more physical symptoms and negative emotions 14 months after a death than those who repressed their feelings.

There is no such thing as 'The Good Grieving Guide'. There is no reason on earth why the bereaved person (ie each and every one of us at some time or another) should become the passive consumer of someone else's advice. We all have our own experience. As Toby Young wrote, after the death of his mother: 'The fact that I was expected to be grief-stricken in public made me even less inclined to be so. I wasn't going to start grieving just because it was the socially acceptable thing to do.'

Tony Walter has argued (in Mortality, March 1996) that people need permission to retain the dead person, not to let them go. Some bereaved people begin to recall more and more memories of their lost spouse, a process described (in Jane Littlewood's delightful phrase) as 'falling in love backwards'. The essence of grieving, Walter believes, is for the community of people that knew the deceased, to discuss and elaborate an accurate and durable 'biography', a shared condensation of the person, to integrate the memory of the person into their lives, mainly through conversation, so as to move on with, as well as without, the deceased. Is it because we do not share memories like this, he asks, that the demand for bereavement counselling has arisen? In Bereavement Care (Spring 1991), he wrote:

> The Jews understand this. Like the Shona, they bury the body within a day or so and then the close family 'sit shiva'. They sit in the living room at home for a week, while friends, relatives and neighbours come to visit, bringing food, talking about the departed. Talking endlessly. Laughing, crying, sharing memories. And then, after that week, the family slowly get back to ordinary life.

Grief is a very active emotion – among other things it contains anger and even aggression, it can be sharply critical, and even has its own sense of humour! Many of the books about bereavement in the Resources chapter are a mixture of impersonal wisdom and highly personal attitudes. Some come from the heart and offer comfort, however idiosyncratic. Others profess vigorous solutions and guidance. Some are biased towards research, others might touch a personal chord in one's own experience. They are all useful. Browse among them, and choose what is to your own taste. Reject what you don't like.

Suicide

Particularly difficult can be facing grief after a murder or a suicide, and this may require specialist help.

Feeling responsible for a suicide

The toughest question to ask Jill Winters is: 'How many children do you have?' Her son James killed himself when he was 34. If she says she has two children, she feels she is denying his existence. If she says she had three but one died, more searching, and unwelcome, questions may follow.

Eight years after her son jumped from a third-floor window, Mrs Winters has finally stopped blaming herself for his death. The sense of liberation has been, she says, remarkable. But it has taken her a long time to accept what happened and to feel at peace with herself again.

The families of those who have taken their own lives have to cope with feelings of distress which go far beyond normal grief. Unlike other deaths, suicide carries with it a heavy social stigma. Those left behind may see it as a violent statement that the love they provided was not enough. Families can become ensnared in a hopeless search to find out why a child, or a parent, felt so desperate; there are profound feelings of guilt to cope with.

'When it happened it was completely unexpected, although looking back I could see it was on the cards,' Mrs Winters recalls. 'We were devastated by it. We were numb to start with. We found it very difficult to talk about; there was a feeling of isolation.'

Her husband came to terms with their son's death better than she did. 'I felt that I hadn't done the right things, that I had been a terrible mother,' she says. 'I wished I had done everything differently. I kept looking for ways that I could have prevented it. I took full responsibility.'

Mrs Winters went to a group for bereaved parents but felt out of place. 'These were people who had lost their children in the normal way. I didn't feel I was one of them,' she says. 'Suicide didn't seem acceptable.'

James was unmarried and had been a solicitor. A psychiatrist had been treating him for schizophrenia. Mrs Winters now realises she was not responsible for his actions. 'I think he was finding life so difficult and stressful that he could not stand it any longer. He was afraid of having another breakdown.'

Support agencies are waking up to the fact that families bereaved in this way often need specialist help. CRUSE, the national bereavement care group, has set up a number of support groups specifically for families of suicide cases and plans to establish more. Forbes Craig, a former nurse and now a counsellor with CRUSE, says that while all families feel loss on the death of someone close, with a suicide there is 'the intensity of the feelings, the inherent violence, the statement being made that whoever is left can't help any more. If it's a natural death we can take it because we all die. But when it's suicide there's a whole history of culture against it.' Suicide was only decriminalised in 1961, she points out. She says that there is no time limit to when someone who has experienced a suicide might need help. One woman sought help nineteen years after her mother killed herself.

Rose Hampton, the director of CRUSE, had a close friend who took her own life many years ago. 'The experience lives with you for years and years,' she says. 'I can still see her now as clear as day. In the end you have to realise that you can't be responsible for other people.'

From an article by Bernadette Friend
in The Independent (Aug. 11th 1992).

The bereaved parent

To lose part of yourself ... Perhaps the loss of a child brings this aspect of grieving into real focus more than any other experience. Here is an account, quoted in full, of the experience of a stillbirth and the fierce reactions it provoked towards our modern attitude to death.

The experience of a stillbirth

Four years ago this summer, I was happy, healthy, seven and a half months pregnant and full of expectations. Within the space of 12 hours, struggling to shake off the effects of a general anaesthetic and an emergency Caesarean section, I was left holding my seemingly perfect stillborn daughter, Laura.

The four days that followed were spent being studiously avoided in a corner of the antenatal ward, desperately trying to shut out the sight of pregnant women and the sound of newborn babies crying. Still quite poorly and in a state of shock, I leapt at the opportunity for the hospital to make all Laura's funeral arrangements for me – anything to have the whole nightmare taken away.

The result was a totally meaningless cremation service taken by a stranger exactly one week to the minute after her birth; there was no gravestone, no special place of hers that I could visit and care for. Most importantly, there was the guilt and regret: I felt I had failed my daughter in the one and only thing I was ever going to be able to do for her.

Four years on, I know that my experience and feelings are not uncommon. I run a local branch of Sands, the Stillbirth and Neo-Natal Death Society. The aim is to support people whose babies die at or around birth by offering a listening ear and a shared experience. I want to make some good come out of the tragedy of Laura's death by trying to ensure that others don't end up with the same regrets as I did.

For example, I had absolutely no idea that I could have asked to hold Laura again a few hours or even a day or more later – at a time when I could have taken her in better and stored my memories of her. As it was, the only time I spent with her I was so dopey that I could barely lift my hand to stroke her face. I had no idea that I could have asked for a lock of her plentiful hair. Things are much better now, professionals much more thoughtful and aware that information may need to be given several times before it sinks in, but there is still room for improvement.

A national Sands survey showed that while some hospitals handle the situation well, others do not. Many foetuses, or 'foetal material', are incinerated with other hospital waste. Parents are not consulted and are totally unaware that they have any choices to make, totally unaware of the fate of their baby's body. Obviously it would be wrong, and in some cases quite inappropriate, to suggest that all babies lost through miscarriage should be held by their mothers. However, babies can be perfectly formed little beings long before they reach 28 weeks; I would suggest that they are most definitely not 'hospital waste fit for incineration only' and it is not the right of hospital staff to decide whether or not a mother should hold her child or decide upon the fate of its body; she should at least be told that she has a choice.

Just as holding your dead child plays an important part in the grieving process, so does saying a formal goodbye in the shape of a funeral or some other social ritual, be it religious or not. It is a way of sharing, of acknowledging the existence of, the child you have lost. This is especially true in the case of babies because society is keen to pretend they never existed ('Oh well dear, you can just have another one' ... 'At least you've got your other children' ... 'As soon as the next one's born healthy everything will be all right'). The more people around me negated Laura's existence, the more they implied that other things would make up for her loss, the more I fought to keep her memory alive.

For women who have had miscarriages or terminations for abnormality, society offers even less opportunity to say goodbye – after all, the baby didn't really ever exist, did it? But a loss is a loss and needs to be grieved for, needs to be acknowledged. Women who lost babies several years ago or more have to live with the fact that they were simply wrapped up and incinerated; there was no choice.

Our society is still singularly bad at dealing with death or allowing for the fact that the grieving process is a necessary part of carrying on with life. In China, they have an annual day set aside for national mourning: people tend graves or simply focus their thoughts on loved ones who have died. God forbid that the stiff British upper lip be subjected to such a public display of emotion!

Feelings of grief (often quite frightening in their ferocity and variety) must be hidden away behind closed doors; until, that is, they burst out, unleashing all sorts of problems and you end up, as I did, crawling desperately to a psychotherapist.

Whenever and however the death of a child occurs, it means shock and disbelief. It may mean regrets about decisions taken at the time; it may mean missed opportunities; it may mean guilt; it may mean anger. One thing is certain; it always means being scarred for the rest of your life.

From 'In Living Memory' by Caroline Jay in The Guardian.

'The Bereaved Parent' by Harriet Sarnoff Schiff and 'Beyond Endurance, When a Child Dies' by Ronald J. Knapp are sensitive explorations of the complex of emotions and realistic living circumstances surrounding the bereaved parent, offering both insight and comfort in great measure. Another book which deals explicitly with this area of loss is 'On Children and Death' by Elisabeth Kübler-Ross. The intensity of grief for the loss of a child is likely to be prolonged and may take half a year to reach its zenith and longer still if it was a violent death. There is an entire subculture of shared feelings created by men and women who have suffered the loss of a child from a wide range of causes. Nowhere is this more fully expressed than in the extraordinary and moving series of pamphlets and newsletters issued by The Compassionate Friends (address under Organisations in the Resources chapter – they even do a special newsletter called Sibbs for bereaved brothers and sisters). Here is an explanation of their policy of 'Befriending, rather than counselling':

Befriending

What do we mean by befriending? The Pocket Oxford Dictionary defines it as 'act as a friend; help in need'. Within The Compassionate Friends it takes on a greater meaning. Befriending is also sharing. We are all befrienders. We all share when we write a letter, make a phone call or talk with another bereaved parent at a meeting. We share when we read the Newsletter. Prayer, meditation and positive loving thoughts are a form of sharing.

The necessity to 'share' and talk about our loved ones and emotions is a need within all bereaved parents that requires to be met. As the pain of grief recedes, so the need to talk endlessly diminishes. We are then in a position to 'share discriminately'. To let the newly-bereaved talk – to be willing to share with a few sentences – to encourage expressions of feelings: 'Yes, I felt that and I also felt...' This is why those who have first contact with the newly-bereaved have been bereaved themselves for at least two years.

Grief is a natural reaction to the death of a loved one/ones. Talking about our dead child/children and the emotion let loose within us is the way forward along the path of grief. Being able to befriend from the time of a death, giving the newly-bereaved permission to grieve, should mean that counselling will be needed by a small minority only: those who become stuck in their grief; people who have other problems within their family; or difficulties within themselves due to past experiences. For these, bereavement counselling is very beneficial and could be viewed as complementary to befriending.

From 'Thoughts on Befriending' by Margaret Hayworth, in The Compassionate Friends Newsletter (Spring 1989).

A child's understanding of death

Young children are curious about death. They have to negotiate the reality of death and fit it into their scheme of things. In a child's world, the loss of a pet can assume enormous emotional significance. When Grandma or Grandad dies, or a parent or a sibling, the loss has to be explained in ways the child can come to terms with. Otherwise there may be a hidden morbid element that will affect development and grownup life. In the following extract, a hospice counsellor helps a father and son to speak about their joint loss. The little boy displays a mixture of childish expression (drawing a picture, as he would at school) and very realistic concerns. These show his awareness of how his dependency has shifted with the loss of his mother.

Coming to terms with a mother's death

A seven year old had been bereaved of his mother a week before. Father sought help for his son. There seemed to be a great deal of apprehension, not just for the boy. However, he happily accepted a large glass of squash – it was a hot day. Father sat slightly apart. In order to understand the outcome of this brief intervention, something of the father's manner and bearing needs to be known. He was a large man who worked with animals. A man who was used to being obeyed by animals and humans alike; this was the tension, I felt. He gave his son instructions to answer my questions honestly. After introductions about who I was and what I did, and the purpose of his visit to the Hospice, I asked about his mother's funeral, including Father in the conversation. Father refused to be drawn, prompting his son instead. The small boy looked at his father as he spoke with a mixture of fear and defiance in his eyes. He spoke of the funeral but quickly went on to say he had visited the grave earlier on his way here. He and his father had discussed the sort of stone they would put on the grave during the drive to the Hospice. I wondered if he would like to draw it for me; he wasn't particularly good at drawing, he said, but he agreed he would have a try when I said I wasn't either.

As he drew, he spoke of his dog which had recently died and the circumstances of its death; 'being put down'. He asked, 'Where was he?' looking all the while at his father. It seemed very hard for the father to be honest about where the body of the pet dog was, though his son did know where his mother's was. This was the theme of the picture. Two tombstones, one a slab and one a cross, drawn very small in the corner of the paper, with a bird in flight above. He spoke very naturally about what was going on the stone and referred to his father for help with the precise detail. I wondered about the cross in the picture.

'Well, that had been part of the talk in the car, about the shape.' The slab seemed to be preferred by the father so that the wording could be better managed.

I wondered what the cross meant.

'That Mummy had gone to be with Jesus.'

'What does that mean for you?' I responded.

'That Mummy no longer suffered great pain and she had left her poor body and was now in Heaven,' he replied.

'Do you know where that is?'

'No – not really.'

I wondered, 'Could you tell me about the bird you have drawn so cleverly?'

He said 'I thought it would make a nice picture. It reminds me of the churchyard in the country with trees around.'

I allowed a pause and then, 'So you are not sure where Heaven is – nor is anybody if they are really honest – none of us is sure – even grownups – but the bird is important to you. Could the bird be Mummy's spirit flying free, out of pain, able to go where she liked to the place we are not quite sure where which is called Heaven?' He liked this idea very much and repeated it.

His father softened and tears ran down his cheeks. His son watched.

I asked, 'Do you and your Dad cry together?'

'Yes,' he said, 'we do when we go to the churchyard, to the grave.'

'That's good,' I said, giving lots more permission in my voice.

There was something in the way he watched his father that prompted me to ask him if there was anything he found very hard to say to his Dad which he might like to say if he found courage here. It seemed as though he had been longing for this opportunity. There was so much, he was worried about his dad working with bulls – he might get hurt; he was worried when his dad drove too fast – he might crash. He didn't want the goats or the calves to be slaughtered, they were his friends and he missed them. He wanted his bedroom to be the same room when he came home, not to be changed around. It was easy to see how insecure, worried and angry this small boy was towards his father, and how he was asking him to take care of himself in order to care for him. A brief interruption allowed him to say more about a visit to the grandparents which was planned and how dad would be in his absence. All his concerns came tumbling out and his anger was acknowledged.

From 'Brief Interventions in Anticipatory Grief and Bereavement'
by Lizette Pugh, in Counselling (Feb. 1992).

Private grief

'We mustn't intrude on private grief,' is a common, jokey saying we use when we want to be a little unkind about the misfortunes of others. Behind the saying, unfortunately, is the assumption that grief is something that should be draped and shrouded from view, and that the rituals of grief are designed to conceal rather than to express feeling. Nothing could be further from the truth.

Listen and be compassionate

My close friends and family were absolutely wonderful when Ernest died. But other people I knew well would cross the road if they saw me coming, and if they did have to speak and ask me how I was, I learned to my cost that I mustn't really tell. They wanted me to say just, 'I'm fine'.

Some people seem to delight in telling me of another bereavement. They asked how my husband died and when I said from a sudden heart attack, immediately told me about a heart attack that killed someone else. I had enough nightmares about my husband's death and I didn't need the harrowing details of anyone else's.

The most helpful thing people can do is listen, just let you talk and be compassionate. People think it will hurt you to talk, but talking keeps the person alive for you. Or they fear they will be reminding you – as if you had forgotten.

It is an absolute safety valve to be allowed to talk, which is why I joined CRUSE, the support group for widows and widowers. There people can cry because everyone understands, but you'll hear gales of laughter too.

Jean Baker, quoted in an article entitled 'Please Don't Say That' in The Sunday Times magazine.

Those who don't know what to say may feel inspired by a lovely Irish tradition, described by Danny Danziger in The Independent (Jan. 27th 1992):

At the very end of the service, before the funeral, the people come up and they hold your hand, and they say a phrase that will ring many bells in Irish ears: that is, 'I am very sorry for your trouble.'

Or, as Elsie Sieben wrote in The Compassionate Friends Newsletter (Spring 1985):

Hug me, tell me you care and that you're sorry this has happened.

Be available to me – often if you can – and let me talk and cry without judging me.

Just love me and I will always remember you as a true friend.

And Virginia Ironside in The Times (July 29th 1992) related how surprised she was to be consoled by letters after her father's death:

I will never let another death go by without dropping the relatives a line. Letters that say things like: 'He will live on for ever in your heart' – trite lines I'd usually wrinkle a lip at – seem to have huge significance, laden with meaning. 'I am down the road if you want an ear,' came from an old schoolfriend I barely know. And a lovely line from my son's godfather: 'These sad deaths are like signposts which direct you into a new and unknown route. I can only wish you well.'

Simply helping the bereaved person with household tasks can be important. Dr Colebrook, who lost his son in a motorbike accident, wrote in the British Medical Journal (Dec 31st 1983) that he felt that he had experienced outstanding support from a local girl, an old college friend of his wife, who simply took over the housekeeping and looked after arrangements at home. Andrew Marshall has suggested that we all consider adopting the Muslim tradition, whereby after a death the mourners do not cook for themselves for 40 days – relatives and neighbours bring food.

Other gestures that have been suggested include sending flowers a month after the funeral to the family of the deceased to let them know they are still in one's thoughts; and to request donations after the death not to charity, as often happens, but to the surviving partner, who may in some cases be reliant only on a state pension. Why, asked Maggie of Cambridge in a letter to the Natural Death Centre, should it be customary for there be gifts for the wedding couple, but not for the funeral partner?

Consolations

Jenny Kander offers consolation of a sort in The Compassionate Friends paper (No. 16) on 'The Death of an Only Child':

> Grief, for a time, can seem larger than life. Your anguish is your response to that, but do not relate solely to your pain; remember your child, however painful the memories at first; recall your lives together, however short or long they were, so that restoration may take place and, in time, you will realise that he or she is still with you in the deepest sense, bonded to you and living within your heart. You are parents of your child for eternity. Nothing can alter that. Nothing can take that away.

At some stages of bereavement the sense that the dead person is present is powerful and disturbing. Of course it is psychologically quite accurate to say that someone we love is within us, an indwelling presence. This is in itself a comfort. But when the longed for appearance of the person in the flesh does not occur, then there is anguish. Where is that physical, substantive presence that we miss? To contain the spirit of the dead person within the self is at once a comfort and an agony, but the bereaved person often wants a larger context for this containment, a context that will take some of the burden away and at the same time be soothing and healing. In this sense the child may feel nearer to a dead person whilst up in an aeroplane because he or she has been told that the spirit is 'up there'. The more sophisticated adult may feel the same soothing presence, inside himself or herself, yet enclosed in something larger, in a religious building for example, within the uplifting and inspiring confines of a cathedral. Or in music which has the same grandeur and peace of containing the spirit. Or in the chanted words of prayer. The bereaved person, then, craves some form of communion within which he or she can share the agony and beauty of containing the spirit of the dead. We may call this religious, or we may call it therapeutic. The distinction only matters to the observer. If the bereaved person is religious, the practice of religion will have a therapeutic effect. If he or she seeks comfort in a conventional therapeutic setting, it is likely to have the intensity of a religious experience. Religion, after all, is largely about reconciling life and death.

Professional mourners, women who attend a funeral service and wail or keen, are traditional in many cultures, and this is one way of sharing the burden of the dead spirit. In Crete this method of joining the living to the dead has been brought to a fine art.

Keening

An essential element in the lament singing is that women identify with each other. Each woman's recollection of her own grief serves to remind and intensify the grief of others. A skilled lamenter has to move her audience to 'ponos' (pain) and thus, symbolically, to lead the living to the dead. The depth of these laments has thus a metaphysical dimension.

> *From a paper by Sonia Greger, sent to The Natural Death Centre,*
> *entitled 'Woman – Man – Peasant – Central Administration'.*

There are many who claim to join the living to the dead in a more direct sense, through psychic guidance and evocations, or through the gift of vision.

Help from the spirit world?

Suddenly I gasped, as a flash of headlights shot over the hill – the old man was going to walk right out in front of a car. But just then, something strange happened – I stood transfixed, as a ghostly gleaming-white mist appeared behind him. It quickly condensed into the radiant form of a middle-aged spirit woman. Strangely unruffled by the gale, her hair was completely unmoved, not a drop of rain had wet it, and her flowing white spirit robes were bone-dry.

All at once she stooped down, drew back her arm and delivered a swift blow to the back of the man's knees. My heart jumped into my throat as he fell backwards like a collapsing house of cards, landing on the pavement with his legs in the gutter. Just a second later, a reckless car hurled around the blind bend at over 50 miles per hour, missing his feet by half an inch – then zoomed past the bus queue, splashing us with muddy water.

Brushing the rain from my eyelashes, I watched the ghostly woman kneel down, kiss the old man's troubled brow, smile, and then vanish into the dark night – fading back into the spirit world, from whence she came.

I've had these psychic abilities from my earliest years, visions of other worlds beyond death.

> *From 'Voices from Heaven' by Stephen O'Brien.*

There is no reliable guide to life after death. Guidebooks abound, but the paths they indicate are varied to the point of confusion. A theologian asks the question, Where do the dead go when they pass over? He reviews the possibilities, beginning with nowhere:

Living in God

Perhaps there is nowhere to go. Perhaps people, burdened with fear, want and sorrow, just dance into the arms of death, as Schopenhauer said, wondering what the tragic comedy of life is supposed to mean – and finding out it ends in nothing. Those who have died are then shadows of the past. Nothing remains of them except for the loving scratches or hideous scar they etched on our world, and our memories.

Then, he considers the opposite option, that of reincarnation:

Perhaps our inner Atman is made of incorruptible stuff, as Hindus maintain. At death the spark of our soul then divests itself of one mortal body to start life again in another disposable shell. Our deceased relatives and friends could then be at any station on the spiralling track of reincarnation. They might even have reached their destination, nirvana, where they merge back into the infinite ocean of Atmas.

Or maybe the dead await judgement:

Perhaps the dead roam as shades in the netherworld, populating the Old Testament *She'ol*. The psalms describe this abyss under the earth as a house of darkness, a bottomless pit, a land of forgetfulness. All the dead can do is bide their time till their fate will be sealed at the universal judgement.

He ends by advocating a truly spiritual understanding:

We can meaningfully speak of heaven and hell, as long as we remember that they are dimensions of life, not locations in outer space. We can say the dead merge back into God if we realise She/He is an ocean of love who does not swamp our littleness. Properly understood, the time-honoured phrase coined by Kohelet puts it rather well: those who have died live in God.

> *From 'Learning to live with life after death' by John Wijngaards*
> *in The Times (Nov. 4th 1991).*

Stephen Levine talks of the comfort to be had in facing up to the worst that human life can bring.

Fierce journey towards freedom

I've been with many people whose grief has been beyond bearing. And in some ways it has been the best thing that ever happened to them. For they come to plumb the depths of their being.

When we experience grief, we are not just experiencing the loss of our son or daughter, our husband or wife, our parent or loved one. We are dropped into the very pit of despair and longing. We are touching the reservoir of loss itself. We experience the long-held fear and doubt and grief that has always been there. It is not an experience that most would choose, though the confrontation with this area of deep holding seems to be an initiation often encountered along the fierce journey toward freedom.

> *Stephen Levine, quoted in Raft, The Journal of the Buddhist*
> *Hospice Trust.*

Sogyal Rinpoche in his helpful book 'The Tibetan Book of Living and Dying' advises helping your dead friend and the healing of your own grief by invoking, perhaps with a mantra, any enlightened being who inspires you, and imagining tremendous rays of light streaming out towards you from that being, filling up your heart. And then: 'Imagine you are sending this blessing, the light of healing compassion of the enlightened beings, to your loved one who has died.'

If the hardest death to bear is an untimely one, and the hardest untimely death is a child's death, and the hardest child's death is one that is accompanied by feelings of great guilt amongst the survivors, then we can surely trust the parents who report their thoughts and feelings in The Compassionate Friends publications. Yes, Margaret Hayworth warns, if death causes *persistent* self-accusatory thoughts, then probably professional therapeutic help should be sought (Newsletter, Summer 1992). But a way that helps is to give yourself permission to forgive yourself, by writing a letter to your child listing regrets and stating your need for forgiveness. For the rest, she shares Kübler-Ross' and Levine's spiritual perspective on suffering as an opportunity for the soul to develop. The American spiritual teacher Ram Dass developed these arguments in a public talk where he was responding to a father whose son had drowned. The father was in despair: 'They say that God is perfect but all I can think is that God made a mistake. I cannot believe there would be any good reason for Him to allow this to happen.' Ram Dass replied, in part:

I feel such pain for the loss you and your wife have suffered. The grief that parents experience over the loss of a child is perhaps the deepest grief of all because it seems to upset the natural order of things.

What I can share with you from a spiritual vantage point cannot really allay your grief. Perhaps however it may allow you and your son to know each other in a new way, and that other way of knowing may give balance to the grief.

Because your son was attractive and was your son, and so warm and vibrant, you got to know him through his uniqueness and his separateness. There is another way of knowing a person, which we know through our intuitive heart. This way of knowing one another is subtle, so it is often hidden behind the more obvious ways of knowing people through senses and thought. But if we know what to look for and cultivate that intuitive way of knowing, we find out for ourselves that we are each indeed more than just bodies and personalities.

The soul has an agenda in taking birth itself as a human being. It has certain work to do and complete while on the earth plane and it uses the body and personality to carry out that work. And when the work is finished it leaves this plane. The wisest beings with whom I have made contact in this lifetime all assure me that a soul leaves the physical plane neither a moment too early nor a moment too late. Human birth is a bit like entering in the fourth grade, and we stay just as long as it is necessary to achieve what we need from that specific grade or form, and then we are naturally ready to go on for further evolution by leaving this plane.

I can sense from the description and pictures of your son, the purity of his heart and the beauty of his soul. And I suspect that though you considered his work on earth just at the beginning, for his soul the work was completed. Even the manner of his leaving was part of his work. For your personality, the pain is shattering and seemingly unbearable. You wake crying and find life now meaningless. Such suffering is what the personality would avoid at all costs if it were able. For your soul, however, it is an entirely different matter. For your soul, suffering is that which forces you to grow spiritually, and brings you closer to awakening to whom you in truth are. I realise even as I say all these things to you, that it is really too much for me to ask of you that you understand the way in which the manner of your son's death was his soul's gift to your soul. I suspect all that seems topsy-turvy to you. But you did ask me how I understand such tragic events, and this is my truth that I am honoured to share with you.

Probably your suffering and attachment to him and sense of loss is felt by his soul. Although he now understands what has happened, why it had to happen the way it did and why you are suffering as you are, I am sure he is surrounding you with healing energy; and as you are able to quiet your mind, I suspect that you will feel it. It of course acts to your benefit even if you don't feel it . To the extent that you are able, sit quietly and just hang out with your son, talking to him as you normally would about the many experiences you shared together. In doing so, look to see the thread of spirit that pervaded each experience. Imagine that you and he are souls who met on earth this time as father and son. How many times in your years together did the love between you nearly rend the veil of mystery that would have allowed you to recognise the truth of soul that lay at the root of your relationship? It takes only a moment for two people to recognise their bond as souls. Souls know no time. And now, even though your son is no longer embodied, you and he can recognise each other.

Chapter 11

THE POLITICS
OF DYING

The Natural Death Centre has drawn up the following provisional Declaration of Rights of the Person Dying at Home. The attainment of many of these rights lies in the utopian future, and would require a fairly drastic redirection of NHS resources and a reanimation of Neighbourhood Care type schemes in both urban and rural areas. The statements that follow are thus perhaps more in the realm of desirable goals than enforceable rights and are limited by how much a family can cope with, since so much of the caring depends on the family at present. Your suggested improvements to this Declaration would be welcomed. It could be made into a more personal declaration by crossing out bits that do not apply to you or by adding others.

A Declaration of the Rights of the Person Dying at Home

• I have the right to sufficient support from the National Health Service and the community to enable me to die at home, if I so wish, whether or not I have relatives to care for me.

• I have the right not to die alone; although with the right to be left alone, if desired.

• I have the right to expect the local priest or other community leader to ask the neighbourhood to support me and those caring for me.

• I have the right to have 'midwives for the dying' or their equivalent to attend to my physical, emotional and spiritual needs.

• I have the right to the same expertise of pain relief as I would obtain if occupying a hospital or hospice bed.

• I have the right not to be taken without my consent to hospital as my condition deteriorates, or, if a hospital operation is required to relieve pain, I have the right to be brought home again afterwards.

• I have the right to have any Living Will I have signed respected and, if not fully conscious myself, to have the wishes of my appointed proxy respected.

• I have the right to reject heart stimulants, blood transfusions or other medical interventions to prolong my life.

• I have the right, to the extent that I so wish, to be told the truth about my condition and about the purposes of, alternatives to, and consequences of, any proposed treatments.

• I have the right to fast as death approaches, if I so desire, without being subjected to forced feeding in any form.

• I have the right to discuss my death and dying, my funeral or any other related matters openly with those caring for me.

• I have the right to as conscious and dignified a death as possible in the circumstances.

• I have the right, if I so express the wish and if the circumstances allow, for my body to remain undisturbed at home after death for a period, and for my funeral to be handled by my relatives and friends, if they so desire, without intervention by funeral directors.

All comments please to The Natural Death Centre, 20 Heber Road, London NW2 6AA (tel 020 8208 2853; fax 020 8452 6434).

Policy changes needed

This book and indeed the above Declaration have implied the need for a number of changes in policies and practices relating to dying and death. These are summarised here:

Education

• Children need less exposure to violent death on television and in the media and yet they need to be more involved in the natural dying of their relatives and friends; to have the opportunities to visit the body if they wish and to participate in the funeral. Teachers in schools can help where appropriate by introducing relevant literature to do with bereavement or, for instance, by helping the children to make Memory Books or Memory Boxes that compile their thoughts and memories and photos of the dead or dying person.

• A number of people learn first aid, which they may or may not ever need to use. But everybody would benefit from learning the basics about preparing for dying and about looking after the dying person, if only to be better prepared for their own death. A one day (or weekend) first-aid-style course in practical care for those who are dying should be popularised, and open to the general public, not just to the nursing profession.

• Death needs to become less socially invisible. Towards this end, the Natural Death Centre promotes an annual English Day of the Dead, along the lines of the Mexican Day of the Dead, both as an opportunity for rituals in remembrance of friends and relatives who have died, with a flavour of festival to it, and also as a chance for debate, discussions and exhibitions related to death and dying. The English Day of the Dead is on the third Sunday in April each year.

The National Health Service and the community

• The natural death movement must be as insistent as the natural birth movement in pressing for changes in the NHS. First, there needs to be a feasibility study leading to a pilot project that would look at the relative costs for a particular region if the policy were to become one of enabling those who are terminally ill to die at home rather than in hospital or elsewhere; and the study would encourage and collect suggestions from carers about how services for those who are dying could be improved. Second, the Marie Curie, Macmillan and other nursing and hospice home-care services need to be adapted, or new organisations founded, for extending services to people dying of other causes besides cancer, motor neurone disease and AIDS. Third, there needs in the long term to be a new holistic profession of 'Midwives for the Dying', trained to look after the physical, emotional and spiritual needs of the dying and their carers; backed up by a nationwide network of volunteer befrienders for those who are dying, who will sit with them, carry out errands for the carers, provide transport, etc. Fourth, we need more take-up of the Canadian experimental brokerage scheme, whereby those with handicaps or those who are terminally ill, together with their carers, identify their own financial and other needs, interviewing and selecting would-be helpers, with generous funding coming from the state. Carers taking time off work should receive an allowance equivalent to their net salary. Fifth, respite breaks for carers should be frequently and flexibly available, preferably through a vast extension of the Crossroads-type arrangements, whereby a replacement carer comes into the home and takes over all the tasks involved. Sixth, night nurses need to be routinely available for all those receiving home palliative care.

• There are many Neighbourhood Watch anti-crime schemes that have provided the foundations for neighbours to get to know each other. There need to be grants for pilot projects to extend these into Neighbourhood Care schemes where neighbours would gradually begin to care for each other in crisis, including helping those who are dying, their carers, and the bereaved. It would be natural in many areas for the local doctor, priest or other respected figurehead to provide the impetus to get such schemes going. For example, Harriet Copperman writes in 'Dying at Home' of an instance where the vicar 'organised a rota of people to sit with a patient who lived alone, in order that he could die at home'. Indeed, a great deal of neighbourhood care already takes place, often under the aegis of church groups, but formalised Neighbourhood Care schemes, receiving funding from Social Services and others, could encourage such activity in neighbourhoods where it is currently lacking.

Spirituality

• There needs to be an English Book of the Dead (there are already several American ones) that would translate Tibetan insights into the experience and psychology of dying and the reports from those who have had Near-Death Experiences into anglicised and even Christian rituals that could become part of a prearranged Dying Service for those wanting it – for instance an elaboration of the 'go towards the light' message whispered into the ear of the dying person, along with breathing and other meditations; and perhaps accompanied by music such as that offered by the Chalice of Repose at a hospice in the United States. People could be encouraged to design their own Dying Plans specifying the kind of material of this nature that they might like.

• People seem to appreciate dying close to nature, as near outdoors as the elements will allow. Either the patient needs to be able to get a taste of the outdoors or nature needs to be brought into the house or even the hospital – not only flowers, but branches, trees and animals.

Hospital

• A hospital palliative care ward should have as much a 'home from home' atmosphere and design as possible – imagine, for instance, a country house hospital with open fires and meals around long tables, with patients' interests accommodated, whether for pets, music or complementary treatments.

• Dr Marie Louise Grennert's excellent palliative care work at the Malmo Geriatric and Rehabilitation Clinic in Sweden deserves copying. To encourage patients to talk freely, she has an informal discussion with each one at the outset and asks: 'What are your most pressing problems right now? What do you want from the care provided here? What is your outlook on the future? Where do you get your strength or inner resources from? How do you feel about entering this palliative care ward?' Next-of-kin also talk with the doctor about anything that is on their mind, not just medical matters – and are invited back to the hospital two weeks after the death for a further talk. Two hours or so after the death, all the ward staff gather briefly to discuss the patient who has died, any problems that arose and any lessons that can be learnt.

• In the hospital setting, the partner needs acceptance as part of the caring team (that is, if both partner and patient would like this). Ideally, just as a parent can sometimes stay with a child in hospital, the partner should be able to share a bed with the dying person, as is possible at home, or to have another bed alongside.

• The medical carers need to maintain reassuring physical contact with the dying. One American hospital renowned for its excellent palliative care was filmed looking after a dying woman who was rigged up to the most high tech equipment. She died with the medical team in full attendance and with an accurate record kept of the exact time of her death. But nobody held her hand or had anything to do with her as a person or even said a word of blessing over her dead body.

• The nursing staff could show carers and visitors simple techniques such as scalp massage and Boerstler's breath relaxation method which can be helpful to the dying person and which give family and friends a feeling of involvement.

• Patients need to be allowed to acknowledge the deaths of fellow patients and to say goodbye in some way – rather than the drawing of ward curtains around each bed, so that no patient is disturbed by seeing the dead body moved away. Dr Elizabeth Lee, in her book 'A Good Death', describes, in contrast, a death in a small Kenyan hospital. The patient's mother stood and, raising one arm above her head, began to sing a hymn. All the other young women on the ward stood by their beds, faces turned to the dead woman, and singing with her mother. They faced her death and bade her goodbye.

• Where it suits their particular style, doctors and nurses in hospital could evolve a brief religious or humanist ritual (depending on their own belief systems and that of the patient) to say together over the body of someone who has just died.

• How to support the dying person and a knowledge of NDEs and of the various kinds of basic information in this Handbook should become an integral and important part of the training of doctors and nurses. (Nurses should not be able to use their 'supernumerary status' to 'opt out' of this subject in their training.) Medical staff need encouragement to recognise the difference between healing and curing, and to acknowledge that a peaceful death is an achievement rather than a failure on their part. All Accident and Emergency department staff should be trained in dealing with those who are bereaved, and each such unit should have a counsellor on call (as suggested in the Nursing Times, Jan. 8th 1992). Counselling help, discussions groups, talks by experts and other support must be available to all personnel caring for the dying (as suggested by Pam Williams, see the booklist).

• Doctors should use tests that are completely reliable indicators of death, for the reassurance of those who are worried that they might be buried or cremated whilst still alive.

• Some hospitals incinerate miscarried foetuses with the hospital waste. A better approach is that of the Aberdeen Maternity Hospital where, since 1985, a service is held at the local crematorium every three months attended by the hospital and those families and friends who wish to come. The main point that parents should have some choice about what happens to the body – and about viewing the body.

• Permission needs to be granted for the resumption of research into the use of the psychoactive and empathogen drugs with the terminally ill – drugs that in the right setting apparently not only relieve pain, depression, tension and anxiety, but help the patient gain a perspective on their situation. Mescaline, LSD, ketamine and MDMA have all produced promising results in these areas. Readers are referred particularly to the Bethesda Hospital work with terminally ill cancer patients written up by Dr Stanislav Grof in 'The Human Encounter with Death', where 71% of the patients rated an improvement in their emotional condition after participation in the experiment.

• Whilst mindful of the exceptions – Mother Teresa, for instance, with her great zest for life, who had a heart pacemaker fitted at the age of 82 – and whilst accepting that the patient's own wishes come first, we believe it would be helpful in some cases if doctors were to take any evidently frail and elderly patients (and their carers) through a detailed series of questions aimed at ascertaining the person's perceived quality of life, before pressurising the patient to accept a major operation and the subsequent stresses and strains of 'maximum recovery' treatment.

• A doctor seeing a very elderly person peacefully dying in a residential home may need to resist the temptation to rush the patient by ambulance to hospital, just so as to guard against claims of negligence.

• When dealing with those who are very elderly and dying, cardiopulmonary resuscitation given by emergency teams should be reserved for those patients who want it, or whose relatives request it on their behalf, or who stand a good chance of surviving and being discharged (currently about 6% of those patients to whom it is given). This routine assault on those who are very elderly and dying should be something a patient has to be 'opted in' for, rather than 'opted out' from as at present. (See 'Whose Life Is It Anyway?' by nurse Pam Williams, an unpublished paper in The Natural Death Centre library.)

• The legal standing of Living Wills should be confirmed by an act of parliament, if only to give more secure legal protection to any medical carer who follows a patient's requests.

• All patients should be offered the opportunity of drawing up a Living Will before entering hospital for serious treatment. Indeed, GPs need to discuss the Living Will concept with all their patients who reach pension age, and should encourage them to lodge a copy of their Living Will at the surgery, and to carry on their persons a summary credit-card-size Living Will card, giving the doctor's phone number. The US government in 1987 concluded that Living Wills could save its health service $5 billion a year ('one out of every seven health care dollars are spent on the last six months of life'). Here then is a reform that would not only save the NHS money, but that would improve the quality of living and dying.

• The hospital should endeavour to leave the body undisturbed for a period after death, if so desired by the next-of-kin, for religious or other reasons.

• The Natural Death Centre backs the proposal made by the A. B. Welfare and Wildlife Trust that postmortems should be performed only in exceptional cases, so as to reduce the trauma for relatives and friends. In cases where the coroner knows that death was natural, bodies should be swiftly released to the families.

• The Anatomy Act 1984 needs amending, to remove the right of hospitals and similar institutions to send unclaimed bodies for anatomical use, irrespective of whether these institutions at present make use of these powers. Under S.4(9) 'in the case of a body lying in a hospital, nursing home or other institution', any person acting on behalf of the management has legal powers to decide whether to send the body for anatomical use. This only applies when no friends or relatives take lawful possession of the body. (Information from 'Green Burial' by John Bradfield, 1994, page 42.)

• Hospitals need to make available leaflets for families explaining how they can organise funerals inexpensively and without funeral directors. All staff need to know that the next-of-kin have the legal right to take possession of the body.

Euthanasia and suicide

The word 'euthanasia' comes from the Greek for 'good death' and in the Shorter Oxford English Dictionary has the definition of 'a quiet and easy death or the means of procuring this or the action of inducing this'. With such a definition it seems hard to imagine who could be against it – even to enter a hospice could count as slow euthanasia. It may reassure relatives of those who have taken their own lives to know that our culture's present stand against suicide and euthanasia has not been shared at other times and in other cultures. For Christians (as The Compassionate Friends outline in a paper on suicide) it stems from a decision of the church Council of Braga in AD 562 to refuse funeral rites to all suicides. This in turn came about because early Christians were killing themselves in worrying numbers – martyrs had all their transgressions wiped out and were glorified by the church, and Christian suicide was very prevalent and acceptable in the fifth century. The Christians had inherited the Roman attitude to suicide. They saw it as a virtuous act if undertaken with dignity, just as the Greek stoics before them viewed death and suicide with equanimity. Plato too felt that if life became 'immoderate' through disease, then suicide was a justified and reasonable act.

The arguments in favour of doctor-assisted active euthanasia include the following: that a small percentage of terminal pain cannot be controlled by drugs; that some patients are either insufficiently mobile or conscious to take their own lives unassisted; that the drugs required for a swift and painless exit are unobtainable without a prescription; and that, as a democracy, we should accept the verdict of the overwhelming majority of people – 82% of respondents to a recent UK survey agreed that 'doctors should be permitted to end a life when someone requests it'.

The arguments against euthanasia include: that pain relief as practised in hospices is a very advanced art; that it is against the Hippocratic Oath for a doctor to kill a patient; that it is not for the doctor to play God and to decide that a patient's time is up; that the soul may have lessons to learn from the body's helplessness, dependency and suffering – the 'labour pains' of dying; and, most powerfully, that it is a slippery slope – once mercy killing is legalised, where will it end?

The Inuits and the Japanese used to practise euthanasia by hypothermia – the elderly person lost consciousness in the freezing cold and died within hours. In nature, some animals who realise their time has come refuse all food, just as, traditionally, American Indians who had decided that 'now is a good time to die' thereafter refused all food. Hindus who are taken to muktibhavans (hospices) in Benaras consider it appropriate and natural not to eat. The *slowness* of this kind of dying seems to be the crux of the matter. Rather than a possibly impulsive decision regretted in the event – a regret implied, for instance, by the positive and almost mystical transformations experienced by those few who survived suicide jumps from Golden Gate Bridge – fasting to death requires commitment and perseverance.

In its early stages, fasting can sometimes have an almost meditative effect, helping people to feel centred and spiritual. If they then change their mind when viewing their condition from this new perspective, they can simply start accepting food again. Death by fasting has been described in this book as a 'gentle way to die' (in the case of Caroline Walker) and as being 'like a leaf falling from a tree' (in the case of Scott Nearing). Da Free John (in 'Easy Death') has talked of it as 'a kind of traditional yoga for conscious death; people who traditionally died in this way were philosophically disposed toward intuitive transcendence and gradual transition'.

President Mitterrand, suffering from terminal cancer, called his wife to his bedside and told her that his end was near – he would take no more medicines and no more food. Such a death can be a slow, orderly and graceful process that allows the person time to come to terms with his or her exit. (Derek Humphry, however, warns in his book 'Final Exit – The Practicalities of Self-Deliverance and Assisted Suicide for the Dying' – £7-19 postage extra from www.amazon.

co.uk; or $13 plus $7 p&p outside USA from the Hemlock Society, PO Box 101810, Denver, Colorado 80250-1810, USA, fax 001 5303 639 1224; web: www.hemlock.org/hemlock_shop.htm#books – that self-starvation can sometimes lead to severe indigestion, muscle weakness, mental incapacity and painful dehydration. Among the self-administered methods he recommends instead are 4.5 grams of secobarbital in combination with brallobarbital, mixed with alcohol and pudding, taken on an empty stomach, followed by a plastic bag secured by rubber band over the head. Hardly a slow, conscious or dignified death.) As a way of dying, fasting is tough on the relatives, watching the patient become more and more skeletal. But perhaps the fact that it is hard on the relatives is an additional safeguard against pressure on the elderly person from potential beneficiaries from the estate. Fasting is also a way that absolves doctors or nurses from ethically problematic involvement, as long as the terminally ill person makes clear his or her rejection of enforced feeding, preferably through filling in a Living Will.

Our tentative conclusions, therefore, are:

• Euthanasia actively assisted by doctor or relative should remain illegal, but judges should be given more scope for leniency in their sentencing, should such cases come to court. We support the recommendations of the Committee on the Penalty for Homicide, chaired by Lord Lane, which called for an end to compulsory life sentences for murder.

• The Natural Death Centre would like to see research into alternatives to active euthanasia, such as better relief of pain, anxiety and depression in terminal care. Our guess is that the breakthrough will come through the use of drugs that enhance the circulation of the neurotransmitter 5-HT.

Funerals and procedures

• Given that our investigations show that few of the mainstream coffin manufacturers will sell a coffin directly to a member of the public and that funeral directors do not see themselves as 'coffin shops' – if they grudgingly sell just a coffin they tend to add an extravagant mark-up – The Natural Death Centre recommends that the Office of Fair Trading issue a requirement that funeral suppliers and directors sell coffins to the general public without undue profit. The Office of Fair Trading has made a move in this direction, writing that 'consumers should be afforded the right to buy a coffin (independently of other funerary goods and services)'.

• Just as funeral directors are required by their associations to offer a basic funeral as one of their options – although only 10 out of 18 in one small study informed the member of the public of this option – so they should also be obliged to offer a basic container for those not wanting a coffin. This could be, as in the United States, either an unfinished wood box or a cardboard coffin or other rigid container (supported by a plank of wood if necessary).

• Given that 97% of people are 'hooked' the moment they contact an undertaker, and do not shop around, The Natural Death Centre recommends the adoption of regulations similar to the 1984 funeral rules of the American Federal

Trade Commission, whereby funeral directors are obliged:

(a) to give a price breakdown over the phone (several of the funeral directors in our survey refused to do so).

(b) to give a written and itemised breakdown of prices to be displayed on the premises and to be readily available for visitors to take away. In 1996, the National Association of Funeral Directors inspected 172 member firms and found that 32.5% were still failing to display a price list, despite the fact that such display is required by the Association's Code of Practice. The Office of Fair Trading should seek a Price Marking Order, legislating as to the composition and distribution of price lists, and making noncompliance a criminal offence. Of the replies to our questionnaire to over 2,000 funeral directors, the most fully itemised price list came from George Brooke of Dewsbury in West Yorkshire (the normal funeral director's price list hides many of the funeral costs behind an inflated price for the coffin). Colin Rogers in Dorset is also to be commended – he offers specific percentage reductions for nine processes that families may wish to do for themselves.

(c) to give an *itemised estimate* before the funeral, so that you can add or subtract items to get what you want.

(d) to charge a fee for embalming only if authorised by the family or required by law – eg for transport out of the country.

(e) to disclose in writing what service fee, if any, is being added by the funeral director to the cost of disbursements, and whether he or she is getting a refund, discount or rebate from the disbursement supplier.

• There should also be an enforcement of the requirement that funeral directors reveal clearly on their paperwork and premises if they are part of a larger firm. (The latter, unlike most chains in other businesses, have pushed up prices, and they will tend to bring about a bland uniformity of style.) One small firm complained in the Funeral Service Journal that 'certain multinationals openly admit they do not display ownership on the premises or paperwork, which is against trading law. Even those that do, go under a pseudonym to fool the public.' Some chains claim to be 'family funeral directors', meaning only that they serve families, a fraudulent use of words which the Disciplinary Committee of the National Association of Funeral Directors has nevertheless explicitly condoned.

• The government should take up Jonathon Porritt's suggestion (reported in the Chapter 4) that Memorial Groves (where a tree is planted by the body) should be included in its Community Forests.

• The A. B. Welfare and Wildlife Trust reports that at present very small nature reserves (intended for burials or other purposes) cannot become wildlife charities, based on precedent court cases. The Charity Commission needs to press for the acceptance of such small nature reserves as charities.

• The Benefits Agency, the Births and Deaths Registrar, the Citizens Advice Bureau and many crematoria should make printed information available to the public about what happens after a death. This information should include the fact that it is possible to organise a funeral without using undertakers and a summary of how to go about it – or at least should refer readers to The Natural Death Centre and similar organisations.

• Local authorities should copy the pioneering efforts in Nottingham and Crewe whereby the councils simply advertise which local funeral director currently provides the least expensive funeral package. Funeral prices have dropped by a quarter in Nottingham as a result. Citizens Advice Bureaux, hospitals, churches, libraries and other community groups could also provide this information.

• The Funeral Service Journal carries fairly regular reprints of news items about funeral directors who have been found guilty of crime or fraud. Whilst we are against the registration of funeral directors – it would tend to leave trade associations such as the National Association of Funeral Directors (NAFD) with a near-monopoly of power – the rules on prepaid funeral plans need tightening. For instance, a funeral director with an unspent record for any crime involving fraud should not be able to take cash from the public for prepaid funeral plans.

• The various funeral directors' associations need to improve their self-policing and in particular their complaints procedure. All complaints should be acknowledged within ten days and dealt with within three months.

• Members of the public do not shop around in the trauma of bereavement. We recommend in this book that they get a friend who is less involved do so on their behalf, so as to find a funeral director that suits their particular requirements. But it would also be of assistance to the public if there were regularly published comparative surveys of price and services, drawn up on a regional basis, naming particular establishments. This book is a step towards such a goal.

• Many people have written to The Natural Death Centre wanting what amounts to a 'disposal service' for their body after death. All local authorities should make agreements with undertakers to supply a cut-rate basic funeral to residents. As an experiment, some might want to go further and offer a 'disposal service', with a simple body container and no hearse, for those members of the public who want this. One correspondent has taken the idea to an extreme and writes that he feels strongly that any such disposal service should not charge 'more than £25 for 60 kilos of rubbish'. This does not fit with the Natural Death Centre's view of the mystery and dignity of death – and of the importance of the rite of physical farewell to a person's body – but we accept that for some people a disposal service is all that they want.

• Funeral directors and funeral shops should make available to the public the type of refrigeration plate that is placed under the deceased's body in rural France, so that the body can more easily be kept at home.

• Local authorities, church authorities or the government should offer financial incentives to churchyards to reopen their graveyards and any impeding legislation should be amended. At the moment it can be to a church's financial advantage to declare a graveyard closed, and to pass its maintenance over to the local authority. Cemeteries too, particularly in London, are running out of space. The Belgian practice, outlined by Tony Walter in 'Funerals and How to Improve Them', needs to be adopted, whereby a short-term grave is bought. We believe that a minimum period of 25 years would be suitable – then if a further 25 years were not paid for, a notice would be pinned to the grave, giving one year's grace before the grave would be made available for reuse. In this way, local burials remain possible and graves are well tended.

• New crematoria buildings should be adaptable, with flexible seating arrangements. Some might like to follow Tony Walter's design proposals for 'theatre in the round' with the coffin stage centre (see Chapter 5 for more on this).

• UK crematoria and cemeteries should offer cardboard and other coffins and shrouds for sale to those who are not using funeral directors, and could consider having a vehicle available for hire for the collection of bodies and cold storage facilities. The Office of Fair Trading should take action against groupings of funeral directors threatening to boycott such places. Likewise, all coffin manufacturers should be willing to sell direct to the public, with the Office of Fair Trading investigating those which are threatened by funeral directors as a result.

• Crematoria, cemeteries and others in the funeral business are urged to adopt the Charter for the Bereaved (published by the Institute of Burial and Cremation Administration), which is more innovative and challenging than the otherwise similar Dead Citizens Charter (published by the National Funerals College).

• Cemeteries should allow family and friends to help dig and fill the graves if they so wish, subject to any safeguards.

• Two doctors have to sign for cremation. In many cases at present, the second doctor neither examines the body nor positively identifies it, yet a second fee is charged. The situation is unsatisfactory and needs to be re-examined.

• There are many commercial opportunities that entrepreneurs could seize on within the UK funeral trade, particularly as the Green movement's sixties generation ages and becomes responsible for organising the funerals of parents and friends. The first undertakers to offer an entirely green funeral might do rather well – one option could consist, for example, of a wheel bier (for short distances) or a horse-drawn cart (as planned at Mole Valley Green Burial Ground in Devon), the body in a cardboard coffin or similar, followed by burial in a wildlife burial ground. Another option would be to offer a posh rentable coffin for display, plus a cheap inner coffin that can be cremated or buried.

• Every local authority should encourage the development of nature reserve burial grounds in its area. Every church, county wildlife trust and environmental charity should set one up and conscientious farmers could do so.

• The d-i-y superstores could offer flatpack coffins. Sainsbury's Homebase wrote to Jane Spottiswoode to say that they would not sell coffins as their stores were intended for family shopping 'based on the future and therefore not associated with death', whereas of course death in the future is one certainty that every family faces! Argos wrote to say that the sale of coffins would require a 'truly personal service' – in fact all that is required is the assurance that the coffin is big enough: two or three standard sizes should suffice.

• Every town needs its funeral shop, similar to the Heaven on Earth shop in Bristol, where inexpensive or artistic coffins can be bought, along with every other funeral item, from body bags to lowering webbing and urns. These need to offer items with lower mark-ups than do the Roc'Eclerc funeral supermarkets in Europe.

• 'At present', writes K. A. Gilchrist to the Natural Death Centre, 'it is far easier to take time off for having a bad cold than for the death of a close relative.' The entitlement of those who are bereaved to adequate leave of absence needs recognition.

• Probate work should no longer remain an expensive monopoly of the banks and solicitors. Others should be able to offer their services, subject of course to effective safeguards against fraudulent practices.

• The rules about the styles of memorial permitted in churchyards, cemeteries and crematoria should be relaxed, with any design or type of stone allowed. The disliked Albert Memorial monstrosities of one era become the much-loved tourist attractions of the future. And as one vicar complained in the journal Funerals: 'I can't tell you how often I deal with clients who are deeply upset because they have set their heart on some appropriate memorial which has then been forbidden'. The Church of England court ruling in 1996 that bereaved families should be allowed to attach photographs of the deceased to their tombstones is a positive development.

• Everyone is entitled to an obituary. Even funerals paid for by the state should include a small fee so that the minister or presiding person can help assemble a brief life story of the deceased for publication – if nowhere else, then at least for putting online in one of the free and permanent 'Gardens of Remembrance' on the Internet (see the Resources chapter). All priests should follow the practice of humanist officiants, who talk before the funeral to relatives, a friend and a colleague, so that at the service they can recount the biography of the person who has died.

Perhaps the next millennium will see the emergence of the new profession described by the science fiction writer Orson Scott Card, that of Speaker for the Dead – memorial service orators who provide catharsis for the friends and relatives by painstakingly assembling the unvarnished truth about the deceased's motivations, intentions and achievements. It could be a suitable job for resting novelists.

• Birthdays are recognised social occasions. Deathdays could be recognised too. On the first anniversary of the death, it could become the accepted practice for there to be a meal for close friends and relatives, and at subsequent deathdays just the simple gesture at mealtime of a toast to the person's memory or those present telling a story or memory about the one whose anniversary it is – thus passing on family lore to the next generations.

This may be the appropriate moment to wish you, dear reader, a peaceful deathday. May death for you be as graceful as Walt Whitman imagined it could be:

Come, lovely and soothing Death,
Undulate round the world, serenely arriving, arriving,
In the day, in the night, to all, to each,
Sooner or later, delicate death.
From 'Leaves of Grass' by Walt Whitman.

Chapter 12

USEFUL
RESOURCES

Booklist

✪✪✪ = *HIGHLY RECOMMENDED from a Natural Death perspective.*
NDC = *Can be ordered through the Natural Death Centre book service.*

• Ainsworth-Smith, Ian and Speck, Peter **Letting Go — Caring for the dying and bereaved**, SPCK, 1999, 176 pp, £9-99, ISBN 0 2810 52255

• **✪✪✪** Albery, Nicholas et al (eds), **Before and After — The best new ideas for improving the quality of dying and for inexpensive, green, family-organised funerals**, The Natural Death Centre (see Organisations below), 1995, 80 pp, £5-95 incl. p&p, ISBN 0 9523280 1 1. Out of print, but available free on the web at www.globalideasbank.org/befaft/contents.html

• NDC**✪✪✪** Albery, Nicholas et al (eds), **Creative Endings — Designer dying and celebratory funerals**, The Natural Death Centre (see Organisations below), 1996, 80 pp, £5-95 incl. p&p, ISBN 0 9523280 2 X.

• NDC**✪✪✪** Albery, Nicholas et al (eds), **Last Aid Manual – For families and palliative care workers**, The Natural Death Centre (see Organisations below), 1999, 108 pp, £5-95 incl. p&p, ISBN 0 9523280 6 2.

• **✪✪✪** Albery, Nicholas et al (eds), **Natural Death and Woodland Burial**, The Natural Death Centre (see Organisations below), 1997, 104 pp, £5-95 incl. p&p, ISBN 0 9523280 5 4. Out of print, but available free on the web at www.globalideasbank.org/ndw/ndwcontent.html

• NDC**✪✪✪** Albery, Nicholas and Wienrich, Stephanie (eds), **The New Natural Death Handbook**, 3rd edition. This present book, published for The Natural Death Centre by Rider, 2000, 384 pp, £12-99 incl. p&p from the Natural Death Centre (see organisations below), ISBN 0 7126 0576 2.

• **✪✪✪** Albery, Nicholas et al (eds), **Sooner or Later – Preparing for dying and family-organised funerals**, The Natural Death Centre (see Organisations below), 1997, 88 pp, £5-95 incl. p&p, ISBN 0 9523280 4 6. Out of print, but available free on the web at www.globalideasbank.org/soonlat/SLTOP.HTML

• Barley, Nigel, **Dancing on the Grave – Encounters with death**, John Murray (London), 1995, 240 pp, £19-99, ISBN 0 7195 5286 9.

• Baum, Rachel R. (ed), **Funeral and Memorial Service Readings, Poems and Tributes**, McFarland (McFarland & Company, Inc., Publishers, Box 611, Jefferson, North Carolina 28640, USA), 1999, 172 pp, £22-50, ISBN 0 7864 0699 2.

• Bell, Lesley, **Carefully — A guide for home care assistants**, ACE Books (Age Concern), 1998, 268 pp, £12-99, ISBN 0 8624 2285 X.

• ✪✪✪ Benefits Agency, **What To Do After A Death in England and Wales**, and **What To Do After A Death in Scotland,** Leaflets D49 and D49 S available free from The Stationery Office, Causeway Distribution Centre, The Causeway, Oldham Broadway Business Park, Chadderton, Oldham OL9 9XD (or order by phoning 020 7712 2171 or 0161 683 2363).

• Benn, June (ed), **Memorials — An Anthology of poetry and prose**, Ravette, 1986.

• Bentley, James, Best, Andrew and Hunt, Jackie, **Funerals – A Guide – Prayers, hymns and readings**, Hodder and Stoughton (Hodder Headline PLC, 338 Euston Road, London NW1 3BH), 1994, 319 pp, £9-99, ISBN 0 3406 1240 1.

• Blackmore, Susan, **Dying to Live — Science and the Near-Death Experience**, Prometheus, 1993, 291 pp, £19-99, ISBN 0 8797 58070 8.

• Boerstler, Richard and Kornfeld, **A Holistic and Meditative Approach for Caregivers and the Dying**, Healing Arts Press (distributed by Deep Books, London, tel 020 8693 0234; e-mail: sales@deep-books.co.uk), $14-95, ISBN 0 89281 329 6.

• Boerstler, Richard, **Letting Go — A holistic and meditative approach to living and dying**, Associates in Thanatology (115 Blue Rock Road, South Yarmouth, MA 02664, USA; web: www.gis.net/~hulenk), 1985, 60 pp, $3-95 plus $2 p&p, ISBN 0 9607928 0 5 T.

• British Medical Association, **Advance Statements About Medical Treatments — Code of practice**, British Medical Association, 1995, 39 pp, £5-95, ISBN 0 7279 09142.

• Buckman, Dr Robert, **I Don't Know What To Say — How to help and support someone who is dying**, Macmillan Papermac, 1996, 247 pp, £8-99, ISBN 0 330 347543.

• Callanan, Maggie and Kelley, Patricia, **Final Gifts – Understanding the special awareness, needs, and communications of the dying**, Bantam Books (New York), 1997, 241 pp, $12-95, ISBN 0 5533 7876 7. 'The subtleties of communicating with those who are dying.'

• CancerLink, **Caring at Home — Caring at home when cancer cannot be cured**, available from CancerLink (see under Organisations below), 1993, 44 pp, £5, ISBN 1 87 0534 67 0.

• Cannon, Geoffrey, **The Good Fight — The life and work of Caroline Walker**, Ebury Press, 1989, 179 pp, £4-99, ISBN 0 7126 3769 9. Out of print.

• Carlson, Lisa, **Caring For Your Own Dead**, Upper Access, 1987, 344 pp, $12-50, ISBN 0 9426 79008.

• Collick, Elizabeth, **Through Grief**, available from CRUSE (see under Organisations below), £6-95 plus p&p.

• Couldrick, Ann, **When Your Mum or Dad Has Cancer**, 1991, 21 pp, ISBN 0 9517 53738, available from OICPC for £2-35 incl. p&p (tel 01865 225896; e-mail: courses@oicpc.demon.co.uk; web: www.oicpc.demon.co.uk).

• Cunningham, James, (ed), **All is Well – Poems and readings in remembrance of loved ones**, HarperCollins (London), 1997, 120 pp, £6-99, ISBN 0 0025 5797 5.

• Davies, Simon, **Death Meditation**, a nonsectarian booklet available from the author at 44 St Gerrard's Road, Lostock Hall, Preston, Lancashire PR5 5TS.

• Diamond, John, **C – Because cowards get cancer too**, Vermilion, 1999, 256 pp, £6-99, ISBN 0 0918 1665 3. The book Diamond says he was looking for himself the night he got the bad news – his personal perspective on: 'How will cancer affect me? What is it like to deal with the pain and the fear and the anger?'

• Dickenson, Donna and Johnson, Malcolm (eds), **Death, Dying and Bereavement**, Sage, 1993, 355 pp, £12-95. This is the reader for the Open University course on death and dying.

• Doyle, Derek, **Domiciliary Palliative Care**, Oxford University Press, 1994, 160 pp, £29-95, ISBN 0 1926 2489 X. Aimed at GPs and community nurses but covering pain, diet, equipment and counselling.

• **✪✪✪** Duda, Deborah, **Coming Home — A guide to dying at home with dignity**, Aurora Press (PO Box 573, Santa Fe, New Mexico 87504, USA, tel 001 505 989 9804; e-mail: Aurorep@aol.com), 1987, 404 pp, £11-95 from Airlift (tel 020 7607 5792), ISBN 0 943358 31 0.

• Dunn, Michael, **The Good Death Guide – Everything you wanted to know but were afraid to ask**, Pathways (How to Books Ltd, 3 Newtec Place, Magdalen Road, Oxford OX4 1RE, tel 01865 793806; e-mail: info@howtobooks. co.uk; web: www.howtobooks.co.uk), 2000, 256 pp, £12-95, ISBN 1 8570 3559 3. Statistics, humour and the practical issues.

• Elkington, Gail and Harrison, Gill, **Caring for someone at home**, Chivers Press, 1998, 304 pp, £14-99, ISBN 0 7540 31055.

• England, Audrey (ed), **Helping Ourselves**, available from The Compassionate Friends (see under Organisations below), £2. For those who have lost a child.

• Enright, D. J. (ed), **The Oxford Book of Death**, OUP, 1983, 351 pp, £18-51, ISBN 0 1928 20133.

• Foos-Graber, Anya, **Deathing — An intelligent alternative for the final moments of life**, Nicolas-Hays, 1989, 397 pp, £11-95 from Airlift (tel 020 7607 5792; web: nowbooks.co.uk), ISBN 0 89254 016 8.

• Fremantle, Francesca and Trungpa, Chögyam (eds), **The Tibetan Book of the Dead**, Shambhala, 1988, 119 pp, £7-99, ISBN 0877730741.

• Garsia, Marlene, **How to Write a Will and Gain Probate**, Kogan Page (tel 020 7278 0433; web: www.koogan-page.co.uk), 1999, 208 pp, £8-99, ISBN 0 7494 3008 7.

• Gill, Sue and Fox, John, **The Dead Good Funerals Book**, Engineers of the Imagination, 1996, 192 pp, £9-50, ISBN 0 9527 1590 2. Good, but unreliable on the law.

• Gold, E. J., **The American Book of the Dead**, Gateways Books and Tapes (PO Box 370, Nevada City, CA 95959, USA, tel 001 530 272 0180; e-mail: info@gatewaysbooksandtapes.com; web: www.slimeworld.org/lrs), 1983, $15-95, ISBN 0 89556 051 8. Describes in plain English how to help the person through and beyond death, with readings, from a Tibetan-style perspective. For UK, see also 'Gold' under Music, Talks and Films, below.

• Gordon, Kate, **A Practical Guide to Alternative Funerals**, Constable (London), 1999, 197 pp, £6-99, ISBN 0 0947 8770 0.

• ✪✪✪ Grof, Stanislav and Halifax, Joan, **The Human Encounter with Death**, Souvenir Press, 1978, 240 pp, £2-95, ISBN 0 285 64874 8. Psychedelic therapy in palliative care. Out of print, alas.

• Grollman, E., **Talking About Death**, Beacon Press (Boston), 1991, £12-99, ISBN 0 8070 23639. For parent and child to read together.

• Grosz, Anton, **Letters to a Dying Friend — Helping those you love to make a conscious transition**, Quest, 1997 (rev), 169 pp, $9-95, ISBN 0 8356 07658.

• Harris, Jill Werman (ed), **Remembrances and Celebrations – A book of eulogies, elegies, letters, and epitaphs**, Pantheon Books (Random House, New York), 1999, 308 pp, $25, ISBN 0 3754 0123 7.

• Henley, Alix and Schott, Judith, **Culture, Religion and Patient Care in a Multi-Ethnic Society – A handbook for professionals**, Age Concern (see under Organisations below), 1999, 602 pp, £19-99, ISBN 0 8624 2231 0.

• ✪✪✪ Hjelmstad, Lois Tschetter, **Fine Black Lines — Reflections on facing cancer, fear and loneliness**, Mulberry Hill Press (2710 S. Washington, Englewood, CO 80110, USA, tel 001 800 294 4714; e-mail: hjelmstad@csd.net; web: www.bookzone.com/mulberry), 1993, 166 pp, $14-95 plus p&p, ISBN 1 9637139 5 7. Includes some fine poems.

• Hockey, Jennifer, **Making the Most of a Funeral**, CRUSE (see under Organisations below), 1992, 54 pp, £0-95 plus p&p, ISBN 0 900321 04 0. Useful suggestions aimed at priests, such as: involve the family, no rushing, use symbols and include the children.

• Huxley, Laura, **This Timeless Moment — A personal view of Aldous Huxley**, Celestial Arts, 2000, 280 pp, $14-95, ISBN 0 8908 79680. Tells the story of his dying.

• John, Da Free, **Easy Death — Talks and essays on the inherent and ultimate transcendence of death and everything else**, Dawn Horse Press, 1991, 431 pp, $14-95, ISBN 0 9188 01303.

• Jupp, Peter and Gittings, Clare, **Death in England – An illustrated history**, Manchester University Press, 1999, 304 pp, £15-99, ISBN 0 7190 5811 2.

• Justice, Christopher, **Dying the Good Death - The pilgrimage to die in India's holy city**, State University of New York Press (CUP Services, PO Box 6525, Ithaca, NY 14851, USA, tel 00 1 607 277 2211; author's e-mail: justice@interlynx.net), $19-95, ISBN 0 7914 3262 9.

• Kamath, M. V., **Philosophy of Death and Dying**, Himalayan International Institute of Yoga, Honesdale, PA, USA, 1978.

• Keizer, Bert, **Dancing with Mister D - Notes on life and death**, Black Swan, 1997, £6-99, ISBN 0 5529 9691 2.

• Kessler, David, **The Rights of the Dying – A companion for life's final moments**, Vermilion (Ebury Press, Random House, London), 1997, 204 pp, £8-99, ISBN 0 0918 6413 5.

• Krementz, J., **How it Feels When a Parent Dies**, Gollancz, 1986. Stories from 18 children.

• Kübler-Ross, Elisabeth, **On Death and Dying**, Routledge, 1990, 272 pp, £15-99, ISBN 0 415 04015 9.

• Kupfermann, Jeannette, **When the Crying's Done**, Robson Books, 1996, £8-

99, ISBN 0 8605 1904 X. Her experience of widowhood; moving and courageous.

• Lake, Dr Tony, **Living With Grief**, Sheldon Press, 1984, 160pp, £6-99, ISBN 0 8596 94267. Sensitively written.

• Lamm, Maurice, **The Jewish Way in Death and Mourning**, Jonathan David Publishers (NY), 1989, 266 pp, $15, ISBN 0 8246 01262.

• Leary, Timothy, Metzner, Ralph and Alpert, Richard, **The Psychedelic Experience — A manual based on the Tibetan Book of the Dead**, Citadel, 1995, 157 pp, $7-95, ISBN 0 8065 16526. Out of print.

• Lee, Dr Elizabeth, **A Good Death – A guide for patients and carers facing terminal illness at home**, Rosendale Press, 1995, 188 pp, £8-99, ISBN 1 872803 16 4.

• ✪✪✪ LeShan, Lawrence, **Cancer as a Turning Point — A handbook for people with cancer, their families, and health professionals**, Gill and Macmillan Publishers (Goldenbridge, Dublin 8, Ireland), 1996, 256 pp, £8-95, ISBN 1 85860 046 4. Highly recommended.

• Levine, Stephen, **A Gradual Awakening**, Gill and Macmillan (see above), 1979, 192 pp, £6-95, ISBN 0 946551 90 1.

• Levine, Stephen, **Guided Meditations, Exploration, Healings**, Gill and Macmillan (see above), 1992, £8-95.

• Levine, Stephen, **Meetings at the Edge**, Gill and Macmillan (see above), 1982, 264 pp, £7-95, ISBN 0-946551 88 X.

• Levine, Stephen, **Healing into Life & Death**, Gill and Macmillan (see above), 1990, 304 pp, £8-95, ISBN 0 946551 48 0. Contains a number of useful meditations.

• ✪✪✪ Levine, Stephen, **Who Dies? — An investigation of conscious living and conscious dying**, Gill and Macmillan (see above), 1986, 336 pp, £8-95, ISBN 0 946551 45 6.

• Lewis, C. S., **A Grief Observed**, Faber & Faber, 1966, 60 pp, £4-99, ISBN 0 5710 66240.

• Litten, Julian, **The English Way of Death — The common funeral since 1450**, Robert Hale, 1991, 254 pp, £14-95, ISBN 0 7090 47770.

• Longaker, Christina, **Facing Death & Finding Hope – A guide to the emotional and spritual care of the dying**, Arrow, 1998, 256 pp, £6-99, ISBN 0 0991 7692 0.

• ✪✪✪ Lunn, Joanne, and Harrold, Joan, and the Centre to Improve Care of the Dying at George Washington University, **Handbook for Mortals – Guidance for people facing serious illness**, OUP (New York) 1999, 242 pp, £14-99, ISBN 0 1951 1662 3. Authoritative and fascinating American book on preparing for dying.

• Magida, Arthur J. and Matlins, Stuart M., **How to be a Perfect Stranger – A guide to etiquette in other people's religious ceremonies (2 vols)**, Northstone (Wood Lake Books Inc., 9025 Jim Bailey Road, Kelowna, British Columbia, Canada, V4V 1R2, tel 00 1 250 766 2778, fax 00 1 250 766 2736; web: www.joinhands.com), 1999, 423 pp, Can$29-95, ISBN 1 8968 3628 3.

• Marie Curie Cancer Care, **Partners in Caring**, booklet, free from Marie Curie

(see Organisations below). Aimed at people caring for a relative at home.
• Mill, Andrew H., **Celebrating Life – A book of special services for use in the Unitarian and Free Christian tradition**, The Lindsey Press (Essex Hall, 1-6 Essex Street Strand, London WC2R 3HY, tel 020 7240 2384, fax 020 7240 3089), 1993, 234 pp, £15-50 incl. p&p, ISBN 0 8531 9041 0. Some suggested readings for funerals and other rites of passage.
• Morgan, Ernest, **Dealing Creatively with Death**, Barclay House, 1990, 167 pp, $11-95, ISBN 0 935016 79 1.
• Morse, Melvyn, **Closer to the Light — Learning from the Near-Death Experiences of children**, Ivy Books (Ballantine, New York), 1991, 237 pp, $5-99, ISBN 0 8041 0832 3.
• Mullin, Glenn H., **Death and Dying — The Tibetan tradition**, Arkana (Penguin US), 1986, 251 pp, $11-95, ISBN 0140 190139.
• Nearing, Helen, **Loving and Leaving the Good Life**, Chelsea Green Publishing Company (Post Mills, Vermont, USA), 1993, 208 pp, £10-95, ISBN 0 9300 31663 6 ; £10 hardback in UK (p&p extra) from Kathleen Jannaway, 47 Highlands, Leatherhead, Surrey KT22 8NQ. The life and dying of Scott Nearing.
• Neuberger, Julia, **Caring for Dying People of Different Faiths**, Austen Cornish, 59 pp, £5-50, ISBN 1 870065 00 X.
• Neuberger, Julia, **Dying Well – A guide to enabling a good death**, Hochland and Hochland Ltd (174a Ashley Road, Hale, Cheshire, WA15 9SF), 1999, 175 pp, £15-95, ISBN 1 8985 0726 0. Includes hints for caring for those of various different religions and ethnic groups.
• Pratt, Mandy, and Wood, Michele J. M., **Art Therapy in Palliative Care – The creative response**, Routledge, 1998, 202 pp, £15-99, ISBN 0 4151 6157 6.
• Putter, Ann Marie, **The Memorial Rituals Book for Healing and Hope**, Baywood Publishing Co Inc (Amityville, New York, USA), 1997, 88 pp, $23-95, ISBN 0 89503 143 4.
• Reoch, Richard, **Dying Well – A holistic guide for the dying and their carers**, Gaia Books (66 Charlotte Street, London W1P 1LR), 1997, 192 pp, £11-99, ISBN 1 8567 5019 1.
• Rees, Dewi, **Death and Bereavement – The psychological, religious and cultural interfaces**, Whurr Publishers Ltd (19b Compton Terrace, London N1 2UN, tel 020 7359 5979), 1997, 258 pp, £19-50, ISBN 1 8615 6012 5. Includes how the different religions and ethnic groups understand death and mourning.
• Riemer, Jack (ed), **Jewish Insights on Death and Mourning**, Shocken Books (New York), 1996, $15, ISBN 0 8052 10350.
• Ring, Kenneth, **Heading Toward Omega — In search of the meaning of the Near-Death Experience**, Quill, 1985, 348 pp, $8-95, ISBN 0 688 06268 7.
• Rinpoche, Sogyal, **The Tibetan Book of Living and Dying**, Rider/Random House, 1994, 427 pp, £12-99, ISBN 0 7126 57525. Spiritual help for the dying, adapted for the Westerner. It gives the background of the teachings, rather than being a prayer book to use. (See also Rigpa in Organisations, below.)
• Rose, Gillian, **Love's Work**, Vintage, 1995, 144 pp, hardback £5-99, ISBN 0 0995 45810. Courageous and passionate memoirs of a philosopher facing cancer.

• St Christopher's Hospice, **Someone Special Has Died**, St Christopher's Hospice (see Bookshops below), £2. An illustrated booklet for children.

• St Christopher's Hospice, **Your Parent Has Died**, St Christopher's Hospice (see Bookshops below), 1991, £2.

• Sanders, Dr Catherine, **Surviving Grief and Learning to Live Again**, John Wiley and Sons Inc (New York), 1992, 240 pp, £13-99, ISBN 0 471 53471 4.

• Schiff, Harriet Sarnoff, **The Bereaved Parent**, Souvenir Press, 1979 (& 1992), 160 pp, £6-99, ISBN 0 285 64891 8.

• Smale, David A., **Davies' Law of Burial, Cremation and Exhumation** (sixth edition), Shaw and Sons, 1993, £29-95, ISBN 0 7219 0064 X.

• Smith Cheryl K. and Docker, Chris G. and Hofsess, John and Dunn, Dr. Bruce, **Beyond Final Exit — New research in self-deliverance for the terminally ill**, The Right to Die Society of Canada (PO Box 39018, Victoria, British Columbia, V8V 4X8, Canada), 1995, 116 pp, ISBN 1 896533 04 3.

• Spottiswoode, Jane, **Undertaken with Love**, Robert Hale, 1992, 175 pp, £5-95, ISBN 0 7090 4979 X. About a funeral without an undertaker.

• Starhawk, **The Pagan Book of Living and Dying – Practical rituals, prayers, blessings, and meditations on crossing over**, HarperSanFrancisco (HarperCollins Publishers, New York), 1997, 353 pp, $17, ISBN 0 0625 1516 0.

• Staudacher, Carol, **Beyond Grief — A guide to recovering from the death of a loved one**, New Harbinger Publications Inc, 1987, 244 pp, £11-99, ISBN 0 9434 986436.

• Stickney, Doris, **Waterbugs and Butterflies**, Pilgrim Press, 1997, booklet, 32 pages, ISBN 0 8298 1180 X. Explaining death to children under 5.

• Stillbirth And Neo-Natal Death Society (SANDS), **Saying Goodbye to Your Baby**, booklet for bereaved parents, available from SANDS (see Organisations below).

• Taylor, Allegra, **Acquainted with the Night — A year on the frontier of death**, Fontana (HarperCollins), 1989, 191 pp, £7-95, ISBN 0 8520 72856.

• Thorpe, Graham, **Enabling More Dying People to Remain at Home**, a paper in the British Medical Journal, October 9th 1993.

• Todd, Jacquelyne, **Living with Lymphoedema — Your guide to treatment**, available from Marie Curie Trading, Unit 10, Dunbeath Court, Elgin, Swindon, Wiltshire SN2 6QF (tel 01793 863463), £6-49 incl. p&p.

• Wallbank, Susan, **Facing Grief — Bereavement and the young adult**, available from CRUSE (see under Organisations below), £9-99 plus p&p.

• Walter, Dr Tony, **Funerals — And how to improve them**, Hodder & Stoughton, 1990, 307 pp, £9-99, ISBN 0 340 53125 8. Out of print.

• Waugh, Evelyn, **The Loved One**, Penguin, 1951, 128 pp, £6-99, ISBN 0 14 018249 7. A satire on the funeral industry in the United States.

• Wells, Rosemary, **Helping Children Cope with Grief — Facing a death in the family**, Sheldon Press, 1988, 112 pp, £6-99, ISBN 0 8596 9559 X.

• Wertheimer, Alison, **A Special Scar**, Routledge, 1991, 256 pp, £15-99, ISBN 0 41501 763 7. Experiences of people bereaved through suicide, excellent for both the bereaved and professionals.

• Which? Books, **Guide to Giving and Inheriting**, Which? Ltd. (tel 0800 252 100), 1999, 240 pp, £9-99 incl. p&p, ISBN 0 8520 27974.

• Which? Books, **Making your Will Action Pack — A practical guide to making your own will (England and Wales)**, Which? Ltd (tel 0800 252 100),1999, 28 pp plus forms, £10-99 incl. p&p.

• Which? Books, **What To Do When Someone Dies**, Which? Ltd. (tel 0800 252 100),1999, 160pp, £9-99 incl. p&p, ISBN 0 8520 28164.

• ✪✪✪ Which? Books, **Wills and Probate**, Which? Ltd. (tel 0800 252 100),1999, 224 pp, £9-99 incl. p&p (or £17-98 incl. p&p if bought jointly with 'What To Do When Someone Dies'), ISBN 0 8520 27710.

• White, John, **A Practical Guide to Death and Dying**, Quest, 1988, 196 pp, $7-50, ISBN 0 8356 0633 3. Out of print.

• ✪✪✪ Wilber, Ken, **Grace and Grit**, Shambhala, 1993, £15-99, ISBN 0 8777 36987. About the death of his wife from cancer.

• Wilkins, Robert, **The Fireside Book of Death**, Robert Hale, 1990, 256 pp, £14-95, ISBN 0 7090 4144 6. Out of print.

• Williams, Pam, **Knowing About Caring for the Dying**, available from author (Lecturer in Nursing, School of Nursing and Midwifery, Humphry Davy House, Health Science College, Golden Smithies Lane, Rotherham S63 7ER, tel 01909 773507 h; 0114 222 9681 w; e-mail: p.williams1@sheffield.ac.uk). How nurses' training is now and how it could be improved.

• ✪✪✪ Willson, Jane Wynne, **Funerals Without God — A practical guide to non-religious funerals**, British Humanist Association (see under Organisations below), 1990, 67 pp, £5 incl. p&p, ISBN 0 901825 14 X.

• Young, Michael and Cullen, Lesley, **A Good Death — Conversations with East Londoners**, Routledge, 1996, 272 pp, £15-99, ISBN 0 415 13797 7.

• Zaleski, Carol, **Otherworld Journeys — Accounts of Near-Death Experience in medieval and modern times**, OUP (New York), 1988, 274 pp, $11-95, ISBN 0 19 505665 5.

BOOKSHOPS: The Natural Death Centre book service, 20 Heber Road, London NW2 6AA (tel 020 8208 2853, fax 020 8452 6434; e-mail: rhino@dial.pipex.com; web: www.naturaldeath.org.uk) sells only the highly recommended books above which are marked 'NDC✪✪✪'. Please add 20% for postage and packing (50% foreign airmail) and make any cheque payable to 'NDC'. Further copies of this present Handbook are also obtainable from the Centre for £12.99 incl. p&p. If urgent, phone your order through for these books, giving your Access, Visa or Mastercard number. Please add the extra 4.2% which the bank charges for this credit card service. Otherwise, probably one of the best bookshops in London for books on dying is **Watkins**, 21 Cecil Court, London WC2N 4EZ (tel 020 7836 2182); sometimes good for American imports is **Compendium Bookshop**, 234 Camden High St, London NW1 8QS (tel 020 7484 8944), or **Airlift** distributors (tel 020 7607 5792 for mail order). **St Christopher's Hospice** have a book service too: 51-59 Lawrie Park Road, London SE26 6DZ (tel 020 8778 9252). Any book in print can also be ordered without paying UK p&p from the **Sunday Times book ordering service** (tel

0345 660 916). UK books can be researched at websites such as **www.amazon.co.uk** (or www.amazon.com for American books) but it is kinder to your local small bookshop to then place the order with them.

Music, Talks and Films

• **Ananda Network Cassette Library**, c/o Ray Wills, 5 Grayswood Point, Norley Vale, Roehampton, London SW15 4BT (tel 020 8789 6170). The Ananda Network has a library of cassettes and videotapes which they will loan for free, with talks on living, dying, death and rebirth, mainly from a **Buddhist perspective**.

• **British Holistic Medical Association** (see Organisations below) — tapes at £9-20 incl. p&p include: **Imagery for Relaxation, Coping with Persistent Pain, Coping with Stress, Introducing Meditation** and **The Breath of Life** (relaxation).

• **Buddhist Death Ritual for Dharmachari Ajita**, on Super VHS, available also on Betacam SP, from Suryaprabha, Lights in the Sky, 39a Lough Road, London, N7 8RH (tel 020 7607 9480; e-mail: surya@budacom.com; web: www.budacom.com).

• **Collick, Elizabeth, Through Grief**, tape available from CRUSE (see under Organisations below), £5-50 plus p&p. Also available as a book (see above). Offers sensible maxims.

• **Levine, Stephen** tapes are available from Gateway Alternatives, the Hollies, Wellow, Bath BA2 8QJ (tel 01225 835127) who will send a free catalogue on request. His tapes (and his schedule of workshops) are also available from Warm Rock Tapes, PO Box 108, Chamisal, NM 87521, USA. Send two international reply coupons for details.

• Long, Barry, **Seeing Through Death**, audiotape from Barry Long Audio, BCM Box 876, London WC1N 3XX (tel 01736 751910; e-mail: prinzpubuk@compuserve.com; web: www.barrylong.org). (Previously published as **May I speak to you of Death?**)

• **Mental Health Media**, The Resource Centre, 356 Holloway Road, London N7 6PA (tel 020 7700 8131) publishes out a catalogue (price £4) of films and videos available for sale or hire in the UK on the subjects of **Death and Bereavement**, many of them aimed at professionals, some about euthanasia, others on Near-Death Experiences, etc.

• **Programme of music for those who are dying**, drawn up by Gilles Bedard (e-mail: inerson@microtec.net). For details see www.microtec.net/inerson/gmi_sep8.html or see pp 33-36 of the 'Last Aid Manual', edited by Nicholas Albery et al (see above under books or available on the web at www.globalideasbank.org/LA/LA-12.HTML).

Useful organisations and individuals

• **A. B. Welfare and Wildlife Trust**, 7, Knox Road, Harrogate, North Yorkshire HG1 3EF (tel 01423 530900 or 868121). Advises dying and bereaved people on any type of funeral in any type of place, anywhere in the country. The Trust was set up by John Bradfield, a social worker, conservationist and author of 'Green Burial - The DIY Guide to Law and Practice' (published by the Natural Death Centre but now out of print). This summarised the authoritative research undertaken for the Trust. This is the only charity in the country able to give sound advice on emotional needs, the full extent of choices, all aspects of the law, environmental health and using burials to promote wildlife. 'Funds are desperately needed to provide the free advice service, train volunteers from all parts of the country and to buy land, so more burials can be arranged in nature reserves. Obtaining advice by telephone may continue to be difficult, unless the Trust is supported with donations and grants.'

• **Age Concern**, Astral House, 1268 London Road, London SW16 4ER (tel 020 8679 8000). Their postal will-writing service, run by a solicitor, can draw up a simple will for £50, based on a self-completion questionnaire. A factsheet (No. 27) on arranging a funeral is available free of charge. Please send an SAE.

• **Alder Centre**, Royal Liverpool Children's NHS Trust, Alder Hey, Eaton Road, Liverpool L12 2AP (tel 0151 228 4811; see Child Death Helpline for freephone helpline). For all those affected by a child's death. Counselling, groups, befriending (see also The Compassionate Friends).

• **Alzheimer's Disease Society**, Gordon House, 10 Greencoat Place, London SW1P 1PH (tel 020 7306 0606, fax 020 7306 0808; e-mail: info@alzheimers. org.uk; web: www.alzheimers.org.uk). Advice given and information on aids and services.

• **Ananda Network**, c/o Dennis Sibley, Flat 1, Laurel House, Trafalgar Road, Newport, Isle of Wight PO30 1QN (tel 01983 526945; web: www.buddhist hospice.cjb.net)

• **Another Way**, c/o South West Environmental Action Project, 17 Castle Street, Kirkcudbright DG6 4JA, Scotland (tel 01557 331993; e-mail: sweapk@ cqm.co.uk). A voluntary organisation providing, for this part of Scotland, information to do with death and dying, help with living wills, public talks and workshops, support with funeral arrangements and support for those who are terminally ill or facing bereavement.

• **Asian Family Counselling Service**, 76 Church Road, Hanwell, London, W7 8LB (tel 020 8567 5616; e-mail: afcs99@hotmail.com).

• **Association of Burial Authorities**, 155 Upper Street, London N1 1RA (tel 020 8288 2522, fax 020 8288 2533; web: www.aba@swa-pr.com.uk).

• **Association for Children with Life-Threatening Terminal Conditions and their Families** (ACT), Orchard House, Orchard Lane, Bristol BS1 5DT (tel 0117 922 1556, fax 0117 930 4707; e-mail: info@act.org.uk; web: www.act.org.uk). Advice and information.

• **Association for Death Education and Counselling**, 342 North Main Street, W. Hertford, Connecticut 06117, USA (tel 001 860 232 4825, fax 001 860 586 7550; e-mail: info@adec.org; web: www.adec.org). Conferences and courses.

• **The Befriending Network**, 20 Heber Road, London NW2 6AA (London and national enquiries: tel 07041 420 192; e-mail: info@befriending.net; web: www.befriending.net. Oxfordshire enquiries: tel 01865 316200; e-mail:

oxford@befriending.net). Trained volunteers who offer support to people with a terminal or life-threatening illness at home, for two to three hours per week. The Befriending Network is currently active in north and west London and in Oxfordshire; and can provide referrals to other similar agencies nationwide.

• **Benefits Agency**: for how to claim benefits, etc, phone your local office, under Social Security or Benefits Agency in your local phone book, or phone their Public Enquiry Office (tel 020 7712 2171). Potentially relevant leaflets to ask for include 'Help when someone Dies' (FB29), 'National Insurance for widows' (CA 09), 'Rates of war pensions and allowances' (MPL 154), 'War widows and other dependants' (MPL 152), 'What to do after a death in England and Wales' (D49), 'What to do after a death in Scotland' (D49 S) and 'Widow's benefits' (NP 45).

• **Bradfield, John**. See A. B. Welfare and Wildlife Trust, above.

• **Bristol Cancer Help Centre**, Grove House, Cornwallis Grove, Clifton, Bristol BS8 4PG (tel 0117 980 9500; e-mail: info@bristolcancerhelp.org; web: www.bristolcancerhelp.org). Holistic treatment and publications. Grief, loss, death and dying workshops, and phone-in service.

• **British Association for Counselling**, 1 Regent Place, Rugby, Warwickshire CV21 2PJ (tel 01788 578328; office 01788 550899; web: www.counselling .co.uk). Has information on organisations, counsellors and therapists nationwide that you can pay to see – although some are free. For information on counsellors in the area and counselling courses please send an SAE.

• **British Holistic Medical Association**, 59 Landsdowne Place, Hove, East Sussex BN3 1FL (tel and fax 01273 725951). Self-help breathing, relaxation, meditation and tapes (see Music, Talks and Films, above) and an informative quarterly called 'Holistic Health'.

• **British Humanist Association**, 47 Theobald's Road, London WC1X 8SP (tel 020 7430 0908). Can provide officiant for non-religious funeral (variable charges, for instance £85 in north west London). See also Jane Wynne Willson under books, above.

• **British Medical Association**, BMA House, Tavistock Square, London WC1H 9JP (tel 020 7387 4499, fax 020 7383 6400; web: www.bma.org.uk). The governing body for the British medical profession.

• **British Organ Donor Society** (BODY), Balsham, Cambridge CB1 6DL (tel 01223 893636; e-mail: body@argonet.co.uk; web: www.argonet.co.uk/body). Information and emotional support for recipients and families of organ donors, and general enquiries.

• **The Buddhist Hospice Trust**, 5 Grayswood Point, Norley Vale, Roehampton, London SW15 4BT (tel c/o Ray Wills 020 8789 6170; web: http:// buddhisthospice.cjb.net). A particularly friendly organisation. 'It was established in 1986 to explore Buddhist approaches to dying, death and bereavement. It is nonsectarian and welcomes both Buddhists and non-Buddhists alike. Its purpose is to bring together, in a creative way, the teachings of the Buddha and the philosophy of modern hospice care.' In fact it confesses that it is at this stage just a network of people, 'a hospice of the heart', rather than a building. Has a biannual magazine Raft (£5 subs.), publishes pamphlets and holds meetings. Volunteers in its Ananda Network (see above) are prepared to sit with and befriend the terminally ill. See also Music, Talks and Films, above.

• **CALL Centre** (Cancer Aid and Listening Line), Swan Buildings, 20 Swan St, Manchester M4 5JW (for national helpline, manned Monday to Thursday noon to 3pm and 7.30pm to 10.30 pm, phone 0161 835 2586; emergencies will be dealt with at any time). Emotional support and practical advice for cancer patients and families.

• **Cancer BACUP** (British Association of Cancer United Patients), 3 Bath Place, Rivington St, London EC2A 3JR. A national charity providing information and counselling for people with cancer, their families and friends. For information on any aspect of cancer call BACUP's Cancer Information Service, staffed by specialist nurses (tel 0800 800 1234 Monday to Thursday 10am to 7pm; Friday 10am to 5.30pm) or write to the address above. Face-to-face counselling is available in London (tel 020 7696 6000) and Glasgow (tel 0141 553 1553) Monday to Friday 9.30 am to 5pm. A minicom textphone is available. All Cancer BACUP's services are provided free of charge and in confidence. Donations are very welcome. Their booklet 'Coping at Home – Caring for someone with advanced cancer' is free to carers.

• **Cancerlink**, 11-21 Northdown Street, London N1 9BN (tel 020 7833 2818; Freephone cancerlink 0808 808 0000; e-mail: cancerlink@cancerlink.org.uk). Now mainly a referral service to other organisations. It also supports local self-help groups and publishes a directory of these – and useful pamphlets on everything from sexuality to complementary alternative treatments and caring for the dying at home.

• **Care for the Carers Limited**, Chandlers Wharf, Railway Lane, Lewes, East Sussex BN7 2AQ (tel 01273 486625; information 01273 486641, fax 01273 486654; e-mail: mary@esussexcarers.freeserve.co.uk). Advice, information and support, primarily for the East Sussex area.

• **Carers National Association**, Ruth Pitter House, 20-25 Glasshouse Yard, London EC1A 4JT (tel 020 7490 8818, fax 020 7490 8824; helpline 0808 808 7777). Advice for carers and former carers. Local support groups.

• **The Center for Attitudinal Healing**, 33 Buchanan Drive, Sausalito, California 94965, USA (tel 001 415 331 6161, fax 001 415 331 4545; e-mail: cah@well.com; web: http://healingcenter.org). Works with children and children facing serious illnesses, and with children whose parents have cancer, etc. Their video 'Under the Sun' (which emphasises that health is inner peace and that the present instant is the only time there is) may be available on loan from the Buddhist Hospice Trust (see above).

• **Chai-Lifeline, Jewish Cancer Support and Health Centre**, Norwood House, Harmony Way, off Victoria Road, Hendon, London NW4 2BZ (tel 020 8202 4567). They work with youth and adults facing life-threatening illnesses, providing support groups, visitors and complementary therapies.

• **The Child Bereavement Trust**, Brindley House, 4 Burkes Road, Beaconsfield, Buckinghamshire HP9 1PB (tel 01494 678088; e-mail: jthomas@thecbt. freeserve.co.uk; web: www.childbereavement.org).

• **Child Death Helpline**, c/o Bereavement Services Department, Great Ormond Street Hospital, London. (Freephone helpline 0800 282986 staffed every night 7 to 10pm, and Monday, Wednesday and Friday mornings 10am to 1pm; administration 020 7813 8551 or 0151 252 5391.) Run jointly by Great Ormond Street Hospital and The Alder Centre, Liverpool. Trained volunteers, virtually all of whom are bereaved parents themselves, offer free telephone counselling and emotional support to anyone affected by the death of a child or young adult.

• **Choice Rites of Passage**, c/o Lorely Burt, Campus House, Albion Street, Wall Heath, Kingswinford, Dudley, West Midlands DY6 OJS (tel & fax 01384 271254). A business helping people in the West Midlands to put together a customised funeral service, using a variety of funeral providers.

• **The Cinnamon Trust**, Foundry House, Foundry Square, Hayle, Cornwall TR27 4HE (tel 01736 757900). Care for pets belonging to the elderly and terminally ill.

• **Citizens Advice Bureau**, free, impartial, confidential advice about death, bereavement, financial and all other matters. See your local phone book or contact the HQ, Myddelton House, 115-123 Pentonville Rd, London N1 9LZ (tel 020 7833 2181, fax 020 7833 4371; e-mail: consultancy@nacab.org.uk; web: www.nacab.org.uk) for details of your nearest branch.

• **The Compassionate Friends**, 53 North Street, Bristol BS3 1EN (helpline tel 0117 953 9639; admin tel 0117 966 5202; e-mail: info@tcf.org.uk; web: www.tcf.org.uk). Befriending bereaved parents and their families. Also a very fine newsletter and a postal lending library for books.

• **Continence Foundation**, 307 Hatton Square, 16 Baldwins Gardens, London EC1N 7RJ (tel 020 7404 6875, fax 020 7404 6876; helpline 020 7831 9831; textphone 020 7831 9831). A continence advisory service.

• **The Cot Death Helpline**, 14 Halkin Street, London SW1X 7DP (e-mail: fsid@sids.org.uk; web: www.sids.org.uk/fsid/). Their 24-hour helpline (tel 020 7235 1721) always get through to a person. They can also arrange 'befriending' for those who have suffered sudden infant death.

• **Counsel and Care, advice and help for older people**, Twyman House, 16 Bonny St, London NW1 9PG (tel 020 7485 1566/0845 300 7585 local rate, 10.30am - 4pm; e-mail: advice@counselandcare.demon.co.uk). Provides advice on finding and paying for residential and nursing care; publishes free factsheets on welfare issues. Publishes books. Undertakes research. Organises conferences and training events.

• **Court of Protection**, The Public Trust Office, Protection Division, Stewart House, 24 Kingsway, London WC2B 6JX (tel 020 7269 7300; e-mail: custserve@publictrust.gov.uk; web: www.publictrust.gov.uk). If you need to apply to manage the financial affairs of someone who has become mentally incapacitated.

• **Cremation Society of Great Britain**, 2nd Floor, Brecon House, 16/16a Albion Place, Maidstone, Kent ME14 5DZ (tel 01622 688292; e-mail: cremsoc@aol.com; web: www.cremation.org.uk). Can tell you the nearest crematorium. Publishes a free booklet on 'What You Should Know About Cremation', and a directory of crematoria (£15).

• **Crossroads-Caring for Carers**, 10 Regents Place, Rugby, Warwickshire CV21 2PN (tel 01788 573653). Trained carers who take over from the regular carer completely in looking after a disabled person at home, so as to give the regular carer a break.

• **CRUSE**, Cruse House, 126 Sheen Road, Richmond, Surrey TW9 1UR (tel 020 8940 4818). Bereavement helpline available on 020 8332 7227. To speak to a counsellor phone 0345 585 565 afternoons or evenings. For all those who have suffered a bereavement: socials and advice, counselling, training courses and excellent publications, including a newsletter for people who are bereaved and a Bereavement Care journal for professional people working with those who are dying and those who are bereaved.

• **Death and Immortality MA Course**, c/o Paul Badham, University of Wales, Lampeter, Ceredigion, Wales SA48 7ED (tel 01570 424810 or 01570 422351; e-mail: badham@lamp.ac.uk; web: www.religious-studies.net).

• **Death and Society MA Course**, c/o Mrs Annette Eley, Dept. of Sociology, Faculty of Letters and Social Science, The University of Reading, Whiteknights, Reading RG6 6AA (tel 0118 931 8519, fax 0118 931 8922; e-mail: deathsoc@reading.ac.uk; web: www.reading.ac.uk/DeathSoc/home.html).

• **DeathNET**, the American Internet site with news of the progress of the euthanasia movement (at www.islandnet.com/~deathnet/).

• **Death Studies Journal**, Taylor and Francis plc, 11 New Fetter Lane, London EC4P 4EE, subs. £27.

• **Disability Information Trust**, Mary Marlborough Centre, Nuffield Ortho-paedic Centre, Headington, Oxford OX3 7LD (tel 01865 227592; e-mail: ditrust@btconnect.com; web: home.btconnect.com/ditrust/home.htm). Their books range from 'Manual Wheelchairs – A practical guide' to 'Hoists, Lifts and Transfers'.

• **Disabled Living Foundation**, 380-384 Harrow Road, London W9 2HU (tel 020 7289 6111, fax 020 7266 2922; helpline 0870 603 9177; textphone 0870 603 9170, helpline and textphone open Monday to Friday 10am-4pm; e-mail: dlfinfo@dlf.org.uk; web: www.dlf.org.uk). National charity offering informa-tion and advice on daily living equipment for people with a disability.

• **Disablement Income Group**, PO Box 5743, Finchingfield, Essex CM7 4PW (tel 01371 811 621). Working to improve the financial circumstances of disabled people.

• **Disaster Action**, Holborn Studios, 49-50 Eagle Wharf Road, London N1 7ED (tel 020 7251 2427). Self-help group for those bereaved following a major disaster such as a plane crash.

• **Exit** (formerly Voluntary Euthanasia Society of Scotland), 17 Hart Street, Edinburgh EH1 3RN (tel 0131 556 4404, fax 0131 557 4403; e-mail: didmsnj@easynet.co.uk; web: www.euthanasia.org). Christopher Grant Docker there is very knowledgeable about the varieties of Living Will texts worldwide and about their shortcomings in practice.

• **The Family Welfare Association**, 501-505 Kingsland Road, Dalston, London E8 4AU (tel 020 7249 6636; e-mail: helen.dent@fwa.org.uk; web – from mid-2000 – www.fwa.org.uk). Gives grants to individuals and families.

• **Federation of British Cremation Authorities**, 41 Salisbury Road, Carshalton, Surrey SM5 3HA (tel 020 8669 4521).

• **Federation of Independent Advice Centres**, 4 Deans Court, St Paul's Churchyard, London EC4V 5AA (tel 020 7489 1800).

• **The Foundation for the Study of Infant Deaths** (FSID), 14 Halkin Street, London SW1X 7DP (tel 020 7235 0965; 24-hour staffed cot death helpline offering information and support to families and professionals 020 7235 1721, fax 020 7823 1986; e-mail: fsid@sids.org.uk; web: www.sids.org.uk). Information, fund-raising for cot deaths research, befriending service, local groups.

• **Funeral and Memorial Societies of America** maintain a site on the Internet with information on American alternatives to costly funerals. The location is http://vbiweb.champlain.edu/famsa

• **The Funeral Ombudsman**, 26-28 Bedford Row, London WC1R 4HE (tel 020 7430 1112, fax 020 7430 1012; e-mail: fos@dircon.co.uk). For complaints about Co-op, SCI, SAIF and non-NAFD funeral directors – in fact, they cover about 70% of all funeral directors in the UK.

• **Funeral Service Journal**, PO Box IW73, Leeds LS16 9XW (tel 0113 284 1177, fax 0113 284 2152; e-mail: info@fsj.co.uk; web: www.fsj.co.uk). Founded 1886. The best of the funeral journals.

• **Garden of Remembrance** on the Internet are numerous nowadays but some charge a great deal, some offer only temporary postings and some are free. One free one which also provides links to the others is to be found at: www.intersource.com/~markh/memorial.html

• **Guild of Soul Midwives**, BCM Soul Midwives, London WC1N 3XX (tel 018657 62807). A pagan-inspired group co-ordinated by Caitlin Mathews and dedicated to the spiritual empowerment of people who are dying and the compassionate support of their friends and family. They can 'shamanically accompany the soul going over'. See also Pagan Federation, below.

• **Helen House – A Hospice for Children**, 37 Leopold Street, Oxford OX4 1QT (tel 01865 728251, fax 01865 794829). There are other children's hospices in Yorkshire, Lancashire, Shropshire, Norfolk, Birmingham, Manchester, Leicester, Barnstaple, Kinross and Cambridge, with more planned.

• **The Hospice Information Service**, at St Christopher's Hospice, 51-59 Lawrie Park Road, Sydenham, London SE26 6DZ (tel 020 8778 9252, Monday-Friday, 8am to 5pm, answerphone during evenings and weekends, fax 020 8776 9345; e-mail: his@stchris.ftech.co.uk). Publishes a UK Directory of hospices and palliative care services (also on the web at: www.kcl.ac.uk/kis/schools/kcsmd/palliative/his.htm). Has international information for health professionals and members of the public caring for people with cancer or other life-threatening illnesses. Also helps patients, families and carers to identify and access appropriate support and resources.

• **Ian Rennie Hospice at Home**, 93 Western Road, Tring, Herts HP23 4BN (tel 01442 890222; e-mail: info@irhh.org; web: www.irhh.org). Provides specialist 24-hour nursing care in the Chilterns area of Hertfordshire and Buckinghamshire. For patients with a terminal illness and also support for their families.

• **In Loving Memory**, Christine Davies, Corner Cottage, 28 Queensway, Old

Colwyn LL29 9ED (tel 01492 514713 and 0948 730322). Christine Davies helps conduct non-religious or non-traditional funeral services and can also help with other aspects such as catering, choice of music and a video record.

• **Institute of Burial and Cremation Administration** – publishes the excellent Charter for the Bereaved (the full 72-page copy costs £25). Order from Ken West, Charter Organiser, Cemetery Office, Richardson Street, Carlisle CA2 6AL (tel 01228 625310, fax 01228 625313). By January 2000, 33 cemeteries and crematoria had officially adopted the Charter.

• **The Internet** holds a vast amount of information on death and dying, including most of the Natural Death Centre's books (at www.naturaldeath.org.uk, where there are many other links). Many libraries and internet cafes can now help you access the Internet. Some other places to start looking include: the Yahoo site (http://dir.yahoo.com/Society-and-Culture/Death-and-Dying); a site on the subject of the sociology of death and dying (at www.trinity.edu/~mkearl/death.html); a free online journal on end-of-life care (at www.edu.org/lastacts/); mainly USA resources (at www.choices-org/links.htm; or at http://dying.about.com/health/dying/mbody.htm; or at www.funerals.org/famsa/links.htm); free Buddhist books on death and dying (at www.buddhist.net/r-booksd.htm); a newsgroup on grieving (accessible using the Netscape browser at: news:alt.support.grief).

• **Jessie's Fund**, 10 Bootham Terrace, York YO30 7DH (tel 01904 658189; e-mail: jessiefund@aol.com; web: www.jessiesfund.org.uk). A charity with music therapists helping sick children in hospices.

• **Jewish Bereavement Counselling Service**, PO Box 6748, London N3 3BX (tel 020 8349 0839 answerphone).

• **John Bell and Croyden**, 50–54 Wigmore St, London W1 (tel 020 7935 5555 ext 212). Chemist for specialist medical requirements, everything from a sheepskin rug to a walking frame.

• **Law Centres Federation**, Duchess House, 18-19 Warren Street, London W1P 5DB (tel 020 7387 8570; e-mail: info@lawcentre.org.uk) can put you in touch with your local law centre which can provide free advice about wills etc for those who are hard-up. Or see the list of law centres on their web site (www.lawcentres.org.uk).

• **Lesbian and Gay Bereavement Project**, Vaughan M. Williams Centre, Colindale Hospital, London NW9 5GJ (tel 020 8455 8894 helpline, 020 8200 0511, office hours; e-mail: LGBP@aol.com). Counselling, support and information on subjects including wills and funerals.

• **LifeRites**, PO Box 101, Aldershot, Hampshire GU11 3UN (tel 01252 341 054; e-mail: info@liferites.org; web: www.liferites.org). National co-ordinator Cheryl Menzies-Runciman. A pagan organisation with information on rites of passage, it can provide celebrants who can conduct services for about £80, and people who work interactively with those who are terminally ill. See also Pagan Federation, below.

• **London Bereavement Network**, 356 Holloway Road, London N7 6PN (tel 020 7700 8134, fax 020 7700 8146; e-mail: info@bereavement.org.uk; web: www.bereavement.org.uk). Supporting and linking London bereavement services.

• **London Lighthouse**, 111-117 Lancaster Road, London W11 1QT (tel 020 7792 1200, fax 020 7229 1238; e-mail: danny@london-lighthouse.org.uk; web: www.london-lighthouse.org.uk). 'A centre for people facing the challenge of AIDS.'

• **Lymphoedema Support Network**, St Luke's Crypt, Sydney Street, London SW3 6NH (tel 020 7351 4480, fax 0171 349 9809; e-mail: lsn@lymphoedema. freeserve.co.uk; web: www.lymphoedema.org/lsn).

• **Macmillan nurses**, c/o Cancer Relief Macmillan Fund, 15-19 Britten St, London SW3 3TZ (tel 020 7351 7811, fax 020 7376 8098; web: www.macmillan.org.uk). The Fund's nurses can help with emotional support, pain and symptom control. It provides financial assistance for some cancer patients and financially supports or helps fund organisations caring for patients with cancer.

• **Malik, Yvonne**, Sweet Briar, Wray, Near Lancaster LA2 8QN (tel 015242 21767). Advice on creating memory or celebration boxes. Interest in NDE.

• **Marie Curie Cancer Care**, 28 Belgrave Square, London SW1X 8QG (tel 020 7235 3325, fax 020 7823 2380; e-mail: info@mariecurie.org.uk; web: www.mariecurie.org.uk) Phone for information about this organisation's hospice centres, and advice about the availability of night nurses, who are free, but normally obtained through your health authority's community nursing manager.

• **Marsden cancer web pages** (at www.royalmarsden.org). 'An authentic source of accurate information' for patients from the Royal Marsden Hospital in the UK, all about cancers and their treatment.

• **Medline**, for all the information your doctor may have neither the time nor the inclination to impart. Abstracts of almost every major medical article are accessible free on the Internet at the location: www.healthy.net/library/search/medline.htm

• **Memorial Messages**, Thom Osborn, 1 Brecknock Road, London N7 0BL (tel 020 7485 2076). Thom Osborn is a film director who charges from £100 to help people make short videotape messages that can be shown after their death, whether for the funeral or for other times.

• **Memorials by Artists**, Snape Priory, Saxmundham, Suffolk, IP17 1SA (tel 01728 688 934, fax 01728 688 411). Nationwide service to put people in touch with designer-carvers who make individual memorials. Any profits are covenanted to their associated Memorial Arts Charity, which is actively seeking to establish a permanent exhibition of memorials; to improve design and lettering skills within the memorial industry; to produce a booklet on epitaphs; to establish workshops and apprenticeships for trainee lettercutters; to give free advice on churchyard rules and regulations for memorials; and to encourage more creative (and consistent) rules in churchyards and cemeteries.

• **Miscarriage Association**, Clayton Hospital, Northgate, Wakefield WF1 3JF (tel 01924 200799; web: www.the-ma.org.uk). Support and information on all aspects of pregnancy loss.

• **Motor Neurone Disease Association**, PO Box 246, Northampton NN1 2PR (tel 01604 250505 or 01604 22269; e-mail: enquiries@mndassociation.org;

web: www.mndassociation.org). Advice, information, equipment loan. Regional advisers and local groups. Financial help.

• **Mortality journal**, edited by Dr David Field, Centre for Cancer and Palliative Care Studies, Institute of Cancer Research, Royal Marsden NHS Trust, Fulham Road, London SW3 6JJ (tel 020 7252 8171 ext 2912, fax 020 7351 9893; e-mail: dfield@icr.ac.uk).

• **National Funerals College**, run by Professor Malcolm Johnson, 3 Priory Road, Bristol BS8 1TX (tel 01179 289 024, fax 01179 741 960; e-mail: malcolm.johnson@bristol.ac.uk). The College issues the Dead Citizens Charter.

• **National Association of Bereavement Services**, 20 Norton Folgate, London E1 6DB (tel 020 7247 1080 referrals; 020 7247 0617 admin).

• **National Association of Funeral Directors**, 618 Warwick Road, Solihull, West Midlands B91 1AA (tel 0121 711 1343; e-mail: info@nafd.org.uk; web: www.nafd.org.uk). Its members' Code of Practice is available free. If complaining about a funeral director, you are supposed to write first to the funeral director for satisfaction, though there is nothing to prevent you going direct to the association or to the trading standards department (see local council's phone number) or to a small claims court. The association's magazine is called 'The Funeral Director'.

• **National Association of Memorial Masons**, 27a Albert Street, Rugby, Warwickshire CV21 2SG (tel 01788 5422 64, fax 01788 5422 76; e-mail: enquiries@namm.org.uk; web: www.namm.org.uk). Code of practice and ethics for members. It issues a list of members, highlighting those who will do individually crafted memorials.

• **National Federation of Spiritual Healers**, Old Manor Farm Studio, Church Street, Sunbury-on-Thames TW16 6RG (tel 01932 783164; referrals 0891 616080, fax 01932 779 648; e-mail: office@nfsh.org.uk; web: www.nfsh.org.uk).

• **National Association of Widows**, c/o 54-57 Allison Street, Digbeth, Birmingham B5 5TH (tel 0121 643 8348). Information sheet, plus local branch socials. A young widows' contact list is also available.

• **The Natural Death Care Project**, PO Box 1721, Sabastopol, CA 95473, USA (tel 001 707 824 0268; e-mail: ndcp@metro.net; web: www.naturaldeathcare.org). An American project with similarities to the Natural Death Centre in London.

• **Natural Death Centre**, 20 Heber Road, London NW2 6AA (tel 020 8208 2853, fax 020 8452 6434; e-mail: rhino@dial.pipex.com; web: www.naturaldeath.org.uk). The Centre edited this present book. Please send any updates to this address – updates are often available on the website. Further copies of this book are available from the Centre for £12-99 incl. p&p.

• **NDC Horizon vzw – Natuurlijk Dood Centrum**, Van Trierstraat 18, B-2018 Antwerp, Belgium (tel & fax 00 32 3 237 81 43; e-mail: Horizon@mail.dma.be; web: http://bewoner.dma.be/Horizon). A death centre in Belgium inspired by the Natural Death Centre in London.

• **NHS Direct**, for free medical phone advice from a National Health Service nurse (tel 0845 608 4455).

• **Office of Fair Trading**, Field House, 15-25 Breams Buildings, London EC4A 1PR (tel 020 7211 8000, fax 020 7211 8000; e-mail: enquiries@oft.gov.uk; web: www.oft.gov.uk).

• **Open University 'Death and Dying' course**, c/o The Course Manager, School of Health and Social Welfare, Walton Hall, Milton Keynes MK7 6AA (tel 01908 653743, fax 01908 654124; e-mail: b.morris@open.ac.uk; web: www2.open.ac.uk/SHSW/).

• **Pagan Federation**, BM Box 7097, London WC1N 3XX (tel 01787 238257; e-mail: President@paganfed.demon.co.uk; web: www.paganfed.demon.co.uk). Defends paganism as a "spiritual way of life rooted in the ancient nature religions of the world", networks pagans and publishes an info pack (£2) and a quarterly journal (£9 subs). (See also two other pagan organisations, Guild of Soul Midwives and LifeRites.)

• **Palliative Care Arts**, c/o Dr Robert Twycross, Sir Michael Sobell House, Churchill Hospital, Old Road, Headington, Oxford OX3 7LJ (tel 01865 225860). Plans for a research post on creativity, arts and music within palliative care, as part of a new International Centre for Palliative Care; and taking over some of the role previously fulfilled by Hospice Arts.

• **People's Dispensary for Sick Animals (PDSA)**, Whitechapel Way, Priorslee, Telford, Shropshire TF2 9DQ (tel 0800 591248). They have a will-making advice pack and provide a re-homing service for the pets of the deceased (if they leave the PDSA money).

• **Pet Bereavement Support Group**, (tel 0800 096 6606), a helpline offering aid to grieving pet owners, run by the Society for Companion Animal Studies. Callers are linked to a befriender.

• **Pets As Therapy (Incorporating P. A. T. Dogs)**, c/o 6 New Road, Ditton, Maidstone, Kent ME20 6AD (tel 01732 848499). Arranges dogs to visit the sick and the elderly.

• **PRISMA**, Fruits of Life Project, c/o Jozef van der Put, Postbus 10346, 5000 JH Tilburgh, Netherlands (tel 0031 13 5441440, fax 0031 13 5440605; e-mail: jput@prisma-brabrant.nl). Helping those who are dying to develop life stories, to draw up the balance sheet of their life and to resolve unfinished business. Josef van der Put is also interested in the concept of those who have had Near-Death Experiences being with those who are dying.

• **Probate Registry**, Principal Registry, Personal Applications Dept, First Avenue House, 42-49 High Holborn, London, WC1V 6NP (tel 020 7936 6939; or 020 7936 6987 for deposit of wills; or 020 7936 6983 for booklets and forms – also on the web at http://www.courtservice.gov.uk/forms/fmenu_prob.htm). Or see your local phone book under 'Probate' for your nearest office.

• **Rainbow Trust**, Rainbow House, 47 Eastwick Drive, Great Bookham, Surrey KT23 3PU (tel 01372 453309; e-mail: enquiries@rainbowtrust.org.uk; web: www.rainbowtrust.org.uk). Help and respite haven for children with life-threatening illnesses and their families.

• **React**, St Luke's House, 270 Sandycombe Road, Kew, Richmond, Surrey TW9 3NP (020 8940 2575, fax 020 8940 2050). Money and equipment for children with reduced life expectancy. Applications via doctor or a professional worker.

• **Red Cross Medical Loans Service**: see local phone book. Branches can supply medical equipment for short term loan – wheelchairs, commodes, etc. Or contact British Red Cross, 9 Grosvenor Crescent, London SW1X 7EJ (tel 020 7235 5454; e-mail: information@redcross.org.uk; web: www.redcross.org.uk).

• **Rigpa**, Spiritual Care Education and Training Programme, 330 Caledonian Road, London N1 1BB (tel 020 7609 7010; e-mail: ukspcare@cwcom.net; web: www.spcare.org). A Buddhist centre which runs courses on death and dying.

• **Rituals for Remarkable Times**, Anja Saunders, 14 Neal's Yard, London WC2H 9DP (tel 020 7836 9404; e-mail: anja@ndirect.co.uk). Anja Saunders can advise a family to design extraordinary and imaginative funerals.

• **Samaritans**, 10 The Grove, Slough, Berks SL1 1QP (tel 08457 90 90 90; e-mail: jo@samaritans.org; web: www.samaritans.org.uk). Or see local phone book. For those in despair or suicidal.

• **Self-help groups**: Lists are maintained by the Patients Association (tel 0845 608 4455); CancerLink (see above); Health Information First (tel 0800 665544); or for families of children with any disability or special need there is either Contact A Family (tel 020 7383 3555; e-mail: info@cafmily.org.uk; web: www.cafamily.org.uk) or In Touch Trust (tel 0161 905 2440; e-mail: worthington@netscapeonline.co.uk). It is also worth making an Internet search – for instance, there are 70 or so online cancer and information groups to be found at www.medinfo.org; and over 250 searchable health and medical newsgroups at www.medexplorer.com

• **Social Security**, see Benefits Agency.

• **The Society of Allied and Independent Funeral Directors (SAIF)**, SAIF Business Centre, 3 Bullfields, Sawbridgeworth, Hertfordshire CM21 9DB (tel 01279 726777, fax 01279 726300; bereavement and medical careline for SAIF clients: tel 08705 234999; legal helpline for SAIF clients: tel 08705 234500; e-mail: info@saif.org.uk; web: www.saif.org.uk). Co-ordinating body for the smaller independent firms. SAIF funeral directors tend to be the best ones to use, in the Natural Death Centre's view.

• **The Starlight Children's Foundation**, 11-15 Emerald Street, London, WC1N 3QL (tel 020 7430 1642; e-mail: starluk@aol.com; web: www.starlight.org.uk). Attempts to grant the wishes of critically, chronically and terminally ill children.

• **The Stillbirth And Neonatal Death Society (SANDS)**, 28 Portland Place, London W1N 4DE (tel 020 7436 5881; helpline 020 7436 7940; e-mail: support@uk-sands.org; web: www.uk-sands.org). Befriending, local groups, information and publications.

• **Support After Murder or Manslaughter (SAMM)**, Cranmer House, 39 Brixton Road, London SW9 6DZ (tel 020 7735 3838, fax 020 7735 3900; e-mail: samm@uk.people.net). Support groups around the UK for those affected by murder or manslaughter.

• **Terrence Higgins Trust**, 52-54 Grays Inn Road, London WC1X 8JU (admin tel 020 7831 0330; helpline 12 noon to 10pm daily tel 020 7242 1010; legal line tel 020 7405 2381; e-mail: info@tht.london.org.uk; web: www.tht.org.uk). A registered charity to inform, advise and help on AIDS and HIV infection.

• **Twins and Multiple Births Association – Bereavement Support Group**, Narnott House, 309 Chester Road, Little Sutton, Ellesmere Port CH66 1QQ (tel 0151 348 0020; e-mail: Tamba@information4u.com; web: www.surreyweb. org.uk/Tamba).

• **Unitarian Churches**, Matthew Smith, Information Officer, Essex Hall, 1-6 Essex St, Strand, London WC2R 3HY (tel 020 7240 2384; e-mail: ga@unitarian.org.uk; web: www.unitarian.org.uk). Unitarian ministers and lay officials conduct personalised funerals – reflecting the life and beliefs of the deceased person – without dogma.

• **Victim Support**, National Office, Cranmer House, 39 Brixton Road, London SW9 6DZ (tel 020 7735 9166; helpline 0845 30 30 900). Trained staff and volunteers in 374 local Victim Support schemes help victims of crime ranging from burglary to murder. Witness Service offers support and information about court proceedings.

• **Voluntary Euthanasia Society** (formerly Exit), 13 Prince of Wales Terrace, London W8 5PG (tel 020 7937 7770; e-mail: info@ves.org.uk; web: www.ves.org.uk). The Society pioneered the Living Will (advance directive) in the UK – a Living Will pack costs £5. Its aim is 'to make it legal for a competent adult, who is suffering unbearably from an incurable illness, to receive medical help to die at their own considered and persistent request'.

• **War Widows of Great Britain**, c/o 11 Chichester Close, Bury St Edmunds, Suffolk IP33 2LZ (tel 0870 2411 305). Advice on pensions, support and friendship for all war widows.

• **Welfare State International**, The Ellers, Ulverston, Cumbria LA12 0AA (tel 01229 581127, fax 01229 581232; e-mail: info@welfare-state.org; web: www.welfare-state.org). They run funeral workshops and courses on rites of passage and they are the publishers of 'The Dead Good Funerals Book' by Sue Gill and John Fox (see above under 'Gill').

• **Yad b'Yad** (Hebrew for 'Hand in Hand'), c/o Louise Heilbron, 8 Grove Avenue, London N10 2AR (tel 020 8444 7134; e-mail: heilbron@cheerful). A Jewish child bereavement project.

Index